£1 = 2·02 francs

£1 = 2·41 mark

£1 = 16·95 schi

Switzerland

Switzerland

A Phaidon Cultural Guide

with over 600 color illustrations
and 34 pages of maps

PRENTICE-HALL, INC.
Englewood Cliffs
New Jersey 07632

Compiled by Niklaus Flüeler
Editors: Niklaus Flüeler, Lukas Gloor, Isabelle Rucki

Contributors: Lukas Gloor, Dorothee Huber, Manfred Jauslin, Christoph Kübler, Paul
Müller, Marc Nay, Sebastian Speich, Adriana Stallanzani

Photographs: Gérard Zimmermann, Geneva; Eduard Widmer, Zurich; Hans R. Schläpfer,
Lucerne; Niklaus Flüeler, Zurich; Fernand Rausser, Bern; Felix Kubli, Sursee; Comet-
Photo, Zurich; Swiss Tourist Board, Zurich

Library of Congress Cataloging in Publication Data

Knaurs Kulturführer in Farbe: Schweiz. English.
    Switzerland: a Phaidon cultural guide.

    Translation of: Knaurs Kulturführer in Farbe:
Schweiz.
    Includes index.
    1. Art, Swiss — Guide-books.   2. Art — Switzerland —
Guide-books.   I. Flüeler, Niklaus, 1934–
II. Title.
N7141.K613   1985   914.94′0473   85-12148
ISBN 0-13-879974-1

This book is available at a special discount when ordered in bulk quantities. Contact
Prentice-Hall, Inc., General Publishing Division, Special Sales, Englewood Cliffs,
N.J. 07632.

This edition published in the United States and Canada 1985 by Prentice-Hall, Inc.,
Englewood Cliffs, New Jersey 07632

Originally published simultaneously in French as *Guide Culterel de la Suisse* and in German as
Knaurs Kulturführer in Farbe: Schweiz
© Ex Libris Verlag AG, Zurich, 1982
English translation © Phaidon Press Limited, Oxford, 1985

ISBN 0-13-879974-1

Translated and edited by Babel Translations, London
Typeset by Electronic Village Limited, Richmond, Surrey
Printed in Spain by H. Fournier, S.A.–Vitoria

Cover illustration: Kühmatt im Lötschental
(photo: ZEFA)

Preface

This guide is a survey of the Swiss cultural heritage: it deals mainly with buildings — churches and chapels, monasteries and fortresses, palaces and ruins, mansions and ordinary houses, and the most important museums. Entire towns and prehistoric or medieval sites, roads like the Schöllenen and bridges like the Salgina bridge near Schiers are also covered.

Criteria of selection. The guide is essentially an inventory, but is itself only a selection from a very large number of significant, remarkable, interesting or charming buildings and places. The individual reader is bound to find that places are missing which he knows very well, or likes very much for some reason, but every opportunity has been taken to make the selection as systematic as possible. The basis for the guide is the list of monuments prepared by the Interior Ministry of the Confederacy in co-operation with responsible officers in the individual cantons; this list includes objects of national, regional and local importance which, in the event of an armed conflict, would be considered in particular need of protection as part of the cultural heritage of Switzerland. Supplementary sources were the volumes 'Kunstführer durch die Schweiz' and 'Kunstdenkmäler der Schweiz', published by the Gesellschaft für schweizerische Kunstgeschichte, and also the 'Burgenkarte der Schweiz'. The most recent research into farmhouses was consulted, and it was borne in mind that industrial buildings and housing estates can today be just as worth seeing and worthy of protection as a baroque chapel or a late medieval monastery.

It was conscious policy not to include a number of buildings which are privately owned and not open to the public, and which may also not be visible from the road; their inclusion would have caused the user of the guide justifiable frustration.

Alphabetical order. The alphabetical order followed in the guide is based on the official Post Office (PTT) index of places, as printed in telephone directories. Thus the reader will find Freiburg under Fribourg and Geneva under Genève. These spellings are also followed in the maps at the end of the guide.

Cross-references. Small towns, parts of parishes and hamlets which are not parishes in their own right are usually listed under the name of the parish to which they belong; thus the reader of the guide requires a certain amount of knowledge of these matters: Acletta is listed under Disentis and Hegi under Winterthur. Wherever possible, however, we have tried to give a cross-reference supplying the name of the parish if the place in question gives the impression of being an independent parish either by its size or by the fact that it is listed on the map. Thus Paradies and its monastery are cross-referenced to Basadingen, and Ittingen to Uesslingen. On the other hand, St.Urban, which is in the parish of Pfaffnau, has an entry of its own, not because Pfaffnau is entirely without interest, but because excessive use of cross-references would have meant that the guide had more cross-references than entries.

Maps. The maps at the end of the guide serve two purposes. On the one hand they enable the reader to locate a place which he has read about in the body of the guide. The maps are numbered, and divided into numbered squares. The abbreviation 1☐E5 means that the place in question, in this case Delémont, can be found on Map 1 in square E5.

The other purpose of the maps is to encourage the user of the guide to visit places which he has never heard of, or to make a detour to somewhere which, unknown to him, has an interesting church, castle, private house or museum. For example, a tourist who is by chance in Wil will discover from Map 3 that there are objects of architectural or historical interest in the surrounding towns or villages underlined in red—Bronschhofen, Wuppenau, Zuzwil, Henau and Münchwilen for example—and can plan his route accordingly.

It should also be mentioned that not all the places referred to in the guide are on the maps, partly because this would have made the map crowded and difficult to use. The places omitted are hamlets or other very small places which are in some cases not even on the 1:25,000 map. A map reference is still provided, however, to give the reader an idea of the area in which Aino, Brechershäusern or Wellnau may be found. For more precise information he will have to turn to locals or others with expert knowledge.

Times of opening. It used to be true that Catholic churches were open all day, whereas Protestant churches were often closed. However, theft of church property has led to many Catholic churches being closed, while Protestant churches of great interest are open even on weekdays. As reliable information on these matters is seldom available, we have not attempted to supply it. The visitor who finds a locked door will have to enquire for a key, either at the priest's house or somewhere else in the community, perhaps at a restaurant. We simply did not have the space to give the opening times of *museums*, which vary so much and in any case are liable to change from time to time; for these the reader is directed to the Schweizerische Museumsführer of 1981 and the local press. Generally speaking, buildings which are *privately owned* are not open to the public, except perhaps by personal recommendation, and nor are those buildings which are now hospitals or prisons (e.g. Hindelbank). In a few cases—some castles for example—the fact that a building is closed to the public is mentioned in the guide, but on the whole this was not possible.

Photographs. The illustrations in the text were largely taken especially for this guide, as so many buildings in Switzerland have been restored or renovated in the past few years, but the very fact that some buildings are being refurbished at the moment has prevented us from taking new photographs (Ittingen, Kappel, Burg Zug). We have also come to the conclusion that it has become more difficult to photograph objects of architectural interest. The view is often spoiled by car parks, obtrusively placed neighbouring buildings or traffic signs. The reader will have to come to terms with this problem.

Mistakes. Despite a conscientious approach and careful checking of dates, figures, names and descriptions it is scarcely possible to avoid mistakes in a guide of this kind. The publishers would be pleased to receive suggested corrections for the new edition.

The editor

Introduction

Material Culture

Ethnographers enjoy using the term 'material culture' to cover the physical objects produced by a people, in order to emphasise the contrast with language, songs, myths and other such phenomena. If applied to Europe and Switzerland the expression 'material culture' includes, in descending order of importance, cities and towns, villages and hamlets, individual buildings and their contents, down to the heating system and the door knob; but the material culture also includes castles and bunkers, bridges and tunnels, power installations of all kinds, from the mill pond to the gas boiler to the cooling tower, and also buildings, equipment and vehicles used in crafts, trade and industry.

Our civilisation affords buildings a special place in the material culture. Like no other cultural phenomenon they are a living part of the past which impinges on us every day; the most banal buildings are often older than the oldest people we know. However, the intention to create a lasting monument can be discerned even in a granary with a date and the builder's initials carved on the doorpost, or in the choice of materials and the strength of the design; this intention shows most clearly in the greatness of our Gothic cathedrals, a greatness which entirely transcends the material.

Thus a guide to the material culture of Switzerland must be a guide to the history of its buildings. The word 'architecture' has not been used, so that our view does not become restricted. The cultured tourist often uses the word 'architecture' to cover a narrow range of buildings on a basis of age, the purpose of the building, and the beauty or strength of its design. This guide cannot and does not intend to overturn the traditional view of architectural monuments, in which the most ordinary Romanesque chapel in a field is rated more highly than the boldest innovation on the alpine railway. It affords pride of place, as is customary, to 'ancient monuments', but it also attempts to broaden the reader's appreciation of aspects of visual culture based on aesthetic enjoyment.

Panorama of Basel and environs, early 19C, perhaps by Maximilian Neustück (Catholic priest's house Oberwil, BL). *The eye is guided from Basel (left) up the Rhine and then into the valleys of the Birs and Birsig; this is a cultural landscape in the original sense of the word: shaped by dairy and arable farming, forestry and market gardening, vineyards and hunting forests.*

Nature and Culture

It seldom strikes us when we drive or walk out into the countryside that the landscape is not something natural, but something cultured in the original sense of the word: shaped by dairy and arable farming, tree and vegetable growing, vineyards and forestry. Only someone who has worked in agriculture or forestry, or who has lived in an area which has undergone great changes, is aware of how much the landscape alters with the way in which it is used, whether he remembers the frantic planting of the Second World War or, a quarter of a century later, the loss of the familiar orchards; whether he regrets the desolation and reduction to infertile steppe of inaccessible farmland in the mountains, or admires the increase of production and rationalisation on the plains, which also affects the landscape: the reorganisation of land into larger units, improvement in irrigation, the building of country roads and paths, and movement from the village to the individual farm in the centre of the cultivated area.

Our maps are full of names which tell of former agricultural methods or point to the pioneering times in which hectare after hectare of pas-

ture, meadow and arable land was wrested from the forest with axe and fire; hence the name 'Rütli' ('gerodetes Land'—'land cleared of trees') for the clearing by Lake Urner where three of the four forest cantons are said to have sworn the Oath of Confederacy. In the seven centuries which have passed since then the population within the present boundaries of Switzerland has probably increased sevenfold.

Since Roman times Switzerland has been a country of roads and bridges. Nowhere do nature and culture interact more clearly than in the architecture and design of systems of transport. Switzerland has seen pioneering work in this field, too: the passes in the Alps and Jura were opened by the Romans, improved in the Middle Ages, and have increased in number ever since. At the end of the 14C the Septimer pass was opened, at the end of the 15C the Viamala gorge was made passable in competition with the Septimer; it was not until the 18C that traffic through the Gotthard was made easier by a road tunnel, and not until 1831 that the post coach replaced the mounted messenger; the great railway tunnel was pierced in 1880, and the Autobahn tunnel opened to traffic a hundred years later. In the 17C the Swiss seemed, like the French and the Dutch, to favour water transport, and indeed started to build a canal intended to join Lake Geneva with the lakes at the foot of the Jura and the Aare, but road transport began to gain the upper hand. Considerable stretches of the modern road system were built for horse-drawn carriages and coaches. The traveller who keeps

View of the Urnerloch (tunnel) near Andermatt, 1773 by Caspar Wolf (Kupferstichkabinett Basel). *The tunnel was bored in 1707 by Pietro Morettini and replaced the Twärenbrücke, a bridge round* *the spur which was suspended on hooks. The gorge, the devil's bridge and the unfamiliar tunnel were an experience of a kind now scarcely imaginable for travellers in the 18&19C.*

his eyes open is reminded of this period by coaching inns and hospices, and also by roads fringed with avenues of trees, embankments protected by massive stone facings, hairpin bends and stone or wooden bridges.

Nature provides the building materials. While roads were poor and transport dear, they came from as near to the site as possible, particularly the stone: granite in the Tessin, grey sandstone in the Mittelland, red sandstone on the high and upper Rhine, white limestone in Solothurn, yellow in Neuchâtel. But as soon as the roads improved, the stone industry developed; in the 17&18C the area around Stans and Saint-Triphon near Ollon supplied a limestone which could be polished like black marble, from the late 18C Solothurn supplied a white limestone for fine wells and fountains, and the area around Alpnach contributed paving stones for roads, particularly in the period between the wars. When it comes to timber, quantity, price and type are heavily dependent on the climate. The fact that much of Switzerland is heavily wooded not only helped the building of wooden bridges in the 18&19C, but also the building of stone bridges, whose scaffolding and arch formworks devour enormous quantities of wood, but also the building of concrete bridges, which are coffered in wood; iron bridges on the other hand were restricted to the railway, and thus to the second half of the 19C.

Switzerland is short of useful minerals. There is little trace of a mining industry, except in a few villages in the Jura, where iron was mined and ore was smelted. But there are links with the building industry: for example, the waters of the river Schüss, which leave the Jura through the Taubenloch gorge near Biel, have been harnessed since the 17C to drive a wire mill, whose products were later used in a famous suspension bridge in Fribourg; the bridge has since disappeared.

It was not the country's mineral wealth but water power which brought early industries, like the Biel wire plant, into being: smithies, wire plants, saw mills, paper mills, hemp mills, later fabric printing and wool and cotton mills, particularly in the canton of Zürich. The numerous ponds, locks and canals bear witness to this source of power; the oldest go back to the Middle Ages, the most recent were intended to run steam engines; their technical successors are the reservoirs, dams and all the other installations of the hydroelectric industry. Buildings remaining from the various stages of industrial development seem to us to be monuments worthy of conservation today.

Areas of the Country

Switzerland is a tiny country, split in two by the Alps and with a small foreland north of the Jura, but its individual regions are as different as it is possible to be. These differences are intensified by the fact that history has settled people from four linguistic groups in the area.

It is not the distance from the northern to the southern foothills of the Alps or the distance from the Atlantic or the gulf stream which determine climate and agriculture, but the enormous and unusual variations in height. Constantly changing economic factors have favoured first one part of the country, then another. This must be remembered when considering the economic factors which have made possible the production of cultural objects. Thus we must assume that the presence in large quantities of early medieval treasures in the alpine valleys is connected with the valuable north–south traffic over the Bünden and Valais passes, which slackened as trade with the Mediterranean subsided. Political powers settle at strategic points; this can be shown by two examples:

The Burgundians were already romanised and Christianised when they conquered west Switzerland in the middle of the fifth century. They chose Geneva as their capital, Saint-Maurice in the Lower Valais was the monastery of their kings; it is therefore not surprising that its treasury is richer than that of any other church treasury in Switzerland. The foundation of the monastery of Müstair in Grisons also has to be seen in a political context. It is a convincing tradition that it must have been founded by Charlemagne, who needed an eastern Rhaetian base and quarters. The wall paintings in the monastery church, presumed to be the work of Italian painters, are the largest cycle of Carolingian frescos to survive in Europe.

In any case the importance of the monasteries in early medieval European culture must never be underestimated. In the Christianisation of the West there was a movement from west to east as well as from south to north. This is the context in which we must consider the Scottish and Irish missionaries who moved over to the Continent from the 6C onwards, and whom Switzerland has to thank for the foundation of many important monasteries. Columban left Ireland with twelve companions *c.* 590. One of them founded the monastery of Saint-Ursanne in the Jura, another the monastery in St.Gallen. The monastery of Moutier-Grandval was founded from Columban's own first monastery of Luxeuil. The oldest abbot's crozier on the Continent comes from here (now in Delsberg).

The areas containing Romanesque art and buildings are clearly delineated, but one must not compartmentalise too much: there are discrepancies based on political and ecclesiastical factors; there are tightly-packed areas and areas of more scattered distribution. Here again are some examples: the Cluniac abbey church of Payerne, set on the northern edge of the kingdom of Burgundy, is built on the pattern of the second building at Cluny, the mother church of the reforming Order; the Minster of All Souls in Schaffhausen, however, is a successor of the church of St.Peter and St.Paul in Hirsau, in the Black Forest. The two reformimg monasteries are only 160 km. apart, although they are also separated by the frontier between the French and German languages. Many other regional schools of building have offshoots in Switzerland, thanks to links between Orders, and trade connections. The Cluniac church of Romainmôtier is part of the Jura-Saône valley tradition; the church of the Benedictine monastery of Muri in Aargau, a Habsburg foundation, shows the influence of the Upper Rhine area; the priory church of Grandson was subordinate to the reforming abbey of La Chaise-Dieu in the Auvergne, and, like an Auvergne church, is vaulted; the Grossmünster in Zürich, the great centre for trade over the Bünden passes, would be unthinkable without the model of Sant'Ambrogio in Milan; finally, the Münster in Basel, in the Middle Ages the second largest town in Switzerland, is an unorthodox synthesis of many regional types (northern Burgundy, Upper Rhine, North Italy). The early Cistercian churches are all North Burgundian too, and the church of Bonmont in the Vaud is one of the earliest of the Order.

The rise of the towns was simultaneous with the rise of Gothic art, and at the same time new centres of art began to form inside and outside Switzerland. No town in Switzerland has ever been more than middle-sized, and none has been a centre of European art for an extended period. This does not mean, however, that no works of art of European rank have ever been created, acquired or collected in Switzerland. It is possible to name with ease a significant work in every century, and it is characteristic of Switzerland that different regions are involved. Thus in the 13C Lausanne cathedral came into being, in the 14C the stained glass in Königsfelden, in the 15C Konrad Witz's Geneva altar, in the 16C the façade of San Lorenzo in Lugano, at the turn of the 17&18C the monastery of Einsiedeln and its church, in the 19C the Hauptbahnhof in Zürich and in the 20C the Salgina bridge at Schiers or Haus Waldbühl near Uzwil.

The Commissioning of Works of Art

The mobility of the greater part of the population in modern times has made us forget that such mobility used to be the privilege of certain classes. Until the Second World War it was not unusual for a farmer or other ordinary citizen never to leave the place of his birth, except perhaps for a day's journey, and then almost always on foot. This was of course not true of craftsmen who travelled for two or three years as part of their training, nor of merchants, mercenaries and soldiers, and things were different again for the patrician classes and the nobility.

The upper classes, the principal commissioners of buildings and works of art, make demands which transcend regional considerations; they measure themselves and their activities against international centres of government, trade and artistic activity. In the Middle Ages the bishops were often members of the nobility, some of them were Princes of the Empire and went to synods of the archdioceses. Thus they were part of a network of connections, a fact which is mirrored in their cathedrals, unless building was dealt with by the cathedral chapter.

Thus it is no surprise that master of works Jean Cotereel and the glass painter Pierre d'Arras (both, as their names suggest, from northern France, at that time in the artistic vanguard) were involved in the building of Lausanne cathedral in the 13C. It may be rather more astonishing that in Vufflens, to stay in the Vaud, there is a massive fortress with a 197 ft. high keep built in brick by Italian craftsmen. This phenomenon of architectural history is easier to understand if one knows something about the man who commissioned it, Heinrich von Colombier; he was the right-hand man of the Duke of Savoy, and ran Piedmont for him from 1405, defeated the Margrave of Montferrat, was dispatched to Jerusalem and concluded the Treaty of Venice with the Duke of Milan on behalf of the Duke of Savoy. It may not be too surprising—to take an Italian building in the German-speaking area —that Lucerne, on the Gotthard road, has a Renaissance Palazzo, but to understand this phenomenon completely one needs to know the glittering personality who commissioned it: Lux Ritter was a saddler by profession, who rose as an officer in France and a politician in Switzerland; in 1551 he was envoy in Lugano, and finally mayor of the town of Lucerne, which continued the building after his death and handed it over to the Jesuits.

If the patron was less well travelled or wished to work on a more modest scale competition was confined to a restricted area. The house of Bruder Klaus in Flüeli-Ranft or the birthplace of the Zürich reformer Huldrych Zwingli in Wildhaus show the modesty of the homes of some of the leading figures of the period of transition from the medieval to the modern period. Country seats also adopted this simple style of building; examples are the 17C Ital-Reding-Haus in Schwyz and the Freulerpalast in Näfels, which was built by French guards officers.

The rich merchants and mercenary leaders in the cities were less modest, as can be seen from the Rittersche Palast in Lucerne. Three more examples from the 16C: the town house of the envoy, captain and merchant Bartolome May in Bern, with a late Gothic oriel; the 'Spiesshof' of the banker, envoy and French officer Balthasar Irmy in Basel, with a Renaissance façade and a late Gothic vaulted hall; the Fribourg 'Hôtel' of the Commandant of the Swiss guard in Lyon, Jean de Ratzé, the work of a Lyon architect.

Patrons who worked in groups are not to be underestimated: religious orders, towns and guilds. At a time when there were still no public buildings in the modern sense they created in embryo the designs of administrative buildings, schools, hospitals, market halls and warehouses, to name just a few examples of buildings which in the 19&20C have been gradually taken over by the state. Many 15&16C Town Halls have open-air staircases leading to their council chambers; the Town Hall in Geneva was the only one to have a tower with ramps for horsemen, in the manner of a French château. This may sound somewhat excessive, but let us not forget the Bundeshaus in Bern, completed at the beginning of this century, with its giant staircase topped by the federal dome. This building was commissioned by a flourishing industrial nation striving to measure up to its larger neighbours: admiring glances were cast at the recently completed Reichstag building in Berlin, and the Swiss architect Hans Auer, who had been working for ten years on the Reichsrat building, was summoned home from Vienna.

Let us return to the assertion that the mobility of individual sections of the population has an effect on the ambitiousness of their buildings: if mobility is low, then ambition will be less, and the architecture more homogeneous. This is certainly true of farmers, and more particularly of farm workers and Tauner (farm labourers paid by the day) until the middle of the last century.

Thus it is clear that within a particular period and region farmhouses will resemble each other more than any other kind of building. It is true that there is a degree of competition even in farm buildings, but the ambition of builder, mason and carpenter is contained on the local plane. Let us consider the 'Jura house' in the canton of Jura and the adjacent areas of France, and of the cantons of Neuchâtel, Vaud and Bern; the thatched houses of the Aargau, although these are restricted to some central areas; the Gommer house in Upper Valais, the Gotthard house, the Engadine house—all clearly defined types, with construction, heating, function and distribution of rooms clear to the attentive eye, even if they are dilapidated, alte:ed to suit modern living or economic requirements, or have been placed in the minority by the modern building industry.

Types of Building

We have so far considered three factors which affect cultural life and the entire material culture: geographical region, historical progress and the social status of the patron. As soon as we turn our attention to the purpose of the building the special position of architecture among the arts becomes clear, at least when viewed through modern eyes: it is only in architecture that form and function are so closely connected.

A tourist who is interested in art must always use his imagination to understand a building from the point of view of its original purpose. He must be able to hear the choristers and monks singing in the choir stalls, see the women and maids on their way to the well, hurry to the walls with the watch, sit at a loom or at one of the thousand typewriters in an office, climb on to the coachman's seat, wipe the soot of a steam locomotive from his face, make paper, expose himself to the deafening racket of a printing press, slip on a frock coat, lace up a bodice, in short, he must be able to think himself into the lives of people from past ages. Best of all, he should eavesdrop on conversations between architect and patron. However, at the very point where there seems to be consistency of function, in churches, confusion creeps in because function has changed so frequently.

The difficulty begins with the discrepancy between the name and the function of the choir in a church. In smaller churches the so-called choir serves as a sanctuary and in older Protestant churches it is where the chairman of the congregation has his place. Collegiate and monastery churches in which the choir stalls have survived, like those in Moudon, Kappel am Albis, Muri im Freiamt, Wettingen, St.Urban or the minsters in Bern and Fribourg, and finally a modern church of

Detail from bird's eye view of Schloss Lenzburg, 1624 by Joseph Plepp (Staatsarchiv Bern). *A set of buildings which has grown very gradually, transcending the demands of terrain and function.*

an Order like the Benedictine church in Sarnen, show that the 'chorus psallentium', the choir of monks and priests, is not always in the same place in a larger church building. The semicircular priests' bench behind the high altar was generally replaced by two parallel rows of choir stalls in the high Middle Ages; a style which had proved suitable for monks' services. After the counter-reforming council of Trent these were gradually replaced with choir stalls behind the high altar, most clearly in the case of the Capucines. In the Cistercian church in Kappel the Gothic choir stalls extend from the transept deep into the nave; in the high and late Gothic period there was a preference for long choirs containing the high altar and the choir stalls, and thus making a clear division from the 'peoples' church', sometimes emphasised by a rood screen—a barrier, higher than a man, which could take almost any form, as can be seen in four churches in Basel, in the churches of Aarau and Burgdorf, in the French church in Bern and some other churches. The fact that the rood screen was retained above all in Protestant areas is connected with the fact that members of the Reformed church liked to use the closed choir as a winter church which could be heated, or as additional space, while in Catholic churches attention was focused on the high altar from the time of the Counter-Reformation. The rood screens were replaced by choir screens; the oldest monumental example in Switzerland goes back to the late Gothic period: the choir screen of St. Nicholas in Fribourg. Since the second Vatican Council many believers have found that even the choir screen is too marked a division between the clerical and lay parts of the church.

If one studies the horizontal and vertical organisation of space in domestic buildings one sees how slowly building habits change. The phylogenesis—origin and history—of a type of building always shows. Large castles, regarded phylogenetically, are agglomerations of individual buildings. For this reason they often consist of sections in which one living room is built above another, and then connected by a spiral staircase, while the horizontal connections are not developed and there are no actual corridors. This is also true of castles which were built quickly and apparently to a uniform plan; it is much clearer in complexes like Schloss Lenzburg which developed gradually, and where a tour of the building shows the differences in level between one section and the next. Not even the battlements are on the same level, but this is often determined by the terrain, as in the three Castelli of Bellinzona.

Monastery buildings come from another tradition; they are based on the Roman atrium. At the centre is the roughly square inner courtyard—the atrium or the cloister—surrounded by open walks on which the individual rooms are placed: chapterhouse, calefactory, refectory and other rooms. In the older two-storey complexes the dormitories and day rooms were connected by doors leading from one room into the next; only in the late Middle Ages were the rooms on all storeys opened up at the same time by building, as it were, one cloister on top of another. North of the Alps this sometimes led to wooden arcades, south of the Alps to arcaded courtyards, which were exported in the 16C along with the Renaissance design which had developed in Italy. The finest examples are the mid 16C Rittersche Palast in Lucerne, which has already been mentioned, and the mid 17C Stockalper Palast in Brig. Significantly, the first monastery with an arcaded courtyard is in the Tessin: the Collegio Papio in Ascona. From the 14C onwards cloisters were gradually glazed; the oldest surviving panes are in the cloister in Wettingen, but even in the 16C the cloister of Muri im Freiamt monastery was unglazed for a good twenty years.

In the large monasteries built in the 17&18C the number of courtyards was doubled or even quadrupled, most impressively in Einsiedeln. Here too the working, living and sleeping quarters are on the outside and the corridors on the four courtyards, with the exception only of the north wing, where sunlight was the deciding factor.

The system of access with which we are familiar, through a central corridor lit from a stair well on the outer side of the building or from windows of its own, is frequently found from the 17C in town houses which are completely detached or detached on three sides. An early example is the Latin School in Bern, opened in 1581, which was built as a boarding school with dormitory, masters' residence and schoolrooms.

In the 19C glass bricks, glass roofs and glass doors were popular for providing light in tenement buildings, until in the 20C, with the spread of electric lighting, the corridor without daylight appeared and was accepted by the building authorities, as for example in the eastern section of the Cantonal Hospital in Bern.

When coach transport became fashionable in the 17&18C most authorities forbade the use of horse and carriage for private transport in the individual towns of the Old Confederacy. At the same time important households had to provide access and passage for coaches, stabling, coach houses and any other necessary provision for state visits. Etiquette not only laid down the number of horses which could be used, but also regulated behaviour during the visit. Three examples from 19C Basel: the Blue House has a spacious main courtyard with a rococo railing and an open-air staircase with two flights; the Wildtsche House had its guests drive up through the Petersplatz and then the equipage disappeared through gates at the side of the house; in the Kirschgarten one drove in through the central *porte cochère*, stopped by the steps in the drive and went directly up to the staterooms, while the coachman used a small turning area behind the house.

After the arrival of the motor car in the late 19C it took architects a long time to stop treating garages like coach houses. It was not until between the wars, when there were more car owners who had to drive into their own garages and unload the luggage themselves, that demand for garages in the house or with covered access began to increase.

Towns

The town as a settlement, a widespread feature of the Roman period, disappeared almost completely from Switzerland at the time of the migration of the peoples. Geneva was the town which most clearly survived the early Middle Ages as an urban community. Roman military camps and towns, royal palaces (Zürich) and monasteries (e.g. St. Gallen) were points of crystallisation for groups of craftsmen and the emergence of markets; they later became walled and were granted charters as towns. Characteristic sites for Swiss towns were loading points for transalpine trade at the ends of lakes: Geneva, Lucerne, Zürich, and also Thun, Zug and Stein am Rhein; the latter was in the shadow of Konstanz.

Numerous towns came into being in the high Middle Ages as foundations of rival noblemen trying to rationalise their dispersed areas of influence and to secure them militarily and economically. Even new towns like this rarely grew up out of nothing, however; they usually made use of a fortified tower or a Burg, or developed from villages. Fribourg, Bern, Thun, Burgdorf and Murten date back to the Dukes of Zähringen, Liestal, Waldenburg, Olten, Aarburg and Zofingen to the Counts of Froburg, Aarau, Lenzburg, Mellingen, Zug, Diessenhofen and Frauenfeld to the Counts of Kyburg and Baden, Bremgarten, Brugg and Laufenburg to the Counts of Habsburg. In West Switzerland the Counts of Neuchâtel established Arberg, Le Landeron and Neuchâtel, the Counts of Savoy Aigle, Morges, Rolle, Romont and Yverdon. The lords spiritual also founded towns: the Bishops of Basel founded Biel, La Neuveville, Porrentruy, Saint-Ursanne, Laufen and Klein-Basel, the Bishops of Konstanz Bischofszell and Neunkirch.

Not all of these foundations were successful, but it is the less important towns, which have remained small, that are most instructive about medieval urban architecture. The system of alleyways and rows of houses, the grading from the market street to the back streets, the situation of castle, town hall and church is more clearly seen in Murten, for example, than in the carefully tended Old Town in Bern; small towns like Murten are also easier to see as wholes than the complexes which have grown beyond their original boundaries. If it is difficult to gain a full impression of an individual building like a castle, it is

Detail from a bird's eye view of Zürich, right bank of the Limmat, 1497 – 1501 by Hans Leu the Elder, completed 1566 – 71 by Hans Asper (Schweizerisches Landesmuseum, Zürich). *This was originally the background of an altar panel portraying the martyrdom of the town's patron saints, but* it was so altered and so many buildings were added after the Reformation that the saints disappeared. It shows the land and water fortifications and the use of the river for transport and to provide power for mills (grain, wood, paper). Many of the houses are directly on the Limmat.

even more difficult when a visitor to a town is not content with enjoying individual views or hurrying to particular buildings mentioned in the cultural guide, but tries to grasp the organisation of the buildings either as a pattern with its own rules or as a mirror of economy and law in the town.

Even today the layout of a town can say a great deal about its origins. Buildings like to spread themselves around churches and monasteries which were there before the town, as in St. Gallen and Bischofszell. If a castle on a hill was the starting point, then the town will be at the foot of that hill, as in Burgdorf and Thun. In other places several originally more or less independent settlements have merged, as in Basel the bishop's seat 'Auf Burg', the craftsmen's settlement at the confluence of the Birsig and the Rhine, the Cluniac monastery of St. Alban with its mills upstream on the Rhine and the canonries of St. Peter and St. Leonhard downstream, and finally on the other bank of the river the village around St. Theodor and the bridgehead settlement—all have grown together over the centuries to create today's modern city. Little towns like Greyerz and Regensberg, but also the formerly walled village of Münchenstein, are like outer works of the Schloss which in each case bears the same name. Rolle and Waldenburg are examples of elongated street towns.

New foundations and planned town extensions in the Middle Ages always have a clearly recognisable system of streets, although the pattern is often dependent on the terrain. Famous examples are the gently curving longitudinal streets of the original town of Bern. In the second half of the 13C, which inclined to regularity even in the design of individual buildings, the Neunkirch rectangle with its four parallel streets came into being; it is the most regular town layout in Switzerland and was helped by the flatness of the site. Agricultural land was also parcelled to a regular, right-angled pattern, as in, to name a less well-known example, the Steinen suburb which grew up to the south of Basel in the 14C. Today, when in Central Europe every building plot is mapped and allocated to one or more planning zones, it is difficult to imagine that towns once grew more or less without any rules, as more and more houses were built along the roads which led out of the town. New town walls often followed rather slowly behind this spontaneous growth, though sometimes they were planned to accommodate an extension of the town. If the walls were built around the outermost tips of the streets, large reserves of land remained available in between, and these were not used up in Basel, a town with generously planned walls, until 1800, while Geneva and Zürich had to resort to building higher. The difference is clear if one compares the height of the buildings on the Nadelberg in Basel, the Grand-Rue in Geneva and the Münstergasse in Zürich.

In the Middle Ages the preferred site for town fortifications was whenever possible a dominating height. Thus we find the Musegg towers, built c. 1400, on the hill north-west of Lucerne; they are functional, but also symbols of defensive capability. This is also true of the town gates, the largest of which is the Spalentor in Basel, also built c. 1400 and extended in 1474. The banks of lakes and rivers were also fortified, as is shown by the water tower and the Kapell bridge in Lucerne. The Lucerne water tower was intended for defence in all directions and thus built on an octagonal ground plan, in the late Mid-

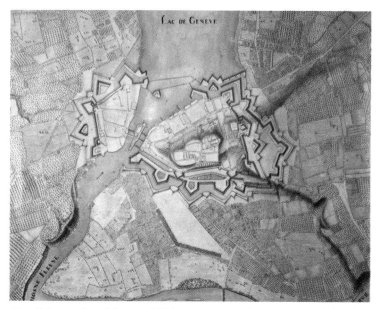

Detail from a plan of Geneva, 1718 by Jacques-Barthélemy Micheli du Crest (Sammlung Gustave Dumur, Geneva). *The giant baroque stars of the fortifications sharply divided town from* *country, and were more restricting than medieval town walls. The plan shows projected extensions to the E. (right), where the terrain shaded in grey was unsuitable for defence purposes.*

dle Ages one often finds shell towers: semicircles in front of the town walls which are open on the town side, as in Fribourg.

From the 16C onwards the town fortifications had to deal with artillery. First of all planners turned to the experience and theories of the Italians. The Basler Turm in Solothurn has a fat round tower with wide gaps for guns on either side. However, the most massive Swiss fortress of the 16C is the Munot, the citadel which towers over Schaffhausen; it is built on a hexagonal base as a cylinder more than 164 ft. in diameter; it hides the vaulting of the casemate and has castellations which could be reached by the guns via the ramp in the adjacent tower.

Well-armed towers like the Basler Tor in Solothurn, citadels like the Munot and bastions like the Elisabethenschanze in Basel could protect the thin shells of the town walls by making room for modern cannons and securing the artillerymen. But the Thirty Years War (1618

– 48) was the point at which it became clear how a town could be devastated by artillery fire. If one wished to keep off siege artillery, it was necessary to use barrage fire. For this one needed a broad firing area ('glacis'), a system of low entrenchments and connecting walls, which survive artillery fire better than high walls. In Geneva and Zürich, which built modern fortifications in the 17C, these structures took up as much land as the towns themselves. The best surviving example of a systen like this is in Solothurn.

In the other Swiss towns the baroque fortifications have largely been removed. This happened in the 19C, for three reasons: the populace outside the capital were beginning to emancipate themselves, and demanded the removal of the walls, which they saw as an outdated privilege from pre-revolutionary days; new developments in the construction of weapons, for example the rifled barrel, reduced the value of baroque forifications; finally the rapid growth of town populations swiftly used up the reserves of land inside the town walls.

This 'defortification' made land available which was used partly for roads around the town, partly for green belts and public buildings and partly for sale to private individuals. Thus after 1830 the right bank in Zürich gained the Hohe Promenade, the Cantonal School on the former Rämi bastion, and the public buildings in the University quarter; the left bank acquired the botanical garden (which has since moved) on the Katz bastion and the tree-lined square on the entrenchment where the river flows out of the lake. The equivalent in Geneva was the Rousseau island, where the entrenchment cladding was retained.

In Geneva it is very easy for the visitor to imagine how the fortified lake harbour was changed into the present park along the bank of the lake. In Basel after 1860 the river fortifications were replaced by the Rheinwege; in Klein-Basel the new road along the river incorporated a culvert to collect the drainage water which had previously reached the Rhine through small gutters. Like most Swiss lake and riverside towns, smaller places like Stein am Rhein, Rheinfelden, Saint-Ursanne and Mellingen do not have promenades along their banks.

The ring and riverside roads like the Limmatquai in Zürich, which came into being on the sites of former fortifications, were at first not able to deal with increasing coach and commercial traffic, but had to be extended, widened and straightened. The Rues Basses in Geneva and the Freie Strasse in Basel were widened, for example; traditional arteries which had to accommodate more traffic as the Old Town became the town centre.

Levelling and the removal of steep inclines, which until the 19C was important for long-distance roads, became necessary in towns as well because of the demands of traffic. The deep cutting in the lower part of the Rämistrasse was built in Zürich and also, about the turn of the century, the Urania cutting, which also required the building of the first major flyover in Switzerland, a device for dealing with traffic problems which became increasingly popular after the Second World War. From the middle of the 19C Bern began to replace the low Nydegg bridge with high-level bridges. Fribourg, which has a similar site, chose to use suspension bridges. In Lausanne the engineers were only able to build a ring road by using two high-level bridges and a tunnel.

Is it not strange that a period which believed so firmly in progress did not found any new towns? The dispersed nature of political power which is so typical of Switzerland did not allow this. The only new town founded in the 18C was the little town of Carouge, outside the gates of Geneva, founded by King Victor Amadeus II of Sardinia, as Lord of Savoy. It was built with absolutely straight streets, as was almost inevitable in that period. La Chaux-de-Fonds, which was largely destroyed by fire in 1794, was built to a strictly rectangular design, despite its sloping site; it favoured horizontal main streets and blocks of buildings parallel to the slope. Glarus was also rebuilt after the fire of 1861 with a network of streets at right angles, but with houses set in squares; a considerable hill had to be removed for the purpose.

Networks of streets at right angles are also the characteristic feature of new districts in old towns. Frequently gardens in front of the houses were prescribed, a means of keeping wide spaces between buildings without any demand on the public purse. An interest in picturesquely curving streets on the other hand does not appear until at the turn of the century villa districts were built on hills with views, under direct influence partly from England, partly from Germany.

Aadorf TG

3 □ C4

Catholic church of St. Alexander: Rebuilt in 1863–5 to the designs of Joachim Brenner and Joh. Christoph Kunkler, incorporating a tower from 1478. Stained glass by Ferdinand Gehr. **Former Cistercian convent of Tänikon:** Now a federal agricultural research institute. First mentioned in 1247, the complex dates in the main from the 15–16C. Today it is in part ruined and a road now cuts through the cloister. Pulpits and altars in the monastery church are in stucco simulating marble — the work of Johann Josef Mosbrugger 1830–1.

Aarau AG

2 □ C5

This town, founded *c.* the middle of the 13C high above the Aare, was part of the Habsburg property seized by Bern in 1415 (Bernese Aargau). The town remained subject to Bern until the Swiss Revolution. The ambitious citizens of Aarau were instrumental in bringing about the collapse of the Old Confederation and it was thought that Aarau would be the capital of the newly-formed Swiss Republic—indeed in the Laurenzenvorstadt district a government quarter was planned. However, history passed over the short-lived Swiss Republic and in 1803 Aarau assumed the more modest role of capital of the new canton of Aargau, a 'patchwork' canton made up of almost a dozen small towns formerly of equal importance together with rural regions. Its role as a seat of government and administration has had a considerable effect on the face of Aarau.

OLD TOWN AND FORTIFICATIONS: Baroque features predominate in the houses e.g. the lavishly decorated eaves. However, the circular layout of medieval Aarau can still be discerned. The town grew up in concentric circles around the intersection of two roads. The course of the old town wall can still be made out in the Graben and Halde areas. Parts to have survived include the **Upper Tower,** whose foundation dates from *c.* 1270 (the upper part with pyramidal roof and little belfry dates from the 16C), the Pulverturm and the Turm Rore, which is the oldest part of the Rathaus. The **Reformed church** occupies the site of an earlier church. Sebastian Gisel built the present basilica in 1471–8 with a nave, two aisles and polygonal apse. The choir screen has seven bays which is typical. The lower part of the tower is older than the church itself; in 1663 Simon Erisman gave the tower two curved gables. **Schlössli:** The oldest building in Aarau, it dates in part from the 11C. There is a keep, a hall from the 13C or 14C, and later additions. Since 1938 it has housed the *Stadtmuseum Alt-Aarau.* The four-storeyed **Rathaus** has a late classical façade. Other parts are much older, e.g. part of the Turm Rore is 13C, baroque alterations date from 1762 and the wings from 1822 – 8 and 1856 – 7. The building was enlarged and restored 1952 –7.

VORDERE VORSTADT UND RAIN: The most striking building is the **Saxerhaus** of 1693 in early baroque style.

SÜDLICHE VORSTADT: Outstanding is the **Regierungsgebäude,** the central part of which was built in 1739 as a residential house and later became an inn. In 1811 – 24 the canton's architect Johann Schneider added the side wings. The **Grossratsgebäude** (parliament building) was built in classical style by Franz Heinrich Hemmann in 1826 – 8. The third prominent building is the **Aargauer Kunsthaus** and the **Kantonsbibliothek** (1957 – 9).

LAURENZENVORSTADT: A street to the E. of the town centre dominated by classical residences and official buildings, including the **Amtshaus,** built by Bern and designed by Carl Ahasver von Sinner in 1784-7 (now local Government Offices), the **Feergut,** built by Johann Daniel Osterrieth 1795 – 7 and much altered 1937 – 9 (now a priest's house) and the

Aarau: view of town, 15C church on the right.

Aarau: neoclassical Säulenhaus with porticoed façade, 1838.

Aarau: the Museum of Old Aarau is housed in the Schlössli.

Säulenhaus, an upper middle-class private residence built in 1838 by Franz Heinrich Hemmann with a four-columned Doric temple front.

Museums: *Stadtmuseum Alt-Aarau* in the Schlössli; *Aargauer Kunsthaus* with a good collection of Swiss art.

Aarberg BE

6☐D3

Small town with rectangular layout founded *c.* 1220 by Count Ulrich III of Neuenburg. The rows of houses along the former street market have a late Medieval

Aarburg: medieval Schloss and later fortifications above the town.

atmosphere although the buildings themselves date mostly from the 18&19C. **Schloss** (Amtshaus): Post Gothic; probably built towards the end of the 17C as a seat for the Landvogt. In the 18C the arrangement of the windows was made regular. Inside, a gallery displays the arms of over 80 Landvogts. **Reformed church:** Late Gothic from 1484 with a tower of 1529; six Renaissance stained-glass windows. In the W. of the town **a wooden bridge** dating from 1568 spans the old River Aare. With four arches and a triangular truss frame, the bridge is supported by stone river pillars which have stood on dry ground since the construction of the Hagneck Canal (1868–70). Grotesques on the arches of the bridge were to ward off the evil water spirits.

Aarburg AG

2☐B5

With its castle and fortress on the hill, rows of old town houses along the bank of the Aare and twin-towered church on the side of the hill, this little town is a prominent feature of the Mitelland and visible for miles. A terrible fire of 1840 destroyed much of the town, a Froburg foundation whose oldest parts go back to the 11C. The **Altstadt** (Old Town) consists of three rows of houses and the town square. The **Reformed church** by Johann Jakob Heimlicher is a neo-Gothic single-aisled building dating from 1842–5 and occupying the site of an earlier church destroyed in the town fire. **Castle and Fortress:** The core of the complex (keep and Great Hall) date from the high Middle Ages. An early baroque residential block was added in the 1621. The seat of a Bernese Landvogt 1415–1798, from 1659 the castle was gradually expanded into a strategic artillery fortress. The castle is now used as a reformatory. **Old Execution Place** in the 'Kloos'.

Aarwangen BE

7☐B1

Reformed church: Built in late Gothic style by Antoni Stab of Zofingen 1576–7. The windows have coats-of-arms, those in the choir dating from the time the church was built. The **'Tierlihaus'** of 1767 belonged to the owner of a travelling menagerie, who had had the façades painted with pictures of exotic animals. At the river crossing stands the **Schloss,** which originally belonged to the Lords of Aarwangen. It was then in the hands of the Lords of Grünenberg and, from 1432 it was the seat of a Bernese governor. In the 16C a knight's house was built alongside the 13C keep.

Abbaye, L' VD
10 □ C1

The site of a former Premonstratensian monastery founded in 1126, of which the Gothic **church tower** and a 16C cloister arcade (rebuilt 1971) have survived.
Les Bioux Reformed church: A wooden building from 1698.

Adelboden BE
11 □ F4

The **Reformed church of St. Anton,** built in 1433, contains modern stainedglass by Augusto Giacometti. On an exterior wall there is there is a late Gothic painting of the Last Judgement (1471).

Adelwil LU
see NEUENKIRCH   7 □ E3

Adligenswil LU
7 □ F3

Catholic church of St.Martin: Built by Franz and Joseph Händle 1825-7, it has classical altars and Biedermeier choir stalls. The **chapel of St.Jodokus** on the Dottenberg is neo-Gothic by Wilhelm Keller and dates from 1863. Altar paintings are by Paul Deschwanden.

Aesch BL
1 □ F4

The stately residential building, parts of the courtyard wall and various outbuildings have survived from the **Schloss,** which was built 1604-7 for the Bishop of Basel, Jacob Christoph Blarer of

Aeschi: the Reformed church has Gothic wall paintings.

Wartensee; today it is the municipal hall. The castle barn houses a *Local History Museum.* **Secondary School:** Unfaced reinforced concrete building by Walter M.Förderer, Rolf Georg Otto and Hans Zwimpfer, 1958-62. At the highest point of the Gmeiniwald there is a Neolithic **dolmen tomb.**

Aeschi bei Spiez BE
12 □ A2

Reformed church of St. Petrus: Flatroofed Romanesque single-aisled church incorporating a 13C choir; altered 1517-20. The wall paintings in the choir date from the mid 14C. Fine features include the Romanesque font, the late Gothic tabernacle, the late Renaissance choir stalls and 3 glass windows dating from 1519.

Aetingen SO
6 □ F2

Reformed parish church: Built in 1502 and enlarged at the end of the 17C, it is one of a charming group of buildings which in-

Aigle: the Château is one of the most important fortresses in Switzerland.

clude the **priest's house** (1654), the **parish barn** (1794) and the **Pfrundstöckli.**

Aeugst ZH

8☐A1

Reformed parish church: Single-aisled church dating from 1667. In the square groin-vaulted choir there is a plaque with a coat-of-arms. The chancel arch and window jambs are painted. Complete renovation in 1967.

Affeltrangen TG

3☐D3

Reformed church: Nave and tower in part 13–14C, choir 15C. Altered in 1882 & 1934. The **Reformed church** NE of Affeltrangen, in MARWIL was built in 1885 by August Keller as a neo-Byzantine basilica.

Agettes, Les VS

See SION   17☐E2

Agno TI

19☐D4

Former priory church of Santi Giovanni e Provino: Built in 1760 on the site of an earlier church. The centrally-planned building is domed and has a neoclassical façade from the late 19C. In an adjoining building there is a small archaeological and local history *Museum.*

Aigle VD

17☐B1

A small market town at some distance from the castle, it has belonged to the House of Savoy from 1076 although its real growth has been from the 13C onwards. The Bernese captured the town in 1476 and ruled it until 1798. **Château:** One of the most important in the canton. The exact date of its foundation is unknown but in the 12C it was administered by the 'Nobles of Aigle', vidames under the House of Savoy. After capture by the Bernese, it was almost entirely rebuilt. The trapezoidal lay out is dominated by 3 round towers and a square keep (apart from the towers and machicolations, this is the oldest part of the castle). Inside are the residential quarters, including the former residence of the Bernese governor, one of whom was Albrecht von Haller (1761 – 3); these quarters now house two museums. Next to the castle is a huge 17C **barn**. In Cloître, the oldest quarter, stands the **Reformed church of St-Maurice**, which was first documented in the 12C and formerly belonged to a now- vanished priory founded by the Abbey of St-Maurice. The Romanesque building was succeeded in the 15C by a Gothic church (17C front tower). In the town, the **German Reformed church of St-Jacques** is medieval in origin with a tower of 1642. Here the reformer G.Farel (1489–1565) preached; he lived at house No. 10 in the street named after him. **Rue de Jérusalem:** Picturesque alley with houses connected by arcades. The Château d'Aigle houses a *Museum of Wine and Salt*.

Allaman: 15&16C Château.

form dates from the 19C; the hotel dates from 1866 and the former toll building from 1838.

Aino GR

See Poschiavo   14☐F4

Airolo TI

13☐B3

A small town which developed with the opening of the St.Gotthard Pass in the 13C and was almost totally destroyed by fire in 1877. **Catholic parish church of Santi Nazario e Celso:** Built in the 12C and first documented in 1224; rebuilt after the town fire in 1879. The tower, crowned by a double row of twin arches, has survived from the Romanesque building. Near the station is the **Memorial for the Victims of the building of the St. Gotthard Tunnel,** a bronze bas-relief by Vincenzo Vela (1820–91).

Gotthardhospiz The St. Gotthard Pass was not used as a connecting route until the 13C at which time the hospice is said to have been built next to the chapel. The latter, which succeeded a small church of the 9–10C, was consecrated in 1230 and rebuilt at the end of the 17C by the Capuchin fathers, who ran the hospice until 1799. The former **Hospice** was destroyed in 1777 & 1779 and in its present

Alberswil LU

7☐C2

The **chapel of St. Blasius** on Burgrain hill dates from 1682 and is Gothic in its proportions. Old coffered ceilings in nave and choir. The **Herrenhaus Kasteln** was built for Heinrich von Sonnenberg in 1682. The T-shaped building with its two garden pavilions is an early example of a baroque country estate in the canton of Lucerne. **Kasteln ruins:** This fortress, which was destroyed in the Peasant's War of 1653, has belonged successively to the Lenzburgs, Kyburgs and Habsburgs. The masonry consists of dressed tufa blocks. *Burgrain Agricultural Museum* (opening hours according to season or by personal application).

Allaman VD

10☐D3

Reformed church of St-Jean: Documented from the 14C; the choir windows and side chapels are late Gothic. **Château:** 15–16C; rebuilt in 18C. Consists of two wings at right-angles to each other and a massive square tower at the SW corner; overlooking the courtyard there is a baroque façade with arches. Near the church is the **Maison de Rochefort,** a fortified building with a round tower, probably of medieval origin.

Allmendingen BE

11 □ F1

Schlösschen: Built in Renaissance style by the Graffenried family at the start of the 17C but only the main building with the staircase tower date from this time. The summerhouse and connecting rooms are baroque extensions.

Allschwil BL

1 □ F3

Typical Sundgau half-timbered buildings are loosely clustered around the **Catholic parish church of St. Peter und Paul,** which is a simple single-aisled church with polygonal apse built 1698–9 on the foundations of earlier buildings. The classical interior dates from 1841; wooden figures of the church's two patron saints have survived from a late Gothic altar. *Local Museum,* Baslerstr.48.

Alpnach OW

7 □ E4

Catholic parish church of St. Maria Magdalena: Built 1812–20. The tower, which is topped by a very pointed spire, dates from 1887. Essentially classical the building has a complicated ground plan and there is a surprising disparity between interior and exterior architectural forms. In SCHORIED, SW of Alpnach, stands the **chapel of St. Theodul,** which was built in 1711. Baroque ceiling paintings inside depict scenes from the life of the saint.

Alt-St. Johann SG

8 □ F2

Reformed church, formerly a chapel, enlarged in 1817 & 1861. The **former Benedictine Abbey** was founded *c.* 1150 and abandoned after a fire in 1626. The former monastery church is today the **Catholic parish church of St. Johann,** which was rebuilt 1869 – 70 by Johann Christoph Kunkler and altered and

lengthened 1939–40. The tower over the N. entrance to the choir dates from *c.* 1770. The **former priory,** now a priest's house, is a wooden building dating from 1626. **Wildmannlisloch** at Selun in the Churfirsten. Resting place for nomadic cavebear hunters; hearths and tools from the Palaeolithic Age; finds of cave-bear bones. E. of Alt-St. Johann, in UNTERWASSER, is the *Toggenburger Senntumsmuseum* of the Bosshard-Frischknecht family.

Altbüron LU

7 □ B2

Chapel of St. Antonius von Padua, built in 1683. Side altars from *c.* 1700.

Altdorf UR

8 □ B5

Capital of the canton of Uri, the town probably dates back to the 10C and became important in the early 13C when the St. Gotthard Pass was made accessible with the bridging of the Schöllenen Gorge. In 1231 the Uri valley became part of the Empire and in 1291 Uri joined with Schwyz and Unterwalden to protect its independence. In 1403, and again following setbacks in 1439, Uri assumed the protectorate of the Leventina valley, thereby securing the southern access to the St. Gotthard Pass. In 1410 the valleys of Uri and Urseren formed a union. In the 15&16C Uri attempted — often without success — to divert Swiss expansionist desires towards the S. The defeat at Marignano in 1515 ended the Confederation's aspirations of being a great power, although Bellinzona remained in the hands of the Old Cantons. In 1798 the Leventina was freed from its bond to Uri. Uri's participation in Schwyz's resistance against the Swiss Republic and its importance as a transit route for foreign armies led to difficulties for Uri *c.* 1800. The extension of the St. Gotthard road in 1830–40, the St. Gotthard railway line (tunnel constructed in 1880) and the St. Gotthard road tunnel (opened 1980) have, however, strengthened Uri's position as a centre of road and rail

Altdorf: the 1895 Tell monument is in front of a former residence tower.

communications in the central Alps. Modern Altdorf has many buildings dating from after the fire of 1799. The **Catholic parish church of St.Martin** was rebuilt 1800–10 by Josef Rey. It is single-aisled with two transept-like side chapels; the classical furnishings have survived and some of the stucco is early 17C. Close by is the two-storey late Gothic **cemetery chapel of St. Anna.** The **Capuchin Monastery,** the first to be founded in Switzerland (1581), owes its existence to the influence of the Milanese Cardinal Carlo Borromeo who wanted to strengthen the Counter Reformation by extending the order N. of the Alps. The church, consecrated in 1585, was rebuilt 1804–7. The **Capuchin Monastery of St.Karl** in the S. of the town and founded in 1677, was one of the few buildings to be spared the fire of 1799, which was spread by a storm. **Rathaus:** Rebuilt in classical style by Niklaus Purtschert 1805–6. Inside there is a splendid collection of Uri's old banners. The medieval **tower** nearby is a residential tower, which was sold to the community in 1517; the dome dates from 1808. In front of the tower is the **Monu-**

ment to **William Tell,** by Richard Kissling (1895). The landscape background, after an original design by Hans Sandreuter, depicts the Schächen valley, his legendary home. The **Fremdenspital,** rebuilt in 1551 and again in 1803, was for the use of impoverished travellers. Its narrow courtyard is bordered by the two main wings and the façade of the 18C chapel. The **Suworow-Haus** owes its name to the Russian General Suvorov's setting up his quarters here in 1799 after his troops had secured passage through the Schöllenen Gorge in spite of bitter French resistance. The house dates from the 16C and is one of the oldest buildings in Altdorf, having survived the town fires of 1693 & 1799. The **Haus von Roll** (today Kantonalbank), built in 1562 for the knight Walter von Roll, was rebuilt in classical form after 1799. Walter von Roll (*c.* 1520 –91) was one of the leaders of the Counter Reformation in Switzerland and a friend of Cardinal Carlo Borromeo of Milan. The detached **Haus im Eselmätteli** (now an administrative building of the Altdorf EW) dates from the 17C and was refurbished in 1764 in rococo style. Above the cemetery, amid terraced gardens, is the **'Oberes Vogelsang',** built sometime after 1815, whose curved gables call to mind the baroque. On a site once occupied by a public scales for butter and salt (documented since the 16C) stands the **'Ankenwaage',** a house of 1824. Attached to the back of the Biedermeier building is the **Hexenturm,** originally the prison. **Dätwyler AG factory building:** Built in 1947 to the plans of Otto von Salvisberg. The growth of the firm in the mid-war period was important for the town after its economy had been seriously threatened by the building of the St.Gotthard railway. The *Historical Museum* is housed in a neo-Gothic building of 1905 in Gotthardstrasse.

Altendorf SZ

8 □ C2

Grouped together in the heart of the village are the 15C **parish church of St. Michael,** the **Ossuary of St.Anna** and the **priest's house.** High above the village lies the **chapel of St.Johann,** which was consecrated in 1476 on the site of the ancestral seat of the Counts of Rapperswil, itself destroyed in 1350. The tower was built in 1483; the belfry with its steep saddle-roof dates from 1891.

Altiroli TI
See GIORNICO   13☐C5

Altishofen LU
                                               7☐C2

The **parish church of St.Martin,** built by Jakob Singer, and the Gothic **castle** of 1575–7 are the main features in this well-preserved and rather straggly village. The castle was formerly the residence of the 'Swiss King', Oberst Ludwig Pfyffer von Altishofen (1524–94).

Altnau TG
                                               3☐F2

The **Landschlacht Chapel** was built on the old pilgrim route from Constance to St.Gallen in the 11–12C on the site of a building from the first millennium AD. The choir was extended to the width of the nave in 14C. Important wall paintings include a Passion cycle on the S. wall from the mid 14C and another from the end of the 15C on the W. wall. In the choir there is a life of St.Leonard from 1432 with prophets, saints and a Crucifixion.

Altstätten SG
                                               4☐B4

Small country town at the foot of the Apenzell massif. The houses, most of which are 18C, have steep, often curved gables. Continuous arcades above street level, particularly on the northern Marktgasse. **Catholic parish church of St. Nikolaus:** Built 1794–8 by Johann Ulrich Haltiner and altered 1909–10; classical furnishing. **Reformed church:** Neo-Gothic, built by Paul Reber 1904–6. **Gut-Hirt church** by the station was built in 1966 by Baumgartner and Bächtold,

Altnau: Landschlacht chapel, fragment of the Passion cycle.

with wall reliefs of Coghuf (by Ernst Stocker) and sculptures by Silvio Mattioli. **Rathaus:** By Hans Burkard, 1959–60. **Reburg** (Rathausplatz 1): Built in 1772 by Johann Jakob Haltiner. **Prestegg:** On the Obergasse. Built in 1488 as the mansion of the St.Gallen representative, von Rappenstein; S. wing 1788, N. part rebuilt in 1867 and now a *Local History Museum.* **Frauenhof** (Marktgasse 56): Built in the 2nd half of the 15C and greatly altered since. Opposite is the **Placiduskapelle,** built in 1646 by the Monastery of St. Gallen. The **Untertor** on Engelplatz is the sole survivor of 4 original gates. In its present form it goes back to the rebuilding of 1823. The **Capuchin Convent of Maria-Hilf** to the S. of the town was consecrated in 1616 and extended 1733–4; the church was altered in 1966 and has a Gothic Pietà (1350–70) and stained glass by Ferdinand Gehr (1966). **Forstkapelle** on the range of hills to the S. of the town is late medieval with stained glass by Ferdinand Gehr (1963). **Castle of Neu-Altstätten:** Documented in 1388 and rebuilt after its destuction in 1404.

Alvaschein GR
                                               14☐B1

MISTAIL. **Church of St. Peter:** Carolingian single-aisled church with three apses from the 2nd half of the 8C. A former convent, it was elevated between 1098 & 1180. Archaeological excavations in 1968 –9 uncovered evidence of several previous buildings, including the N. convent building, an early medieval tomb building in the S. (shelter), as well as a former N. annex of the church. Tower and sacristy date from *c.* 1400, the ossuary is later. The most recent restoration dates from 1967– 79. The horseshoe apses have 3 Carolingian altar slabs. Flat wooden ceiling from 1645. Remains of Carolingian wall paintings on the nave walls and in the apses are thematically related to those in the Carolingian church in Müstair (GR). Gothic wall paintings: the flattened dome of the central apse has Christ in a mandorla with the Evangelists' symbols and the 12 Apostles in a row below. Beneath this are St. George and the Dragon, knight saints and an Adoration of the Magi (early 15C). Paintings on the N. wall include a large St. Christopher and above the side portal St. Gallus, the consecration of the church with St. Peter and the so-called Feast Day Christ.

Alvaschein: Carolingian church of St. Peter in Mistail, with three apses.

Amden SG

8 □ E2

Catholic parish church of St. Gallus: Founded in the 13C, nave extended in 1794, restored in 1923. Elongated nave with tower over the choir. **Gmür-Haus** in Vorderächern: Toggenburg-style mansion built in the early 19C and the family home of a branch of the Gmür family. Inside are 17C family portraits. **Strahlegg ruin:** (In Betlis, S. of Amden near the bank of the Walensee.) A Habsburg tower from the 14C, which was originally a Roman watch tower.

Amlikon TG

3 □ D3

Picturesque village square with **half-timbered buildings.** In Leutmerken is a **non-denominational church** first mentioned in 1275. Rebuilding in 1462 and later. Nave is Romanesque up to the height of the window ledges, above this it dates from 1634 like the choir. Tower 1556.

Alavaschein: Feiertagschristus inside St. Peter, Mistail.

Amsoldingen: the Reformed church is the largest Ottonian basilica in the region.

Ammerswil AG

2 □ E5

Reformed parish church: Late Romanesque single-aisled church with a closed choir added in 1640; late Gothic saddle-roofed tower. The church is part of a group of buildings which include the classical **priest's house** (1783) by Carl Ahasver of Sinner. Two-storey **tithe barn** with covered gallery (1685).

Amriswil TG

3 □ F3

The industrialization of the 19&20C has clearly left its mark on the town. **Reformed church:** Built in 1892 by August Hardegger in neo-Gothic style. Interior conversion in 1922 & 1943–4. **Catholic church:** This concrete building, built by Paul Büchi in 1939, was one of the first modern churches in the canton. Stained glass by Otto Steiger, frescos by Carl Roesch. **Half-timbered buildings** nearby include: No. 13 in Rüti (late 17C), the Hubhof in Mühlebach (1813) and the half-timbered house in Moos, which projects

above a front portico on turned wooden columns (1737). The **Gasthaus zum Goldenen Löwen** in OBERAACH, built in 1711, is one of the most lavish half-timbered houses in Switzerland. The courtroom and ante room on the first floor have coffered ceilings with intarsia work. HAGENWIL Schloss Hagenwil, SE of Amriswil. Built in the early 13C by the Crusader Rudolf von Hagenwil, it is a moated castle with drawbridge (1741), 13C keep, Great Hall from *c.* 1551, E. wing 1786, 16C chapel. It was altered in 1786 and refurbished. Since 1830 there has been a restaurant in the gallery.

Amsoldingen BE

11 □ F2

The **former priory church of St. Mauritius** is one of a group of churches with Lombard characteristics (see S. Ambrogio in Mailand) built on the bank of the Thunersee around the turn of the millennium. Like the church in Spiez this one is a transeptless pillared basilica with 3 apses and elevated choir above the crypt. Later alterations, particularly to the E. end, include the Gothic saddle-roofed tower. The outside of the apse is articulated with pilaster strips, a frieze of round arches and a ring of niches.

Amsteg UR
13 □ B1

Zwing-Uri ruins: Substructure of a castle tower built at the end of the 13C and apparently destroyed before completion. The castle is reputed to have been begun by Governor Gessler; Friedrich Schiller, in his play 'Wilhelm Tell', transferred Zwing-Uri to Altdorf according to an older tradition.

Andeer GR
14 □ A2

Reformed church: Baroque building of 1673, incorporating a choir tower from a previous building (*c.*1580, the same date as the late Gothic font inside the church). **Haus Pedrun:** Probably built in 1501 and completely covered in sgraffiti dating from *c.* 1560–70.

Andelfingen ZH
3 □ B3

Capital of the Zurich wine-growing region, it has been a market town since the 13C. The **town centre** oozes with history and abounds in interesting old buildings, including the **Schloss** of 1780–2 (now an old people's home) and neighbouring buildings like the **Alte Kanzlei** of 1697 and the **Gasthof Löwen,** the oldest parts of which go back to the 16C. **Reformed parish church:** This single-aisled church was rebuilt 1666–7 on the site of a previous church mentioned as early as 1260. In 1860 it was enlarged following the removal of the old choir tower and Johann Caspar Wolff built the distinctive neo-Gothic tower in 1861 - 2. **Covered wooden bridge** over the Thur to Kleinandelfingen dates from 1814–5.

Andermatt: the Rathaus was rebuilt after a fire in 1762.

Andermatt UR
13 □ A/B2

Main town of the Urseren valley, which was settled by people from Goms in the 11&12C. Part of the E-W connection in the Central Alps, it was for centuries within the Disentis Abbey's sphere of influence. **Catholic parish church of St. Peter und Paul:** Built in the early 17C and converted to baroque by the local architect Bartholomáus Schmid. It replaced the oldest parish church in the valley, the **Catholic church of St.Kolumban,** at the N. exit of the town, which may date back to a Carolingian foundation. The latter is a simple late Romanesque building from the 13C with a rectangular late-Gothic choir. **Pilgrimage chapel of Maria-Hilf:** This baroque chapel from 1739–42 has a little tower and is visible from afar because of its elevated setting. **Rathaus:** A stone building of 1767 built following a village fire, it includes parts of a 16C building. Now the administrative centre of the Urseren Corporation, the successor to the old valley community which, when joined with the Uri Valley in 1410 preserved its independence for centuries.

Andiast/Andest GR

13☐E1

Catholic parish church of St. Julitta und Quiricus: Rebuilt in baroque style in 1707; extended W. and renovated in 1939. 11C Romanesque tower. High altar (1669–70) by Joh. Baptist Wickart from the parish church of Boswil (AG).

Andwil SG

3☐F4

Catholic parish church of St. Otmar: Built 1731–2 by Joh. Pfister; lengthened and renovated by Albert Rimli 1932–3. **Former Gasthaus Hirschen,** to the E. of the church was built in 1732 by Johann Grütter. One of the bedrooms has rural rococo paintings.

Angenstein BE

1☐F4

Not far from Aesch, enthroned above the narrow end of the Birs Valley, is **Schloss Angenstein,** a 13C fortress built by the Bishops of Basel and later in the possession of the Counts of Thierstein. An earthquake of 1356 and fires of 1494 & 1517 resulted in extensive 16C rebuilding, e.g. the chapel and residential buildings right next to the gutted tower.

Anzonico TI

13☐C4

Catholic parish church of San Giovanni Battista: Late 17C, single-aisled building with rectangular choir. S. side altar from 1791; late 18C furnishings.

Appenzell AI

4☐A4

Main town of the half-canton of Appenzell-Innerrhoden, it was first mentioned in 1071 as Abbacella when it had a bailiff's court and parish church. After 1200 Appenzell was divided into Rhoden (tax and military districts). Originally belonging to the Prince-Abbot of St. Gallen, the individual communities formed the Appenzell in 1378. 1401–8 Appenzell Wars of Independence. In 1411 the Monastery of St. Gallen relinquished all claims to power. Appenzell became part of the Confederation in 1513. During the Reformation the inner Rhoden remained Catholic while the outer ones adopted the Protestant doctrine and in 1597 it was divided into the Catholic Innerrhoden and Protestant Ausserrhoden. For the Ausserrhoden the economic base was hand-weaving, while the Innerrhoden remained mainly agricultural. Under the Swiss Republic the half-cantons were joined with St. Gallen to form the Canton of Säntis. Before 1848 the Innerrhoden tended to be conservative, although they did not join the Sonderbund. Appenzell is notable for buildings dating from after the fire of 1560. Wooden houses, partly brightly painted with curved or stepped gables, give it its special character, which is particularly visible in the row of houses in the **Hauptgasse.** The **Landesgemeindeplatz** with the old court linden tree is unevenly lined with tall and low buildings. The **Catholic parish church of St. Mauritius,** occupies an elevated position above the left bank of the Sitter. It has a W. tower, polygonal apse, crypt from *c.* 1513 and parts from after 1560. Nave by Enoch Breitenmoser, 1823. Inside there is a broad classical nave with double galleries, neo-baroque ceiling paintings (1891) by Franz Vettiger and high altar by Bartholomáus Cades, 1622. The late Gothic choir has wall and vault paintings from the 16,17&18C, including a view of the village by Moritz Girtanner, *c.* 1620. **Reformed church:** Built 1908–9 by La Roche and Stähelin. **Heiligkreuzkapelle** on the Hauptgasse was built in 1561 with a portal of 1787 and stained glass by Ferdinand Gehr installed in the renovation of 1963 – 5. The **Capuchin Monastery of Mariä Lichtmess** at the W. entrance to the village was founded 1586–7. The *church,* with early baroque altars, was rebuilt in 1688, the *monastery* in 1925 by Hans Burkard.

Appenzell: typical painted house of the Appenzell type.

The church's high altar has a Descent from the Cross by Giulio C.Proccaccini, 1605. The right side altar has a Virgin with Saints(1610 – 20); the left side altar has Mariä Lichtmess (1935) by Johann Hugentobler. **Capuchin convent of Maria der Engel is to the** S. of the Hauptgasse. The *church* was built in late Renaissance style 1621 – 2 by the Misox masters Giovanni ('Altern') and Andrea Toscano; coffered barrel vault within. The *convent buildings* were built 1679 – 82 by Jost Mosbrugger and Christian Zünd based on a model by Father Marquard Imfeld. **Rathaus:** Late Gothic building of 1561 – 3 by Hans Bilchenfelder. Façade frescos with depictions from the history of Appenzell by Aug. Schmid, 1928. The council chambers have wall paintings by Caspar Hagenbach the Younger, 1567. **Landeskanzlei:** Built 1914 by Adolf Gaudy with a new wing by Hans Burkard (1954). Next to the Capuchin convent stands the so-called **Schloss**, a patrician's house built 1563– 70 in late-Gothic style with Renaissance features. Also predominantly Gothic, but with a classical extension, is the **Haus Ebneter-Kölbener,** No.183. The ground floor has wall paintings of the 8 Virtues by

Caspar Hagenbach the Younger, *c.* 1580. **Houses** typical of the local style are the 'Kreuz', No.242, 'Raben', No.238 and numbers 223 – 8 on the Hauptgasse, as well as the uniform group of houses comprising Dr. Breitenmoser/Leo Linherr/Gasthaus Falken/J.Brülisauer on Gaiserstrasse. The *Bruno Bischofberger Collection* includes Appenzell peasant painting.
W. of the village is the **chapel of St.Anton** in Rinkenbach, built in 1661 with an early baroque high altar from 1666, Knorpelstil pulpit of 1673 and 18C side altars. N. of Appenzell, in Mettlen auf der Steig is the **chapel of St.Karl** built in 1620. Also in Mettlen is the **covered wooden bridge** over the Sitter, built *c.* 1766 by a member of the architect family Grubenmann. The **chapel of Maria in Sonnenhalb,** S. of Appenzell, dates originally from 1796 with rebuilding in 1861; rural late baroque altar with a Gothic Pietà in the Soft Style from *c.* 1400. N. of Appenzell lies the castle hill with the **Clanx ruin,** built in 1219 under Abbot Ulrich VI of St.Gallen. Its destruction in 1402 by the rebellious peasants triggered the Appenzell wars of independence in 1401. Excavated 1949.

Arbedo: the Catholic parish church has fragments of Gothic frescos.

Aquila TI

13□D4

Catholic parish church of San Vittore Mauro: Documented since 1213 and rebuilt in 1728. Remains of medieval features on the S. façade and in the lower part of the tower, rest baroque. The furnishings are mainly 18C. The triumphal arch has a 15C wooden crucifix.

Arare GE

16□E2

Fortified House: Typical seat of a local lord, it was built *c.* 1500 and is rectangular with a semicircular staircase tower in the middle of the main façade.

Arbedo TI

19□E2

Suburb of Bellinzona (famous for the defeat which the Confederacy suffered at the hands of the Milanese in 1422). In the old part of the village is the **Catholic parish church of Santa Maria Assunta,** which is medieval in origin and has been enlarged and rebuilt from 1625 onwards. The choir has frescos by Baldassare Orelli from *c.* 1700. Stucco decoration in the side chapels and Gothic frescos on the N. wall of the nave. Close to the station, near the oil tank,

is **San Paolo,** known as Chiesa Rossa. The Swiss who fell at Arbedo are buried in the graveyard. The first church dating from the 8C was rebuilt in the 12–13C around the surviving Romanesque tower. The building was enlarged after 1422 when it acquired its definitive form. Inside, the nave has a wooden ceiling of 1540; the walls have 15&16C frescos.

Arbon TG

4□A2

The area has been settled since the Neolithic Age and there are early Bronze Age lake dwellings around Bleiche. During the 4C the Roman post station *Arbor Felix* was extended into a fort in the area today occupied by the church and castle. In the 13C the town acquired first a market, then a charter. The former enclosure of the **fort** with its semicircular towers is preserved in the castle fortifications. On the substructure of the fortress wall and the SE tower is the **Galluskapelle,** possibly founded in the 7C. In the wall to the left of the entrance a boulder bears the 'footprint of St.Gallus', who built the embankment here in 612. Romanesque nave, polygonal apse from 1768. Inside remains of 14C frescos reveal the style of the Lake Constance School. **Catholic parish church of St.Martin:** The present complex stands on the site of a Romanesque basilica. Nave 1786–9, choir 1490, tower 1457, Tudor style spire 1895. Inside, late Gothic figure of the Virgin Mary. **Schloss:** Mid-13C keep with top storey from 1520; high entrances on the town side and to the E; domestic quarters *c.* 1515. **Catholic priest's house** formerly the Rotes House, was built in 1704 and altered in 1783 in the style of the late rococo. The old quarter to the W. of the castle contains the **Rathaus,** a half-timbered building from 1791. The **Stadthaus** on the Hauptstrasse was formerly the seat of a linen baron. It was altered for the Alberti linen barons 1768–9 and converted into a town hall by Oskar Linner in 1941. The *Town Museum* in the castle has a local history collection.

Ardez: the ruined Burg Steinsberg is on a hill E. of the village.

Arconciel FR
See **ILLENS**   11 □ C1

Ardez GR
                                                  15 □ A3

Houses decorated with sgraffiti or paintings abound in this village and make it a
superb example of an Unterengadine settlement. **Reformed church:** First mentioned in the 12C, the tower was rebuilt in
1445, the church was rebuilt 1576-7 and
restored in 1948. This double-aisled gallery church is typical of the Reformed
church and in style reflects the transition
from late Gothic to Renaissance.
Steinsberg Castle ruins: Probably
founded in the 12C, the castle was destroyed by the Austrians in 1499. Parts to
have survived include the keep, remains of
the enclosing wall and the ruins of the
former Chapel of St.Luzius, (a Romanesque single-aisled church with semicircular apse).
SUR EN: Reformed Filialkirche: This unarticulated Romanesque single-aisled church
was probably built in the early 13C. The
tower in the NW corner of the nave is late
17C.

Ardon VS
                                                  17 □ D2

Catholic parish church of St-Jean:
Neo-Gothic, built in 1892 by Emile
Vuilloud; front tower 1525. The (still visible) excavations of 1959-60 revealed remains of preceeding buildings, the oldest
of which goes back to the 5 or 6C.

Arenenberg TG
See **SALENSTEIN**   3 □ D2

Argnoud VS
See **AYENT**   17 □ E1

Arlesheim BL
                                                   2 □ A4

The residence of the chapter of Basel
(1679 - 1792) comprises the **Collegiate
Church, canons' houses** and the **Cathedral Square,** laid out to the designs
of the Misox architect Jakob Engel in
1679-87. The façade and interior of the
church were altered in splendid rococo
style by Franz Anton Bagnato, 1759-61;
the stucco is the work of Francesco Pozzi

Arlesheim: baroque collegiate church with rococo interior.

after a model by Johann Michael Feuchtmayer. Wall, ceiling and altar paintings are by Giuseppe Appiani and the organ was made by Johann Andreas Silbermann. It has been the Catholic parish church since 1812. The **Reformed church,** built to plans by Emanuel La Roche 1911–12, displays numerous styles which combine to create an unorthodox overall effect. The **Bezirksstatthalteramt** (district governor's office), a former canon's house beyond the residence, dates from 1761 when the cathedral was altered. Also built by the chapter, but somewhat earlier, is the house at Domstrasse 2, which was converted into a patrician's house with an English garden 1812 & 1851. Between the **Andlauerhof,** an aristocratic seat of 1616 (conversions before 1754 and 1815) which has superb furnishings, and the **Birseck Castle ruins,** originally 13C, stretches the **Eremitage,** an artistic landscape garden with a mill, gardener's house, caves, grottoes and hermitage, designed with a romantic love of nature by Balbina von Andlau-Staal and Canon Heinrich von Ligertz; extensions and alterations date from before 1793 and 1810–12.

Arogno TI

19 □ D4

Catholic parish church of Santo Stefano: Baroque, built in 1638 with an apse of 1839. The choir has a classical high altar and Renaissance wall tabernacle from the early 16C. 18C frescos in the dome. On

Arosio: Catholic parish church with important 16C wall paintings.

the N. side is the stucco-adorned chapel of the Madonna of the Rosary and the chapel of St. Antony with trompe l'oeil frescos of 1730. Nearby is a baroque **ossuary.** 2 km. from the village towards Rovio lies the **church of San Michele:** Romanesque, baroque conversion.

Arosio TI

19 □ D3

Opposite the cemetery stands the **Catholic parish church of San Michele:** Built 1640 – 7 it incorporates part of a 14C building. 18C porch on S. side. The church has a nave, two side chapels with stucco and a rectangular choir which was formerly vaulted. The walls of the nave and choir have important frescos from the early 16C by Antonio da Tradate and his workshop; also fragments of 14C frescos.

Arth SZ

8 □ A3

This town became important as the port

serving the old St.Gotthard route. **Catholic parish church of St. Georg und Zeno:** Built by Jeremias Schmid 1695-6, it was one of the first large baroque churches in central Switzerland. The tower, connected to the nave by a vestibule, comes from an earlier building from the 14C. The interior has wall pillars with pilasters on which the heavily-stuccoed vault ribs rest. **Chapel of St.Georg,** built 1652-4 on the site of the town's oldest parish church, it is now a cemetery chapel. In the 17C on the site of a second parish church dedicated to St. Zeno, a **Capuchin church and monastery** were built. The Capuchins were invited in 1655 when the discovery of a secret Protestant community in Arth necessitated the protection of the Catholic faith. On the **Dorfplatz** (village square), in front of the parish church, stands the **Rathaus,** built in 1721.

Arzo TI

19 ☐ D5

In the middle of the village is the **Catholic parish church of Santi Nazario e Celso,** which is probably 16C. It has a nave, two aisles, rectangular choir and entrance atrium. The interior furnishing are made of local marble. 18C high altar. The N. side altar has an 18C statue of the Virgin Mary; the S. side altar a 15C crucifix. S. of the village stands the church of **Santa Maria del Ponte;** an octagonal building from the 17C. A niche in the façade has a stucco statue of the Virgin Mary of the same date. On the street leading to the bridge is the 18C **Haus Allio** , which has an elegant portal beneath a two-storey loggia.

Ascona TI

19 ☐ C2

In the Middle Ages Ascona, which was already settled in prehistoric times, was protected by four castles, all of which have now disappeared. It has been the home of numerous artistic families. In the middle of the village is the **Catholic parish church of Santi Pietro e Paolo.**

Ascona: Casa Serodine with 17C stuccoed façade.

Ascona: two-storey arcade in the 16C Collegio Papio.

Documented since 1264, it was rebuilt in the 16C and has a nave, two aisles, polygonal chancel and an elegant bell tower in the S. The choir vault has frescos by P.Francesco Pancaldi, known as Mola, *c.* 1770; the high altar has a painting of the Coronation of the Virgin by Giovanni Serodine (1599-1630); two further paintings by the same artist can be seen on the W. wall. On the Via Bartolomeo Papio, next to the college of the same name, is the church of **Santa Maria della Misericordia,** built in 1399-1422 and containing an important late Gothic fresco cycle. The choir walls have scenes from the Old and New Testaments (15C); the walls of the nave and the triumphal arch have frescos from the 15–16C. At the choir entrance there is a Renaissance polyptych by Antonio de Lagaia (1519). Next to the church is the **College,** founded by Bartolomeo Papio and built from 1584 onwards. There is an elegant Renaissance courtyard and a bas-relief of 1602 on the N. entrance. Near the church of Santi Pietro e Paolo is the **Casa Serodine**, built *c.* 1620 by Cristoforo and G.Battista Serodine. The 3-storeyed façade is richly decorated with stucco: historical friezes and recumbent figures crown the windows with the Virgin and Child in the middle. Near the town exit towards Losone there are remains of the castle of San Materno, one of Ascona's vanished castles. A Romanesque **chapel** with round apse and a fresco with a depiction of Christ have survived.

Assens VD

10□E2

Non-denominational parish church of St-Germain: Used up to and during the last century by both Catholics and Protestants. This single-aisled building with a rectangular choir of two bays dates from 1454, the front tower from 1717. The nave walls have Gothic frescos. A wrought-iron grille of 1696 divides the nave from the choir which contains a baroque altar with an altarpiece of 1649–50 by the sculptor J.F.Reyff of Fribourg.

Attalens FR

11□A4

Mentioned in 1274 when it was a property of the Lords of Oro. Since that time Attalens has had several owners before it was acquired by Fribourg in 1615 and made into a Vogtei. The **Château,** thought to date from the 12–13C, was partly rebuilt after 1615; drastic alterations in the 19C have completely changed its appearance.

Attinghausen UR

8□B5

Haus Schweinsberg, visible for miles, was probably built in the 14C by the Barons of Attinghausen-Schweinsberg, who came to the region and were a family with many branches. The nearby **castle ruins** underline the rapid decline of this once-mighty line, which played a considerable part in the setting up of the Confederation. The family held the title Landammann of Uri for more than 50 years, when it would seem the castle was besieged and destroyed in an unchronicled uprising of the valley population.

Attiswil BE

7□A1

Heimatmuseum, Dorfstr.5. A small collection of local interest housed in an 18C 'Heidenstock'.

Au SG

4□B3

Catholic parish church of Mariä Geburt: Built 1924–5 in neo-baroque style by Albert Rimli. Ceiling painting of 1950 by Siegfried Herforth. The **Reformed church** was built by Max Künzler in 1953.

Au Peninsula ZH

See WADENSWIL   8□B1

Aubonne VD

10□D3

Finds from the Hallstatt period, Roman architectural remains and Burgundian tombs indicate a continuous settlement. The first château was built in the 11 or 12C by the Lords of Aubonne and the settlement developed around this; a charter of 1234 awarded significant liberties. Power changed hands several times, until it was sold to Bern in 1701; government from Bern up to 1798. In the still extensive and

Aubonne: the Château has an important baroque arcade.

well-preserved **Old Town** there are remains of the former fortifications, including two gates. **Château:** Built in the 11&12C and extensively rebuilt in the 17C by the traveller J.B.Tavernier and Admiral H.Duquesne. The former was responsible for the baroque palace and round tower with onion dome built on the foundations (still visible) of the old square keep. The latter added the arcaded courtyard inside the palace. In the courtyard there is a Roman bas-relief of two gladiators, and a milestone; the courtroom has a painted ceiling of 1670. **Reformed church:** Originally the chapel of St.Etienne from the early 14C, it has been enlarged several times and joined with another chapel to form a church. The Gothic choir of two bays has consoles carved with symbolic motifs and also the tombstone of Admiral Duquesne; remains of a 14C fresco on the right of the choir. On the S. side there is a Flamboyant chapel with 17C paintings. The **Hôtel de Ville,** also called Grenette, stands on the Place du Marché. Originally a corn exchange, it was built on open arcades in 1770–80. Rue Tavernier No.3 is a 16C **hall** with a vaulted passageway. **Maison d'Aspre,** Rue du Chêne 20, is a private house and orangery from the 18C.

Augst: Roman museum, statuette with gold jewellery, perhaps Venus.

44 BC. Scenic theatre, amphitheatre, forum with basilica, 3 temple precincts, thermal baths, residential and commercial buildings as well as plumbing systems have been revealed. Finds are displayed in the *Roman Museum*.

Ausserbinn VS
12☐D5

Baroque **chapelle du Rosaire** built in the 17C. The façade niche contains a stone sculpture by Johann Ritz from 1702.

Augst BL
2☐A3

Excavations since the 16C have expanded our knowledge of the **Roman town of Augusta Raurica,** which was founded as a trading centre by Munatius Plancus in

Auvernier NE
6☐B4

Prehistoric excavation site famous for its lake dwellings from the Neolithic and Bronze Ages. Today the village specializes in fishing and viticulture. The **Reformed**

Auvernier: the Château is a unified 16C complex.

church, in the upper part of the village was originally a chapel dedicated to St. Nicholas (1478), which was enlarged in 1598 & 1709 (the irregular groundplan can be attributed to the various alterations). The 16C **Maison dite de l'Hôtel de Soleure,** Rue de la Roche 1, consists of two wings on either side of a staircase tower which has a Renaissance portal of 1570. The *Grand-Rue,* which runs through the village is lined with numerous houses from the 16–17C, a period of great prosperity for the community. Of particular interest is house No. 1 with a portal of 1615, Nos. 3,4,24 & 46 are also interesting. Below the village is the **château,** built for the commissioner and collector Blaise Junod. The main building, flanked by two towers, dates from 1559 with late-17C extensions; a gallery was added to the N. part in 1746. 18C wrought-iron grilles in the garden. Rue de la Bala No. 6 is a Renaissance **residence** built in 1574 for Jean Jacques de Bonstetten, Governor of Neuchâtel.

Avenches VD

6☐B/C5

Capital of Roman Helvetia, it was founded at the start of the 1C AD and elevated to the rank of colony by the Emperor Vespasian. Aventicum, as it was then known, achieved great prosperity in the course of the 1&2C, when it numbered 20,000 inhabitants and was surrounded by a wall 4 miles long. In 260 & 354 the town was attacked and destroyed by the Alemanni and never really recovered. In the 4–6C Avenches was a bishop's seat; when this moved to Lausanne some time before 594 the town was deprived of what was left of its importance. Today's town now only covers a small part of the area occupied by the Roman one and consists principally of the hill which was fortified in the mid 11C. In 1536 Avenches fell to Bern and became the seat of a governor.

The Roman town was used as a quarry from the Middle Ages onwards and as a result its buildings have been almost entirely eradicated. Since 1885 there have been systematic excavations and attempts at conservation. Much remains of the walls, with their four gates and 75 semicircular towers and the E. Gate, part of the wall and one of the towers, the **Tornallaz,** have been rebuilt. In the lower part of the town there are remains of the **Baths, Capitol, Theatre** and the **Cigognier Temple,** so-called after the column, nearly 40 ft. high, which still stands and once bore a stork's nest. Beside the entrance to the medieval town is Switzerland's best-preserved **Amphitheatre,** which had a capacity of 12,000 spectators. From medieval times part of the fortifications with two 14C towers have survived; in the S. the **Benneville Tower,** in the NW the **Vuilly Tower.** On the edge of the amphitheatre there is an 11C fortified **tower** which was probably part of the original town fortifications and is now a *Roman Museum.* In the NE corner of the market-place stands the **Château,** originally the bishop's residence and converted and enlarged by the Bernese governor in the 16C. The Renaissance façade of 1565 is by the architect Antoine Ballanche; 18C N. wing. On the Grand-Rue stands the **Reformed church of Ste-Marie-Madeleine.** Built at the end of the 11C, it was extended in Gothic style and altered 1709 – 11. Let into the S. façade of the church there are two fragments of old timberwork (now used as benches); Romanesque round apse on N. side. Opposite the church is the **Hôtel de Ville,** built by N.Hebler in 1753. A 3-storeyed structure on arcades, the façade is surmounted by a sculpted triangular gable in which two moors hold the town's coat-of-arms. In the same street is the **Hôtel de la Couronne** and other interesting houses. The **Tour de Montauban,** Rue du Jura

Avenches: the Roman museum is in the tower by the amphitheatre.

No. 3, has a polygonal staircase tower and is all that remains of a baronial seat from the 15C. Rue des Alpes Nos. 3 and 5 are late Gothic houses. The *Musée Romain* has a collection of excavation finds from Avenches.

Avers-Cresta GR
14☐B3

A collection of isolated farms some 6,700 ft. up, the influence of the Walser migrations from the 14C onwards is still apparent. **Reformed church:** Late Romanesque with polygonal apse and tower of 1764; restored 1844 & 1980. The inner W. wall has a 15C painting of St. George and St.Christopher.

Avry-sur-Matran FR
11☐C1

The **château,** an 18C mansion built for the Buman family, stands in the middle of the old village.

Avully GE
16☐D2

Left of the road from Espesses is the **Maison Mottu,** built *c.* 1780; to the right

Avenches: Château altered in Renaissance style in 1565–8.

the **Maison Desbaillet,** flanked by two interesting 18C farm buildings.

Ayent VS
17☐E1

This community comprises several hamlets. ARGNOUD: The chapel of Ste-Marie-Madeleine was probably founded in the 11C and altered at the end of the Middle Ages. It is a small building with a round apse and an altar of 1729. ST-ROMAIN occupies the site of a priory founded in the 11C and later dissolved. The **Catholic parish church of St-Romain** dates from 1860-2 and has a 15 –16C tower built on the foundations of the old priory tower. 16C **priest's house.**

Azmoos SG
See WARTAU
9☐A2

B

Baar ZG

8 ☐ A2

Catholic parish church of St. Martin:
14C church; nave altered in baroque style
in 1771–7. Inside, late Gothic wall paintings (16C) and baroque stucco and ceiling paintings. Nearby is the **cemetery
chapel of St. Anna** with a carved wooden
ceiling of 1508. The **Reformed church**
was built by Ferdinand Stadler 1866–7.
The **Rathaus** on the Hauptstrasse, a half-
timbered building on a masonry base, dates
from 1676. On the road to Sihlbrugg
stands the **Spinnerei an der Lorze,** a
spinning mill with two main buildings
dating from 1852–7. Together with the
workers' settlement behind, the buildings
are typical of many erected during the early
years of industrialization. **Wildenburg
Ruins:** SE of Baar. Former seat of the
Knights of Hünenberg.

Bad Ragaz SG

9 ☐ B2/3

Catholic parish church of St. Pankraz:
Built in 1703–5 by Ulrich Lang to the
plans of an architect from Bregenz, it incorporates a medieval tower; the porch
dates from 1908. Ceiling painting by Martin Leonz Zeuger. **Chapel of St.
Leonhard:** Rebuilt 1410 – 12 below
Freudenberg Castle. Choir painted 1414
–18; the Italianate style of the painting is
without parallel in Switzerland. In 1945
–6 the narthex was converted into a room
commemorating the Confederacy's victory
at Ragaz in 1446. **Reformed church,**
built 1889–90 by Johann Vollmer. **Hof:** Today the old part of the spa hotel, it was formerly the residence of the governor of the
Pfäfer monastery. Rebuilt in 1774, it was
converted into hotel in 1841 according to
the plans of Felix Wilhelm Kubly. Open
timberwork construction in the dining-

room. **Quellenhof,** by Bernhard Simon
the younger, 1880–90. The **Bad- und
Trinkhalle,** built by Johann Christoph
Kunkler, 1866 – 8 is a single-storied
building with round-arched columned
hall. The **Freudenberg ruins** NW of
Ragaz date from the 13C and belonged to
the barons of Wildenberg; destroyed by
confederates in 1437.

Baden AG

2 ☐ E4

Baden's hot springs were already in use in
Roman times. The town's strategically important setting in the deeply carved Limmat valley led to the early building of the
castle and fortification complex of Stein
under the counts of Lenzburg. The little
town of Baden did not develop until the
13C because of Habsburg domination of
the region. In 1415 Baden was incorporated into the Confederation as a subordinate area and after 1712 (Villmergen
War) into the reformed cantons. Baden was
the preferred assembly place of the Old
Confederacy. The fine architecture of the
Altstadt survived 19&20C industrialization mostly undamaged.

ALTSTADT AND FORTIFICATIONS: Survivors
of the old fortifications include the foundation walls of **Castle Stein** (dismantled
1712), the late Gothic **town gate** from the
15C with coloured, glazed roof tiles
(restored 1925–6) and a fragment of the
battlement walk by the chapel of St.
Sebastian. The **Catholic town church of
Mariä Himmelfahrt und St. Damiøn,**
a late Gothic basilica with nave, two aisles
and choir closed on three sides; was built
by Rudolf Murer and Konrad Zobrist in
1457–60. The substructure of the tower
dates from 1364. Church interior altered
in baroque style in 1613–17 and 1696–7,
with classical alterations made by Johann
Joseph Mosbrugger 1813–14. The **Sebastianskapelle** has two storeys: crypt with
ribbed vaulting dates from 1480–1; upper
chapel (1505) has a late Gothic fresco. The
Landvogteischloss (governor's
residence), a castle-like building by Jakob
Hegnauer (1487 – 90) with a late

Baden: 15C town gate, part of the former town fortifications.

Balerna: Renaissance triptych of 1500 in the baptismal chapel near the church.

Renaissance portal of 1580, stands on the right bank of the Limmat. It is now a *Historical Museum.* **Stadthaus:** Actually a whole group of buildings, the oldest part of which—the central building—contains the **Assembly Room,** (rebuilt 1497) with a richly-carved ceiling. BÄDERQUARTIER (spa quarter): Inns and hotels from several centuries.

Bagnes VS
17☐D3

A valley community made up of several villages. LE CHABLE is the main town of the Vallée de Bagnes. **Catholic parish church of St-Maurice:** Late Gothic, built 1520-4; tower of 1488 with dormer windows. The church has a nave, two aisles and polygonal apse; the choir is closed by a wrought-iron grille dating from 1683. The high altar has a 19C copy of the Last Supper by Leonardo da Vinci. 18&19C furnishings. The **Ossuary,** built in 1560, contains an interesting group of 17C baroque statues. S. of the church is the 16–17C **priest's house.** Near the bridge is the Ab-

baye, the former summer residence of the Abbot of St-Maurice, which was built in the start of the 15C and altered in the 17C. Square porch with columns.

VILLETTE: Beautiful group of traditional wooden houses and mill. In the middle of the village there is a small local history *Museum.*

COTTERG: The village square has a monolithic **fountain.**

MAUVOISIN **Chapel:** Built *c.* 1730 on the ruins of a former watch tower. The dam was built in 1950–58. Louvie and Giétro are typical **Alpine meadows.**

Balerna TI
19☐D5

Collegiate church of San Vittore: Documented since 789 and rebuilt in the 12C from which time the Romanesque apse has survived. Extended and rebuilt in the 16&19C. The baroque façade dates from 1744. Choir and transept chapels are decorated with 17–18C stucco and frescos. The N. chapel contains remnants of Renaissance frescos and a 16C crucifix; the

Ballenberg: Madiswil farmhouse and Kiesen storehouse in the museum.

S. chapel has a terracotta statue of the Virgin Mary from 1676. The **baptistery** next to the church was altered in 1820 and contains a 16C fresco of the Virgin and Child and a Renaissance triptych from *c.* 1500. N. of the church there is a baroque **ossuary** (1759) and the **Bishop's Palace** (1706). The former **Nuntiatur** behind the choir, is 18C.

Balgach-Heerbrugg SG
4☐B3

Catholic parish church of the Hl. Drei Könige (Three Kings): Built 1825–6 by Josef Simon Mosbrugger and sons. **Reformed church:** Documented since 1419, this late medieval complex has a new (S.) building. Late 15C relief of the head of Christ in the choir. **Former Rathaus:** Built in 1566. Late Gothic stone building, corn store converted into banqueting hall by David Zollikofer in *c.* 1596; Renaissance paintings. The **Gasthaus Rössli,** at the entry to the village, was built *c.* 1640 and altered in 1754 & 1834. Near the Catholic church in the middle of the village there are painted wooden 17&18C houses. **Haus Nüesch,** S. of the village, a long building with a small gable at the side dates from 1787. **Schloss Grünenstein,** on a height SW of Balgach, is documented since 1270. It was rebuilt in *c.* 1776, probably by Johann Jakob Haltiner in collaboration with Conrad Schindler, the son of the owner. Late baroque complex; the lower part of the tower comes from the preceding building. HEERBRUGG, NE of Balgach, is the site of

the **fortress** built by Ulrich III von Eppenstein, Abbot of St. Gallen, in 1078. Rebuilt by Bartholomäus Schlumpf in 1774 after a fire. The 3-storey baroque building with 6 bays has a curved central gable; the tower dates from 1911.

Ballenberg BE
12☐D1

Swiss open-air museum of rural architecture and home decoration: This museum is in the process of being set up but when complete it will illustrate many aspects of rural culture, including types of houses and settlement, building materials and methods, modes of furnishing and decoration, as well as historical and social differences.

Balliswil FR
see DÜDINGEN   6☐D5

Ballwil LU
7☐E2

Catholic parish church of St. Margaretha: Built in 1847–9 by the Munich architect Johann Seidl in a romantic style with round arches; this is the first ecclesiastical building to be built in historical style in central Switzerland.

Balm bei Günsberg SO
6☐F1

Grottenburg: Ruins beneath overhanging rocks; the castle was built by the former lords of Balm, probably in the middle of the 11C.

Balm bei Messen SO
6☐E3

The **little mountain church** with its detached bell tower (*c.* 1400 & 1691) possibly belonged to **Burg Balmegg,** of which a few remains can still be seen on the ridge above the village.

Barberêche: the Château in Petit-Vivy with keep and wooden gallery.

Balsthal SO

2☐A5

Former **Catholic parish church of Unserer Lieben Frau:** Built on top of the remains of Roman and early medieval walls, the church in the main dates from the 16–18C. The **chapel of St.Antonius,** not far from the church, has baroque vault paintings from the early 17C. **St. Ottilien-Kapelle,** founded in 1511, is still visibly Gothic in spite of extensive rebuilding in 1662. The **Herrengasse** has a provincial air and interesting buildings such as the early classical Old Amtshaus, the early baroque Gasthof zum Kreuz, the Biedermeier 'Rössli' and the former granary by Paolo Antonio Pisoni. A *Paper Museum* is housed in the **mill** (1773).

Baltschieder VS

18☐B1

Muttergotteskapelle from the 17–18C; baroque altar.

Barberêche FR

6☐C5

Petit-Vivy: **Château**: Built in the 13C; the local lords are documented since 1153. Oldest parts include the square keep, remains of the ring wall, a wooden gallery running along the top of the wall and the 16C residence.

Grand-Vivy: **Château**: Built in 1616 by the Praroman family on the site of a medi-

eval castle. The rectangular building has a semicircular staircase tower in the middle of the façade; beside it is a 19C chapel.

Bargen SH

3☐A1

Gasthaus Löwen: Large country house from the 2nd half of the 18C with a gable and saddle roof.

Basadingen TG

3☐B2

Non-denominational church of St. Martin: Built in 1840–1 in classical style to the plans of Jean Ruch. In UNTERSCHLATT, to the W. of Basadingen is the **former Convent of St. Clare,** founded in the mid 13C by Count Hartmann the Elder of Kyburg. The convent of Schaffhausen had been forced to adopt the new doctrine in the course of the Reformation but reconstituted itself in 1578. Rebuilt in 1588, the church was converted to baroque 1726–7; the convent wing was renovated and converted 1950–1. It is currently owned by Georg Fischer AG who in 1948 set up a library in the W. wing devoted to the history of iron production.

Basel BS

1☐F3

On both sides of the Rhine the remains of military and trading stations of the Romans, Alemanni and Franks among others testify to the almost continual settlement of this area around the 'knee' of the Rhine since the 1&2C BC (finds in the History Museum). In the 11C the city and its ruler, the Bishop, passed from Burgundian to Imperial power. With the building of the bridge in 1225 Basel established its position of importance in European trade. The emancipation of the citizens from bishop and nobles, principally by the craftsmen who were organized into guilds, was a lengthy process. In 1356 a serious earthquake destroyed large parts of the city. The Council (1431–48), the opening of the

Basel: Münsterplatz and Münster with towers dating from 1430 and 1500.

University (1471) and the presence of humanists meant that Basel was important not only economically but also culturally. When Basel became part of the Swiss Confederation in 1501 the city's interests changed. The Reformation (1529) brought about a period of isolation from outside and concentration on internal development. The Swiss Assembly (1789) was effectively a bloodless dissolution of the Ancien Régime. Following the loss of the long-independent area in the civil war-like separation turmoil of 1833, the contours of the townscape, then still predominantly medieval, began to dissolve under the demands of traffic and industry.

GROSSBASEL

THE ALTSTADT WITHIN THE 12C RING WALL: Until the second city wall was built in the 2nd half of the 14C, Basel was divided into the fortified city and the various suburbs which had grown up over the years. The city itself lies on Münsterhügel, Leonhards- and Petershügel and the area in between.

Münsterhügel with Rittergasse, Münsterberg and Münsterplatz (Minster Square), Schlüsselberg and Stapfelberg, Augustinergasse and Martinsgasse, as well as the Rheinsprung, still abound in official residences and mansions belonging to the nobility, patricians and the clergy.

Minster: The oldest parts date from the beginning of the 9C and just after the Magyar onslaught of 916. Of the earliest building the foundations of the choir under the present crossing have survived. A later building was consecrated in 1019 in the presence of Emperor Henry II. After rebuilding and restorations in the 11C the present late Romanesque/early Gothic basilica was built, using parts of the crypt and the N. façade tower and comprising, transept, ambulatory, two front towers, two choir towers, a crossing tower, galleries and vaults. The W. end was first rebuilt after a fire in 1258. Bishops and nobles immediately began adding burial chapels along the sides resulting in an aisle-like extension. An earthquake of 1356 destroyed vaults, spires and crypt. During the rapid rebuilding the choir clerestory was built in a contemporary style heralding the late Gothic by Johannes (Parler), master of the works. The (S.) tower of St. Martin was completed *c.* 1400; *c.* 1430 the (N.) tower of St. George was finished. With the assimilation of St. Martin's tower the cathedral was completed in 1500. The large and small cloisters were built in the course of the 15C.

The carved decoration and tomb sculpture, like the building itself, date from High Romanesque to Late Gothic. The Apostle and Vincentius slabs (*c.* 1090?) are high to late Romanesque; the capitals in the choir exhibit Lombard influence. The Gallus Gate, which takes the form of a triumphal arch, and the Wheel of Fortune date from the third quarter of 12C; the statues and archivolt figures of the W. façade from the 13–14C; the tomb figures are 14–15C; and the spires, pulpit, net vaults and the window tracery in the cloister stand as model examples of late Gothic masonry. The **Niklauskapelle,** a two-storey building between the small cloister and the choir, was the meeting place of the cathedral chapter, *c.* 1270 & 1400. The **Reformed church of St. Martin,** probably the city's oldest parish church, was built over foundations dating from sometime after 1356 and incorporates the old tower. The choir was consecrated in 1398, the sacristy *c.* 1450; the late Gothic pulpit with falchion tracery dates from 1495. In the **Haus zur Mücke** (14–15C, 1549) Pope Felix V was elected in 1439. 1671–1849 it housed the city's library and the public art collection based on the Amerbach cabinet. The **Bischofshof** has had a complicated history, but in the main owes its present appearance to Bishop Arnold of Rotberg (mid 15C). After successful negotiations with the city, Bishop Jacob Christoph Blarer of Wartensee had the **Domhof** built in 1578; renovation by Christoph Riggenbach in 1841. The **Museum in Augustinergasse** was built privately to the designs of the classical architect Melchior Berri (1844–9). During the late 19C it housed the city's collections, the library and the university. External features of the **Hohenfirstenhof** date from the rebuilding of 1583. The **Ramsteinerhof** was designed by Johann Carl Hemeling, an architect in the service of the Margrave of Baden, 1727–32. As a whole the building is symmetrical and has a small central gable. The tree-lined Münsterplatz has a **fountain** with a quatrefoil basin and classical column by Paolo Antonio Pisoni, 1789.

The commercial quarter lay along the *Birsig valley* which has since been dammed. Buildings on Freie Strasse, Gerbergasse, Falknerstrasse, on the Marktplatz and in the Fishmarkt date in the main from the 19C & early 20C. From 1231 Franciscan monks, who had the support of the bishop, preached in Basel and the first monastery church was built 1253–6. This was succeeded by a larger building following a fire of 1298 and the present **Barfüsserkirche,** with flat-roofed nave, choir formerly with stained glass and chapel screens was built. The overall simplicity of the building encompasses fine proportions and careful treatment of small details. 19C rebuilding was to some extent reversed in the restoration of 1978. Since 1894 it has been the Historisches Museum. The **Zunfthaus zum Schlüssel** has a baroque façade and was built in several phases (13C, 1485, 1730, 1762). The 3-storeyed building which forms part of the **Rathaus** in the market place dates from 1503–7; the higher part on the left from 1606–8, the right tower from 1898–1904. Lavish late Gothic and Renaissance details include carvings, panelling, furnishings, wall paintings and stained glass. The unknown architect of the **Geltenzunft,** who was obviously familiar with the writings of Italian architects, created a façade which stands out from other buildings nearby in its pretension. The **Stadthaus,** commissioned by the merchants' guild, was built to the plans of Samuel Werenfels in 1771–5 and has reliefs and colossal pilasters on the façade. On the site of the former trading house (two portals of 1572 have survived in the passageway) Johann Jacob Stehlin the Younger built the neo-Gothic **Hauptpost** (main post office) in 1852–3. This building was extended to the Rüdengasse by Friedrich von Schmidt of Vienna in 1877–80. The Gothic tower-like **Fischmarktbrunnen** (fountain; *c.*1380) has figures of saints and prophets.

Leonhards- and Petershügel: Within the wall (pre 1206), along Kohlenberg,

Leonhardsgraben and Petersgraben, many medieval buildings have survived, particularly in Leonhardskirchplatz and Leonhardsstapfelberg, Heuberg, Gemsberg, Spalenberg, Nadelberg, Imbergässlein, Totengässlein, Petersgasse and Blumenrain.

Reformed church of St.Leonhard: Part of a former Augustinian foundation, the present building was built in 1480–1520 above a Romanesque crypt and in place of a church rebuilt after the earthquake of 1356 (choir remains) as a pure late Gothic hall church. From the hexagonal pillars ribs spread into an organized stellar vault which is striking in both colour and material used. The Heilsspiegelaltar (parts in the Art Museum) dates from the time of the Council of Basel and was probably intended for the high altar.

Frequently rebuilt and restored since Carolingian times, the present building of the **Reformed church of St.Peter,** once the seat of secular canons, dates mainly from the 14&15C; wall paintings in the choir chapels and in a pointed-arched niche in the S. wall (Mocking and Burial of Christ, late 14C). Between the Nadelberg and the inner city wall fine 13C mansions have façades rebuilt in baroque style. The **Shönes Haus** has a Gothic window arrangement and painted wooden ceiling. Nearby, to the S., is the **Zerkindenhof,** rebuilt 1603 – 8. Most notable about the **Spiesshof,** is the bold use of contrasting colours in the main façade overlooking the courtyard. Built in two styles, the three lower storeys date from 1550 – 60 and the fourth from *c.* 1589 (Daniel Heintz).

SUBURBS (Vorstädte): With the building of a second city wall in the late 14C both old and new suburbs were incorporated into the city; large areas of open space left within this wall allowed building to continue into the 19C.

The **St. Alban-Tal** and *St. Alban-Vorstadt* is probably the oldest quarter outside the first fortification. The **Reformed church of St.Alban** belonged to a priory founded by the Bishop in 1083 and later assigned to the Cluniac order. The N. wing of the Romanesque cloister has survived from the 11C. The Gothic

The 13C church of the barefooted friars, historical museum since 1894, reopened 1981.

Detail of the façade of the Rathaus (1503–7) with painting of 1824–8.

Romanesque crypt under the Leonhardskirche.

church (choir begun in 1270) was reduced to its present size in 1845, an act which

Spiesshof, main façade in the courtyard, built in two different periods.

Ramsteinerhof (1727–32), near the Münster terrace above the Rhine.

Haus zum Kirschgarten (1775–80), now part of the historical museum.

separated it from the monastery buildings to the N. The commercial district, the 'Albanteich', on the canal leading off the Birs grew up to the W. of the partly reconstructed **Letzimauer** and the Mühlegraben, which ran from the Rhine (Letziturm 1676) to the St. Albantor (1360–70). The production of paper, which has been carried out here since *c.* 1450, is documented in the **Gallizianmühle**, the Swiss Museum of the History of Paper; the house dates from the 16–17C, the commercial building from 1788. In contrast to the early industrial architecture is the **Museum für Gegenwartskunst** designed by Katharina and Wilfried Steib in 1980. The St. Alban-Vorstadt has rows of attached, originally medieval houses, now partly baroque or historicized; **Zum Hohen Dolder,** house of the suburban community of the same name, is later than 1500. The **Kunstmuseum** (art museum) was built 1932–6 to the designs of Rudolf Christ and Paul Bonatz amid some controversy.

The **Reformed church of St. Elisabeth** was founded by Christoph Merian and built by Christoph Riggenbach to the plans of Ferdinand Stadler, 1857–66. The recent classical accentuation of the building contrasts with the perfectly copied individual Gothic forms. The **Haus zum Raben,** three buildings around a courtyard, dates from 11763–5. Johann Rudolf Burckhardt had the well-proportioned and lavishly furnished **Haus zum Kirschgarten** built for himself by Johann Ulrich Büchel in 1775 –80 (now part of the History Museum). The idea of a cultural centre on a generously planned (triumphal) street was expounded by Johann Jacob Stehlin the Younger with his buildings on the Steinenberg: Kunsthalle (1872), Stadttheater (1875) and Musiksaal (1876). In 1972 the Stadttheater was replaced by a new building by Felix Schwarz and Rolf Gutmann. The Fasnacht Fountain in front of the theatre is by Jean Tinguely, (1977). The **Spalentor** forms the boundary of the **Spalen-Vorstadt.** Much of the gate survives in its original form: the massive square central part is flanked by two round battlemented towers. The 3 sculptures on the outside date from the time of the gate's

The museum of contemporary art, designed by Katharina and Wilfrid Steib, 1980.

Elisabethankirche, a pure neo-Gothic building of 1857–66.

construction *c*. 1400. To the N. and formerly outside the walls, stands the **Riegelhaus der Stachelschützen,** built in 1546 & 1626; wings in 1707&1729. In 1277 canons from the nearby abbey planted the first trees on **Petersplatz,** a square within the fortress walls which later was the scene of both fighting and festivals. The **Wildtsche Haus** on the N. side, an important example of rococo architecture, was built by Johann Jacob Fechter for a Basel trade magnate in 1762–3. Opposite, on the site of the former arsenal, stands the **university lecture hall** built by Roland Rohn in 1937–9.

Of particular note in the *Neuen Vorstadt,* today's Hebelstrasse, is the **Markgräflerhof,** the occasional residence of the margrave of Baden-Durlach, built to the plans of an unknown architect of the French school in 1698–1705. The **Holsteiner Hof** was begun in 1696 for the wife of the Margrave and rebuilt in 1743–52. The first building of the **Catholic preacher's church** was built in connection with the Dominican house, itself founded in 1233. The extension of 1240 – 50 was followed by the distinctive building of 1261–9; nave and two aisles, polygonal apse and fine screens in the chapels. The 'Dance of Death' on the inside of what was formerly the cemetery wall is one of old Basel's main curiosities; by Konrad Witz or a similar artist it dates from 1435-40 and was severely damaged in 1805.

The *St.Johanns-Vorstadt* has generously proportioned baroque mansions like the Erlacherhof, Formonterhof and Antönierhof. The third surviving gate in the outer ring of walls, the St.Johanns-Tor of 1360–70, stands on the Strasse ins Elsass.

KLEINBASEL

Kleinbasel was released from the Habsburgs as the first in a long line of acquisitions by Grossbasel. The smaller town enjoyed swift growth in the early 13C. A wall with two gates, the Riehentor and the Bläsi-Tor, defended the grid-like settlement. The Rhein-, Uten- and Rebgasse running parallel to the Rhine, as well as the districts around the Klingental and St. Theodore, still exhibit the original building pattern and house types. The **Reformed church of St.Theodore,** the first parish church in Kleinbasel, was originally built before the earthquake on the site of earlier buildings (consecrations in 1277, 1377 & 1435). The flat-roofed basilica is concluded by a fine choir, which once had lavish stained glass. Opposite the Dominican monastery on the S. bank of the Rhine Dominican nuns set up the **Klingental Convent** after 1273. The consecration of the church took place in 1293; the exceptionally long choir adjoins a more moderately proportioned nave. The former convent buildings were sacrificed for barracks in 1860 (architect Johann Jacob Stehlin the Younger). Now all that remains of the earliest buildings is the **Kleine Klingental,** which is now the City and Cathedral Museum, and a national monu-

ment. The **Catholic church of St. Clara**
was at the centre of the former convent of
Poor Clares who resided in Basel from
1266. The 14C church had the long choir
so typical of the Mendicant order and a
short nave. Misappropriated and neglected
after the Reformation, the church was
rebuilt 1858-9 as a parish church in keeping with the Gothic building. The former
Charterhouse goes back to a foundation
by Jacob Zibol in 1401; the church was
consecrated in 1416. In the years following both civil and religious foundations endowed the monastery with valuable works
of art. Parts of the small cloister and
secular buldings have survived; it is now
a municipal orphanage. The **Hattstät-
terhof,** a stately building on the
Lindenberg, was built in 1576-85 and has
a massive hip-roof and little corner towers.
The three Kleinbasel honorary
establishments, Zur Hären (Wilder
Mann), Zum Rebhaus (Leu) and Zum
Greifen (Vogel Gryff), built their
clubhouse, the so-called **Café Spitz,** on
the bridgehead to plans by Amadeus
Merian in a romantic classical style, 1838
-41.

*The neoclassical Sommercasino, built in
1823.*

*The Antoniuskirche, a pioneer reinforced
concrete building.*

BASEL ENVIRONS
QUARTERS OUTSIDE THE FORMER FORTIFICA-
TIONS: Before industrialization the growth
of Basel's population was barely discernible but during the first half of the 19C it
nearly tripled. With the dismantling of the
walls and the levelling of the ditches after
1859 building activity began on a completely new scale. Far-sighted urban
development under Councillor Karl
Sarasin and the architect Jacob Stehlin the
Younger led to the creation of public parks
(under Karl von Effner, head gardener
from Munich) in the area contained within
the former fortifications. At the same time
new districts developed on all sides; these
varied architecturally depending upon the
economic base and social structure of the
area.
The growth of the city's industry drew
many workers from the countryside into the
city. In order to accommodate the growing
population the Society for Welfare and
Community Service held a competition for
building inexpensive workers' accom-

modation. The **Siedlung in der Breite,**
built in 1855 to plans of Johann Jacob
Stehlin the Elder, inspired a series of
similar projects. In 1823 the amateur architect Johann Georg Von der Mühll, commissioned by the municipal authorities,
built the **Sommercasino** on the Birstal
road as a community social club. **St.
Jacobsdenkmal** (St. James monument,
1872) by the sculptor Ferdinand Schlöth,
commemorates the battle of 1444. The
precise contours of the **Lonzahochhaus,**
by the architects Suter and Suter 1960-2,
rise from an elongated hexagonal groundplan. The **Catholic Heiliggeistkirche** in
the Gundeldingen district was built in
1911-2 in romantic late Gothic style by
Gustav Doppler and Max Merkel. **Untere
Mittlere Gundeldingen** was the country
seat of the humanist Thomas Platter in
1549. The **Bundesbahnhof** (station),
1905-7 by Emil Faesch and Emanuel La
Roche, stands out with massive solemnity.
The **Reformed church of St. Paul** was
built by Robert Curjel and Karl Moser in

The Badische Bahnhof is by the same architect as the Antoniuskirche.

Beaker with lid made for Erasmus of Rotterdam, 1531, historical museum.

neo-Romantic Art Nouveau style, with the intention of creating an effect from a distance (1898–1901). The neo-Byzantine **synagogue** was built by Hermann Gauss in 1867; Paul Reber enlarged it to twice its original size in 1893. The **Feuerschützenhaus** (Arquebusier house) was built outside the wall in 1561 – 4; painted windows depicting arquebusiers by Hansjörg Rieher and Ludwig Ringler (late 16C). The **Catholic church of St. Antonius** was built in unplastered reinforced concrete, unusual in 1926 – 7, by Karl Moser. KLEINBASEL: The **Reformed church of St. Matthäus,** built in 1892–

6 to plans of the Breslau architect Felix Henry, who won a competition, stands in the middle of a tree-lined square of apartment houses built in historical and Art Nouveau styles. The **Sandgrube,** built by Johann Jacob Fechter 1745–6 for a Basel ribbon manufacturer, has an extravagant central projection. Karl Moser conceived the **Badische Bahnhof,** 1910–13, as the focus of the Mittlere Rheinbrücke-Clarastrasse and the Johanniterbrücke-Feldbergstrasse axes; historical styles have been used to create a most individual building. Fountain with 'Rhine' and 'meadow' by Carl Burckhardt. The architects Hermann Baur, Franz Bräuning and Arthur Dürig built the **Allgemeine Gewerbeschule** (universal technical school) in 1956; 4 dissimilar buildings are arranged around a square which has a stele designed by Hans Arp. Restrained elegance and refinement characterize the **Hoffmann-La Roche Building** by Otto Rudolf Salvisberg, 1935-6. Spacious housing estates, which became models for social residential architecture include, **'Hirzbrunnen'** (by Hans Bernoulli, Hans Von der Mühll, Paul Oberrauch and August Künzel, 1924–30), **'Schorenmatten'** (by Paul Ataria and Hans Schmidt, 1929) and **'Eglisee'** (by 13 architectural firms for the Swiss Housing Exhibition of 1930).
Museums: *Antikenmuseum,* (Antiquities) St.Alban-Graben 5. *Basler Papiermuseum,* (Paper). St. Alban-Tal 35/37. *Gewerbemuseum* (Commerce), Spalenvorstadt 2. *Historisches Museum,* Barfüsserkirche; Haus zum Kirschgarten, Elisabethenstr.27; Collection of Old Musical Instruments, Leonhardstr.8. *Kunstmuseum,* St.Alban-Graben 16. *Museum für Gegenwartskunst* (Modern Art) St.Alban-Tal 2. *Museum of Natural Science and Folklore,* Augustinergasse 2. *Swiss Folk Museum,* Augustinergasse 2. *Swiss Sports Museum,* Missionstrasse 28. *Klingental Municipal and Cathedral Museum,* Unt.Rheinweg 26, *Jewish Museum,* Kornhausgasse 8.

Basse-Nendaz VS
see NENDAZ   17□D2

Bassins VD

10 ☐ C3

Reformed church of Notre-Dame:
Church of a priory, which no longer exists
but which was once attached to Payerne.
The building, probably Romanesque in
origin, was rebuilt in Gothic and modern
times. 15C tower and chapels.

Bätterkinden BE

6 ☐ F2

Reformed parish church: Built in 1664
in Gothic style by Abraham I.Dünz, who
was also responsible for the stone pulpit.
Decorative works come from the workshop
of Albr. Kauw.

Bauen UR

8 ☐ A4

Catholic parish church of St. Idda:
Built 1808–12 in classical style. Amongst
the numerous wooden houses in the village
the **Obere Baumgarten,** built in 1678 for
Councillor Aschwanden, stands out. A
monument of 1901 commemorates Pater
Alberik Zwyssig, composer of the
Schweizerpsalm, who was born in Bauen.

Baulmes VD

5 ☐ E5

This village has become known for
prehistoric finds which have recently been
discovered in the rocky terrain above the
settlement. **Reformed church of St-
Pierre:** Documented since 1228, rebuilt
in 1821 and extended in 1871. Romanesque elements have been integrated in the
present building and the substructure of
tower is possibly Romanesque; Gothic
windows. Part of the tower has a Roman
altar dedicated to Apollo. Baulmes once
had a second church, part of a 7C priory,
of which a fragment of an 8C Carolingian
ambo is preserved in the local museum.
The Grand-Rue has a late 18C **Archive
Tower** , whose roof is surmounted by a

*Baulmes: Roman altar dedicated to Apollo
in the tower passage.*

small belltower. On the Rue du Theu, the
former Maison de la Dime from the
17C is now the *Musée du Vieux-Baulmes*
(local history museum).

Bavois VD

10 ☐ E1

Reformed church of St. Léger:
Documented since the 12C. The present,
partly Romanesque, partly Gothic
building is of interest for its central
belltower, between nave and choir. The N.
side of the choir has a 16C chapel. The
castle above the village is of medieval
origin and was rebuilt in the 19C.

Beatenberg BE

see SUNDLAUENEN   12 ☐ B2

Beckenried NW

8 ☐ A4

The classical **Catholic parish church of
St.Heinrich:** was built in 1790–1807 by
Niklaus Purtschert. The **pilgrimage**

chapel of **Maria im Ridli** was built in 1700–1 and is a landmark high above the lake. Stairway with seats for sermons.

Begnins VD

10☐C4

Reformed church of Notre-Dame: Founded in the 11C, this single-aisled building has a square choir surmounted by a 15C bell tower. On the S. side 3 chapels date from the 14&15C; façade, 1932. S. of the church is the **Château du Martheray,** now a hotel but formerly the residence of the lords of Begnins. Greatly altered in the 19C, the building includes a staircase tower of 1671. The **Château de Rochefort** or 'de Menthon', is a late medieval mansion, which was rebuilt in the 16–18C.

Beinwil AG

7☐F1

Catholic parish church of St.Peter and Paul: Baroque hall church of 1619–20 with high choir and spired tower (1645). The nave has Louis XVI stucco and ceiling paintings by Joseph Anton and Johann Nepomuk Messmer. **Schloss Horben:** Baroque mansion with little onion-domed towers, built around 1700 as a rest home for the monastery of Muri. Paintings by Caspar Wolf.

Beinwil SO

1☐F5

Former Benedictine monastery: Transferred to ▷ Mariastein in 1648. The monks who remained were built a simple new church with wooden ceiling in 1668.

Belfaux FR

11☐C1

Church of St-Etienne: Documented since 1138, it was completely rebuilt in 1841–52. This monumental building has a nave, two aisles and a semicircular apse;

Begnins: Le Manoir, rebuilt in 1631 in the Bernese style.

Beinwil: Schloss Horben, built as the sanatorium of Muri monastery.

Bellelay: interior of the monastery church, a baroque building by Franz Beer.

13C wooden crucifix in the choir. In front of the church stands the **Auberge du Mouton** (1579). Along the road to Misery, on the right, there is an 18C **patrician's house;** somewhat further along on the left there is a house with interesting windows and a portal dated 1630.

Bellelay BE

6 □ C/ D1

Former Premonstratensian Abbey:
Founded in 1136 by Prior Siginand of
Moutier-Grandval. The church was rebuilt
in 1709–14 along the lines of the so-called
Vorarlberg scheme (▷ St. Urban). The
baroque abbey buildings surround a courtyard. It is now a mental hospital.

Bellikon AG

2 □ E/ F5

Castle: Late Gothic building with spiral
staircase and stair gables. The chapel,
dating from 1676, is not open to the public.

Bellinzona TI

19 □ D2

Capital of the canton of Ticino, Bellinzona
lies in the the the upper Ticino, which was
already settled in the Bronze and Iron
Ages. The town occupies a strategic position where N-S routes (to Nufenen, St.
Gotthard, Lukmanier, Greina and San
Bernardino) and the E-W route of San Jori-
Centovalli converge. Bellinzona was
already fortified in Roman times—Gregory
of Tours referred to Bellinzona as 'castrum'
in 590. After the Romans the area came
under the influence first of Lombardy,
then the Franks. The town was then controlled by a succession of diferent
overlords: the bishop until 1231, then the
town of Como, from 1396 by Milan, from
1402 by the counts of Sax, the Visconti
(after 1426), then the Sforzas, the French
(1499) and finally from 1501 onwards, the
Confederation. After the St.Gotthard Pass
became accessible with the opening of the
Schöllenen Gorge at the start of the 13C
trade and traffic N-S increased and with
it came the need to secure trade routes in
the S. In 1403 the Swiss of Uri and Ob-
wald occupied the valley of the Leventina.
After the defeat of Arbedo in 1422, the victory at Giornico in 1478 finally secured the
Leventina for Uri. In 1496 Uri, Schwyz
and Unterwalden occupied the Blenio

*Bellinzona: Castel Grande with Torre bianca
(right) and Torre nera (centre).*

*Interior of the collegiate church, redesigned
in the baroque style in the 17&18C.*

valley, in 1499 the Riviera and in April
1500 Bellinzona. In 1512 the Confederation captured Lugano, Locarno and the
Maggia valley and in 1512 Mendrisio. The
regions to the S. of Bellinzona were thenceforward administered as common territories by the 12 Old Cantons, while the
governorship of Leventina, Blenio, Riviera
and Bellinzona came under Uri, Schwyz
and Nidwalden. During the Swiss
Republic the cantons of Lugano and
Bellinzona joined the Confederation and
became the canton of Ticino under the
M diation. Until 1878 the cities of Bellinzona, Lugano and Locarno in turn acted
as capital of the canton for six years at a

Fresco on the rood screen in Santa Maria delle Grazie, late 15C including Crucifixion.

time. The **fortifications and castles,** which were laid out in the 13C and continuously extended until 1500, are amongst the most important medieval fortifications in Switzerland. The complex is made up of 3 castles interconnected by ramparts, of which numerous parts, such as the Sforza's famous 'Murata', have survived. The oldest castle is the **Castel Grande,** also called 'Castel Vecchio' or 'Castle of Uri', which was built over a Roman fortress. The core dates back to the 12–13C and includes the 'Torre Bianca', a square keep, and the 'Torre Nera', a rectangular residential building; the buildings surrounding the main courtyard are of a later date. Within the walls surrounding the castle (a place of refuge in times of trouble for the local population) once stood the parish church of San Pietro and two other churches. The **Castello di Montebello** (Castle of Schwyz) dominates the E. of the city; it was begun at the end of the 13C and added to until the late 15C. The oldest part, built *c.* 1300, consists of a rectangular five-storey keep surrounded by a polygonal wall. A second surrounding wall was built *c.* 1400. At the end of the 15C the complex was fortified on the E. side by the gate

tower and the wall which is equipped with machicolations and which connects the castle with the city. The **Castello di Sasso Corbaro** (Castle of Unterwalden) is a massive building on a square ground-plan, built in just a few months in 1479 by the Milanese, who after the Battle of Giornico in 1478 feared a new attack by the Confederation. Left to decay from 1798, it was restored 1933–4.

Piazza Collegiata, **collegiate church of Santi Pietro e Stefano.** Mentioned in 1424, rebuilt between 1517 and 1565 by the architect Tomaso Rodari, foreman of works on Como cathedral, altered in the 17&18C. The church is an interesting example of Renaissance architecture with baroque additions: it consists of nave, eight side chapels and a polygonal choir. The façade became more elaborate in the baroque period, the main portal dates from 1640, the side portals are 16C; the interior has lavish 17&18C stucco. On the high altar paintings by Simone Petrazana dating from 1568, in the nave carved choir stalls of 1784 and marble aquamanile, formerly a well (1460). By the collegiate church 17&18C **Oratorium Santa Maria.** Trompe l'oeil painting in the vault (1762).

Opposite the cemetery is **Santa Maria delle Grazie,** former church of the Franciscan monastery dissolved in 1848. The church was built in 1481-5, and is a plain building with a single aisle and three N. side chapels; the choir is separated from the nave by a rood screen with a large late-15C fresco of the Crucifixion and 15 scenes from the Life of Christ. In the chapel S. of the rood screen Death of Mary, fresco, school of Gaudenzio Ferrari, in the first N. chapel red chalk drawing of St. Bernardino of Siena, in the choir Annunciation, fresco of the Lombardy school. Two squares in the Altstadt have retained their original character: the Piazza Collegiata, with mainly 18C buildings, including No. 1, the **former priest's house** of 1722 and No. 7, **Casa Chicherio** with rococo portal; and the Piazza Nosetto with 15C porticoes in the Lombardy style, No. 5, **Palazzo Civico,** built in 1924 on the foundations of the 15C town hall; and Via Nosetto 1, **Casa Rossa** of 1860 with neo-Gothic terracotta exterior. In the Via Teatro **Palazzo del Governo,** former monastery dating from 1738, altered and enlarged in the late 19C.
RAVECCHIA Now a suburb of Bellinzona. **San Biagio.** Built in the 13C on the site of an earlier church. Nave and two aisles and three rectangular apses. Massive St. Christopher on the façade, and in the lunette Madonna with St. Peter and St. Blasius, late-14C frescos by the 'Master of San Biagio', who also painted the frescos in the choir vault; the other pictures and statues on walls and pillars are 15C. In the S. aisle painting with a Madonna dating from 1520, the work of Sursnicus of Lugano.
Museums. Castello di Sasso Corbaro, *Museo dell'arte e delle tradizioni popolari del Ticino.* Castello di Montebello, *Museo civico,* archaeology and local history.

Bellmund BE
6☐D3

Refugium Knebelburg: An oval castle plateau surrounded by a moat and situated on the Jäissberg to the E. of the village. Its age is unknown but it probably dates from the 10-12C. The interior structure was probably extensively wooden (▷ Studen).

Bellwald VS
12☐D4

A community of several hamlets. FÜRGANGEN: 17C **chapelle de la Vierge** The late Gothic altar in the choir has a depiction of the Coronation of the Virgin (*c.* 1500). The **chapel of St. Anna** above the village dates from 1684.
BODMEN: 17C **Chapelle de la Vierge** with a baroque altar (1684) and a 16C crucifix on the choir arch.
RIED: The **Chapelle de la Vierge** was built in 1686 with an altar from 1750.
EGGEN: 17C **Chapelle de la Vierge**: The central group of figures on the retable dates from 1750.
BELLWALD: **Catholic parish church of Sept-Allégresses-de-la-Vierge** (7 Joys of the Virgin): Built in 1690 and restored in the 19C. Lavish baroque interior furnishings include the high altar of 1704 by the sculptor Johann Sigristen. The **ossuary** of 1733 has an 18C baroque altar.

Belp BE
6☐F5

Reformed church of St. Peter and Paul: This essentially Romanesque building has late Gothic wall paintings in the nave dating from *c.* 1455-60. The frescos are related to those in ▷ Büren, ▷ Kleinhöchstetten and ▷ Kirchlindach. **Altes Schloss** (Local Government Offices): In *c.* 1636 Johann Rudolf Stürler added the main building on to the N. 16C building. The **Neues Schloss,** a baroque building of 1740 built for the historian Alexander von Wattenwyl. The gardens of the country seat of **Oberried** have an early classical gloriette, probably built by Niklaus Sprüngli.

Benken SG
8☐D2

Catholic parish church of St. Peter

*Berg: 16C Kleiner Hahnberg, rebuilt in 1751
(privately owned).*

und Paul: Built 1792–6; extended and
altered in neo-baroque style in 1917. The
late baroque layout has a semicircular apse.
Pilgrimage church of Maria Bildstein:
Built by Hans Burkard in 1966 replacing
an earlier building from the 19C. Of the
former **Wandelburg Castle** to the S. of
the village there are no visible remains. In
the so-called **Kastlet** on Benken Hill traces
of prehistoric settlements have been
revealed in archaelogical excavations.

Berg SG

4□A3

Catholic parish church of St.Michael:
Rebuilt in 1775–6 by Johann Ferdinand
Beer incorporating the medieval tower
(made higher in 1931). The hall church has
a rectangular choir and a new arcaded
vestibule. **Schloss Pfauenmoos,** to the E.
of the village was built c. 1564 by the
Seckelmeister of St. Gallen, Leonhard
Zollikofer; altered at the end of the 18C.
The three-storeyed building has a ceiling
painting of 1585 in the hall. **Grosser
Hahnberg,** N. of the village, is the former
seat of the Zollikofer family. Built c. 1616,
it was rebuilt c. 1770. Gabled building
with staircase tower on the S. side, Art
Nouveau stucco ceiling on the 1st floor.
Kleiner Hahnberg: Built in the 16C for
the Zollikofer family; rebuilt c. 1751. Half-
timbered building with brick ground floor,
staircase tower in the S. gable and stucco
reliefs over the portal and on the windows.

Berg TG

3□E3

Reformed church: Late Gothic building
with late Romanesque choir tower; the
nave was lengthened in 1735-7. **Catholic
church of St.Mauritius:** Built by Adolf
Gaudy in 1938. The **schloss** was altered
or rebuilt c. 1600 and has been an old people's home since 1953. The castle chapel
dates from 1619; alterations in 1667 and
18C.

Berg am Irchel ZH

3□A3

Schloss Berg: Rebuilt in 1642 as the seat
of law lords. The Renaissance hall has
panelling and a coffered ceiling. The tower
oven is by Hans Heinrich Pfau (1705);
other ovens are 18C. **Schloss Eigenthal,**
a small country seat built in 1588, is approached along an avenue.

Bergün/Bravuogn GR

14□C1

The **townscape** of Bergün is typically
Engadine (▷ Guarda). The **Reformed
church** has Romanesque nave walls and
tower (1188), late Gothic polygonal apse,
a richly embellished flat ceiling and a spire
from c. 1500. Also from c. 1500 date the
interior wall paintings, probably the work
of a Lombard artist, which were heavily
restored in 1930. The **Catholic daughter
church of St.Maria** at the lower end of
the village, was built in 1958 and has
stained glass by Ferd. Gehr. The **Platz-
turm,** built in the 12C as a bailiff's tower,
stands out above the roofs of the village
with its 17C baroque dome. **House No.
114** in the upper part of the village probably dates from the 15C and has 17C additions. The gable front has oriels and
façade paintings in rococo style (1786).
STULS/STUGL: The **Reformed church**
has splendid wall paintings (restored 1955).
Outside, on the N. wall, there are St.
Christopher, John the Baptist (c. 1310-20),
and St.George and the Dragon (1360-70).

Stugl: Christ in the Mandorla (detail), wall painting c. 1360–70.

Inside there is a painted vault (by the painter of St.George). A central mandorla has Christ with symbols of the Evangelists and the four church fathers. Besides this, the W. wall has the Burial of the Virgin, Baptism of Christ, Last Supper and 5 scenes from the Passion.

Berlingen TG

3 □ D2

Reformed church: Built in 1842 by Johann Nepomuk Keller, it is one of the fist neo-Gothic buildings in Switzerland to incorporate classical architectural elements.

Bern BE

6 □ E4

In 1191 Duke Berchtold V of Zähringen founded the city of Bern. When the Zähringen line died out the city became free and, finding itself increasingly threatened by the Kyburgs and the Habsburgs, formed an alliance with Savoy in 1255. The victory against Fribourg and the Burgundian nobles at Laupen in 1339, as

well as its admission into the Confederation in 1353, fostered Bern's policy of expansion, which reached its height with the annexation of the Aargau in 1415. The first parts of the Vaud were obtained in the Burgundian War and following its complete occupation in 1536 Bern was the largest city state N. of the Alps. Revolts by the peasants (1653) and burghers (1749) failed to bring the absolutist Patriziat (the patricians) to its knees. Its fall did not come until the invasion of the French in 1798, which resulted in Bern losing its Aargau posessions and the Vaud, although Bern was promised the former Prince-Bishopric of Basel (Jura) instead, at the Congress of Vienna. Bern became federal capital in 1848.

ALTSTADT (Old Town) *City layout and fortifications:* The Altstadt, naturally protected on 3 sides by the Aare, is rectangular, with streets running lengthways. The **Gerechtigkeits-, Kram-** and **Marktgasse** form the central axis, which stands out from the parallel side streets for being broader. The city developed in stages with the lengthening of these streets westwards. Exit was via **Burg Nydegg** (built by the Zähringens at the end of the 12C) at the apex of the bend in the Aare to protect the river crossing (ferry). Of this fortress, a massive keep (destroyed *c.* 1270) a corner projection and the Sodbrunnen (reconstructed) are still visible. The *first layout* of the city adjoined the Kreuzgasse to the W., with walls and a gate tower, which have now disappeared. The *first expansion of the city (1191-1256)* took in the area from the Kreuzgasse up to the **Zeitglockenturm**, the new W. gate. Originally (late 12C) open towards the city, the structure is now the result of rebuilding from the 15–18C. The clock, by Kaspar Brunner (1530), along with the Marktturm in Solothurn and the Hoher Turm in Aarau, is one of the oldest great clocks in Switzerland. The hour striker in the little bell tower, the two tower clocks, the jack-o'-the-clocks and the astronomical clock are all driven by a central mechanism. The calendar displays the time of day, the day of the week and month, the month itself, the zodiac and phases of the moon. The *second expansion (after 1256)* extended the city

Bern: aerial view showing the layout of the 12C Zähringen town.

The Gothic decoration on the main portal of the Münster dates from 1490–1500.

as far as the **Käfigturm.** This, the third W. gate (1641–4), takes the form of a triumphal arch, an example of Italian Mannerism (late Renaissance) in the N. The *last city expansion (1344–6)* pushed the boundary back to the site of today's railway station. In the underpass excavated remains of the walls and the foundations of the **Christoffelturm,** (removed in 1865) are visible. There are also fragments (copies) of the tower's statue, a wooden figure of St.Christopher some 29ft. 6 ins. high. The N. end of the fourth ring of walls is formed by the **Blutturm,** (at the foot of the Lorraine Bridge) a semicircular tower open to the E., with a ring of battlements and spire. The medieval defences were strengthened

during the baroque (1622–42) by a ring of **entrenchments.** The University now stands on the site of the Great Entrenchment. The Small Entrenchment to the W. of the Bundeshaus has been a promenade since 1873. The **removal of the fortifications** began in 1807 with the dismantling of the outermost W. belt, and ended in 1917 with the removal of the Münztor. In spite of the various styles of façade, the city preserves remarkably uniform **groups of streets,** not least because of the unifying effect of the **arcades,** which have a combined length of *c.* 4 m.

Ecclesiastical buildings: The late Gothic **Minster** (St. Vincent) owes its richness of vault forms to a long building history. Begun in 1421 under the direction of Matthäus Ensinger, the interior was not completed until 1571–3 when the central aisle was vaulted. The tower, based on the tower of Ulm Cathedral, was completed in 1892. Erhard Küng, a Westphalian created the main portal with the Last Judgement. Inside: late Gothic stained glass and Renaissance choirstalls. **French Church** (Predigergasse): The church of the former Dominican monastery, it was built at the end of the 13C in the simple Gothic style typical of the Mendicant order. The rood screen, dating from the time of construction has paintings dated 1495 by the Bernese 'Nelkenmeister'. The building acquired a baroque W. front in 1753. The **Nydegg Church** rises at the E. end of the Aare peninsula on the site of the 13C Reichsburg, of which the remains of walls are still visible below the choir. The present building is a late Gothic hall church from the end of the 15C, with a W. extension in the same style dating from 1864–5. The late Gothic **Antonierkirche** on Postgasse was the hospital church of the Antonines, whose duty it was to attend to those suffering from ergotism ('St. Anthony's fire'); it is now deconsecrated. **Heiliggeistkirche** (by the station) was built in baroque style by Niklaus Schiltknecht in 1726–9 and is the most important Protestant building in Switzerland. Inside, between colossal columns, galleries rest on net vaults, a curious resurgence of late Gothic. The upper vaults are adorned by Régence stucco by Joseph Anton Feuchtmayer of Wessobrunn. The **Catholic church of St.Peter und Paul,** near the Rathaus, was built in Romanesque/early Gothic style to plans of French architects, as a result of an international competition.

The Heiliggeistkirche, the most important Protestant baroque church in Switzerland.

State buildings in chronological order. **Rathaus:** Late Gothic, built in 1406–17; 19C neo-Gothic additions were removed in 1940–2. A double flight of steps leads to the council rooms on the upper floor. The ground floor hall with its beamed ceiling supported by round pillars was formerly a granary. The **Kornhaus** next to the **Stadttheater** (1903), a high baroque

Late Gothic Rathaus with double flight of steps.

building from the early 18C was converted into a trade museum in 1895. Vaulted cellar and pillared hall with former granaries above; the outside is articulated by colossal pilasters. The **Burgerspital** (next to the main station) was built in 1734–42 based on French models (e.g. Hôtel des Invalides in Paris). The basic concept of a rectangular courtyard linked to a semicircular one was conceived by Niklaus Schiltknecht, the details are by Joseph Abeille. In the courtyard there are urn fountains of 1739–42 in 'sepulchral style'. The **Stiftsgebäude** on Münsterplatz, now the seat of the cantonal government, is a late baroque building by

Albrecht Stürler; it occupies the site of the Deutschordenhaus (Teutonic Order), which became a canonical foundation in 1485. The **Stadtbibliothek** (library) near the neo-baroque **Kasino,** was built in 1755 as a corn exchange and converted into a library in 1787–94 by Niklaus Sprüngli and Lorenz Schmid. The complex is horseshoe-shaped; classical interior decoration. The late baroque façade of the **Bibliotheksgalerie,** built by Niklaus Sprüngli in 1772–5, was reconstructed as the backdrop to a fountain on Thunplatz after the building was pulled down in

1912. The **Hauptwache** of 1768, with parterre and colonnaded portico, attic and mansard roof, was also built by Sprüngli as the S. end of the Theatre Square. **Waisenhaus,** now a police station, was built in 1783–6 and has Louis XVI ornamental detail. **Alte Hauptpost,** Kramgasse 20. This post-Gothic trading house, which is now the canton's police H.Q, was converted in classical style in 1832–4. The **Kunstmuseum** is a neo-Renaissance building by Eugen Settler, 1876–9. The **Bundeshaus** was built in two main phases. The W. wing was built in the Maximilian style of Munich by Friedrich Studer in 1852–7. Later came the Parliament building and the E. wing, both by Hans Wilhelm Auer, who based the E. wing on the W. wing. The modest quattrocento wings contrast strongly with the neo-Renaissance domed building.

Public buildings: **Rathaus des äussern Standes,** Zeughausgasse 17. Built in 1728–30, probably by Albrecht Stürler; rebuilt in 1905. The façade reveals French influence. The **Hôtel de Musique,** on Theaterplatz, was built in 1767–70 to the plans of Niklaus Sprüngli. The Grande Société building was equipped with a theatre, despite drama being forbidden, and indeed it was not to serve its purpose as a municipal stage until after the fall of the Ancien Régime (1799–1900). The '**Museum**' on Bundesplatz was converted into the Cantonal Bank of Bern in 1906.

Residential buildings: Despite a few intrusions, the *Gerechtigkeitsgasse* has preserved its intricate late Gothic character as the oldest part of the main axis of the Zähringen city. A few buildings are essentially 16C, of which nos. 19,30,34 and 60 each have an old staircase tower. No. 33 has a front courtyard and a spiral staircase in late Renaissance style. *Junkerngasse* is mainly late Gothic with unobtrusive baroque, such as No. 59, **Von Wattenwyl-Haus,** built for Samuel Frisching in 1706–9 incorporating older parts. There are good reasons for thinking that the designer was Joseph Abeille, for a French love of balance expresses itself in the clear articulation of the S. front, from which a terrace leads towards the Aare. **Erlacherhof,** No 47, built for the Mayor

Hieronymus von Erlach (▷ Hindelbank and Thunstetten) was begun by Albrecht Stürler in 1746 and is the only example of a palace in the form of a horseshoe in the French style in Bern. In contrast the arcaded side of the main courtyard reflects local character. Most of the houses in the *Kramgasse* acquired baroque façades over the old arcades in the 18C (nos. 16,54 and 72 are by Stürler). The **Mayhaus,** *Münstergasse 6,* has a Renaissance façade. **Diesbachhaus,** No. 2 in the same street, is late baroque. The **Tscharnerhaus,** *Münsterplatz 12,* has a façade decorated in Régence style. **Marcuard-Haus,** *Amtgasse 5,* built for Governor Johann Rudolf Fischer *c.* 1763–5, later belonged to Marcuard. The building, attributed to Niklaus Sprüngli has a wrought-iron staircase and stucco in Louis XV style.

Bridges: The **Untertorbrücke** is the oldest and, up until 1844 was the only fixed river crossing. In 1461 the original wooden bridge was replaced by a new stone construction. Well into the 18C the bridge had battlemented walls, walkways and gates above the bridge pillars but it has since been reduced to its basic structure. Of the two bridgeheads the gate tower on the right bank known as the **Felsenburg,** has survived from the 13C. The **Grosse Nydegg bridge,** built in 1841–4 as Bern's first high-level bridge, stands some 82 ft. above the water. A massive plain structure with granite supports, it expresses a classical architectural approach. Other high-level bridges include the **Railway Bridge** (1941, in reinforced concrete) and the **Lorraine Bridge** (also reinforced concrete, finished in 1930) by Maillart and Klauser.

Fountains: Of the 11 Renaissance fountains with figures built around the middle of the 16C, 10 have preserved their original figures, although basins and columns have in many cases been replaced. E—W they are: The **Läuferbrunnen** at Nydeggstalden, whose classical trough of 1824 is structured like an antique basin and whose figure dates from 1545. The **Gerechtigkeitsbrunnen** (in the Gasse of the same name) has a figure personifying Justice (1543: Justitia, with bound eyes and ears, holds the executioner's sword and scales) and is probably by Hans Gieng of

Statue of Justice on the Gerechtigkeits-brunnen, 1543.

Kindlifresserbrunnen by Hans Gieng of Fribourg.

Fribourg. Half figures at Justice's feet (pope, sultan, emperor, mayor) are allegories of four types of government, theocracy, monarchy, autocracy and republic. The **Vennerbrunnen** in front of the Rathaus has a Bernese soldier in full armour carrying a banner (1542). The **Mosesbrunnen** near the cathedral was rebuilt in 1790-1 and has a Louis XVI-style basin and a figure in 16C style; it may have been made by Niklaus Sprüngli. The figure of the **Simsonbrunnen,** sculpted by Hans Gieng in 1544, is modelled on the Solothurn fountain of the same name. The **Zähringerbrunnen** by the Zeitglocken-turm was built in 1535 as a monument to the city's founder Berchtold von Zähringen. The fountain's column has Bern's heraldic beast depicted in a tournament. **Kindlifresserbrunnen,** Kornhausplatz.The monogram HG declares the work of Hans Gieng. The child-devouring giant probably represents an old Fasching (carnival) figure. By the same artist is the figure of the **Schützenbrunnen** at the E. end of the Marktgasse. The archer found its successor in Michael Wumard's banner carrier on the Bieler Ring-Brunnen. The **Anna-Seiler-Brunnen** by the Käfigturm was incorrectly named after the founder of the island

hospital in the 19C. In fact the townswomen mixing water and wine represent the Virtue of Temperance. The column is probably Roman. The **Pfeiferbrunnen** in the Spitalgasse is another work by Hans Gieng. The significance of the bagpiper is not known. **Ryfflibrunnen,** Aarbergergasse, was named in the 19C after Ryffli, the legendary crossbowman of Burgiswald. *Monuments:* **Zähringen Monument,** Nydegghöfli. The bronze statue by Karl Emanuel von Tscharner (1844–7), commemorates the city's founder. The **Equestrian statue of Rudolf von Erlach** on Kornhausplatz depicts the victorious army commander from Laupen. Like the Zähringen Monument, the work, which was begun by Josef Volmar in 1839, represents the romantic leaning of Swiss monumental sculpture. **Baubenberg Monument,** Hirschengraben. By Max Leu, 1892-7. On the Kleine Schanze is the monument to the flyer **Oskar Bider,** by Hermann Haller (1924). In the same place is the **World Post Monument** (1908). Near the university is the monument to **Albrecht von Haller** by Hugo Siegwart.

OUTER DISTRICTS: **Dreifaltigkeitskirche** (Holy Trinity) Taubenstrasse: Building in historical style (Lombard-Romanesque).

Pauluskirche in the Länggasse Quarter, built by Curjel and Moser in 1903, is Art Nouveau. **Friedenskirche,** in the Mattenhof, is a neoclassical building by Karl Indermühle. The **History Museum** in Helvetiaplatz was built in the romantic 'Burgenstil' in 1892–4. To the S. lie the **Natural History Museum** (1932) and the **Landesbibliothek,** built in 1928–31 by Oeschger, Hostettler and Kaufmann in the 'Neue Bauen' style. Opposite is the neoclassical **Neue Gymnasium** (Great Hall with frescos by Cuno Amiet). Pre-war Functionalism is represented by the **Loryspital,** the **Kantonale Säuglingsheim** in Elfenau, the **new buildings of the university**—all by Salvisberg and Brechbühl — as well as the **Gewerbeschule** by H.Brechbühle. The **Siedlung Halen** at Stuckishaus, by the 'Atelier 5' in 1959–61 includes over 75 standardized family houses, the owners of which are also co-owners of the communal complexes (swimming-pool, restaurant, sports complex, etc.). Not far from the estate, which is situated in a clearing in woods, is **Neubrück** , some 295 ft. long over the Aare. This strut and truss-framed bridge dates from 1466. **Schloss Holligen:** In the 13C this was probably a fief of the nearby royal court of Bümpliz; rebuilt in the 16C by Christoph von Diesbach. **Schloss Wittikofen** belonged to the monastery of Interlaken in the 13C and was later the residence of the Bernese historian Johann Ludwig von Wurstemberger. **Morillongut** (Köniz): While the Altstadt is overwhelmingly 18C, the architecture of the surrounding residential districts includes historical styles, Art Nouveau and 'Heimatstil'. **Museums:** Several are in Helvetiaplatz: No.1, *Kunsthalle (art);* No.2, *Berner Schulwarte;* No.4, *Schweizerisches Alpines Museum* and *Schweizerisches PTT Museum;* No.5, *Bernisches Historisches Museum* and *Völkerkundliche Sammlung.* Not far away is the *Schweizerisches Schützenmuseum* (Bernastr.5) and the *Schweizerische Theatersammlung* (in the Landesbibliothek). The *Gewerbemuseum* occupies the Kornhaus, Zeughausgasse 2, which also houses the *Schweizerische Berufsmuseum für Buchbinderei* (book-binding) and the

Cup of the Gesellschaft zu Webern, 1712, in the Historisches Museum in Bern.

Schweizerische Gutenbergmuseum. Kunstmuseum, Hodlerstr.12. *Bernische Abgusssammlung,* Mattenenge 10. *Einstein-Haus,* Kramgasse 49. Also: *Botanischer Garten,* Alltenbergrain 21. *Bärengraben; Tierpark Dählhölzli,* Dalmaziquai 149. *Bundesarchiv; Staatsarchiv.*

Berneck SG

4☐B3

Catholic parish church of Unsere Liebe Frau: Founded in the 9C, rebuilt probably in the 12C; choir 1449, Sebastianskapelle 1468. Nave lengthened *c.* 1500. Baroque conversion in 1760 – 70; renovated by Hans Burkard 1937–8. Inside there is a wall painting from the 15–17C. S. of the church is the **Heiligkreuzkapelle,** built in 1759 by Johann Martin Ilg as a quatrefoil centrally-planned building. **Rathaus:** Imposing gabled building on the village square, mentioned in 1501, rebuilt in 1591 and converted by Hans Burkard in 1943. **House No.43** is painted and has gables and an arcade at the side from the early 18C. **House No.604 – 5:** Built *c.* 1700, half-timbered building with decorative painting.

Beromünster: The oldest printed matter in Switzerland was produced in the so-called Schloss in 1470.

Chlösterli, on the E. edge of town, probably dates from the 15C and was formerly a mill attached to the Convent of St. Catherine in St.Gallen. **Fürstenhaus,** at the foot of the castle hill, is a stone building with a steep gable; over the round arch of the portal there are the arms of Abbot Josef von Rudolfi, (1729).

Bernhardzell SG
see WALDKIRCH   3 □ F4

Beromünster LU
7 □ D/E2

The **college for canons** is thought to have been founded by a count called Bero as a funerary chapel for the counts of Aargau and later of Lenzburg. The loosely organized group of collegiate buildings from the 16–18C contrasts with the regular street arrangement at the foot of the hill on which the college stands. The **Collegiate Church of St.Michael** was built c. 1030 as a columned basilica. It was altered in baroque style by Jeremias Schmid, a chaplain, at the end of the 17C and again in 1773–5. The tower dates from the 13C. The original early Romanesque complex is still visible from the outside; the crypt is a special form of the gallery type. Of interest amongst the furnishings are the Renaissance choir stalls (1601–10). The

church treasure, one of the finest in the country, includes a silver book cover from an early 14C Evangelistary. **Gasthaus Hirschen,** former college administrative building, was built by Hans Murer and Hans Riner in 1536. This late Gothic building has a stepped gable like the somewhat older priest's house of Hochdorf (LU) by the same architects. The so-called **Schloss,** now a *Heimatmuseum* local history), was formerly a 14C residential tower. The oldest Schweizer Druck (a theological dictionary) was produced in the printing works of Helias Helie here.

Bertiswil LU
see ROTHENBURG   7 □ E3

Betschwanden GL
8 □ D4

Reformed church: Documented since 1370 and repeatedly altered; tower above choir.

Betten VS
12 □ D5

BETTMERALP **Chapelle Notre-Dame-des-Nieges** built in 1697 with a 17C altar from the workshop of Johann Sigristen (Virgin Mary by Johann Ritz).

Bettingen BS
2 □ A3

St. Chrischona: The first church was reputedly the burial place of St.Christine of the legendary 11,000 virgins. The present structure was built in three stages. The W. tower dates from c. 1450–60, the choir 1503–9 and finally, the nave incorporating the tower, 1513–16. Church of the Pilgrim Mission since 1840.

Bettlach SO
6 □ E2

The residential tower and Great Hall of the **ruined castle of Grenchen,** perched on

Bever: 14&15C paintings on the exterior wall (including fight with the dragon).

a high ridge to the N. of the village, date from the mid 12C.

Bettmeralp VS
see BETTEN   12☐D5

Beurnevésin JU
                                              1☐C

Catholic parish church of St-Jacques:
A nave was added to the late Gothic choir (fine groin vaulting and window tracery) which was probably itself once a chapel with a tower attached at the front.

Bevaix NE
                                              6☐A4

Reformed church: Built in 1605. The W. portal has Romanesque decorative elements from the church of a former Benedictine priory (founded in 998), which lay to the E. of the village. Next to the church is the **Hôtel de Commune,** an 18-19C building. The **Château,** Rue du Château 1, a baroque mansion of 1722, has a sculpted gable on the main façade with the arms of the Chambrier-Jeanjaquet family. The **Maison Chambrier,** Rue du Temple 19, dates from 1746-7.

Bever GR
                                              14☐D2

The **Reformed church** was rebuilt using older building materials by Giov. Caserin and Franc. Pancera in 1665-7. Tower,

1669-73. On the exterior of the W. wall remains of wall paintings date from the late 14C and early 15C); restoration 1968.

Bévilard BE
                                              6☐D1

The **Reformed church,** rebuilt 1715-16, incorporates a front tower with an onion dome. Inside, wooden ceiling with octagonal panels.

Bex VD
                                              17☐B1

Originally in the possession of the bishops of Sion, from the 12C it belonged to the counts of Savoy. In the 16C Bex enjoyed moderate prosperity due to exploitation of the saltworks by the Bernese. In the 19C it was a bathing resort. The **Reformed church of St. Clément** is documented since 1193. Choir and nave were built in classical style in 1813, while the massive front tower with late Gothic portal dates from 1501. The **Hôtel de Ville** in the main street dates from 1746. On a hill S. of the town stand the **Tour de Duin** and ruins of the castle of Bex, founded in the 12C. *Local History Museum.*

Biasca TI
                                              13☐D5

The **collegiate church of San Pietro e Paolo,** stands in a dominating position above the village. Probably built between the end of the 11 and the 12C, the Romanesque basilica has a nave, two aisles, round apse and a S. staircase tower of 4 storeys. The flight of steps and the porch in the W. façade date from 1685; the S. polygonal chapel from 1600. The interior, most sober since the restoration of 1955-66, contains a rich collection of frescos from the 13-17C. The oldest frescos are those in the choir vaults; the others, adorning walls and pillars, are in the main 15C. The S. wall has a depiction of the Life of San Carlo Borromeo by Alessandro Gorla, *c.* 1620. In the aisles there are fragments of Romanesque carving. The **Catholic parish church of San Carlo,** a massive structure over a Greek cross groundplan with octagonal dome, is early 20C.

Biberist SO
6 ☐ F2

Schlösschen Vorder-Bleichenberg: The summer residence of the von Roll family, it was built at the start of the 17C and converted into a 'Türmlihaus' (tower house) in 1678–80. *Picture Gallery of the Moos-Flury Foundation.*

Bichelsee TG
3 ☐ C/D4

Set amid beautiful lakeland scenery, the **Reformed church** was built by Edwin Rausser in 1960 using Le Corbusier's 'Modulor' unit of measurement. Doors carved by Rolf Lehmann; stained glass by Köbi Lämmler.

Biel/Bienne BE
6 ☐ D2

The town was founded at the beginning of the 13C by the Bishop of Basel as a stronghold against Nidau Castle and the Counts of Neuchâtel.

ALTSTADT: The heart of the town is formed by the **'Ring'** (the marketplace), the town church and the Unter- and Obergässli. The rest of the town radiates from this centre. The first expansion was the Unter- and Obergässli in the late 13C. The oldest part of the town defences are the three **Towers on Rosiusplatz,** built *c.* 1405 with material from the town castle which had been destroyed in 1367. In **Obergasse** German and French architecture meet: late Gothic houses on the S. side have arcades in the Bernese manner and ground-floor entrances, while those on the N. side have flights of steps leading up to raised entrances. The **Reformed church of St.Benedikt** is a late Gothic building from the mid 15C; tower, 1483–1549. Stained glass in the upper choir windows

Biasca: round apse and tower of the 11&12C collegiate church.

is dated 1457 and depicts Christ's passion and the life of the church's patron saint. Stylistically the windows are similar to those of Bern Cathedral. In the Burgplatz are the **Rathaus,** in Flamboyant style (1530–4), and the **Zeughaus** (once an arsenal, now a theatre) of 1590. The **Zunfthaus zu Waldleuten,** built in the Ring in 1559–61, has stepped gables, Gothic windows and corner oriel surmounted by an onion dome. Renaissance elements are apparent in the detail, e.g. shell decoration. The latter building's architect, Michael Wymard, was also responsible for the **Ring Fountain** (Bannerherr) and the **Obergassbrunnen.**

NEUSTADT (New Town): With the growth of the clock industry in the 17&18C the town expanded towards the lake. Elegant dwellings were built along the newly laid-out promenades. **Rockhall,** Seevorstadt 103. Vautravers, Rousseau and Cagliostro number among the famous residents of this baroque country seat, built in 1692–4. **Museum Schwab,** built by Friedrich de Rutté in 1871–3, houses an important *archaeological collection* which includes finds from the settlements of La Tène and Petinesca. **Landhaus Elfenau,**

Biel: market-place, known as the 'Ring'.

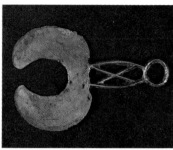

Biel: bronze razor from Cortaillod in the Musée Schwab.

Schüsspromenade 14, built in neo baroque style 1861–2. In *c.* 1930, following a competition, numerous buildings in the style of the 'New Architecture' were built in the **Bahnhofquartier.** Notable contemporary architecture is represented by the **Kongresshaus** (1961–6) and the **Neue Gymnasium** (1976–9) on the Strandboden, both by Max Schlup.

Biel VS

12☐E4

Catholic parish church of St.Johannes Evangelista: A simple 13C chapel, it was enlarged in 1654 and rebuilt in the 18–19C. The single-aisled building with rectangular choir has a high altar (1715) by Johann Ritz; statues on side altars are from Ritz's workshop. The S. wall of the nave has a Gothic crucifix and an 18C Pietà by Johann Baptist Lagger.

Biglen BE

7☐A4

Reformed church: Built in 1521 on the site of a Romanesque basilica with 3 apses. The wooden ceiling is decorated with carvings of fabulous creatures, grotesques and foliage.

Bignasco TI

13☐B5

In the old part of the village an **arched bridge** spans the river Maggia. The **chapel of San Rocco** nearby dating from 1597 was altered in baroque style. The **chapel of Santa Maria del Ponte** stands on a hill and has frescos from the time it was built (1512).

Bilten GL

8☐D2

On the slope behind the church stands the **Herrenhaus Milt,** the gable of which houses a richly furnished banqueting hall. The mansion was built in 1608 for Heinrich Elsener, known as Milt, the richest inhabitant of Glarus at the time. Further up the mountain, is the **Miltsche Ritterhaus,** dated 1724 in the gable.

Binn VS

12☐D5

The valley community comprises several hamlets. ZENBINNEN: The **chapelle St-Sébastien,** a baroque building of 1725, has an altar of 1675.
SCHMIDIGENHAUSERN: The **Chapelle St-Antoine,** a baroque building of 1690, has an altar of 1692 by Johann Ritz. A bridge dating from 1564 spans the Binna.
WILLERN: The **Catholic parish church of St-Michael,** medieval in origin, was rebuilt in the 16&18C. The façade has a Renaissance portal of 1561. The high altar by the sculptor Peter Lagger dates from 1767; 18C side altars by Anton Sigristen.
IMFELD: Beautifully preserved hamlet

with traditional wooden buildings. The **chapelle St-Martin** dates from the end of the 17C. Baroque altar (1700) by Johann Ritz; painted leather antependium (1763).

Binningen BL
1☐F3

The **Reformed parish church of St. Margaretha,** on a hill to the E. of the Birsig, was built by Jacob Meyer in 1673 on older foundations. It is part of the St. Margaretha estate (17&19C). The **Schloss,** originally surrounded by water, dates back to the 13C; altered in baroque style in the 17C and reduced in size in the 19C.

Biolay-Orjulaz VD
10☐E2

The village has interesting **granaries,** including a remarkable stone granary with a Renaissance window (1720), another stone granary with an oven (1680) as well as 17C wooden granaries.

Bioux, Les VD
see L'ABBAYE
10☐C2

Birgisch VS
18☐C1

Chapelle St-Jean-Baptiste: Founded in 1477; baroque altar with 14C crucifix.

Birmensdorf ZH
2☐F5

Reformed parish church: Church with nave and two aisles built in 1659 on the site of a church mentioned as early as the 9C; Romanesque tower.

Birmenstorf AG
2☐E4

Cemetery Chapel: The Romanesque choir of the former parish church has a late Gothic fresco cycle (with prophets,

Bironico: the Casa dei Landvogti, seat of the Landvogts until the late 18C.

apostles, Sts. Leodegar, George and Martin), uncovered in 1937.

Bironico TI
19☐D3

Catholic parish church of Santi Giovanni Evangelista e Martino: Documented since 1205, it was probably built in the 13–14C. Additions of various dates, e.g. tower 1931. The baroque interior is single-aisled with 8 side chapels, a richly-decorated triumphal arch and a high altar dating from 1625; 17C Crucifixion on the W. wall. The **Chapel of Santa Maria del Rosario** next to the cemetery is early 17C.
BRICCOLA: The **chapel of San Pietro** dates from 1653 and has a stuccoed façade. The **Casa dei Landvogti** of 1576 was partly rebuilt in 1966; the courtyard has two storeys with loggias and coats-of-arms on the walls. A first floor room has a fine fireplace and decorative paintings.

Birwinken TG
3☐E3

Reformed church: Rebuilt in the 14C as a simple nave; tower and polygonal choir date from 1485, last storey of tower and pointed spire date from 1809.

Bischofszell TG
3☐E/F4

This little country town above the con-

Bischofszell: the Rathaus has extraordinary wrought ironwork.

Bischofszell: impressive bridge over the Thur, 1487.

fluence of the Sitter and the Thur was founded and fortified before 1000 by the Bishops of Constance as a stronghold against St. Gallen. The oldest part is the court district with castle and canonical foundation, the enclosing wall of which gradually became a ring of houses. After the demolition of the E. suburb in the Appenzell War and a fire in 1419, the suburb was rebuilt and fortified in 1437. A severe fire in 1743 in the area of the Markt-, Kirch- and Tuchgasse destroyed some 70 buildings. The town which had grown prosperous from the linen trade, was then rebuilt to plans by the Grubenmann brothers.
Catholic parish church of St. Pelagius: Originally the collegiate church of the canonical foundation. The basilica has a nave, two aisles, choir and 14C Allerheiligen (All Holy) chapel; nave rebuilt 15C. The sacristy was added to the E. end of the choir in 1708–9. 15C tower; choir altered to baroque *c.* 1770. Inside, there are fragments of late Gothic wall paintings and an early baroque high altar (1639–40). The **chapel of St. Michael,** a free-standing building N. of the Catholic church, was built at the beginning of the 15C and has a late Gothic painting of St. Michael dated 1731. The **Reformed parish church of St. Johann,** is by Benedikt Huber (1968–9). The **Rathaus,** by Gaspare Bagnato 1747–50, has a façade divided into 5 parts linked by pilaster

strips, with a front gable and a double flight of steps. **Schloss:** Originally a fortified bishop's palace. The lower part remains from this 13C residence, the upper part dates from sometime after 1419; the E. part was added in 1813. In the court area, 4 of the free courts (whose privileges go back to before the founding of the market settlement) have survived: the **Bürklersche Freihof** to the E. of the castle (Kirchgasse 35), the **Helmsdorfische Freihof** (Hofplatz 27), the **Blarerhof** (Schattengasse 12) and the **Grüne or Von Anwilische Hof** (Kirchgasse 25). Rebuilding after the fire of 1743 followed the Grubenmann brothers' (Ulrich, Jakob and Johann) overall plan. They also built several houses themselves, such as the **Doppelhaus zum Rosenstock und zum Weinstock** (Marktgasse 7 – 9) built 1743–5 in Wessobrunn stucco. **Bogenturm:** Once the E. outer work, it became a clock and bell tower after the fortification of the suburb in 1437; new ridge crest, 1743. **Thurbrücke,** a stone bridge with 8 arches, was completed in 1487 and is one of the most important late medieval bridges in Switzerland. The *Local Museum,* Marktgasse 4, has a local history collection.

Bissone TI

19☐D4

Birthplace of the architect Francesco Borromini (1599–1667). The **Catholic parish church of San Carpoforo,** at the end of the village, is documented from 1148 and was completely rebuilt at the end of the 17C. The façade dates from 1759 & 1784. It has a nave, two aisles, six side chapels and a rectangular choir. It is richly decorated inside with stucco and 17C frescos. The 16C high altar is probably the work of Tomaso Lombardo da Bissone, pupil of Sansovino. The **church of San Rocco** N. of the village, is medieval in origin and was rebuilt in 1630. Baroque façade adorned with three statues. 17–18C furnishings inside. The main street has arcaded houses typical of the area. **Casa Tencalla,** No. 10, a 16C patrician's house is now a *Museum.*

Bissone: façade of the parish church of San Carpoforo dating from 1759 and 1784.

Bitsch VS

12 □ C5

WASEN: **Chapelle de la Présentation-de-la Vierge** built in 1657 with 17C altar and 16&17C statues.

Bivio/Beiva GR

14 □ C3

The **Catholic parish church of St. Gallus** has a very fine late Gothic/Renaissance winged altar. The carvings seem to be stylistically related to late works from the Strigel workshop, e.g. the altar of ▷ Brienz (GR). Remains of two columns, one on either side of the road through the JULIERPASSHÖHE remind the traveller that it was the Romans who opened this Alpine pass.

Blankenburg BE

see ZWEISIMMEN   11 □ E3

Blatten LU

7 □ E3

The **pilgrimage church of St.Jost** was founded *c.* 1370. Tower and E. parts of the nave survive from the original building, which was consecrated in 1391. The remainder dates from the 16–18C. The baro-

Blatten: pilgrimage church of St. Jost, frequently extended and altered.

que high altar (*c.* 1680) is by Michael Hartmann. Side altars have carved figures in biblical scenes by Hans Ulrich Räber.

Blatten LU

12 □ B5

A village typical of the Lötschen valley with wooden chalets, barns and granaries. The neo-Gothic church was built in 1878. EISTEN: Small hamlet with traditional buildings. **Muttergotteskapelle,** baroque building of 1672.

Blonay: often extended and altered after 1175.

KÜHMATT: Chapel of Mariä Heimsuchung, built in 1654. Inside, 18C altar attributed to Johann Sigristen; 18&19C exvotos.

Blattenbach ZH
see WALD   8☐C1

Blonay VD
11☐B4

The **château,** to the W. of the village was built by Guillaume II de Blonay in 1175 and, apart from one short interruption, has been in his family's hands ever since. The oldest part of the building is the square keep, which was later incorporated into a set of buildings around a courtyard. Four corner towers, two of which have survived, defended the complex. Important alterations were carried out on the castle in the 18–20C; in the 19C the moat was filled in.

Blumenstein BE
11☐F1

Reformed church of St. Nikolaus: Gothic building of the 14&16C with a 13C Romanesque tower. The late Gothic wooden ceiling is borne by two wooden supports. The stained-glass windows in the choir have depictions of saints and are similar to the windows of ▷ Köniz and ▷ Münchenbuchsee.

Bodmen VS
see BELLWALD   12☐D4

Bois, Les JU
6☐B2

The **Catholic parish church of Ste-Foy,** built in 1832–3 and influenced by the churches of the Franche-Comté (cf. Ste-Madeleine in Besançon). Empire furnishings.

Bolligen BE
6☐F4

The **Reformed church** has a fine Louis XVI organ and a Renaissance pulpit (1628). The tithe barn next to the church houses a small local *Museum.* The late Gothic **priest's house** of 1581 has a room with grisaille paintings. **Thalgut** in IT-TIGEN was built in 1668, probably by Samuel Jenner. This country mansion has symmetrical groundplan and a window arrangement typical of the Renaissance; the roof is typically Bernese. The **ruins of Geristein** NE of Bolligen are what remains of the ancestral castle of the lords of the same name; documented since 1131.

Boncourt JU
1☐C4

Catholic parish church of St-Pierre-et-Paul: Rebuilt in 1920–1, retaining the Gothic choir and the front tower. The high baroque furnishing is by the Breton brothers (1725–30).

Bondo GR
14☐B4

Catholic church of San Martino: Romanesque hall church consecrated in 1250, with semicircular apse and tall bell tower with a pointed spire (15C). In the 17C the sacristy was added, the nave vaulted and the windows repositioned. Restoration 1960–1. Wall paintings by a N. Italian artist date from *c.* 1480–90 and include a Last Supper on the S. wall of the nave. **Palazzo Salis:** Lord's seat in the Italian mansion style, 1765–74 by Pietro

Blumenstein: church with early-13C stained glass.

Bondo: Palazzo Salis below the village with view over the Bergell.

Martocco and Martino Martinojo for the envoy to Grisons, Count Hieronymus von Salis-Soglio. The building has a broad front divided into three, and a hip roof. On the W. front symmetrical flights of steps lead to a geometrically laid-out garden. Inside: rococo and Louis XVI stucco, portraits and stylistically matching furniture combine to form a tasteful whole (not open to the public).

Bönigen: BE
12☐C2

Numerous buildings from the 16–19C dominate the town. The 16C buildings, with their fluted window frames, astragals and circle ornaments, differ from those of the 17C, which are decorated with cube and lozenge friezes. The equally richly carved 18C façades are colourfully decorated and have painted mottos.

Boningen SO
2☐B5

The **Wirtshaus St. Urs,** built in 1644, has a reception room with painted glass panels and a coffered ceiling dating from the time it was built. The **Tanzhüsli** nearby dates from 1789.

Bonvillars VD
5☐F4

Reformed church of St-Nicolas: Documented in 1148 as being in the

possession of the Abbey of Payerne, this single-aisled building has pointed barrel vaults in the choir and 15C S. side chapels. An interesting fragment of sculpture depicts what seems to be a carpenter and an angel. The **Résidence La Cour,** a former nobleman's seat, dates from the 15–18C.

Borgonovo GR
see STAMPA 14☐B4

Boscéaz, La VD
see ORBE 10☐E1

Boscero TI
see CORZONESO 13☐D4

Bosco Gurin TI
19☐A1

Highest village in Ticino (4,940 ft. above sea level) and the only German-speaking village in the canton. The inhabitants originally came from Valais in the 13C and having settled here have preserved their language and customs ever since. The **Catholic parish church of St.Jakobus and Christophorus** is 13C, was rebuilt in 1581 and altered in the 17&19C; S. chapel with a rococo retable with a statue of the Madonna. Some of the houses and farm buildings are built in Valais style.

Bösingen FR
6☐D5

Church of St-Jacques: Documented

since 1226 and rebuilt in the 18&19C, this single-aisled church has a rectangular choir and a medieval bell tower; 18–19C furnishing. A chapel dating from 1836 has three Roman columns. Opposite the church there is a **granary** dating from 1690; house No. 27 in the village is interesting as it was formerly a **granary** (dating from 1732) and bears an inscription.

Boswil AG
2□E5

Former parish church of St.Pankraz: A fortress church with a late Gothic tower dating from the 17C; stucco redone in the 18C. The church was deconsecrated in 1913 and since 1953 it has served as a concert hall of the 'Alte Kirche Boswil' foundation. The **former priest's house** (18C) is now an artists' home.

Bottmingen BL
1□F3

The **Weiherschloss** has its origins back in the 13C; alterations date from the mid 17C (under the direction of Johann Christoph von der Grün) and 1720 (under Johann Deucher). The previously formidable complex was transformed into a country seat both inside and out, according to French taste.

Böttstein
2□E3

Castle and Castle Chapel: Group of early 17C buildings arranged around a courtyard. The chapel, which is dedicated to St.Anthony, has two towers and follows Italian baroque models with its lavish interior furnishing.

Boudry NE
6□A4

Of the fortifications which formerly enclosed the market town there remain

Bottmingen: moated castle altered as a country seat in the 18C.

only the **Tour Marfaux,** a round tower rebuilt in 1548, and the **Porte des Vermondins,** which was rebuilt using old material in 1741. Above the village stands the **castle,** which was founded in the 13C and whose oldest parts date from the 14C; it is now a *Wine Museum.* The **Reformed church** was built in 1645–7 and has a 19C façade. In front of the church stands the **Gerechtigkeitsbrunnen** (Fountain of Justice), which has a statue dating from 1610.

Bourg-St-Pierre VS
17□D4

Since ancient times Bourg-St-Pierre has been a staging post on the road to Mont-Joux. However, it did not develop until the 13C when the settlement received an enclosing wall (whose course can still be discerned) and two castles. The **Catholic parish church of St-Pierre** was first built by the Carolingians in the 8C along with hospice and monastery. It was destroyed in 972 and Bishop Hugo of Geneva built a new church *c.* 1000—from this time the interesting *bell tower,* with twin windows and Lombard blind arcades, has survived. The tower acquired an an octagonal spire in the 16C. The church was rebuilt in 1739 when the Romanesque N. chapel and the triumphal arch were retained. The S. wall has a 15C fresco depicting St.

Böttstein: detail of the baroque interior of the Schloss chapel.

Apollonia. 18 – 19C interior furnishing. Next to the church stands the former priory building. In the graveyard wall there is a Roman *milestone* which dates from the time of the Emperor Constantine. Two **houses** which belonged to the Challant family (15–16C) stand on the main street. S. of the village, near the Roman and medieval road, are the **ruins of Schloss Allinges.** Of the castle, documented since 1323 and destroyed in 1475, there remains just a massive shell of walls. Another castle, which belonged to the lords of Quart, stood on the site of the present Botanical Garden. N. of the village is the **baroque chapel of Notre-Dame de Lorette,** which was built in 1663.
GRAND-SAINT-BERNARD: The pass of the former Mont-Joux (from the Latin Mons Jovis) was an important crossing point in Roman times. A small temple to Jupiter Penninus and a shelter for travellers was built at the head of the pass. In the 11C St. Bernard of Aosta founded the present **Hospice,** which has borne his name since 1149 and was run by Augustinian canons from the end of the 12C onwards. With the exception of the unaltered cellar, the original building was altered and enlarged in the 16,17&19C; it now consists of the priory building, the St. Louis hospital building of 1786 and the morgue. The **convent church of St-Bernard** was built in 1686 on the foundations of a late medieval building. The richly decorated choir

Bourg-St-Pierre: hospice buildings on the Great St. Bernard.

has a frescoed 17C vault, a high altar in marble dating from 1689 and carved choir stalls of 1681. The sacristy houses the *church treasure* which has a 13C reliquary of St-Bernard. The hospice *museum* documents the history of the pass since Roman times.

Bourgillon FR
see FRIBOURG   11 □ D1

Le Bouveret VS
see PORT-VALAIS   11 □ A5

Bramois VS
                                                          17 □ E2

The river Borgne is spanned by an old stone bridge dating from 1550. The **bridge chapel of Ste-Catherine** dates from 1650 and contains a painting of the Last Judgement. Above the gorge through which the Borgne flows there is the **Longeborne Hermitage,** founded in 1521 and run by the Benedictines. Inside: Way of the Cross; the chapel of Notre-Dame and that of St-Antoine have baroque altars; interesting collection of votive images.

Brechershäusern BE
see WYNIGEN   7 □ A3

Breil/Brigels GR
                                                          13 □ E1

Catholic parish church of St. Maria: Late Gothic church built *c.* 1486 on a site of

Brigels: pilgrimage church of St.Sievi with exterior and interior wall paintings.

Bremgarten: bridge (1544–9) and view of the town with the Muri-Amtshof.

earlier buildings; nave rebuilt in 1963 by Georg Berther. The **pilgrimage church of St.Sievi** (Eusebius) on a height to the N. of the village has interesting wall paintings. On the S. outer wall there is a St. Christopher (*c.* 1400) and inside a large fresco with the Adoration of the Magi (*c.*1450–60). The church of **St.Martin** has a graceful winged altar (1518) from a S. German workshop.

Bremgarten AG

2☐E5

This little town on the Reuss, documented since the mid 12C, has an astonishing number of medieval and baroque buildings. Bremgarten received its charter from Rudolph of Habsburg in 1256, and expanded greatly in the 14&15C. In 1443, however, it was captured by the Confederacy and remained a subordinate town up to the Swiss Revolution.

The town is clearly divided into an Upper (E.) and a Lower (W.) town. The **Spittelturm**, by Albrecht Murer (1556–9) with its striking Renaissance coat-of-arms, the **Hexenturm** (14C) and the **Hermansturm** (1407) survive from the old fortifications. The **Catholic church of St.Nikolaus,** a late Gothic building with two aisles is documented since the 13C. The N. aisle was added in the 15C, while the choir dates from *c.* the end of the 14C. The **chapel of St. Anna,** dating from 1487 and lengthened in 1645–6), is now a baptistery. Within, there is an unusual baldacchino-covered shrine with Calvary group and Passion relief by Gregor Allhelg

(1646). **Muttergotteskapelle:** Dating from the early 15C and converted to baroque in 1757, it contains a late Gothic fresco cycle which was uncovered in 1957–8; rococo altar with anchorite Madonna by Johann Baptist Babel (1767). The **chapel of St.Klara** and former nunnery (abandoned 1798) is an early baroque hall church by Hieronymus Kuster (1625) and Kilian Stauffer (1687–8). Late Renaissance high altar, 1627. The **church of the former Capuchin monastery** is part of a group of buildings on the left bank of the Reuss. A hall church built by Viktor Martin in 1618–21, it has late baroque furnishing. The monastery has been a chidren's home since 1889. **Former Muri government building:** Richly furnished, late Gothic (16C) building with stepped gables; 19C neo-Gothic extensions. Privately owned. **'Schlössli':** An early baroque town house with lavish interior furnishing, dating from *c.* 1640. **Reuss Bridge:** Wooden construction rebuilt 1953–7 on four pillars dating from 1544 –9; two corbel chapels on the third pillar.

Bremgarten BE

6☐E4

Ramparts and tombs from the La Tène period on the **Enge Peninsula** indicate a fairly large Celtic settlement. The ruins of a bath, an amphitheatre, two temples and other buildings have survived and indicate a Roman street settlement. The **Reformed church of St. Michael** is essentially a Romanesque building with a Gothic choir and dates from just after

1306. The glass in the choir windows is by Louis Moilliet (1924-5). The **Schloss,** NW of the church is a medieval castle which was converted in the 2nd half of the 18C into a rococo country seat; classical wing added in 1840. Inside, one late rococo room in particular is lavishly decorated with paintings and stucco.

Bretonnières VD

10 □ D1

The **Reformed church** was probably built at the end of the 11C. The nave is Romanesque, while the Gothic choir was built in the 15C on the site of a round apse. Arcaded tower (1906).

Bretzwil BL

2 □ A5

In 1786-7 the chapel of St. Maria was replaced by the **Reformed parish church,** a simple hall with an oriel-like E. end. Before that the Basel architect Johann Jacob Fechter had produced plans for the **priest's house.** S. of the village remains of a keep and a residential building are thought to be evidence of the former seat of the lords of **Ramstein.**

Brouloux, Loo JU

6 □ B/C2

Catholic parish church of St-Pierre-et-Paul: A stepped hall church built in 1852-5 in late classical style. As in the church of ▷ Les Bois, the high altar is in the form of a sarcophagus.

Brévine, La NE

5 □ E3

The **Reformed church** was built in 1604 and has a rectangular nave with a front tower; wooden interior.

Bricola TI

see BIRONICO   19 □ D3

Brienz: ruined Burg Belfort, destroyed in the Swabian War in 1499.

Brienz BE

12 □ C1

The **Reformed church** has a Romanesque tower dating from the early 12C. Late Gothic frescos on the outer walls of the nave include Descent from the Cross and Lamentation of Christ (on the side facing the mountain) and a St. Christopher, the patron of sailors (towards the lake). The **Brunnengasse** in Aenderdorf is surrounded by predominantly 19C buildings, whose façades are embellished with carved friezes. *Ballenberg Open-Air Museum:* ▷ Ballenberg.

Brienz/Brinzauls GR

14 □ B1

Catholic parish church of St.Calixtus: Rebuilt in late Gothic style in 1519 and revaulted in 1874; restored in 1939 & 1979-81. The polygonal apse has a late Gothic winged altar with lavish carved decoration and neat crowning; it dates from *c.* 1519 and comes from the Strigel workshop (▷ Bivio). **Ruins of Belfort castle** (above Surava): Originally built in the 12C, the castle was extended several times until it burned down in 1499. In 1939 the remains of the two towers, the residential buildings, the defensive wall and the outer ward were secured.

Brig VS

18□C1

Brig, already settled in the Stone Age and documented since 1215, is traditionally held to have been the capital of the Uberians. A trading centre at the N. foot of the Simplon Pass, it became the principal town in the area. In the 17C the fortunes of the town flourished thanks mainly to mining and the entrepreneurial abilities of Kaspar Jodok von Stockalper (1609–91). **Stockalperpalast,** was built in 1658–78 by K.J. von Stockalper. A spacious residence of generous proportions, it is the most important baroque palace in Switzerland. Arcaded buildings of different heights surround a courtyard which is dominated by three towers (bearing the names of the three kings, the highest is called Kaspar) topped with gilded spheres. The palace is connected to **Peter Stockalper's house** by a two-storey arcade, built in 1533 and enlarged in the 17C when a wing in the S., a chapel and an arcaded courtyard were added. The **Catholic collegiate church of Spiritus Sanctus,** on Simplonstrasse, was built in 1675–85 in the style of German Jesuit churches, probably to the designs of M.Koller and H.Mayer. A single-aisled building with a polygonal apse, the sober interior contains a high altar and side altars in serpentine by J.M.Schuster (1691–3). **Chapel of St. Antonius Eremita:** Rebuilt in 1304 and altered in the 15&18C. Groin-vaulted nave, baroque choir. The high altar has a Gothic statue of the saint. **Catholic Ursuline Church of the Dreifaltigkeit (Holy Trinity):** This sober building of 1732 is a faithful scaled-down copy of the collegiate church. The **chapel of St.Sebastian,** on the square of the same name, was built in 1636. The façade has two Gothic statues and a porch; the square nave is crowned by an octagonal dome. **Catholic parish church of the Hl. Herz Jesu:** Built in 1967–70 by the architects Jean and Nadine Iten. The **Kollegium Spiritus Sanctus,** near Simplonstrasse, dates in part from 1663. The **Marienheim** near the chapel of St. Antony was formerly the Wegener-Haus,

Brig: courtyard of the Stocker palace with arcades.

and dates from 1709. Opposite the Stockalperpalast is the **House of Fernanda Stockalper,** which was built in 1727 and has a carved coat-of-arms on the entrance portal. At Simplonstrasse 29, is the 17C **Wegener-Haus;** 19C façade and tower. Opposite is the **Theiler-Haus.** The *Oberwalliser Local History Museum* is housed in the Stockalperschloss.

Brione-Verzasca TI

19□C1

Catholic parish church of Santa Maria Assunta: Founded in the 13C, enlarged in the 14&17C and rebuilt in 1840. The façade has frescos of St. Christopher and two founders (14C). Inside, on the S. and W. walls, there are important Gothic frescos of scenes from the Life of Christ (interesting Last Supper) which show the influence of Giotto. **Castello Marcacci** on the church square is now a restaurant. This 17C residence, on a rectangular groundplan with four corner towers, is surrounded by a wall which itself has four small towers.

Brissago TI

19□B3

The **Catholic parish church of Santi Pietro e Paolo,** in the middle of the village, was built in Renaissance style in 1526–1610 by the architect Giovanni Beretta. The single-aisled building has a domed ante-choir; choir lengthened in the 19C. 17-18C furnishing. S. of the village, on the edge of the lake, is the **church of Santa Maria di Ponte:** Documented since the 13C, it was rebuilt by Giovanni Beretta in 1526 – 8. A single-aisled Renaissance building, it has a rectangular choir, beautiful dome and lantern above the crossing; the portal dates from 1594. The interior has unfortunately been robbed of its furnishing as a result of the restoration of 1953–8. The modern chapel on the N. side has a marble baroque altar dasting from 1686. Above Brissago stand the chapels of Sacro Monte and **Santa Maria Addolorata,** a baroque building of 1767. In the village on the edge of the lake stands the **Palazzo Baccalà,** a baroque palace built by the Branca family (1740–50).

Brissago Islands: The main island has an exotic park; the **Villa** dating from 1927 is now an *Ethnographic Museum.* The **church of Sant'Apollinare** on the smaller island dates from the 11–12C.

Bristen UR

13☐B1

At the opening of the Maderaner valley, E. of Bristen, there is a reconstruction (set up 1966) of a **casting furnace** used in the 17C for casting the iron mined here. As early as the 16C Peter Madran, an entrepreneur who came originally from Madrano in the Leventina, exploited the iron deposits in the valley subsequently named after him.

Broc FR

11☐C3

The **Château-d'En bas,** a fortified house documented from the 14C, stands at the entrance to the village. A square building, it has mullion windows and small modern tower on the roof, an arched bridge in front of the house was built in 1580 and rebuilt in the 18&19C. The 17C **tower** behind the house belonged to a now vanished church. In the woods on the Route du Juan, stand the ruins of the **Castle of Montsalvan,** founded in the 12C by a branch of the Counts of Gruyère and abandoned in

Bristen: early iron-smelting kiln.

Bronschhofen: baroque pilgrimage church of Our Lady of Dreibrunnen near Wil.

1671. The imposing remains of the keep have survived.

Bronschofen SG

3☐D4

Marienwallfahrtskirche Dreibrunnen: (W. of Wil). The former parish church, it came into the possession of the monastery of Rüti in 1280. Extensively rebuilt in 1672 and painted inside in 1761, this elongated baroque building has a loggia-like porch. Ceiling painting by Jakob Joseph Müller depicts battles—with the Turks at Lepanto (1571) and at Vienna (1683). The high altar has a late Gothic (early 16C) miracle painting.

Brontallo TI

13☐B5

Catholic parish church of San

Giorgio: A single-aisled building with two side chapels and a 16C polygonal apse. The façade has a fresco of St.Christopher; inside 17&18 stucco. The **graveyard chapel** next to the church has 16C frescos. In the village there are numerous **granaries**, both wooden and stone.

Brugg AG

2□E4

The Habsburgs, whose ancestral castle is nearby, founded this little town at the start of the 12C, at the point where the Aare could be bridged and with access to the Bözberg-Jura crossing. Expansion was thwarted; at the critical time Brugg was unable to exploit this excellent site on important routes, as it was one of the Habsburg possessions captured by Bern in 1415 and was thenceforward under Bernese rule. Until industrialization Brugg was a self-satisfied little provincial town. The **Altstadt** consists of two almost equal quarters on either side of the main street leading to the bridge. The **Schwarze Turm** (substructure mid to late 12C, superstructure with oriel and hip roof 16C), the Archivturm near the town church and the Storchenturm have survived of the old **fortifications. Reformed Town Church:** The oldest part is the tower. The church itself was founded in 1220 and has undergone many alterations over the centuries, including baroque alterations in 1734–40. Nave and choir share the same roof.

Impressive choir furnishing (altar table, font, pulpit, priest's seat) in the 'gnarled' style (1641–2). **Former Latin School:** Built on to the church, it includes the former headmaster's house (late Gothic) and a baroque wing from 1638–40. Architectural and allegorical wall paintings on the E. façade are by Rudolf Schwerter (1640). **Former Rathaus:** Built in 1579, this late Gothic gabled building stands SW of the Schwarzer Turm. **Hofstatt:** Picturesque square in the E. quarter with former Zeughaus (arsenal), now *Heimatmuseum* (local history), former Salzhaus (salt store) and former Kornhaus. **Schlösschen Altenburg:** Late Gothic

Brontallo: typical wood and stone storehouses with stone roofs.

Brugg: former Latin school with allegorical wall paintings on the E. façade.

tower house with stepped gable on a bend in the Aare, W. of the town; now a youth hostel. Adjacent on the W. side of the building is a 30 ft. high Roman wall, part of a late Roman river fort (4C). *Vindonissa Museum:* Exhibits include finds from the Roman army camp Vindonissa (▷ Windisch), as well as the canton's prehistoric collection.

Brülisau AI

4□A4

(SE of Appenzell in the district of Rüte.) The **Catholic parish church of St. Sebastian** was rebuilt in 1879 by

Klemens Steiner; processional cross *c.*
1500. **Bergkapelle Maria Heimsuchung** (on Plattenbödeli, next to Säm-
tisersee): Built in 1939 by Johann
Hugentobler, who also altered the **chapel
of St.Magdalena** in Steinegg (consecrated
1590) in 1946. **Bleiche,** E. of Appenzell,
built in the 16C for the Bleichermeister of
the Appenzell canvas company; façade
painting, 1804.

*Brunnadern: Türmlihaus with characteristic
oriel turret.*

Brunegg AG
2☐E4

Schloss: An outpost of the Habsburgs, it
dates back to the 13C. The present complex is a 19C rearrangement (not open to
the public.

Brunnadern SG
3☐E5

Reformed church: Built in 1763-5 by
Johann Ulrich Grubenmann. Single-aisled
with tower over the choir. Pulpit and font
from the time of building. **Priest's house:**
Wooden building topped by a painted cross
from 1820-30. **House No.196** in Spreiten-
bach, SE of Brunnadern, is a Blockbau of
1616. Curved baroque gable and weather-
board are probably 18C. **Oberes
Türmlihaus** in Furth, built by Josef
Brunner in 1614, small oriel tower on the
SE corner. **Unteres Türmlihaus** from
1620, is a gabled Blockbau on stone base
with a little oriel tower on SE corner.
House No.520: Gabled building with side
arcades, it probably from 1672.

Brunnen SZ
8☐A4

Village chapel: Built in 1632-5 in a style
heralding the baroque (most clearly seen
in the entrance façade).

Brusio GR
14☐F5

Catholic parish church of St. Carlo

Borromeo: A clearly arranged early baroque building rebuilt in 1617. The buttresses and lightly tapered window jambs
recall the late Gothic. The **Reformed
church** dates from 1645 (rebuilt 1727) and
has a rococo organ with a carved gallery
(built in 1786). VIANO: Terraced alpine
village.

Bry, Le FR
11☐C2

PONT-EN-OGOZ on this small island in the
artificial Lac de Gruyère has the remains
of a château and a chapel, although the
village has itself disappeared. The
château, which controlled a crossing over
the Sarine, had already declined in the 15C
and, apart from remains of walls, two
square towers have survived. The 13C
chapel of St-Théodule is documented
from 1300.

Bubendorf BL
2☐A4

The **priest's house,** extended several
times from the 16-18C, has a panelled ceiling with Biblical scenes painted by Mat-
this Faust (1695). The **Dinghof,** former
seat of the prior's steward was built in 1600
with stepped gables and richly decorated
windows.

Bubikon ZH
8☐C1

Ritterhaus (former Commandery of the
Knights of St.John of Malta): Founded in

1192 for the Knights of St.John and rebuilt following its destruction in the Old Zürich War. It survived the Reformation thanks to an arrangement between the Order and Zürich and the latter thenceforward appointed Protestant stewards. Extended *c.* 1570, the complex now comprises the old monks' house, the *chapel* (Romanesque single-aisled church with remains of frescos), the convent house, the new monks' house, the Knights' Hall and the Sennhaus (a farm building), all of which surround a courtyard on three sides. The commandery, which has been kept up by a 'Ritterhausgesellschaft' (an association for the preservation of commanderies) since 1936, houses the richly endowed *Museum of the Knights of St. John.*

Buchberg SH
3☐A3

Reformed parish church: A Neo-Romanesque building (1848–50) by Tobias Hurter, rebuilt after a serious fire in 1972. Together it and the priest's house make a striking impression.

Buchegg SO
6☐F2

Foundation walls and a 16C tower (which now houses a *Local History Museum*) survive from the **Schlösschen** of the lords of Buchegg, which goes back to 1267.

Buchrain LU
7☐E3

Former parish church of St.Agatha: Rebuilt in 1748 and lengthened in 1932. The **priest's house,** an early 18C Blockbau, was formerly the seat of the governor of Lucerne.

Buchs SG
9☐A1

Catholic church of Herz Jesu: Founded in 1880, the building was newly built in

concrete (1964–5) by Justus Dahinden with sculptures by Albert Wider. **Reformed parish church:** Built in 1931-2 by Wilh. Schäfer and Martin Risch.

Bühler AR
4☐A4

Reformed church: Built in 1743 by Lorenz Koller and Jakob Grubenmann; tower rebuilt in 1828. The former **Rathaus of Trogen** dates from 1598 but was brought to Bühler in 1842 (the upper part of the Blockbau was dismantled and rebuilt in Bühler on a new brick base). It is now used as a residence. The village street has numerous **manufacturer's houses** from the 18&19C, including the late baroque **Türmlihaus** from *c.* 1790.

Bülach ZH
3☐A3

One of the old Zürcher Landstädtchen (country towns subordinate to Zürich), now a provincial capital in the Zürcher Unterland with a historical town centre. The town, officially documented as early as 811, received its charter from the Habsburgs in 1384. The oldest buildings (with very few exceptions) date from after the third and last disastrous town fire (1506).
In the W. of the **Altstadt** quite large parts of the town wall, which once surrounded the town in an oval, survive in the form of houses. The **Reformed church,** documented as the church of St.Laurentius in the early Middle Ages, was rebuilt in late Gothic style in 1508-17, altered in neo-Gothic style in 1838-9 and thoroughly modernized inside in 1969 - 70 (Fritz Schwarz). **Rathaus:** Rebuilt in 1672-3 incorporating older parts and completely renovated in 1958-9. Now a local government building, it is richly furnished and has a panelled baroque council chamber. The **Gasthof 'zum goldenen Kopf',** a massive half-timbered building, was faithfully rebuilt after a fire in 1965-6; the 'Goethe-Stübli' is decorated with panel paintings by Dutch and German artists

Bulle: 13C Savoyard Château with keep on the left.

and a ceiling painting by Stöffi Kuhn (1737-97). The **Gasthof 'zum Kreuz'** is a classical building of 1820.

Bulle FR

11 ☐ C3

The present capital of Gruyère, it was first officially documented at the start of the 9C, although it is actually considerably older and was already settled in Roman times. Into the 16C Bulle was ruled by the Counts of Gruyère and the Bishops of Lausanne, who built the first defences. In 1536 Bulle came into Fribourg's sphere of influence. In 1805 it was almost totally destroyed by a fire.

Of the former market town there remains only the regular layout around the market. **Schloss:** Built in the 2nd half of the 13C in the style which Peter II of Savoy (d. 1268) had introduced into the Pays de Vaud. The château is a typical 'carré savoyard', with the 108 ft. high round keep on the SW side. The other corners of the square building are crowned by turrets. The building was altered several times under the Fribourg governors after 1537. **Church of St-Pierre-aux-Liens:** Rebuilt after the town fire in 1812-16 and enlarged in 1931; stained glass by Albert Cingria. Near the castle is the church of **Notre-Dame-de-Compassion,** the former chapel of the now-vanished hospital, which has been in the care of the Capuchins since 1665. The first church building dates back to 1350; the present building was rebuilt in 1454 after a fire. Carved wooden doors date from 1662; the baroque high altar in the choir is by Pierre Ardieu (1692). In-

teresting collection of votive pictures on the aisle walls. Next to the church of St-Pierre is the **Hôtel des Trois Couronnes,** a former covered market hall on wooden columns, rebuilt sometime after 1805. The *Musée Gruérien* is a local history museum.

Bünzen AG

2 ☐ E5

Catholic parish church of St. Georg: Neo-Gothic single-aisled church by Caspar Joseph Jeuch (1860-1).

Buochs NW

7 ☐ F4

Catholic parish church of St-Martin, built by Niklaus Purtschert in 1802-8 on the site of an older church (burned down in 1798), using parts of the earlier buildings. SW of Buochs, on the Ennerberg, lies the **Loretokapelle,** founded in 1713 by Landammann Johann Jakob Achermann after his victorious battle against Bernese troops at Sins (AG), the only successful action by the Catholic cantons in the 2nd Villmergen War (1712). Inside: painting of the battle; also a copy of the Casa Santa of Loreto. Next to the chapel, a former **patrician's house** from the early 19C.

Buonas ZG

7 ☐ F2

Old Castle: Built in 1494-8 on the site of an earlier building from the 11C (not open to the public).

Büren an der Aare BE

6 ☐ E2

This small medieval **town** was formerly surrounded by a moat. The triangular town centre is enclosed by two streets, one of which is very urban in character, while the other is more rural. **Reformed church:** The early Gothic choir has capitals decorated with figures and slighter

Burgdorf: 12C Schloss, one of the earliest brick buildings in Switzerland.

later paintings in the vaults. The late Gothic nave, with a carved and painted wooden ceiling, was erected in 1510. The **Rathaus,** built *c.* 1500, has a panelled Renaissance room from 1640. **Landvogteischloss** (governor's castle), at the W. entrance of the little town, was built around 1620 by Daniel Lerber, Daniel Heintz and others. The façade, framed by massive projecting towers and round gables, has Gothic stepped windows. *Heimatmuseum Spittel,* Spittelstr.36 (open by appointment)

Burg im Leimental BE

1 □ E4

Castle: Of the several castles formerly occupying Schlossberg there remains only Biederthan, so called after former owners. The gabled wing on the E. side (rebuilt in the 15–16C) is probably the oldest part.

Burgdorf BE

6 □ F3

The town was probably founded by Duke Konrad of Zähringen, who built a fortress guarding the entrance to the Emmental in

the early 12C. Like Bern the town developed with parallel streets along an E.–W. axis. With the end of the Zähringen line the castle village fell to the Kyburgs in 1218, who sold it to Bern in 1384; the latter sent its governor to the castle until 1798.

Reformed church: Built by the Bernese cathedral architect Niklaus Bierenvogt in 1471–90 on the site of the previous Zähringen church. The screen dates from 1511–12 and is one of the finest examples of late Gothic masonry. **Schloss:** Keep and residential quarters from the 2nd half of the 12C are amongst the earliest brick buildings in Switzerland. The residential quarters include a Romanesque baronial hall and a chapel with frescos from *c.* 1330. The other buildings come from the long period during which Bern governed. In 1798 Heinrich Pestalozzi founded his elementary school here. The castle houses the *Local History Collection* of the Rittersaalverein. The **former Siechenhaus** (hospital for incurables) in the Lorraine Quarter is a late Gothic ashlar building dating from 1472. Of note amongst the houses on the Hohengasse are the **Haus zum Ochsen** (No.35) with Renaissance and Gothic features, probably built to the plans of Paulus Nater; the baroque **Diesbacherhaus** (No.19) and the classical **Gasthof zu Metzgern** (No.12). The *Folk Museum* stands on the Kirchbühl, near the **Stadthaus** (1746–50). The **inner Wynigen Bridge** dating from 1764 is a late example of a truss-frame construction.

Bürgenstock NW

7 □ F4

Important health resort which attracted visitors from all over Europe, particularly after the opening of the Kehrsiten cable railway in 1889. To accommodate the visitors a series of hotels were built, including the **Grand Hotel,** the **Palace Hotel** as well as luxuriously furnished houses. Next to the Palace Hotel stands a neo-Gothic **chapel** of 1897. On the S. slope above Ennetbürgen is the much-rebuilt pilgrimage chapel of St.Jost, going back to in 1346.

Burgistein BE

11 □ F1

Castle: From 1500–1714 this belonged to Wattenwyl, thereafter to Graffenried. Built in 1260 by the knight Jordan of Thun, the fortress made way for a more residential castle in the 16C.

Bürglen TG

3 □ E3

Castle: Ancestral castle of the barons of Bürglen in the 12 - 13C, it has been a schoolhouse since 1888 - 9 and was extended and converted in 1950-1. The keep dates from the 12 - 13C. **Reformed church:** Former castle chapel. Mostly late Gothic; altered and enlarged in 1684-5. The tower, dating from 1864-5, was made higher in 1970-1.

Bürglen UR

8 □ B5

Two medieval towers dominate the village. The **Meierturm** was probably the 13C

Bürglen: 13C Wattigwilerturm with Tell museum.

seat of the Meier (bailiff) of the Zürich Fraumünster abbey, to which the village belonged until 1426. The **Wattigwiler-turm** houses the *Tell Museum.* Remains of two other residential towers now form the foundations of the Pfarrhaus and the Gasthaus Tell. **Catholic church of St. Peter und Paul:** Built in 1682-5 to plans of Johann Jakob Scolar, who was parish priest in Bürglen. The church of ▷ Dallenwil (NW) is also attributed to Scolar, who is also thought to have participated in the building of the monastery church of ▷ Seedorf (UR). The early baroque building stands on the site of a Romanesque church, from which crypt and substructure of the tower have survived. The **Ölbergkapelle,** built in 1693, and the ossuary in the graveyard are also by Scolar. On the site of William Tell's supposed house there now stands the **Tellskapelle,** dedicated to St.Sebastian, patron saint of archers (founded in 1582; rebuilt in 1758). Opposite the Wattigwiler-turm stands the massive **Haus in der Spielmatt,** built in 1609 for the Landammannn Peter Gisler, who had made his wealth in the service of France and Venice. Just outside the village in the direction of the Schächental is the **Loretokapelle,** built in 1661, with wall paintings typical of this type of chapel.

Bursins: keystone of the Gothic vaulting in the side chapel.

Buttisholz: baroque pilgrimage church of St. Ottilien SE of the village.

Büron LU
7□D2

Catholic parish church of St. Gallus: Rebuilt in 1640 retaining the medieval E. section. The choir has Gothic frescos from the first part of the 14C.

Bursinel VD
10□C3/4

Château: Originally it belonged to the Lords of Bursinel. In 1527 the 'Confrérie des gentilshommes de la Cuillier', a league of Savoyard nobles allied against Geneva, was founded in the castle. The present structure dates principally from the 18C, the towers are medieval in origin.

Bursins VD
10□C3

Reformed church of St. Martin: Part of a priory, documented since 1011 and annexed to Romainmôtier in 1329. The Romanesque church, of which the N. apse has survived, was much altered 14–16C; the Gothic choir was built first and then the Romanesque-style tower. The nave,

shortened on the W. side, was extended towrds the S. where a chapel was built in Flamboyant style with carved keystones. Next to the church is a former priory building, now the priest's house. To the E. stands the **château,** an 18C ruler's house with a late Gothic tower. N. of the church is **Château Rosay,** a late medieval building with round towers. To the S. of the church stands an 18C mansion.

Büsserach SO
1□F5

Ruins of Thierstein Castle: This fortress was probably built c. 1200 under Rudolf I of Thierstein as a watch-station at the entrance of the Lüsseltal gorge. The residential tower with Gothic windows has survived.

Bussnang TG
3□E3

Reformed church: Rebuilt probably in 1423; tower superstructure 1694, nave extended in 1787. **Catholic church:** Trefoil building with round tower built in 1934 –6 by Gustav auf der Maur to the plans of Otto Linder. Stained-glass windows depic-

ting Stations of the Cross by Andreas
Kübele.

Bütschwil SG

3☐D5

Weisses Haus: Built in the mid 17C.
Small staircase tower on the N. side. 18C
furnishing.

Buttenberg LU
see Schötz   7☐C2

Büttikon AG

2☐E5

Koch-Haus: Large Freiamt farmhouse of
1791 with lavish exterior painting.

Buttisholz LU

7☐D2

Classical village layout. **Catholic parish
church of St. Verena:** Built in baroque
style in the mid 18C. The baroque
pilgrimage church of St. Ottilien SE of
the village was built in a unusual form of
the centrally-planned building by amateur
architect Jost Melchior of Gilgen in 1669.

C

Cabbio TI
19☐E5

Catholic parish church of San Salvatore. A single-aisled baroque building dating from 1780 – 95 with transept and semicircular choir and 19C decoration and furnishings.

Cademario TI
19☐D4

Former parish church of Sant'Ambrogio, just below the village, near the cemetery. The first place of worship, with one aisle and a semicircular apse, was built in the 12C; the bell tower and a second S. aisle were added in the 13C. Baroque additions were removed in the course of restoration in 1968. The church has remarkable wall paintings: in the apse Christ in Glory, Apostle and Saint Ambrose and Agnus Dei, Romanesque paintings dating from the 1st half of the 13C. In the S. aisle are 15C paintings, including a Crucifixion, Martyrdom of St. Bartholomew and the Last Judgement. In the village is the **Catholic parish church of Santa Maria del Popolo,** built in the early 17C and redecorated in baroque style at the end of the 18C.

Cadro TI
19☐D3

Catholic parish church of Sant'Agata, mentioned since 1366, altered in 1603. The interior was renovated in the rococo style *c.* 1770 and has fine stucco decoration; the finest features are the trophies on the choir walls, the work of the Reali brothers from Cadro.

Camignolo TI
19☐D3

On a hill S. of the village late Romanesque **chapel of Sant'Ambrogio,** altered in 1719. The frescos in the interior include a Christ in a Mandorla in the apse and St.Ambrose on the S. wall, probably early-14C. Near the chapel is the **ruin** of the castello Sant'Ambrogio, destroyed in 1518.

Camischolas GR
See TAVETSCH
13☐C2

Camp GR
See VALS
13☐E2

Campione TI
19☐D4

Italian enclave in the Tessin. **Pilgrimage church of Santa Maria dei Ghirli,** first mentioned 874, rebuilt in the 13&14C, porch added in the 18C. In the church important 14&17C wall paintings. On the S. wall is a painting of the Last Judgement, the last work of Franco and Filippolo de Veris, *c.* 1400. In the interior, on the walls of the nave and the W. wall, 14C Gothic paintings of scenes from the life of John the Baptist, the work of an anonymous painter. In the choir, rebuilt in the baroque period, and on the chancel arch paintings by Isidoro Bianchi dating from 1634. In the village square is **San Zenone,** now deconsecrated, first mentioned in 777, rebuilt in the Romanesque period and altered in the 17C. In the interior are a tabernacle and carved Renaissance reliefs.

Campo TI
19☐A1

This parish in the Vallemaggia includes several picturesque villages.CAMPO At the entrance to the village **Catholic parish church of San Bernado,** medieval in origin, with a 16C bell tower. In the interior, in very bad condition, side chapels with 17C stucco, and in the choir, enlarged in 1748, baroque painting by G.Mattia

Cademario: late Gothic wall paintings (15C) in Sant'Ambrogio.

Carona: 15C relief sculpture in the Catholic parish church of San Giorgio.

Borgnis of the Stations of the Cross. In the village **chapel of Santa Maria Addolorata** dating from 1767, and next to it the **Palazzo Pedrazzini**, built in the 18C with religious wall paintings on the façade, dating from 1724 and 1748. On the other side of the river, which divides the village into two, is a second **Palazzo Pedrazzini** dating from the same period, connected by a covered corridor to a chapel dedicated to St.John the Baptist and built in 1749; there are paintings by G.Mattia Borgnis in the interior.

CIMALMOTTO The 17C **Catholic parish church of Santa Maria Assunta** was enlarged in 1749, porch painted by G.Mattia Borgnis. Nave and choir have 17&18C painting and stucco.

Carona TI

19 □ D4

Catholic parish church of San Giorgio, of medieval origin, completely rebuilt in the 16C, tower with baroque crown. The Renaissance building consists of a nave and two aisles with groin vaulting and a rectangular choir with domed ante-choir. Lavish interior: on the choir walls paintings of the Crucifixion, the Last Judgement and All Saints by Domenico Pezzi, dating from 1584&5. In the N. aisle 17C font, a Renaissance triptych depicting the Madonna with two saints, a marble Madonna and Child, 16C, and an 18C marble side altar. In the S. aisle 15C Gothic triptych, a Renaissance crucifix, and statuette, 1650, of John the Baptist on the side altar. Above the village **Catholic church of Santa Marta,** medieval in origin, enlarged during the baroque. The original building is the atrium of the present church, and has frescos dating from 1486, attributed to the Seregno master. The baroque building consists of a nave and rectangular choir. The furnishings are 18C. Near the church of San Giorgio is the **Loggia del Commune,** built in 1591. Elegant portico on the ground floor, and trompe l'oeil paintings and coats-of-arms of the first 12 cantons on the façade. Houses in the village with decorated façades in very good condition, above all in the Via della Costa the Adami, Solari and Lucchini **houses**, and in the small square the **casa Constanza** with 18C paintings, and, by the post office, the **casa Andreoli** with 16C windows. W. of the village in the wood, **pilgrimage church of Santa Maria d'Ongero**. The church was built in the 17C on the site of a 1515 chapel. The building is cruciform, with a pendentive dome. Interior stucco mainly by Alessandro Casella, 1646–8. On the marble high altar fresco of 1515 with a Madonna: the two frescos of the Presentation in the Temple and Jesus in the Temple are by Giuseppe Antonio Petrini, 1750.

TORELLO 45 minutes from Carona, on the W. flank of Monte Arbostara, **Santa Maria Assunta di Torello**, built 1217 by Guglielmo della Torre, Bishop of Como, at the same time as an Augustinian monastery, dissolved in 1389 and now a private house. The Romanesque church consists of a porch with gallery, a nave and a square choir with a straight end. On the façade fragments of 13&16C paintings. S. of the choir is the semicircular apse of a 10&11C chapel.

Carouge: neoclassical façade of the Catholic church of the Ste-Croix, completed 1824.

Carouge with Geneva and was built by the engineer Nicolas Céard in 1810–17.

Carouge GE
16 □ E2

This little town adjacent to Geneva is separated from the city by the river Arve; it was founded in the late 18C by Victor-Amédée III of Savoy as a new town to compete with Geneva's fair and market. There were 5 plans for Carouge in all, by Piedmontese architects, and they are most interesting examples of 18C town planning. The **Catholic church Ste.Croix,** was designed in 1777&8 by the Piedmontese G.B.Piacenza, but not completed; the transept, choir and façade were built in 1824. Stucco decoration and 16C statues of the Apostles. **Reformed Church,** built in 1818 – 22, neoclassical. **Théâtre de Carouge** and Salle des Fêtes built 1970–2. **Tours de Carouge,** built 1958–63. Interesting features of the town are the typical rows of houses, the **Place du Marché** with an 1866 fountain and the **Place du Temple**. The **Pont Neuf** connects

Cartigny GE
16 □ D2

Reformed church, Rue du Temple. Built in 1772 on the site of a medieval church, connected to the vicarage in the NE. **Château,** Rue de la Vallière. Built in the 18C and altered in the 19C. The façade is decorated with fluted pilasters and has a pediment. There is a neoclassical pavilion in the park, and there are various 18C houses in the village.

Casaccia GR
14 □ C4

Towards Majola, **pilgrimage church of San Gaudentius,** in ruins since 1739. Rebuilt 1514–18, possibly by Bernhard von Poschiavo. Dignified, consistent, late Gothic building with wall sarcophagus of the patron saint in the choir. Above the village **hospice,** c. 1520.

Castagnola TI

19☐D4

Above the village **Catholic parish church of San Giorgio,** a medieval building, altered in the 17C. Cruciform with two N. and one S. chapel and 17C stucco and paintings. 18C interior. At the edge of the village, on the bank of the lake, **Villa Favorita,** built 1687 and extended in the 20C; it contains the *pinacoteca* of Baron Thyssen-Bornemiza, one of the finest private collections in Europe.

Castaneda GR

19☐E1

Burial ground with over 100 graves, some with various items of jewellery, ceramic grave goods and bronze vessels, including a spouted jug with an Etruscan inscription. Finds from the **Golasecca culture,** remains of Iron Age and late Neolithic settlements and traces of late Neolithic ploughing.

Castel San Pietro TI

19☐D/E5

At the centre of the old village baroque **Catholic parish church of Sant'Eusebio,** built in 1670–8 by the architect Agostino Silva; choir and façade added by Francesco Pozzi in 1736. Lavish interior with paintings framed in rococo stucco in the choir vault, paintings by C.I.Carlone 1759, high altar 1760. In the second N. chapel wooden crucifix dating from 1600 and fine stucco altar with Crucifixion by G.Battista Barberini, 1689. In the second S. chapel lavish 18C stucco altar. Below the village, in the wood, **Catholic parish church of San Pietro,** known as the Chiesa Rossa (red church); built 1343–4 by Bonifacio da Modena, Bishop of Como. The church gets its nickname from a legend which says that on Christmas night 1390 about a hundred people were massacred here. The building, a plain rectangular nave with a semicircular apse, contains an important cycle of

Castel San Pietro: important Gothic paintings in the Chiesa Rossa.

early Gothic paintings dating from the late 14C. Geometrical ornamentation on the walls of the nave, on the choir wall an Annunciation, Madonna and Child and three Saints, and in the apse scenes from the life of St. Peter.
OBINO On a hill **chapel of San'Antonio,** a medieval building mentioned in 1578. Part of the church has been turned into a house. On the S. portal 15C relief of St. Anthony, and in the interior 16C frescos. LOVERCIANO **Palazzo Turconi,** 18C house, now a religious institution.

Castelletto TI

See MELANO 19☐D4

Castelrotto TI

19☐C4

Catholic parish church of San Nazzaro, baroque, dating from 1635–70.

Casti GR

14☐A1/2

Reformed church. 12C Romanesque single room with semicircular apse and massive S. tower. Wall paintings by the Waltensburg master *c.* 1340: on the left choir wall Angel of the Annunciation and Christ in Majesty in the apse.

Castro TI

13☐D4

On the S. edge of the village **Catholic**

parish church of San Giorgio, rebuilt 1867. In the interior 12C stucco statue of apostle. In the centre of the village baroque **chapel of Sant'Antonio di Padova,** altered in 1730. The choir was painted in 1732 by Carlo Biucchi. Next to it so-called **Casa dei Balivi** with painted façade (1642).

Cavagno TI
13 □ C5

SEGNO **Chapel of Sant'Ambrogio,** late Romanesque, built in the 13C. Nave with semicircular apse and bell tower with twin windows. 15C wall painting in the interior.

Cazis GR
9 □ A5

Convent of St.Peter and Paul, founded in the 8C, Dominican convent since 1647. **Parish and convent church.** This late Gothic church of 1504 with a polygonal choir is the largest building by Andreas Bühler. Groin vaulting in the nave added after a fire in 1768; the tower dates from 1871. Dedicatory painting over the W. portal (1504). W. of it **chapel St.Wendelin,** a plain Romanesque church with semicircular apse and stone belfry over the new roof. Gothic wooden statues: Madonna 1330–40, St.Anne with the Virgin and Child *c.* 1500. Below the village is the **old parish church of St. Martin.** Single-aisled, the oldest parts are presumed to date from the early Middle Ages; the exterior has blind arches. N. of the village is the **Petrus hill,** a plateau with a late Neolithic settlement. SW of the village, in **Cresta** are remains of a Bronze-Iron Age settlement in a 16 to 19 ft. rock channel with eight zones of settlement.

Celerina GR
14 □ D2

St. Gian. Romanesque single-aisled church with square choir dating from the 11&12C and tower of the same period. The nave extension, the beamed roof with sten-

Celerina: the great tower of San Gian was struck by lightning in 1682.

cil painting, the choir vaulting, and the campanile, damaged by lightning in 1682, date from 1478. Wall painting: late medieval fragment of a picture of St.Mauritius on the S. wall of the choir; late 15C by the master of Pontresina: cycle on the life of St.John the Baptist on the choir walls, on the chancel arch Annunciation, under it on the left St.Sebastian, St.Margaret and St.Barbara, on the right Madonna with St.Jerome.

Céligny GE
10 □ B4

Geneva enclave in the canton of Vaud. Near to the church **château de Garengo,** built 1722 and enlarged in the 19C. On the road to Crans is **l'Elysée,** an 18C baroque-neoclassical house with a wrought-iron gate.

Cerentino TI
19 □ A1

On a hill in the direction of Bosco Gurin **Catholic parish church of Santa Maria,** a baroque building with a 1707 fresco over the portal. Next to it **ossuary** with a representation of Purgatory.

Cergnat VD
11 □ C5

Reformed Church (St-Maurice), mentioned in 1279, subordinate to the abbey of St-Maurice. The oldest part of the church is the choir, the façade tower with

Cerentino: Santa Maria on a hill above the village.

Gothic portal and roof lights are late Gothic. On the edge of the village, below the church, 17C wooden **storehouse.**

Cerlatez, Les JU
See SAIGNELEGIER   6☐C1

Cerniat FR
          11☐C/D2

Carthusian monastery of La Valsainte, founded 1295, destroyed by fire in 1381 and 1732. It was dissolved in 1778 and housed Trappists and Redemptorists from France until 1824, when it was abandoned and allowed to fall into disrepair. In 1863 the Carthusians returned from La Part-Dieu (see Gruyères) and rebuilt the monastery. The buildings, dating mainly from 1734, form a remarkable group, even though almost none of them is original. The *monastery church* is dedicated to Our Lady and dated 1868, the *chapel of Notre-Dame de Compassion,* the only section open to the public, contains an altar by J.F.Reyff.

Cernil, Le BE
See TRAMELAN   6☐C1

Cevio: Casa Respini, once the seat of the Confederate Landvogts.

Cevio TI
          19☐A/B1

At the N. end of the village **Catholic parish church of Santa Maria Assunta e San Giovanni.** First mentioned in 1253, rebuilt in the 16C and altered between the 17&19C. Neoclassical façade with porch. S. of the church free-standing bell tower of 1565 and portico with **ossuary,** the latter with allegorical paintings dating from 1741. Near the church are **houses** belonging to the Franzoni family; a fine 17C portal leads to a courtyard with three houses with decorated façades, one of which houses the *Museo di Vallemaggia* (local history museum). In the village square **casa Respini,** the former residence of the Landvogts; it has a small curtain wall with two little towers, pierced by a lavishly decorated 18C doorway. Next to it is the **pretorio,** a three-storey building with coats-of-arms of the Landvogts, mostly dating from the 17C.
ROVANA On the edge of Cevio in the Campo direction, near to an arched bridge, **pilgrimage church of Santa Maria del Ponte,** built in 1615. A plain, single-aisled building with vestibule and lavish interior stucco and painting.

Châble, Le VS
See BAGNES   17☐D3

Chalais VS
          17☐F1

On a hill on the edge of the village ruined

13C tower, the only remaining feature of a château once owned by the lords of Chalais.

Cham ZG
7☐F2

Catholic parish church of St. Jakob, built in 1783-94 by Jakob and Johann Anton Singer; the Gothic tower behind the choir with spire of 1853 was part of an earlier building. **Schloss St. Andreas.** The Schloss, mentioned for the first time in 1282, is probably on the site given to the college of the Zürich Frauenmünster by King Ludwig the German in 858. The Schloss has been much altered. The **St. Andreas chapel** dates from 1488&9, and was altered in baroque style in 1675.

Cham: St. Jakob, late baroque building by Jakob and Johann Anton Singer.

Chamoson VS
17☐D2

Catholic parish church of St-André. This neo Gothic building dates from 1929&30, the tower from 1751. In the interior mosaic, paintings and stained glass by Edmond Bille, 1928–30.

Champvent: the 13C Château is of the 'carré savoyard' type.

Champéry VS
17☐A2

Catholic parish church of St-Théodule, rebuilt 1966; the baroque bell tower has survived from the church of 1725.

Champvent VD
5☐E5

The little estate and church of Champvent, first mentioned in the early 11C, were inherited *c.* 1225 by Henri von Grandson, who had the **château** built as the centre of his domain. In 1336 domain and château passed to Count Louis de Neuchâtel, in 1377 to the Burgundian de Vergy family, and after 1536 finally into the hands of Bernese patrician families; it is now privately owned, and not open to the public. The 13C château has survived largely intact, with the exception of the keep, which was shortened by 49 ft. in the 18C; it is a particularly fine specimen of a so-called 'carré savoyard', a castle on a square ground plan with round corner towers. Champvent is also remarkable because the château was not built on flat ground, the normal practice for Savoy castles, but on a hill.

Chamues-ch GR
See PUNT.LA
14☐E2

Charmey FR
11☐D3

St-Laurent, mentioned for the first time in 1228, rebuilt 1735-8, choir 1937. In the

Charmey: typical 18C farmhouse.

interior 17C carved choir stalls and 19C altars. Near the Kantonstrasse **house** No. 27 with a decorated façade dated 1716. In Les Arses 18C **farmhouses**, Nos. 111–114.

Charmoille JU

1☐D4

The **chapel** of the former Augustinian priory (founded in the 12C) in MISEREZ is a late Gothic single-aisled building with a stellar-vaulted polygonal choir and a massive façade tower.

Château-d'Oex VD

11☐C4

Reformed church (St-Donat), built on the site of a former château destroyed by fire in 1800. The Gothic choir is 15C and so is the tower; its lower parts were once part of a fortress tower. *Musée du Vieux-Pays-d'Enhaut.* Fine local historical and applied art collections.

Châtel-St-Denis FR

11☐B3

St-Denis. Built in 1872–6. Neo-Gothic building, nave and two aisles with polygonal choir, interior decoration from the period of the building of the church, modern high altar. By the church is the **château**, now an office, dating from the late 13C. Only the lower part of the square keep of the original château has survived; it was incorporated into the new buildings

in the 18C. The two towers in the walls date from the same period. FRUENCE On the edge of the village fine 15C double farmhouse with a Gothic doorway.

Châtillens VD

11☐A3

Reformed church (St-Maurice and St-Pancrace), first mentioned in the 13C, present building essentially 14C. In the interior carved choir stalls dating from 1621 and a capital from the former abbey of Hautcrêt, whose ruins are near to the village of Les Tavernes.

Chaux-de-Fonds, La NE

6☐A2

In 1794 the town, at that time still very much a village, was completely destroyed by fire. Rebuilding began immediately to Moïse Perret-Gentil's plan based on a central square with streets in a grid pattern; the engineer Charles-Henri Junod worked out a master plan of the street layout, which was accepted in 1835, and gave the town its characteristic appearance. **Reformed church,** built on an oval ground plan in 1794–6 by Moïse Perret-Gentil; the interior was badly damaged by fire in 1919, and rebuilt in 1921. Interior and exterior bas-reliefs by Léon Perrin. The Place de l'Hôtel de Ville was the core of rebuilding in 1794. The **Hôtel de Ville** of 1803 is very restrained; the façade has a roof light with clock; in the square bronze **monument to the Republic** by Charles l'Eplatennier, 1910. In the Rue des Musées the **Musée international de l'horlogerie**, devoted to clock-making, is an underground building built by P.Zoelly and G.J.Haefeli in 1971–3. The **Musée des Beaux-Arts** was built in 1925–6 by R.Chapallaz and Ch.L'Eplattenier; there is a bas-relief of the latter on the façade. SW of the town is the **Museée paysan**, housed in a remarkable 1612–14 farmhouse, with panelled rooms and a vaulted kitchen with an open fireplace and column dating from the 16C.

La-Chaux-de-Fonds: the Musée historique et médaillier, established in 1923.

La-Chaux-de-Fonds: clock collection in the Musée international de l'horlogerie.

Museums. *Musée international d'horlogerie* (clock-making); *Museée des Beaux-Arts* (fine art); *Musée d'histoire et Médaillier* (history and medals); *Musée paysan et artisanal* (farming and trades).

Chavornay VD
10□E1

Reformed church (St-Marcel), late medieval building with a late Gothic choir and a remarkable nave with a wooden roof and wooden pillars dating from 1971. Tower with clock in roof light. There are some fine 16&17C **houses** in the Bernese style in the **Grand'Rue**, particularly No. 61.

Chêne-Bougeries GE
16□E/F2

Protestant church in the Place Audeoud, built in 1756-8 by Jean-Louis Calandrini, a baroque building on an oval ground plan. The severe façade has a columned portico,

the interior is laid out like an amphitheatre. **La Gradelle,** a residential quarter built in 1963-7 by J.Hentsch and J.P.Zbinden.

Chêne-Pâquier VD
5□F5

Reformed parish church on an oval ground plan, built in 1667 by the Bernese architect Abraham Dünz. It is the first example in Switzerland of a church specifically designed for Protestant worship; it is based on the Temple du Paradis in Lyon, built in 1564 and destroyed shortly afterwards. Exterior with four tracery windows with round arches and a Renaissance portal. The interior is very plain and without division, and has a wooden roof with four wooden pillars. Near to the village of Chêne-Pâquier is the **tower of St-Martin du Chêne,** a massive square keep, the only fragment of the 13C château, built by the local lords, who also founded the village, which is now in ruins.

Cheseaux-s.-Lausanne VD
10□E2

10 Route de Genève, **nouveau château,** a 17C house, enlarged in the 18C with additional outbuildings.

Chéserex VD
10□B4

2 km. from the village, at the foot of the Jura, former **abbey of Notre-Dame de Bonmont;** originally a Benedictine monastery, affiliated to the Cistercians as a daughter-foundation of Clairvaux in 1131, and thus the first Cistercian monastery in Switzerland. Bonmont reached its peak in the 14C, was secularised in 1542, and turned into an estate. The monastery buildings have been destroyed, only the *abbey church of Sainte-Marie* has survived. The church, built between 1131 and 1150, is a typical example of Cistercian architecture; the ground plan is T-shaped, the nave has barrel vaulting, the aisles have transverse barrel vaulting, the rectangular

choir has now been reduced in length. There is a square tower over the crossing. The portal and rose window in the W. façade date from the late 12C. S. of the church is the **château,** built in 1738 on the foundations of the monks' hospital.

Chessel VD
11 □ B5

Reformed church (St-Nicolas), probably founded in the 10C. The present single-aisled building with a round apse is Romanesque. In the N. a chapel and a tower with a Gothic crown.

Chevroux VD
6 □ B5

Reformed church (St-Jean-Baptiste), built in the 15C and altered in the 18C. It has one aisle and a square choir with rib vaulting. Wooden **storehouse** opposite the church.

Cheyres FR
11 □ A1

St-Nicolas, built 1749–52 on the site of a 15C chapel. In the interior 14C Virgin Mary. **Château,** built 1773–4; it has a carved façade gable with the arms of Fribourg.

Chiasso TI
19 □ D5

Catholic parish church San Vitale, first mentioned in 1237, the present monumental basilica with nave and two aisles was built in 1934; there are baroque altars in the interior. **Magazzini Generali SA,** warehouses built by Robert Maillart in 1924–5.

Chiésaz, La VD
11 □ B4

Reformed church (St-Légier), probably

Chêne-Pâquier: the Reformed church of 1667 is set on the diagonal and oval in plan.

Chéserex: the former abbey church of Sainte-Marie was built in the 12C.

founded in the 12C. Two apses, S. apse part of the first Romanesque church. The N. apse originally a chapel, built by Amadeus von Blonay in 1223. The single-aisled church with a façade tower dates from the 16C. In front of the church is a 17C **priory.**

Chiggiogna TI
13 □ C4

Catholic parish church of Santa Maria Assunta, first mentioned in 1229; the present building dates from 1524, but is based on older buildings. The six-storey 11&12C bell tower and the remains of pilaster strips and blind arches are evidence of the Romanesque origins of the first building. A second aisle was added later and there has been much alteration in the interior. In the N. choir is a late Gothic retable dating from 1510–20, which originated in S. Germany; next to it is an early 19C Pentecost group.

Chiggiogna: late Gothic triptych, c. 1510–20, in the parish church.

Chillon: the 13C Savoyard castle is on a rock in the lake.

Chillon VD

11 □B5

Château. One of the finest and best-known Swiss medieval fortresses. The rock of Chillon supported a settlement from ancient times, and has been fortified since the 9C. It was owned first by the vassals of the bishop of Sion, then acquired in the 12C by the counts of Savoy. Extensions began in 1189 under Thomas I of Savoy, and continued for a century, as the château had become one of the preferred residences of the counts. Chillon acquired its distinctive design from 1255, under the architect Pierre Meinier, commissioned by Peter II of Savoy; Meinier created the defensive system on the E. side by the addition of semicircular flanking towers, an innovation for the period. After 1442 the lords of Savoy stopped living in the château, from 1536 it was occupied by the Bernese, and from 1803 it was owned by the canton of Vaud. The château, famous through the work of Byron and Victor Hugo, was completely restored at the end of the 19C. The

Chironico: the 14C Torre Pedrini towers over the village.

buildings of Chillon are arranged around four courtyards; the centre of the rock is dominated by the keep, the oldest part of the château. The most powerful defensive buildings are on the land side in the E., while the residential buildings on the W. and N. sides were protected by the lake and the fleet stationed there. Parts of the château which deserve particular mention are: the vaulted cellars, which were used as a prison—the most famous inmate was F.Bonivard of Geneva—,the Gothic chapel of St.George with wall paintings, the so-called salle des chevaliers with the coats-of-arms of the Landvogts of Bern, and the Duke's room with 14C paintings.

Chironico TI

13□C4

In the middle of the village **Santi Ambrogio e Maurizio,** one of the oldest churches in the Leventina valley, mentioned for the first time in 1227. The present Romanesque building, based on a place of worship dating from the year 1000, has a particularly wide nave with a double apse. Interior wall paintings of various periods; the oldest date from 1338, the rest are 15&16C. Near the church 14C **Torre Pedrini**.

Choëx VS

17□B2

Catholic parish church of St-Sylvestre, built 1706, baroque building with single aisle and polygonal choir, rococo altar 1750. By the church **priest's house,** built by Abbot Bernadin de Kalbermatten in 1736.

Choully GE

16□D2

On the road from Satigny to Bourdigny 1735 **house** built for Michel Lullin of Châteauvieux.

Chur GR

9□B4

The capital of the canton of Grisons. The oldest documented settlement goes back to the Neolithic *c.* 2500 BC. It was on the left bank of the Plessur, in what is now Welschdörfli. Remains of Bronze-Age, Iron-Age and Roman buildings have also been discovered there. In the Roman period Chur was the principal town of the Raetia Prima, which extended well beyond the present boundaries of the canton. Chur was a bishopric by the end of the 4C, in the 6C Rhaetia became part of the Frankish empire. Under Charlemagne, *c.* 800, Churrätien became part of the Holy Roman Empire. With the immigration of Valais citizens, who founded free Walser communities, the German language arrived in the previously pure Rhaeto-Roman area (13&14C). To keep the peace after the collapse of the Empire the Gotteshaus alliance was formed in 1367, the Graue Bund (Grey League) in 1395 and 1424 and in 1436 the Zehngerichtebund (Ten Courts League). In alliance since 1471, they formed, until the Helvetian Republic in 1798, the 'Free State of the Three Leagues'. In 1497 and 1498 the Free State entered into alliance with the Confederation under increasing threat from the Habsburgs. Territorial enlargements followed with the acquisition of the Bündner Herrschaft in 1509 and of Veltlin, which was later lost again, in 1512. The period of conflict of the faiths threatened to break up the state, which was still a very loose formation. In 1803 Grisons became a canton in the Confederation and Chur its capital. In the 19C the pass roads were extended and the Rhaetian railway was built. Parts of the fortifications (Obertor) and the network of narrow streets remain of the **medieval town.** The town is dominated by the episcopal court, which had its own fortifications (Marsöl and Tor towers). The **Cathedral St.Maria Himmelfahrt** is a heavy, late Romanesque building built in 1150–1272. It is a pillared basilica without a transept and with three bays, a square presbytery and a rectangular sanctuary over a bipartite crypt of the same shape. The tower with its baroque dome dates from *c.* 1600. The portal already has Gothic capitals. Late Gothic carved high altar (1486–92) and tabernacle by Jakob Russ. At the entrance to the first crypt four early-13C Apostle columns. Capitals with figures in the nave and the choir (Daniel capital) contemporary with the main building. The *Laurentius chapel* has net vaulting (1467). In the *Dommuseum* are parts of the church treasure. To the S. in the complex of the new cantonal school **former church of St.Stefan.** There are remains of an early Christian square tomb (Bishop's mausoleum) with barrel vaulting *c.* 500. On the walls fragments of paintings of Apostles, with traces of decorative paintings on the side walls. In the porch late antique granite sarcophagus, in the rebuilt

Chur: general view from the E., St. Luzius on the right, cathedral centre.

The interior of the cathedral has outstanding ornamentation.

apse of the early Christian single-aisled church (early 6C) remains of its floor mosiac. **Reformed parish church of St. Martin.** Former Carolingian single-aisled church rebuilt after the fire of 1464; late Gothic polygonal choir with stellar vaulting added at the same time by Steffan Klain. Windows by Aug.Giacometti 1917–19. **Reformed parish church of St. Regla.** Late Gothic single-aisled church with stellar vaulting built 1494–1500 after the town fire by Balthasar Bilgeri. The modern windows were added by Hans Studer in 1973. **Former monastery church of St. Luzius.** The very high ante-choir (1150) leads from the nave

Carolingian ring crypt under the choir of St. Luzius.

with its flat ceiling, rebuilt after a fire in 1811, into the inner choir (1200), which has three aisles and vaulting and a square sanctuary (*c.* 1250). The original choir with three apses can still be discerned in the present building. Under the ante-choir Romanesque hall crypt with three aisles (1150), leading to a Carolingian ring crypt (early-8C). In the apex to the W. is the passage to the grave of the patron of Grisons St. Luzius, and to the E. the

passage to the hermitage grave. The **Bishop's Palace** in the courtyard was built to an irregular design in the 17&18C, using parts of the medieval building. The baroque W. façade has three bays and stucco dating from 1732&3, in the interior monumental staircase and Renaissance stucco from the same period. Below the courtyard is the **Rätische Museum,** the former Haus Buol, a cubic building of 1675–80, with a saddleback roof. By the Plessur, at 16 Jochstrasse is **Haus Schwarz** auf dem Sand, a two-storey villa with a hipped roof, built *c.* 1700. In the Bärenloch, 12–14 Kirchgasse, is the so-called **Hasenzimmer** with wall painting (*c.* 1600). In the Poststrasse is the **Rathaus,** made up of three late-medieval cubic buildings. It has a large, trapezoid roof with a ridge-turret dating from 1560. The *Rathaushalle* is incorporated in the central section, with groin vaulting dating from *c.* 1540. At 14 Poststrasse is the **Altes Gebäu,** built from 1727–30 for Peter von Salis-Soglio with baroque gardens; it is a plain, rectangular building with a hipped roof; in the interior are ceiling paintings by G.P.Ligari of mythological scenes, framed in Renaissance stucco. At 6 Rabengasse is **Haus Pestalozza,** built in the late 16C. It has a vaulted lower storey with broad Gothic windows, three upper storeys and a roof with a hipped gable. An der Reichsgasse, opposite Regierungsplatz (Vazerol monument of 1881 in memory of the joining of the Three Leagues) is the **Neues Gebäu,** today a government building, a four-storey house with a hipped roof, built 1751&2 by Joh.Grubenmann for Andreas von Salis-Soglio. 28 an der Reichsgasse, **Haus Braun** with 16C façade painting. 2 Planaterrastrasse, **Haus Capol.** Former city Burg (1533) with a polygonal staircase tower and a three-sided oriel. **Haus zum Brunnengarten** 1 Obere Plessurstrasse, a late neoclassical building by Martin Hatz (1848); the façade has a two-storey portico with pediment. The **Catholic Heiligkreuzkirche** was built in 1967–9, the architect was M.Förderer.
Museums. *Kunsthaus,* in the former Villa Planta (1874–6) am Postplatz; largely Bünden art of the 18–20C and temporary

exhibitions. *Rätisches Museum* (Haus Buol) with collections on the history and ethnography of Grisons. *Naturhistorisches Museum,* 31 Masanserstrasse; natural history.

Churwalden GR
9□B5

Former Premonstratensian monastery, founded *c.* 1140. *Monastery Church of St. Maria and St. Michael,* late Gothic building dating from 1477-1502. Hall with nave and two aisles, net vaulting and rood screen; square monks' choir with a polygonal sanctuary, late Gothic triptych (1477). On the E. wall of the N. aisle, part of the earlier Romanesque building, Gothic Coronation of the Virgin by the Waltensburg master.

Cimalmotto TI
See CAMPO   19□A1

Cinuos-chel GR
See S-CHANF   14□E1

Clarens VD
See MONTREUX   11□B4

Clées,Les VD
10□D1

Château on the hill which dominates the town; mentioned in 1130, and first owned by the counts of Genevois, after 1250 by the counts of Savoy. It commands an important crossroads on the road to the Jougne pass; it was destroyed in 1475. The square 13C keep has survived, and was restored in the 19C.

Clugin GR
14□A2

Reformed church. 12C Romanesque single-aisled church with semicircular apse and wall paintings from three periods. Waltensburg master *c.* 1340: in the apse dome Christ in Majesty and symbols of the Evangelists, Apostle frieze below them. On

Clugin: apse painting by the Waltensburg master in the Reformed church.

Collombey: Château built in the 17C for the Du Fay family.

the left choir arch wall Angel of the Annunciation and saint bishop, on the N. wall of the nave two martyrs; Rhäzün master after 1350: outline drawing on the N. wall; master *c.* 1400: St.George and Crucifixion on the S. wall.

Coldrerio TI

19☐D5

Near the cemetery 17C **Santa Apollonia** with 18C wall paintings in the interior. VILLA On the cantonal road 16C **Catholic church of Santa Maria del Carmelo** with a 19C semicicular apse. In the interior, in the N. side chapel, vault painting and picture by Pier Francesco Mola (1612–1666).

Collombey VS

17☐B1

On the hill which dominates the village **convent of the Bernadines,** former château of the lords of Arbignon, changed convent from 1643. The massive 13C keep of the château has survived in the SW corner. The convent buildings date from the 17C, as does the **St-Joseph chapel,** a plain building with a single aisle with an 18C baroque altar. On the cantonal road is the **manoir Du Fay de Lavallaz,** in the 14C the property of the Châtillon-Larringes family. The present château was built after 1650; the entrance portal is dated 1633.

Cologny GE

16☐E2

The traditional home of the Geneva bourgeoisie. **Reformed church,** built in 1709 on the site of a medieval place of worship in the style of the churches of Geneva. 18C **Maison d'Espine,** with wrought-iron balustrade, now a parish hall. **Maison Diodati,** Chemin de Ruth. 18C building, Lord Byron stayed here in 1816. *Fondation Bodmer,* Chemin du Guignard, collection of books and manuscripts.

Colombier NE

6☐B4

Reformed Church, neoclassical, built in 1828&9. **Château.** Little is known of the history of Colombier, the lords are only mentioned from the 13C; the first château was presumably built on the site of a Roman villa, whose foundations are still visible. The château acquired its present form in the course of major rebuilding in the 17&19C, when it was the parade ground of the Confederation. The principal buildings are set around a courtyard, entered through a portal dominated by a tower with machicolations of 1543. The old château in the SE corner of the courtyard dates from the 15&16C. The late-16C Porte des Allées connects the château with the buildings in the N. of the complex. Rue Haute, numerous 18C **houses. Le Pontet,** Chemin du Pontet, 17C house in which Madame de Charrière lived. In the vineyard W. of the town is **Vaudijon,** an Empire-style country seat built in 1800–7 by J.P.du Pasquier. The principal façade

Colombier NE: the Château houses a military and fabric museum.

is visible from the cantonal road and has a rotunda decorated with bas-reliefs. In the château are a *Musée militaire* (military museum) and a *Museé de toiles peintes* (printed fabric).

Colombier VD
10□D2

Reformed church (St-Martin), first mentioned in 1228, present building essentially 15C. On the S. side is the late Gothic chapel of St-Jean-Baptiste dating from the 16C. Near the centre is the so-called small château, and behind it the 18C **Manoir Loeffel,** with a Gothic staircase tower and a fresco featuring Anti-Pope Felix V.

Comano VD
19□D3

Catholic parish church of Santa Maria, first mentioned in 1359, enlarged in the 16C and rebuilt during the baroque. In the choir are notable stucco, 1625 by G.A.Marchi of Comano and 17C paintings attributed to Isidoro Bianchi; the altar has an 18C Presentation in the Temple.

Combes NE
See LANDERON.LE   6□C3

Commugny VD
10□B5

Reformed church (St-Christophe), built on the site of a Roman villa. The earliest

church in Commugny dates from the 6C. As can be seen from the excavations still visible in the choir, the original chapel had a number of successors. The present church was rebuilt in the 15C, the square choir is dominated by a bell tower in the Romanesque style built in 1481. The nave has side chapels, in the N. choir chapel are earlier, finely-carved capitals which have been incorporated into the later building.

Comologno TI
19□A2

Catholic parish church San Giovanni Battista, built 1688, altered in the 18&19C. Ossuary and chapels of the Stations of the Cross 1807, with modern painting. In the village 18C houses built by members of the Remonda family; the most important is the 1770 **Palazzo della** The **commandery** of the Knights of the Order of St.John of Jerusalem functioned until the French Revolution. The château, built from 1425, is on a square ground plan and is flanked on the S. by a round stairtower and in the N. by a square tower. Two annexes with round towers were added in 1626. It now houses the parish hall and a small *museum of the Order.*

Concise VD
5□F4

Reformed church (St-Jean-Baptiste), probably built in the late 11C, first mentioned in 1228. The semicircular apse and the bell tower are Romanesque, the Gothic parts of the building were built in the late 15C and altered in the 17&19C. In the N. chapel carved consoles and a Gothic pew. In the upper village interesting 16C **house.** Above Concise, on the road to Provence, tablet and a stone commemorating the battle of Grandson (1476).

Confignon GE
16□E2

Catholic church Sts-Pierre-et-Paul, mentioned in the 12C, choir early 16C,

Coppet: the magnificent entrance to the Château which has a cour d'honneur.

Corbières: Château with distinctive Bernese roof.

nave late 17C, tower raised in 1871. N. of the choir 16C chapel with Italianate frescos dating from 1714.

Conthey-Bourg VS

17 □ D2

An important fortified settlement from the 13–15C; it was used by the lords of Savoy as a base for their military expeditions against the bishop of Sion. The little village was surrounded by a wall and protected by two fortresses. The lower part of the semicircular 13C keep and a section of the curtain wall with the **porte St-Séverin**, parts of the château built by Peter II of Savoy, have survived on the vine-clad hill. **St-Georges chapel**, rebuilt in the 17C, baroque altar of 1730. Near the chapel **maison Germanier;** its door is framed with marble slabs with Gothic inscriptions.

Coppet VD

10 □ B5

This little town founded in the 13C owes its distinctive appearance to its arcade houses. **Reformed church,** formerly the church of the Dominican monastery founded by Amedée de Viry, Lord of Coppet, in 1490. Built *c.* 1500 in the Flamboyant style, W. façade and bell tower altered in 1774. The interior has 16C carved choir stalls, by Suzanne Necker in memory of her parents. Glass by Charles Clément, 1945&55. **Château,** built in 1767 on the site of a medieval predecessor

and acquired in 1784 by Jacques Necker, Louis XIV's minister of finance. His daughter, Madame de Staël, established a salon here. The château is entered through a courtyard with an orangery and stables; the horseshoe-shaped main building opens on to a French park. In the interior the rooms of Madame de Staél and the Necker family, with the surviving furniture, can be visited. In the Grand-Rue the Hôtel du Lac has an 18C sign, and the Hôtel d'Orange has one dating from 1680; **Maison Michel.** Late Gothic building, now *musée régional*

Corbières FR

11 □ C2

Château in the centre of the village. The Corbières family, first mentioned in 1115, originally had two castles, of which only one has survived; it was rebuilt in 1560 and altered in 1750. Rectangular building with Gothic windows and a Bernese roof, surrounded by a low wall.

Corcelles NE

6 □ A4

Reformed church (Sts-Pierre-et-Paul), mentioned in 1092, part of a priory dependent on Cluny. Tower and part of the choir Romanesque, nave and S. chapel 15C; the **priest's house,** adjacent to the church in the E., is built over the former priory and dates from the 16–18C. Generally speaking the Grand-Rue has survived intact; **house** No. 31–3 dates from the 16C, windows and doors the Renaissance style; **house** No. 35 has 16C windows and 18C roof timbering.

Corcelles-près-Concise VD

5☐F4

Beyond the village, at the foot of the Jura, is a **group of menhirs** unique in Switzerland. A megalith which disappeared in the 18C was replaced in 1843.

Corcelles-près-Payerne VD

6☐B5

Reformed church (St-Nicolas), built in the 11C, part of the Payerne monastery from the 12C. It has a single aisle with a round apse and a Romanesque bell tower; the W. façade is Gothic. There are numerous wooden and stone **storehouses** in the village.

Corippo TI

19☐C1

A characteristic Val Verzaca village on the right bank of the artificial lake; the village has survived in very good condition. **Catholic parish church of Santa Maria del Carmine**, built in the 17&18C.

Corminboeuf FR

11☐C1

Fine **farmhouses** on the cantonal road; No. 59 dates from 1718 and No. 62 from 1653; there are also 17C wooden **storehouses**.

Cormondrèche NE

6☐A4

Château, Rue du Château. 16C building, probably altered in the 18&19C. At 25 Grand-Rue is the so-called **priory,** built in 1550–2 for Claude Baillod; used by the priors of Val-de-Travers to store their wine harvest; **House** No. 28 dates from the

Corcelles-p.-Payerne: the Reformed church is a Romanesque building with late Gothic W. façade.

16&17C; the group of buildings at No. 56, known as **le Manoir** were built in the 16 –18C.

Cornaux NE

6☐B3

Reformed church (St-Pierre), mentioned in 1228, 14C choir tower; 3. of the nave is the 1500 Chapelle Clottu. Rue de Fontaines, group of 18C houses; No. 27 **maison la Cour,** elegant 17C façade. In the Rue du Vignoble some 15C houses have survived; Nos. 1 and 5 are particularly notable.

Corsier-sur-Vevey VD

11☐A4

Reformed church (St-Maurice), first mentioned in 1079. The present building, built on Romanesque foundations, was enlarged and altered in the 15C. The Lombardy bell tower is N. of the church; there are 15C wall paintings in the choir: angels bearing crosses, Christ in Glory and symbols of the Evangelists.

Corsier-s.-Vevey: 15C wall paintings in the choir of the Reformed church.

Cortaillod: Hôtel de Commune with richly articulated façade.

Cortaillod NE

6☐A4

Reformed church, originally in 1505 a chapel dedicated to S.Nicholas, enlarged and altered in 1722; façade tower 1611. Opposite the church is the **Hôtel de Commune** of 1761. Elegant two-storey façade with two gables in the form of segments of a circle decorated with carved motifs. Rue de Coteaux. 16 – 18C **houses,** particularly remarkable are Nos. 10, 29, 34. By the lake, near the modern Cortaillod cable factory, **Fabrique Neuve,** calico factory from the 18C industrial complex; several buildings and the owner's house have survived.

Corzoneso TI

13☐D4

Catholic parish church of Santi Nazario e Celso, first mentioned in 1211, altered in 1671. The façade has a portico-

Corzoneso: Romanesque stucco Apostle figures in San Remigio chapel.

like chapel, frescoed all over in 1587. In the interior 17C high altar, the N. chapel has 1679 stucco and the sacristy 15C frescos by the masters of Seregno.
BOSCERO On the left after leaving Dongio take the road to Boscero and the **San Remigio chapel.** A building with two aisles and a double apse, built in the 11C, enlarged in the 12C and altered in the 17C. Interesting 13&15C paintings inside the

Courrendlin: the clock tower was originally built as a prison.

apse and on the interior walls of the nave, and on the W. wall Tarilli frescos dating from 1600. There are two 12C stucco Apostle figures on the reconstructed altar.

Cossonay VD

10 □ D/E2

The town was the seat of a powerful family in the high Middle Ages; when they died out it came under the control of the dukes of Savoy in 1421 and in 1536 of the dukes of Bern. The former château of Cossonay has completely disappeared; the characteristic concentric plan of the town has survived, however, while the area built in the 18&19C developed along a straight road out of the town. **Reformed church** (Saints-Pierre-et-Paul), first mentioned in 1096. A church with three apses was built in the 9–11C on the site of the original 8C place of worship; this was followed in the 13C by a basilica with a nave and two aisles. In 1250–60 the three Romanesque apses were replaced by a square choir. The imposing tower N. of the choir had a watch-tower added in the 15C. In the Place du Temple is the 19C **Hôtel de Ville** with a neoclassical façade and the **Hôtel du**

Cerf with a doorway dated 1666. In the Rue du Prieuré is the **château,** now the prefecture, an 18C house on the site of the medieval château. 9 Petite Rue, **Café des Bains,** a late Gothic house. Opposite is a former school building, with a clock tower which was originally on one of the town gates.

Cotterg VS
See **Bagnes** 17 □ D3

Courfaivre JU
1 □ D5

Catholic parish church of St-Germain-d'Auxerre dating from 1702 and 1856 with modern decoration; glass 1954 by Fernand Léger, high altar 1954 by Remo Rossi, choir tapestry 1957 by Jean Lurçat.

Courrendlin JU
1 □ E5

Catholic parish church of St-Germain-et-Randoald, single-aisled building with façade tower; the three baroque altars are identically built: two columns with Corinthian capitals support a gable and form a frame for a painting. In the **church treasury** is a late Gothic monstrance in the form of a tower. The **tour de l'horloge,** a late Gothic prison and archive tower with step gables, has a clock dating from 1697.

Couvet NE
5 □ E/F4

Reformed church, built 1657, façade tower 1756–66. Grand-Rue No. 27, **Hôtel de l'Aigle** of 1778, a spacious building with semicircular wooden framing under the gables; No. 38 **Hôtel Communal** of 1739, a small portico supporting a balcony on the façade. **Maison de l'Ecu de France,** 2 Rue du Clos, built in 1690. On the road to Môtiers is **le Marais,** an 18C house with outbuildings.

Crans-p.-Céligny: 18C Château, built to a French design.

Crans-près-Céligny VD
10☐B4

Rue A.Saladin, **château;** house built in 1764–7 for Antoine Saladin of Geneva on the site of a medieval château and designed by the French architects Jaillet and Léonard Racle; it consists of a main building and two wings around a courtyard. The façade visible from the cantonal road has a semicircular protruding central section with a balustrade.

Cresciano TI
19☐D1

Catholic parish church of San Vincenzo, first mentioned in the 13C, rebuilt in the 16C or 17C. Fine 13C Romanesque bell tower, restored in the 19C.

Cressier NE
6☐C3

The **Catholic church,** built 1873–5 in neo-Gothic style, contains remains of the interior decoration of the former church of St-Martin, now deconsecrated (renamed château Jean-Jaquet) and of a rosary chapel destroyed in 1872, on the site of which it stands. The **château,** now a parish hall and school, was built in 1609 for Jacob Vallier, Landvogt of Neuchâtel; it extends over a spacious site surounded by a wall with a Renaissance portal. Main façade with two rectangular towers topped by a massive roof. In the upper part of the centre of the old village **maison Vallier,** built for Pierre Vallier, the governor of Neuchâtel. The protruding corner turret is decorated with the coats-of-arms of the Vallier and d'Affry families and dated 1572; Renaissance-style portal and windows. By the house are a 1654 **stone cross** and a 1584 **lion fountain;** the fountain basin dates from 1578. Rue Sans-Soleil, **group of 16&17C buildings.**

Cressier-sur-Morat FR
6☐C5

Saint-Jean, mentioned in the 12C and rebuilt in 1842–44. It has a single aisle, façade tower and portico. Opposite the church is the **château,** rebuilt in the 17C by J.F.von Diesbach on the foundations of an earlier building, altered in the 18&19C.

Creux-de-Genthod GE
See GENTHOD   16☐E1

Croglio TI
19☐C4

Catholic church of San Bartolomeo, of medieval origin, with a semicircular apse. In the interior are frescos signed and dated 1440. Near the church is the 18C **casa Conti,** with loggias in its façade.

Cudrefin VD
6☐B4

Small town, fortified in the 13C, when it belonged to Savoy. Only one **tower** has survived of the former curtain wall, and this has been incorporated into a church. In the square is a **justice fountain** with 1605 statue.
MONTET **Reformed church** (St-Théodule), late Gothic, built in the 15C. In the choir vault are coats-of-arms of the bastard Humbert of Savoy, in the S. chapel keystone with Lamb of God and paintings in the vault spandrels. By the church is the 15C **priest's house,** vicarage, built at the time of Humbert of Savoy, altered and enlarged during the baroque.

Cressier-s.-Morat: 17C Château, much altered later.

Cully: the Maison Muriset, a semi-detached house of 1684.

Cugnasco TI
19□D2

On the cantonal road is the **Santa Maria delle Grazie chapel,** first mentioned in 1463. It has a single aisle and a polygonal choir; the interior is decorated with 15&16C paintings.
CUROGNA **Santi Anna e Cristoforo chapel,** a medieval building enlarged in the 16C. In the interior in the apse and on the walls of the nave late-15C wall paintings in the style of the masters of Seregno, on the W. façade paintings by Alessandro Gorla, 1601.
DITTO **San Martino chapel,** of medieval origin, subsequently enlarged. In the interior are 15C paintings, including a remarkable Last Supper by the masters of Seregno; in the extension of the nave paintings by Alessandro Gorla, 1603.

Cully VD
10□F3

Reformed church. Neo-Gothic, built 1865-6 on the site of a medieval church, of which the 15C tower has survived. In the **chapel of the former Infirmary** (Rue de l'Hôtel de Ville), in the back room of a former shop, paintings of the Judgement of Solomon dating from 1570-80. 7 Rue du Temple, **house of Major Davel.** Nos. 8 - 10 Rue de la Justice, **Muriset house** with double portal dating from 1684. **Maison jaune** with portal of 1641. 8 Route de Vevey, 17&18C **house** and **justice fountain** with 1643 basin and statue of Justice personified.

Cumbels GR
13□E1

Catholic parish church of St.Stephan. Late Gothic building, extended to the E. and W. in 1689. In the interior wall paintings from the second half of the 16C.

Cunter/Conters GR
14□B2

Catholic parish church of San Carlo Borromeo. Baroque single-aisled church of 1677 with polygonal choir and 2 side chapels, on the S. side two rows of windows. The furnishings date from the time of the building of the church.

Curaglia GR
See MEDEL
13□C2

Curtilles: Reformed church with Romanesque nave and late Gothic choir.

Cumbels: the originally late Gothic St. Stephan was redesigned in the baroque style in the 17C.

Curogna TI
See **Cugnasco** 19 ☐ D2

Curtilles VD
11 ☐ A2

Curtilles was founded in the 11C as a market town by the Bishop of Lausanne, who built walls and a château, which was given up again in the 13C. Only an earth mound at the N. end of the town survives of this château, which is not to be confused with the present **château,** a late Gothic building. **Reformed church** (Notre-Dame), founded in the 11C and rebuilt *c.* 1230. The Flamboyant rectangular choir was built in the 16C. On the N. wall of the nave are fragments of stained glass *c.* 1500, including arms and portraits of the Bishop of Lausanne, Aymon de Montfalcon.

D

Dallenwil NW
7 ☐ F4

Catholic parish church of St. Laurentius, built 1697–8 to plans by the priest Johann Jakob Scolar of Bürglen (UR). The interior stucco is probably by Italian masters.

Damvant JU
1 ☐ B5

The single-aisled Catholic parish church of **Saint-Germain,** (1747) has a tower above the façade. Side altars (1775) and pulpit rococo, high altar neoclassical.

Dardagny GE
16 ☐ D2

Reformed church. Baroque-neoclassical, built 1723 at the expense of Jean Vasserot. **Château.** The largest in the canton, now a parish hall and school, largely rebuilt for Jean Vasserot in 1723. Rectangular ground plan, baroque-neoclassical monumental façade with gable, four square corner towers, the only remains of a château of 1655.

Därstetten BE
11 ☐ F2

Reformed church of St. Maria, the place of worship of the former priory founded by the lords of Weissenburg in the late 12C. The building, often rebuilt, contains frescos from the first half of the 14C. **Haus Knütti** im Moos is considered one of the finest farmhouses in Europe. The first storey above the whitened cellar is built on the Ständerbau principle, the loft storeys are Blockbau. The gabled frontage

Dallenwil: St.Laurentius, a baroque building by the priest J.J.Scolar.

Därstetten: Haus Knutti, a lavishly decorated 18C farmhouse.

is decorated with symmetrical rows of windows and carved and painted friezes. The 'Sunday room' in the interior is rococo. The central kitchen has an open fireplace. The **farmhouses in Wiler,** E. of Därstetten, are, like the Knuttihaus, typical Simmertal houses with a stone substructure with mixed (Ständer- and Blockbau) storeys above them.

Davos GR
9 ☐ D4

DAVOS DORF The Gothic single-aisled **Reformed church,** 1514, with late Gothic wall paintings on the ground floor of the tower. *Heimatmuseum* (local history) in the former prebend's house dating from the 17C.

DAVOS PLATZ **Reformed parish church.** The polygonal choir (after 1500) leads to a nave with two aisles of 1909 – 10 with

Davos: Reformed church in Frauenkirch with avalanche deflector in the W.

massive entrance tower (1481) and small tower from an earlier building (after 1280). **Rathaus,** built 1564 by Hans Ardüser with *'Grosse Stube',* the state room of the Zehngerichtebund. **Alexanderhaus,** built 1907 as a sanatorium. **Eishalle,** a wooden rotunda with saddleback roof (1979).
FRAUENKIRCH The **Reformed church,** built *c.* 1500 has a polygonal choir and a wedge-shaped avalanche deflector on the W. wall.
MONSTEIN *Bergbaumuseum* (mining) on the Schmelzboden.
WILDBOGEN **Memorial** to the painter Ernst Ludwig Kirchner who lived here from 1923–38.

Degersheim SG

3☐E5

Catholic parish church of St.Jakobus. The earlier building of 1818 was replaced by a neo-baroque building by Danzeisen and Hunziker in 1923 – 4. **Reformed church.** Jugendstil building, 1908 by Robert Curjel and Karl Moser.

Deggio TI

See QUINTO 13☐B4

Deitingen SO

7☐A2

The neoclassical nave of the **Catholic parish church of St.Marien** with its late Gothic choir and tower dates from 1816– 19. The moated former **Schlösschen**

Wilihof was altered in 1680 as a 'Türmlihaus'.

Delémont JU

1☐E5

Principal town in the canton of Jura. The canton goes back to the Basel Bishop's State which came into being in 999 as a gift of the King of Burgundy. In the 14&15C Bern concluded treaties with the S. regions of the Prince-Bishopric and later introduced the Reformation there; the S. Jura is associated with Bern politically, denominationally and linguistically. In 1815 the Congress of Vienna forced Bern to accept the former Bishop's State as a substitute for the Vaud and parts of the Aargau. The occupation of the N. Jura by Bernese troops (1836 and 1873) as a result of conflicts with the Catholic church deepened the gulf between N. and S. When in 1747 the Bernese Grosser Rat withheld the building department from the Jura Regierungsrat Moeckli the Comité de Moutier was formed, which aimed for partial autonomy, whilst the Rassemblement Jurassien, founded in 1948, aimed to establish a new canton. On the 24 September 1978 the people of Switzerland voted in support of a canton of Jura, essentially embracing the areas Delémont, Porrentruy and Franches-Montagnes.
The town of **Delémont,** founded by the Bishops of Basel in the 13C, is almost rectangular in plan and has two main axes with four roads running across them. The **Tour des Archives** in the NE corner of the Old Town is part of the former fortifications. The **Porte de Porrentruy** (1756– 9) and the **Porte-au-Loup** (1775) are the only town gates to have survived; they are post-medieval reconstructions. 16C fountains with statues include the **Fontaine de la Vierge** by Hans Michel of Basel and the **Saint-Maurice** and the **Sauvage** fountains by Laurent Perroud. **Catholic church of Saint-Marcel,** built in 1762 –6 to plans by Pierre-François Paris and Paolo Antonio Pisoni. The polychrome altars are still rococo, but the architecture shows the more sober lines of early

Delémont: Hôtel de Ville, a dignified baroque building by G.G.Bagnato.

The former bishops' palace is a horseshoe-shaped 18C building.

neoclassicism. **Hôtel de Ville,** built 1742 – 5 by Giovanni Gaspare Bagnato, and raised by one storey in the 19C. The interiors of this baroque building have lavish stucco ceilings (some by Francesco Pozzi) and panelling. The former bishop's **château** was used as a summer residence by the church dignitaries of Basel. The main courtyard of this horseshoe-shaped complex has a Louis-XIV-railing at the front. All the interior rooms have Régence stucco ceilings. The *Musée Jurassien* by the Porte de Porrentruy has an important regional collection. The Abbot's crozier of

Seated figure of St.Marcel (1508) by Martin Lebzelter in St-Marcel.

Moutier-Grandval is a particular treasure. W. of the town is **Château Domont,** built by the Vorbourg family in 1560. NE of Delémont, across the Soyhières Cluse, remains of the early medieval **Château-Fort du Vorbourg** can be seen. The **Sainte-Marie pilgrimage chapel** incorporates a surviving fortress tower and was consecrated in 1049 by Pope Leo IX, and later much rebuilt. The high altar has a 16C Madonna.

Delley FR
6☐B4

At the end of the village is the **château,** built in the 18C for the de Castella family; in the park is the **Saint-Antoine de Padoue chapel,** built 1710, with small 18C stained-glass panes.

Démoret VD
5☐F5

Reformed church (Saint-Maurice), one of the oldest churches in the canton of

Vaud. The archaeological excavations (1964–5) visible under the nave have proved the existence of a 7–8C church, later extended and rebuilt *c.* 1000. The present one was built in three stages: the rectangular choir with barrel vaulting in the 13C, the nave in the early 15C.

Densbüren AG

2□C/D4

Ruined Burg Urgiz. The fortress NE of the village, presumably 13C, was destroyed by an earthquake in 1356. The keep and parts of the curtain wall have survived.

Diemtigen BE

11□F2

The village has several dignified farmhouses: **Haus Kernen** in the Bächlenmatte with a Gothic façade probably late 15C. The **Grosshaus,** built in 1805, is a mixture of masonry and Ständer- and Blockbau; it has taken over the semicircular wooden decoration under the gables from the Unterland. The S. gable of the **Haus Klossner** (1751) has carved friezes and painted ornaments. In Selbezen: **Haus Karlen** (1738) with painted figures of David's victory over Goliath on the façade.

Diepoldsau SG

4□C4

The **Reformed church** (1728) was altered in 1839 and a new tower was built in 1931. **Catholic parish church of St. Antonius,** rebuilt 1880, altered 1920.

Diesbach GL

8□D4

Haus Sunnezyt in Dornhaus, built 1773 for Landseckelmeister Adam Schiesser. The sides have curved gables.

Diessenhofen: medieval town with Rhine bridge.

Diesse BE

6□C2/3

The **Reformed church of St. Michael** has a Romanesque nave and a Gothic choir with a lateral tower with a steep saddleback roof.

Diessenhofen TG

3□B2

Diessenhofen was built around a castle of the Counts of Kyburg and was granted its charter in 1178. The bridge town has numerous secular Gothic buildings. Several parallel streets with the broad Marktgasse at the centre are intersected by a single diagonal street. **Reformed church of St.Dionysius,** first mentioned in 757, rebuilt in the 12C as a Romanesque basilica, modified as a hall church in the 14&15C. It was throughly renovated in 1838&9 by Jean Ruch and Johann Nepomuk Keller, including transformation into a neo-Gothic barrel-vaulted hall. **Unterhof** (15 Obere Kirchgasse). A 12C fortress of the High Stewards of Diessenhofen, altered in the 14C and the 16–19C. 14C wall painting on the ground floor of the palas. **Siegelturm,** built as an inner gate by Martin Heünsler in 1545–6. **Vorderes or Konstanzer Amtshaus** 7 Schwaderloch). Acquired by the Konstanz cathedral chapter in 1489, extended by Lorenz Reder in 1518&19, rebuilt in baroque style in 1762. **Hinteres or Peterhauser Amtshaus** (11 Museum-

Disentis: Benedictine monastery of St. Martin above the valley.

Late Gothic carved altar by Ivo Strigel in the parish church of St. Johann Baptist.

sgasse). New building started in 1558, in the hands of Petershausen monastery from 1586, raised by one storey in 1840. **Oberhof** (47 Hintergasse), dating from 1520–7. Interior painting by Thomas Schmidt, 1527. **Rhine bridge,** first mentioned in 1292. Frequently rebuilt wooden bridge destroyed by the Russians in 1799, rebuilt 1814–18, rebuilt in 1945 after American bombing. In the *Ortsmuseum* in the Hinteres Amtshaus museum of fabric printing and paintings from the Carl Roesch endowment.

ST. KATHARINENTAL **Former Dominican convent of St. Katharinental** near Willisdorf, founded in the 13C. Convent rebuilt in 1715–18 by Franz Beer, convent church rebuilt in Vorarlberg-Swiss baroque in 1732–5 by Johann Michael Beer of Blaichten to plans by Franz Beer influenced by Caspar Mosbrugger. *Former convent church.* Almost square hall-like nave with two bays and pendentive domes. In the W. bay organ gallery. Narrower sanctuary, behind it nuns' choir of the same width. Decoration contemporary with the

building with paintings by Jakob Karl Stauder, Régence stucco presumably by Niklaus Schütz.

Dietwil AG
7 □ F2

The late baroque-early neoclassical single-aisled Catholic parish church of **St. Jakobus and St. Barbara** by Vitus Rey (1780–1) is lavishly decorated and forms an integrated group with the **ossuary chapel** (1780) and the **priest's house** (1821).

Dinhard ZH
3 □ B3

Reformed parish church. The late Gothic church built in 1511–15 on the site of an earlier building mentioned in 1275 is in the same precinct as the **vicarage** (16C, rebuilt in 1831).

Dino TI
See SONVICO   19 □ D3

Disentis GR
13 □ C2

Benedictine monastery of St. Martin, founded after 700. *Monastery church of St. Martin,* built in 1712 to plans by Caspar Mosbrugger. Baroque pillared hall of the so-called Vorarlberg design with surrounding galleries and twin-towered façade. Early baroque high altar 1655, Régence choir screen 1737, Castelberg altar 1572. In the N. wing of the monastery building are the *Marienkirche* with three medieval apses and the *Klostermuseum* with a historical collection (both being rebuilt at the time of writing). In the courtyard remains of an early medieval monastery. **Catholic parish church of St. Johannes Baptist,** built 1640–3. Baroque single-aisled church with Gothic elements, late Gothic triptych 1489 by Ivo Strigel in the porch.

In ACLETTA **Chapel of St. Maria,** 1680 baroque building with paintings (1731) by

*Domat-Ems: the old parish church of St.
Johann Baptist was originally a fortress
church.*

J.J. Rieg and altarpiece of the high altar by
Carlo Francesco Nuvolone *c.* 1655.

Ditto TI
See CUGNASCO   19☐D2

Domat-Ems GR
9☐A/B4

Old Catholic parish church St. Johann
Baptista. Single- aisled nave 1515 with narrower, polygonal, Gothic high choir (1504)
and crypt-like lower storey. The tower remains from the original fortified complex
(1st half of the 12C). Late Gothic triptych
of 1504, at the end of the choir
Marienkapelle c. 1700. N. of this is the
chapel of the Holy Sepulchre (former
ossuary), built 1693, with late-13C early
Gothic Sepulchre. **St. Peter chapel,**
Carolingian rectangle *c..* 800 with
horeshoe-shaped apse.

Dombresson NE
6☐B3

Reformed church (Saint-Brice), built

1696–8, mentioned since 1178; the Romanesque tower with twin windows survives
and is incorporated in the present building;
barrel-vaulted nave with trompe l'oeil paintings. By the church is a **vicarage** dating
from 1730.

Donatyre VD
6☐C5

Reformed Church (Saint-Etienne),
square 11C Romanesque hall with
horseshoe apse and belfry, Gothic alterations. It is built of stones from the town
wall of Avenches. Inside, on the W. wall,
a stone slab from an antique sarcophagus,
in the apse modern copy of the Montcherand frescos.

Dornach SO
2☐A4

**Former Catholic parish church of
St. Mauritius.** A new nave was added to
the late Gothic choir with saddleback-
roofed tower in 1784; it was designed by
Paolo Antonio Pisoni, and is now the
Heimatmuseum (local history). E. of
Dorneck is the **ruined Burg Dorneck**,
which dates back to the 11C. In 1499, after
the victory at Dornach, Hans Gibelin
began to extend the fortress, which was
Solothurn's main N. bulwark until it was
sacked in 1798. **Goetheanum.** The
buildings of the anthroposophic centre are
important examples of architectural expres-
sionism. The main building was erected
from a model by Rudolf Steiner in 1924
– 8 after the earlier wooden one burned
down.

Dübendorf ZH
3☐B4

The early-13C Romanesque former
Lazarite **church of Gfenn** was refurbished
in 1961–7 after more than 400 years as a
barn; it is now used for ecumenical functions. The small convent formerly part of
to the complex burned down in 1828; a
farmhouse was built on its site.

Dornach: Goetheanum, built 1924–8 on anthroposophical principles.

Düdingen FR

6☐D5

Parish church, mentioned since 1228, rebuilt 1834–7. In the apse paintings including the Stans Landtag of 1906.
St. Wolfgang **St. Wolfgang chapel,** 15C.
Jetschwil On the cantonal road, 18C house built by F. de Boccard
Balliswil **Château,** mentioned since 1555, owned by the Diesbach-Torny family.
Uebewil (Villars-les-Joncs) **Château** built 1765 for Rodolphe de Castella.

Duillier VD

10☐C4

Château, spacious building with hexagonal staircase tower; the various parts of the building date from the 16&17C.
Grange des Dîmes, 17C tithe barn.

Dürnten ZH

8☐C1

Reformed Church. The tower of the late Gothic church (1517 – 21) is 13C, the wooden ceiling in the nave has painted carving.

Dürrenroth BE

7☐B3

Reformed church of St. Laurentius und Maria, built 1486, later rebuilt in baroque style. Barrel vaulting was added in the nave. The Gasthof **Bären** with a hipped roof and the Gasthof **Kreuz** with a mansard roof are baroque buildings from the 2nd half of the 18C.

Dusch GR
See Paspels
9☐A5

Ebikon LU

7 □ F3

Tierweltpanorama und zoologisches Museum (panorama of the animal kingdom and zoological museum) 63 Luzernstrasse, open in the afternoon. RATHAUSEN. **Former Cistercian convent,** founded in 1245, dissolved in 1848. The Renaissance cloister of 1591 has survived in part and is related to that of the Wesemelin monastery near ▷ Luzern.

Ebnat-Kappel SG

8 □ E1

Reformed church in the centre of Ebnat, built in 1762 by Johann Ulrich Grubenmann. Single-aisled church with façade tower. **Haus Steinfels,** built in 1667 under Hans Jakob Bösch. The building is Gothic in concept with baroque detail. **Haus Edelmann** in the so-called Acker. Built in 1752 in Füberg, rebuilt in 1951 in Ebnat for Albert Edelmann (1886–1963), who founded the *Heimatmusuem* here. In Eich typical **Toggenburg wooden houses** (Nos. 16,18 and 19) have survived. **Haus Felsenstein** in Kappel (No. 15), dating from 1624; saddle-roofed building with late Gothic windows and groin-vaulted rooms.

Echallens VD

10 □ E2

Château, built 1273 by Amadeus of Montfaucon and destroyed in 1475, later rebuilt as residence of the Landvogts of Bern and Fribourg. Two medieval round towers have survived in the S., the N. wing dates from 1719. Near the château is the **Hôtel de Ville,** built in 1781; it has steps and a carved façade gable on one side and

Echallens: Hôtel de Ville (1781) with carved gable.

Echandens: Château, completely altered in the 16&17C.

a clock tower on the other. In the main street **maison Bezençon** with a carved façade gable and the 18C Mestrezat coat of arms. On the edge of the town towards Yverdon is the 17&18C **Hôtel des Balances.**

Echandens VD

10 □ E3

In the N. of the village **château** of medieval origin, radically altered in the 16&17C. The building has numerous towers which are merely decorative; polygonal staircase tower with Renaissance portal.

Eclépens VD

10☐E1

Reformed church (St-Pierre), first mentioned in 1228, building late medieval, tower 1735. By the church is the **château d'Enhaut,** rebuilt 1781–9 as a residence for Alexandre de Gingins.

Eggen VS
See BELLWALD   12☐D4

Eggersriet SG

4☐A3

Catholic parish church of St. Anna, built in 1649 by Johann Hofer, nave rebuilt in 1738 by Johann Jakob Grubermann. Sigmund Hilbi extended the nave in 1811 –12 and replaced the choir and the tower. The **priest's house** was built in 1796 as a late baroque building in the style of the Grubenmann patrician houses.

Eglisau ZH

3☐A3

This little town with a bridge over the Rhine had a crossing point even in ancient times and probably dates in its earliest sections (fortified bridgehead of Seglingen on the left bank of the Rhine) from the 11C. The original town, on the right bank of the Rhine, dates at the earliest from the early 13C and was owned by the lords of Tengen, who had their seat here. In 1496 the town was sold to Zürich and used by the canton as a Landvogt's seat until the collapse of the Old Confederation. The building of the power station in Rheinfelden (1916) raised the level of the Rhine to the bottom of the façades of the houses on the river and meant that the bridge had to be moved from the church in the E. to the W. edge of the town. The town consists essentially of two long streets (Untergasse and Obergasse) with Gothic, Renaissance and baroque façades. **Reformed parish church.** The surviving baroque building dating from 1716&7 is attached to the Gothic choir of the earlier church (c. 1350).

The interior (hall with nave and two aisles, side galleries with wooden pillars) is modelled on St.Peter in Zürich. The choir contains late Gothic frescos (c. 1490, presumably by Hans Fischer and Hans Ott).

Eichberg SG

4☐B4

Reformed Church, single-aisled church (1713), stained glass 1939 by Ulrich Hänny and 1961 by Köbi Lämmler.

Eigenthal LU
See SCHWARZENBERG   7☐E4

Einigen BE

12☐A2

Reformed church of St.Michael. The little single-aisled building is one of the 'Lake Thun churches' which came into being in the 10&11C, and of which the most famous examples are the basilicas in ▷ Amsoldingen and ▷ Speiz. These early Romanesque buildings all have exterior pilaster strips and round-arched friezes. In the interior late Gothic font and tabernacle.

Einsiedeln SZ

8☐B2

A little monastic community developed on the spot where St.Meinrad was martyred in 861; it adopted the Rule of St.Benedict in 934. The **Benedictine monastery** which developed from this became a significant force when it was granted imperial status by Otto I, and it maintained its importance until the Schwyzer took over the monastery in 1424. The buildings burned down on many occasions in the course of the centuries and in the 18C were extended to become one of the most splendid monasteries in Europe. The square, built in 1748&9 to plans by a Milanese architect, makes the main façade of the monastery part of the theatrical effect of the whole complex. In the centre is the façade of the *monastery church,* consecrated in

Eglisau: buildings at water level on the river front.

1735. It was built in 1719–35 to plans by Brother Caspar Mosbrugger and included Hans Georg Kuen's baroque choir. It combines the traditional longitudinal building with the idea of a rotunda, which is the basis of the octagonal area surrounding the Gnadenkapelle in the E. The decoration of the church is of a quality to match its rank as a pilgrimage church since the 15C. Stucco and ceiling frescos in the nave are contemporary with the building of the church and are the work of the Asam brothers of Munich; the ceiling paintings in the choir date from 1746. The chief object of veneration is a late Gothic *miraculous image* of the Madonna, which is kept in the *Gnadenkapelle*, built in 1815–17.

Eischoll VS

18☐B1

Catholic parish church of Mariä Himmelfahrt, neo-Romanesque, built in 1886 by the architect Joseph de Kalbermatten.

Eisten VS

See BLATTEN   12☐B5

Elgg ZH

3☐C4

Almost square late medieval town with ecclesiastical buildings in the centre, founded in 1370–1 by the Habsburgs, part of the canton of Zurich since 1425. **Reformed parish church.** Late Gothic church with a nave and three aisles dating from 1508 –18 on the site of earlier churches which can be traced back to the 8C. The tower must have been built *c.* 1370. There is a crypt under the choir. Some of the wall paintings are from the older church (1370), the majority date from 1514–18 and are attributed to Matthäus Gutrecht the Younger of Konstanz. **Schloss.** Originally a dairy founded *c.* 1000, then a court, frequently altered and extended. In the possession of the Werdmüller family since 1712; lavish interior decoration, mainly early 18C (not open to the public).

Elm GL

8☐E4

Slate-mining caused a landslip in 1881,

Einsiedeln: the Benedictine monastery is one of the finest baroque buildings in Europe.

The Gnadenkapelle in the E. of the collegiate church is the goal of the pilgrimage to Mary.

Elgg: the Reformed church is a late Gothic building with a tall spire.

which covered up part of the village. The 15C late-Gothic **Reformed church** is illuminated twice a year by sunlight shining through a natural window in the rock in the Tschingelhörner. Elms, like the rest of Glarus, has a multiplicity of houses of different kinds: the **Grosshaus** of 1585&6 is a wooden building on a masonry base, the type of house found in the Swiss interior, whereas the **Suworow-Haus** is built of stone and shows the influence of the Bünden building method. The house was the last quarters of the Russian General in Switzerland, before he reached the Rhine valley with his troops.

Embrach ZH

3□A3

Reformed parish church. Almost square single-aisled church dating from 1779&80 (David Vogel) with semicircular projections.

Emmetten NW

8□A4

Hl.Kreuz chapel in Sagendorf, built 1791. On the rear interior wall is a 1710 panel painting with a Dance of Death.

Ems GR
See DOMAT-EMS 9□B4

Endingen AG

2□E3

Synagogue. The Jews were allotted the Surba valley villages of Endingen and Lengnau by the Diet in the 18C. The place of worship was built in 1845 in the neoclassical-Moorish style to plans by Caspar Joseph Jeuch.

Engelberg OW

7□F5

The village formed around the **Benedictine abbey** founded in 1120 as the centre of a small spiritual community which included the upper Engelberg valley and was independent until 1798. The present *monastery church* and the *monastery buildings* were rebuilt by Johannes Rueff after a fire in 1730 – 7; they form a unified whole which was completed by the extensions to house the school built for the monastery in the 19&20C. In the *treasury* are a few pieces from the monastery's first heyday in the 12&13C, including the reliquary cross of Abbot Heinrich. The examples of Engelberg book illumination in the *library* date from the same period. In front of the monastery church is the **ossuary,** built in 1608 to a late Gothic design; it is the oldest of the five chapels in the Engelberg valley.

Endingen: W. façade of the synagogue with unusual step gable.

Engelberg: interior of the baroque collegiate church with numerous altars.

Below the village is the chapel of **St.Jakob in Espen,** consecrated in 1648. The **Maria im Holz chapel** was built in 1715&16 to replace an earlier 16C building threatened with flooding. At the so-called 'End of the World' is the **Maria im Horbis chapel,** extended in 1630-5; the choir dates back to a building of 1490. The **Maria ad fontem chapel** in the Schwand, dedicated in 1683, was extended in 1951; the coffered ceiling was painted by Father Karl Stadler in 1953.

Engollon NE

6☐B3

Reformed church (St-Pierre), 13C choir, 17C nave, tower 1803. In 1923 the most important 14&15C wall paintings in the canton were discovered in the choir. In the vault Christ in Glory, surrounded by the symbols of the Evangelists, on the walls scenes from the Life of Christ.

Ennenda GL

8☐E3

Ennenda has a large number of 19C buildings, and is thus a particularly good example of the effects of industrialization on towns and villages in Glarus. The older buildings are mainly near the **Reformed church,** built by Jakob Messmer in 1780 – 2, for example the **Doppelhaus Sunnezyt,** with two lavishly carved doorways. The row of houses in the **Kirchweg** dates from the 19C and is striking for its unity. The **factory and house of Jenny & Co** date from the same period. The proximity of factory and owner's house which we see here was abandoned in the second half of the century: the **Villa Freuler** (1888), the **Villa Fontana** and the **Villa Wartegg** (1890) are set in large gardens; they are built in the same style as the **parish hall,** (1888–90), which has a spacious ballroom in its upper storey.

Ennetbürgen NW

See Bürgenstock   7☐F4

Ennetmoos NW

7☐E4

St. Jakob chapel. Destroyed chapel rebuilt 1803 – 7, tower and aisles 20C. **Winkelried chapel** (dragon chapel) in Allweg, built in 1671&2 on the site on which a member of the Winkelried family is said to have killed a dragon. The **obelisk** erected near the chapel in 1900 commemorates the defeat in 1798 of 16,000 French by 2,000 Nidwaldners. N. of the Allweg is the **Rotzberg ruin,** a Habsburg

Entlebuch: parish church St. Martin, a baroque building by Niklaus Purtschert.

seat built in 1231, apparently destroyed by the Confederates in 1291.

Enney FR

11☐C3

St-Nicolas de Flüe, built in 1619–24. A small building with one aisle with a polygonal choir and façade tower. In the interior altar (1717) and wooden ceiling (1618).

Entlebuch LU

7☐D4

The **Catholic parish church of St. Martin,** begun in 1776, is a baroque country church in the Singer-Purtschert style (▷ Ruswil). Side altar paintings by Paul Deschwanden.
Finsterwald **Catholic parish church Herz Jesu,** reinforced concrete and masonry building dating from 1935.

Epalinges VD

10☐E/F2

On a hill SE of the village **church des Croisettes,** built in 1661&2.

Epesses VD

10☐F3

In the vineyard belonging to the parish of Puidoux is the **tour de Marsens,** mentioned since the 12C; battlemented rec-

Erlach: 11C Schloss with 13C round tower.

tangular tower, fully restored in the last century.

Erlach BE

6☐B3

The town was founded by Burkhard von Fenis, Bishop of Basel, when he built a **castle** here *c.* 1100. The Rittersaal with its beamed roof on late Romanesque carved pillars is the most striking feature of the medieval building which remains. The fortress later became the seat of a Landvogt; the painter-poet Manuel Deutsch worked here. The **Junkerngasse**, which runs steeply down from the Schloss is lined with late Gothic houses with continuous arcades. The **Rathaus**, built *c.* 1500 and the **Stadttor** are at the end of the Junkergasse. The **Ulrichskirche**, altered in 1679, has a Romanesque tower.

Erlen TG

3☐F3

Reformed church, built in 1764 by Johann Ulrich Grubenmann. Broad hall tending to a centralized plan, façade tower. In Erlen and the surrounding villages of Engishofen, Kümmertshausen and Buchackern are 17–19C **half-timbered buildings.**

Erlenbach BE

11☐F2

Striking **village** with wooden buildings in the Dorfstrasse built largely after the fire of 1765. As well as Simmental houses (Ständer/Blockbau with protruding saddleback roof) there are also Blockbau buildings with circular panelling under the gables and steep saddleback roofs. **Reformed church.** The nave dates back to a 10C early Romanesque complex. Instead of the original apse a rectangular choir tower was built in the 13C. The interior contains a large late Gothic fresco cycle. The sequence of pictures on the N. wall dates from the early 15C and shows attempts to master perspective; it also suggests the influence of Italian Quattrocento painting, and comparisons with Basel book illumination and Angers tapestry also suggest themselves.

Ermatingen TG

3☐E2

Kehlhof. Built in 1694 and extended in 1811. Half-timbered building with N. arcades, courtrooom inside with painting dating from the 3rd quarter of the 18C. On the hillside is **Schloss Hard,** dating from 1520. Altered and rebuilt by the Zollikofen family 1720–24, then in 1829 by Thomas Lindsey and in 1848 by George F. Thomas. Saddleback roofed building with curved gables and turrets (pulled down in 1982). **Schloss Wolfsberg,** core *c.* 1571, altered after 1731 and in 1800. S. section extended under Colonel Parquin in 1825, then a meeting-place for the Bonapartists. **Schloss Lilienberg,** built in 1830 for Count Zappe. **Schloss Hubberg,** near Fruthweilen. Built in 1596, upper storey half-timbered.

Ernen VS

12☐D5

Formerly principal settlement of the Goms, one of the most interesting villages in the Valais because of its numerous 15–18C houses. **Catholic parish church St.Georg,** built in 1510–18 by Ulrich Ruffiner on the site of an 11C church with three apses. The present building consists of a nave and a polygonal Flamboyant

choir. Very lavish interior furnishings: in the choir rococo high altar of 1761 and carved choir stalls (1666) by H.Siegen and G.Matig, 1518 crucifix on the triumphal arch, baroque side altars. On the S. wall of the nave fragments of a Gothic retable (1527) and statues of saints. On the N. wall portable altar with figures of the auxiliary saints (1480), 14C Gothic Pietà and a late Gothic sculpture of St.George the Dragonkiller. Fine group of houses in the village square. **Zendenrathaus,** stone building built 1750 – 62, paintings by Henri Boissonnas (1953) on one façade wall. **Tellenhaus,** 1576, frescos of the William Tell legend on the ground floor walls; there is a wooden storehouse next to it. 18C **Wirtshaus St.Georg,** group of sculptures including St.George on the façade (original in the church). **Haus Jost-Sigristen,** built in 1581 by Martin Jost and renovated in the 18C. 16&17C **School house,** paintings by Henri Boissonnas (1943) on the façade. **Wirtshaus zur Linde,** built in 1552. By the church 1733 **priest's house,** some parts of the building are older. **Haus Kreyg,** built in 1677 by Landeshauptmann Johannes Kreyg. On the edge of the village in the direction of Mühlebach on a hill to the left of the road are posts of the **former gallows.**
ERNERWALD In the wood SW of Ernen **Mariä Heimsuchung chapel,** built in 1693–1709. In the interior high altar of 1693 by J.Sigristen and M.Bodmer and 18C paintings of the Madonna and the pilgrimage to the chapel; numerous votive pictures.
NIEDERBERNEN **St. Antonius chapel,** baroque building of 1684. In the interior vault paintings (1780) and high altar (1684) by J.Sigristen and M.Bodmer.

Ernen: lavishly carved side altar in the early 18C Catholic church.

Ernetschwil SG

8☐D1

Catholic parish church of St.Karl Borromäus. Neoclassical building, built in 1846 by an architect called Huttle; five-storey choir apex tower. A Blockbau house (No. 487) with small roofs over the windows and doorway survives of the **former Stegmühle** (mill; 2nd half of the 18C).

Erschmatt VS

18☐A1

Catholic parish church of St.Michael, 18C baroque building. In the interior high altar of 1770. Outside the village to the left of the road **Hohe Brücke,** an old arched bridge.

Erstfeld UR

8☐B5

Just outside the centre of the present village is the **Jagdmattkapelle** in a meadow on the bank of the Reuss, built in 1637&8 on the site of a place of worship mentioned in 1339 to commemorate a wondrous incident during a hunt. The legend is illustrated on the façade.

Eschenbach LU

7☐E2

Cistercian convent, founded in 1285 by the Freiherren of Eschenbach. Convent buildings largely 16&17C, convent church and parish church neo-baroque by August Hardegger.

Estavayer: Château Chenaux, founded under the Savoyards.

Eschenbach SG
8☐C1

Catholic parish church St.Vinzentius.
Mentioned in 885, tower built and church renovated in the 13C, in 1496 the choir and tower were rebuilt in the Gothic style and the choir was adapted to the baroque in 1665. Nave rebuilt 1723-6 by Hans Georg Schueler, baroque modification 1753&4 by Joh. Jakob and Joh. Ulrich Grubenmann. Nave lengthened 1874-6 by Karl Reichlin, in 1955 modern extension in the W. **Kusterhaus,** also called Landrichterhaus (Nos. 88&9), built in 1771 by Landamman Josef Anton Kuster. Gabled house with open steps and carved portal. The so-called courtroom on the gable storey has a stucco ceiling, painted alcoves and wall cupboards and is considered the finest rococo room in the lake area. Archaeological excavations in **Balmenrain** near the Schmerikon boundary have proved that the area has been settled since the Hallstatt period. The finds from the grave mounds (dishes, funeral urns, bronze and iron implements of the early iron age, 8–7C) are in the Uznach Heimatmuseum. **Castel** near Bürg, also called Chastli. The name of this plateau, SE of Bürg in Aabachtobel, dates back to a Roman fortress. The channels of an under-floor heating system have been excavated.

Eschenz TG
3☐C2

Former Roman bridgehead settlement of Tasgetium. **Catholic church Mariä Himmelfahrt.** Built 1737&8 by Franz Singer of Messkirch, extended to the W. and façade tower by August Hardegger 1896, rebuilt 1950 by Felix Schmid. Inside modern panes illustrating the Stations of the Cross, the last, unfinished work of Heinrich Danioth (d. 1953), completed by Eduard Renggli. **Freudenfels,** SE of the village. Former residence of the vicar of Einsiedeln, renovated from 1692 under Caspar Mosbrugger, largely rebuilt by Franz Singer in 1747.

Escholzmatt LU
7☐C4

The Catholic parish church of St. Jakob, built 1892–4 by August Hardegger, neo-Gothic hall church with interior in the same style.

Estavayer-Le-Lac FR

6☐A5

Estavayer began to develop in the late 11C, the lords of Estavayer are mentioned in records in the first half of the 12C, the town is first mentioned in 1241. From 1245 to 1536 Estavayer was noticeably under the influence of Savoy, in 1536 Fribourg took over part of it, and controlled it completely from 1635. Estavayer originally had three châteaux. The first was in the W., the second, of which the so-called Savoy tower has survived, in the SE and the third, that of Chenaux, in the N.; this is the only one to have survived. The village which grew up between these three châteaux was provided in the 13C with a wall which has largely survived; it is pierced by four gates. **Château de Chenaux,** late 13C, built in the period of Savoyard dominance, partially destroyed in the 15C and rebuilt after the Burgundian wars. The Savoy-style fortress was originally a square, with entrance secured by a round keep. In the 15C the barbican and the fortified passage were added. **Collegiate church of St-Laurent,** Gothic, built 1379–1525 on the site of an earlier place of worship. The monumental staircase dates from 1859. Church with nave and two aisles and rectangular choir, between choir and nave the bell tower with bartizans. In the choir, which is separated by a wrought-iron screen, high altar by J.F.Reyff with painting by Pierre Crolot 1638–40, and carved choir stalls by J.Mattelin of Geneva, 1522-4. In the Grand-Rue **Dominican convent,** founded 1316, rebuilt in the 18C, and *Dominican church,* dedicated to Our Lady, built 1697. Elegant building with nave and two aisles and groin vaulting; in the interior opposite the entrance, retable of 1571. **Chapelle de Rivaz,** dedicated to Our Lady and St. Margaret. Gothic building, built 1449 and altered 1539. Outside the walls, **Chapelle de l'Institut du Sacré Coeur,** neo-Gothic, built 1904&5. Various notable buildings in the town. In the Grand-Rue, **house** No. 6, 16&17C, 1645 carved coat-of-arms on the façade; **Hôtel du Cerf,** built in the 16C for Philippe d'Estavayer-

Etoy: house, c. 1700, SW of the church with three-storey loggia.

Molondin. Rue du Musée, **Maison de la Dîme,** (tithe barn) built in the 15C for the bastard Humbert of Savoy, now *musée d'histoire locale.* In the place de l'Eglise a **house,** built in 1775 for J.F.Grangier. No. 142 Rue Motte-Châtel, 15C **house,** last residence of the Estavayer family.

Etagnières VD

10☐E2

Catholic church of St-Laurent with façade tower. Nave 1768 and 13C choir. In the interior baroque altar, 1654 by the Fribourg Reyff brothers.

Etoy VD

10☐D3

Reformed church (St-Nicolas), formerly church of a priory mentioned in the 11C, rebuilt in the 13C and heavily altered after the Reformation. A massive façade tower protrudes from the central axis, in the interior 13C triumphal arch. Behind the church, on the site of the former priory, 15C **château,** rebuilt in the 18C. In front of the church elegant **résidence** with 17&18C three-storey arcades.

Ettiswil LU

7☐C2

Catholic parish church of St. Maria and St.Stefan, built 1769–71 by Jakob Purtschert in the baroque style incor-

Ettiswil: moated Schloss Wyher, 1510, much altered subsequently.

Etzel: the wooden roof of the 12C Tüfelsbrugg was probably not added until the 19C.

porating older parts of the building. In the interior altars with figures by Johann Baptist Babel. **Sacrament chapel.** In 1450 -2 an expiatory chapel was built on the spot where a woman had abandoned a host stolen from the parish church. In the interior Gothic wooden ceiling from the time of building. **Schloss Wyher,** S. of the road to Grosswangen, was once moated. Main building dates largely from *c.* 1510.

Etzel SZ

8☐B2

St. Meinrad, the founder of Einsiedeln, settled temporarily on the rounded summit of the Etzel. The **St.Meinrad chapel,** built in 1697&8 on the site of his cell, is similar in design to the Gnadenkapelle in Einsiedeln, which is also on the site of Meinrad's cell. The **Gasthaus** rebuilt in 1758 and the **Tüfelsbrugg** (bridge) over the Sihl, dating back to the 12C, are clear signs of the large number of pilgrims who visited the place.

Evolène VS

17☐F3

Characteristic village of the val d'Hérens, still largely intact, with interesting wooden and stone houses; the doors and windows are framed in stone and the façades decorated with paintings. **Catholic parish church St-Jean-Baptiste,** rebuilt 1852-5, late medieval tower. Cotter, typical alpine pasture.

LA GARDE **Notre-Dame chapel,** 1620, small porch and 18C rococo altar.

LANA Circular hamlet with traditional buildings. **St-Laurent chapel,** built 1711, with arched porch. In the interior late-18C baroque altar.

LA SAGE In the village **Ste-Trinité chapel** of 1848. On a terrace in the precinct **St-Christophe chapel,** baroque building of 1670, modern wall paintings by R.Martin. Tsaté, typical alpine pasture.

LA FORCLAZ Village in excellent condition, wooden houses with carved façades and storehouses on supports. **St-Georges chapel,** 1705, with 18C altar.

LES HAUDERES Interesting village with typical three and four storey 18&19C val d'Hérens wooden houses.

Eyholz VS

18☐C1

By the road baroque **Mariä Himmelfahrt chapel,** late 17C. Single-aisled building with rectangular choir and porch. In the interior high altar of 1680-90, S. side altar with Gothic statues of the same period; organ with 18C painted panels. By the church fine **house** (1673).

F

Fahr AG
See WÜRENLOS   2☐F4

Faido TI
13☐C4

Catholic parish church of Sant'Andrea, rebuilt 1830, medieval bell tower. S. of the village Capuchin monastery founded in 1607 and **monastery church of San Francesco,** built 1608 and altered in the 18C. In the interior neoclassical high altar with painting (1680), in the N. chapel Renaissance retable. On the main road **casa del Gottardo,** fine wooden building of 1582 with bas-reliefs on religious themes.

Faido: the Casa del Gottardo has a decorative frieze on the façade.

Falera GR
13☐F1

S. of the village **Old Catholic parish church of St. Remigius.** Single-aisled church with late Gothic polygonal choir and 13C tower. Wall paintings: by the wall tabernacle St. Jodokus, late 14C; in the choir 4 medallions with half-figures, late 16C; choir completely painted 1623; on the N. side of the nave, Last Supper, early 17C. E. of the church **prehistoric cult site and refuge,** from which stone vessels and a row of six blocks of rock have survived.

Farvagny-le-Grand FR
11☐C2

St-Vincent, neo-Gothic, built 1888–92, interior of the same period. Opposite the church **château,** former Vogt residence, built 1616–18 by Fribourg. Round staircase tower and portal (1617) with carved coat-of-arms.

Farvagny-le-Grand: St-Vincent, a late-19C neo-Gothic building.

Féchy VD
10☐D3

Pretty village with winemakers' cottages. **Reformed church** (St-Sulpice), mentioned from 1188 and altered later. Single-

Feldbrunnen: Schloss Waldegg is reminiscent of Fontainebleau.

Fenin: Château, a late Gothic country house with three corner turrets.

aisled building with rectangular choir, chapel (1518) under the bell tower. On the Geneva-Lausanne cantonal road, country house **la Gordanne,** built in the 19C, interesting example of Palladian architecture in Switzerland. Cylindrical building with a dome and columned portico with a gable. Orangery in the park.

Felben-Wellhausen TG
3 □ D3

Schloss Wellenberg. Original seat of the lords of Wellenberg, mentioned in 1204, 1669 and 1694 residence of the Zürich Vogts. Keep 13C, gabled building 16C staircase tower 1768.

Feldbrunnen SO
6 □ F2

Schloss Waldegg, built in 1682-4 for Mayor Johann Viktor Besenval. This is one of the best examples of the Solothurn-style 'Türmlihaus', based on French château architecture. The narrow promenade in front of the main façade was originally laid out like an Italian baroque garden, but later redesigned as an English park.

Feldmeilen ZH
See MEILEN   8 □ A1

Fenin NE
6 □ B3

Above the village, near the wood, **Reformed church** (St-Laurent). Nave and choir 15C, tower and portal 1736. In the choir early 16C stained glass of St. Leonard and St.Laurence; in the nave the Tables of the Law, a painting of 1773. By the road **château,** a late Gothic residence; main façade with two turrets, portal (1561) decorated with figures.

Ferret VS
See ORSIERES   17 □ C5

Fousisberg SZ
8 □ B2

Catholic parish church of St. Jakob, built 1780-5. Curved designs mark the transition from the nave to the choir on the Singer-Purtschert model (▷ Ruswil).

Fex-Crasta GR
See SILS I. E.   14 □ C3

Fiesch VS
12 □ D5

St-Augustin chapel, built 1722 on the site of a chapel of the monastery of Gnadenberg. Rococo furnishings.
WICHEL im Fieschertal. Baroque Padua chapel, built 1688. On the façade statue of

Filisur: typical Engadine house with decorated gable façade.

Fischingen: former Benedictine monastery with Idda chapel in the NW corner.

St. Antony by J. Ritz. Altar 1691 by J. Ritz and Chr. Ritter; wooden screen 1731.

Filisur GR

14☐C1

Long ribbon village on the way to the Albula pass. House design (▷ Guarda) is influenced by the nearby Engadine, see house No. 49; broad façades with Sulèr doors, sgraffito, painting, oriels and window grilles. **Reformed church.** Vaulted Gothic single-aisled church with narrower polygonal choir (*c.* 1495). In the interior wall painting *c.* 1500; on the chancel arch Annunciation, Baptism of Christ and Man of Sorrows, on the S. wall of the nave

Mount of Olives. **Parish hall,** built 1975-7 by Robert Obrist. Above the village **Greifenstein ruin,** three-storey Burg complex with 12C house chapel. Tiefencastel direction **Landwasser-Viadukt** (1906-9), 295 ft. high arched bridge, the largest rubble-built bridge on the Rhätische Bahn.

Filzbach GL

8☐E2

Roman watchtower near Voremwald, built in the early stages of the Roman colonisation of Switzerland at the end of the 1C BC.

Finsterwald LU

See ENTLEBUCH   7☐D4

Fischbach-Göslikon AG

2☐E5

Catholic parish church of Mariä Himmelfahrt in Göslikon. Single-aisled church built 1671, interior altered in the rococo style in 1757-60; frescos by Franz Anton Rebsamen. The church, the **Rochus chapel** (1709) and the **priest's house** form a unified whole.

Fischingen TG

3☐D4

Former Benedictine collegiate foundation, founded in 1133-8 by Bishop Ulrich II of Konstanz, dissolved in 1848, now a reformatory. Oldest parts 16C. *Monastery church,* built 1685-87, presumably to plans by Caspar Mosbrugger. Five-bay barrel-vaulted nave with gallery in the W. and equally wide choir in the E. Upper choir added 1753 by Johann Michael Beer of Bildstein, arch (1795) in the lower choir with life-size stucco statues in the crown. Choirs painted in the second half of the 18C, choir stalls in the upper choir 1687 by Chrysotimus Fröhli. *Iddakapelle,* built on to the N. side of the church by Christian Huber under the influence of Mosbrugger 1704-8; three arches open on

Fischingen: late Gothic sarcophagus of St. Idda in a niche of the Idda tomb altar.

to the nave. High baroque rotunda with transepts and false dome; Dominkus Zimmermann was involved in the decoration. OBERWANGEN The **St. Martinsberg chapel** dates from the 10C, was much altered, and extended in 1693 and 1727 by the addition of a domed building by Johann and Jakob Grubenmann, probably influenced by Caspar Mosbrugger.

Fislisbach AG

2☐E4

Catholic parish church of St. Agatha. Late neoclassical single-aisled church (1828) by Fidel Obrist with stucco by Johann Joseph Mosbrugger and Michael Huttle.

Flawil SG

3☐E4

Reformed church, built 1909–11 by Robert Curjel and Karl Moser as a neobaroque building with Jugendstil elements. Last Supper by Hermann Meyer. **Catholic church of St. Laurentius,** 1943–5 by Karl Zöllig. The

Flawil: Cistercian monastery of Magdenau, a 13C foundation.

Künishaus in the village square dates from the early 18C and is a town house with rural design elements.

In OBERGLATT, E. of Flawil, is the **Gasthaus zum Hirschen** of 1771–7, a baroque building with mansard roof and staircase tower. Opposite is the **former customs house** by the bridge over the Glatt, built 1742&3. **Mesnerhaus,** former priest's house; timber-clad Blockbau, *c.* 1740.

In BURGBAU, S. of Oberglatt, 17C **timber buildings. Rathaus,** built on to the farmhouse (1632) of the Moosberger family in 1639 by Ammann Peter Moosberger. On the N. side half-timbering and an arcade.

MAGDENAU, S. of Flawil. **Former parish church of St. Verena,** rebuilt *c.* 1500. Late Gothic building with saddleback-roofed tower in the N. choir entrance. **Cistercian convent** of Magdenau, founded 1244, church and convent largely rebuilt *c.* 1600, additional buildings and farm buildings 18&19C. *Convent church,* rebuilt 1953 by Karl Higi. Early 14C choir stalls in nuns' choir.

Flims GR

8☐FE

Reformed church, built in 1512 by Andreas Bühler. **Schlössli,** built 1682 Bünden Schloss type from the second half of the 17C with lavish decoration: stucco panelling, stoves. In Flims-Waldhaus: apartment house **Las Gaglias,** 1960 by R. Olgiati.

Flüelen UR

8☐B4

Important port on the old Gotthard route; customs duty was paid here in the Middle Ages on goods transported on the lake. The **old parish church St. Georg und Nikolaus,** built 1665–6, is no longer used; its role was taken over by the **new Catholic church,** built on an eminence in the neo-baroque style in 1910&11. The **Schlösschen Rudenz,** a medieval keep extended as a residential house in the 19C, used to have a courtyard extending to the lake, and was used as a customs point. The **iron sculpture 'Schwurhände',** created for Expo 1964 by Werner Witschi now decorates the plot by the lake.

Flüeli-Ranft OW

7☐E5

Home and hermitage of Brother Niklaus of Flüe (1417–47), the only Swiss to have been canonised (1947). In FLÜELI, the original home of the saint, are his **birthplace,** and the **house** in which the von Flüe family lived until the 19C. The birthplace has sections dating from the 14C and is considered the oldest timber building in Switzerland; it is typical of a certain kind of inner Swiss farmhouse, with a shallow saddleback roof and arcade on one side; the 15C family house is of the same type. In nearby RANFT, to ⁄hich Niklaus von Flüe withdrew in 1467, are three pilgrimage chapels: the **upper Ranft chapel,** built for brother Klaus in 1468, rebuilt after an earthquake in 1693–1701; the hermit's cell in its original condition is adjacent. The **lower Ranft chapel,** built 1501–4, has an interior decorated throughout the centuries to a high standard, showing the honour in which brother Klaus was held. On the slope on the other side of the Melchaa is the **Müsli chapel** (Müsli, Mösli = little peat moor), built in 1484 for Brother Ulrich, a pupil and companion of Brother Klaus. The chapel here is also adjacent to the hermit's cell. The lavishly carved late Gothic ceiling friezes in the chapel are probably the work of

Flims: Schloss, now parish hall, a cubic building with residence tower.

Flüeli-Ranft: the Upper Ranft chapel, one of the three pilgrimage chapels in the Ranft.

Peter Tischmacher of Uri; on the Carved keystone of the rib vaulting in the choir is the coat-of-arms of Obwalden.

Flums SG

8☐F3

Since the 15C the main site for the smelting of Gonzen ore, as is shown by the **Eisenherrenhaus** (ironmasters' house), bu lt in 1567. The centre of the village is by the former parish church of St.Justus, under the choir of which is an Alemannic

Flums: ruined Burg Gräpplang on a hill above the Seez valley.

necropolis. **Former parish church of St.Justus.** Rebuilt in the 12C, choir added and tower raised in the 15C, choir painting and Crucifixion in the Romanesque lunette above the portal, 2nd half of the 15C. **Catholic parish church of St. Laurentius,** built in 1861–3 in the neo-Byzantine style to plans by Felix Wilhelm Kubly, rebuilt with a nave and two aisles in 1905–6 by August Hardegger. S. of the church of St.Justus in the village square is the former **dower house** of the Tschudis of Gräpplang, built 1524. Nearby is the **Haus Zingg** of 1624. **St.Jakob chapel,** on the slope between Flums and Gräpplang, partially rebuilt *c.* 1360, wall paintings *c.* 1300. **Ruined Burg Gräpplang,** NW of Flums. Mentioned in 1249 as the administrative seat of the Chur Hochstift, 1528–1767 seat of the Gräpplang Tschudi family, acquired by the parish in 1928.

Font FR

6 □ A5

Catholic church of St-Sulpice, nave 1560 and tower 1823; altered in the 19C. Opposite the church is the **château,** built in the 16&17C, former residence of the Landvogts. Only a few walls remain of the medieval château of Font, the oldest Fribourg fortress, mentioned from 1011.

Fontaines NE

6 □ B3

Reformed church (St-Maurice), late Gothic. Fine vaulting (1530) in the choir and painted scenes from the Holy Scriptures dating from 1680.

Fontenais JU

1 □ C4/5

The **château,** built around the middle of the 18C, is a serene rococo building with onion domes on round towers.

Forclaz,La VD
See Sepey,Le   11 □ C5

Forclaz,La VS
See Evolene   17 □ F3

Fosano TI
See Vira-gambarogno   19 □ C2

Franex FR

11 □ A1

St-Nicolas chapel, mentioned from 1625. On the altar thirteen polychrome wooden statues of Christ and the Apostles. On a hill N. of the village **tour de la Molière,** impressive 12C square keep, only surviving feature of the château built by the lords of Font-Molière and destroyed in the 16C.

Fraubrunnen BE

6 □ F3

Schloss. The Cistercian convent founded in 1246 was seat of the Bern Landvogts from 1528–1798 after its dissolution. It was rebuilt as a baroque Schloss in the 18C.

Frauenfeld TG

3 □ C/D3

Capital of the canton of Thurgau since 1803. Founded in the mid 13C, as a result of the building of the Burg by the Counts of Kyburg, who — followed by the Habsburgs—were also Counts of Thurgau in Swabia. The quarrel between the Hapsburgs and the Confederation, par-

Frauenfeld: Catholic church (1904–6), reminiscent of S. German baroque.

The 18C Luzernerhaus now houses the Naturhistorisches Museum.

The 13C keep is one of the oldest parts of the Schloss.

ticularly the ostracism of Duke Friedrich in 1515, because of which the Habsburg rights fell to the empire and then to Konstanz, led to the collapse of Austrian dominance. In 1460 the Confederates conquered the whole of Thrugau and made it into a domain of 7, later 8, towns and villages, at which time Frauenfeld became the seat of the Confederate Landvogts. The Reformation quickly spread from Zürich, but was brought to a standstill in 1531 by the Battle of Kappel and forced back by various waves of the re-establishment of Catholicism, supported by the Catholic areas of the Swiss interior. Thus the Thurgau was exposed to the cultural influence of S. Bavarian baroque. Equal rights for the denominations were not established until the 2nd Villmergen War of 1712. In 1798 the Thurgau was declared free by the threatened Confederate towns even before the French revolutionary armies marched in. The Helvetian Republic (1798 – 1803) created the basis of state organisation; the actual composition of the new canton was established in the Mediation (1803-14).

The Old Town of Frauenfeld is dominated by buildings from the period after the fires of 1771 and 1788, which reduced the number of medieval houses in the town to those between the Rathaus and the Reformed church. Tower and gatehouses were demolished in 1830–40, the town wall had already been incorporated into rows of houses in the 16C. **Catholic church of St. Nikolaus,** built in 1904-6 by Albert Rimli in neo-baroque style, with some Jugendstil elements. The interior is by Karl Glauner among others, wall paintings by Karl Manninger. **Reformed church,** nave rebuilt 1927-9 by Hans Wiesmann, façade tower from the earlier building 1664-5. In the choir window glass by Augusto Giacometti, 1930. **Rathaus.** Neoclassical building by Josef Purtschert built 1790-4 with three entrances in the main façade. The central axis is emphasised by ashlar pilasters and a portico with a balcony. Frontispiece with Justitia and Sapientia 1793 by Johann Wirtensohn. Rear precinct and Rathaus tower 1905&6 by Otto Meyer. The **Schloss** stands on a sandstone rock above the bank of the Murg. Massive keep and base of the palas date from the early 13C, half-timbered upper building late medieval. Late 18C linen panels with Romantic-Arcadian landscapes and decorative figures, presumably the work of Heinrich Wüst. **Alte Landeskanzlei or Landschreiberei** (180 Zürcherstrasse), built in 1771 under Reding von Biberegg, seat of cantonal government from 1806-67. **Haus zum Licht** (4 Freie Strasse) dating from 1598. Late Gothic façade with stepped windows on the first floor, above them domed windows, Gothic windows and portal on the ground floor reconstructed 1969-70. **Luzernerhaus** (Haus Reding, 24 Freie Strasse), built after 1771 as residence of the Lucerne ambassador. **Former Gasthaus zum Schwert** (6 Freie Strasse) dating from 1630-2, until 1690 seat of the Zürich Diet envoy. Façades 1912 with hints of baroque. The **Bernerhaus zum Geduld** (5 Bankplatz) of 1771 was the residence of the Bernese delegate. In the façade is a copy

of the old sandstone portal. In Kurzdorf, on the road to Schaffhausen is the **Reformed church St. Johann,** built in 1915&16 by Joachim Brenner and Walter Stutz in the 'Heimatstil' of the period. The SE corner of the sanctuary of the earlier building with wall paintings in the Soft Style c. 1400 has been incorporated in the building. **SBB station** dating from 1855 to plans by Johann Georg Müller. **Guggenhürli** (No. 36), S. of the Landstrasse. Built c. 1720 as a country house, extended in 1791. Half-timbered building with saddleback roof and outlook turrets. In Oberkirch, NE of the Old Town **nondenominational church St. Laurenzen,** cemetery and mother church of Frauenfeld. W. section 9-10C, central section 10-11C, choir 1st quarter of the 14C. In the choir important high Gothic windows c. 1330 with Annunciation and Crucifixion. Contemporary Gothic frescos in the window jambs have been completed by later hands.
Museums. *Kantonales Historisches Museum* in the Schloss with primeval collection. *Naturhistorische Sammlung* (natural history) in the Luzernhaus. *Öffentliche Kunstsammlung,* with works by modern Thurgau masters in the Bernerhaus.

Frauenkirch GR
See Davos   9◻D5

Frauenthal ZG
                                             7◻F2

Cistercian convent, founded 1231 in a secluded setting in a loop of the Lorze. The present convent buildings date largely from the 17C; the 14C **church of our Lady** was also altered in the 17&18C.

Freienbach
                                             8◻B2

Catholic parish church of St. Adalrich, rebuilt 1672-4, extended and altered on various occasions. In the only vineyard of the canton Schwyz, the Leutsch, a baroque

Frauenthal: Cistercian convent with four wings.

winegrower's house which belonged to the monastery of Einsiedeln, dating from 1762–4.

Frenkendorf BL

2☐A4

Neu-Schauenburg, built in the 13C on cleared land, was acquired in 1502 from the nearby monastery and gradually fell into decay. In 1813 a lookout pavilion was built in the ruin. **Auf der Fluh,** excavated foundations of a fortified Gallo-Roman hill shrine with a square temple.

Fribourg FR

11☐C/D1

The earliest traces of human habitation in the canton go back to the neolithic period; there are numerous other finds from the Bronze and Iron Ages and the Roman period. The area which later became the canton was under Frankish rule from 534 and part of the Kingdom of Burgundy from 888–1032. In the 11&12C a series of larger and smaller feudal systems grew up. The town of Fribourg, founded in 1157 by Berchtold IV of Zähringen, played a major role in the development of the canton; it was in the possession of the Counts of Kyburg from 1218 and acquired by the Habsburgs in 1277. Between the 12&15C the town, which was constantly in conflict

with Bern and Savoy, gradually made successful claims for the adjacent areas, though it was temporarily under the rule of Savoy in 1452. After the Burgundy Wars Fribourg became a member of the Confederation in 1481, in 1536, after conquering the Vaud, the territory of the present canton was more or less established. From the 16C to the 18C Fribourg developed nominally into a republic, in fact into an aristocratic oligarchy, and with its call to the Jesuits in 1580 it became a centre of the Counter-Reformation. The all-powerful patriciate was strongly resisted in some quarters in the 17&18C and had to give up its claims in 1798. Attempts to restore the former state of affairs began in 1815 and finally collapsed in 1847 when, in the course of the Sonderbund War, Fribourg was taken by Confederate troops. In 1857 the canton acquired a new constitution.

TOWN AND DEFENCES The town founded in 1157 grew up on the site of the present suburb of Bourg, and was protected by a château, and a ring wall which has now disappeared. The town grew in stages: first to the E. by the inclusion of the present Quartier de l'Auge and the part of the town on the right bank of the Saane, later to the N. and W. and finally to the S. by taking in the Quartier de la Neuveville. In the course of its development Fribourg was provided with an important fortification system; the town wall completed in the 15C was improved and altered until the end of the 18C. Its partial removal in the 19C permitted enlargement of the town, but with its 2 km. of wall defended by 14 towers Fribourg still has the most important medieval defensive system in Switzerland. The walls in the E. and S. of the town have survived in particularly good condition; in the second E. town wall on the right bank of the Saane the **tour-porte de Berne,** the **tour des Chats,** the **tour Rouge,** an important 13C square tower, and the **tour de Dürrenbühl** have survived. In the N. of the town a section of the 14&15C fourth W. wall and numerous towers are still standing: **Tour-porte de Morat** of 1410. **Tour des Rasoirs** of 1411, so-called **tour des 'Curtils novels'** and the **Grand Boulevard,**

Fribourg: part of the former fortifications in the NE of the town.

View of the Quartier du Bourg with Hôtel de Ville and St-Nicolas cathedral.

Important Entombment (1443) in the Chapel of the Holy Sepulchre in the cathedral.

an imposing semicircular bastion dating from 1490 and the **tour Henri,** 1415, also semicircular.

QUARTIER DU BOURG Oldest part of the town founded in 1157. **St-Nicolas Cathedral.** The present church, built on the site of a 12C Romanesque place of worship, was built between 1283 and 1490, the side chapels were added between the 16&18C and a new choir was built in 1630. It is a Gothic church with a nave and two aisles, a façade tower and a polygonal choir with two bays. The main portal is in the massive façade tower; its tympanum is decorated with a late-14C representation of the Last Judgement. The archivolts have busts of angels, prophets and patriarchs of the same period. On the portal jambs are 14&15C statues (originals in the museum). The 1330–40 S. portal has the Three Kings and male and female saints. In the interior, in the chapel of the Holy Sepulchre, is a very fine 1433 Entombment, showing Burgundian influence. 1498 font and 1516 choir stalls in the Flamboyant style. On the beam of the triumphal arch wooden polychrome Crucifixion of 1430. The choir screen dates from 1474, the carved choir stalls are

the work of Antoine Pency (1462–4). The high altar dates from 1877, most of the other churches are baroque. Modern glass by the Pole Joseph de Mehoffer (1869–1946). *Church treasury* in the sanctuary. Place de l'Hôtel de Ville. This was the site of the Ducal Schloss, destroyed in the 15C. **Hôtel de Ville,** built 1501–22 by Gylian Aetterli and Hans Felder the Younger; the clock tower was altered in various ways in the 16&17C. The trapezium-shaped building has a flight of steps built in 1776 in front of it; the ground floor, enclosed with baroque railings, was originally a corn hall. The entrance portal is framed by two arch reliefs by Charles Iguel, 1881. In the interior 'salle des pas perdus' ('Hall of the lost steps') with Gothic windows and crucifix by Martin Gramp, 1508. Salle du Grand Conseil with Louis XIV panelling and cantonal courtroom with 18C furnishings and panelling. By the Town Hall is the **maison de ville,** built in 1730&1 by Hans Fasel, a baroque-neoclassical building with wrought-iron balcony. **Gendarmerie,** built 1783 in Louis XIV style, with a gabled peristyle. In the square **fontaine Saint-Georges** with sculpture by Hans Geiler, 1525, **tilleul de Morat** (lime tree), planted in 1470, replaced in 1981, the columns by it date from 1756. 118 Rue des Bouchers, **Chancellerie d'Etat,** baroque-neoclassical building, built 1734 – 7 by Hans Fasel. On the ground floor windows with wrought-iron grilles (1737), carved heraldic motif over the door. In the middle of the street is the **poste,** the former customs house, a pavilion in Louis XV style built in 1756-8. Behind the cathedral **fontaine de la Vaillance** with sculpture by Hans Gieng, 1549&50. The **Grand-Rue,** the main traffic artery of the Quartier du Bourg, backbone of the 12C town and also the site of the former market, has a very fine group of 16–18C houses. No. 37, **Direction de l'Edilité,** 17C, combining Gothic and Renaissance elements; at the corner of the building column and niche with 18C statuette. No. 55, **maison Castella,** built in 1780 for J.Antoine de Castella, elegant façade decorated with trophy and coats-of-arms. No. 56, **baroque building,** built 1675 – 80. No. 66, **les Tournalettes,** Restaurant Schweizerhalle, late Gothic building built 1611 – 13 for Pierre de Gottrau, with polygonal staircase tower and corner oriel. Nos. 96&7 Rue Zaehringen, **maison Techtermann,** oldest residential building in the town, first mentioned 1359, but presumed to be older. Property of the Velga family, then the Englisberg family and in the Techtermann family from 1553; façade in Louis XV style, No. 99, **Hôtel Zaehringer,** elegant building built for the Lenzburg family in the 18C.

OBERSTADT Former infirmary quarter. **Notre-Dame,** built in the 12C shortly after the foundation of the town, altered in 1785-7. Only the bell tower of the original building has survived. The present building, with baroque-neoclassical façade, has a nave and two aisles, with a polygonal choir and Louis XVI decor. Under the bell

The façade of Notre-Dame, built in the course of alterations in the 18C.

tower 13C Romanesque-Gothic chapel, in the choir stalls of 1506 and marble statue of the Immaculate Conception of 1787. By the church is Hans Gieng's 1547 **fontaine de Samson** (original in the museum). Rue des Cordeliers. Monastery and **Franciscan church.** The monastery was founded in 1256 and the church was in existence by 1281. It has a remarkable polygonal three-aisled choir; the nave and façade date from 1735-46. Very lavish interior furnishings: in the choir, on the high altar, retable by the Fribourg Nelken master (1480), a masterpiece of Swiss 15C painting; the 1280 standing choir stalls are among the oldest surviving choir stalls in Switzerland; fragment of the retable of St.Antony by Hans Fries, 1506, and tomb of Elisabeth von Kyburg, 1275. In the first S. chapel wooden retable, carved 1509-13, Alsatian work and gift of Jean de Furnos. In the surviving part of the old cloister are frescos of *c.* 1440 with representation of the Madonna and remains of a 1608 Dance of Death. Rue de Morat, monastery and **church of the Visitandines,** built 1653 – 6 by the architect and sculptor Hans Reyff. It is a rotunda with an octagonal tambour, and has a slightly bulging façade, pierced with a lavishly decorated portal, an interesting architectural creation, combining Gothic and Renaissance elements with baroque design. Place St-Michel, **College and Church of St-Michel.** The college was founded 1580-2 and the Dutch Jesuit Petrus Canisius was appointed as its director; the buildings date from 1584-96. The church of 1604 – 13 is a late Gothic building; its interior was altered 1756-71 and has lavish stucco and painted rococo

The Church of the Visitandes is an early baroque rotunda with drum dome.

Interior of St-Michel with exuberant rococo décor.

decor. High altar of 1766, altered in 1942 to accommodate the reliquary of St.Petrus Canisius. In the side chapels 18&19C altars. By the church Renaissance-style *college building*. The two earlier sections date from 1584–95, the third from 1660; the school was built 1829–38. 92 Rue de Lausanne, convent and **church of the Ursulines.** The convent built in 1677–9 was restored and enlarged in the 19C, the church was built 1653–5 by the architect J.E.Reyff. The building is a mixture of Gothic and Renaissance elements, and consists of a nave with a single aisle and a rectangular choir with rib vaulting. Rue Pierre-Aeby, **Hôtel Ratzé,** *Musée d'Art et*

d'Histoire. Private house, built in 1581–5 by the French architect Jean Fumal for Jean Ratzé, the commandant of the Swiss Guard in Lyon. The Renaissance building consists of a main building with staircase tower, connected to a second tower by a gallery. In the garden is a porter's lodge; its carved façade of 1518 comes from a house in Rueyres-St-Laurent. No. 190, **house,** of Louis d'Affry (1743–1810), first Landammann of Switzerland. 17C building with an 18C mansard roof. No. 191, 17C **house** with square 16C staircase tower incorporated in the façade. No. 192, **Ecole Ménagère,** built in 1767 for Jean de Castella, with rococo façade. No. 233 Rue de Morat, **Ecole Normale Ménagère.** Private house, built in 1737 by G.Fasel for Tobie de Gottrau, side portals with carved heraldic animals above them. No. 259, late Gothic **house,** built in the 16C. No. 262, **house** in Louis XV style, built in 1740 for the Ammann family. Beyond the Porte de Morat the **château de la Poya,** visible from the Zaehringer bridge. The building was inspired by Palladio and built in 1699–1701 for F.P. de Lanthen-Heid, the mayor of Fribourg. Rue de Lausanne, with very fine group of 16–18C houses. No. 32, **house** in Louis XV style, built in 1768 for N.Féguely, with carved window keystones. No. 37, **maison de Gottrau,** built in the 18C by architect Charles de Castella; lavish Louis XVI façade with fluted pilasters. No. 39, **house,** built 1730–40 for Ph. de Gottrau; Louis XV façade with a portal with two putti. No. 80, 18C **house** with baroque-neoclassical façade. No. 86, **episcopal palace,** built 1842–5. Rue de l'Hôpital, former **Hôpital des Bourgeois,** built 1681–9, with 18C outbuildings. In the middle of the complex is an interesting circular **church.** Rue des Alpes, **Etat Civil,** (Registry Office), neoclassical building built at the end of the 18C for the French banker A.Forestier; portal with double flight of steps. No. 54 **maison Vicarino,** post Gothic building dating from the 17C.

QUARTIER DE L'AUGE This quarter developed at the same time as the market and village started in 1157, and contains a remarkable group of buildings. **Augustinian monastery and church,** founded in the 13C. The *church* is dedicated to St. Maurice and was built between 1255 and 1311 and frequently altered in the 16&18C. Nave and three aisles with a polygonal choir, main façade with 1684 portico. The interior was refurbished in 1783 in Louis XVI style and has very lavish furnishings: high altar with monumental carved retable by the Spring brothers, 1602. 17C side altars from the Reyff studio; on the side aisle walls 4 altars by D. Angerhoffer, stone sedilia dating from 1594. By the church is the *former Augustinian monastery*, now the State Archive. The present buildings date from the 17&18C. The monastery was dissolved in 1842 and used as a prison. In the interior former summer refectory with 1748 baroque painting. In the Rue Stalden, which connects the Bourg and Auge quarters, **house** No. 14 is 16C and has fine windows. 2 Rue de la Lenda, **maison de maître**, built in 1765 for F.N. Kuenlin; elegant baroque façade with very fine rococo railings. 16 Rue de la Samaritaine **Gothic house**, built in the 15C for the Reyff family; the windows of the first floor have guilloche moulding. Opposite is the **fontaine de la Samaritaine**, the work of Hans Gieng 1550&1 (original in the museum) with a representation of Christ and the Samaritan leaning on a fountain. No. 36 **Gothic house**, probably 14C. 13 Rue d'Or, roomy 16C **late Gothic house** with fine windows. No. 24, **Hôtel de la Cigogne**, 1771 painting on the façade. Place du Petit-St-Jean. Fine group of buildings, No. 29 is particularly striking. **Fontaine Sainte-Anne** with sculpture by Hans Gieng, 1559&60 (original in the museum). **Pont du Milieu**, leading to the Planche area, a 1720 stone bridge with four arches. **Pont de Berne**, wooden structure with masonry piers (1653). In the Rue des Forgerons and the Rue de la Palme are fine groups of Gothic houses. 2 Rue de la Palme, 15C **maison Mooses. Fontaine de la Fidélité** with column by Hans Gieng, 1552, and statue by Stephan Ammann, 1606 (original in the museum.

NEUVEVILLE AND PLANCHE Fine collection of Gothic buildings. Rue de la Neuveville, **église de la Providence** 1749–62, elegant Louis XV façade, three baroque altars in

the interior. **House** No. 1, in the Place du Pertuis, built in the 17C, statue of St. Christopher on the corner of the house, 1612. **Houses** Nos. 46–8, probably built in the 16C, very fine façades, the windows have guilloche moulding. Opposite is the **fontaine de la Force** with statue and column by Hans Gieng 1549&50 (original in the museum). The Quartier de la Planche is reached via the **Pont St-Jean,** built 1746. In the large triangular square are the **Commandery and Church St-Jean,** founded by the Hospitallers of St. John of Jerusalem. The *church* of St-Jean was consecrated in 1264 and much altered in 1885 and 1951. In the choir 1712 high altar and tombs of Knights of the Order Pierre Englisberg (d.1545) and Jacques Duding (d.1716). In the S. part of the baldachin gallery 14C frescos, next to them a chapel dating from 1600. Beyond the Anna chapel (1514) is a Hans Gieng crucifix (1525). By the church around a courtyard are the 16&17C buildings of the former commandery. **Caserne de la Planche,** former storehouse built 1708&9 and adapted as a barracks in 1821. The main façade with a stepped gable is decorated with the coat of arms of the canton. **Fontaine Saint-Jean** 1547 by Hans Gieng. **Cistercian abbey of Notre-Dame de la Maigrauge.** The nunnery of Maigrauge was first mentioned in 1255; united in 1261 with the Cistercian Order as a daughter foundation of the abbey of Hauterive. The *convent buildings* were rebuilt after a fire in 1660–6. The *abbey church* was consecrated in 1284, the body of the church was shortened and the nave raised *c.* 1350, the gallery was built in 1610. Despite the modifications the square choir is a fine example of Cistercian architecture. In the interior is a remarkable representation of the dead Christ in polychrome wood, under an archway which is painted with a Wailing over the Body of Christ. In the gallery wooden stalls dating from 1378 – 1400. Chemin de Lorette, **Montorge monastery,** built 1626–8, occupied by the Tertiaries of St. Francis. The convent church is dedicated to St. Joseph and was consecrated in 1635. Plain building with a single aisle with a striking 1668 choir screen. High altar and side altars by J. Reyff and his studio, *c.*

1635. Choir stalls 1660, ascribed to the same artist. **Loreto chapel,** built 1647&8 by J.Reyff, copy of the Santa Casa di Loreto. The chapel walls are decorated with statues (originals in the museum), in the interior 1648 Madonna statue from the Reyff workshop, and figure of an angel. By the chapel rampart and 14&15C **porte de Bourguillon.**

NEW QUARTERS **The Université Miséricorde** on the Route du Jura, built 1938–41 by the architects F.Dumas and D.Honegger, consisting of three sections.

Cistercian abbey of Notre-Dame on the Saane peninsula.

In the central section Grosse Aula and Senatc Hall with 17C tapestries. In the vestibule 14–17C statues from the collection of the Musée d'Art et d'Histoire, near the chapel Roman mosaic of Theseus and the Minotaur. Quartier de Gambach. Villa quarter with interesting late 19C and early 20C buildings. Quartier de Pérolles. On the Boulevard **église du Christ-Roi** built 1951-3 by F.Dumas and D.Honegger; interesting triangular concrete building. Avenue du Midi. **château de Pérolles** and **chapel.** The château has been mentioned since 1259 and was rebuilt in 1508-22 by C. de Diesbach, at the same time as the **chapelle Saint-Barthélémy,** a fine example of the Flamboyant style. In the interior collection of Renaissance glass painting by Lukas Schwarz, 1529-3. 1520 terracotta statues and crucifix by Hans Geiler.

Polychrome figure of St.Christopher in the chapelle Saint-Barthélémy, Pérolles.

BOURGILLON Suburb of Fribourg. **Notre-Dame,** built 1464-6; single-aisle building with rectangular choir. In the interior on the walls of the nave marble votive pictures, in the niche of the high altar 14C wooden statue of the Madonna and Child. **Museums:** *Musée d'Art et d'Histoire* in the Hôtel Ratzé; important art collection, archaeological and historical collection. *Musée d'histoire naturelle;* museum of natural history.

little hill above the village in 1716. It has a domed tower, nave with aisles and a polygonal choir with domed vaulting. The high altar is said to have been a gift from the Empress Maria Theresia. **Cemetery chapel** 16C with Crucifixion by the brothers Heinrich and Melchior Fischer.

Frick AG

2☐C3

Catholic parish church of St.Peter and Paul. This spacious baroque church replaced a medieval fortress church on the

---

Frienisberg BE

6☐D/E3

The **former Cistercian abbey,** founded in 1131, was rebuilt as a Landvogt's Schloss in the 16C. The plan of the church, which has survived in part, is related to those of ▷ Bonmont and ▷ Hauterive.

Fruence FR
See CHATEL-ST-DENIS   11☐B4

Frutingen BE
                                       12☐A3

Reformed church St. Quirinus. This
late Gothic building of 1421 was rebuilt
in the baroque style, incorporating some
older sections, after a fire in the 18C. S.
of the village are the ruins of the **Tellen-
burg,** which burned down in 1885; its
keep is probably 12C.

Ftan GR
                                       15☐A3

In the W. part of the village is the **casa
Vulpius,** built in 1674 with gable frontage and raised entrance. In Ftan-Pitschen

a group of farmhouses in excellent condition form a picturesque hamlet.

Fürgangen VS
See BELLWALD   12☐D4

Fürstenau GR
                                       9☐A5

Formerly a small fortified town with
customs point (Fürstenaubruck), rebuilt in
village style after a fire in 1742. **Unteres
Schloss** (former Episcopal Palace).
Rebuilt 1709–11 incorporating the 1272
defensive tower; it protrudes slightly under
the unified hipped roof of the NE section.
Oberes (former Schaustein-Schloss),
built 1660–7 with integrated medieval corner tower on the street side. In front of the
portal façade is a baroque terraced garden
ending in gently climbing terraces on the
other side of the road.

G

Gächlingen SH

3☐A2

Houses. Some of the step-gabled half-timbered houses, most of which are in good condition, date from the 16C. The old parish hall was built in 1571.

Gachnang TG

3☐C3

Reformed church of St. Pankratius. The choir and tower were rebuilt 1493–5, and the hall-like nave 1747–9, in place of a Romanesque pillared basilica which had collapsed. **Catholic church** by Adolf and Paul Gaudy, 1952. The **Schloss** was built in 1767 by Brother Caspar Braun as a hermitage chapel of ease. It has nine sections; the central one is articulated with pilaster strips and has a portal and flight of steps. KEFIKON NW of Gachnang, **former moated Burg.** Numerous modifications in the 16, 18C and the 00C. The keep has some adjacent residential buildings and stands on the historic boundary-line between Zürich and Thurgau. ISLIKON **Greutersche Fabrikanlagen,** former dyeing and fabric printing works. First building 1777, followed by more than thirty more in Empire and Biedermeier styles. The main building, No. 25, surrounds an enclosed courtyard with vehicular access on all sides. Neoclassical façade.

Gais AR

4☐A4

The village has traditional timber houses with curved gables and some imposing stone buildings, and dates largely from after the fire of 1780. The houses around the village green and in the Webergasse up to the Schwantleren in the NE form the core of the village. **Reformed church,** built 1781-2 by Hans Ulrich Haltiner. Interior rococo stucco, school of Andreas and Peter Anton Mosbrugger (1782). **Haus zum Ochsen** in the Dorfplatz with domed tower at the rear, built by Konrad Langenegger in 1796. In the N. row of houses in the Dorfplatz **Haus Eisenhut** (No. 168), with a fine curved gable. The detached **house,** No. 177, combines a late baroque sense of design with the vernacular style and was built in 1783 for Jakob Gruber, the Landeshauptmann of the time. It has a high transverse gable with a double curve above the central section, the upper storey is articulated with an enormous pilaster, rococo doorway. **Schlachtkapelle am Stoss** E. of Gais, built in the 15C in memory of the victory of the Appenzellers over an Austrian army in 1405. Altered in 1955 by Johann Hurgentobler.

Gaiserwald SG

3☐F4

Large parish W. of the Sitter without a town or village of the same name. In Abtwil **Catholic parish church of St. Joseph,** built by August Hardegger in 1901/5 as a neo Gothic hall church. In Engelburg **Catholic parish church of the Guardian Angels,** built in 1768 by Johann Ferdinand Beer. Baroque building with axial entrance tower, rococo altars by Franz Anton Dirr, 1779. **Wooden bridge** over the Sitter in St.Josephen, built in 1779 by Johann Ulrich and Andreas Thaddäus Schefer of Rotmonten.

Galgenen SZ

8☐C2

Catholic parish church of St.Martin, built 1822-6 by the Zürich cantonal architect Hans Conrad Stadler. The 1804 tower was incorporated into the façade, which is strongly neoclassical, with three arches opening into the vestibule. **St.Jost chapel.** The Gothic building consecrated in 1398 was rebuilt in 1622-3; the wall

Gais: village square with unusual gables.

paintings on the street side date from the same period.

Gampelen BE
6☐C4

The **priest's house** of 1668–71 is a two-storey building with a hipped roof with carved ends. On the gable above the entrance portal is a Carved Erlach coat-of-arms.

Gams SG
4☐A5

Catholic parish church of St.Michael, rebuilt 1868 by Carl Reichlin in neo-Gothic style.

Gamsen VS
18☐C1

W. of the village remains of the **Gamsen wall,** which has survived over a length of several hundred metres. The origin and purpose of this wall, presumed to date from the 14C, are uncertain; it probably served to protect the village from attacks from the W.

Gandria TI
19☐D4

Charming village in excellent condition with narrow alleyways and characteristic houses. **Catholic parish church of San Vigilio,** first mentioned 1563; baroque building with 19C façade. *Museo doganale svizzero,* a little collection on smuggling and the Swiss customs.

Galgenen: Catholic church of St. Martin, a neoclassical building by H.C. Stadler.

Gänsbrunnen SO
6☐E1

The **Catholic parish church of St. Joseph** was built in 1627 in neo-Gothic style. The **priest's house** built c. 1720 has half-timbered gables, atypical for the region.

Ganterswil SG
3☐E5

Reformed Church, mentioned 1245, rebuilt 1438, 1488, 1820. Essentially late Gothic wall paintings in the choir c. 1460–70 and probably 16C. **Catholic church St. Petrus und Paulus,** built 1939–40 by Hans Burkard. Glass by August Wanner, altar paintings by Karl Peterli.

Garde,La VS
See. EVOLENE
17☐F3

Gebenstorf AG
2☐E4

Reformed parish church. Neo-Gothic

single-aisled church by Paul Reber (1889 –91).

Geiss LU

7☐D3

The **parish church of St. Jakobus the Elder,** altered on numerous occasions, has 1783 late rococo altars contemporary with the nave. The ceiling and altar paintings are by Josef Anton Messmer.

Gelfingen LU

7☐E2

Schloss Heidegg. Built for the Lords of Heidegg in the 11C or 12C. Rebuilding in 1618 transformed the Burg into a baroque country seat; the addition of three residential storeys with large windows removed much of the war-like appearance of the keep. The ballroom was decorated by artists from the Tessin.

Gelterkinden BL

2☐B4

Village square with late 16C fountain, 1821 priest's house and **Reformed parish church** forming a fine group; the church and its W. tower are visible for miles, both late 15C; late Gothic cycle of wall paintings.

Genève/Geneva GE

16☐E2

The old Genava, city of the Allobroges and seat of an oppidum has been inhabited since the neolithic period and was part of the Roman Empire from 120 BC. It became Christian in the 4C, fell to the Burgundians in 443, to the Franks in 534 and became an imperial city and bishopric in 1033. For five centuries the bishops and lords of the area, above all the Lords of Savoy, fought for dominance of the town. In the 16C two important factors determined the fate of Geneva: the first alliance with the Confederates, 1519 with Fribourg

Gelfingen: Schloss Heidegg, extended and redesigned in the baroque style in the 17C.

and 1526 with Bern, and the Reformation, which began to impinge in 1536. The fact that Jean Calvin made his home in Geneva brought about a radical change in the political and social life of the town and altered its spiritual image. The independence of the 'Protestant Rome' was not yet secure, however; in 1602 the Duke of Savoy tried once more to conquer the town, on the night of the Escalade, but without success. The influx of French Protestants in the 17C helped the economic development of Geneva, particularly in the fields of industry and banking. In the 18C, when Rousseau and Voltaire were citizens of the town, Geneva began to feel the consequences of the new ideas which were causing so much confusion and activity. After the French Revolution Geneva was annexed by France from 1798–1813, and after achieving independence, became the twenty-second Swiss canton. Since the second half of the 19C the international importance of Geneva has been enhanced by the foundation of the Red Cross in 1864, the establishment of the League of Nations in 1919 and of the United Nations in 1945. LEFT BANK OF THE RHONE **Old Town,** the historical centre of Geneva, where a Gallic oppidum was followed by the Roman and then the medieval town. **Cathedral of St-Pierre** (Reformed church). The present building, on the site of a 6C basilica built by the Burgundians over an earlier 4C church, is Romanesque-Gothic in style and was built between 1150 and 1225. The polygonal choir has two side towers and a central spire. The church is entered via a neoclassical portico, built in 1752–6 to plans by the Piedmontese architect

Genève: Rhône quay and view of St-Pierre cathedral.

Maccabees chapel in the S. of the cathedral, much altered 1878–88.

The Arsenal, a former 16&17C corn exchange, now houses the State Archives.

Benedetto Alfieri. The interior is cruciform, nave, choir and transept have a triforium, the columns are decorated with numerous capitals forming a remarkable sculptural ensemble. In the S. transept is the tomb of Henri de Rohan (1579–1683), in the N. aisle is the so-called Calvin throne, in the S. aisle 15C choir stalls. On the S. side of the cathedral is the Maccabees chapel, built in 1406 by Cardinal Jean de Brogny, a fine example of the Flamboyant style. By the cathedral is the **Auditoire de Calvin.** This theological lecture hall in which Calvin, Knox and Bèze taught was in the 13C former parish church of Notre-Dame-de-la-Neuve, which was altered in the 15C and took over the site of the earliest church, which dated from the 5C. **Saint-Germain,** Old Catholic since 1873, built in 1460 on the site of a 5C basilica. In the interior an altar has been reconstructed from early Christian carved fragments (copies). **Lutheran Church,** Bourg-de-Four. Built 1762-6 for the Prince of Hessen, externally like a neoclassical town house. **Hôtel de Ville,** built from the 15C to the late 17C. Street façades 1617-30 in Renaissance style. In the peristyle courtyard is a square tower with a gently sloping paved ramp, built in 1556-78; it is entered through a remarkable Renaissance portal; by the ramp and visible from the Promenade is the **tour Baudet,** built in 1455. In the interior 15C salle des Pas-Perdus, council chamber with 15-17C paintings, and Alabama chamber, where the Red Cross agreement was signed in 1864 and where the court of arbitration on the Alabama conflict of 1871&2 held its meetings. **Arsenal,** opposite the Hôtel de Ville. Former 16C corn hall, altered 1629 -34, arsenal from 1720, now state archive. The hall on the ground floor has arcades on three sides and contains five 17&18C cannons; on the walls are three mosaics dating from 1949 by Alexandre Cingria. On the exterior of the first floor is a frieze dating from 1893 by Gustave de Beau-

Maison de Saussure, an early 18C private house.

mont, which tells the story of Geneva in pictures. **Maison Tavel,** Rue du Puits-St-Pierre. Oldest residential house in the town, mentioned in 1303. The Gothic façade with carved heads has a round tower in the NE corner; façade altered in the 8C, two vaulted 13C cellars. **Maison Turrettini,** 8 Rue de l'Hôtel de Ville, palais in Renaissance style, built 1617–20 to plans by Faule Petitot, entrance portal with triangular gable, courtyard surrounded by columned arcades on two sides. **Maison Cayla,** 10 Place de la Taconnerie, 1750 private house, façade with rococo balcony consoles. **Maison Mallet,** Cour St-Pierre. Baroque-neoclassical private house, built in 1721 by French architect Jean-François Blondel for Gédéon Mallet. The façade has a flight of steps and windows with carved lintels. Group of houses in the **Grand-Rue,** built between the 15–18C, notable particularly are No. 11 (1743) and No. 15 (17C). **Maison de Saussure,** 24 Rue de la Cité, an example of a private house in the French style ('entre cour et jardin') executed with considerable grace by the French architect Joseph Abeille in 1707–12 for Jean-Antoine Lullin, later the home of the Geneva scholar Horace-Bénédict de Saussure. **Rue des Granges,** built in 1719 on private initiative; on the odd-numbered side a row of French-style private houses of great stylistic unity; the run of façades is visible from the Place Neuve. **Bourg-de-Four.** Main square of the Old Town, on the site of the former Roman forum, in the 13C most important trade centre of the town. In the square **Palais de Justice,** former infirmary built in 1717–12 by Jean Vennes on the site of a monastery. **Collège**

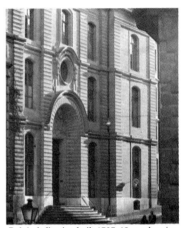

Palais de Justice, built 1707–12 as a hospice, court building from 1857.

Reformed church of La Madeleine, rebuilt in the first half of the 15C.

Calvin, Rue Théodore de Bèze, founded by Jean Calvin and built 1559 – 62 by Pernet Desfosses. Mixture of Gothic and Renaissance styles. **Palais Eynard,** Rue de la Croix-Rouge. Neoclassical building, built in 1821 by the Florentine architect Giovanni Salucci for the banker and graecophile Gabriel Eynard. The Palais, built on two different levels, is supported by the former town rampart, the street façade has an Ionic peristyle. In the same street **Palais de l'Athénée,** built in 1864

Russian church, with numerous 16–20C icons.

by Gabriel Diodati as the seat of the Société des Arts on the basis of a donation by J.G.Eynard.

Les Rues-Basses. The quartier was established in the 14C and completely redesigned in the 19&20C. Place de la Madeleine, **Reformed church of La Madeleine.** The present Gothic building is on the site of three older churches, built after 500 above a 5C memorial building; the remains of the earlier buildings are visible under the present nave. **Temple de la Fusterie,** built 1713–15 by Jean Vennes. The baroque building was inspired by the famous 'Temple' of Charenton, destroyed by Louis XIV. In front of the church is a 773 **fountain. Place du Molard.** Once the economic centre of the town, a fine traffic-free square with 1591 **tower** and 7C former **market halls.** Place Longemalle, 1774 **fountain** by Louis Favre. In the Jardin Anglais **national memorial,** bronze group by Robert Dorer 869.

Place Neuve and Bastions. Part of the own which developed in the 19C. **Sacré-Coeur,** Rue Henri Dunant, built 1857–0 as a freemasons' lodge, Catholic church nce 1873, enlarged in 1939. Place Neuve, uilt on the site of the former fortifications. **Musée Rath.** One of the earliest museums

in Europe, built 1824&5 by Samuel Vaucher in neoclassical style. **Grand-Théâtre** of 1874–9; the building was inspired by Charles Garnier's Opéra in Paris. **Conservatoire,** neoclassical building 1857&8 to plans by J.B.Le Sueur, façade decorated with statues and niches. **Memorial for General Dufour,** 1879–94, bronze equestrian statue by Alfred Lanz. **Rue de la Corraterie.** The odd-numbered houses were built in 1827&8 on state initiative; severe restrictions were imposed on the design of the buildings; plans by Samuel Vaucher. Place Bel-Air, **Crédit Lyonnais** of 1830, originally a covered market hall. In the Parc des Bastions **University,** neoclassical building dating from 1868–72. In the Quartier des Tranchées, Rue Toepffer, **Russian church,** built in 1863–9 to plans by the architect Grimm of St.Petersburg. **Musée d'Art et d'Histoire,** built 1909&10 by J. and M.Camoletti.

Rive and Eaux-Vives. Parc de la Grange, neoclassical **house,** built 1766&7 for the Lullin family, villa and park presented to the city in 1917 by William Favre. **Maison Carté,** Rue A.Lachenal. Residential house, designed 1930–2 by Le Corbusier and Pierre Jeanneret.

Bridges. **L'Ile.** The Rhône island facilitated river crossing from the earliest times and helped the development of the city. **Tour de l'Ile.** Only surviving part of the 13C episcopal château, thoroughly restored in 1898. At the foot of the tower monument (1919) for the Geneva patriot Philibert Bertelier, beheaded here in 1519. **Ile Rousseau, bronze statue** of Jean Jacques Rousseau by Jean Pradier, dating from 1835.

RIGHT BANK OF THE RHONE *Quais.* There is a row of large hôtels on the Quais. **Hôtel des Bergues** 19&20C. **Palais Wilson,** former Hôtel National, built 1873–5, seat of the League of Nations from 1920–6. **Brunswick Monument,** Quai du Mont-Blanc. Mausoleum, built to resemble the Scaliger tombs in Verona in 1877–9 by Duke Karl II of Brunswick, who died in Geneva and left his fortune to the city.

St-Gervais, St-Jean, Cornavin. St-Gervais is the oldest quarter on the right bank. There were a palace with chapel and fortifications here from the 9C; the fortified suburb attached to it was radically altered in the 19&20C. **Reformed church of St-Gervais,** Rue du Temple. The present building dates from the 15C and was built over a 10&11C church, which in its turn stood on the site of an older place of worship. The Romanesque crypt is still visible and contains Carolingian remains. In the interior 15C wall paintings, probably from a Piedmontese studio, choir stalls and Escalade memorial (1895) in memory of the sacrifice of 1602. **Priorat St-Jean,** Pont Sous-Terre. Important Geneva monastery, subject in the 11C to the abbey of Ainay, destroyed in 1536. The excavations of 1967–70 have revealed the foundations of a massive Romanesque basilica, also those of the cloister and a chapel; archaeological tour and small *museum.* **Catholic church of Notre-Dame,** Place Cornavin. Neo-Gothic, built 1852 –9 to plans by A.Charles Grigny. Behind the church **Ecole des Arts Industriels** of 1876. **Les Délices,** 25 Rue des Délices. 1730–5 house, in which Voltaire lived from 1755–65; now *Institut et Musée Voltaire.* *International organisations.* **Perle-du-Lac,** Villa Bartholoni. Neoclassical building dating from 1828&9, home of the *Musée de l'histoire et des sciences.* **Musée de l'Ariana,** Purpose-built in 1877–84 in Italian Renaissance style to house the collections of Gustave Reveillod, who left them to the city in 1890. **Bureau International du Travail** (BIT), Route de Lausanne. Present home of GATT, built in 1924–6 by Georges Epiteaux; in the garden sculpture by James Vibert, 1935, L'Effort humain. **Palais des Nations,** European home of the United Nations Organisation, built 1929 – 37 by five architects of different nationalities. The largest building in Europe after the Palace of Versailles. In the interior conference hall with paintings by E.Vuillard, R.Chastel, M.Denis and K.-X.Roussel. Council chamber with paintings by José Maria Sert. Bronze armillery sphere in the garden. The important international organisations based in Geneva all have their buildings around the Palais des Nations. **Museums.** *Musée d'Art et d'Histoire;* art

Musée d'instruments anciens de musique, with 16–19C instruments.

collection, archaeological, historical and numismatic collections. *Musée de l'Ariana;* ceramics. *Musée d'histoire naturelle;* natural history. *Musée de l'horlogerie et d'émaillerie'* clocks and enamel. *Musée d'ethnographie;* collections from Africa, Oceania, America and Europe. *Musée d'instruments anciens de musique;* old musical instruments. *Petit Palais;* 19&20C painting. *Musée Baur;* Art from the Far East. *Musée de l'histoire des sciences;* museum of the exact sciences. *Musée des Suisses à l'étranger;* collections on the Swiss abroad

Genolier VD
10☐B/C

Reformed parish church (Notre-Dame), first mentioned 1110 and rebuilt in the late Gothic period. Single-aisled with two side chapels and a square choir with tall bell tower. 1526 façade, with baroque vestibule 1832 fountain in the village square.

Genthod GE
16☐E

Château, medieval seat of the lords of Genthod. The present building is essentially 17C. Opposite, **maison de la Rive** built 1730, home of the natural scientist and philosopher Charles Bonnet. CREUX-DE-GENTHOD **Maison de Saussure,** built in 1723–33 for Amédée Lullin by the French architect Franço

Gentilino: Sant'Abbondio, with scrolled gable façade.

Blondel, who also designed the gardens. The elegant house was the home of Horace-Bénédict de Saussure. The main façade has a triangular gable decorated with the coat-of-arms of the Lullin-de Saussure family. The sculptural decoration is by J.-F. Funk and K. Haag.

Gentilino TI
19☐D4

Outside the village in the direction of Montagnola **Catholic parish church of Sant'Abbondio**, mentioned from 1372, altered in the 16&17C. Nave and three aisles with polygonal choir, free-standing bell tower to the S. Choir lavishly decorated with 18C stucco; high altar 1700. In front of the church is an **ossuary** with baroque wall paintings, painted Station of the Cross niches on the cemetery wall.

Géronde VS
see SIERRE
8☐A4

Gersau SZ
8☐A4

Politically independent from 1390 to 1798 and thus the smallest republic in the world; annexed by the canton of Schwyz in 1817. **Catholic parish church of St. Marcellus,** built 1807–12 by the Einsiedeln Brother Jakob Nater. The single-aisled building with narrow transepts contains neoclassical stucco with altars and furnishings in the same style. Among the surviving Blockbau buildings in the town the most striking are the **'Gerbe'**, dated 1577 and the 16C **Gasthaus Schiff**. There are various French-looking 18C stone houses including the **'Hof'** in the Dorfstrasse, built *c.* 1790 for the last abbot of Einsiedeln and the **Familienhaus Camenzind** by the church, which stood directly by the lake until the lake road was built in the 19C.

Gerzensee BE
6☐F5

Altes Schloss, built 1518 for mayor Jakob of Wattenwyl. House with a steep hipped roof, with 13C wall oriels. The central section of 1772 has a ballroom in Louis XVI style. The **Neues Schloss** is a baroque building in the French style dating from 1690.

Geschinen VS
12☐E4

St. Sebastian chapel, built 1750, bell tower raised 1893. In the interior high altar (1756) from the Peter Lagger studio, 16C stone tabernacle in the choir. In the village very fine group of 16&17C houses and a group of wooden farm buildings, barns and storerooms of which one, near the chapel, dates from 1609.
WILER On a hill in the direction of Ulrichen **St. Katharina chapel,** built 1686 and 1704. In the interior 1697 high altar by Joh. Sigristen, on the triumphal arch trompe l'oeil painted medallions; altars dating from 1777. 18&19C votive pictures.

Gersau: parish church with neoclassical stucco.

Geuensee LU

7☐D2

The **St. Niklaus chapel** contains wall paintings dating from the last quarter of the 16C and the first half of the 17C. By the chapel is a **storehouse** dating from 1743.

Giez VD

5☐E5

Charles the Bold camped near the village before the battle of Grandson. **Reformed church** (St-Pierre). The building consists of a partially Romanesque choir with a tall tower, and a late Gothic nave which has been altered. By the outer wall of the present church are remains of a ruined chapel built in 1500. By the church is the **château,** built in the 15&16C for the de Pierre family and acquired in 1613 by Etienne Bourgeois. The L-shaped building consists of two sections connected by a square keep and adjacent polygonal staircase tower. Opposite the church **maison des Tourelles,** with a staircase tower (1635) on the façade side.

Gilly VD

10☐C3

VINCY **Château de Vincy,** started in

Gilly: 18C Château Vincy with French park.

1724 under Jean de Vasserot and completed in 1793. Lamartine stayed here in 1815. The courtyard façade has two low side wings and a pediment with the coat-of-arms of the Vasserot family and a portico with balcony above it.

Gingins VD

10☐B4

Reformed parish church (St-Laurent), first mentioned in 1211; the originally Romanesque building was enlarged in the Gothic period and acquired a façade tower. Later enlarged and altered. Adjacent 18C **priest's house. Château** S. of the church. The square building has three towers, the oldest parts of which date back to the 15C.

Giornico TI

13☐C5

Famous since the Roman period, know[n] for the victory of the Confederates over th[e] Milanese in 1478. Since the high Middl[e] Ages Giornico has been an extremely im[-] portant spiritual centre and still has si[x] churches and chapels. **San Nicolao,** th[e] most important Romanesque building i[n] the Tessin. The church has been men[-] tioned since 1210, was built in the first ha[lf] of the 12C and was subordinate to [a] Benedictine monastery which has sinc[e] disappeared. A building with a single a[i]sle; the square choir has a semicircul[ar] apse. The outer walls have Lombardy a[r] ches and the main and S. portal are decorated with sculpture. The raised choir is above a three-aisled crypt; its columns have carved capitals with geometric and representational motifs. In the apse 1478 wall paintings by Nicolao da Seregno. 12C font decorated with bas-reliefs in the nave. By San Nicolao is the **Catholic parish church of San Michele,** Romanesque in origin, altered in the 17&18C, 1861 bell tower. In the interior late Gothic retable of 1574. On a little hill is **Santa Maria di Castello,** by the ruins of a Milanese castle destroyed in 1518. The church is probably 12C and originally consisted of a nave with a semicircular apse; later a second nave with a shallow apex was added. In the interior painted 1575 coffered ceiling, in the S. choir interesting wall paintings by the masters of Seregno. In the village, on the bank of the river, a fine group of houses and two stone bridges. The 16C **casa Stanga** was originally a hostel. On the façade are coats-of-arms of travellers who stayed here, dating from *c.* 1589. The building now houses a small **museum** of local history. ALTIROLO **Pilgrimage church of San Pellegrino,** on the old Gotthard route. The single-aisled building with polygonal choir and side chapel was consecrated in 1345 and enlarged in the 16C. In the interior important wall paintings (1589) by G.B.Tarilli and D.Caresano of Lugano with the Last Judgement, the Apostles and the Vices and Virtues.

Giornico: Santa Maria di Castello with 12C Romanesque bell tower.

Burg mound as protection from the floods of the Laui brook. The baroque building was rebuilt in neoclassical style in 1823. The remains of 13C **Burg Redenz** were once part of the fortifications at the foot of the Brünig pass, to which the **ruined tower** in Kleinteil also belonged. There are various characteristic farmhouses and storehouses between Kleinteil and Grossteil.

Gipf-Oberfrick AG

2 ☐ C4

Alt-Tierstein ruin. Family seat of the Counts of Tierstein, lived in until the 15C. The ruins were excavated and made safe in 1934&5.

Giswil OW

7 ☐ D5

Catholic parish church of St. Laurentius, built 1630–5 on a former

Giubiasco TI

19 ☐ D2

In the centre of the village **Catholic parish church of Santa Maria Assunta,** mentioned since 929. The single-aisled building with rectangular choir was often altered and dates essentially from the 17C. 17C stucco in the choir and 15C wall painting on the nave and choir walls. By the cemetery **Catholic church of San Giobbe,** 1627, lavish stucco decoration and 17C painting of the Trinity by Alessandro Gorla in the choir. By the church **Sant'Anna chapel** with 16&17C wall paintings.

Givisiez FR

11 □ C1

12 Route de l'Epinay, **château.** Built in 1539 for the d'Affry family, radically altered in the 17C. The main façade has a portico and square staircase tower. Opposite the church 18C **house** No. 33.

Glarus GL

8 □ D/E3

Principal town of the canton of Glarus. The town developed from two settlements which formed around the old parish church and a farm belonging to the monastery of Säckingen. The monastery was for a long period the most important landowner in the area; the founder of the monastery, St.Fridolin, is still depicted on the Glarus flag. In 1352 the valley was conquered by the Confederates, thus ending the dominance of the Habsburgs, who had ruled Glarus as Reichsvogts. In 1388 in Näfels the people of Glarus defeated an Austrian attempt to reconquer the valley. It was not until 1450, however, that they achieved parity of status in the Confederation. In the Reformation the majority of the people of Glarus joined the side of the reformer Zwingli, who had been a priest in Glarus for a time; a Catholic minority made its presence felt in certain areas. Thanks to the ready availability of water power in the valley there was some industrialisation even in the early 18C, and this increased rapidly in the 19C. The most important industry was fabric dyeing, and this product had a world-wide market for a time. From 1807 to 1816 the marshes of the Linthe plain were drained, opening the canton to important Swiss transit routes; a railway link followed after 1879. The town of Glarus was completely rebuilt, particularly in the N. area, after a fire in 1861, and the houses on a grid pattern still show the unified architecture of their period of origin. The central point of the N. section is the **Spielhofplatz,** which broadens into an imposing green area; around it are grouped the **house** built for the subsequent Bundesrat Joachim

Giubiasco: late Gothic wall painting of St. Veronica in Santa Maria.

Heer in 1862, the **courthouse** built in 1864, the **cantonal school** of 1872 and a unified row of houses. The courthouse, distinguished by its breadth and a central projection, is on the site of the old parish church before the fire of 1861. The new **Reformed church,** used by both denominations until the building of the Catholic church in 1964, stands to the W. of the town centre; it was built in 1864–6 to plans by Ferdinand Stadler and shows Romanesque and Renaissance influence. In the centre of the town in the Rathausplatz the dominant building is the **Rathaus,** (1862–5), with its broad façade; from here a street leads past the **parish house** (1837) to the **station,** built in 1903 in neo-Gothic castle style. S. of the Town Hall is the older part of the town; it is grouped mainly around the **Landsgemeindeplatz,** in which the Glarus Landsgemeinde (community) meeting still takes place each year. Some of the houses around it still have characteristic curved gables. The **Haus Brunner im Sand** has the same kind of gable; it was built 1770&1. Various houses outside the centre survived the fire of 1861, including the **Haus Leuzinger-Paravicini,** c. 1560, the **Iselihaus,** also c. 1560, altered c. 1800 and the **Haus in der Wies,** built in 1746–8

Glarus: view of Ferdinand Stadler's church of 1864–6.

Haus in der Wies, built 1746–8 for J.H.Streiff, the textile magnate.

for Landmajor Johann Heinrich Streiff, the founder of the Glarus textile industry. The **Catholic Burg chapel St.Michael** also survived the fire; it was built in 1762 on the mound of the former seat of the Vogts. By the **Stadtpark,** created 1874–8, the 'Volksgarten', is the *Kunsthaus,* which has collections of art and on scientific subjects.

Glis VS
18☐C1

Catholic parish church de l'Assomption, founded in 615, according to legend.

The present building dates from various periods: the 1519 transept and 1539 choir are the work of Ulrich Ruffiner, the nave and vestibule of 1642–59 of the brothers Peter and Christian Bodmer; the bell tower with Romanesque lower section was rebuilt in 1968. Church with nave and two aisles on a cruciform ground plan with rectangular choir; in the N. Porte d'Or, 1519, by Ulrich Ruffiner. The entrance portal by the vestibule is lavishly decorated with polychrome statues; there is also a 16C crucifix. In the choir and the transept chapels very fine Flamboyant vaulting. On the high altar 1480 triptych with modern sections. In the N. chapel, dedicated to St.Anne and founded by Georg Supersaxo, is a fine Gothic triptych of the founder and his family. Baroque cemetery portal. Behind the **chapel of St.Joseph** and ossuary crypt with 1729 Crucifixion by A. Sigristen.

Gnadenthal AG
See NIEDERWIL   2☐E5

Gnosca TI
19☐D1/2

On the edge of the village are the ruins of **San Giovanni Battista,** Romanesque, probably dating from the 12C, bell tower 13&14C. **Catholic parish church of San Pietro Martire,** mentioned since the 13C, altered in the baroque period. Marble Renaissance tabernacle in the choir.

Goldach SG
4☐A3

Catholic parish church of St. Mauritius. Nave rebuilt 1670&1, choir and S. tower late medieval, rebuilt and extended as an octagonal domed area by Adolf Gaudy 1929&30. **Schloss Sulzberg** or Möttelischloss, S. above Goldach. Built *c.* 1230, in the possession of the Mötteli family from 1474 – 1571. Residential building often altered. High-medieval tower, barrel-vaulted Burg chapel.

Glis: elaborately decorated entrance to the Catholic parish church.

Gnosca: ruined Romano-Gothic San Giovanni Battista.

Goldingen SG

8☐D1

Catholic parish church of St.Nikolaus. Built 1679–81, choir and nave rebuilt in late baroque style in 1784 by Marx Schob, incorporating the tower of the earlier building. **Maria zum Schnee chapel** in Gibel, built 1722. Madonna statue, presented in the late 17C by the Einsiedeln foundation.

Goldswil BE

See RINGGENBERG   12☐B2

Golino TI

See INTRAGNA   19☐B2

Gommiswald SG

8☐D1

Catholic parish church of St.Jakobus the Elder, founded 1500, rebuilt 1789 probably by Brother Jakob Natter in late baroque style. E. façade with curved gable and Louis XVI portal. **Premonstraten-sian monastery of St.Loreto** on Mount Sion. Founded 1761 by Josef Helg, church consecrated 1772. Long sequence of buildings with church in the W. Loreto chapel (1765) adjacent to the church in the E.

Gondo VS

18☐D2

Suste, warehouse and place of refuge, built

c. 1670 at the time of Jodok von Stockalper, who owned gold-mines in Gondo. Massive building with step gables and a defensive tower.

Gonten AI

3☐F5

Catholic parish church of St.Verena. Built 1863, neo-Gothic. 17C statue of the Madonna on the left side altar. Processional cross (1595) in the sacristy with crucifix *c.* 1320. **S'Rot Hus,** now cantonal bank, was originally painted red (its name is a dialect version of 'red house'). Built in the 18C as a four-storey family house. Wall paintings in one room.

Gordevio TI

19☐C2

VILLA **Catholic parish church of Santi Giacomo e Filippo,** first mentioned in 1334 and altered *c.* 1600. The interior is decorated with 1853 wall paintings. Adjacent **ossuary,** with 1753 wall paintings by G.Antonio Felice Orelli.

Gorgier NE

6☐A5

E. of the village, on the Road to Bevais, **château.** Mentioned from 1299, first owned by the Lords of Estavayer, then the Counts of Neuchâtel. The building was enlarged in the 19C but some 16C sections remain.

Gormund LU
See NEUDORF   7☐E2

Göschenen UR
                                               13☐A2

N. exit of the road and rail tunnel under the Gotthard massif. The **Alte Zollbrücke** (old toll bridge) is a reminder of the history of traffic over the pass; a bridge toll was levied at its tower well into the 18C.

Göslikon AG
See FISCHBACH-GÖSLIKON   2☐E5

Gossau SG
                                                3☐F4

Ribbon village by the Chellen brook. In the centre of the village **Catholic parish church of St.Andreas,** built in 1732 by Jakob Grubenmann. Extended to the W. and renovated in 1925 by Karl Zöllig. Single-aisled church with transept and narrower choir, oval pendentive crossing dome. **Reformed church.** Rotunda, built 1899–1900 by Otto Pfleghard and Max Haefeli. **Schloss Oberberg,** E. of Gossau, built mid 13C, rebuilt in 1406 after being destroyed in the Appenzell war. Late Gothic building, SE masonry high medieval, modern chapel on the ground floor.

Gossau ZH
                                                3☐F4

Reformed parish church. Neoclassical single-aisled church of 1820–1 designed by Johann Jakob Haltiner with stucco by Gotthard Geissendorf.

Gottlieben TG
                                                3☐E2

Tiny village with a fine square containing the **Drachenburg** (dragon castle), so called because of the dragon gargoyle added in 1884; it was originally built as the Oberes Steinhaus in 1674 and combined

Göschenen: 16C Häderlis bridge at the lower end of the Schöllenen.

with the Unteres Steinhaus in 1716. The Oberes Steinhaus has two oriels, one with two storeys. **Schloss,** built in the 13&14C, partially destroyed in 1352. E. and N. wing 15C, residential section rebuilt after 1836 by the later Emperor Napoleon III in neo-Gothic style. In the W. tower was a prison in which the reformer John Huss and the deposed Pope John XXIII were kept during the Council of Constance. The moat of the former moated Burg was filled in in the 19C.

Goumoens-la-Ville VD
                                                10☐E1

Reformed parish church, mentioned since the 12C, altered in the 15&16C and in 1848. In the interior heavily restored 14C Gothic wall paintings. On the road to Orbe **château** of medieval origin, with three square towers incorporated into 17&18C buildings.

Grabs-Werdenberg SG
                                                9☐A1

Werdenberg lies below the Burg of the same name and is the oldest surviving timber-built settlement in Switzerland, systematically redeveloped and restored since 1960. Characteristic arcades below

Gottlieben: medieval moated Schloss, redesigned in the neo-Gothic style in the 19C.

Grabs-Werdenberg: Schloss on the hill above the village.

street level in the Hauptgasse, which broadens to form the market-place in the centre of the village. **Schloss,** founded *c.* 1230, with keep (12&13C), palas in the N. (early 15C), staircase wing (late 15C) and the Glarus building (1695) in the SW. **Rathaus** (No. 31), late Gothic stone building with round-arched passageway. **House** No. 24–5 of 1583 is a half-timbered building on three massive pillared arches which dominates the square, **Drachenhaus** W. of the village; 17C Blockbau with decorative 18C painting around the windows and below the roof.

Grafenort OW

7☐F5

Heiligkreuz chapel, built 1689. The building is in three sections: an octagonal main interior space leads to a longitudinal choir with adjacent sacristy, a design which suggests the influence of the Einsiedeln monastery architect Caspar Mosbrugger. The nearby **Herrenhaus,** built 1689&90, originally the summer residence of the Abbots of Engelberg, is in poor condition.

Grafenried BE

6☐F3

Reformed church, built 1747. In the interior baroque pews and font contemporary with the building and modern stained glass by Max Brunner in the choir. Baroque **priest's house** (1736).

Grand-Lancy GE

16☐E2

Château, now parish hall, built 1817&18 for the diplomat Charles Pictet-de-Rochemont. Small 18C pavilion in the park.

Grand-Saconnex GE

16☐E1

Catholic parish church of St-Hippolyte. Building with nave and bell tower of 1837, 12&13C choir and two 15C chapels. In the interior 15C Italian triptych.

Grand-St-Bernard,Le VS
See BOURG-ST-PIERRE 17☐C5

Grand-Vivy FR
See BARBERECHE 6☐C5

Grandcour VD
6☐B5

On the edge of the village **château,** buil 1337–41 for Abraham Sinner; it consist: of a main building with two wings. RESSUDENS **Reformed parish churc** (Notre-Dame), built in the 13C on the sit of an early medieval church. The buildin; is an irregular rectangle, medieval be tower N. of the façade. An important cy cle of wall paintings was discovered in th choir in 1922; it is the most complete ex ample in the Vaud. The paintings depic

Grafenort: Heilig-Kreuz, one of the few baroque rotundas in Switzerland.

scenes from the Life of Christ and a Madonna and were commissioned in 1376 by Guillaume de Grandson.

Grandson VD

5⬚F5

The history of the town is closely linked with that of the lords of Grandson, who played an important role in W. Switzerland from the 10–14C until the line died out with Otto III in 1397 and power fell to Savoy. The market town around the Schloss burned down in 1466. It was immediately refortified, and played a decisive role before and during the Battle of Grandson, which was decided near ▷ Concise. After the Confederate victory over Charles the Bold, Grandson came under the joint administration of Fribourg and Bern. The **château,** on a mound by the bank of the lake, is one of the largest fortresses in Switzerland. First mentioned in 1050, the present castle is essentially 13C. It is built as an irregular square and is a variant of the 'carré savoyard', protected by three round towers to the E. and S. and in the W. by two semicircular towers. The battlements run around the entire castle and date from the 16C. Interior: in the chapel 16C painting by Jan Metsys, salle des chevaliers (1620) with choir stalls, armoury. **Reformed parish church,** (St-Jean-Baptiste). From the 11C Grandson was the seat of a Benedictine priory subordinate to the Abbey of La Chaise-Dieu in the Auvergne from 1146. The monastery was dissolved in 1555 and disappeared,

only the church has survived. The present church, heavily influenced by Auvergne Romanesque, is essentially a 12C building on the foundations of a 10&11C church. The square choir and part of the transept were rebuilt in the 14C, a funerary chapel was built in the S. c.. 1500. The main façade was renewed in 1896. The church is cruciform in shape, the aisles have tunnel vaults and the nave has a round barrel vault supported by columns with capitals. The Romanesque columns have carved Romanesque capitals which are among the finest in Switzerland. Most notable are St. Michael subduing the Devil, the Madonna with St.Hugo of Cluny and the representation of Hell. In the transept a 15C carved late Gothic sedilia. In a niche in the S. transept Entombment, 1410–20 wall painting, in the S. chapel tomb of Prior Guillaume Bourgeois, d.1508. By the church former **Hôtel de Ville,** with town arms of 1779 on the triangular gable of the façade. 11 Rue Haute, **Maison du Bailli,** 18C house; flight of steps and wrought-iron balcony in front of the façade. Behind the church **fountain** with basin dating from 1637. **Menhir** on the road to Fiez. In the château *museum* with historical collection, furniture, weapons and a collection of cars. *Institut suisse d'armes anciennes* (institute of ancient weapons).

Grandvaux VD

10⬚F3

In the village square **vieille tour,** bell tower of the former church of St-Nicolas, dating from the 14C. **Maison Buttin de Loës,** an interesting 17&18C complex, now *museum of local history.* 16C **Maillardoz houses** with late Gothic windows.

Grandvillard FR

11⬚C3

St-Jacques, built 1935–7 to replace a 16C building. In the village, one of the most interesting in the area, a large number of 17C houses have survived. Above the settlement **maison du banneret,** built 1666 for Pierre de la Tinnaz, banneret of Mont-

Grandson: the five-towered Château is essentially 13C.

servant; the door in the two-storey façade has an inscription and a date above it. By the banneret house is the **house** of Lucien Raboud, built in 1641 for the Zürich family; door and windows have a Christ monogram. Notable **houses:** No. 31 (1631), No. 64 (1640), No. 68 (1662) and No. 94 (1636–430). NW of the village, at the place called La Daudaz, **Notre-Dame de Compassion chapel,** built in 1701.

Grange-Canal GE
16 ☐ E2

62 Route de Chêne, **La Grande Boissière,** now International School, built in the 18C for Gaspard Boissier. Neoclassical buiding, much altered in the 19C, outbuildings now used as flats.

Granges VS
17 ☐ E/F1

In the Middle Ages the village belonged to the Counts of Grange, one of the oldest families in the Valais, mentioned from the 11C. On the hills which dominate the town are the **ruins** of three castles, destroyed in

Grandson: important Romanesque sculpted capitals in the interior of the Reformed parish church.

1375 and 1417. At the SW end of the village **maison Tavelli,** a fortified building, built in the 15C and altered after 1747. Covered well in the courtyard.

Granges-p.-Marnand VD
11 ☐ B1

At the S. end of the village **Reformed parish church.** The present building, with nave and rectangular choir, was built on the foundations of three earlier buildings; this was established by excavations in 1970–2. The oldest, which pro-

Granges-p.-Marnand: Romano-Gothic parish church with 19C tower.

bably dates back to the 7C, was built over a Roman building. The church has Romanesque and Gothic sections from the 12&14C, the N. chapel is 15C; in the choir and on the N. wall of the nave remnants of 15C paintings. House No. 144, former 16C **monastery** with Gothic windows.

Gränichen AG
2☐D5

Reformed parish church. The rectangular single-aisled church without a choir was designed by Abraham Dünz and is considered a copybook example of an Aargau Protestant church. The tower has a clock gable with unorthodox curves. **Schloss Liebegg.** The former double Burg was replaced by a striking late Gothic house (1561&2) and a farm building (1617&18) with a neoclassical residential section (1817).

Granois VS
See SAVIESE   17☐E1

Greifensee ZH
3☐B5

Historic small town on the lake of the same name, founded in the 12C by the lords of Papperswil. **Reformed parish church.** Small early 14C high Gothic church with oriel-like pointed turrets. The rear wall with Gothic windows was part of the town wall. **Schloss.** The Burg built *c.* 1100 was largely destroyed in the Old Zürich War (1444) and rebuilt *c.* 1520. Seat of the

Landvogts of Zürich, including Salomon Landolt 1780 – 6, the model for the character in Gottfried Keller's Novelle 'Der Landvogt von Greifensee'. It is now owned by the canton and let to private individuals.

Grenchen SO
6☐E2

Catholic parish church of St.Eusebius, built in the neoclassical style 1806–12, probably by Niklaus Purtschert. The **Kapelle Allerheiligen** is a neo-Gothic building of 1682. **Parktheater,** brick building by Ernst Gisel 1949–55.

Greng-Dessous FR
6☐C4

On the Murten-Avenches cantonal road **château** and agricultural buildings, built in the late 18C to plans by Charles de Castella.

Grengiols VS
12☐D5

Catholic parish church of St. Peter, neo-Romanesque, built 1913 by the architect Adolf Gaudy. In the interior rococo high altar of 1760–70, in the N. aisle cross altar from the workshop of A.Sigristen, 18C.

Greppen LU
7☐F3

The **Catholic parish church of St. Wendelin** was built 1645–7 by Moritz Salebacher. The high altar is contemporary with the building and is an early work in the 'gnarled' style.

Grimentz VS
17☐F2

Eifisch valley village in excellent condition. The hamlet stretches along a narrow street lined with timber and stone houses and characteristic storehouses and barns. The **maison bourgeoisial** dates from 1550; collection of pewter mugs in the parish hall. By the church built in 1950&1 are three stone wine cellars.

Grimisuat VS

17☐E1

Catholic parish church of St-Pancrace, first mentioned 1193, rebuilt in the 17&18C, enlarged 1948. In the interior in the choir and the nave fragments of paintings (1626) and 18C baroque high altar. **Priest's house.** Former residence of the lords of Grimisuat. Square 12&13C building with 15C façades with step gables.

Grindelwald BE

12☐C/D2

The village burned down in 1892 and is now dominated by tourist buildings. **Reformed church of St.Maria.** Built in 1793 with tower of 1875. The church has a painted flat ceiling. By the church are the **priest's house** of 1785 and the *Heimatmuseum* (local history).

Grône VS

17☐E1

Parish house, a square building with a rectangular staircase tower built in 1565 on the site of the medieval château of the lords of Morestel.

Grono GR

19☐E1

Catholic parish church of San Clemente. Long nave with rectangular choir and adjacent sacristy. The present church goes back to 17C alterations. Romanesque tower. The **Santi Rocco e Sebastiano chapel** is on an exposed site in the S. Bernardino village square. Baro-

Greifensee: country town on the lake of the same name.

Grengiols: neo-Romanesque parish church with 18C interior.

que chapel with shallow tunnel vaulting and rib vaulting with stucco over the choir, which is the same width as the nave and separated by a choir screen set well into the nave, built 1615. **Torre Fiorenzana.** Five-storey 13C residence tower. **Cà rossa** (Pallazzo Togni). This stately patrician house, built 1721, now houses the Misox *cultural centre.*

Grono: parish church San Clemente with lavishly decorated baroque choir.

portant work of the building contractor Wilhelm Keller, who was responsible for numerous historicist buildings. **St.Gallus und Othmar chapel** in Oberroth. Built late 17C. The late Renaissance high altar contains figures from an earlier altar *c.* 1500.

Grub AR
4☐B3

Reformed church, rebuilt 1752 by Jakob Grubenmann, renovated 1943 and 1952. Font and body of pulpit 1691. **Priest's house,** built 1786 by Jakob Kriemler, double curved gable. **Haus Schläpfer,** now Rechsteiner (No. 50), dates from 1765, repainted in 1797 in Louis XVI style. Blockbau over a masonry ground floor with flight of steps and round-arched sandstone portal. Hamlet of Riemen, SW of Grub. This is one of the oldest settlements in this part of the parish, and was mentioned in 1325 as 'hof zen Riemen'.

Grossaffoltern BE
6☐E3

Reformed church of St.Stephan, built in late Gothic style in the early 16C. The end of the choir has three sides with tracery windows. Stained glass 1524&5. The **village square** is lined with greenish-grey and brownish painted half-timbered buildings.

Grüningen ZH
8☐B1

A country town on a hill, founded in the early 13C by the Freiherren of Regensburg; it has belonged to Zürich since 1408. **Reformed parish church.** A neoclassical single-aisled church built on to the Schloss in 1782&3, presumably designed by David Vogel. Burned down in the great fire of 1970; interior redesigned by Markus Dieterle (1973). **Schloss.** The early 13C Burg was the seat of the Zürich Landvogts from 1798. In the 19C parts of it were pulled down; the smaller building has since served as priest's house. Badly damaged in the fire of 1970. The Schloss contains a *historical collection.*

Grossdietwil LU
7☐C2

The **Gasthaus Löwen,** built in 1810, has gables on all four sides with semicircular wooden decorations and thus shows Bernese influence.

Grosswangen LU
7☐C2

Catholic parish church of St.Konrad, built 1863–6 as a neo-Gothic pillared basilica with nave and two aisles; it is an im-

Grüsch GR
9☐C3

Houses of the Salis and Ott families, in-

Grüningen: view of the medieval town with church and Schloss.

Grüsch: Haus zum Rosengarten, a 17C residence.

cluding the **Haus zum Rosengarten,** built *c.* 1650. It houses the *Talmuseum* with historical collection and temporary exhibitions.

Gruyères FR

11 □ C3

The counts of Gruyère were mentioned for the first time in the late 11C; from then until 1554 the family ruled the town and the large hinterland, partially in feudal dependence on Savoy. Graf Michel was in debt in 1554 and had to sell his rights, which were split between Fribourg (Gruyères) and Bern (Pays d'Enhaut). The small market town started to develop in the 13C and has retained its medieval appearance and a large part of its town wall. The fortifications in their present form are

largely 15C; in the S. are the rectangular partially 12C **tour-carrée Chupia-Bârba,** and the 15C barbican known as **le Belluard.** The **château** is on the top of the hill and existed as early as the 12C and was almost completely rebuilt after 1480; the round Savoy keep dates from the 13C. The château, from 1555 seat of the Fribourg Landvogts, was sold to the Bovy family in 1848 and bought back by the state of Fribourg in 1938. In the courtyard is a 14C chapel dedicated to St.John the Baptist, partially rebuilt after 1480, 15C stained glass. In the château salle de Bourgogne, and salon with landscapes by J.B.Corot and B.Menn. **St-Théodule,** founded in the 13C, façade tower 1680, nave 1860 and choir 1731. In the village fine group of 15–17C houses, in the main street so-called **maison de Chalamala,** the house of a 14C court jester of the Counts of Gruyère. The house was built in 1531 and has an elegant façade. In the middle of the road is a Calvary by Pierre Ardieu, 1705.

LA PART-DIEU **Former Carthusian monastery,** founded in 1307, rebuilt in the early 19C, dissolved 1848. The monastery buildings have almost completely disappeared; only the church and one spacious building have survived.

Gsteig BE

11 □ D5

The Gothic **Reformed church of St. Theodul** has a carved ceiling. Of the furnishings the late Gothic font and baroque pulpit of 1713 are notable. The **Gasthof Bären** built in 1756 is a Ständer- and Blockbau on a stone ground floor. Its façades are lavishly decorated with carved and painted friezes.

Guarda GR

9 □ F5

Ribbon village, formerly on the main road through the Lower Engadine. The village is in superb condition and has typical Engadine houses. House and stable were united under one roof in the 14C; the

Gruyères: Château on the hill, now a museum.

Guarda: one of many typical Engadine buildings.

Engadine house developed in the 17C: behind the round-arched doorway is the Sulèr, which serves partly as a passageway to the built-in barn, and partly as an anteroom to the house. From this one reaches the wood-panelled Stüva (living room in the façade corner), the Chadafö (kitchen with open fireplace) and the Chaminada (larder). Stüva and Chadafö and the Chambra (bedroom) above them make up the part of the house which can

be heated. The façades are decorated with sgraffito and wall paintings and also have oriels, window grilles and heraldic beasts. *Information* on the way into the village.

Gubel SG
See JONA   8 □ C1

Gubel ZG
                                            8 □ A2

On the summit of the Gubel is the **Mariahilf chapel,** built in memory of the battle which decided the first Kappel war (1531) in favour of the Catholics. On the ceiling is a painting of the battle renewed after a fire in 1780. By the chapel is the **Capuchin monastery** built on the occasion of the three hundredth anniversary of the battle in 1843-7.

Guggisberg BE
                                            11 □ E1

The **Reformed church of St. Mauritius** is a late Gothic single-aisled church with rectangular choir and tracery windows. The furnishings were partially renewed when the church was rebuilt in 1783 and 1823.

Gümlingen BE
                                            6 □ F4

Schloss, built 1735&6 for Postherr Beat Fischer of Reichenbach. The country house in Louis XV style was presumably designed by Albrecht Stürler, who took Schloss ▷ Hindelbank, designed by his father (Daniel) as a model. In the French garden the columns and fountains form a 'point de vue'. There is also an 18C hen house. Fischer also commissioned the **Hofgut** in 1741. The main façade and farm buildings are decorated with trompe l'oeil façade paintings. The Hofgut, known as the 'Trianon of Gümlingen' because of its fine garden, is the last building on the courtyard pattern in the Canton of Bern. S. of the Pourtalèsstrasse, in Muri, is the

Guggisberg: Reformed church St.Mauritius, a plain Gothic building.

Gurtnellen: St. Anna chapel on the old footpath to the Gotthard.

Mettlengut. This 17C country house was rebuilt *c.* 1780 by Karl Ahasver in neoclassical style.

Guntalingen ZH

See **WALTALINGEN** 3☐B2

Gurtnellen UR

13☐B1

In Wiler is the 17C **St.Anna chapel;** the old pack route over the Gotthard formerly passed through the porch.

Guttannen BE

12☐E2

Kristallmuseum. The private crystal collection of E.Rufibach includes cairngorms, pink fluorspar, adularia and amethysts from the Hasli valley.

Gwatt BE

12☐A2

Bellerive country house (Bonstettengut), built largely *c.* 1780 and in the early 19C to a neoclassical design. The Régence ceilings from the earlier building have survived.

H

Habsburg AG

2☐D/E4

Schloss. Only the W. half of the family castle of the Habsburg dynasty has survived; the keep dates from the time of foundation (1020), but the battlements were added in the last century. The plain palas is essentially 12&13C. The Habsburg now houses a popular restaurant.

Habsburg: 12&13C palas and keep (c. 1020) of the Schloss.

Hagenwil TG
See AMRISWIL

3☐F3

Häggenschwil SG

3☐F3

In the centre of the village is the **Catholic parish church of St. Notker,** built in 1728 by Johann Jakob Grubenmann, altered in 1780 by Ferdinand Beer. Baroque building, choir narrower than the nave with polygonal apse, choir apex tower. Ceiling paintings by Josef Anton Dick, rococo stucco by Joh. Jakob Rüest, neoclassical furnishings. Ruined **Burg Ramschwag,** W. of the village on the banks of the Sitter (11C or 12C), keep with Gothic twin windows and E. curtain wall with round-arched tower have survived. bNeuramschwag Burg site 3 km. up river; remains removed to build the church in Häggenschwil. In the **Waldburg,** a wooded area in the loop of the Sitter S. of Häggenschwil, is an early-historic refuge. Excavations are proceeding.

Häggenschwil: ruined Burg Ramschwag above the right bank of the Sitter.

and pulpit by Joseph Mosbrugger. In 1951 a late Gothic fresco cycle was revealed in the ground floor of the tower.

Hägglingen AG

2☐E5

Catholic parish church of St. Michael. Single-aisle church, choir narrower than the nave with polygonal apse built in 1739–42 by Franz Xaver Widerkehr, using parts of earlier buildings. Three altars

Haldenstein GR

9☐B4

Reformed church, built 1732. Single-aisle building without separate choir; polygonal apse. **Schloss Neu-Haldenstein,** built 1544–8, extended in the 18C. Rectangular complex with courtyard and short side wings. Coat-of-arms of the French ambassador who commissioned the building on the main portal. Above the Schloss is

Haldenstein: parts of the tower and of the palas have survived of the former Burg.

the 12C ruined **Burg Haldenstein,** remains of a tower and adjacent palas. Further N. above a steep rock wall is the **Lichtenstein ruin,** also 12C. Threestorey tower with adjacent palas. Below it, and presumably once part of it, is the cave fortress **Grottenstein,** with remains of the façade wall.

Hallau SH

2☐F2

This wine-growing community has a long tradition of extraordinary political freedom. The movement to give parity of status to the town and Land of Schaffhausen started there in 1831. **Reformed mountain church of St. Moritz.** This church on a hill above the village was built in 1491 as a simple hall church. The side aisle was added in 1598. Three decorative Gothic keystones in the late Gothic net vaulting: church patron St. Moritz, four soldiers of the Theban legion, coat-of-arms of Otto IV, Bishop of Konstanz. Entirely renovated in the late seventies. **Reformed village church of St. Moritz.** Built in

Halten: the former Zähringen residence tower now houses the Heimatmuseum.

1753 on the site of an earlier chapel. The top of the present tower was added in 1834. The wood panelling from the neighbouring **priest's house** is in the *Heimatmuseum* (local history) in the church schoolhouse.

Hallwil AG
See SEENGEN   2☐E5

Halten SO
7☐A2

Defences with ditches and later Zähringen keep, housing the *Heimatmuseum Wasseramt* (history of the water authority). The **storehouses** in the Burg ditch were brought here from various other places.

Hasle BE
7☐A3

Reformed church, built in 1678–80 as a baroque hall designed to emphasise the importance of preaching. The 15C frescos of the legend of St. Benedict are from an earlier building. The **wooden bridge** N. of Hasle over the Emme near Wintersei has a span of 190 ft. and is the longest bridge of its type in Switzerland. It was designed in 1839 by Joh. Daniel Osterrieth (neoclassical portals).

Hasle: 16C Heiligkreuz pilgrimage church, extended in the18C.

Hasle LU

7 ☐ D4

The Gothic **ossuary** of the parish church contains a painted Dance of Death.
HEILIGKREUZ, in the Middle Ages a mystics' settlement, became a place of pilgrimage after a hailstorm in 1588. The **church** built shortly after that was redesigned in the baroque style and extended in 1753 by Jakob Singer. Frescos have survived from the late Gothic period.

Haslen AI

4 ☐ A4

Catholic parish church of Maria Hilf. Built in 1901 by August Heidegger, neo-Romanesque. The miraculous image of Maria Hilf (*c.* 1650) is a copy of the Passau Madonna. There are baroque statues from the earlier building of 1649.

Haslen GL

8 ☐ E4

In Zusingen is the **Stüssihaus,** apparently the family home of the Zürich mayor Rudolf Stüssi.

Haudères,Les VS

See EVOLENE   17 ☐ F3

Hauptwil TG

3 ☐ F4

Oberes Schloss, at the foot of the Bischofsberg, surrounded by manufacturing and warehouse buildings. Built in 1664&5 for the Gonzenbach family of manufacturers and magistrates, old peoples' home since 1953. Early baroque country house design; stucco on the ground floor from the building period, rococo and neoclassical Steckborn and Winterthur stoves on the upper ground floor. Old **Schlosstaverne zum Trauben,** dated 1665. Three-storey half-timbered building with transverse gables. **Untere Walche or Farb,** now known as 'Spittel', half-timbered house with transverse gables, 1735, indigo dyeworks from 1787, rebuilt 1920&1.

Hausen ZH

See OSSINGEN   3 ☐ B2

Haute-Nendaz VS

See NENDAZ   17 ☐ D2

Hauterive NE

See POSIEUX   11 ☐ C1

Hauterive NE

6 ☐ B3

In the village square **former school house,** a 15–17C three-storey building on arches. **Maison Court,** 10 Rue de Chasses-Peines. Built 1577 for Siméon Péter; the façade of the first floor has gabled windows; next to it 16C house. **Maison Clottu,** 16 Rue de la Rebatte. Spacious 17&19C building.

Heerbrugg SG

See BALGACH   3 ☐ F3

Hefenhofen TG

3 ☐ F3

Haus zum Roten Öpfel, in Sonnenberg. Half-timbered building, built in 1811 by master carpenter Knup.

Heiden: Reformed church, a neoclassical building by Felix W.Kubly.

Herdern: the Schloss was extended to its present size in the 17C.

Heiden AR

4 ☐ B3

The village square was laid out as a rectangle with church and simple Biedermeier houses after the fire of 1838. The **Reformed church** was rebuilt by Felix Wilhelm Kubly in 1839&40 and rebuilt in 1937&8 with altered interior alignment after a fire. Late neoclassical rectangular building with columned portico and tower in the middle of the rear end. **Catholic church** (1965). The **Rathaus** opposite the Reformed church has the date 1840 on its façade. Built on seven axes with doors with archivolts in the façade axes, flight of steps on the three middle axes. **Kursaal,** 1956–7 by Otto Glaus.

Heiligkreuz LU

See Hasle 7 ☐ C/D4

Heimiswil BE

7 ☐ A3

Village centre with fine farmhouses. **Reformed church of St.Margaretha.** Baroque hall designed to emphasise the importance of preaching, built 1703&4 by Samuel Jenner. The contemporary **priest's house** has a saddleback roof.

Hemberg SG

3 ☐ E5

Mountain village in a picturesque situation. **Catholic parish church of St. Johannes der Täufer und Andreas,** founded 1214, nave and choir rebuilt 1781–2 under Ferdinand Beer. Lower parts of tower medieval, onion dome and lantern baroque. **Reformed church,** built 1779 by Johann Jakob Haltiner. Single-aisled building with façade tower, interior stucco and Louis XVI gallery. In Schwanzbrugg **house,** dated 1776, gable façade with rococo paintings.

Hemmental SH

3 ☐ A1

Reformed parish church. Single-aisle church with ridge turret. The oldest parts of the building are presumed to be 12C; rebuilt 1723.

Henau SG

3 ☐ E4

Catholic parish church of Mariä Himmelfahrt. Nave rebuilt 1875 by Karl Reichlin. The old choir tower (now baptismal chapel) is considered the finest Gothic tower in St.Gallen.

Henggart ZH

3 ☐ B3

Reformed parish church. 1820 neoclassical single-aisle church (Johann Volkart) with two-tier ridge turret.

Herisau: Haus Wetter, restored in 1980.

Herisau: typical panelled wooden houses in the Schmiedgasse.

Herdern TG

3☐C/D2

Schloss. The building is in four sections; it was originally the seat of the Bettler of Herdern, and its (keep) dates from the 13C. Living quarters 1601&2, altered in the late 17C to designs by Caspar Mosbrugger.

Hérémence VS

17☐E2

Catholic parish church, 1967–70 concrete building by the architect Otto Förderer.

The Rosenburg W. of Herisau was destroyed in the Appenzell wars.

PRALONG **St-Barthélemy chapel,** founded 1604; the present timber building dates from 1929; late Gothic altar. **Grande-Dixence dam wall.**

Hergiswald LU
See KRIENS 7☐E3

Herisau AR
3☐F5

Principal town of the canton Appenzell-Ausserrhoden. First mentioned in 837 as subject to the monastery of St. Gallen as part of the Mark Gossau, church founded and market rights granted in the 10C. Under the Helvetic Republic district capital of the canton Säntis, from 1876 seat of the Kantonsrat and of government (for history of the two Appenzells see Appenzell). The textile trade became increasingly important from the 15&16C onwards.

The layout of the village square dates back to the time before the fire of 1559. The town developed from this central square along the four approach roads. **Reformed Church** E. of the square. Rebuilt 1516–20 by Lorenz Reder in late Gothic style, tower 14C, new belfry and neo-Gothic spire (1741) by Johannes Grubenmann. On the N. side of the nave late Gothic side chapel, the so-called 'Schwätzchörli', now baptismal chapel. In the narrower choir

late Gothic net vaulting and rococo stucco by Andreas Mosbrugger (1782). Pulpit and font in stucco marble, also by Mosbrugger. The **former priest's house** (2 Oberdorfstrasse) S. of the church was rebuilt by Jakob Mittelholzer in 1606 after the village fire. Corner oriel and stucco on façade 1926. Adjacent **former Rathaus** (No. 2A) pulled down 1826, rebuilt 1827&8 by Johannes Alder, designed by Stadler. Stucco and round arch on the ground floor 1926, *Historisches Museum* since 1946. The **former arsenal** (13 Poststrasse) was built 1836–8 by Joh. Konrad Bischofberger and designed by Felix Wilhelm Kubly in Florentine Renaissance style. **Former Realschulhaus** (secondary school, 12 Poststrasse), built 1867&8 by Daniel Oertle, late neoclassical. The **parish house** (16 Poststrasse) is in the same style, built 1876–8 by Johann Jakob Schäfer. **Cantonal Bank and administrative building** (5 Oberdorstrasse), built 1912–14 by Bollert and Herter to a neobaroque design influenced by the Jugendstil. **Walsersches Doppelhaus** (1/2 Platz), 1779, N. of the square. Transverse gable with stucco relief (allegories of War and Peace), two rococo portals. **Haus zur Rose** (6 Platz) on the W. side of the square, built 1737 by Jakob Grubenmann, interior Régence stucco. **Haus Wetter** (12 Platz), also 1737 by Grubenmann. Interior Régence stucco with allegorical representations, in the vestibule on the third floor allegory of Life and Death. **Haus zum Tannenbaum** (1 Oberdorfstrasse), 1780. S. of the church in the fruit market, Louis XVI portal. **Alte Bleiche** (93 Oberdorfstrasse), 1666 by Debus Frischknecht. Shingle Blockbau with gable on the street side. The **Schlösschen Steinegg** 1778 on the Alte Landstrasse is a half-timbered building with a neoclassical veranda added *c.*1913.
NW of Herisau is the hamlet of **Schwänberg,** the oldest inhabited area in the town. So-called **Rathaus, (No. 1329)** *c.* 1627, half-timbered. The name is presumed to come from an earlier building. **Bürgerhaus** (No. 1328), stone building from the 1st half of the 17C. Near Schwänberg a **covered wooden bridge** over the Wissenbach, built in 1782 by

Johann Knellwolf. Second **wooden bridge** over the Urnäsch by Hans Ulrich Grubenmann, 1780. The same architect built the **wooden bridge** over the Herisau Tobel. Ruined **Burg Rosenberg** to the N., **Rosenburg** or Ramsenberg to the W. and **Urstein** E. of Herisau, all 13&14C

Hermance GE
16☐F1

Town and port were founded in 1247 by Aimon de Faucigny and annexed to the canton of Geneva in 1815. The former fortified village grew into a formally designed lower town and the upper town dominated by the Schloss, of which the round **keep,** built 1337–9, has survived. **Catholic church of St-Georges,** founded in the 13C, façade tower and nave 1679. **Ste-Catherine chapel** (1471) N. of the church and joined to it by a double arch. Several 15&16C houses indicate the prosperity of that period. By the church **maison Mestral,** tower and foundations 15C, the 16C former **Auberge de la Couronne.**

Hermetschwil-Staffeln AG
2☐F5

Former Benedictine convent. The complex was built in the early 17C on the site of a 12C building. The monastery church, now **Catholic parish church St.Martin,** was built 1603-5 in the Gothic style with lay nave and nuns' choir; the early baroque high altar (1657–9) is by Gregor Allhelg. The **convent building** (the convent was dissolved in 1841) of 1624–5 is now used as a reformatory. Lavish interior decoration.

Herrliberg ZH
8☐B1

Landhaus Schipf. Imposing baroque building on Lake Zürich with 1617 residential building and 1732&3 ballroom building; very lavish 16–19C interior. The estate is in a well-known vineyard and may

1718&19 by Johann Pfeiffer. The dome paintings are the work of Johan Adam Wieland and Francesco Antonio Giorgioli.

Herzogenbuchsee BE
7☐A2

Reformed church of St.Petrus, built in 1728 by Johann Jakob Dünz, incorporating Gothic parts. The building is above a Roman villa. The decoration includes 20 coats-of-arms (1728&9) and a Biedermeier wooden pulpit. The former **corn exchange** of 1581&2 is a three-storey rubble building with saddleback roof and roof lights. *Ortsmuseum* (local museum) in the Gasthaus zum Kreuz with lake village finds from Lake Burgäschi.

Herzwil BE
See **KÖNIZ**
6☐E4

Hildisrieden LU
7☐E2

Catholic parish church of St.Maria, built 1901-3 by August Hardegger in neo-Gothic style.

Hilfikon AG
2☐E5

Schloss. Rectangular Schloss largely rebuilt 1650 – 60 with medieval keep; privately owned. **Schloss chapel.** Built 1750; rococo interior with altar by Johann Baptist Babel and ceiling paintings by Franz Anton Rebsamen.

Hilterfingen BE
12☐A1/2

Reformed church of St.Andreas. Built 1727&1888. The late Gothic tower and some of the furnishings have survived from an earlier building, including the 1476 stained glass, reminiscent of that in the Münster in Bern. **Schloss Hünegg,** built 1863 in the style of French Renaissance châteaux. It is organised as a *museum of*

Hermance: nave and tower of St-Georges, rebuilt 1697.

Herznach: parish church of St.Nikolaus with oval choir added 1718&19.

be visited in the summer for public concerts.

Herznach AG
2☐C/D4

Catholic parish church of St.Nikolaus. This church on a hill forms, with its ossuary and priest's house, a walled church precinct; the buildings date from 3 periods: the tower with steep saddleback roof is late Gothic, the nave with stucco by Giovanni Giacomo Neurone is dated 1691&2, and the domed oval choir was added in domestic life in the neo-Renaissance and Jugendstil periods. The *Martin Lauterburg foundation*, with works by this artist, is also housed here.

Hindelbank BE

6 ☐ F3

Reformed Church, rebuilt 1911&12 by Karl Indermühle. Notable for the 1751 tombs of priest's wife Langhans and mayor Hieronymus of Erlach by Johann August Nahl. Hieronymus commissioned **Schloss Hindelbank,** built 1722 – 5, a baroque country seat on a horseshoe plan, similar to Schloss Thunstetten, also built for Hieronymus. Hindelbank was built under Daniel Stürler to designs by the French architect J.Abeille and shows the transition from Louis XVI to the Régence. Interiors with lavish wall decoration, including trompe l'oeil painting in the ballroom, (women's prison since 1896).

Hinterrhein GR

13 ☐ E/F3

Alte 'Landbrugg' by Peter Zurr, 1692. Packhorse bridge to the St.Bernard pass, rebuilt 1935.

Hinwil ZH

8 ☐ C1

Reformed parish church. 1786–87 baroque church by Franz Schmid on the foundations of a Romanesque building; the tower is 15C; rococo stucco in the interior.

Hitzkirch LU

7 ☐ E1

The early baroque St.Pankratius was built 1679–80 by the dilettante builder-chaplain Jeremias Schmid. **Former Commandery of the Teutonic Order,** founded 1236, built 1744ff. by Giovanni Gaspare Bagnato. The complex is influenced by baroque monastery and Schloss architecture. In the ballroom of the

Hochdorf: the Catholic church, an example of the so-called Singer-Purtschert scheme.

Hohenrain: former commandery of the Knights of the Order of St.John with 14C 'Roten' tower.

S. section Régence stucco, 1745. *Baldeggersee-Museum* in the seminary (opened on request).
RICHENSEE **Ruined Richensee tower.** The keep built in the 11C of megalithic blocks formed the centre of the town founded by the Kyburgs in 1237 and destroyed in 1386.

Hochdorf LU

7 ☐ E2

The **Catholic church of St.Martin** was rebuilt by Jakob Singer in 1757&8 incorporating the tower of an earlier building. The baroque church, **ossuary** and **priest's house** of 1534 form an impressive group of buildings.

Hofen SH

3□B1

So-called **Holländerhaus.** House built 1687 for Tobias Holländer, mayor of Schaffhausen. Relief coat-of-arms above the main portal. Interesting outbuildings: barracks for the bodyguard, bath house.

Hofstetten SO

1□F4

The **St. Johannes chapel** with 13&14C choir has a late Gothic fresco cycle.

Hofstetten ZH

3□C4

So-called **Doktorhaus.** 1708 half-timbered building with three-storey oriel tower; paintings on the façade and in the interior.

Hofwil BE

See MÜNCHENBUCHSEE   6□E3

Hohenrain LU

7□E2

Fomer Commandery of the Knights of St. John. The oldest parts of this castle of the Order founded c. 1180 date back to the early 14C; the 'Roten' keep has in its timber upper storey a Gothic panelled room with 15C vaulted beam ceiling. The present baroque church of 1694 is a triconchate building, unlike the earlier church, which had a rectangular choir.

Hohentannen TG

3□E/F3

Schloss Oettlishausen, NW of the village. Founded by the 'fratres de

Hombrechtikon: Haus Egli in Lautikon, a picturesque 17C half-timbered building.

otilehusen', mentioned in 1176. A new residential section was added to the 12&13C keep c. 1590; later much altered. **St. Michael Schloss chapel,** 12&13C Romanesque building. Frescos in the sanctuary by Hans Haggenberg, c. 1500, wooden ceiling also c. 1500.

Hohle Gasse SZ

See KÜSSNACHT   7□F3

Holderbank SO

2□A5

Alt-Bechburg ruin, on a rocky ridge S. of the village. Family seat of the Counts and Freiherren of Bechburg and Falkenstein (11&12C); like Neu-Falkenstein it was a double Burg.

Hombrechtikon ZH

8□B/C1

Reformed parish church. A rococo church built by Jakob Grubenmann in 1758&9; the tower was part of a late Gothic church. Outstanding **rural houses and farmhouses** in various outer hamlets, especially in SCHIRMENSEE (former Gasthaus 'Rössli'), FELDBACH (late Gothic-baroque houses of the Bühler family), LÜTZELSEE (**Menzi** house, imposing half-timbered building c. 1680),

LAUTIKON (**Egli** house, painted half-timbered house, 1665&6) and LANGENRIED (**Dändliker** house, 1683).

Homburg TG
3 ☐ D2

Catholic parish church of St. Peter.
Rebuilt 1754, neoclassical restoration after a fire in 1784.

KLINGENBERG **Moated Schloss** between Homburg and Wigoltingen. The old 13&14C building was pulled down in 1859, while the lower Schloss, dating back to a 1446 complex, was largely rebuilt in the 18C. The Schloss chapel, partially rebuilt in 1695 and 1772, is in the W. section of the Schloss. Oratory cut into the rock nearby.

Honau LU
7 ☐ F2

St. Eligius chapel, built 1647. Three Renaissance altars from the studio of Niklaus Geisler.

Horgen ZH
8 ☐ A1

Reformed parish church. The rococo church built by Jakob Haltiner (1780–2) is almost oval in ground plan. The interior has a mirror vault. The stucco is the work of Andreas Mosbrugger. The **priest's house** is an early neoclassical building by Johann Meyer (1784&5). **Landhaus Bocken.** 1675 country estate. It was the scene of bloody battles in 1804 between peasants in revolt and the Zürich forces of law and order. ('Bocken war').

Horn TG
4 ☐ A2

Enclave in the canton St.Gallen. **Catholic church of St.Franz Xaver.** Neo-Gothic building with vernacular elements by Albert Rimli, 1910–11.

Hornussen AG
2 ☐ C/D4

Houses. Post-Gothic gabled houses, including the **former Säckingen Amtshaus** of 1595.

Hospental UR
13 ☐ A3

Catholic church of Mariä Himmelfahrt, built 1705-11 by Bartholomäus Schmid. The baroque building has exterior blind arches, like the same architect's parish church in Andermatt. The same articulation is seen in the **prebendary's house** with **St.Karl chapel** of 1719, also by Schmid. The **tower,** built in the 13C for the Hospental family, first mentioned in records about the same time, dominates the village and is a reminder of the importance of the valley as a link in the central alpine E.-W. communications system.

Hundwil AR
3 ☐ F5

Since the late 16C Hundwil has alternated with Trogen as the seat of the Ausserrhoden Landesgemeinde. Historic centre is the Dorfplatz, between the church and the Gasthaus zur Krone. Building in the 17&18C shifted emphasis to the Landsgemeindeplatz W. of the church. The **Reformed church** is a 13C late Romanesque building, altered in 1750 by Hans Ulrich and Jakob Grubenmann. The tower was rebuilt in 1894 by the Oertly brothers to August Hardegger's design. In the jamb of the Romanesque window behind the pulpit is the oldest surviving painting in the canton: St. Catharine and a bishop saint, c. 1400. **Priest's house and former Rathaus** (No. 12) NW of the church, built 1607&8, rebuilt in late baroque style in the 18C. Panelling and colossal articulation on the façade, c. 1840. In the former Ratsstube 17C councillors' arms. **Gasthaus zur Krone** (No. 7), built 1599 by Master Debus Bohl. Pilastered façade (probably 1828). The Stube is painted in late rococo style, dated 1815. **Heidenhaus im Tobel** (No. 72), dated 1568, shallow saddleback-roofed building with roof side to the street, barn dated 1614. **Concrete bridge** over the Hundwil Tobel, built 1925 to design by engineer Ritter.

Hünenberg ZG

7□F2

The Catholic church St. Wolfgang, N. of Hünenberg, a former pilgrimage church, was built 1473–5 by Hans Felder the Elder. Late Gothic tabernacle in the choir, probably by Ulrich Rosenstain of Lachen. In the present parish **Hünenburg ruin,** the family seat of the Knights of Hünenburg, destroyed in 1386.

Hüswil LU

See Zell   7□B/C2

Hüttikon ZH

2□F4

Only surviving house in the canton of Zürich with **straw thatch** (1652).

Huttwil BE

7□B3

The village grew into a town in the 13C and burned down in 1834. Its unified appearance is due to the rebuilding of church and houses in the neoclassical style. *Heimatmuseum* (local history) in the old Nyffel school house, SE of the town.

Hüttwilen TG

3□C2

Catholic church of St. Franziskus. Rebuilt 1964&5 by Justus Dahinden.

Horgen: 1780–2 Reformed parish church on an unorthodox ground plan.

Frescos transferred from the earlier (mid-15C) building and crucifix from the Charterhouse of Ittingen, mid-17C. In Stutheien remains of a **Roman villa;** finds on show in the Historical Museum in Frauenfeld.

Kalchrain **Former Cistercian convent,** training institution since 1848. Completely rebuilt 1703–23 by Johann Mosbrugger the Elder and Younger and Michael Rueff, designed by Caspar Mosbrugger. Strictly symmetrical building; the original interior design has been spoiled by unthinking restoration.

Nussbaumen, NW of Hüttwilen. The **Reformed church** has frescos of the Passion, *c.* 1325.

Hutzikon ZH

See Turbenthal   3□C4

IJ

Igels GR
13 □ E2

Catholic parish church of Mariä Himmelfahrt. Gothic single-aisle church with polygonal apse (1504), late Gothic winged altar *c.* 1520. SW of the village chapel of **St.Sebastian.** Rebuilt 1494; three *c.* 1741 carved altars, choir altar based on a late Gothic carved altar by Ivo Strigel, 1506.

Igis-Landquart GR
9 □ B3

Reformed Church in Igis. Late Gothic single-aisle church with wall paintings from the first half of the 15C. **Schloss Marschlins.** Only moated Burg in Grisons with corner towers, built mid 13C. The present building dates mainly from the 17C.

Ilanz GR
13 □ F1

This town on the upper Rhine developed from a former estate of the Viktoriden family. Of the older town the **Rotes Tor** (1715 – 17, with curved gable) and the **Obertor,** rebuilt after a fire in 1513, have survived; upper storey with hipped roof added in 1717. On the town side the arms of the founder, Schmid von Grüneck, and of the Cantons of Zürich and Bern, which assisted in the extension of the town walls in 1715-17. On the outside the arms of the city of Ilanz and the three Bünde. **Reformed parish church of St. Margarethen.** The late Gothic building with net vaulting was rebuilt after the fire of 1483; presumably school of Steffan Klain. Vault painting in the nave, 1518. A former keep and defensive tower has served as bell tower since 1438. **Monastery of St. Joseph,** rebuilt by W.Moser, 1969.

Igels: late Gothic triptych from a Swabian studio in the Catholic church.

Casa Gronda, built 1677. Cubic building with staircase tower. In the Casa Carniec **volkskundliches Museum** (ethnography). Above the road to the Lugnez **St. Martin.** Adjacent to the trapezoid hall with integral NW tower an antechoir with rectangular sanctuary and two E. facing side chapels attached to this. Built *c.* 1000 and much Altered until 1662. 14C wall paintings on the tower and in the interior.

Illens FR
11 □ C1

N. of the village on the left bank of the Sarine, ruins of the **château of Illens.** This important fortress, built at the beginning of the 13C, was subject along with ARCONCIEL to the Lords of Glâne; the château of Arcenciel no longer exists; i stood on the right bank of the Sarine. The former château of Illens was destroyed i 1425; the remains of a rectangular buildin; and adjacent staircase tower built in th 15C by the de la Baume family hav survived.

Igis: Schloss Marschlins is a square moated castle with inner courtyard.

Ilanz: late Gothic St. Martin with interior paintings.

Ilanz: Obertor, decorated with inscribed tablets and coats-of-arms.

Illens: remains of the keep and staircase tower of the former Schloss.

Imfeld VS
See BINN   12 □ D5

Indemini TI
                                            19 □ C3

Interestingly sited village at a height of 3,051 ft. with numerous traditional houses with wooden galleries.

Inden VS
                                            12 □ A5

Catholic parish church of la Vierge-du-Bon-Conseil, 1767 late baroque building. Rococo altar and furnishings. **St-**

Antoine-l'Ermite chapel, late medieval building, partially rebuilt in 1670. 1670 baroque altar and 16C statue of St.Antony. Near the hamlet of Rumeling stone **bridge** over the Dala, built in 1539 by Ulrich Ruffiner and restored in the 18C.

Ingenbohl SZ

8□B4

Catholic parish church of St. Leonhard. Essentially early baroque building of 1656–61. Vaulted 1788 with ceiling paintings by Josef Ignaz Weiss. Furnishings neoclassical.

Ins BE

K6□C4

In the Schaltenrain NE of the village are several **grave mounds** from the Hallstatt period (Old Iron Age). Finds suggest that the dead were buried with their carriages and lavish gold gifts, for which reason the graves are also called 'princes' graves'. Contact between Greeks and Celts via the colony of Marseille led to an early Celtic feudal culture. **Reformed church of St. Maria.** Built early 16C in late Gothic style. The nave has a coffered ceiling.

Interlaken BE

12□B2

19C hotels dominate the town. The **former Augustinian priory,** first mentioned 1133, was used as the Landvogt's seat after the Reformation. The high Gothic choir of the monastery church of St.Mary, the E. walk of the 1445 cloister and the chapterhouse have survived of the original buildings. The **Landvogteischloss** next to them is a horseshoe-shaped baroque building dating from 1748 and designed by Albrecht Stürler.

Intragna TI

19□B2

Catholic parish church of San Got-

tardo, built 1722 – 38, has the highest church tower in Ticino (213 ft.), built in 1765. High altar with rococo retable at the end of the choir; trompe l'oeil marble balustrade, 1764.

GOLINO Pretty village in excellent state of conservation. **Catholic parish church of San Giorgio,** baroque building with a single aisle and rectangular choir; four fine 18C altars.

VERDASIO Picturesque village with fine group of buildings. **Catholic parish church of Santi Giacomo e Cristoforo,** rebuilt in the 19C. Next to it the 17C **casa Tosetti**.

Inwil LU

7□F2

The **Catholic parish church of St.Peter und Paul,** built 1777&8 by Jakob Singer, extended in 1923, is one of the numerous examples of the Singer-Purtschert scheme (▷ Ruswil). S. of the road to Gisikon is the **St.Katharina chapel,** built in 1659; its predecessor belonged to the convent founded by the Lords of Eschenbach. Further S. by the Rotbach are traces of the outer Burg and fortifications of **Eschenbach.** The little town was probably founded in the 13C and was destroyed by the Austrians in 1309 as a result of the participation of Walter IV of Eschenbach at the regicide at Windisch.

Irgenhausen ZH
See PFÄFFIKON

3□C5

Isérables VS

17□D2

Below the village in the Combe de Teure group of **granaries,** typical wooden buildings for storing sheaves and threshing grain.

Isle,L' VD

10□D2

Château, built in 1696 for Charles de Chandieu, now a school and parish house.

Fine rectangular building, inspired by French models, with two wings surrounding the main courtyard. The main façade is defined by a projection at either end and has a triangular gable with the arms of the owners; behind is a garden with fountains dating from 1710. **Reformed parish church,** built 1732&3. Late Gothic round-arched portal of a church which no longer exists under the façade tower.

Islikon TG
See GACHNANG   3☐C3

Isola GR
See STAMPA   14☐C3

Itingen BL
                                      2☐B4

T-shaped village with 16–19C **domestic and farm buildings** with their roof edges to the street.

Ittigen BE
See BOLLIGEN   6☐F4

Ittingen TG
See UESSLINGEN   3☐C3

Jaun FR
                                      11☐D3

The Jaun territory was founded in the 13C by the von Korbers (Corbières) family. The château, which survives only in **ruins,** was destroyed in 1407. Below the road is the **former church,** first mentioned 1228. The tower, presumably medieval, was over the choir; the nave dates from 1808–11.

Jegenstorf BE
                                      6☐F3

The **Reformed church of St.Maria,** an early 16C late Gothic building. Much glass has surviving from the 16–18C. **Schloss.** In the 1720s Albrecht Friedrich von Erlach had the medieval Burg rebuilt as a baroque country seat. The square building with corner pavilions and central keep

Jegenstorf: the core of this baroque Schloss is medieval.

Jenaz: stellar vaulting (1483) in the choir of the Reformed church.

houses a *Museum für Wohnkultur des Alten Bern* (Bernese domestic culture).

Jenaz GR
                                      9☐C3

Typical Prättigau houses, including **Haus**

Valär in the Platz, built 1728. **Reformed church.** Choir with stellar vaulting, 1483, nave rebuilt 1485. **Schlössli** in the Kirchweg, built 1822.

Jerisberghof BE
6☐D4

Bauernmuseum Althus, 1 km. S. of Gurbrü. The contents of the furnished farmhouse include implements for the treatment of hemp, flax and wool, milk and cereals and also for the cultivation of arable land.

Jetschwil FR
See DÜDINGEN   6☐D5

Jona SG
8☐C1

Catholic parish church of Mariä Himmelfahrt und St. Valentinus. Rebuilt 1488–90, late Gothic choir and lower part of the tower have survived. In 1852 nave rebuilt and tower raised by Augustin Helbling, new tower top 1925. 1936 extension to the W. by Josef Steiner. **Villa Grünfels** with French garden, built on the edge of Rapperswil in 1822 in neoclassical style by Jakob and Rudolf Braendlin. **Catholic church of St. Martin** in Busskirch, SW of Jona. Rebuilt 1482–4, extended 1848, tower raised 1853. Refurbished in Biedermeier style with late Gothic choir and tower.WURMSBACH On the lake, SE of Jona, **Cistercian convent of Mariazell,** founded 1259. *Monastery church:* rebuilt *c.* 1600, tower raised 1767 by Johannes Grubenmann. *Convent buildings:* refectory 1578, guesthouse 1588, new abbess's section and cloister *c.* 1612. **St. Dionys chapel,** former Wurmsbach parish church. Mentioned 1217, renewed in the 15C, reconsecrated 1493. Late Gothic wall paintings and remains of rococo wall paintings.

The **Haus zum Tiefen Graben** in GUBEL, with symmetrical lake-side gardens, dates from 1802. Biedermeier wall paintings in the salon. S. of Wagen, in SALET, the foundations of a Roman villa were discovered; numerous individual finds in the Historisches Museum in St. Gallen. Other traces of Roman settlements were found in KEMPRATEN; remains of a Roman vicus with narrow single-roomed or multi-roomed houses, one suggesting an owner of some status. Ceramic finds and coins.

Jonen AG
7☐F1

Jonental pilgrimage chapel. Built 1734–6 by Hans Georg Urban, cruciform church with barrel vaulting, transepts and choir. The miraculous image is a 16C late Gothic statue of Mary.

Jonschwil SG
3☐E4

In Schwarzenbach, N. of Jonschwil, **Schloss Schwarzenbach.** Mentioned 1221, from 1483 seat of the Obervogts of the Monastery of St. Gallen, renovated 1960. **Gasthaus Rössli.** Strickbau, built 1732 over a medieval cellar, neoclassical wall painting in the Wirtsstube.

Jussy GE
16☐F2

Reformed Church (Ste-Marie-Madeleine). Founded in the 9&10C, extended in the 11&12C and in the 16C, tower 1726. Choir stalls with arms of Cardinal de Brogny, dating from the 15C. In the vineyard **château du Crest,** presumed built in the 13C, destroyed 1590. The present building, with the exception of the 1880 square keep, was built by Agrippa d'Aubigné in 1621.

Kaiseraugst AG

2☐A3

Old Catholic parish church of St. Gallus. In 1960–1 a cycle of late Gothic paintings with scenes from the Life of Mary and the life of St. Gallus was discovered in the rectangular Gothic choir of the otherwise baroque single-aisled church. It must date from *c.* 1460 and is ascribed to the school of Konrad Witz. The church is successor to a larger early Christian apsidal church. The walls of the 4C or 5C *baptistery* of the latter building were revealed in 1964&5. **Roman citadel wall.** The Castrum Rauracense dates from the year 300 and was the successor settlement to the town of Augusta Rauracorum (▷ Augst). A large section of the trapezoid curtain wall has been revealed.

Kaiseraugst: lid of a Roman sarcophagus in the church.

Kaiserstuhl AG

2☐F3

This little bridge town on the Rhine, founded in the mid 13C is built on a striking triangular plan and has almost completely retained its medieval character, although there are a very few baroque and rococo buildings. **Old Town and defences.** The Hauptgasse runs quite steeply direct to the Rhine bridge from the S. point of the fortified triangle, the **Obere Turm,,** which the Freiherren von Kaiserstuhl had built even before the town was founded; the bridgehead on the German bank is Schloss Röteln. The town wall has survived in part, also the Storchenturm in the W. and a fragment of the Wörndli tower in the E. **Catholic parish church of St. Katharina.** Gothic single-aisle church with vaulted choir tower, extended in 1609 and refurbished in baroque style in 1755. The furnishings include a carved rococo pulpit by Franz Ludwig Wind (1756). **Haus zur Linde.** 1764

Kaiserstuhl: small medieval town on the Rhine.

country house with rococo coat-of-arms cartouche. **Former Amtshaus of the Monastery of St. Blasien.** Large late Gothic building with double step gable (1562 – 4). **Mayenfisch- or Marschallhaus.** built in 1764 as a tripartite 'hôtel' in the French style for Marschall Johann Jakob Mayenfisch. **Nepomuk-Statue** on the bridge by Franz Ludwig Wind (1752).

Kalchrain TG

See H**ÜTTWILEN** 3☐C2

Kaltbrunn QG

8☐D1

Catholic parish church of St. Georg, built 1820&1 by Heinrich Ladner. Single-aisled church with choir apex tower, interior double gallery. On the **Schlossbüchel,** on the N. outskirts of the Gaster wood, are traces of a prehistoric settlement.

Kandergrund BE

12☐A3

The **Felsenburg ruin** diagonally above the Blausee-Mitholz station is a presumably 12C combination of keep and palas.

Kandersteg BE

12☐A4

The **Rüedihaus,** built in 1753, a Blockbau with overhanging saddleback roof, is decorated with carved friezes and painting on the outside.

Kappel am Albis ZH

8☐A1

Former Cistercian abbey. The monastery complex built in the 13&14C was badly damaged in the Old Zürich War (1443), by a fire in 1493 and in the 1529–31 religious wars. The buildings around the church were altered in the 16, 17&19C and finally used as an old peoples' home; after a referendum among the members of the Reformed denomination entitled to vote in the Canton, Kappel has now been extended as a 'house of quiet and reflection'. The former **monastery church of St. Maria** with its cruciform ground plan is one of the most important Gothic church buildings in Switzerland. The present building is thought to date from between 1250 and 1310; the straight-ended choir is possibly a little older. There are two side chapels on each side of the choir. In the choir itself is a sedilia let into the wall,

Kappel: former Cistercian abbey, a 12C foundation.

lavishly decorated early Gothic masonry. The *stained glass* in the windows of the N. wall of the nave is of outstanding quality; they are all that remains of a cycle which once included all the windows in the church. Five of the six windows are early 14C, the sixth is the work of Johann Martin Usteri and Franz Hegi and dates from the 19C. In the choir is Max Hunziker's 1964 window 'Christ the Saviour of the World'. In the side chapels, the choir and the nave 14C wall paintings have been discovered. **Näfenhäuser.** Former dairy of the monastery; 16C half-timbered building.

Kefikon TG

See Gachnang

3☐C3

Kehrsatz BE

6☐F4

Lohn. Country house built 1780-3 by Karl Ahasver von Sinner for Beat Emanuel Tscharner. The neoclassical design is at its most striking in the façade: four colossal Ionic pilasters under a broken gable articulate the central projection. The park is partly English, partly French (owned by the Confederation, parts open to the public).

Kehrsiten NW

7☐F4

Maria in Linden Chapel, built 1758 by Johann Anton Singer on the site of a 17C building; rebuilt 1799-1801.

Kappel: early Gothic sedilia in the former monastery church of St.Maria.

Kerns: so-called Steinhaus with richly profiled late Gothic windows and door frame.

Kilchberg: Reformed church, a fine example of neo-Gothic use of space.

Kempraten SG
See J<small>ONA</small>   8 □ C1

Kerns OW
7 □ E5

Catholic parish church of St.Gallus. The Jakob Singer baroque building was restored after a fire in 1813. The **Steinhaus,** built in the first half of the 16C, is considered to be one of the oldest stone residential buildings in the canton. The house was probably originally occupied by the Obwalden statesman Andreas zum Hofen. The windows have lavishly carved surrounds. NE of Kerns, in Wisserlen, near a former place of execution, is the **St.Katharina chapel** built in 1641 and dedicated to the patron saint of the gallows. The vaulting in the nave and choir rests on consoles supported by putti. N. of Kerns, in Siebeneich, is the **chapel of the 'blutweinenden Muttergottes von Pocs',** (weeping Madonna of Pocs) built 1729 and extended 1745.

Kerzers FR
6 □ D4

Reformed church, single-aisled building with polygonal apse, bell tower in the S. In the late Gothic choir 16–18C wall paintings and glass and 1684 gravestone.

Kiesen BE
11 □ F1

The *Milchwirtschafliche Museum* (dairy museum) in Bernstrasse illustrates cheese manufacture by means of apparatus, pictures and an audio-visual presentation.

Kilchberg BL
2 □ B4

Rudolf Zwilchenbart, who became prosperous in England, endowed the **Reformed parish church of St.Martin** in memory of his father, who is buried here, in 1866. The neo-Gothic church was designed by Paul Reber.

Kippel VS

12□B5

Kippel, in the Lötschen valley, is one of the most beautiful villages in the Valais. **Catholic parish church of St.Martin,** a single-aisled building with polygonal choir and vestibule. The church was rebuilt in 1779 and enlarged in 1915 and has 16C sections by the architect Roman Ruffiner. In the choir high altar (1747) by J.M.Albasino and 16C Renaissance tabernacle. By the church is the **ossuary,** built in 1556 by R.Ruffiner; in the interior 18C Pietà. The old part of the village has fine 17&18C wooden houses, often with inscriptions. In the Dorfplatz is the 'Grosse Haus', built 1665&6 for Melchior Werlen. Numerous wooden storehouses and barns.

Kirchberg BE

6□F3

The late Gothic **Reformed church of St. Martin** has early 16C stained glass. The **priest's house** is a late Gothic building of 1636. **Tschiffeligut** (Kleehof). The Bernese choral writer and economist Johann Rudolf Tschiffeli commissioned this country seat in Louis XVI style after 1765. The arrangement of the octagonal side pavilions is similar to that of the library gallery in Bern and tends to confirm the ascription of the design to Niklaus Sprüngli.

Kirchberg SG

3□D4

Catholic parish church Heiligkreuz. Nave and choir rebuilt 1748–51 by Johann Michael Beer of Bildstein, rebuilt after fire of 1784 by Johann Ferdinand Beer. **Alttoggenburg ruin,** near Mühlrüti SW of Kirchberg, family seat of the Counts of Toggenburg.

Kirchbühl LU

See Sempach   7□D2

Kippel: Catholic church of St.Martin, altered in the 18&20C.

Kirchlindach BE

6□E4

The **Reformed church of St.Elegius** is a Gothic building with 14&15C wall paintings, altered in the baroque style in 1672. Abraham I. Dünz created the communion table at the same time.

Kleindietwil BE

7□B2

Kleindietwil was settled in prehistoric times, as is shown by the remains of two **refuges** in the Hunzen mountain forest and **ramparts** on the Betzlis mountain.

Kleinhöchstetten BE

6□F5

The **former pilgrimage church of St. Maria** is a pre-Romanesque hall with a

Klosters: lavish Gothic stellar vaulting in the choir of the Reformed church.

Knutwil: Josef Singer's neoclassical Catholic parish church.

single apse and niches on the exterior wall. There are fragments of frescos in the late Gothic extension.

Klingenberg TG
See Homburg   3☐D2

Klingnau AG
                                     2☐E3

Old town. This little town, founded in 1239 by Ulrich von Klingen, consists essentially of a single street broadening to a square in the NW. Interesting features are

the **Schloss** (recently renovated), the former **priory** of the monastery of St. Blasien (1746–53), now used as a school, and the early baroque former **Amtshaus** of the Zursach canons, with step gables (1641).

Klosters GR
                                     9☐D4

The name Klosters goes back to the foundation of a filial of the monastery of Churwalden in the early 13C (Kloster= monastery). **Reformed church,** former monastery church with Romanesque tower. The baroque nave was built on to the choir, (itself built in 1493 by Andreas Bühler) after a fire in 1621. 1493 wall paintings in the stellar vaulting of the choir. Windows by Augusto Giacometti (1928): Jacob's dream. **Nuttlihüsli** (1565), in the Monbiel direction, now *Heimatmusuem* (local history).

Kloten ZH
                                     3☐A4

Reformed parish church. This late rococo church was built 1785&6 by Johann Jakob Haltliner; the tower is by Johann Grubenmann the younger (1788–90).

Klus SO
                                     7☐A1

This **township** at the foot of a crag seems to have been founded by the Counts of Falkenstein for the Froburgs. **Burg Alt-Falkensrein** with *Heimatmuseum* (local history). Built in the 12&13C, presumably by the Froburgs, to secure the route to the Oberer Hauenstein pass.

Knonau ZH
                                     7☐F1

Reformed parish church. This church was built in the early 16C on the site of earlier churches proved by excavations to have existed since the 8C; the interior was radically altered in 1769&70. The greenish and reddish stucco is by Lucius Gambs (1769). **Schloss.** Early 16C step gable building; seat of Landvogts until 1798. Interior partially 18C.

Knutwil LU

7☐D2

Catholic parish church of St.Stephan and Bartholomäus, built 1821–6 by Josef Singer. The neoclassical hall building is based on French models.

Koblenz AG

2☐E2/3

Roman observation point. The fragments of walls in the E. of the village, by the so-called 'oberen Laufen' rapids, on the Rhine were put under protection in 1932.

Königsfelden AG

See WINDISCH   2☐E4

Köniz BE

6☐E4

Reformed church of St. Peter and Paul. The church of the former Augustinian priory was taken over in 1226 by the Knights of the Teutonic Order. The Romanesque nave has a painted wooden ceiling dated 1503. The three apostle windows in the Gothic choir are stylistically related to those in ▷ Königsfelden. 1398 frescos between the windows. The former commandery was rebuilt as a **Schloss** in 1610. **Morillongut,** built in 1832 for Friedrich Ludwig of Wattenwyl to a design by Daniel Osterrieth. The late neoclassical country house is built on a Greek cross plan with imposed square. In the interior monumental staircase and Empire decoration. HERZWIL, W. of Köniz has 8 farms with outbuildings. The Ständerbau buildings have arcades and carriage entrances on the longer side and are the older form of the Bernese Dreisässen house. The **Bauernhaus Burren** was built in 1783

Köniz: St.Peter und Paul, originally part of an Augustinian priory.

in MENGESTORF, SW of Köniz, and has ornate façades: arcades and windows are decorated with carving and painting. The Stöckli is a 1779 half-timbered building.

Koppigen BE

6☐F2

The former 'Bären' in the hamlet of **Friedau,** E. of Koppigen, was built in 1824; it has a mansard hipped roof and roof lights. The 1645 corn house is a late Gothic building with wooden arcades.

Kottwil LU

7☐C2

Granary, not far from the Gasthaus 'Post'. This 1600 building is constructed of 'Hälblinge': circular timbers cut longitudinally.

Krauchthal BE

6☐F4

Schloss Thorberg, a reformatory since 1848. The women's guesthouse and the chapel with fragments of late Gothic frescos remain from the Carthusian monastery founded in 1399. The baroque Schloss was built in the Vogtei period.

Kreuzlingen: lavish rococo décor in the church of the former Augustinian Stift.

Kriens: Maria Loreto pilgrimage church in Hergiswald with Loreto chapel.

Kreuzlingen TG

3☐E2

Former Augustinian monastery, now teachers' seminary. Founded 1125, present building 17&18C. Partially rebuilt and renovated on historical principles. **Former monastery church of St. Ulrich and St. Afra,** built 1650–3 by Stephan Gunertsrainer and Melchior Gruber. Lavish 18C decoration with polychrome stucco, ceiling paintings by Franz Ludwig Herrmann, choir screen by Jakob Hoffner. **Mount of Olives chapel,** 1760. Ceiling painting by Franz Ludwig Herrmann, 1761, miraculous cross with 'genuine' hair, late 14C; crib figures and Calvary with over 300 stone pine statues, of which *c.* 250 are original; they date from 1720 – 30 and are from a SE alpine workshop. **Monastery buildings** *c.* 1660 by Michael Beer von Au and Jakob Sayler. In Egelhofen *Heimatmuseum* (local history) in **Haus Rosenegg,** 17&18C.

Kriegstetten SO

6☐F2

The **Gasthof zum Kreuz** was built in 1774 by Paolo Antonio Pisoni in neoclassical style.

Kriens LU

7☐E3

Schloss Schauensee, with its 13C round tower, is one of the few castles in the canton to have survived in good condition. HERGISWALD The **pilgrimage church of Maria Loreto** was rebuilt 1651-62. As frequently occurs in rural baroque churches the plain exterior contrasts strongly with the exuberant interior. The Loreto chapel is a copy of the 'Casa Santa' in Loreto.

Krinau SG

3☐D5

Nucleated village in a deep valley with 16-18C **wooden buildings**.

Krummenau SG

8□E1

The village is notable for its old Toggenburg **timber buildings**.

Küblis GR

9□C/D3

Reformed church, late Gothic building of 1472 on the site of a former church. The polygonal choir with stellar vaulting and the net vaulting in the nave are by Steffan Klain, stained glass with Apostle figures by August Giacometti, 1921.

Kühmatt VS

See **BLATTEN**   12□B5

Küsnacht ZH

3□A5

So-called **Höchhus.** Romanesque keep, later extended as a stately home. **Former tithe barn.** The striking feature of this building in the Albis, built in the 13C by the Cistercian abbey of Kappel, is the unusual cycle of spiritual frescos in the Soft Style (*c.*1410).

Küssnacht SZ

7□F3

The development of the village was determined by its position as a port on the old Gotthard route, which here crossed the road from Lucerne to Schwyz. By the former harbour the **Catholic parish church of St.Peter und Paul.** Originally built with nave and two aisles in 1708 and altered in 1963 into a hall church with one aisle. The church is surrounded on one side by the unified group of **Pfarramt, old school house** and **Rathaus,** built in 1728; on the other side of the buildings is the road from the lake to the Hauptplatz in the village. There are various large inns on this road; in the Hauptplatz the **Gasthaus Engel** with a fine half-timbered façade. Several Diets are said to have met

Küsnacht: the 'Höchhus', a keep altered in the late Middle Ages.

in the older, rear part of the house. Behind the church the *Heimatmuseum* (local history; open on Sundays from Whitsuntide to mid September). E. of the village ruins of the so-called **'Gesslerburg'.** HOHLE GASSE On the old road from Küsnacht to Immensee, which linked Lake Lucerne and Lake Zug, is the **Tellskapelle** in the 'Hohle Gasse' (sunken lane); here Landvogt Gessler is said to have met his death through 'Tell's shot'. The altar image by the subsequently famous alpine painter Caspar Wolf (1735 – 98) shows the Fourteen Auxiliary Saints.

Kyburg ZH

3□B4

Schloss Kyburg. Family seat of the Counts of the same name, who were highly influential in the Middle Ages; the original 11-13C building has largely survived. The Kyburg has been in the possession of the canton of Zürich since 1917 and is now used as an historical museum, giving a vivid impression of life and social conditions in the feudal period. The Burg is set on a rock above the Töss and is surrounded by ditches and built around a central courtyard. The buildings include a keep, the so-called Grafenhaus (used as Landvogt's seat in later centuries), battlements, a guest house (Ritterhaus) and a Burg chapel with Gothic wall paintings.

Laax GR

8 □ F5

Catholic parish church of St.Othmar und Gallus: Baroque single-aisle church with narrower rectangular choir (1675–8) by Domenico Barbieri of Roveredo; ossuary built in 1685. In the old alpine dairy is a *Heimatmuseum* (local history) with a folk-lore collection.

Lachen SZ

8 □ C2

Catholic parish church zum Heiligen Kreuz, built 1707–10. Two-storey articulation, semicircular apse with onion dome. Interior on the Vorarlberg pattern; deep pilasters, side galleries. Next to the church early-19C **schoolhouse;** nearby 1836 **Rathaus,** with wall paintings. E. of the village centre **'im Ried' pilgrimage chapel,** built 1679–84 to house a miraculous image saved from the lake at the time of the Reformation.

Laconnex GE

16 □ D2

The square **fortified house** with polygonal staircase tower dates from the 15C; parts altered in the 16–17C.

Lain GR
See VAZ/OBERVAZ   14 □ B1

Lana VS
See EVOLENE   17 □ E/F3

Landecy GE

16 □ E2

Fine **village** with typical 16–18C houses.

Lachen: baroque church by Johann Peter and Gabriel Thumb.

Le Landeron: Laurent Perroud's fontaine de Saint-Maurice, 1574.

Landeron, Le NE

6 □ C3

Long fortified market town, built between 1325 and 1344 by Rudolph IV of Neuchâtel. Main street with a gate at each end and lined with houses on both sides (E. and W.). In the N. the town has a 1499

Langenbruck: Romanesque portal sculpture on Schönthal monastery church.

outer work, the **clocktower,** rebuilt 1631, and the 14C **château** to the W. of the tower; in the S. is the former gate, the **Portette,** rebuilt 1596. **Catholic church,** situated outside the town walls, built in neoclassical style in 1828–32. **Hôtel de Ville** and **Ten Thousand Martyrs chapel** are in the same building; 16C façade with two portals. One, with the inscription 'Domus Domini', leads to the 15C chapel with a polychrome wooden Pietà of 1520–5, attributed to the studio of Hans Geiler; the other portal leads into the Hôtel de Ville, which occupies the two upper storeys. The houses in the main street date mostly from the 18C; at each end of the street is a fountain by Laurent Perroud, in thc N. the **fontaine du Vaillant,** in the S. the **fontaine de St-Maurice.** Outside the town walls, towards La Neuveville, is a group of 16&17C houses called La Russie.
In COMBES is the 17C **Sainte-Anne chapel** containing late 19C statues of the Virgin Mary and saints.

Langenbruck BL
2 □ B5

NE of the village, where traces of the **Roman road** to the pass still survive, isolated former **Benedictine monastery of Schönthal.** Founded in 1145, it passed to the Basel Spital after the Reformation, then in 1907 into private ownership; the partly dismantled church, consecrated 1187, W. façade with sculptures, and

residential and farm buildings have survived.

Langenthal BE
7 □ B2

Heimatmuseum, 11 Bahnhofstrasse. The collection includes ancient and early historical finds, documents on the Oberaargau textile industry and a late 18C country doctor's pharmacy.

Langnau BE
7 □ B4

Village centre with randomly arranged houses and inns; **Neuhaus** and **Engelhaus** are stone houses with semi-circular timber decoration under the gables and half-hipped roofs. The **Hirschenstock** has a curved rococo roof, while the **Biedermeier houses** have low hipped roofs. **Reformed church,** built by Abraham I.Dünz in 1673. Notable furnishings include the pulpit and font, both with lavish baroque carving. The **Chüechlihaus** is a 16C Blockbau with a high saddle roof. The *Heimatmuseum* housed here contains a collection of Old Langnau ceramics and Flüeli glasses, and documents on local personalities. The **Moosbrücke** (now by the open-air swimming-pool), built in 1797, is supported by a triple trapezium truss.

Langwies GR
9 □ C4

Reformed church: The 1384 single-aisle nave and the 1477 narrower polygonal choir were provided with a late Gothic vault by Steffan Klain and Andreas Bühler in 1488. Late 14C wall-paintings.

Lantsch/Lenz GR
14 □ B1

W. of the village **St. Maria.** Late Gothic single-aisle church, built by Petrus Bamberg in 1505, using the nave walls of an earlier building. Wall paintings: on the W. wall St.Christopher, early-14C, next to it the Adoration of the Magi and saints, mid-14C. On the S. wall Genesis, Childhood and Passion of Christ by the Master of Rhäzüns, 2nd half 14C. 1749 late Gothic winged altar. Towards Lenzerheide **St. Cassian chapel.** Pre-Gothic building with narrower rectangular chancel, vaulted around 1513. On the opposite side of the street striking early medieval buildings. **Bot da Loz,** remains of a settlement, probably a late Celtic watch station of the late La Tène period (1C BC).

Lantsch/Lenz: Bot da Loz, with remains of a settlement, 1C BC.

Lauenen BE

11 ☐ E5

Reformed church St.Petrus, built to a late Gothic design in 1520–1. Nave with wooden ceiling in polygonal sections, choir with tracery windows and rib vaulting. Wooden Ständer-Blockbau houses on masonry lower storeys in the **centre of the village.** The 1796 **Jägerhaus** has carving, landscape paintings between the garret windows and a hunting scene on the gable. The 1765 **Mühlehaus** is also lavishly carved and painted.

Läufelfingen BL

2 ☐ B5

The **Reformed parish church,** altered in 1491, the priest's house built at the same time and the 17C sexton's house form a church hamlet high on the E. side of the village. **Burg Homburg,** 13C seat of the Froburgs, was destroyed in 1798.

Laufen BE

1 ☐ F4

The centre of the town, founded by the Bishop of Basel in 1295, is the main street, with the **Obertor** and **Untertor** at either end. The lower part of the **Wassertor** at the E. end of the street of the same name is part of the first fortification of *c.* 1300. Over 400 yards of the **town walls** are still extant. **St.Katharina** by the Untertor, a baroque building begun in 1698 with 1755

rococo stucco by the Mosbrugger brothers. Notable furnishings include a late Gothic Madonna, the 1688 wooden pulpit and the Régence altars. Adjacent is the *Heimatmuseum des Laufentals* (local history). Former **Rathaus** by the Obertor with neoclassical façade. The **Amtshaus** (or 'Hof'), built in the early 17C, was once an episcopal administrative building of the Dinghof, independent of the town and known as 'Vorstadt' (suburb) since 1482. 1809 **Martinskapelle** in the cemetery E. of the Vorstadt, containing the furnishings of the earlier baroque building.

Laufen-Uhwiesen ZH

3 ☐ A/B2

Reformed parish church. This church, mentioned in 1155, was considerably enlarged in 1492, new choir 1516. A thorough alteration was carried out in 1895 (heightening of the nave, porch, new interior furnishings). The **priest's house** of 1760 is in the church precinct. **Former Uhwiesen chapel.** This small church, deconsecrated since the Reformation, contains remains of frescos from the immediate pre-Reformation period. **Schloss Laufen** on the Rhine falls, not mentioned until 1123, came under Zürich in 1544 and served as a Landvogt's seat; it now houses a youth hostel and a restaurant.

Laufenburg AG

2 ☐ C/D3

Small medieval bridge-head town on the

Laufenburg: town founded by the Habsburgs with Rhine bridge.

Laufenburg: altar in the ossuary chapel showing the death of St. Joseph.

Laupen: the Schloss is the oldest surviving stone building in the canton of Bern.

Rhine, founded *c.* 1207 on the site of older fishing settlements by Rudolf II of Habsburg. Seat of the Counts of Habsburg-Laufenburg; later an Austrian possession until the separation of 1802: Gross-Laufenburg on the left bank of the Rhine went to the canton of Aargau, while Klein-Laufenurg went to the Grand Duchy of Baden. **Old Town and defence systems.** The small town is set on a rocky hill of Schwarzwald gneiss. Of the once spacious **Schloss** on the Burg mound there remain only the 12C keep and parts of the defence walls. The old **town wall** is still visible in places; of the gates and towers the **Schwertlisturm, Wasenturm** and **Pulverturm** still stand. **Catholic church St. Johannes Baptist:** This was built in the 15C, on the site of an older church dating from before the town's foundation, and was redesigned in the baroque style in 1750-3. Interior in light rococo style with stucco by Hans Michael Hennevogel and ceiling paintings by Anton Morath. In the **ossuary chapel** below the N. aisle is a carved altar by Hans Freitag (1727). **Gerichtsgebäude** (court building) of 1525, later redesigned in the baroque style. In the renovated court-room rococo stucco and portraits of Austrian rulers.

Laupen BE

6☐D5

This small town, founded by the Zähringens in the 13C at the confluence of the Saane and Sense was, as an important border town, always a bone of contention. In 1339 Bern victoriously defended the town, which it had acquired 15 years previously, against a coalition of nobles. The French suffered a defeat here in 1798. **Schloss,** probably built by King Rudolf II of Burgundy around 930 to defend the E. border of his empire. This would make the castle one of the oldest stone buildings in Switzerland. A late Gothic Landvogt's castle was built to the N. of the great hall, incorporating the former keep. At the W. end is the 1662 'Chefiturm' with remains of outer works.

Lauperswil BE

7☐A4

Reformed church, late Gothic building, *c.* 1518. The stained glass, transitional between Gothic and Renaissance, was donated by various benefactors in 1518-20. The

Lausanne: Notre-Dame cathedral in the centre of the Quartier de la Cité.

Kalkmatthöfe NW of Lauperswil are an intact ensemble of rural architecture from the 18C to the early 19C. **Haus Grunder** (No.597) in **Wittenbach** has residential accommodation, stable and threshing floor under one roof. The galleries of this 1788 baroque building are decorated with openwork carving. 18C oven-house.

Lausanne VD

10 □ E3

Capital of the canton of Vaud. The canton was inhabited in the Palaeolithic era and numerous settlements sprang up after the Neolithic period and during the Bronze and Iron Ages, particularly on the shores of the lake. In 58 BC the Helvetians, a Celtic tribe, were defeated by Caesar at Bibracte and forced to return to their homeland in the Swiss interior. The area was then swiftly Romanized; the first town founded by the Romans was Nyon, *c.* 45BC. In the 1C Avenches became capital of Helvetia. After 250 the Roman Empire was threatened by the onslaughts of the Alemans. In the 5–6C the area became part of the Kingdom of Burgundy, then of the Frankish Empire; it was integrated into the

Holy Roman Empire in 1032. From the 11C the territory of the canton was divided among various feudal lords, amongst whom the Bishops of Lausanne played a dominant role until the Counts of Savoy came to power in the 13C. The whole of the Vaud was taken over by Bern in 1536 and divided among 12 Landvogts. Under Bernese rule the Reformation, which had been preached since 1530 by Guillaume Farel and Pierre Viret, was finally introduced. Bern maintained its supremacy over the area until 1798. In 1723 Major Davel's attempt to persuade the council of Lausanne to revolt against Bern failed.

THE TOWN The original Celtic settlement began to develop in the 3C, after the Roman settlement of Vidy was abandoned. In the 6C Bishop Marius or St.Maire made Lausanne a bishopric, and gradually the city became the centre of the bishops' secular power. In the 12&13C Lausanne enjoyed a period of great economic and spiritual growth. In 1234 the citizens managed to obtain partial autonomy and in 1336 the city had its own council, and Savoy actively supported the citizens in their struggle against the bishops. In 1476 Lausanne was occupied by Burgundian troops and then plundered by the Confederates. In 1525 Lausanne formed a coalition with Bern and Fribourg. With the occupation of the Vaud Lausanne too fell under the rule of Bern, thereby losing all political importance. Not until 1803 did Lausanne become capital of the Vaud, which had declared its independence in 1798.

QUARTIER DE LA CITE Heart of the original city, site of the Roman 'castrum', over which the first fortified castle and the cathedral were later built. **Cathedral of Notre-Dame,** now Reformed church. The cathedral, which replaced the old 6C church of St.Maire, was first mentioned in 814. This Carolingian basilica was replaced by a Romanesque building around 1000. In 1173 Bishop Landry de Durnes commissioned the present church, which was consecrated in 1275. In the 16C Bishops Aymon and Sébastien de Montfalcon carried out various architectural alterations in the cathedral, including the Martyrs' Chapel and the Portail des Montfalcon. After the Reformation the cathedral was again altered. In 1873 a comprehensive restoration was begun under Viollet-le-Duc; the excavations, which can still be seen, date from 1904–14. Lausanne Cathedral is the most beautiful Gothic building in Switzerland. The cruciform church has a nave and two aisles, polygonal apse with ambulatory and semicircular apex chapel; the transept has a crossing tower and two side towers. The main façade has one complete and one incomplete tower. The porch, into which two side-apses open, was greatly altered in the 16C by the building of the Portail des Montfalcon. The portals of the cathedral have interesting sculptures, the S. portal, 'Portail peint' dates from the beginning of the 13C. The sculptures, which depict the Coronation of the Virgin Mary by Christ Enthroned (tympanum) with the Burial and Raising below, and Apostles and Prophets (jambs), have survived in their original colouring; restoration work has been going on for many years and is now coming to an end. The Flamboyant W. portal dates from 1515–32, the sculptures are 19C copies. On the inner portal are three damaged statues c. 1275. The interior of the church is of great stylistic unity. The

Interior with triforium.

Schloss St-Maire, a compact sandstone and brick building.

groin-vaulted nave consists of six bays and a double bay in the W. A triforium with a gallery and tall windows above it runs round the whole interior. In the S. transept is a chapel of the Virgin Mary with polychrome Gothic décor. In the rose window of the S. transept, stained glass is attributed to Pierre d'Arras, probably dating from before 1235 and restored in 1894. 13C carved choir stalls, among the oldest in Switzerland, and 1509 choir stalls. At th

16C former Académie with protruding staircase tower.

N. entrance of the choir ambulatory is the tomb of Otto von Grandson, who died in 1328. In the cathedral square on the N. side (No. 15) are the remains of the **Gothic chapter-house**. **Château St-Maire,** former seat of the Bishop, was built under Bishop Guillaume de Menthonay from 1397 on the site of the Priory of St.Maire, to which the 6C church of the same name (formerly St. Thyrse) was subordinated. The castle was enlarged and converted in the 16C. After 1536 the building was seat of the Bernese governors and altered several times before the end of the 18C. The castle is a massive cubic construction topped by a brick storey with machicolations and four corner towers. On the S. façade is an monument (1898) to Major Davel. Inside, on the ground floor, are late-15C allegorical wall paintings. On the first floor is the 'chambre de l'évêque' with 16C painted ceiling and fireplace. Near the castle is the **baâtiment du Grand Conseil,** built by A. Perregaux in 1803–6. Classical façade with wall columns and triangular gable. Rue Cité-Devant, **former Academy,** built in 1579–87 and restored in 1920. Rectangular building with a square staircase tower on the façade and step gables on the side façades. Place de la

Cathédrale No.2, **Ancien Evêché,** now *museum.* Group of buildings from several epochs. The episcopal palace was founded in the 11C; all that remains from this period are the core of the central building, which was rebuilt in the 18&20C, and parts of a chapel dedicated to St.Nicholas. On the E. side is the 14C Guy de Prangins wing with an early 15C brick extension and the Jacquemard tower of 1360–80, probably originally part of the city fortifications. Rue de la Mercerie, **ancien Hôpital** (now secondary school), built in 1766–71 by Rodolphe de Crousaz on the site of a medieval hospital. The building, which is on two levels, is arranged in a horseshoe around a court of honour. Place de la Cathédrale No. 6 is the prefecture, **former maison Gaudard,** 1670 façade with staircase tower. The **escaliers du Marché,** which connect the districts of Cité and Palud, are of interest for their covered flights of steps. **House** No.17 with Gothic windows.

QUARTIER DE LA PALUD The market quarter, one of the first to develop after the Cité. **Hôtel de Ville,** built in 1672–5 by the architect Abraham de Crousaz on the site the 15&16C Town Hall, converted and enlarged in the 18–19C. The Renaissance façade on the Place de la Palud consists of two storeys over an arcade and is surmounted by a bell tower. The central section has a gable with pilasters. On the bell-tower clock is an allegory of Justice, painted by Hans Ulrich Fisch II in 1684 and restored in 1867. Place de la Palud No.2, **former maison de Seigneux** (police station), baroque-early neoclassical building of 1731–2. No.4, 18C **maison de Crousaz.** 16C **fontaine de la Justice,** (original in the museum). Place de la Riponne. **Palais de Rumine,** built in 1898 – 1906 by the French architect Gaspard André. The neo-Renaissance building was built thanks to a bequest by Gabriel de Rumine (1841 – 71). It was designed to accommodate the university, the library and the museum. On the same square is the **former musée Arlaud,** built 1836–9 by Louis Wenger.

QUARTIER DU BOURG Documented since the 10C. The heart of the quarter is the Place St-François, which was redesigned

Place de la Palud and façade with tower of the Hôtel de Ville.

Palais de Rumine, housing various cantonal museums.

Monastery church of St-François, adapted as a Reformed church in the 16C.

in the 19&20C. **Reformed church of St-François.** Only surviving part of the Franciscan monastery founded in 1258. The single-aisle church with polygonal apse and groin vaulting was built in 1270, the chapelle de Billens in the 14C. The church was rebuilt after a fire in 1368. The bell tower and further chapels were added in the 15C; alterations in the 18–19C, particularly on the W. façade, which was rebuilt in 1860. Inside are interesting choir stalls by Jean de Liège, 1387. Organ by

Samson Scherrer, 1777. In the square is an interesting group of early 20C buildings. Rue du Bourg No. 26, **maison Vullyamoz-Constant,** small private house, built in 1667.

Quartier St-Laurent First mentioned in 1000. In the street of the same name is the **tour de l'Ale,** one of the last remnants of the city fortifications. This 13&14C round tower protected the entrance to the St-Laurent quarter. **Reformed church of St-Laurent,** built in the 18C. A first church from the 11C fell into ruin in the 16C and was replaced by Guillaume Delagrange's building of 1716–19. This was altered in 1761–3 by Rodolphe de Crousaz and the baroque façade added. In the Place du Grand-St-Jean is a 1777 **fountain.**

Outer Districts Avenue de l'Elysée, **maison de l'Elysée,** built 1780–3 under the direction of the architect Abraham Fraisse. Elegant mansion with gabled façades. Avenue de la Gare, **gare centrale,** built 1908–16 to plans by Alphonse Laverrière. Avenue de Cour, **Ecole polytechnique fédérale,** enlarged in 1962 by the architect Jean Tschumi. No.41, **Mutuelle Vaudoise,** built by Jean Tschumi 1959–61. Quartier Maupas-Beaulieu, Avenue des Bergières. **Château de Beaulieu,** built in 1765. Jacques Necker and his daughter Mme de Staël lived here after 1784. **Palais de Beaulieu,** congress and exhibition centre, built in 1920. Quartier Béthusy. 18C **Château de Béthusy.** Avenue Mon-Repos No.1, **maison Villamont,** classical building of 1791–3. **Palais de Mon-Repos,** 18C mansion, rebuilt in 1817 to plans by French architect Louis Damesme, who also designed the adjacent buildings. The park, designed by the Parisian Mon-sailler, contains an octagonal pavilion of 1780. **Tribunal fédéral,** neo-classical, built 1922–7 by the architects L.-E.Prince, J.Béguin and A.Laverrière.

Ouchy Traditional harbour of Lausanne, site of an episcopal palace since the 12C. Of this palace only part of a keep remained by the 19C, and this was incorporated into the **Hôtel du Château d'Ouchy,** a neo-Gothic building by Francis Isoz, 1889–93. In the Place du Port is the **Hôtel d'Angleterre,** formerly Auberge de l'Ancre, built in 1775–9 to plans by Abraham

Maison de l'Élysée with projecting gabled sections picked out in colour.

The Musée Olympique is housed in the Palais de Mon Repos.

Neoclassical Federal Court building (1922–7) in Mon-Repos park.

Fraisse and converted in 1880. Adjacent is the **maison Panchaud,** an elegant building of 1802-3. **Hôtel Beau-Rivage,** 1858-61. Avenue Denantou, **Villa and Château Denantou,** built for William Haldimand in 1820-32. In the park are 19C sculptures and neo-Gothic 1830 **tower ruins** on the quay.

VIDY Route de Chavannes, archaeological park with remains of Roman buildings, a temple and a forum. Small *Roman Museum.*

MONTHERON **Reformed Church,** built

Lausen: Mid-15C Crucifixion on the E. wall of the choir of the Reformed church.

1590-2, enlarged, converted and baroque façade added by Abraham Fraisse in 1776 -8. The church was erected on the ruins of the Abbey of Montheron, which was founded in the 12C; remains uncovered by excavations in 1911. Next to the church is a 16C **hostel.**

Museums: The Palais de Rumine houses various museums, including the *Musée cantonal d'archéologie et d'histoire,* collection of excavation finds from the canton of Vaud; *Musée cantonal des beaux-arts,* collection of art-works by Vaud artists, small collection of Swiss, French and Dutch art; *Cabinet des médailles. Collection de l'art brut* (Château de Beaulieu), collection of works of art by the mentally handicapped and others not integrated into society. *Musée des arts décoratifs de la Ville,* collection of applied art (not on display), temporary exhibitions. *Musée de l'Elysée,* collection of engravings and photographs. *Musée de la cathédrale et de l'Ancien Evêché,* local history collection.

Lausen BL

2 ☐ B4

After a fire in the mid 15C the **Reformed parish church** was rebuilt as a single room and the choir covered with paintings of scenes from the life of Christ and the legend of St. Nicholas; sexton's house and

Lavin: completely painted choir of the church, Upper Italian, c. 1500.

barn (15&16C) added as a W. extension of the church.

Lauterbrunnen BE
12 □ C3

The old schoolhouse contains the *Heimatmuseum der Talschaft* (local history) and the *Balloon Museum* of the International Spelterini Society.

Lavertezzo TI
19 □ C1

Catholic parish church of Santa Maria degli Angeli, built in the 17&18C. Late baroque façade of 1780. Bridging the Verzasca is the **Ponte dei Salti,** an elegant stone bridge of medieval origin with an 18C chapel.

Lavin GR
9 □ F5

Reformed church, built around 1500. Flat-ceilinged room with narrower, vaulted polygonal apse. Wall paintings by an Italian master (*c.* 1500) in the choir and on the choir arch wall.

Léchelles FR
6 □ B/C5

On the cantonal road **château,** a rec-

tangular building restored in the 18C by Nicolas de Gottrau. Trompe l'oeil paintings on the E. façade.

Leggia GR
19 □ E1

Catholic church of Santi Bernardo e Antonio: This 1513 building, altered in 1610, is an embryonic version of the baroque pilastered nave. **San Remigio chapel.** Medieval single-aisle church with semi-circular apse built into the hillside.

Leibstadt AG
2 □ D3

1672 **Loreto chapel** in the district of Bernau. Originally the Schloss chapel of a family seat which has disappeared.

Lengnau AG
2 □ E3

Synagogue. Lengnau and Endingen were the two Surbtal villages allocated to the Jews by federal Diet. The neoclassical-neo-Gothic building was built by Ferdinand Stadler.

Lens VS
17 □ E1

Catholic parish church of St-Pierre. Monumental building dating from 1843; the bell tower and choir of the previous late Gothic building, built by Ulrich Ruffiner in 1535–7, have survived; the choir is now the sacristy. Adjacent are the **priory buildings** of the monks of Great St. Bernard, rebuilt in 1835–7. W. of the church is the **manoir,** a 16C stone house. On Mont Châtelard (4, 100 ft.) is a monumental statue of Christ dating from 1935.

Vaas **Former hostel,** built in 1565 for Antoine Gilloz. Interesting building, the façades of which are painted with agricultural and hunting scenes and an inscription in French dialect: 'Qui ne aur

Lenzburg: massive Schloss on a hill above the town.

d'or, argen, ni credit, ni abit de lanne, quil hale bioere a la fontanne'.

Lenzburg AG
2 □ D5

The visual charm of Lenzburg still lies in the combination of massive hill-top Burg and huddled Old Town. The town itself was founded relatively late, around 1240, by the Kyburgs, the heirs of the mighty dynasty of the Counts of Lenzburg. A terrible town fire in 1491 destroyed most of the old buildings, which is why baroque design predominates in the Old Town. A number of dignified houses were built outside the former ring wall in the 18C. **Reformed church.** Single aisled church with no choir built in 1667; the tower dates from 1601&2. The interior is mainly 17&18C. Stucco ceiling by Jakob Mosbrugger in Régence and rococo style. **Schloss Lenzburg.** This spacious complex, the oldest parts of which are high medieval, was the ancestral castle of the Counts of Lenzburg. When their line died out it passed first to the Kyburgs and then to the Habsburgs. After Lenzburg had been taken by Bern in 1415 the castle became the seat of the Landvogt until the collapse of the Old Confederation. In 1956 the canton of Aargau and the community of Lenzburg bought the castle, making it

public property. It now houses the *cantonal historical collection* and, in the so-called Berner- or **Philipp-Albert-Stapferhaus,** a meeting-place of the Pro Helvetia and Pro Argovia foundations, as well as the Neue Helvetische Gesellschaft. **Rathaus:** Baroque building constructed in two stages, 1677 and 1692, with a three-part façade; central tower with clock gables. **Ruins of a Roman street with semicircular theatre complex** on the Lindfeld, discovered during government road-building in 1964–5 and conserved in 1970. **Neolithic necropolis** on the Burg mound.

Lessoc FR
11 □ C4

St-Martin. Built in 1627 – 35. Façade tower, 19C interior. In the village beautiful **houses** and farms, the façades of which are decorated with poyas, depictions of the Alpine pageant. In the middle of the village is a 1796 **fountain** with an onion dome. N. of Lessoc, in a place called Le Buth, is the **Du Roc chapel** or Notre-Dame des Neiges, an interesting polygonal building of 1684 containing a baroque altar. Next to it is the 1688 **farmstead** of La Grange Neuve.

Leuk/Loèche VS
18 □ A1

This place, already settled in pre-Roman times, belonged to the abbey of St-Maurice in 515 and from 1138 to the Bishop of Sion. Until 1411 the lords of Raron held the position of vidame; after 1420 the office was held by citizens of the town. The original town fortifications have now disappeared, only a 14C tower near the bridge over the Dala survives. **Bishop's Palace,** former seat of the Bishop's administrators. First mentioned in 1254, the building was destroyed around 1415, then rebuilt and later frequently altered. The square tower dates partly from the Romanesque epoch and the residential wings have 13C windows, including a particularly elegant one on the S. front. **Former château des vidames,**

Leuk: 16C former vidame tower, now used as Town Hall.

Leuk: baroque Ringacker chapel with unusual arcaded porch.

now Rathaus. Residence of the vidames from the 13C onwards, destroyed around 1415 and rebuilt in 1541–3 by Ulrich Ruffiner, reusing the older parts. Pentagonal building with step gables and four corner turrets. On the ground floor is a spacious room with groin vaulting and a monumental fireplace; courtroom with 16C coffered ceiling. **Catholic parish church of St-Stéphane,** late Gothic, begun in 1497, with a very beautiful 12C Romanesque bell tower, the sole surviving part of the earlier building. The church has a nave, two aisles and polygonal apse. On the main façade is a 16C crucifix. Inside is a 1679 carved pulpit, on the S. side of the choir is a 1668 baroque altar and on the N. side fragments of a 16C painted Gothic retable. In the ossuary under the church are 16C paintings with a depiction of the Dance of Death. On a flat area of ground below the village is the **Ringackerkapelle,** built 1690–4, one of the most beautiful baroque buildings in the Valais. Single-aisled church with polygonal apse, façade with protruding section supported on columns. Lavish interior stucco decorations, monumental high altar by Joh.Ritter and Joh.Sigristen, completed in 1705; 1722 baroque organ. In Kreuzgasse is the **house** of Baron de Werra, an interesting set of 17&19C buildings. On the road to Varen is the **former manoir de Werra,** an imposing 16&17C complex, surrounded by a wall with watchtower. The oldest part of

the house is rectangular with 1532 hexagonal staircase tower; the later part of the building dates from 1626.
SUSTEN At the village exit **château de Werra,** now an old people's home. The building consists of two different parts, the older of which, with a round staircase tower, dates back to the 15C and was built by the Perrinis, the vidames of Leuk; the other part of the building dates from around 1800.

Leukerbad VS

12☐A5

Catholic parish church Maria Hilfe der Christen, rebuilt in the 18C; the choir survives from the earlier building and is now the baptistery. Inside is a 1760 rococo altar.

Lichtensteig SG

3☐E5

Founded around 1200 by the Toggenburgs on a spur of rock on the River Thur. Owned by the abbey of St. Gallen from 1468, regional capital of Neutoggenburg from 1803. The end of the Altstadt nearest the hills is semicircular and was originally protected by ditches and walls. Gates dismantled in 1828. In the main street are **half-timbered houses** with picturesque arcades. **Catholic church of St.Gallus.** 1969&70 concrete building by Walter M.Förderer, which replaced a neo-Gothic church. **Former Rathaus,** mentioned in 1534, altered in the 17C. Imposing stone building in the S. ring of houses. **Türmchenhaus and 'Glocke',** originally belonging together as a late Gothic mansion on the main street. Dated 1583, converted 1766. Stairway at the back of the 'Glocke'. **Loreto chapel** N. of the town, built in 1677–80. Baroque building with narrower turreted porch. **Mösli-Haus** below Grueben on the left side of the valley, with oriel, portal dated 1615. *Toggenburger Heimatmuseum* (house No.191) with local history collection.

Lichtensteig: country town on a triangular plan with half-timbered buildings.

Liddes VS

17□D4

S. of the village is the baroque **St-Etienne chapel,** built in 1752. Baroque altar (1654) with painting. N. of the village is the **St-Laurent chapel,** built in 1505, converted in the 17C; Renaissance frescos on the façade. In the main street there are interesting houses, such as the 1627–30 **maison Massard,** with staircase tower and wrought-iron balcony. RIVE-HAUTE **Notre-Dame chapel,** small baroque building, 1735, containing a Régence altar.

Lieli LU

7□E2

The **Burg ruin,** seat of the lords of Lieli in the 13C, has an irregular, nine-sided ground plan, hence its local name 'Nünegg'.

Liestal BL

2□A/B4

Capital of the canton of Basel-Land. Traces of Roman and Frankish settlements are indicative of Liestal's importance on the road from Augusta Raurica over the Upper Hauenstein into central Switzerland. The town was officially founded by the

Froburgs around the mid 13C. After their decline the charter was acquired by the Bishop of Basel, who lost it to the city of Basel by 1400. As the seat of one of the seven Landvogts Liestal was part of the urban area subject to Basel. It was not until the time of the Helvetian Republic that the rural population achieved equal status with the citizens of the town. As a result of the confusion after the separation from Basel Liestal became capital of the newly created canton of Basel-Landschaft. The names of such writers as Georg Herwegh, Carl Spitteler and Joseph Viktor Widmann are connected with Liestal.

OLD TOWN The extent of the medieval town can still be clearly discerned from the arrangement of the houses. The Rathausgasse, former medieval street market and main traffic artery until very recently, connects the **Obertor** in the S., which originated as part of the first fortifications from the time of the town's foundation, with the N. town exit (the Untertor was removed in 1827). The main axis has two parallel side-streets, the outer edges of which, with houses of mostly Gothic character, were once part of the fortifications. It was not until the 19C that the town outgrew its medieval limits. Streets where the old buildings have survived include the Rathausgasse, Kanonengasse, Fischmarkt, Kirchplatz. **Reformed church** in the Kirchhof, with tightly-packed houses. At the time of the town's

Lieli: remains of 13C 'Nünegg' castle.

Liestal: the E. section of the late Gothic Rathaus dates from 1938.

foundation a church with a nave and two aisles was built over earlier 9 – 13C buildings. In 1506 – 7 it acquired a new chancel and in 1619–20 a tower on the S. flank of the chancel. The aisles were removed in 1652 to form a single room. The late Gothic **Rathaus,** rebuilt in 1568, has 1901 façade paintings by Wilhelm Balmer, while the E. extension, rebuilt in 1938, has scenes from the town's history by Otto Plattner; on the first floor is the Burgundy glass of Charles the Bold, a trophy from the Battle of Nancy, 1477. The **Olsbergerhof,** a delicately articulated late Gothic patrician's house dating from 1571, was the seat of the Schultheiss and later sanctuary of the Convent of Olsberg. The 17C former **Zeughaus** (arsenal) was also used as a granary for a time. The **priest's house** in Kanonengasse bears the date 1743. The **Regierungsgebäude** (government building) was built above the former Freihof by Samuel Warenfels in 1779. Installed in the W. wing, added in 1850, is the *Kantonsmuseum.* The late classical **Amtshaus** is its counterpart in municipal architecture.
OUTSIDE THE FORMER TOWN WALLS The **Feldmühle,** already mentioned around 1300, was used for a while as the country seat of wealthy Basel families after rebuilding in 1588. The **Berri-Gut** was built in the style of French châteaux in 1768 as a country seat for Samuel Ryhiner, an indienne manufacturer from Basel. The

Pfrund (old people's home) was built as a hospital to plans by Benedikt Stehlin in 1852-4. **Villa Gauss,** built in 1864-6 by Johann Jacob Stehlin the Younger. The former **Postgebäude** was built in the style of a Renaissance palazzo by Hans Wilhelm Auer, the architect of the Bernese Bundeshaus, in 1892.
MUNZACH This settlement to the N. of Liestal was abandoned around the middle of the 15C. Excavations in 1952 uncovered a Roman complex with a farmstead, temple and water pipes; notable mosaic pavement in the villa.
Museums: *Kantonsmuseum Baselland,* reopened in the Altes Zeughaus in 1982; natural and cultural history of the canton. *Dichtermuseum* in the Rathaus commemorating Georg Herwegh and others.

Ligerz BE

6 □ C3

The façades of this ribbon village have arched doorways and windows set in rows. In the vineyards above the village **Reformed church of St. Imer und Theodul,** a 1470-5 late Gothic building. The nave has a carved wooden ceiling and the choir stellar vaulting. The polychrome interior paintwork dates from 1669 (renewed). Plaques with coats-of-arms *c.* 1520. Housed in the **Hof,** a 1545 Gothic mansion, is a *Rebbaumuseum* (viticulture).

Lignon, Le GE

16 □ E2

Satellite town: 2,800 dwellings, built 1962 – 70 by the architects G.Addor, P.Juillard, J.Bollinger and L.Payot.

Ligornetto TI

19 □ D5

Catholic parish church of San Lorenzo, first mentioned in 1209. The present single-aisle building with square, domed choir dates from 1735–9. In the dome 1777 trompe l'oeil paintings, in the choir marble high altar and three paintings by G.B.Colombo, 1788. In the N. chapel is a crucifix dating from 1600. On the street beside the church is the **Osteria Circolo Operaio** with a stuccoed portal of 1780. **Museo Vela,** installed in the villa built for the sculptor Vicenzo Vela (1820 –91) in 1863-5. Lavish *collection* of plaster casts and originals by the artist.

Limpach BE

6 □ F3

The **Reformed church,** built in 1808, is a neoclassical church designed to emphasise the importance of preaching with an integral façade tower. Empire-style furnishings.

Linthal GL

8 □ D4

The **Reformed church** of 1728 replaced a 17C building threatened by flooding. The **Catholic parish church Mariä Himmelfahrt** was built by August Hardegger in 1906&7 on the site of a church built in 1283, the tower of which is still standing.

Locarno TI

19 □ C2

Locarno has been inhabited since Roman

Ligerz: St. Imer und Theodul with late-Gothic stellar vaulting in the choir.

times and belonged to the Archbishopric of Milan in the 9C. In the 11C it came under the rule of the Bishop of Como and was administered by the Orelli family. In 1342 the Viscontis, as new lords of the town, transferred their power to the noble Ruscas. From 1516 to 1798 Locarno was joint ruler of the 12 Old Cantons, and from 1803-78 was alternately capital of Ticino with Lugano and Bellinzona. Important holiday resort since the 19C. **Castello.** Little is known of the origins of the first castle of Locarno, the present building being officially documented for the first time in 1342. Important fortification works were carried out on the castle and its harbour by the Rusca family in the 15C; the Confederates destroyed the fortress buildings in 1532. Outer castle walls rebuilt in 1924-9; older parts have survived inside. The 15C residential section has an elegant courtyard with portico and loggias in the Lombardy Renaissance style. In the piazza Sant'Antonio is the **Catholic parish church of Sant'Antonio,** built in 1664–92 and partly rebuilt in 1863. The domed building has a cruciform ground plan. The interior is mostly 19C; the 1742 trompe l'oeil paintings by Giuseppe

A.F.Orelli in the S. transept chapel are an exception. In the piazza San Francesco **monastery and church of San Francesco:** According to tradition the monastery was founded in 1229 and the church consecrated in 1316, although the present building was built from 1538, probably by the architect G.Beretta. Basilica with nave and two aisles, square choir and three polygonal apses; 17C side chapels, façade inspired by the Romanesque-Lombard style. On the walls of the aisles are 1761-5 trompe l'oeil paintings, in the apse chapels 18C marble altars and balustrades. The monastery, now a school, was partly rebuilt in 1893; in the former refectory are paintings by A.Baldassare Orelli. In the via Cittadella **Catholic church of Santa Maria Assunta,** known as Chiesa Nova, consecrated in 1636. On the façade is a massive stucco figure of St.Christopher, statues of St.Rochus and St.Sebastian in the niches and the Orelli coat-of-arms above the portal. The single-aisle interior with polygonal chancel contains very beautiful painted stucco; statues of St.Anne and St.Veronica in the nave. Next to the church is the **casa dei canonici,** built around 1600. Three-storey building with loggia façade overlooking the garden. Via Vallemaggi, in the cemetery, **church of Santa Maria in Selva,** 15C building; only the choir survives, important wall paintings in the Soft Style. The paintings, which depict scenes from the Life of Christ and the Virgin Mary, were executed by various artists, including the master of Santa Maria in Selva, who painted the Virgin of the Protecting Cloak, the Annunciation and the vault decorations, *c.* 1400. The Burial of the Virgin Mary was painted by Jacobino de Vaylate around 1450. The late 15C studio of Antonio da Tradate is also represented. In the **cemetery** are interesting 19C tombs. Of interest among Locarno's secular buildings is the **Casorella** near the castle, a 16C house built for Melchior Lussy with a small stuccoed loggia. Via Sant'Antonio 3, a 16-18C **house** with an interesting inner courtyard; No.11, **palazzo Rusca,** a group of houses from various epochs, altered in the 18C. Via Borghese 14, **casa del Negromante,** 14C house; 16C paintings

by the entrance, portico and gallery on wooden columns in the court. The Piazza Grande totally changed its appearance in the 19&20C. 14C **torre del Comune,** probably part of the former fortifications. **Municipio,** community centre, 17C former palazzo from the 17C, rebuilt in 1896&7. In the castello is the *Museo civico.* Archaeological collection and museum of modern art.

SOLDUNO **Catholic parish church of San Giovanni Battista,** baroque building, built 1778-89 next to a church of 1385, the choir of which survives. The interior has paintings dating from 1848; 1794 high altar. 1630 stucco in the choir of the former church. ▷ also Muralto and Orselina.

Locle, Le NE

After the fire of 1833 the town centre was rebuilt under the directions of Charles-Henri Junod, who designed La Chaux-de-Fonds in similar geometrical form. 1321 **Reformed church,** originally Chapel of Ste. Marie-Madeleine; enlarged and façade tower added in 1521-5; the tower is all that remains of the original building; nave rebuilt in 1758&9; interior creates a theatrical effect. Former **Hôtel de Ville,** Grand-Rue 11. Classical building of 1839 -41. Rue du Crêt-Vaillant No.28, **house** of 1786. In front of the façade is a double flight of steps. Above the town is the **château des Monts,** mansion built by the architect Gabriel de la Grange in 1785-90 which houses the *Musée d'horlogerie et d'histoire* (watches and clocks and history and the Maurice Sandoz *collection of automata.*

Lohn SH

Reformed parish church: The oldest parts of the nave probably date from the 10C; the tower dates from the 13C. Late Gothic tabernacle (*c.* 1525) with Agnus Dei.

Locarno: 1742 Descent from the Cross in a side chapel in Sant'Antonio.

Locarno: Santa Maria Assunta with lavish early baroque stucco.

Locarno: vault painting c. 1400 in the choir of Santa Maria in Selva.

Löhningen SH

3 □ A2

Spitaltrotte: 17C agricultural building (Renaissance memorial plaque dated 1603) with massive wine press. The traditional Trottenfest (wine-pressing festival) is held here annually.

Lommis TG

3 □ D3

Catholic parish church of St. Jakob, first mentioned in 1214, altered in the late Gothic period, medieval nave. **Reformed church,** built by Willy Kräher and Karl Jenni in 1966.

Losone TI

19 □ C2

San Giorgio, mentioned since 1331, rebuilt in 1799. The choir of the original building has survived; now the sacristy, decorated with early 16C wall paintings.

Lostorf SO

2 □ C5

Schloss Wartenfels. The original fortress of the Barons of Wartenfels, named in 1250, no longer exists; the present building consists of parts of the 16–19C palas, converted into a patrician's house *c.* 1700.

Lottigna TI

13 □ D4

Catholic parish church of San Pietro e Paolo, mentioned since the 13C, enlarged and altered in 1632. Single-aisle building with two side chapels and polygonal apse, bell tower partly Romanesque. Baroque interior, 17C altars and stucco in the choir and chapels. On the S. wall of the nave is a 17C terracotta statue of the Virgin Mary. **Palazzo del Pretorio** or casa dei Landvogti, seat of the Landvogts of the

Le Locle: Château des Monts with clock museum and collection of automatic machines.

Blenio valley from 1550 to 1798. 16C rectangular building by G.Domenico Cima. Façade decorated with coats-of-arms. Now a *museum* with a small local history collection and an important collection of arms. Below the village, at the bottom of the valley, is a **chapel** with interesting 1445 frescos by Cristoforo da Seregno and Lombardo da Lugano.

Lotzwil BE

7 ☐ B2

Reformed church of St.Johannes der Täufer, built in 1682 as a baroque hall designed to emphasise the importance of preaching. Architect was Abraham I.Dünz, who also made the sculpted communion table and the font.

Loverciano TI
See CASTEL SAN PIETRO   19 ☐ D/E5

Löwenburg JU
1 ☐ D4

Löwenburg ruins: Initially owned by the lords of the same name, in the possesssion of the Münch family of Basel from *c.* 1360. After acquisition by the monastery of Lützel in 1526 it gradually fell into disrepair. The 13C complex consisted of the great hall, the courtyard to the W. of it with a round keep, cisterns and oven, outer walls and two gatehouses. **Former provostry** of the monastery of Lützel, built in the late 16C as a fortified farm-

stead, extended in the 18C. Residential and agricultural buildings, church, gatehouse and defence walls make up a picturesque group of post-Gothic buildings. In the cheese dairy is a *museum* with excavated finds from the ruins, farm and church.

Lucens VD
11 ☐ A2

First mentioned in the 10C, site of an episcopal château since the 13C. From 1542–1798 Lucens was the residence of the Bernese governor of Moudon, and the little town developed considerably in this period. **Château.** One of the canton's most impressive castles, built by the Bishops of Lausanne in the 13C, set on fire in 1476 and rebuilt a little later. Developed and extended in the 16C. Built on a ridge overlooking the Broye valley, the castle consists of two parts. The older part lies to the N. and is dominated by a stately round keep of the Savoy type (85 ft. high). The later part was built by the Bernese and extends over the rest of the plateau; it consists of an extensive palas on an irregular ground plan. A double ring wall with three oriel turrets surrounds the castle, which now serves as a *museum*. **Reformed church,** former Ste-Agnès chapel. 14C Gothic building; in the choir is a 15C votive painting, probably of Jean de Baulmes and his family.

Luchsingen GL
8 ☐ D4

Homogeneous village; the S. part, Adlenbach, is particularly attractive.

Ludiano TI
13 ☐ D4

Catholic parish church of San Secondo, mentioned since 1293, rebuilt in 1780. Beautiful classical façade with stucco. The interior is decorated with paintings and stucco by L.Peretti, *c.* 1800. Motto **San Pietro,** single-aisled Romanesque church with semicircular apse, buil

Lottigna: Landvogts' coats-of-arms on the façade of the Palazzo del Pretorio.

Lucens: 13C Château above the Broye valley.

Löwenburg: ruined castle excavated and restored in 1965.

in the 13C and altered in the 16&17C. 15C frescos in the apse.

Lüen GR

9☐B4

Reformed church. Irregular rectangular single room dating from 1084. Wall paintings *c.*1350 by the Waltensburg Master or his studio. On the E. wall is a depiction of the Apostles, on the S. wall scenes from the Life of Christ, on the N. wall the Passion.

Lugaggia TI

19☐D3

SUREGGIO **Catholic parish church of Santi Pietro e Paolo,** built in the Romanesque epoch on the foundations of a two-apse building which was probably Carol-

Lugaggia: Sureggio Catholic church with important Romanesque frescos.

ingian. 12&13C bell tower with twin arches. On the interior walls of the nave are important Romanesque paintings dating from the 2nd half of the 12C with scenes from the Life of Christ and a stylized view of the city of Milan.

Lugano TI

19☐D4

This city, mentioned by Gregory of Tours in 590, belonged to the bishopric of Como in the 9C, was part of the Duchy of Milan in the 15C and in 1499 came under the temporary rule of France. From 1516 to 1798 it was seat of the Landvogts of the Twelve Cantons and from 1803–78 it alternated with Locarno and Bellinzona as capital of Ticino. Since the 19C it has been an important tourist centre.

Cathedral of San Lorenzo, first mentioned in 818. Still essentially Romanesque, the church was enlarged in the 13 –14C, given a new façade in the 16C and side chapels in the 17&18C; in 1905 it was renovated and altered. The façade of 1500-17 is a masterpiece of the Lombardy Renaissance. It is divided into two horizontal parts and articulated by four pilasters. It has a round window and three portals, richly decorated with sculptures. Inside, on the W. wall, are fragments of 13C paintings, on the nave pillars are paintings from the 13 – 15C. In the second baroque S. chapel, built in 1774, is a fine altar with a 1632 painting by G.B.Carloni. Beautiful rococo statues (personified Virtues) on the walls. In the chapel to the S. of the chancel is a 16C font and next to it a sculpted stone tabernacle of the same period. At the entrance to the choir is a 17C marble high altar and in the choir are 1764 trompe l'oeil paintings by the Torricelli brothers. In the chapel to the N. of the choir is a 1430 font and next to it a 16C organ front. In the Piazza B.Luini **Santa Maria Degli Angioli,** formerly the church of a Franciscan monastery founded in 1490 and dissolved in 1848. The monastery church was built in 1499 – 1515; single-aisle building with four N. chapels. The choir is separated from the nave by a rood screen with three openings. This is decorated with a monumental wall painting, the work of Bernardino Luinis, 1529, depicting the Passion and Crucifixion of Christ. Depicted on the pillars are St.Sebastian, St.Roch and six prophets. By the same artist are the Last Supper on the S. wall, the Lamentation over Christ with St.Francis and St. Bernardino on one of the side-chapel pillars and the Virgin Mary with Child in the first chapel. In the second chapel is a painting of St.Francis by G.Antonio Petrini, 1728. On the walls of the fourth chapel are paintings with scenes from the Life of the Virgin Mary by

Lugano: San Lorenzo cathedral with Renaissance façade.

Lugano: Passion in S.Maria degli Angioli

Domenico de Pet, 1520 - 30. Under the rood screen arches are 16C paintings notably a View of Jerusalem. Piazza Dante **Catholic church of Sant'Antonio Abbate,** built in 1633 – 52, façade 1915 Single-aisle building with a semicircular apse. Inside is a 1734 high altar, in the chancel vault a St.Antony by G.Antonio Petrini, 1730. In the side chapels are three paintings by the same master. Via Nassa, **Catholic church of San Carlo Borromeo,** built in 1640-2. 17&18C interior. Painting behind the high altar of the Delivery of the Keys to St.Peter, attributed to G.A.Petrini. Via Loreto, **Catholic church of Santa Maria di Loreto,** built in 1524. Two-storey baroque porch with painted groin vault. Inside the church is a chapel, a copy of the Santa Casa di Loreto dating from 1728. Via Canova, **Catholic church of San Roco,** built in 1592-1602, 1909 neo-baroque façade. Inside are 17C wall paintings, vault paintings by Carlo Carlone, 1760, painting by the same master in the second chapel, stucco by Muzio Camuzzi. The city is no longer dominated by interesting old buildings. Amongst the more interesting buildings are: Piazza Cioccaro, 18C **Palazzo Riva,** trapezoid building with arcades on two sides; Piazza della Riforma, **Municipio,** town hall, built in 1844-5. In the court is a statue of Spartacus by Vincenzo Vela, 1848; Piazza A.Manzoni, **Palazzo Riva,** headquarters of the National Bank, elegant 18C brick baroque building; Via Pretorio No.7, 18C **Palazzo Riva,** portal with balcony above it; Via della Posta, **Poste centrale,** interesting building with corner tower, built by the architect T.Gohl in 1910; Parco civico, **Villa Ciani,** built by Luigi Clerichetti for G.Ciani in 1840. Next to it is the **Palazzo dei Congressi** by Rolf Otto, 1965-75. In the park 19C sculpture. Lungolago, Hotel **Splendid-Royal,** built in 1887 and enlarged in 1902. **Museums:** Villa Ciani, *Museo civico di belle arti,* painting collection. *Museo cantonale di storia naturale.*

Lumbrein GR

13☐E2

Catholic parish church of St.Martin. Rebuilt 1646&7. Baroque single room with narrower polygonal choir, beneath which is the ossuary. Paintings in the choir vault and stations of the rosary by Joh.Rud.Sturm, 1661. On the W. wall is the Last Judgement by Nicolao Giuliani,

1694. **St. Maria Magdalena chapel,** built in 1844, containing a late Gothic winged altar by Bernhard Strigel, 1490. Below the street is the **residential tower** of the Lords of Lumbrein, c. 1200. The upper storey, Blockbau with a shed-roof, was probably added in the 18C. In the hamlet of Sontg Andriu is the baroque **St. Andreas chapel,** built c. 1660, painted throughout by Joh.Christoph Guserer of Bavaria, 1695; on the N. chancel wall St. Placidus and St.Sigisbert, and picture of the monastery of Disentis before it was rebuilt. In Silgin is the **St. Sebastian chapel,** altered in 1643 with façade paintings dating from the 2nd half of the 18C. In **Crestaulta,** near Surin, is a Bronze Age settlement with adjacent burial ground on a flat-topped hill, 1400–800 BC.

Lungern OW

12☐D1

Catholic parish church of Herz Jesu, built to a neo-Gothic design by Wilhelm Josef Tugginer (1891-3).

Luthern LU

7☐C3

Catholic parish church of St.Ulrich, built by Jakob Singer and Johann Josef Purtschert. The design of interior, created here for the first time, dominated the church architecture of Central Switzerland for a whole century (▷ Ruswil).

Lütisburg SG

3☐D/E4

Catholic parish church of St.Michael, on a castle mound above the River Thur. Rebuilt 1810 – 11 using stone from Lütisburg Castle. Parts of the tower 1472. The **Ölbergkapelle** can be reached from the church through the former tower sacristy and a late Gothic portal. S. of the village is a covered **wooden bridge** over the Thur, built by Johann Ulrich Haltiner in 1790.

Lutry: Tour Bertholo, originally the residence of the Mayor family.

Lutry VD
10☐F3

Former possession of the bishop of Lausanne, fortified between 1212 and 1220; from the 11C it was the seat of a priory subordinate to the Abbey of Savigny en Lyonnais. **Reformed church** (St-Martin). Excavations uncovered the remains of the Romanesque priory church, which was incorporated into the present building; choir and polygonal apse 1260, nave and N. side chapels 14&15C, tower 1544. In 1570 the carved Renaissance portal was added to the W. façade. The nave and choir vaulting was painted in mannerist style by the Flemish painter Humbert Mareschet, 1577. **Château.** 15&16C, originally the residence of the episcopal administrator Mayor von Lutry. The massive entrance gate with echauguettes and machicolations on the Rue du Bourg dates from the 16C, decorative coats-of-arms 1640. In the vineyard above the village is the **tour Bertholo.** Residence from 13C of the Mayor family until the building of the château in the town. Interesting circular military building with a 17C house next to it. SAVUIT Huge 18C 'Roman scales' in the square.

Lützelflüh BE
7☐A4

The late Gothic **Reformed church** has a 1785 baroque organ. The **priest's house** is a 1655 Renaissance building. Ad-

jacent is the *Gotthelf-Stube* with memorabilia of the writer.

Luzein GR
9☐C3

Reformed church. Late Gothic single-aisled church by Steffan Klain, 1487, with late 15C wall paintings. The village is dominated by 8 **houses** of the Sprechers of Bernegg. In Putz, to the W. of Luzein, **Castels ruin,** probably 12C.

Luzern/Lucerne LU
7☐E3

Capital of the canton of the same name, it originally belonged to the monastery E. of the town, which was subordinate to the monastery of Murbach in Alsace in the 9C. With the establishment of its own parish in 1178 the town achieved a certain autonomy, which is why that year is considered the date of the town's foundation. In 1291 the Abbot of Murbach sold the important trade centre to King Rudolf I of Habsburg. With Lucerne's accession to the Confederation in 1332 an alliance of peasants and townsfolk was formed against the Habsburgs, which led to the decisive victory at Sempach in 1386. In the succeeding years Lucerne conquered most of the present area of the canton. During the Counter Reformation it was in the front line of the Catholic cantons, a position it maintained until its defeat in the 2nd Villmergen War in 1712. In 1798&9 Lucerne was briefly the seat of the Helvetian government and later led the Sonderbund of 1847.

MEDIEVAL TOWN Despite being a monastic foundation, the town did not develop around the monastery precinct, but evolved from a fishing and farming village on both sides of the Reuss. Thanks to its slow development within the ring of walls, until they were largely dismantled in the 19C, the town has maintained its medieval plan: enclosed squares—the Weinmarkt is probably the oldest—are integrated into a primarily longitudinal street system. The **Mühletor,** mentioned in 1314 and the

Lucerne: Old Town with Kapell bridge and water tower, Musegg in the background.

oldest surviving part of the fortifications, was part of the inner ring of walls on the right bank, which ran from Löwengraben to Grendel. Over 2800 ft. of the outer ring, the *c.* 1400 **Museggmauer** are still standing. All nine towers were originally open on the town side, as the 'Luegisland' still is. Only reconstructed fragments remain of the fortifications along the Hirschgraben on the left bank. **Kapellbrücke with Wasserturm:** Built around 1300 this is the oldest wooden bridge in Europe. (The even older Hofbrücke connecting the town with the monastery was dismantled in the mid 19C.) Lucerne's wooden bridges were, as covered wall passages, part of the town fortifications. In the case of the Kapellbrücke this can be seen from the higher cladding on the lake side and the approximately contemporary tower. Apart from defence, this was also used as an archive, prison and town treasury. In the roof truss of the bridge is an important cycle of pictures, painted in late Renaissance style from 1614 onwards under the direction of Heinrich Wägmann. In 1626–35 the much-rebuilt **Spreuerbrücke** was also decorated with pictures, a Dance of Death series by Kaspar Meglinger.

Town centre on the right bank **Stift im Hof:** The Benedictine monastery, mentioned in the 8C, was turned into a secular canonical foundation in 1455. **Collegiate church St. Leodegar und Mauritius.** The earlier Romanesque church was burnt down in 1633. A new building was then begun by the Jesuit brother Jakob Kurrer of Ingolstadt, incorporating the late Gothic W. towers, which had survived the fire. The pillared basilica, consecrated in 1644, is one of the few large late Renaissance churches N. of the Alps. The stylistically uniform interior is the work of Niklaus Geisler of Schweinfurt. In the choir is the earliest example of a perspective grille. In the **Collegiate treasury** (visits by appointment only!), the so-called Eschenbacher Plenar, a chased gold Romanesque book-cover, and a Romanesque chalice plundered from the Burgundians. The **St. Leonhard ossuary chapel** was built *c.* 1480. The church precinct is enclosed by the tomb-halls of 1639; their Tuscany arches are a variation on a Renaissance motif popular in Lucerne. **Propstei,** N. of the church, built in 1535, rebuilt to an early neoclassical design by Josef Singer in the late 18C. To the S. is the **Leutpriesterei,** a Gothic building of 1594.

The baroque **Marienbrunnen** dates from the 2nd half of the 17C. The **Rothenburgerhaus,** a 15C Blockbau, is the oldest wooden house preserved in its entirety in Switzerland. **Kapellkirche** (St. Peter's chapel) at the N. end of the bridge named after it. The oldest church within the town walls, it was structurally altered several times from the 12-18C. **Former Ursuline convent of Mariahilf,** built in 1676–81 by Heinrich Mayer. The unconventional E. end of the church is based on Bavarian-Bohemian baroque. To the E. of this church is the **Old Catholic church** on early Christian models. **St. Matthäus** behind the 'Schweizerhof', built in neo-Gothic style by Ferdinand Stadler in 1860-1. **Rathaus:** Built by Anton Isenmann of Prismell in 1602–6, retaining the medieval tower. While the façade was influenced by the Florentine early Renaissance, local tradition shows in the hipped saddleback roof. Inside is a splendid panelled Renaissance room. The 'Neue Kanzlei' of 1698 was influenced by monastery libraries. **Museggmagazin,** built 1685–6. This former corn and salt store room follows the pattern of Gothic functional buildings, as exemplified by the Altes Zeughaus in Pfistergasse. **Casino of the 'Herren zu Schützen'** at Löwengraben. This former Pfyffer summerhouse of 1719 was extended into a neoclassical single room building by Josef Singer in 1807. In 1755 Anton Schlegel designed the column of the **Mühlenplatzbrunnen;** its chinoiserie is an example of the rococo passion for exotic design. Notable amongst the **'Im Zöpfli'** group of houses below the Reuss bridge are the **Sonnenberghaus,** probably built by the amateur architect Thüring von Sonnenberg in 1787, and the **Roncahaus** (im Zöpfli No.3) of 1777. The latter's interior marks the transition from late rococo to Louis XVI. In 1595 the **Häuser unter der Egg** by Anton Isenmann were replaced by uniform stone buildings, rebuilt after the fire of 1833, retaining the old **Markthalle.** The Hotel des Balances and houses Nos.7 and 9 in Hirschplatz have neo-Renaissance **façade paintings** by Seraphin Weingartner. The **Göldlinhaus,** Hirschplatz No.12, built in

Spreuer bridge, with a series of Dance of Death pictures in the rafters.

Hofkirche, rebuilt from 1633 using the late Gothic towers.

1524-5, has a columned courtyard, *c.* 1600, inspired by the Regierungsgebäude. Also influenced by the same building is the **Am Rhyn-Haus.** This building, attached to the Rathaus, consists of two parts connected by a Tuscan bridge. The N. part, built as a Renaissance palazzo in 1616-18, houses a *Picasso collection.* The S. part was redesigned in classical style by Josef Singer

Rathaus, built in the Upper Italian Renaissance style.

in 1785–6. Kapellplatz: **Zurgilgenhaus** (No.1) rebuilt in 1507–10. Converted to baroque in 1731-2, with the exception of the tower, which used to be part of the town fortifications. The tower houses the oldest private library preserved in situ in Switzerland, with the books of the humanist Ludwig Zur Gilgen, who died in 1577. On the upper floor is a cycle of frescos after a series of woodcuts by Hans Burgkmair the Elder. The **Engelbergerhaus** (No.2) of 1532 originally belonged to the monastery of Engelberg, baroque conversion 1769. **Balthasarhaus** (No.7), now Willmann Stiftung (open to the public), rebuilt at the start of the 17C. Inside is a room with 1690 panelling. Schweizerhofquai: **Kreditanstalt**, neoclassical building of 1922. The neoclassical **Schweizerhof** was built in 1845 as the first grand hotel after the quay was redesigned in its present form. **SBB Building,** built to a neo-Renaissance design in 1887–9. Tourist buildings on the Halde: **Hotel National,** French-influenced neo-baroque, much toned down by later alterations (pilasters instead of columns). **Kursaal,** built in 1882, neo-classical conversion in 1910.

Hotel Palace of 1904–6 with art-nouveau architectural ornamentation. **Panorama** in Löwenplatz. Enormous round painting by Edouard Castres, depicting the crossing of the Bourbaki army into Switzerland in 1871. The **Löwendenkmal** (Lion Monument) is the oldest surviving statue monument in Switzerland. It commemorates the self-sacrifice of the Swiss Guard during the Tuileries Riot in 1792. The idea came from Carl Pfyffer of Altishofen, who escaped the fate of his brothers-in-arms thanks to being on leave. The lion was carved from the rock wall of a quarry by Lukas Ahorn in 1821, influenced by the Dane Bertel Thorwaldsen. The nearby **Gedenkkapelle** is a classical domed building of 1819.

TOWN CENTRE ON THE LEFT BANK **Former Franciscan church in der Au,** now parish church. Built around 1270–80 the church is a plain elongated building without a transept and with a ridge turret instead of a bell tower, following the mendicant order's ideal of poverty. The chapels, added later, were decorated with stucco by masters from Ticino in 1626 and from Wessobrunn in 1673. Lavish mannerist pulpit by Niklaus Geisler (▷ Hofkirche). The **Spitalbrunnen** by the church once stood in the courtyard of the old Bürgerspital. It is a copy of the original of 1651. **Jesuit Church of St. Franz Xaver,** built in 1666–77. It is not certain who designed this, Switzerland's first large baroque church, but it may well have been the Jesuit father Heinrich Mayer, who later built the local Mariahilf church and the Jesuit church of ▷ Solothurn. The stucco was certainly designed by him and is the first example of the work of the Wessobrunn School in the whole of Switzerland. The **Reformed Lukaskirche** is a concrete building of 1935, stained glass by Louis Moilliet. **Station,** built in 1894–6, partly burnt down in 1971. Adjacent is the **Kunst- und Kongresshaus,** built by Armin Meili 1930–3. The collection of the *Kunstmuseum* housed here covers art from the 16C to the present day, concentrating on the 19C and early 20C. Temporary exhibitions of contemporary art. The **Rossebändiger,** set up in front of the Kunsthaus in 1934, and the

*Lion memorial, 1821, with inscription
'Helvetiorum fidei ac virtuti'.*

*Detail from the circular 'Bourbaki painting'
(1889) in the Panorama.*

Schwingergruppe of 1905 on the nearby
'Inseli' are the work of Hugo Siegwart.
Regierungsgebäude (Ritterscher Palast).
Built under the influence of the Florentine
early Renaissance by Ticino architects
from 1556, this residential palace was
given to the Jesuits by the town in 1577,
following the death of the architect
Schultheiss Lux Ritter. Rustic façade and
Tuscan columned court show the town's
attachment to the South and were copied
in a number of buildings, such as the
Rathaus and Göldlinhaus. In the court is
the **Weinmarktbrunnen** (copy on the
original site in the Weinmarkt). The late
Gothic fountain, made by Konrad Lux of
Basel in 1481, has 1737-9 Régence additions. **Staatsarchiv** (state archive), opposite the Regierungsgebäude. The former
Jesuit College is a block-like baroque
building with arcades and mansard roof.
Former Kantonsbibliothek (cantonal library), now Finance Department, built in
1846-9 to a late neoclassical design by the
Munich architect Johann Seidl. The **Kor-
porationsgebäude** am Reusssteg (No.7),
former patrician seat of the Sonnenberg
family, was originally two houses converted
in 1670 - 3. Inside is an 11 ft. long
panorama of the town dating from 1820-
5. **Former Zeughaus** (arsenal), built in
1567. As the shape of the windows reveals,
this building is still entirely late Gothic.
In Kasernenplatz is the **former
Waisenhaus** (orphanage), built by Josef
Singer, 1808 - 11. This sober classical
building houses the *Natur-Museum* with
ancient history and natural history collections. Opposite lies the **Anderallmen-
dhaus** of 1679. The similarity of this

*Lavishly sculpted pulpit (1628) in the
Franziskanerkirche.*

half-timbered building to the slightly older
Spitalmühle in Pilatusplatz suggests that
they were built by the same architect.
Former Spital zum Heiligen Geist,
now municipal police station, built 1654
-60 on the pattern of a baroque monastery.
The main façade was altered by Josef
Singer in 1783. **Krienbachschulhaus,**
late classical building of 1857.
Gewerbeschule, Heimbachweg No.12,
reinforced concrete construction of 1956
- 8. Albert F.Zeyer built the
Dulaschulhaus in 1931-3 in the style of

Jesuit church (1666&7) the first large baroque building in Switzerland.

Tuscan columned court inside the Rittersche Palast.

the 'new functionalism'. **Kellerhof** (Kino Moderne), completed in 1883. This castle-like complex was the seat of the building contractor Wilhelm Keller, whose buildings dominate the entire Hirschmatt quarter. The **Liebenauhaus** in Franciskanerplatz contains a room with a Régence stucco ceiling. **Fideikommishaus von Segesser,** built 1751-2 by Hans Georg Urban. This rococo palace still belongs to the family and is articulated by a central projection and pilasters. The **Grundhof** in Obergrundstrasse (No.11) is a classical mansion. The country seat of **Himmelrich** on the same street (No.61), a rococo palace built for Franz Placidus Schumacher, who pursued his optical studies here. The construction on the roof was his observatory.

OUTER DISTRICTS In the **Catholic church of St.Paulus** in Obergrund, built by Karl Moser in 1911 - 12, characteristic neo-Gothic features are combined with art nouveau. **Sentikirche** in Baselstrasse. The church of the former infirmary was rebuilt in 1662 and acquired a classical façade designed by Josef Singer in 1817-19. Cath-

olic church of St.Karli by the bridge of the same name. Built by Fritz Metzger in 1932-4, it was the first concrete church in central Switzerland. Nearby is the **St. Karli chapel,** built *c.* 1630, with decorative interior paintwork. **Capuchin monastery auf dem Wesemlin,** founded by the Order in 1583, followed by enlargement of the existing pilgrimage church and the erection of the monastery buildings. The church is still late Gothic, while the cloister, built at the same time, is already Renaissance in design. **Schloss Steinhof,** built by Marschall Thüring von Sonnenberg in 1759. As was common in the baroque, the client for whom the house was built was also its designer. **Landhaus Tribschen** was the home of Richard Wagner from 1866-72. In memory of the composer there is a *museum;* exhibits include a collection of old musical instruments and the original manuscript score of the 'Siegfried Idyll'. The **Dorenbach mansion,** mentioned in 1446 was altered in the mid 18C. The contemporary painting in the panelled rooms is an example of a device popular in country houses in Lucerne of transposing French ornamental engravings into colour. A few rooms in the **Landhaus Oberlöchli,** built for Ludwig Pfyffer of Altishofen in 1754, are similarly decorated. The **country seat of Utenberg** houses a *costume museum.* Erected by Jakob Singer in 1758, the building departs from the pattern of the

Former orphanage, rebuilt in its original form 1975&6 in the Kasernenplatz.

Observatory on top of the Himmelrich house, 1772.

mansions mentioned above with its lighter roof structure. Two outstanding examples of historicist houses are the **Villa Bellerive** (Bellerivestr.19), built in 1888 in Italian neo-Renaissance style, and the **Villa Dreilinden** (Conservatory), built in 1890–1, which shows the influence of the English cottage style.
Museums and collections: *Staatsarchiv.* Oldest documents 11–12C. The *Stadtarchiv* (now 6 Industriestrasse) was established when the state records were split in 1803. The *Zentralbibliothek,* opened in 1951, has a picture archive. *Historisches Museum* (collection currently in storage). *Kunstmuseum* in the Kunst- und Kongresshaus (see text). *Natur-Museum* in the Waisenhaus (see text). *Verkehrshaus der Schweiz* with planetarium.

St.Karli, the first concrete building in inner Switzerland.

Largest transport museum in Europe, covering all areas of transport and information technology. Adjoining the Verkehrshaus is the *Hans Erni Museum* with over 300 works by the artist. *Schweizerische Trachten- und Heimatmuseum* (national costume and local history) in Utenberg. *Richard-Wagner-Museum* in the Tribschen mansion. *Panorama* in Löwenplatz. Holes worn in the rock by glacial water are a geological curiosity to be admired in the *Gletschergarten.* Also collection with geographical and ethnographic exhibits. *Picasso-Sammlung* (Donation Rosengart) in the Am Rhyn-Haus. *Collegiate treasury* of the Hofkirche.

Luziensteig GR
See **Maienfeld** 9☐B2

Lyss BE
6☐D3

Old church of St. Johannes Evangelista, built in 1612 retaining Romanesque sections. The choir stalls of 1675 (and the pulpit, now in the new church) date from the later baroque conversion.

M

Madiswil BE

7☐B2

Reformed church of St.Blasius, built in 1778, tower 1810. Baroque, flat-ceilinged hall designed to emphasise the importance of preaching, with wooden pulpit of 1779. The 1607 **priest's house** has a half-hipped roof and semicircular wooden decoration under the gables.

Magdenau SG
See FLAWIL

3☐E4

Maggia TI

19☐B1

On a hill above the village **Catholic parish church of San Maurizio;** very old original building, altered in the 19C. Single-aisle building with square choir, two side chapels with 17C stucco and statues. Monumental staircase, 1881. Outside the village is the **Santa Maria delle Grazie 'di Campagna' chapel,** rectangular building with semicircular apse, built *c.* 1510 above an older chapel and repeatedly extended. The chapel contains a series of interesting wall paintings, mostly early 16C. In the apse Coronation of the Virgin Mary, Crucifixion and Apostles, on the S. wall of the nave scenes from the Life of St.Anne and the Life of the Virgin Mary. In the N. side chapel frescos and stucco dating from 1625-6.

Magliaso TI

19☐D4

Catholic parish church Santi Biagio e Macario, built *c.* 1680; rotunda, oval dome with lantern. In the choir marble high altar, 1680; in the side chapels 18C altars. Next to the church medieval **casello** with 17C extension.

Maggia: Coronation of Mary in the apse of the Santa Maria delle Grazie chapel.

Maienfeld GR

9☐B2

This small medieval town, which had oval walls with 3 gate towers, developed on the site of a Roman bridge garrison from a royal court named as 'curtis lupinis' in the Carolingian land register. The town is dominated by **town houses and mansions** such as the **Rathaus,** a former Gothic residence with a staircase tower, altered in 1589, and the **Brügger-Haus** opposite, a building dating from 1643 with corner projections, 16C core. To the N. is the **Reformed church,** the only transverse church without a choir in Grisons, built in 1720-4 with contemporary Régence stucco ceiling. S. of this is **Schloss Brandis,** which developed from a medieval castle formerly outside the town walls. Of the older buildings the 13C residential tower and the 'neues Schloss' of 1465 have survived. In the former residential storey of the tower early Gothic wall paintings (1320) have been revealed, early works by the Master of Waltensburg:

inn scenes, scenes from the Dietrich Saga and the Life of Samson. Above the town **Schloss Salenegg**. The present 17&18C complex has an elongated façade articulated by pilasters and projections overlooking the valley. To the E. in front of the Schloss, on the longitudinal axis, baroque gardens with corner pavilions connected by arcades with vines. In the Steigwald is the **Heidibrunnen** in memory of Johanna Spyri's fictional character. LUZIENSTEIG **St. Luzius**. Replaced a Carolingian building with semicircular apse. The present church has a single aisle (before 1457) with narrower late Gothic polygonal apse. Wall paintings from two periods: on the N. wall and in the tower are fragments from the early 14C, Last Judgement on the N. wall and Legend of St. Luzius on the long W. wall, 1457.

Maienfeld: Schloss Brandis has paintings by the Waltensburg master.

Malans: Schloss Bothmar, with baroque garden in the W.

Mairengo TI

13 ☐ C4

Catholic parish church of San Siro, one of the oldest churches in the Leventina valley, mentioned in 1170, but probably dating back to the 11C; altered in the 16C and later. Tower rebuilt in 1574-5. Two aisles with rectangular choirs. Façade with blind arches, late Gothic winged altar from a German workshop, 1510-20; interesting 1558 wall paintings by Gerolamo Gorla da Milano and 17C paintings.

Malans GR

9 ☐ B3

This wine-growing village is dominated by 17C **town houses,** including the 1685 **Rathaus** with panelled council chamber, and stove by David Pfau, 1690. The **Reformed church** was built in the Gothic period (1469). Porch and gallery were added in 1773 and the vaults, in particular, were decorated with rococo stucco at the same time. The **Planta-Häuser** are grouped around an inner courtyard with farm buildings and dairy, built in the course of the 17C. Lavish furnishing: stoves, panelling, stucco. Above the village **Schloss Bothmar,** central building 16C,

side buildings and tower 18C; late baroque interior. Adjacent to the W. is the finest surviving French baroque garden in Switzerland. To the N. **Wynegg ruin.**

Malters LU

7 ☐ E3

Catholic parish church of St. Martin, built by Fidel Obrist in 1833-5. The porch of this neoclassical building is integral with the nave and thus adds to the block-like impression given by the exterior.

Malvaglia TI

13 ☐ D5

Catholic parish church of San Martino. Original building mentioned in the 13C. Single aisle with two side chapels and polygonal apse. Nave rebuilt 1525 and extended in 1602&3. Very beautiful 12C Romanesque tower with dwarf gallery and double and triple windows. On the main façade 16C frescos, including an enormous St.Christopher. Inside numerous 16C wall paintings and in the chapels 17C stucco. Next to the church **Santi Enrico e Apollinare chapel** with 1551 wall paintings.

Malval GE

16 □ D2

Outside the village **Reformed chapel** (Ste-Marie-Madeleine). Founded in the 10C, rebuilt in the Gothic period, 1932 tower with arches.

Mammern TG

See STECKBORN   3 □ C2

Marbach SG

4 □ B4

Catholic parish church of St. Georg. Rebuilt after 1466, nave rebuilt in 1852 by Felix Wilhelm Kubly, tower still partly Romanesque. **Schloss Weinstein,** mentioned in 1375, rebuilt in 1479, now a restaurant. Massive substructure and projecting half-timbered upper storey, late medieval.

Mariastein SO

1 □ F4

The **Benedictine monastery** was transferred from ▷ Beinwil in 1648 to the pilgrimage shrine of Our Lady 'im Stein'. The monastery church, built at that time in the Gothic style, was given a neoclassical façade in 1830–4. Neo-baroque interior.

Mariazell LU

See SURSEE   7 □ D2

Marly FR

11 □ C/D1

St. Peter und Paul, first mentioned in 1294, rebuilt in 1785 and altered in the 19C; 17C font, 19C high altar. Adjacent

Malvaglia: San Martino has the highest Romanesque tower in the Tessin.

Märstetten: the impressive 16C Schloss Altenklingen.

is the 18C **priest's house.** In the middle of the village, next to the **St. Sebastian chapel,** first mentioned in the 16C, is **Haus Gottrau,** a massive 19C building with a mansard roof.

Märstetten TG

3 □ D2/3

Reformed church St.Jakob: Mentioned in 1155, choir tower 13&14C, nave lengthened and tower superstructure 1487–9, sacristy 1525. **Hohes Haus,** built as a tithe house in 1613. Half-timbered building with projecting upper storey and N. arcade. **Schloss Altenklingen,** in the Kemmen valley N. of Märstetten. Founded around 1200 and rebuilt in 1587, since when it has belonged to the Zollikofer family of St.Gallen. The complex consists

Marthalen: group of half-timbered buildings in the village square.

of two late Gothic gabled houses at right angles to each other. Inside are plaques with pictures and coats-of-arms, ancestral portraits and ornamental tapestries from the Renaissance and baroque periods.

Martigny: imposing ruin of the medieval Château La Bâtiaz.

Marthalen ZH

3☐B2

Attractive farming village in the Zürich wine-growing district with superb 16, 17&18C **half-timbered buildings.**

Martigny VS

17☐C3

As an important station on the road to the Great St.Bernard Pass, Martigny was the site of a Celtic 'oppidum' in 57BC. Under the Romans Octodurus, as it was then called, was elevated by Emperor Claudius (41–54) to the rank of Imperial market town. Around 381 Martigny was the seat of Theodor (St-Théodule), first bishop of the Valais, and remained episcopal seat until 585, the approximate date of the transfer of the bishopric to Sion. From 1384 it belonged to Savoy, in 1475 it was again under the control of the bishop. Important development of the town in the 18&19C. Little survives of the Roman settlement; in the SE of the town are remains of an **amphitheatre** and the foundations of a Gallo-Roman **temple,** discovered in 1976, which are now in the *Römermuseum.* On a hill in the N. of the town, dominating the Drance valley, is the **château de la Bâtiaz,** one of the most impressive surviving medieval buildings in the Valais. The

Martigny: 'Le Manoir', built in 1730 for the Bannerhauptmann.

strategically important position was presumably defended by a tower even in Roman times; a first castle was probably built in the 13C by the Bishop of Sion. Peter II of Savoy, owner of the castle from 1260–8, commissioned the remarkable circular keep, which still stands; surrounding wall and residential sections were later added by the bishops of Sion. La Bâtiaz was sacked in 1475 and set on fire in 1518. MARTIGNY-VILLE **Catholic parish church of Notre-Dame-des-Champs,** baroque building, built 1645–87 on the foundations of a medieval church. Nave and two aisles with polygonal apse, marble main entrance with broken gable and very beautiful carved door, side portals with similar doors. On the outside of the choir is a Roman milestone. 1700 baroque high altar, choir stalls 1684; in the niches in the upper part of the nave are Gothic statues of Apostles by Jean Boular, 15C. Behind the church is the **Provostry,** built in the 16C and altered in 1753; Napoleon stayed here in 1800 on the way to Marengo. Rue de l'Hôtel de Ville, **Hôtel de Ville,** building on arches, 1866&7; on the staircase stained glass by E.Bille, 1949. Rue du Collège, **Collège,** formerly Auberge de la Tour, 17C, portal dated 1669. 1 Rue des Alpes, **maison Supersaxo,** the oldest house in the town, built by Ulrich Ruffiner in the 16C, later completely altered. Nearby, at Place Centrale, No.7, is **la Grande-Maison,** a 17C building, much altered; former inn, guests included Goethe and Alexandre Dumas. Lower down **le Manoir,** a spacious square building, built by J.-J.Ganioz, capitaine of Martigny, in 1730.

LA BATIAZ This part of the town is reached by a covered **wooden bridge** dating from 1830. On the left bank of the Drance is the **Notre-Dame-De-Compassion chapel,** founded in 1595 and rebuilt in 1617 and 1748. 1755 rococo altar and fine collection of 18&19C votive pictures.

MARTIGNY-BOURG Traditional old market town. On the Rue Centrale, lined with low houses, is the **former Parish Hall** (No.35), building on arches, 1645. In the square is the **Hôtel des Trois Couronnes,** former residence of the Bishop's vidame, built in the 17C and altered in the 18&19C.

LE BROCCARD Above the village are the **ruins** of the former episcopal château of la Crète or Saint-Jean, mentioned in the 13C, which is probably on the site of the Celtic 'oppidum'. **Saint-Jean chapel,** Romanesque in origin, rebuilt in the 17C.

Märwil TG
See AFFELTRANGEN 3□D/E3

Maschwanden ZH
7□F1

Reformed parish church. Late Gothic

Mathod: 18C horseshoe-shaped Château.

church *c.* 1500 with nave and choir. Parts of the original interior (windows and carved wooden ceiling) are now in the Schweizerische Landesmuseum; the church contains copies.

Maseltrangen SG
See SCHÄNIS 8□D/E2

Massongex VS
17□B1

The former Roman settlement of Tarnaiae was a staging post on the route to the Great St. Bernard pass. In the restaurant au Caveau Romain, above the former thermal springs, is a **Roman mosaic** depicting two men fighting. On the façade of the 19C **Catholic parish church of St-Jean-Baptiste** is a Roman inscription by a certain Sectus Varennuns Priscus, 2C AD.

Mathod VD
5□E5

On the cantonal road in the direction of Yverdon, **château,** a very beautiful building, commissioned by the Dutchman Gaspard Burman in the late 18C, incorporating older sections. The elegant main façade with two side wings is influenced by Palladian architecture.

Mathon GR
14□A1

Ruined church of St. Antonius: Nave walls and lower storey of the tower Romanesque, rectangular choir with barrel vaulting and belfry, late Gothic, evidence of a pre-Romanesque semicircular apse.

Matt GL
8☐E4

Reformed church, altered in 1758, retaining substantial parts of an earlier building dating from 1261. In the nave, late Gothic wooden ceiling of 1497.

Mauensee LU
7☐D2

The **Schloss** on Mauensee Island was built in 1605–8 for Michael Schnyder, Mayor of Sursee.

Maur ZH
3☐B5

Reformed parish church. Built in its present form in 1507–12; the neo-Gothic tower dates from 1874&5. **Priest's house** of 1563 with late Gothic beamed ceiling in the drawing room. So-called **'Schloss',** greatly altered residential tower of medieval origin.

Mauvoisin VS
See **Bagnes**
17☐D3

Mayens-de-Sion VS
See **Sion**
17☐E2

Medel GR
13☐C2

Platta **Catholic parish church of St. Martin.** baroque, 1774, incorporating the earlier building. In Sogn Gagl **St.Gallus chapel.** Flat-ceilinged and rectangular, probably built in the 11C or 12C. On the end wall Italian style early Gothic wall painting dating from the first half of the 14C. The **farmhouse** No.3 in Curaglia has a 1510 façade picture by Antonius da Tradate with a Crucifixion and two female saints.

Mauensee: 17C Schloss on an island in the lake of the same name.

Medel: baroque parish church in Platta with paintings from an earlier building.

Meggen LU
7☐F3

Catholic parish church, built by Franz Füeg in 1964 – 6. Vordermeggen. **Neuhabsburg ruins,** built c. 1240 by Rudolf III of Habsburg, destroyed by the 4 forest cantons in 1342. **Schlossvilla Neuhabsburg,** built in picturesque castle style in 1868–71. **St.Niklaus chapel,** on a little island near Meggenhorn. From the lake side of the building one can see the patron saint of mariners, an early 14C statue of St. Nicholas of Myra. **Schloss Meggenhorn:** Heinrich Viktor von Segesser redesigned this country seat on the pattern of a French Renaissance château in 1886–99. The **castle chapel,** also by Heinrich Viktor von Segesser, is a gem of neo-Gothic architecture.

Meierhof GR
See **Obersaxen**
13☐E1

Meggen: neo-Gothic chapel in Schloss Meggenhorn, 1888.

Meierskapell LU

7☐F2

The **Vorderspichten farmhouse** is a Blockbau on a stone substructure, built in 1765, with a large flight of steps on the entrance side.

Meikirch BE

6☐E4

Reformed church. Late Gothic single room, converted to baroque in 1747. On the S. side Romanesque tower articulated with pilaster strips and blind arches. Neoclassical **priest's house** of 1795.

Meilen ZH

8☐B1

Principal town of the region on Lake Zürich with several opulent country houses. **Reformed parish church.** The present building of this ancient church (*c.* 700) consists principally of sections added in major conversions in *c.* 1493–5 (choir and tower), 1683 (nave) and 1786 (extension). Inside late rococo stucco. **Landgut Seehalde,** rococo alteration 1767 – 8, presumably by David Morf; lavish rococo

interior. **Landgut Seehof.** Rococo mansion by David Morf (1767). The famous wrought iron by Sixtus Kambli, Hans Jakob Ochsner and Johann Heinrich Daelliker is partly here and partly in the Schweizerische Nationalmuseum. The author Conrad Ferdinand Meyer lived in Seehof from 1872-6. **Landgut Mariafeld** in **Feldmeilen.** Large 17C complex, converted in part in neo-Gothic style. The 'Round Table of Mariafeld', whose members included Georg Herwegh, Gottfried Keller, Franz Liszt, Richard Wagner, Gottfried Semper and Wilhelm Mommsen, used to meet here. Residence of General Ulrich Wille.

Meiringen BE

12☐D/E1

Reformed church of St. Michael, rebuilt in 1684 to plans by Abraham I.Dünz. The sanctuary walls of the previous late Gothic church were incorporated into the new building. The Romanesque lower church, with a nave and two aisles, contains fragments of wall paintings from *c.* 1300. In the detached late Romanesque **tower** is the oldest dated bell (1351) in canton Bern. The two-storey **graveyard chapel** contains frescos *c.* 1500. *Museum der Landschaft Hasli,* by the church (local museum).

Melano TI

19☐D4

At the edge of the village **Catholic parish church of Sant'Andrea.** Rotunda with an octagonal dome, built by Luigi Fontana in 1850. Next to it is the baroque tower of the earlier church. In the piazza 17C **casa Canavesi.** On the portico is a 1668 frieze with pessimistic aphorisms.

Above the village, in CASTELLETTO, a way of the cross leads to the **cappella della Madonna,** a 1634–44 baroque building containing lavish stucco decoration, marble high altar with a 15C picture of the Virgin Mary. Beautiful collection of 17– 20C votive pictures.

Melchnau BE

7☐B2

The **Reformed church of St. Georg** is a baroque room designed to emphasise the importance of preaching dating from 1709&10. Inside is a 1582 late Gothic font. The rest of the furnishings date mainly from the time of constuction. The **priest's house** is a baroque hip-roofed building of 1749. A small *Ortsmuseum* (local museum) is housed in the Haus der alten Ölpresse (by the station). The keep, remains of the palas and the outer works are still recognisable among the **Grünenberg Burg ruins,** to the E. of the village.

Mellingen AG

2☐E4

Old Town. Founded by the Kyburgs in the mid 13C. Parts of the town walls and some towers and gates still survive, in particular the **Reusstor,** the medieval **Hexenturm** in the N. and the **Lenzenburgertor,** also called the **Zeitturm** (1544–7) in the W. **Catholic parish church of St. Johannes Baptist.** Early baroque single room of 1657 with 1830 neoclassical interior. The tower dates from 1523; on its ground floor is a baptistery with late Gothic frescos.

Mels SG

9☐A2

Storage town for Gonzen iron ore, iron forges mentioned in 1412. The village square, which served as the Landsgemeindeplatz (annual community assembly area) from 1831–61, is the only square in the Sargans area which has survived in its original form. **Catholic parish church of St. Peter und Paul.** Rebuilt in 1727–32 by Hans Georg Schueler and Martin Masügger, neo-baroque conversion by Adolf Gaudy, 1922–3. **Capuchin monastery,** built 1651–4 by Jakob and Peter Lang. S. convent wing extended by Felix Schmid in 1869–72. The **priest's house,** a three-storey gabled building, was built in

Mellingen: country town on the Reuss founded by the Kyburgs.

1748. The **Gemeindeverwaltung** (local government building), formerly Haus Good, was built in neoclassical style in 1842 to plans by Felix Wilhelm Kubly. Built by the same architect is the **former Armenhaus** (poorhouse), now house of retreat, 1838&9. **Drogerie Reichlin,** old Gasthaus Schlüssel, with the finest half-timbering in the Sargans region. The group of houses running from **Haus Lendi** to the **David-Nagler-Haus** are characteristic 17C wooden buildings. In Heiligkreuz, opposite Mels station, is the **Heiligkreuz chapel,** a late Gothic building with wall paintings dating from the last quarter of the 15C (transferred to canvas). **St. Antonius of Padua chapel** in Butz-Hintersberg, SE of Mels. Built in 1938&9 by Albert Scheier, frescos by Ferdinand Gehr. **Schlösschen Nidberg** was built to the W. of Mels in the style of a 17C town house in 1604 to replace a 13C Burg. The hill of **Castels,** NW of Mels, is the site of pre- and early historic settlements, finds from the Bronze Age and Hallstatt period, the Melnau and la Tène cultures, also from Roman times; Alemanic graves.

Meltingen SO

1☐F5

Catholic parish and pilgrimage church of Maria im Hag. Late Gothic choir and tower, new nave *c.* 1730. Interior

Mendrisio: the Catholic priory church is a monumental 19C rotunda.

Mendrisio: Romanesque San Martino articulated with blind arches.

features include stained glass depicting the Crucifixion, related to the glass in the Münster in Bern.

Mendrisio TI

19☐D5

Mentioned in 793; in the Middle Ages it was governed first by Como and then Milan, and administered by the famous Della Torre family. In 1512 it was occupied by the Confederates and became a Landvogt's residence until the end of the 18C. In a dominant position above the town is **Santi Cosma e Damiano,** built in 1863–75 to plans by Luigi Fontana. Monumental rotunda with octagonal dome and lantern; façade with portico. Inside 1670 high altar and a 15C polychrome wooden figure of the Virgin Mary. Piazzetta dei Serviti, **former Servite monastery,** mentioned in 1251, dissolved in 1852. *Former monastery church of San Giovanni,* rebuilt in baroque style in 1722–38; 16C tower. Lavish interior stucco and 18C paintings, in the choir statue of the Virgin Mary in a stucco frame. N. of the church

is the *cloister* of the former monastery, 17&18C. In the corner of the Via Ginnasio is the **Santa Maria delle Grazie chapel,** probably 13C. Baroque interior with stucco and paintings, on the altar 15C fresco of the Virgin Mary. Via Sta Maria, **Santa Maria in Borgo chapel,** originally medieval, rebuilt in the baroque period. Part of the Romanesque tower of the earlier church remains. The N. side chapel of 1656, dedicated to San Carlo, with small lantern dome; marble altar with terracotta statues by Agostino Silva, 1662. N. of Mendrisio, near the motorway, is the **Catholic church of San Martino,** first mentioned in 962. The present 12&13C Romanesque building was built over three earlier churches, the oldest of which was probably pre-Carolingian. The Romanesque nave with blind arches has survived; the choir with belfry and various extensions was built in 1695. 17&18C interior. In the piazza is a **medieval tower,** a massive fortress-like rectangular building, possibly 12C, later used as a bell tower. Via Nobile Torriani No.1, **Palazzo Torriani,** an extensive baroque residence, built for A.N.Torriani in 1719-20. **Hospital:** classical building with monumental portico, built by Luigi Fontana in 1853. On the opposite side is the **Villa Argentina,** a beautiful 19C building in the Palladian style by the architect Antonio Croci. Mendrisio also has numerous interesting late 19C and early 20C buildings.

TORRE Small township on the heights above Mendrisio, where the castello of the Della Torre family once stood, destroyed in 1350; the present **palazzo** dates from the 17C. **Catholic church of San**

Sisinio, first mentioned in 1276. 19C interior painting.

Mengestorf BE
See KÖNIZ   6 ☐ E5

Menzingen ZG
8 ☐ A2

Catholic parish church of St.Johannes der Täufer, rebuilt in 1624-5. Tower and vault ribs in the choir are from the previous late Gothic building. High altar in the style of the late Renaissance, 1639. **Institut Heiliges Kreuz,** the mother house of the Sisters of the Holy Cross, who work principally as nurses. The *church* with its massive dome was built by August Hardegger in 1895-7. W. of Menzingen, in the hamlet of EDLIBACH, is the **Staub** residence, built around 1768, which transfers urban design to a rural half-timbered building.

Merenschwand AG
7 ☐ F1

Gasthaus zum Schwanen. This building, partly 16C, is the most lavishly decorated half-timbered building in Aargau. Innkeeper Heinrich Fischer (1790-1861) played an important role in the history of Aargau in the 19C.

Meride TI
19 ☐ D5

In the village square is the **Catholic church of San Rocco,** first mentioned in 1578, rebuilt in baroque style in 1770-2. On the N. wall of the interior is a painting of St.Lucia by Pietro Gnocchi, 1595. In the cemetery is the **Catholic parish church of San Silvestro,** first mentioned in 1483. Nave and two aisles with rectangular choir, 19C portico on the S.side, columns set on medieval capitals. Interior choir painting by F.Antonio Giorgioli, 1690, pulpit 1595. The fine village has numerous interesting **houses.** Hauptstrasse, No.45, **Gemeindehaus** (parish

Meride: fine village in the Tessin with interesting fossil museum.

hall) and *Fossilienmuseum* (fossils), three-storey gallery in the courtyard. At the E. end of the same street is the **casa Oldelli,** built in 1740-60, court with two-storey gallery, very beautiful rococo balustrade opposite.

Merishausen SH
3 ☐ A1

Reformed parish church. This church was rebuilt in 1838 on the site of a church of St.Martin mentioned as early as 846; the tower dates from 1589. **Gemeindehaus** (parish hall). Late Gothic step-gabled house, built in the late 16C. Striking farm buildings: **Zehntscheune** (tithe barn) or **Spitalscheune** of 1560 (now a farmhouse) and **Abtscheune** by Lorenz Schreiber (1704).

Merlischachen SZ
7 ☐ F3

The **farmhouses** on the mountain side of the village street are Blockbau on a brick base; some have small canopies above windows and doors.

Mervelier JU
1 ☐ F5

Catholic parish church of St.Rémy, built in 1770-2, altered in 1841. The façade

Mesocco: Santa Maria del Castello with tall Romanesque campanile.

Mesocco: remains of the citadel with ruins of San Carpoforo.

is transitional from late baroque to early neoclassical and shows the influence of Pisoni.

Mesocco GR

13 ☐ F5

Catholic parish church of Santi Pietro e Paolo, Unarticulated baroque building, extended in the first half of the 17C. **Catholic church of San Rocco,** built in the 16C, Capuchin hospice since 1668. **Lower casa a Marca,** 1668. **casa Maggiorasca** or **upper casa a Marca** (No.97), 1597. **Catholic church of Santa Maria del Castello:** Six-storey Romanesque tower *c.* 1100, nave lengthened and choir rebuilt by Giov. Battista Viscardi. Interior painted by the da Seregno brothers *c.* 1460: On the N. wall of the nave are scenes from the Passion, pictures of saints and the cycle of the months. 1757 ceiling with beams, Gothic niche tomb *c.* 1320 on the S. side of the tower. **Ruins of Castello di Mesocco:** former refuge castle, extended by the Barons of Vaz in the 11&12C. **Santa Maria** was incorporated in the outer works. Large courtyard with wall and 5 towers; fortified buildings with keep. To

the N. is the **ruined church of San Carpoforo.** Small single-aisled building with horseshoe-shaped apse (11C). The campanile has twin round-arch windows in the five upper storeys. SAN BERNARDINO San Bernardino chapel *c.* 1450. **Catholic church of San Bernardino,** neoclassical rotunda based on S. Carlo in Milan, 1867. Between Mesocco and San Bernardino **impressive section of the Nationalstrasse 13.**

Mettau AG

2 ☐ D3

Catholic parish church of St. Remigius: Late baroque single room of 1773–5 with rococo interior. Stucco by Lucius Gambs, ceiling paintings by Franz Fidel Bröchin. Interior renovated 1978&9.

Mettmenstetten ZH

7 ☐ F1

Reformed parish church. Built largely 1520&1 on the site of an older church (mentioned in 998). Carved late Gothic

Mex: late-18C farmhouse of the Château in massive masonry.

wooden ceiling by Jakob Winkler and 17C paintings in the choir arch.

Mex VD

10□E2

In the centre of the village 16C **château,** enlarged around 1650 for Jean-François de Charrière. The main façade overlooking the park has three galleries, one above the other, and two towers.

Meyriez FR

6□C4

Reformed church. Single-aisled building with polygonal apse, main portal 1670.

Mézières FR

11□B2

By the church **château,** a rectangular building with a polygonal tower, probably built over an earlier building. On the main façade arms of the Diesbach family.

Mézières VD

11□A3

Reformed church, built in 1706–7, entrance tower 1731. Inside is a stone pulpit

Mezzovico: San Mamete, built in various phases in the 11–15C.

dated 1712. The **Théâtre du Jourat** on the cantonal road, founded by René Morax in 1903, is an interesting wooden building by the architects Robert Maillart and Chal dating from 1907–8.

Mezzovico TI

19□D3

In a dominant position above the village **Catholic parish church of Sant'Abbondio,** first mentioned in 1426 and altered in the 16&17C. 14&15C tower built on Romanesque lines. Below the village, on the cantonal road, **San Mamete,** built between the 11&15C. The first church had one aisle and a semicircular apse; it was later extended and refurnished. The Romanesque tower dates from the 12&13C. The choir contains interesting 16C frescos depicting the Crucifixion, Last Judgement, Church Fathers and Evangelists.

Middes FR

11□B

Former château, now farmhouse, with polygonal tower. The front door is dated 1676. Opposite is the **château,** built for Nicolas de Griset, Vogt of Bulle, in 1748&9; elegant residence with mansar roof.

Miécourt JU

1□C/D

Catholic church. Built 1769–72 incor

Middes: 16C former Château, now used as a farmhouse.

Miglieglia: San Stefano with late Gothic paintings in good condition.

porating parts of the earlier Gothic building. Rococo main altar and pulpit, Augsburg chalices in the church treasury also rococo.

Miglieglia TI
19 □ C4

In the cemetery above the village medieval **Catholic parish church of Santo Stefano al Colle,** first mentioned in the 15C; Romanesque tower. The single-aisle building with rectangular choir contains interesting late Gothic wall paintings, those in the choir dating from 1511. Below the church, among stone haylofts, 15C **ossuary.** In the village **Catholic parish church of Santo Stefano,** built in 1634, altered in the 18C. High altar with a splendid 18C tabernacle.

Minusio TI
19 □ C2

In the Rivapiana quarter **Catholic church San Quirico,** first mentioned in 1313, rebuilt in the 18C. Baroque interior, on the S. wall fragments of 13C Romanesque paintings. Next to the church is an imposing 13–15C bell tower, formerly used as a watch-tower. On the shore of the lake **Cà di Ferro,** a former barracks, built by Peter A. Pro of Uri in 1560 as a training centre for mercenaries. Opposite is the **Santa Maria dei Sette Dolori chapel,** a 17C baroque building.

Miraniga GR
See Obersaxen   13 □ E1

Miserez JU
See Charmoille   1 □ D4

Mistail GR
See Alvaschein   14 □ B1

Mitlödi GL
8 □ E3

Schoolhouse, built as a private house in neoclassical style in 1829 – 30. **Textile printing works.** Characteristic 19C complex with a 'Tröckniturm', on which the length of printed material were hung up to dry. Above the village **Schönenbergerhaus,** a half-timbered building with lavish façade paintings, probably dating from the 16C.

Mogelsberg SG
3 □ E5

Gasthaus Rössli, 18C Blockbau with mansard roof and curved gable. In Hofstetten, S. of Mogelsberg, is a group of 17C **Blockbauten,** Nos. 617–20, 594–7, 604.

Möhlin AG
2 □ B3

Celto-Roman complex on the 'Bürkli'

on the banks of the Rhine: ramparts and (probably late Roman) gate ruins.

Mollens VS

17☐F1

S. of Mollens **Catholic parish church St. Maurice-de-Laques.** Of the late Gothic church, built by Ulrich Ruffiner in 1531, the rectangular choir and the bell tower survive; the nave was rebuilt by J. de Kalbermatten in 1893–4, stained glass by Alexandre Cingria, 1929.

Mollis GL

8☐E3

In the choir of the **Reformed church,** built by Johann Ulrich Grubenmann in 1761, is a neoclassical monument of 1830 –40 to those who died at the battle of Näfels (1388). The monument is combined in an unusual way with the pulpit, which is of the kind commonly found in Protestant churches. Just outside the centre of the village is the former **Haltli** house, built to plans by the architect Conrad Schindler in 1772–84 (now a school for mentally handicapped children). The baroque house has a farm building with curved gables on either side. **Haus Hof** and the neighbouring **Höfli,** both built in 1786 – 7, are incorporated into the present old people's home; in the gardens is an *Orangery.* Among the uniform houses is the **Zwickyhaus** of 1621 with a tall gable. On the road to Netstal is the **Fabrikhof,** a semi-detached house with three curved gables on the road side, built around 1760.

Mon/Mons GR

14☐B1

Catholic parish church of St. Franziskus. Baroque single room church with narrower choir and polygonal apse, built in 1643 – 8 by Giulio Rigaja of Roveredo. Above continuous beams articulated tunnel vault and half dome in the choir. Wall painting in the choir *c.* 1660. **Santi Cosmas e Damiano** below the

Mollis: main façade of the former house of the Haltli family with neoclassical gable.

Mon: the dome on the tower of the Catholic parish church was added in 1911.

village. Early Romanesque single room church with semicircular apse, massive tower *c.* 1400. Wall paintings on the N. and S. wall dating from the 2nd half of the 14C. in the apse and on the S. choir arch 2nd half of the 15C.

Monstein GR
See **D**avos

9☐D

Montagny-les-Monts FR

11☐B

The ruins of the **château** of the Lords o Montenach, who were mentioned from

1146 and ruled the area into the 15C, tower above the church. Control of the area was assumed by Fribourg, which made it a Vogtei. Only the 13C round tower of the château has survived. **Catholic church de l'Immaculée Conception,** built in 1760 and enlarged in 1926. Single-aisle building, the 14C Gothic choir of which was adapted from the former château chapel, first mentioned in the 13C. In the choir 17C wall paintings and a stone Madonna with Child, 1500.

Montbovon FR

11□C4

Catholic church of St-Grat, neo-Romanesque, built in 1896–8. Below the church, on the old road, is an interesting group of houses, in particular a chalet-style **wooden house,** built in 1725 for A.Jordan, banneret of Montbovon; later used as an inn. On the façade is a very long inscription, which includes the names of the owners.

Montcherand VD

10□E1

Reformed church (St-Etienne), built in the 10C as church of a priory subordinate to Payerne; the present single-aisle building with semicircular apse dates back to the 11C. The apse contains interesting 12C wall paintings. These were discovered in 1903 and portray a barely discernible Christ in His Glory and seven Apostles.

Monte Carasso TI

19□D2

Catholic parish church of Santi Bernardino e Girolamo, originally part of a monastery founded in 1450 which has since disappeared. The 15C building was completely altered in the 20C; late medieval tower. On the façade 16C wall paintings, fine 1746 painted organ inside. On the hill above the river is the baroque **Catholic church of Santa Trinità.** On the mountain is the medieval **Catholic**

Montcherand: Romanesque wall paintings in the choir of the Reformed church, probably 12C.

church of San Bernardo, extended in the 20C. Chapel and tower date from the 16&17C. On the façade 1582 frescos. Inside is an important cycle of of wall paintings; those in the nave are attributed to the Seregnese family and date from the 15C, those in the apse date from 1607.

Montet FR

6□B5

Catholic church of the Ste-Trinité, built in 1663, altered in the 19C; high altar and side altars baroque.

Montet VD
See CUDREFIN
6□B/C4

Montfaucon JU

6□C1

Catholic parish church of St-Jean Baptiste. Built in 1831 – 64 as a neoclassical single room with a square tower. The high altar is in the form of a sarcophagus.

Montheron VD
See LAUSANNE
10□E3

Monthey VS

17□B1

From the 11C the town was under the House of Savoy and was administered by vidames and majors. From 1536 to 1798 power was exercised by Landvogts from the Upper Valais. **Catholic parish church of Notre-Dame-de-l'Immaculée-Conception,** neoclassical basilica with a gabled portico and two-aisle nave, built by E.Vuilloud in 1851. 19&20C interior. Rue du Château, **nouveau château,** first mentioned in the 15C, completely rebuilt by the Landvogts of the Upper Valais in 1663-4. The building, which incorporates a medieval tower, consists of three sections around an arcaded courtyard. Rue de Bourg-aux-Favres, **arsenal,** former medieval tower, altered in the 17C. Place de l'Hôtel de Ville, baroque **Notre-Dame-du-Pont chapel,** rebuilt in 1775, oval building with portico, inside rococo altar with a 15C Pietà. Next to the chapel is a hillock, upon which the old 13C castle and the original market town of Monthey used to stand, both mentioned in 1329. Over the Vièze is a covered **wooden bridge** of 1809 and a **figure** entitled 'La Vièze déchaînée' by the sculptor J.Casanova, 1917. Rue du Commerce, **maison Delacoste,** built above a former defensive building in the 17C for Bishop Hildebrand Jost. Avenue du Crochetan 10-12, **Le Crochetan,** former defensive building, the property of the Du fay family until 1875. Of the medieval building there remain the ring walls with two corner towers and a gate with machicolation. The residential section dates from 1734. In the châtaeu is the *Musée du Vieux-Monthey,* local history collection.

Montlingen SG
See OBERRIET   41 ☐ B4

Montorge VS
See SION   17 ☐ E2

Montreux VD
                                                  11 ☐ B4

This health resort on the Vaud Riviera developed considerably in the 19C. In the old market town above the hill is the late Gothic **Reformed church of St-Vincent.** The 1495 choir and the 1507 nave have groin vaulting, the façade tower is dated

Montreux: Grand-Hôtel, an important late 19C-hotel building.

1470. Next to the church is the former ossuary of the 16C **Catholic church.** Neo-Gothic, built in 1883-5. In the town interesting 19C and early 20C buildings, particularly the hotels. On the quay is the **Montreux-Palace,** built by Eugène Jost in 1904. In TERRITET **Grand-Hôtel,** built by Maillard in 1887. In CLARENS **Villa Karma,** built by Adolf Loos in 1904-6, his first private house, developed from an earlier building. Among the vineyards above Clarens **Châtelard,** a castle built by Jean de Gingins as a place of refuge in times of peril for the inhabitants of Montreux. Partly destroyed by the Confederates in 1476 and then rebuilt. The building is dominated by a massive square keep, influenced by contemporary N. Italian architecture. The *Musée du Vieux-Montreux* has a local history collection.

Montricher VD
                                                  10 ☐ D2

Village with market founded in the 13C by the Lords of Grandson, who had previously built a château here. The village was rebuilt after the fire of 1828. **Reformed church,** former château chapel, built near the town wall, which has since disappeared; a surviving tower from the wall was converted into a bell tower. Above the portal Flamboyant tracery window.

Montsalvan FR
See BROC   11 ☐ C.

Morbio Inferiore: oval drum dome in Santa Maria dei Miracoli.

Morcote: late Gothic paintings on the wall of the choir of Sant'Antonio Abate.

Morbio Inferiore TI

19☐E5

Catholic parish church of Santa Maria dei Miracoli, built in baroque style in 1595–1613. Cruciform building with drum dome above the crossing; inside fine 18C stucco by members of the Silva family. In the choir 1770 high altar and statues by F.Silva, four terracotta medallions by A.Silva. In the N. transept chapel 17C altar with 15C fresco of the Virgin Mary and copper medallions painted by Isidoro Bianchi, 1620–30. In the S. chapel 17C altar and painting by G.Antonio Petrini. By the cemetery is the **old parish church of San Giorgio,** first mentioned in 1309. Nave, two aisles, semicircular apse, late medieval tower. Inside interesting 15&16C wall painting.

Morbio Superiore TI

19☐E5

Above the village **Catholic parish church of San Giovanni Evangelista,** built in neoclassical style in 1783 – 9; 18&19C interior. Below the village **Sant'Anna chapel,** baroque building of 1703–5; 18C paintings inside.

Morcote TI

19☐D5

Very old town, first mentioned in 926, now an important tourist resort. On a terrace

Morcote: 1483 Casa Paleari with rusticated arcade.

above the village **Catholic parish church of Santa Maria del Sasso,** probably founded in the 13C, rebuilt in 1462, altered and refurbished in 1758. Originally medieval tower, raised in the 16C. Inside interesting 16&17C paintings. In the old choir, partly concealed by the organ, 1513 paintings attributed to Domenicus Sursnicus. In the sanctuary 1591 stucco and 1611 paintings. The chapel opposite contains 18C trompe l'oeil architectural painting. Baroque high altar of 1758. Next to the church is the **Sant'Antonio da**

Padova chapel, an interesting octagonal baroque building with dome, built in 1676. The choir contains stucco by A.Paleari, 1682. **Graveyard** with interesting 19C tombs. Below the church **Sant'Antonio Abate chapel,** an unusual, originally medieval complex, containing 15C frescos by the Master of Seregno, with later frescos on the end wall of the choir. Morcote has remained a handsome town; on the Hauptstrasse alongside the lake is a beautiful row of houses with porticoes. Torre del Capitano, originally medieval tower, the upper part of which has been removed. **Casa Paleari,** an elegant dwelling of 1483, altered in 1661. Façade stucco by Abbondio Paleari.

Morgarten: the Letziturm is the remains of a valley fortress built c. 1322.

Mörel VS

12☐D5

The **Catholic parish church of St. Hilarius** is of medieval origin; the nave was rebuilt in the 17C and enlarged in 1942-3. In the late Gothic polygonal choir 16&17C paintings, 18C baroque altars. On the cantonal road towards Brig **Kapelle der Muttergottes von Hohenflüh,** a baroque building of 1730. Inside three interesting altars by Anton Sigristen, 1732, painted by J.K.Leser of St.Gallen, 1733.

Morgarten SZ/ZG

8☐B3

On the site where the men of Schwyz annihilated the advancing Austrian army in 1315 is a **memorial chapel,** rebuilt in 1603. Not far away the remains of a **Letzimauer** (defensive wall) and **tower** of 1322 are a reminder that this is a key defensive position. In canton Zug, on a spot mistaken in the 19C for the site of the battle, stands the **battle memorial,** built in 1906-8.

Morges VD

10☐E3

The château and market town of Morges originated in 1286 as a Savoyard founda-

Morges: the Château is a 13C foundation of the Counts of Savoy.

tion, built to oppose the bishops of Lausanne. The town quickly developed thanks to its favourable site and the freedoms awarded to its townsfolk (autonomous community from 1375); in 1536 Morges came under Bern. The **château,** built in 1286 – 91, served as residence, first of the castellans of the Counts of Savoy then, after 1536, of the Bernese Landvogts. The building is of the 'carré savoyard' type, modelled on Yverdon, with four round corner towers, including the keep, which towers up to the NW of the town. 16&17C interior and alterations, restored in 1948, now the *Musée militaire vaudois.* The **harbour** opposite the château was built by the Bernese in 1696 as base for their fleet and has two jetties with square pavilions. **Reformed parish church,** built in 1769-71 to plans by the Bernese architect Erasmus Ritter

Morges: early neoclassical Maison Monod (1768) in the Rue Louis-de-Savoie.

Morrens: 17C birthplace of Major Davel by the church.

partly rebuilt 1772–6 by Léonard Roux of Lyon in collaboration with Rodolphe de Crousaz. The baroque building has strong neoclassical elements. It is built on a Greek cross plan with a tower incorporated into the façade. Inside elegant galleries on three sides, wooden choir stalls in the apse, designed by R.de Crousaz. Place de l'Hôtel de Ville, **Hôtel de Ville,** late Gothic building of 1518–20 with a staircase tower pierced by a 1682 baroque portal. Adjacent is the Renaissance **poste de police,** built in 1620 as an extension of the Hôtel de Ville. Grand-Rue No.94, **building** with 17C pilastered façade. Next to it is the **Hôtel de la Couronne,** with a hotel sign

c. 1800. Nos. 70–2, **Confiserie Vernet,** late Gothic windows. No.54, **Musée Alexis Forel,** 16C former maison Blanchenay, redesigned in the baroque style in 1670; arcaded inner court. The building was acquired in 1919 by the collector and engraver A.Forel. Rue Louise-de-Savoie No.11, elegant **house,** built for E.Monod in 1768. **House** No.74 has a fine portal with a gable dated 1665.

Möriken-Wildegg AG

2☐D/E4

Schloss Wildegg. Residential Burg dating from the 13C, later converted to baroque. For over 400 years it belonged to the von Effinger family and was bequeathed to the state in 1912. Now a *Wohnmuseum,* annexe of the Schweizerische Landesmuseum.

Morrens VD

10☐E2

Reformed church of St-Maurice. Building of medieval origin, façade with porch and square tower. Next to it is the 17C **priest's house,** birthplace of Major Davel. **Parish hall,** 1696 portal, built by the de Saussure family.

Mörschwil SG

4☐A3

Catholic parish church of St.Johannes Baptist, rebuilt in 1699–1704 by Peter and Johann Haimb, vaulted by Johann Ferdinand Beer in 1783, lengthened and restored by Oskar Müller in 1957–9.

Mosnang SG

3☐D5

Catholic parish church of St. Georg. Choir rebuilt in 1463, nave in 1731, lengthened and refurbished in 1798. N. tower from the earlier Romanesque building, *c.* 1200. **Hof Spilhusen,**

Môtiers: fine inner courtyard of the priory dissolved in 1538.

residence of the sculptor Josef Anton Grob (1745–1807). On the façade sundial and a wooden portrait-bust of the artist, 1755.

Môtier-Vully FR

6 □ C4

Reformed church (St-Pierre), probably founded in the 11C. The present building consists of a 15C Gothic choir, a nave of 1824 and a 12&13C Romanesque bell tower. In the village is an attractive **group of houses,** particularly Nos.133 and 200, 18C.

Môtiers NE

5 □ E4

Reformed church. Gothic, rebuilt in two stages, the two-aisle nave and private chapels in 1460–90, the choir and façade tower in 1669–79. Next to the church **priory.** Mentioned in 1107 as the property of the French abbey of La Chaise-Dieu, it was secularized after the Reformation. In the course of the centuries the priory was extensively altered; in the N. is the late-15C former *St-Pierre,* partly Romanesque. The site of the former convent buildings is now occupied by a 16–18C house. **Hôtel des Six Communes,** former market hall of 1612. Main façade with five round arches, Gothic windows on the first floor. Grand-Rue. **Maison Boy de la Tour,** Régence-style house, built in 1720–3 to plans by the French architect N.Aubry for the banker Abraham d'Ivernois. **Maison Girardier** or 'des Mascarons', named after the 18C

sculpted heads on the windows; now *musée régional.* Adjacent is the 'maison Rousseau', housing a small *museum* dedicated to the famous writer, who lived here in 1762–5. Two thirds of a mile from the village is a **château,** mentioned since the 14C. The oldest part is the N. tower, called La Diesse.

Motto TI

See LUDIANO   13 □ D4

Moudon VD

11 □ A2

Moudon is Celtic in origin and was important in the Roman period as a staging-post on the road from Avenches to the Great St. Bernard. The medieval town of Moudon was first mentioned in the 12C; it was fortified and had a château. From 1219 it was ruled by Savoy, and received its charter in 1285. After the Vaud was conquered it fell to the Bernese and diminished in importance when the Bernese Vogts took up residence in the château of ▷ Lucens.

Moudon still looks like a medieval town, although town wall and château have disappeared. In the town only the **tour de Broye** has survived; it was built under the Zähringen family in the 12C. **Reformed church** (St-Etienne), after Lausanne cathedral the most important Gothic building in the Vaud. The church was first mentioned in 1305 and was built in the late 13C on the site of a Roman cemetery. Nave and two aisles with polygonal apse, rib vaulting throughout, N. chapels 15&16C. The 15C bell tower was part of the town fortifications. In the interior numerous fragments of 13–17C paintings, including 14C statues of Peter and Paul and Crucifixion in the choir, scenes from the Life of Christ in the S. aisle. 1695 stone pulpit an very fine carved choir stalls by Rudol Pottu and P. and M.Vuarser, 1499–1502 In the lower town, near the church **arsenal,** former corn hall of 1774&5. On the other side of the river, 6 Rue Mauborger, **former Hôpital de Malte** remarkable 1556 building. In the Rue d Grenade interesting group of 17&18

Moudon: Reformed St-Etienne, an impressive Gothic pillared basilica.

Moudon: Maison d'Arnay with protruding roof, 1646.

houses. No. 8 so-called **maison du Chasseur,** 18C, façade decorated with heads and Carved motifs. No. 34, **maison de Cerjat,** built 1698 for Loys de Villardin. Grand-Rue, 1835–42 **Hôtel de Ville,** Roman votive altar under the arches. **La Grenette,** former corn hall of 1861. **Fontaine de la Justice** with 16C figure, probably by L.Perroud. The Quartier du Bourg, the oldest part of the town, occupies the whole of the hill above the Broye. In the Rue du Château **tour de Broye** and **maison des Etats du Pays de Vaud,** small late Gothic building *c.* 1500, in which the representatives of the Etats

Moutier: choir of Chalières chapel with Romanesque frescos.

vaudois are held by an inaccurate legend to have met during the period of Savoy rule. The **maison d'Arnay,** (No. 34), essentially 14C, rebuilt in the 16&17C. Large overhanging roof dated 1646. No. 21, buildings of the 15&16C. former prison. No. 50, **château de Rochefort,** now *Musée du Vieux-Moudon,* spacious square building with façade turrets and S. portal dated 1595. Adjacent to this **fontaine de Moïse,** 1557 figure by L.Perroud and 1697 basin. No. 47, **château de Carrouge,** a late medieval building, completely rebuilt in the 18&19C. In the NW corner elegant 1780 portal with arms of Bernhard Gottlieb Diesbach. At the end of the garden square medieval **watchtower.** On the edge of the town interesting group of 15&16C late Gothic houses. Outside the town 17&18C **château de Billens.**

Moutier BE

6☐E1

Moutier was a centre of medieval monastery life. The former abbey of Moutier-Grandval was founded *c.* 640 by Germanus, a disciple of St. Columba. The **Reformed church** now stands on the site of the Romanesque abbey church. The basilica with flat ceiling and three apses is, with the exception of the westwork, a copy of the earlier building, demolished in 1858. **Chapelle de Chalières,** SW of the town. The interior of this Romanesque single room was decorated *c.* 1020 with frescos in the style of Reichenau manuscript illumination: in the apse Apostles under arches and Christ in Glory between the symbols of the Four Evangelists; on the triumphal arch Cain and Abel (or Abraham and Melchisedek) beside medallion with face of Christ. **Hôtel de Ville,** built in the early 19C in the 18C French style. At 9 Rue de l'Hôtel de Ville *Musée jurassien des beaux-arts.* The **Préfecture** is a 1738–42 baroque building with late medieval outer walls and four round towers.

Muhen: 17C 'Strohhaus', now a farmhouse museum.

Muggio TI

19☐E5

Catholic parish church San Lorenzo, first mentioned 1578, rebuilt 1760 by the architect Giuseppe Fontana; elegant baroque façade. 1760 trompe l'oeil painting on the inner surfaces of the dome. Opposite the church **casa Cantone-Fontana,** 18C house.

Muhen AG

2☐D5

Strohhaus. 17C Ständerbau with thatched roof. Rebuilt after a fire in 1961 and now a *bäuerliches Wohnmuseum* (museum of agricultural life).

Mühlebach VS

12☐D5

Birthplace of Cardinal Matthäus Schiner. **Chapel of the Holy Family,** 1676 baroque building, 1680 high altar. **Schiner's birthplace,** one of the oldest wooden buildings in the Valais, recently restored.

Mühlebach: birthplace of Cardinal Schiner, one of the earliest wooden buildings in Switzerland.

Mühleberg BE

6☐D4

Reformed church of St.Martin, rebuilt 1523 to a late Gothic design. The Romanesque tower of the earlier building has survived; it is articulated with pilaster strips and a frieze of round arches. W. of Mühleberg **former town of Gümmenen,** first mentioned 1262. The picturesque buildings on either side of the road show the old pattern of the urban farmstead. The **Gasthaus Kreuz** is a neoclassical building with semicircular timber decoration under the gables dating from 1839. Covered **wooden bridge,** built 1555 and 1732–9. The bridge has six bays and is supported by four stone piers (18C) and a timber-clad wooden pillar.

Mühlehorn GL

8□E2

The **hammer mill** in the Meerenbach gorge shows techniques of iron-founding in the early industrial period in the second half of the 18C; it is water powered, and still in operation.

Muldain GR
See VAZ/OBERVAZ 14□B1

Müllheim TG

3□D2

Catholic Muttergotteskirche, built 1966–8 by Bächtold and Baumgartner. In the choir baroque crucifix, Witnesses of the Crucifixion 1757 by Anton Feuchtmayer.

Münchenbuchsee BE

6□E3

Reformed church of St. Johannes der Täufer. The church of the former commandery of the Knights of the Order of St. John is a 13C Gothic building with triangular apse. The flat-ceilinged interior has important late-13C stained glass. The founder's window is older in style than the Passion window. N. of the church are the buildings of the **commandery of the Knights of the Order of St. John,** founded by Cuno von Buchsee in 1180: residence of the commander (now priest's house), cells, monastery building. Adjacent is the baroque **Landvogteischloss. Landsitz Hofwil,** E. of Münchenbuchsee. This early neoclassical house with English gardens was built 1784 to plans by Carl Ahasver von Sinner. Emanuel von

Münchenstein: Ehinger country house, an early neo-Renaissance building by M. Berri.

Fellenberg later established his educational establishment here and built a larger building, the present **Seminar,** not far away; neoclassical with hipped roof and roof lights.

Münchenstein BL

2□A3

The **hammer mill** is prominent among the industrial buildings on the St. Alban pool because of its striking proportions. The **Bruckgut** was built 1759–61 to plans by Samuel Werenfels as the country seat of a Basel businessman. Fine chinoiserie by a Frankfurt manufacturer in the interior. The **Brüglingen estate,** now run by the Christoph-Merian-Stiftung, includes Unter-Brüglingen, (16–19C) the former Vorder-Brüglingen estate and the Merian-Villa (1711, altered 1858 by Johann Jacob Stehlin the Younger) in an English park. The neoclassical **Ehlinger** country house was built 1829–31 by Melchior Berri while influenced by his journey to Italy as a student.

Münchenweiler BE

6□C4/5

Schloss. The former Cluniac priory was made into a house in 1537–53, retaining the E. sections of the 12C church. The lower parts of the roof and the triumphal arch on the W. side of the crossing tower are the parts of the nave which have survived. Extensive grounds.

Münchwilen TG

3☐D4

St. Margaretha chapel in St. Margarethen; 1641 with three baroque altars contemporary with the building, probably from the studio of Adam Thörig. In Oberhofen-Freudenberg **workers' accommodation.** Detached house, Nos. 51&2, built 1820. The window balustrades consist of large strips of timber.

Münsingen BE

6☐F5

Hallstatt **burial mound** (near Tägertschi station, excavated 1856) and a Celtic grave field of the la Tène period (500 yards S. of the village, discovered 1904). Remains of a **Roman villa** probably c. AD 100 were discovered E. of the parish church in 1941. Marine morifs on the mosaics in the bath house. **Schloss.** The 1316 Burg was much altered in the 16&18C.The **Blumenhaus,** which was part of it, is a late Gothic one-storey building by Niklaus Sprüngli. The **Gasthof Bären,** built 1579, a Ständerbau with hipped roof, has a guest room with panelling c.1700.

Münster VS

12☐E4

Catholic parish church of St. Maria, first mentioned 1309. The present church dates from various periods: Romanesque bell tower 12&13C, choir 1491, nave, side chapels and porch 1664–78. In the porch 1743 wooden Crucifixion by Peter Lagger, and sculptures of Mary and a saint dating from the 17C. In the choir high altar with late Gothic retable by Jörg Keller of Lucerne, 1509, 1491 wall tabernacle and 17C painting. On the triumphal arch and in the upper part of the nave 1751 paintings by J.G.Pfefferle. Four fine 17&18C

Münster: choir of St.Maria with late Gothic triptych.

baroque altars, 1670 carved choir stalls. On the wall of the S. aisle 1509 Gothic crucifix, font with 1670 basin and carved upper part by J.Sigristen, 1698. By the church **priest's house,** built 1509, altered 1745; in the interior small *museum* containing the church treasure. By the cantonal road **St. Peter chapel,** first mentioned 1309, altered in the 17C. In the choir 1642 – 5 paintings and 1642 altar by M.Mangolt. On a hill above the village **St.Antonius von Padua chapel,** built 1680–4 and enlarged in the 18C; in the nave 1772–5 vault painting, in the choir 1683 high altar and votive pictures; 18C side altars. In the village interesting **houses,** of which the oldest are 15&16C. Traditional storehouses and barns.

Münsterlingen TG

3☐F2

Former Benedictine nunnery. According to legend the convent was founded by the daughter of the English King Edward I, who was shipwrecked here. The *convent church* is an example of Vorarlberg baroque Tunnel-vaulted nave, shallow domes over crossing and choir, groin-vaulted sanctuary. Régence stucco by Wessobrunn masters 1719 – 22, ceiling paintings by Jakob Carl Stauder from the same period. *Nunnery buildings,* 1703-9 by Franz Beer.

Munteiler FR

6 ☐ C4

Large 18C **château** in the middle of the village.

Muolen SG

3 ☐ F3

Catholic parish church of St. Joseph, rebuilt 1863, altered by Hans Burkard 1963-4. Sculpture by Otto Rausch, stained glass by Walter Burger, wrought iron by Josef Tannheimer, all 1963&4.

Muotathal SZ

8 ☐ B/C4

Behind a compact group of timber houses **Catholic parish church of St. Sigismund und Walburga,** built 1786-93. The spatial effect of the interior is achieved by the manipulation of perspective: the three principal areas move in decreasing order of height and width towards the choir; the impression of greater depth thus achieved is heightened by the chamfered choir arch, which seems like another bay. Rococo stucco by Peter Anton Mosbrugger, ceiling painting by Josef Anton Messmer. **Franciscan nunnery of St. Joseph.** First mentioned mid 13C; present building 1684-93. The convent building has canopies over its windows in the manner of the local farmhouses.

Muralto TI

19 ☐ C2

Collegiate church of San Vittore: The church was already in existence in the 9C; first mentioned in 1061. The Romanesque complex was built between 1090 and 1110, the tower was built in 1524 and completed in 1932. The building was radically altered

Muotathal: late-17C Franciscan nunnery.

in the 17&19C, restoration currently in progress. The collegiate church of Muralto is a basilica without transepts with a nave, two aisles, three semicircular apses and a crypt below the choir. The façade (with the exception of the porch) and the exterior of the choir have retained their Romanesque character. On the tower there is a marble relief of St. Victor by Martino Benzoni of Milan, 1460-2. Inside fragments of 12C Romanesque paintings and, in the choir, wall paintings by one of the Seregno family, 1467. Very fine Romanesque crypt with a nave and two aisles, columns with richly carved capitals.

Muraz VS

17 ☐ B1

Catholic church of St-André, neo-Gothic, built in 1898. Massive façade tower of 1657. Adjacent is the priest's house of 1768.

Muri AG

7 ☐ F1

Former Benedictine abbey. This monastery, founded in 1027 and dissolved in 1841, was one of the great centres of religious art in Switzerland. The *monastery church* is essentially a Romanesque basilica with a nave, two aisles and square choir above a hall crypt, also with a nave and two aisles. Under Prince Abbot Placidus Zurlauben Giovanni Bettini and Caspar Mosbrugger undertook decisive conversion work in 1695-7: the nave was opened up to accommodate an octagonal

Muralto: hall crypt with carved capitals in the collegiate church.

Murten: general view with Château and parts of the medieval fortifications.

Muri: church of the former Benedictine abbey, redesigned in the baroque style in the 17C.

Murten: Porte de Berne with clock tower, built in its present form 1777&8.

dome 82 ft. high, abutted by barrel-vaulted side chapels to the N. and S. The extremely lavish interior is one of the major works of Swiss baroque. Stucco by Giovanni Bettini, ceiling paintings by Francesco Antonio Giogioli (1696 – 7). The former *monastery buildings* (now hospice, nursing institution and *monastery museum*) date in their present form from the 16C at the earliest. The Loreto chapel in the N. walk of the former cloister has served as family vault of the Habsburgs since 1971. The three other cloister walks were restored in 1953–7; at the same time the *Renaissance stained glass*, which had been stored in Aarau, was put back.

Murten FR

6 ☐ C4

Around 515 Murten was a walled court (muaratum), in the 11C it had a fortress, but was totally destroyed in 1033–4 and lost all importance. It was not until its foun-

dation by Berchtold von Zähringen (between 1157 and 1177) that the town started to develop. After 1255 Murten was ruled mostly by the Dukes of Savoy. In 1476 Murten, which already had an eventful history, was the scene of the battle which brought the Confederacy its first victory over Charles the Bold. Until 1798 Murten was under the joint rule of Bern and Fribourg.

The town has a typical Zähringen rectangular plan and is split by a broad street, which is also the market-place. The château is in the SW. Below the town are the districts of du Ryf and the harbour, both built in the 13C. The fortifications, built in several stages in 1238, have survived as well as any in Switzerland. They were raised in the 14C and restored after the Battle of Murten and again in the 20C. The ditches were filled in the 16C. The **town wall,** with battlements built in the 15C, is strengthened with 12 towers of varying shape and size. Two main entrances gave access to the town, one of which, the **porte de Berne,** has survived and dates in its present form from 1777–8. The **château,** now prefecture, was rebuilt the Savoyard period. It consists of a massive square keep, perhaps older, which stands within the curtain wall and is strengthened by semicircular towers. The building was radically altered in the 18C. In the Deutsche Kirchgasse is the **German church,** former chapel of Sainte-Marie, first mentioned in 1399. Of this original building there remain parts of the choir. Vault and paintings date from 1682–5, the nave was built in 1710–13. Massive choir tower, integrated into the town wall, rebuilt on an older substructure in 1683. Inside is a beautiful carved pulpit of 1484 and choir stalls of 1494–8, organ of 1748. On the S. façade of the church interesting carved tombstones. Opposite the church is the **German priest's house,** a beautiful building in the 18C Bernese style. The writer Jeremias Gotthelf was born here. In the Rathausgasse is the **French church,** originally the chapel of Sainte-Catherine, built in 1478–80, with an 18C nave. Next to the church is the **French priest's house** of 1732. **Hôtel de Ville:** This building, first documented in the 15C, was rebuilt several times. The arcades, which lead to the lake and the Portette, date from 1588–9, the main façade from 1832. The main street has very beautiful covered walks from the 16C; most of the houses have 17&18C façades. No.16, the so-called **zum Rübenloch** house, dates back to the 16C and has a beautiful late Gothic façade with windows with ogee arches, Bernese roof 1672. In the Speichergässlein interesting granaries and stables. In the district of Ryf are Gothic tradesmen's houses and shops. Outside the town walls **Haldenhof,** a mansion built around 1740 for Jean-Théodore Chaillet. Below the château is a **mill** of 1578, which now serves as *local history museum.*

Müstair GR

15☐B/C4

According to tradition Charlemagne founded a monastery around 780–90 at the S. end of the Ofen pass. This was con-

Müstair: Benedictine nunnery with Carolingian church with three apses.

verted into a **Benedictine convent** in the 12C. The convent buildings, still mostly medieval, are grouped around two inner courts, with the *convent church of St.Johann* adjacent on the E. side. Formerly Carolingian single room with three apses, converted into a late Gothic hall church with a nave and two aisles by the addition of two rows of columns and a net vault. Carolingian wall paintings *c.* 800: parts of a Biblical cycle have survived; they read from top to bottom and run in 5 bands from the S. wall across the W. wall to the N. wall. The top row, with scenes from the life of David, is now in the Schweizerische Landesmuseum, including 3 rows with scenes from the childhood, life and Passion of Christ. In the lowest strip is the crucifixion of St.Andrew. The W. wall ends with a cycle depicting the Last Judgement. In the apses are Romanesque paintings, Romanesque statue of Charlemagne in front of them. In the W. section of the convent is the *double chapel of St. Ulrich und Nikolaus;* in the choir of the lower chapel Romanesque vault stucco. By the road to the S. is the **Heiligkreuzkapelle,** a trefoil building with horseshoe-shaped apses and

Müstair: paintings in the S. apse of the church, martyrdom of St. Stephen.

Muttenz: St. Arbogast with castellated walls.

Müstair: Romanesque Heiligkreuz chapel built on a trefoil ground plan.

a flat, carved ceiling of 1520, unique in Switzerland. *Convent museum* with Carolingian marble fragments. Opposite the convent is the **Chasa Chalvaina,** the oldest part of which dates from the era of the fortress. The present building is an alteration of *c.* 1500. The façade picture, painted in Italian style *c.* 1467, depicts the Virgin Mary and St. Rochus.

Muttenz BL

2☐A3

At the centre of upper village, from which the streets radiate, is the church precinct of **St. Arbogast,** which is enclosed by a battlemented ring wall. An uncompleted Romanesque complex on the site of several earlier buildings was rebuilt after the earthquake of 1356. The rebuilding of the choir, tower and ring wall took place in 1420–30. In the choir pictures from the legend of St. Arbogast and St. Nicholas (14C), in the nave scenes from the life of Christ, the Virgin Mary and the Apostles (1507); in the ossuary Last Judgement (1513). On the road to Basel is the **Siedlungsgenossenschaft Freidorf,** a pioneering achievement of social residential architecture by Hannes Meyer, 1919–24.

N

Näfels GL

8□D3

Catholic parish church of St.Fridolin und Hilarius, built by Jakob Singer in 1778-81 in imitation of the parish church of Schwyz by the same architect. The breadth of the single-aisle interior is exaggerated by the convex curve of the central bay. Behind the church is the **Schlachtkapelle** in memory of those killed at the Battle of Näfels against the Austrians in 1388. The **Capuchin monastery of Maria-Burg,** built in 1675-9 on the site of the Burg of the Austrian rulers, destroyed in 1352, recalls the importance of the town as an outpost of the religious communities of Glarus who remained Catholic. **Freulerpalast,** built in 1645-7 by Hans Fries for Oberst Caspar Freuler, who became rich in the service of the French. The building, with its numerous external Renaissance elements and baroque interior furnishing is now the *Museum des Landes Glarus.* This contains, apart from numerous early documents, a collection of Glarus printed textiles, an important source of overseas trade, particularly in the 19C. Near the old, partly-preserved **Letzimauer** (defence wall) is the **Schlachtdenkmal,** built in 1888; 11 **memorial stones,** some old, recall the stages of the battle.

Naters VS

18□C1

This former property of the Bishop of Sion, administered by majors and vidames, played an important role in the Upper Valais wars of independence. In the upper village, by the river, are the ruins of **Schloss Auf der Flüe** or Supersaxo, seat in the 13C of the Manegoldis, called de Saxo, administrators of the Bishop of Sitten; the building was the property of the

Näfels: 1645-7 Freulerpalast, now Glarus cantonal museum.

Näfels: magnificent Renaissance portal on the main façade of the Freulerpalalst.

Bishop from 1339. The remains of the 13C square residential tower are still visible. Opposite the Schloss is the **Ornavasso tower,** former seat of the Bishop's vidame, built in the 13C. At the start of the 14C it belonged to the Ornavasso family and later to the Rarons and the von Plateas. The building was radically altered when converted into a schoolhouse in 1899. **Catholic parish church of St. Mauritius,** founded in the 12C and rebuilt in 1659-61 by Peter and Balthasar Bodmer, altered 1755. Remaining from the original church is the very beautiful Romanesque bell tower with Lombardy ar-

Naters: Romanesque tower of the parish church with louvres.

Naters: baroque side altars of the Ritz school.

ches. Single-aisle church with polygonal apse, baroque furnishings. The chancel contains a high altar of 1667 and carved choir stalls of 1665 by Hans Siegen. On the triumphal arch Crucifixion (1664) four baroque side altars. Next to the church is the **ossuary,** built by U.Ruffiner in 1514. Inside 18C Mount of Olives and on the right a crucifix with a Romanesque head, 12C. Opposite the church is the 15–17C **Rathaus Junkerhof,** and the **priest's house,** a large building with a loggia, built in several stages from the Middle Ages to the 19C. In the Schulhausgasse **Haus Lergien,** 1599 and 1631, window with ogee arch on one of the façades.

Navone TI
See SEMIONE   13☐D5

Negrentino TI
See PRUGIASCO   13☐D4

Nendaz VS
                               17☐D2

BASSE-NENDAZ **Catholic parish church**

of **St-Léger,** built in 1880, altered in 1970. Beneath the nave is a chapel with some Romanesque masonry, part of the original church with a semicircular apse over which the present church was built. Below the main street is the **majorie,** built in 1505 by U.Ruffiner for Gabriel de Bertherinis, Castellan of Conthey. Massive building with saddleback roof and two step gables. HAUTE-NENDAZ Below the main street and surrounded by old wooden granaries is the **St-Michel chapel,** of medieval origin, rebuilt 1856, paintings by Charles Brun, who was called 'Le Déserteur'.

Nenzlingen BE
                               1☐F4

The **Birsmatten cave** was inhabited in the Mesolithic period by hunter-gatherers, as the finds (including flint artefacts) indicate.

Nesslau SG
                               8☐E/F⁵

Reformed church, rebuilt in 1811. The lower part of the N. side tower is probably medieval. In the Kirchplatz neoclassical **houses.**
NEU ST.JOHANN **Former Benedictine**

*Nesslau: former Benedictine abbey in Neu
St. Johann, founded in the 12C.*

abbey, founded around 1150 in Alt St.
Johann, transferred to its present site in
1626. The *church* was begun in 1641–4 by
Alberto Barbieri and completed in 1680
after an interruption. The hall church,
with a polygonal sanctuary, combines
elements of late Gothic and baroque architecture. Furnishings in the 'gnarled'
style, 1644–5. **Haus zur Mauer.** On the
ground floor of this half-timbered building
are Renaissance paintings *c.* 1630.

Netstal GL

8 ☐ E3

Reformed church, built in 1811–13. The
pulpit side of the transept has a domed
tower. **Catholic church Dreikönige,**
built by Otto Willi in 1933–4. The exterior
of the building is fortress-like, while the interior impresses by the contrast between
the simple concrete architecture and the
strongly coloured light from the stained-
glass windows.

Neu St. Johann SG

See NESSLAU   8 ☐ E1

Neubrück VS

See STALDEN   18 ☐ B2

Neuchâtel NE

6 ☐ B4

The present canton has been settled since
the palaeolithic period; Auvernier and
Cortaillod are important neolithic sites,
and the second Iron Age owes its name to
the excavations at La Tène on the Lac de
Neuchâtel. Other finds provide evidence
of the settlement of the region in the
Roman period. In the 5C the area was incorporated into the first Kingdom of
Burgundy. The mighty family of the
Counts of Neuchâtel began to exert its influence over the region in the 12C. The last
Count of Neuchâtel died in 1373 and the
region was then ruled by the Counts of
Freiburg im Breisgau, the Hochbergs and
the House of Orléans-Longueville. The
latter had difficulty sustaining claims to
power in the 16C and was unable to hin-
der the Reformation, which was adopted
between 1530–6 thanks to the efforts of
Guillaume Farel. In 1707 the people of
Neuchâtel offered their principality to the
King of Prussia, who ceded it to Napoleon
in 1806; he in turn gave it to his Marshall
Alexandre Berthier. In 1814 Neuchâtel
became the 21st canton of the Confederacy,
while still remaining a Prussian principality. In 1848 the canton detached itself
from Prussia and provided itself with a
new constitution.

COLLINE DU CHATEAU Little is known of
the origins of the town of Neuchâtel. It was
first mentioned in 1011 as the residence of
the Kings of Burgundy. After 1033 it
passed to the Lords of Fenis and after 1147
it was the seat of the mighty dynasty of the
counts of Neuchâtel. In 1214 the town acquired a charter. The oldest part of the settlement developed on the hill, which still
dominates the town. The first fortifications
may date back to the 10C. Of the ring walls
there remain the west front and the **keep**
at the NE corner. This dates in its present
form from 1439–65. Also surviving is the
prison tower, the lower part of which probably consists of spoils from the 10–11C,
while the middle part was built in the 13C
and the upper part in the 15C. To the SE
of the hill is the 12&13C **tour de Diesse,**
partly rebuilt in 1715. The **château** was
built as the seat of the counts of Neuchâtel
between the 12&15C, altered in the 19C
and restored in 1905–34. It consists of a
group of buildings arranged around a large
court. The partly Romanesque S. wing has
an interesting, decorated façade, articulated
by a gallery with twin columns, Carved

Neuchâtel, 12–15C Château, once the seat of the counts of Neuchâtel.

Collegiate church Notre-Dame, at the point of transition from Romanesque to Gothic.

gable areas. The window below also has carved masonry. A 15C portal, framed by two castellated towers, leads into the château. In the interior salle Marie de Savoie with fragments of 15C paintings and salle des Etats, entirely covered with 17C painted coats-of-arms, restored in the 19C. **Collegiate church of Notre-Dame,** now Reformed church. Beautiful Romanesque-Gothic building, built in the 12&13C, partly destroyed by the fire of 1450. The church was greatly altered after the Reformation. Numerous alterations were undertaken during the restoration of 1867–70; the church acquiring, amongst other things, a N. tower. The collegiate church is a basilica with a nave and two aisles, transept, and choir with three apses. On the S. side is the Romanesque Saint-Pierre portal with modern sculpture. The interior of the nave is Gothic. In the Romanesque choir carved capitals and consoles. *Cenotaph* of the Counts of Neuchâtel begun in 1373 for Louis de Neuchâtel This remarkable monument contain 14&15C painted statues. N. of the church is the cloister, reconstructed in 1873–5 The older parts of the building are supported by the church wall.

Town The town developed to the E. of the hill from the 13C onwards. The diversion of the River Seyon in 1839–4 greatly

Tomb of the counts of Neuchâtel in the choir of the collegiate church.

Banner carrier in Renaissance armour on the Venner fountain, by L.Perroud.

increased the area of the town in the 19C. In the Old Town, Rue du Pommier No.1, **Hôtel judiciaire** (court house), built as residence for Jonas Chambrier in 1719. Balcony with Louis XV wrought-iron railings. **Fontaine du Griffon,** sculpture by Jonas Favre, 1664, basin 1776. On the Place de la Croix-du-Marché is the **Hôtel du Banneret,** Renaissance building, erected for Jean Marval in 1609. The entrance door and the first-floor windows are richly embellished. **Fontaine du Banneret,** statue by Laurent Perroud, 1581, basin 1804. Rue du Trésor, built in 1637–9 to plans by Abraham Sire to house shops and storehouses. The back of the building has a beautiful Empire façade of 1836. 2 Rue du Trésor, elegant **house** with Régence façade, built by Moïse Jeannin in 1743. Rue des Moulins, **house** No.21, very beautiful baroque building built in 1685 by Jacques Borel for J.-P. de Montmollin. The three-storey façade is flanked by pilasters, above the portal are the arms of Montmollin-Petitpierre, borne by two wild men. Place des Halles, **Maison des Halles,** built in 1569–75 by Laurent Perroud under the direction of Léonor d'Orléans-Longueville. Splendid

Renaissance building, the ground floor of which was designed for selling corn, the upper floor for cloth merchants. The S. side has a polygonal staircase tower and projecting corner turrets. On the E. façade are very beautiful, richly embellished doors, above which are the arms of Léonor d'Orléans. Running around the whole building is a carved frieze. The **Puits des Halles** were built in 1681. On the Place Numa-Droz is the **Collège latin,** built in 1828–35 to plans by Anton Frölicher. Rue du Temple-Neuf, **Temple du Bas,** built in 1695–6 to plans by Joseph Humbert-Droz, altered 1703. Rectangular building, galleries on three sides inside. **Fontaine du Lion,** statue by Jonas Favre, 1664, basin 1655. Place de l'Hôtel-de-Ville, **Hôtel de Ville** (town hall), built in 1784–90 to plans by the French architect Pierre-Adrien Paris and financed by David de Pury. Beautiful neoclassical building with monumental façade. Above the Doric colonnade is a gable with the carved depiction of an allegory of War and Peace. Inside is the salle du Conseil général with panels by J.-B.Boutry and Fayence stoves. **Hôtel communal** (parish hall), built in 1724–9. **Bâtiment des Services industriels,**

S. Façade of the Maison des Halles with staircase tower and corner oriel.

Hôtel DuPeyrou, magnificent house with gardens in the French style.

former hospital of 1780 – 1. Massive building with turrets on the gables. Rue de l'Hôpital, 18C houses and **fontaine de la Justice,** statue by Laurent Perroud, 1545–7.

Faubourg De L'Hopital Street and residential quarter with a beautiful row of 18&19C private houses. Nos.8, 14, 19, 21 and 24 are notable. **Hôtel DuPeyrou,** built around 1765 – 7 to plans by the Bernese architect Erasmus Ritter for Pierre-Alexandre DuPeyrou. Splendid Louis XVI mansion. The main façade overlooks the French garden, which may also have been designed by Ritter. Avenue

The domed central section of the Musée de l'art et de l'histoire.

du Premier-Mars, **poste centrale,** built in 1893-6 by Jean Béguin. Quai L.-Robert, **Musée d'art et d'histoire,** built in 1882-5 by L.Châtelain. Inside are frescos by Paul Robert, 1886 – 94. Avenue de la Gare, **Grande Rochette,** 18C mansion, enlarged and altered in the 19C.
Museums: *Musée d'art et d'histoire;* collection of paintings, historic documents, clocks. *Musée cantonal d'archéologie;* important Stone Age finds. *Musée d'ethnographie;* collections from Africa, Oceania and Asia.

Neudorf LU

7☐E2

Catholic church of St. Agatha, rebuilt in 1677 – 8 retaining the Gothic tower, lavish interior contemporary with the rebuilding. In the **ossuary** is a 1633 stone retable with a Renaissance Crucifixion. On the Gormund hill, **pilgrimage church of Maria Mitleiden,** rebuilt in 1612 incorporating the old choir. Inside the building, which still looks Gothic, late Renaissance trompe l'oeil wall-paintings. **Kaplanei** (chaplaincy) at the foot of the hill, 1627 Blockbau, Lucerne farm-house type.

Neuhausen: Schlösschen Wörth was once a customs point for shipping on the Rhine.

Neuendorf SO

7 □ B1

Fine ribbon village with 17&18C farmhouses.

Neuenegg BE

6 □ D/E5

Reformed church of St. Maria. Late Gothic building with Gothic font, Renaissance pulpit and 1516 stained glass with coats-of-arms. Adjacent is the baroque **priest's house.**

Neuenkirch LU

7 □ E3

ADELWIL **Pilgrimage church of St. Gallus und Einbeth:** When the relics of St. Einbeth were transferred from Strasbourg (1624) the church acquired a cycle of paintings depicting the legend of the patron saint by Kaspar Meglinger. WARTENSEE The Gothic **Schloss** at the S. end of the Sempachersee was built by Peter Zukäs, Mayor of Lucerne.

Neuhausen / Rheinfall SH

3 □ A2

Industrial suburb of the town of Schaffhausen by the Rhine falls; popular for ex-

cursions. **Schlösschen Wörth.** Moated castle W. of the falls, formerly toll-house for Rhine shipping, now a restaurant. The oldest parts of the building possibly date from the 12C. **Aazheimerhof:** Summer residence of the abbots of Rheinau, some two miles W. of the township. This late Gothic step-gabled building was built in 1598 and has been much altered. **Villa Charlottenfels:** This Schloss-like neo-Renaissance complex was built in 1850–4 for an industrial magnate. Broad terrace with covered walks and pavilions; in the S. pavilion four wall paintings by Hans Bendel (subjects from Swiss history).

Neuheim ZG

8 □ A2

Catholic parish church of Our Lady, built on the site of an older church in 1504, nave extended in 1663–4. Next to the church is the 1724 **St. Josef und Maria graveyard chapel.**

Neunkirch SH

3 □ A2

This Klettgau country town, founded in the last third of the 13C by the Bishop of Konstanz, is a particularly attractive example of medieval urban architecture, thanks to its regular design, based on a rectangle running from E. to W. with four parallel streets. It still looks medieval, even though a few striking Renaissance elements were added in the 16&17C. Of the former fortifications there remain parts of the town wall and, in particular, the **Obertorturm. Reformed Bergkirche.** This church, mainly late 14C, can be seen for miles on its eminence to the S. of the town. It replaced a much older church dedicated to the Virgin Mary. The tower was built in 1484, the S. aisle in 1598. **Schloss or Oberhof.** This partly medieval complex, greatly extended in the 16C, takes up the whole of the NE corner of the medieval town. The 'Schloss' was the seat of the town Vogt, first from Konstanz then, after the Reformation, from Schaffhausen. The complex now serves as *Ortsmuseum* (local history). **Parish hall.** This late Gothic step-gabled building of 1565 has a large vaulted passageway allowing traffic to pass between the two parallel main streets. **Rietmannsches Doppelhaus.** Two houses with a large farm building in the middle (1762–3). Above the barn door rococo shield and sundial. **Fountains.** At each end of the Vordergasse there is a fountain with column by Johann Stamm with a model church (1767 and 1769).

Neuveville, La BE

6□C3

Founded in 1312 by the Bishop of Basel. The almost square town has three parallel streets and a diagonal street of modern origin. The **tour Rouge,** the **round tower** (tour de Rive) and the **porte du Lac** (Seetor) were all part of the former fortifications, built at the time of the town's foundation. By the Seetor is the **French church,** built in 1720. The **Eglise blanche** to the E. of the Old Town, built in 1345 and enlarged in the 15C, contains a wooden ceiling and 14&15C Gothic frescos. The façades of the houses date from the 16–19C but are built in late medieval style. The **Hôtel de Ville** (Rathaus), rebuilt in 1541 – 69, houses the *Musée historique,* collection including Landolt ovens and the Burgundian cannons plundered in 1476. **Maison des Dragons,** built in 1757–8. This house, named after its dragon gargoyles, is a baroque building with a mansard roof with lights. The **Bernerhaus** was the autumn residence of the abbots of Bellelay. Built in 1631, later provided with a staircase tower (knocked down). On the ground floor are a wine cellar and pressing room. The **Rue du Faubourg,** N. of the old town, is lined with rows of 16 – 19C houses, notably the Hôtel de Gléresse (Préfecture), built in 1578–1605, with a Renaissance portal in the staircase tower. The Rue du Faubourg came into being when the agricultural buildings were moved outside the town walls. **'Schlossberg'.** Built in 1283 by Heinrich von Isny, Bishop of Basel as a fortress against the Counts of Neuchâtel, extended in the 15C and aban-

Niedergesteln: largely intact old village dominated by the parish church.

doned in 1531; it was made habitable again as a Romantic 'ruin' in 1885. Renovated in 1931–2.

Nidau BE

6□D2

Founded by the Count of Neuchâtel-Nidau in 1338. **Rathaus,** rebuilt 1756–60, Neuchâtel-style yellow plaster and consoles. **Schloss.** The lower parts of the keep, the Kefiturm and the ring wall were part of the former moated castle *c.* 1180. Most of the present building dates from 1627–36.

Niederbüren SG

3□E4

Catholic parish church of St. Michael, rebuilt in 1761-2 by Johann Michael Beer von Bildstein. Baroque building with side projections and choir tower. **Haus Holenstein** (No.91). This panelled Blockbau was built, according to an inscription, by Moritz Hug in 1730.

Niderernen VS

See ERNEN

12□D5

Niedergesteln VS

18□B1

Catholic parish church of St. Maria, first mentioned in 1282. 16C bell tower by Ulrich Ruffiner, nave 1838. On the rocky heights above the village are the **Gestlenburg ruins** (Tour-Châtillon). The powerful de la Tour family settled in the area around 1170. The castle, first mentioned in 1235, was destroyed by the people of the Upper Valais in 1384. In the village is a row of 16–18C **houses.**

Niederhäusern VS
See Visperterminen   18 □ C1

Niederhelfenschwil SG
                                        3 □ E4

Catholic church of St.Johann Baptist, mentioned in 903, rebuilt 1786–7 by lay brother Paul Wuocherer. Baroque building with imposing dome vault, gallery with mirror vault. Ceiling painting by Josef Anton Büellacher. **Schloss** in Zuckenriet, W. of Niederhelfenschwil. From the 12C onwards in the possession of the abbot's officials on the Zuckenried estate, privately owned since 1807. Substructure probably high medieval, chapel *c.* 1500.

Niedermuhlern BE
                                        6 □ E5

Bachmühle (mill by the river). Rococo trompe l'oeil paintwork dating from 1773: balustrades on the gallery panelling and marble on the half-timbering.

Niederösch BE
                                        7 □ A2

The **mill** of 1813 and the 1797 **mill annexe** are two-storey plastered buildings with sandstone frames.

Niederteufen AR
See Teufen   4 □ A3

Niederurnen GL
                                        8 □ D2

Above the village, in the middle of a vineyard planted in 1640, are the remains

of **Burg Oberwindegg,** captured by the people of Glarus in 1386.

Niederwald VS
                                        12 □ E4

Catholic parish church of St.Theodul, 1666. Single-aisle baroque building with porch and polygonal choir, lavish baroque interior. High altar of 1787 by J.B.Laggers, on the choir wall is a Crucifixion of 1687. 18C side altars, 1671 font with 18C carved upper section. In the village interesting group of houses, storehouses and traditional barns.

Niederwil AG
                                        2 □ E5

Former Cistercian convent of Gnadenthal. Founded in the 13C, although most parts of the complex date from the 17C. The **church** was converted to baroque in 1687. Dissolved in 1876, the convent is now a nursing home.

Noirmont, Le JU
                                        6 □ B1

Old Catholic church of St. Hubert. Built in the early 16C as a basilica with nave, two aisles and Flamboyant façade tower. High altar *c.* 1720, probably from Bellelay abbey.

Nottwil LU
                                        7 □ D2

Schloss Tannenfels dates from 1688; rectangular country house with a hipped roof, the customary design until the mid 18C. In the hamlet of **St.Margarethen** is the **chapel** of the same name, which was rebuilt or altered in Gothic style in 1479.

Novazzano TI
                                        19 □ D5

Catholic parish church of Santi

Quirico e Giulitta, first mentioned 1330, rebuilt 1776–9. Of the original building there remains the tower, probably 12C, and a chapel. The present cruciform church is baroque; the interior dates mainly from the 19–20C. In the chapel of the old church wall paintings by G.Battista Tarilli *c.* 1584, including a Last Supper reminiscent of Leonardo; lavish baroque altar, 1711.

Nürensdorf ZH

3☐B4

St.Oswald chapel with wall paintings *c.* 1400, uncovered and restored in 1920: Apostles, St.Christopher, St.Oswald and St.Ulrich, the Life of the Virgin Mary, the Passion of Christ. The date of the Romanesque building is uncertain. **Roman earth fort, 'Heidenburgen',** from the time of Emperor Valentinian (4C).

Nussbaumen TG
See Hüttwilen   3☐C2

Nyon VD

10☐C4

The garrison town of Colonia Julia Equestris, founded by the Romans after 58 BC on the site of the Celtic Noviodunum, was the first town to be founded by the Romans in W. Switzerland. In the 5C Nyon disappeared under the onslaughts of the Burgundians. The medieval town had a new start under the Lords of Prangins in the 11–12C, in 1293 it found itself within the Savoyard sphere of power and in 1536 it fell to Bern. From 1781 to 1813 it was the home of a porcelain manufacturing company of world renown.
From Roman times the town has the remains of the **basilica,** which were discovered in 1974 and are now in the Roman museum, and three **columns** from the former forum, which now stand at the entrance of the town. The Old Town of Nyon kept more or less to the Roman layout, medieval houses frequently being built on the antique foundations. In the Middle Ages the Lords of Prangins probably pro-

Niederwald: St. Theodul has a lavish baroque interior.

Nyon: Château on a plateau above the lake.

vided Nyon with a château and a fortification system, part of which was the **tour de César** or tour de Rive in the street of the same name. The origins of the present **château,** which was rebuilt by Ludwig I of Savoy at the end of the 13C, are obscure, as are those of the ring wall which surrounded the town, parts of which still survive in the SE. The château, at the NE end of a mound, is square with side towers. It was extensively altered in the 16–18C. Rue du Temple, **Reformed church** (Notre-Dame). Former priory church, built in the

Nyon: detail of Whitsuntide picture (c. 1300) in the choir of the Reformed church.

Nyon: 18C building, originally a porcelain factory.

12C on the site of an early medieval complex (before 700), itself on Roman foundations. The nave was built in the 14C, vaulting and side chapels in 1471 – 81. Numerous alterations in the 18&19C, bell tower rebuilt in 1934. The choir, with flat apex with two round-arch windows framed by little columns, has survived from the 12C Romanesque church, as have paintings on the inner N. wall: Miracle of Pentecost, 13&14C. Grand-Rue, 18C

porte **Sainte-Marie** and next to it, No. 41, **maison Bonnard** with a 15C tower. Place du Marché No.1, 16C late Gothic house with staircase tower; on a pillar is a fragment of a bucrane (carved ox-skull). Place du Château, **Hôtel de Ville** or maison Lancaster dating from the 16C, converted in 1733; on the façade 18C sundials. Rue Maupertuis, **Manoir,** 16C building, portal with earlier sculpture. 33 Rue du Collège, **former Collège,** classical building of 1784–92. No.3, late Gothic **house** with ogee-arch windows and a portal dated 1569. Rue de Rive, **fountain of Maître Jacques** with a baroque basin of 1763 and a figure of 1546 (original in château). Rue de la Porcelaine No.13, 18C building of the former porcelain factory. **Museums:** *Musée historique et des porcelaines. Musée romain. Musée du Léman.*

Oberaach TG
See Amriswil   3☐F3

Oberägeri ZG
                                       8☐B2

**Catholic parish church of St. Peter
und Paul.** The neo-Gothic basilica, built
1906 – 8 to August Hardegger's design,
replaced an earlier 15C building, which
was the source of parts of the choir. 16C
tower on Romanesque substructure.
Nearby is the **St. Michael ossuary,** consecrated in 1496, with late Gothic wall
paintings. **Zurlaubenhaus,** on a bend in
the main road. Built in 1574 for a member
of the powerful Zug army family and used
for the hiring of mercenaries.

Oberbalm BE
                                       6☐E5

Reformed church of St. Sulpitius. The
interior has late Gothic frescos *c.* 1470-80:
on the W. wall the Last Judgement, on the
side walls the Passion and legends of the
saints.

Oberbipp BE
                                       7☐A1

Reformed church. Baroque hall
designed to lay emphasis on preaching
built in 1686 with late Gothic façade tower.
Fragments of the following earlier
buildings can be seen under the floor: 2-
3C Roman villa, graveyard of the 7C Carolingian church, 11&12C Romanesque
pillared basilica.

Oberbüren SG
                                       3☐E4

Catholic parish church of St. Ulrich,

*Oberdiessbach: Neues Schloss (1666–8) with
important interior.*

rebuilt 1858-62 by Felix Wilhelm Kubly
incorporating the medieval tower. 1925
ceiling paintings by August Bächtiger. So-
called **Grosses Haus** W. of the church,
built in 1807 in neoclassical style.
Schülerheim Thurhof, built as an inn
and customs house on the Thur bridge in
1778 by Johann Ferdinand Beer. **Benedictine monastery of St. Gallusberg** near
Glattburg, N. of Oberbüren, mentioned
1167. *Church and living quarters* by Simon
and Georg Schratt under the supervision
of Paul Wuocherer in the 18C.

Oberbütschel BE
See Rüeggisberg   6☐E5

Oberdiessbach BE
                                       7☐A5

Altes Schloss, built after 1546 for Niklaus
von Diesbach. A few yards S. is the **Neues
Schloss,** built 1666 – 8 for Albrecht von
Wattenwyl, and still in the possession of
the family. The high hipped roof with roof
lights and long chimneys and the arcades
of the central section mark the building as
a late product of the French Renaissance.
The interiors are contemporary with the

Oberdorf SO: church hill with pilgrimage church and cemetery chapel.

building and 18C (Gobelins). SE of the village centre is the baroque country seat of **Diessenhof,** dating from the 1st half of the 18C.

Oberdorf BL
2 ☐ B5

The **Reformed parish church** between the upper and the lower village, the first church in the Waldenburg valley, was rebuilt in the 15C on the site of an older building and extended 1633&4; priest's cottage 1716.

Oberdorf SO
6 ☐ F1

Pilgrimage church of Our Lady. An orientated church was built *c.* 1420 on the site of a chapel and hermit's cell, and this church was incorporated into the new building of 1604 with choir in the S. The barrel-vaulted single-aisled church is richly decorated with Wessobrunn stucco by Michael Schmutzer. In the cemetery late Gothic **Michael chapel** (1613).

Oberegg AI
4 ☐ B3

An Innerrhode exclave in the Ausserrhode

foreland. **Catholic parish church of Maria zum Schnee.** Rebuilt 1870&1 by Karl Reichlin, substructure of tower 17C, likewise Peter and Paul statues on the high altar and monstrance. The **Schmid and Manser farmhouses** are shallow hipped-roof buildings with the roof side to the street, so-called Heidenhäuser. Oldest house type, mentioned since the 16C.

Oberentfelden AG
2 ☐ C5

Reformed parish church. Late neoclassical-neo-Romanesque building by Ferdinand Stadler (1864–6).

Oberflachs AG
2 ☐ D4

Schloss Kasteln. This early baroque Schloss was built in 1642–50 on the site of the medieval double Burg of Kasteln-Ruchenstein. Used as a reformatory since 1855.

Oberhelfenschwil SG
3 ☐ E5

Ecumenical church of St. Maria, Dionys und Jakobus. Mentioned 1336, choir rebuilt *c.* 1500, nave extended 1833. Substructure of tower probably medieval. **Neutoggenburg.** Burg site on a rock N. of the Wasserfluh, founded 1271 by the counts of Toggenburg, remains of walls visible.

Oberhofen BE
12 ☐ A2

Schloss. Oberhofen once belonged to Walter IV von Eschenbach, who, together with other conspirators, murdered King Albrecht of Habsburg in 1308. The oldest building in the group is the 12C keep, surrounded by 15C palas with chapel. Extensions in the baroque period and in the 19C. In 1952 the Schloss became a *branch of the Bernese historical museum* and was partly freed of historicist accretions. **Wichterheergut.** 17C buildings in extensive parkland, also called Oberes Schloss. The **Klösterli,** a house with hipped roof and staircase tower, was built by the Landvogt of Interlaken in 1627.

Oberhofen: Schloss, now the Historisches Museum.

Oberlunkhofen AG

2☐F5

Catholic parish church of St. Leodegar. Single-aisled church with choir built on the site of a medieval church in 1685. The 12C Romanesque tower survived. Interior partially rococo.

Oberrieden ZH

8☐A1

Reformed parish church. Single-aisled church by Johann Ulrich Grubenmann (1761) with rococo stucco.

Oberschönenbuch SZ

8☐B4

St.Katharina chapel, built 1691–3. Wall and ceiling paintings in the interior with scenes from the lives of the saints in trompe l'oeil stucco frames.

Oberschönenbuch: trompe l'oeil ceiling painting, St.Katharina chapel.

Oberwald VS

12☐E/F3

Catholic parish church Heilig Kreuz, 1710 baroque building. Single-aisle chruch with polygonal choir and avalanche deflector. Lavish baroque interior, high altar 1716 with Crucifixion by Johann Ritz. N. side altar of 1716, perhaps from the workshop of J.Sigristen, S. side altar 1717. Fine 1725 font by Anton Sigristen. Pulpit 1710.

Oberwangen TG

See FISCHINGEN   3☐D4

Oberwil BL

1☐F3

The Catholic parish church of St. Peter and Paul, a neo-Romanesque basilica, was built in 1896 by Josef Tugginer on the foundations of three earlier buildings (7&14C, 1696). Interior refurbished by Hanspeter Baur in 1964&5. In the **priest's house,** built 1785, a cycle of wall paintings was discovered in 1970 with a panorama of the town of Basel and the Birsig and Birs valleys, *c.* 1820. NE of the village is the **Weiherhof,** a neoclassical farm dating from *c.* 1820.

Oberwil ZG

8□A2

St.Nikolaus chapel. Extended to its present size in 1619, emblem 1730. Late baroque and neoclassical interior. On the road to Zug **St.Karl Borromäus chapel,** built 1637&8, with polygonal tower over the sacristy. The chapel is part of the former **St. Karlshof** (Salesianum School of Domestic Science), a baroque stately home in which Alberik Zwyssig composed the Swiss anthem in 1841.

Oberwil bei Büren BE

6□E2

Reformed church of St. Maria. Late Gothic choir *c.* 1507. On the S. side of the nave, rebuilt in 1604, is a Romanesque tower with double round-arched windows, pilaster strips and arch frieze. The free-standing belfry in the churchyard probably also goes back to the Middle Ages. **Priest's house,** built 1534.

Oberwil im Simmental BE

11□E2

The **Reformed church of St.Mauritius** is a late Gothic single aisled building with baroque modifications in the nave. The ceiling and font are late Gothic.

Obino TI

See CASTEL SAN PIETRO 19□D/E5

Obstalden GL

8□E2

Reformed church. A medieval building, extended 1836; interior 14C fresco cycle.

Ocourt JU

1□C5

NW of Ocourt is the **ruined château-fort de Montvoie** with the remains of a round keep and a 10&11C palas; also the foundations of a 15&16C building.

Oensingen SO

7□A1

The **Catholic parish church of St. Georg** is a single-aisle building with façade tower built in the 15C and later extended. Next to it is the rustic **priest's house** of 1764. The 1604 **Pflugerhaus,** not far from the church, is an early baroque stone building. **Neu-Bechburg.** Built *c.* 1200 and later extended; seat of the Landvogts of Solothurn from the 15C to the end of the 18C.

Oeschgen AG

2□C3

Schlösschen. Built 1597&8 as seat of the lords of Schönau, altered in the 19C. Completely renovated 1977, now parish hall.

Oftringen AG

2□C5

Hintere Wartburg ruin. Medieval fortress destroyed by the Bernese in 1415. The remains excavated in 1966&7 show the outlines of the complex very vividly.

Olivone TI

13□D3

Catholic parish church of San Martino, mentioned 1136, rebuilt in the 17&18C. A fine Romanesque bell tower with dwarf gallery and bi- and tripartite windows has survived. Lavish 1654&5 stucco in the choir, probably by Carlo Terugio da Dumenza; 17C wall paintings. In the village of **Centralone** is an interesting neoclassical building with rotunda and lantern, built 1839 for Carlo Poglia. Opposite the church **Cà da Rivöi,** 17C farmhouse, now *museo di storia locale* (local history).
SCONA **San Colombano chapel,** first mentioned 1205, one of the oldest in the

Olivone: the Romanesque tower of the first church of San Martino has survived.

Ollon: detail from the 15C painted Apostle frieze in the Reformed church.

Ollon: remains (apse) of the Chapelle de la Sainte-Vierge in St-Triphon.

village on the basis of its patronage. The chapel was rebuilt in the baroque period, but has retained its tower and Romanesque sections. Fragments of 15C paintings in the interior.

Ollon VD

17□B1

Reformed church (St-Victor), first mentioned 1244, rebuilt in the 15&17C. Carved 16C busts of saints in the corners between nave and choir, next to them a 1735 sundial. In the choir 15C painted frieze with pictures of the Apostles; wall paintings by L.-F. Rouge, and Roman milestone from Charpigny. By the church **Hôtel de Ville,** massive building with Bernese roof dating from 1772. 1892 **sign.** In the main street interesting houses and fountains dated 1683, 1720 and 1812. 1891 **sign** of the Café Au Mouton.
PANEX The first Swiss salt mine was in Panex, exploited from 1554 to 1797. The **Maison des Salins** can still be seen, along with the former reduction house and a mining level cut into the mountain.
ST.TRIPHON **Ruined château** of St-

Triphon at the top of the hill, first mentioned in the 12C, since 1232 in the possession of the lords of Saillon, destroyed 1476. A very fine square 59 ft. high keep has survived of the château, with stone consoles at the top to support the battlements. N. of the keep ruins of a double chapel. The older aisle, dedicated to St.Blasius, dates from the 11C, the later square one from 1311.

Olsberg AG

2□B3

Former Cistercian convent. The church was rebuilt after a fire in 1427 and altered to a baroque design in the 17&18C. The building has been a reformatory since 1840.

Olten SO

2□B/C5

The bell-shaped plan of the old town

Olten: 1807 neoclassical pilastered church.

Oltingen: typical Oberbaselbiet village in excellent condition.

Onnens: Reformed church with important high Gothic wall paintings in the choir vaulting.

follows the lines of the Roman citadel. There are records of a bridge on the site of the present early 19C **wooden bridge** as early as 1295. The **church,** built in 1807 to plans by Niklaus Purtschert, transformed the baroque pilaster system to a neoclassical design. The **tour municipale,** built in 1521, used to be part of St. Martin, which has been pulled down. **Museums.** *Musée des beaux-arts* (fine art) with the Martin Disteli collection and natural history section. *Musée historique* (local history).

Oltingen BL

2☐C4

Reformed parish church of St. Nikolaus on the edge of this fine Oberbaselbiet farming village, surrounded by priest's house, barn and ossuary. The church was radically renovated in 1474 and the nave extended to the N. in 1852; cycle of late Gothic wall paintings (Mary legend, Last Judgement, Apostles and saints).

Onnens VD

5☐F4

Reformed church (St-Martin), rebuilt 1722, with a 14C choir possibly on the site of a Romanesque predecessor. In the Gothic vault of the choir important Gothic frescos with the Entombment, and St.Peter at the Gates of Paradise and Hell.

Orbe VD

10☐E1

The former Roman town of Urba fell first to the Burgundians, and then to the Franks and began to expand from the 11C when it came into the possession of the counts of Burgundy. The medieval town of Orbe was founded in the 13C by Amadeus III of Montfalcon, who built a ring wall and granted the town a charter. Orbe was destroyed in 1475 because of its connection

Orbe: View from the Château of the roofs of the town and the Reformed parish church.

Orbe: fountain outside the Hôtel de Ville with 1543 banner carrier.

with Charles the Bold, and later taken over by Bern.

Château. The hill above the town was fortified from the 9C. Only the round keep of 1255–9 and a square wall tower have survived of the château built by Amadeus III of Montfalcon in the 13C. The town wall was destroyed in the 17C; a round tower survives near the school. **Reformed Church** (Notre-Dame). The medieval church, at that time one of six in Orbe, was destroyed by fire in 1407. The present Flamboyant building was built in the 15C. The choir was established in a tower which was part of the town wall, the tower itself was turned into a bell tower and capped with four bartizans. The nave, aisles and three side chapels were rebuilt 1521–5; the number of side chapels was increased in 1887–90, and they were enlarged to form two supplementary aisles. The façade has a 1407 Gothic portal with a Carved frieze and a fine Flamboyant tracery window. The interior vaulting is lavishly decorated with corbels supporting carved pendant keystones. Remains of 15C paintings on the jambs of the choir windows, very fine

17C carved tomb in a chapel in the S. nave. Place du Marché. **Hôtel de Ville,** built 1786–9 by Samuel Jeanneret to a design by the French architect César Gasquet. Two-storeyed building with arcades; the main façade is articulated with pilasters and is surmounted by the coat-of-arms of the town between two balustrades. In the square **fountain** with 1753 basin and banner-carrying figures dating from 1543, ascribed to Pierre Lagniaz. 3 Grand-Rue, **priory,** now a chemist's, built 1758–60 by Gabriel Delagrange, carved framework on the façade. No. 16, **maison Grandjean** of 1781, fine façade with carved decoration in Louis XVI style. Rue du Grand-Pont. **Hôtel des Deux Poissons,** former monastery of St. Clare, founded 1426 and rebuilt in the 16C. The building has been refurbished in the baroque style and has a 16C tower. 2 Rue de la Tournelle. **Ancien Hôpital,** built 1778, façade with carved gable. At the end of the Rue du Moulinet **Pont du Moulinet** of 1421.
LA BOSCEAZ N. of the town in the direction of Yverdon four little pavilions with the most important **Roman mosiacs** in

Switzerland. The mosaics were discovered in 1841; they were the floor decoration of an extensive Roman villa dating from the early 3C AD. Mosaic of gods with sections depicting various gods in a frieze of running animals. Mosaic fragment showing a four-wheeled cart pulled by two oxen, mosaic of a labyrinth and mosaics with geometrical patterns.

Ormalingen BL

2☐B4

The **Reformed parish church** is essentially 14C, altered 1626, 1756. Gothic wall painting cycle *c.* 1360–70 on the interior N. wall (Feiertagschristus). On an eminence E. of the village ruins of the **Fransburg,** built in the 14C as seat of the Counts of Thierstein.

Orny VD

10☐E1

Reformed church (Notre-Dame), first mentioned 1177, altered and enlarged in the 14&16C, reorientated in 1815. The present church is entered through the former choir, which like the nave is part of the Romanesque building; late medieval bell tower. The Gothic chapels are 15&16C. On the former end wall of the choir 16C wall tabernacle. S. of the church **château,** now a hospice, stately home built in the 18C for Victor de Gingins.

Oron-le-Châtel VD

11☐A3

Château, now *museum,* late 12C or early 13C built by the lords of Oron, later owned by the counts of Gruyère. The château was sold to Bern in 1555, and from 1557 seat of the Bernese Landvogts. The building is almost oval in plan and fortified by a 13C round keep; the living quarters were altered on numerous occasions between the 14C and the 18C. Inside is the great hall, now a library, with fine late Gothic coffered ceiling; monumental fireplace in the kitchen.

Orbe: very fine Roman mosaics in La Boscéaz.

Oron-le-Châtel: Château with museum and library.

Oron-la-Ville VD

11☐A3

Reformed Parish church, built 1678 by Abraham I.Dünz. Interesting building on a transverse oval plan reminiscent of ▷ Chêne-Pâquier. 1678 carved pulpit in the interior.

Orpund BE

6☐D2

Former Gottstatt monastery. Premonstratensian abbey founded 1255; like many other Bernese monasteries it became a Landvogt's seat after dissolution in 1528. Church late Romanesque-early Gothic; monastery buildings in the customary arrangement around a cloister S. of the church. Refectory with late Gothic stellar vaulting.

Orselina: pilgrimage centre of Madonna del Sasso on the Sacro Monte above Locarno.

Orselina: Renaissance altar with late Gothic sculptures in the pilgrimage church.

Orselina TI

19☐C2

Madonna del Sasso, Sacro Monte, pilgrimage place in the N. Italian tradition, founded 1480. The church is reached along a Way of the Cross and was built in the 16&17C; it was radically altered in the 19C. Terracotta figures which used to decorate the chapels of the Way of the Cross have survived: Last Supper, Pentecost, Birth of Christ, all early 17C and probably by Francesco Silva. In a new chapel notable 15C wooden Holy Sep-

ulchre figures. In the **chapel dell'Annunziata** 1522 Renaissance fresco. **Pilgrimage church of Santa Maria Assunta** dating from the 16&17C, completely altered 1903-25. In the interior 17C stucco and frescos by Alessandro Gorla, 1792 high altar with miraculous image of the Madonna of 1485-7. In the S. aisle 1520 painting of the Flight to Egypt by Bramantino. In the second N. chapel carved Wailing over the Body of Christ, late 15C and a painting of the Annunciation. In the third chapel Entombment picture by Antonio Ciseri, 1870. Numerous votive offerings.

Orsières VS

17☐C4

Catholic parish church of St-Nicolas. 1896 neo-Gothic building by J. von Kalbermatten. The fine 13C bell tower with projecting carved animals on the corners has survived from the original church. Charming 1691 font in the interior.
FERRET **Notre-Dame-des-Neiges chapel,** 1707 baroque building, baroque altar.

Orvin BE

6☐D2

The baroque **Reformed church,** designed to emphasise the importance of preaching, was built in 1638, rebuilt 1660 and 1722. The three coat-of-arms tablets of the Thellung family in the interior bear the same dates.

Osogna TI

19☐D1

Village in a good state of conservation with interesting buildings. **Catholic parish church of Santi Felino e Gratiano,** originally medieval, altered in the baroque. S. portal with heavily weathered 15&16C sculptures. The late medieval **Santa Maria del Castello chapel** is on a hill above the village. In the interior fine 1494 carved winged altar by Yvo Strigel.

Osogna: Santa Maria del Castello chapel with late Gothic triptych.

Ossingen ZH

3☐B2

Dignified farming village in the Zürich wine-growing area with numerous high-quality half-timbered buildings; there are particularly fine 16–18C houses around the **Reformed parish church** (1651). **Hausen Reformed church.** The parish church of Ossingens used to stand in the hamlet of HAUSEN in the medieval period; it was first documented in 1112. The present building is essentially late medieval in design; the interior was redesigned in 1578. **Schloss Widen.** Originally late medieval Burg complex, extended in the 15C. Badly damaged and rebuilt after a US bomber crashed here in 1944; privately owned.

Osterfingen SH

3☐A2

Klettgau wine-growing village with striking farmhouses, including the centrally sited **Doppelhaus Ochsen-Hirschen. Bergtrotte.** These old farm buildings in the vineyards are the scene of the wine festival each autumn, the last of the Klettgau wine festivals. **Osterfingbad.** Old bath complex SE of the village, now a country inn. **Ruined Burg Radegg.** Parts of the keep, the outer Burg and part of the moat survive of the seat of the Freiherren von Radegg, built in the 12C and destroyed towards the end of the 13C.

Otelfingen ZH

2☐F4

Lower Mill or Klostermühle. late Gothic step-gabled building with panelled living-room.

Othmarsingen AG

2☐E4

Reformed parish church. This twelve-sided building dates from 1675; the tower was added in 1895.

Ouchy VD

See LAUSANNE   10☐E3

Oulens-sur-Echallens VD

10☐E2

Reformed church. Originally Roman-esque building; choir rebuilt 1529&30 in Flamboyant style. 19C façade. The choir is separated from the nave by a wrought-iron choir screen and contains corbels, carved keystones and a wall tabernacle.

PQ

Palagnedra TI
19 □ B2

Catholic parish church of San Michele, first mentioned 1231, rebuilt 1663–6, incorporating part of the original church. In the former choir, now a chapel, there are notable late 15C Gothic wall paintings, attributed to Antonio da Tradate, in the vaulting Majestas Domini with symbols of the Evangelists, on the walls scenes from the Life of Christ, Apostles and pictures of the months. In the village interesting **houses** with decorative painting and the **casa Mazzi,** built in the 18C for Petronio Mazzi.

Pampigny: late 15C Reformed church, a plain groin-vaulted single-aisled church.

Pampigny VD
10 □ D2

Reformed parish church (St-Pierre), single-aisled building with 15C square choir, 1736 façade. 15C paintings in the choir, Christ Enthroned, symbols of the Evangelists and St.Peter and St.Paul on the E. wall. By the church, **château** now a school, built in the 18C on the old substructure.

Panex VD
See OLLON   17 □ B1

Paradies TG
See BASADINGEN   3 □ B2

Parpan GR
9 □ B5

Parpan: mid-16C Schlössli on a cruciform ground plan.

Reformed church, late Gothic building with narrower polygonal choir 1489–1510/20, tower 1633. **Schlössli.** Three-storey rectangular building with crossed saddleback roof and onion tower, *c.* 1550.

Part-Dieu,La FR
See GRUYERES   11 □ B

Paspels GR

9 □ A5

N. of the village on a rock is the **St.Lorenz chapel.** Romanesque single-aisled church with blind arches (formerly vaulted) and rectangular choir (formerly semicircular apse) and 13C entrance tower. Late Romanesque wall paintings in the sanctuary and elsewhere: Majestas Domini with symbols of the Evangelists and Apostles; early medieval marble altar-slab. **Schloss Paspals,** built *c.* 1695, altered in 1893. S. of the Schloss **ruined Burg Alt-Sins.** Remains of a four-storey keep with ring wall (late 12C). Lavatory oriels in the upper storeys. SE on the lake of the same name **Canova ruin,** a round tower with adjacent living quarters 13C. DUSCH In the Trans direction is the **St. Maria Magdalena chapel,** a Romanesque single-aisled building with semicircular apse and ridge turret. In the interior early Gothic wall painting by the Waltensburg master (*c.* 1350): in the N. wall Raising of Lazarus, Magdalena in the House of Simeon and other scenes from the lives of the saints, and a picture of the founder (Premonstratensian). **Casa Buol** (von Albertini), built 1664.

Payerne VD

6 □ B5

The name of the town came from the influential Roman Paterni family. In 587 Bishop Marius of Lausanne had a chapel and presumably a house built here. The history of Payerne has been linked with the history of the abbey since the 10C; the latter, according to an apocryphal document, is said to have been founded by Queen Bertha in 962. In 999 the abbey was presented to Cluny, and flourished, thanks to the generosity of the kings of Burgundy; the town became part of the empire in 1033. After various changes it came to the house of Savoy in the 13C. The inhabitants of Payerne were in alliance with the Bernese in the Burgundian war, and accepted the Reformation in 1536, the monastery was given up and turned into a barn in 1686;

Paspels: former Burg Alt-Sins, destroyed in 1451 and abandoned in the 16C.

it has been continually restored since 1926. **Former abbey church of Notre-Dame,** one of the finest examples of Cluniac architecture in Europe. The 1958 excavations revealed the history of the earlier buildings. The first church was built in the 10C on the foundations of a Roman villa, perhaps belonging to Bishop Marius; this church contained the probable grave of Queen Bertha. The present building was started in the 11C at the wish of Odilo, the abbot of Cluny. It is a pillared basilica with nave and two aisles and a large semicircular apse, with apsidioles on either side. In the W. two-storey section with narthex and Michael chapel. The barrel-vaulted nave and groin-vaulted aisles are impressive in their scale and their use of contrasting materials. In the transept interesting carved cushion capitals; they have an archaic look and date from the beginning of the 11C; the capitals in the choir are also 11C and show the influence of Burgundy. There are contemporary frescos in the 15C Grailly chapel. In the narthex early 13C paintings, including depictions of Christ and the elders of the Apocalypse. Of the monastery buildings only the 16C chapterhouse in the S. remains. Four 13&14C towers have survived of the medieval town wall. Behind the parish church **Reformed parish church** (Notre-Dame), built in the 13&14C, presumably on the foundations of Bishop Marius' chapel, and altered in the 16C. The church has a nave,

Payerne: abbey church, one of the most important Romanesque churches in Switzerland.

Payerne: interior of the abbey with impressive yellow and grey ashlar.

two aisles and a rectangular choir. In the S. aisle 16C wall painting of Christ's shroud. In the N. aisle 1817 tomb containing the supposed bones of Queen Bertha. Next to that **court room,** a late Gothic building of 1571&2 with a double staircase. Two door knockers on the entrance portal in the form of lions' heads. In the courtroom secular wall paintings by Hubert Mareschet, 1576. **Banner carrier fountain** with 1542 figure and 1864 basin. By the abbey church **locksmiths' fountain** with 1533 figure (original in the museum). **Museums.** In the E. wing of the abbey *local history collection* and *General Jomini museum;* Jomini was born in Payerne.

Perroy VD

10☐D3

Reformed church (Ste-Marie), church of a priory mentioned in 1172.The nave was altered in 1828; the rectangular choir with rib vaulting and two tracery windows sur-

vive from the medieval building. Gravestones on the end wall of the choir. On the edge of the village in the Allaman direction 16&17C **château.** In the village interesting **group of houses.**

Peseux NE

6☐B4

Reformed church, 1737 tower and 1899 nave; in the interior two windows by Charles l'Eplattenier, 1933. **Château,** Rue du Château, dignified building with three polygonal towers, built in 1531 and 1574 for Jean Merveilleux and his son, on the E. side Renaissance portal dating from 1474. **House** No. 13 – 15 Grand-Rue, Renaissance windows with carved heads, 1597; 1 Rue des Granges, similar window 1600.

Petit-Vivy FR
See **Barbereche**

6☐C

Pfäfers SG

9□B3

The **former Benedictine Abbey** was founded 730–40 and was one of the earliest and most important monasteries in Rhaetia. *Former monastery church.* The 1688–93 building designed by Georg Kuen was the first large church in Switzerland to follow the so-called Vorarlberg scheme. Tunnel-vaulted pilaster hall with galleries on double arches, stucco by Giovanni Bettini and Antonio Peri, ceiling paintings by Antonio Giorgioli, 1701 high altar by Franz Bislin. The *former monastery buildings,* now a sanatorium, are adjacent to the church in the W. The S. and W. sections 1672–4 are by Giovanni Serro and Giulio Barbieri, N. section probably 1698. The warm spring of **Bad Pfäfers** in the Tamina gorge was already in use as a medicinal spring in 1242. The present spa buildings are by Andreas Mefenkopf and his son and date from 1704–18. **St.Georg Chapel** on the rock by Burg Wartenstein. Rebuilt *c.* 1430, painted wooden ceiling 1713. **Wartenstein ruin,** built 1206 as a bastion against the enemies of the monastery. Remains of a keep, a fortress and ring walls. **St.Martin chapel** in the Calfeisen valley, W. of Vättis, mentioned 1432. Wooden crucifix from the first half of the 14C. The **Drachenloch** on the Drachenberg near Vättis, at a height of 8021 ft., is a palaeolithic resting place of the nomadic cave bear hunters.

Pfäfers: the former monastery church is a baroque pilastered hall with galleries.

Pfäffikon ZH: Irgenhausen citadel, the largest Roman defensive site in Switzerland.

Pfäffikon SZ

8□C2

A fortified **keep** was built here by the lake in the 13C to house the administrative section of the monastery of Einsiedeln; it was extended as a moated Burg in the 14C. Late Gothic chapel refurbished in the baroque style in 1780–5.

Pfäffikon ZH

3□B/C5

Reformed parish church. Built 1484–

8 on the site of an earlier church probably dating from the 7C. Late Gothic frescos on the choir arch, presumably by Hans Haggenberg. **Roman citadel of Irgenhausen.** This extensive complex dating from the end of the 3C is in a good state of conservation; it was excavated between 1898 and 1908. The walls enclose roughly 1213 sq. ft.

Pfaffnau LU

7□C1

The **parish church of St.Vincentius** was built in 1810–12 by Niklaus Purtschert; it is a hall church with nave and two aisles. The centre of the nave is emphasised by means of a pendentive dome over the second bay. The **priest's house** was built by the Purtscherts as the summer residence of the abbots of St. Urban. The cubic building is rococo only in its detail.

Pfeffikon LU

7 □ D1

The **Catholic church of St.Mauritius,** built on the site of a medieval church from 1524, was refurbished in the baroque style by Joseph Purtschert after 1770. In the **ossuary,** the upper storey of which was formerly a granary, is a mid-17C early baroque Pietà. The **priest's house** is an 18C building.

Pfeffingen BL

1 □ F4

This former dairy S. of the Burg was rebuilt by Fritz Stehlin in 1899 using some older sections as **Schlossgut,** a neo-baroque stately home; now an open-air school. The core of the **Burg** is 12C, a first extension took place in the 13C by the counts of Thierstein; it was removed after 1761 to be used as building material.

Pfyn TG

3 □ D3

Built under Diocletian (284–305) as the Roman town of Ad Fines on the Rhaeto-Helvetic border. The old curtain wall was used as the base of the N. side of the 'Städtli'. In the area of the former citadel **ecumenical parish church of St. Bartholomäus,** a cruciform building parts of which are early medieval. Sanctuary after 1361, numerous alterations until the 20C. Neo-Romanesque arches 1930–1. In the school house *local museum* with finds from a neolithic moor hut settlement of the Michaelsberg culture in the Breitenloo.

Pieterlen BE

6 □ E2

The **Reformed church of St.Martin** has an essentially Romanesque nave. The fur-

Pfeffingen: ruins of a 12&13C fortress, abolished in the 18C.

nishings of the Gothic choir built shortly after 1300 include sedilia, tabernacle and grave niche.

Pitasch GR

13 □ F1

Reformed church. Single-aisle church with semicircular apse dating from the mid 12C. Interior wall paintings *c.* 1420; on the S. exterior wall St. Martin and St. Christopher by the Waltensburg master *c.*1340.

Platta JU
See **Medfi**

13 □ C2

Pleujouse JU

1 □ D4

Château-fort. The fortress founded by the lords of Pleujouse (Blitzhausen) became the property of the bishop of Basel in the late 14C, and he presented it in fief to many noblemen. The round keep with its high entrance is the oldest part of the complex after the ring walls.

Pont-en-Ogoz FR
See **Bry,le**

11 □ C2

Ponte Capriasca TI

19 □ D3

Catholic parish church of Sant'Am-

Pleujouse: ruined Château, given up in the 18C and allowed to fall down.

Ponte Capriasca: copy (1550) of Leonardo da Vinci's Last Supper.

brogio, rotunda with semicircular apse, built in 1835 over a medieval church; partially Romanesque tower. In the interior on the left 1550 picture of the Last Supper, a copy of Leonardo da Vinci's Last Supper of great documentary value, on the right carved Crucifixion, and Resurrection picture dating from the 16C. On the entrance wall detached wall paintings, 1500. In the village numerous interesting houses.

Ponto Valentino TI

13 ☐ D4

Catholic parish church of San Martino, single-aisled baroque building with semicircular apse, originally medieval, rebuilt 1733-40. By the church **ossuary** with façade paintings. On the road to Aquila **old bridge** with high arch.

Pontresina GR

14 ☐ E3

Reformed church of St. Maria. Post-Romanesque single room (1450) with flat lath ceiling (1496), semicircular apse and integral Romanesque tower from an earlier building. Wall paintings from two epochs. On the W. wall, which was part of the earlier building are paintings dating from c. 1230: Epiphany, baptism of Christ and Last Supper. On the choir arch wall Annunciation, Maria Magdalena and two Madonna pictures. On the S. wall, beginning above the highest strip of the W. wall

Ponte Valentino: baroque San Martino with ossuary.

Pontresina: St. Maria has frescos dating from c. 1230 and 1495.

and running to the N. wall: scenes from the Life of Christ, concluding with the Last Judgement on the S. wall again. On the lower strips of the W. wall Magdalena cy-

Porrentruy: Château with 13C keep over the Old Town.

cle; seven of these pictures were removed in the course of restoration work in 1962 –76 and placed low on the N. wall.

Porrentruy JU

1 □C4

The capital of the Ajoie must have been important even in the 11C because of its good position, as it had two churches even then. It was later owned by the counts of Ferrette, then the counts of Montbéliard and came to the bishop of Basel in 1271. Despite a charter granted by Rudolf von Habsburg in 1283 Porrentruy became more and more dependent on the church. After the Reformation the château became the residence of the prince bishops of Basel (until 1792).

The **Old Town** is naturally protected by a fork in the river and forms a long, thin rectangle. Set diagonally to it is the **Faubourg,** which contains the only notable section of the town fortifications to have survived, the **porte de France** built in 1563. The **Catholic parish church of St.Pierre** is a mid-14C Gothic basilica. The remarkable late baroque side altars are the work of Urs Flüeg. In the

church treasury late Gothic goldsmiths' work, including pieces by Georg Schongauer, brother of the famous painter. **Catholic church of St.Germain,** E. of the Old Town. Built at the beginning of the 13C to a late Romanesque design; the nave was lengthened and painted in 1698. The late Gothic font is a striking feature of the furnishings. In the S. of the Old Town is the **former Jesuit church,** now the Aula of the cantonal school, built 1597–1604. Octagonal tower of 1701. The interior is decorated with early baroque stucco of the Wessobrunn school. The **church of the Ursulines,** consecrated in 1626, is a gellery church with a 1702 rectangular choir. Neoclassical altars in the interior. **Château.** The oldest section is the tour Réfouse (refuge), dating from the early 13C. E. of this the Basel Prince Bishop Christoph Blarer had the Résidence, the Chancellerie and the tour du Coq (with the bishop's emblem of a cock) built in the late 16C. Ornament from the period of building occur only on the portals; the stucco window heads are Régence (18C). S. of this is the pavilion of Princess Christine of Saxony (1697), and at the end of the pavilion are the tour de la Monnaie (1591) and the lavishly stuccoed Roggenbach chapel (17C). **Hôtel de Ville,** built 1761–3 by Pierre-François Paris. The exterior in the Rue Pierre-Péquignat combines the restraint of French architecture (façade) with the lively detail of S. German baroque (bell tower). The same is true of the former **Hôpital** by the Hôtel de Ville, built 1761–5 by the same architect on a double-horseshoe plan. Now a *museum* with modest collections on local history and pharmacy. The **Hôtel des Halles,** also shows the influence of Paris; it is a French-style late baroque building dating from 1766–9. The building was originally used as a trading hall and as overnight accommodation for the bishop's guests. **Hôtel de Gléresse** (Archiv), built *c.* 1750 for Baron de Ligurz by an unknown architect. The articulation of the façade with banded pilaster strips and shallow moulding is related to that of the Hôtel de Ville. The building contains a library with an important *collection of books and manuscripts* (with the finest on permanent exhibition). The **fontaine de la Samaritaine** near the Hôpital, by Laurent Perroud, 1564, is modelled on its namesake in Fribourg. **Fontaine du Suisse,** 1558, Rue des Malvoisins. On the base by the banner carrier is a boar, the animal from the Porrentruy coat-of-arms. The *botanical gardens* of the cantonal school were founded in 1795 by the revolutionary Lémane; plants classified on the A.L. de Jussieu system.

Museums and collections. ▷ Text.

___

Port-Valais VS

11 □ A5

LE BOUVERT **Hôtel de la Tour,** former château and storehouse, first mentioned in 1544.

___

Poschiavo GR

14 □ E/F4

Extensive nucleated settlement with urban character. The actual centre is the italianate *Piazza,* surrounded by cubic patrician houses with shallow stone slab roofs. The **Collegiate church of San Vittore** is in

Porrentruy: Old Town seen from the Château terrace.

Porrentruy: Fontaine du Suisse (1518) with banner carrier and boar.

this square. The choir was rebuilt in 1497 by Andreas Bühler, the nave was extended and vaulted in 1503. The portal and the tracery on the rose window and the windows in the N. aisle wall are from the same period, baroque alterations 1653. S. of this is the **Oratorio Sant'Anna,** rebuilt 1732. Baroque single-aisled church with nave, sanctuary and a retro-choir behind the altar of 1770. The individual areas have domes which decrease in height towards the S.

Poschiavo: 19C Spaniolen quarter at the S. end of the village.

Poschiavo: baroque Santa Maria Assunta.

Trompe l'oeil ceiling painting (1770) in the nave. E. of the collegiate church **monastery chapel of Santa Maria Presentata,** built late 17C. Single-aisle church with three bays, tapering towards the choir bay. Ridge turret with a slender, un-Italian

onion dome. N. of the Rathaus **Reformed church.** Rectangular room without a choir, built 1642–9. High tower with polygonal upper storey and dome. In the piazza **casa Comunale,** a building which owes a lot to nearby Italy; it has a surrounding wall and a Romanesque keep, raised in 1668. Also in the square **Hôtel Albrici,** built 1682. Broad cubic building with polygonal lintel. In the interior tunnel-vaulted corridors and lavishly decorated 'sala delle Sibille' with coffered ceiling. S. of the piazza **Landolfi houses** (Nos. 130, 131) built *c.* 1565. In No. 131 saletta with decorative early Renaissance painting. On the S. edge of the village is the **quartiere spagnolo,** built *c.* 1830 by emigrants returning from Spain; the houses are very colourful and have lively façades. In Surcà on the other side of the river is the expansive **casa Mengotti,** which consists of a S. and a N. section (*c.* 1655 and early 18C) and a W. wing, which, together with the older S. section, forms a single façade articulated with tower-like projections. The lavish interior houses the *museum* with a collection on the history of the region. On the road to Sta Maria Assunta is the **San Rocco chapel,** built 1516, with a representation of the patron of the church on the entrance (1516) and on the altar (*c.* 1600). S. of Poschiavo **Catholic church of Santa Maria Assunta.** The choir is to the E. and the nave to the W. of the central, square crossing with a dome on an octagonal drum and transept-like side chapels. Built 1692 and 1708&9. Trompe l'oeil dome painting 1719 with Assumption and Holy Trinity by Giovanni Prino of Como. The rectangular pulpit, formerly in the collegiate church, is first-class Renaissance work and was made in 1634, presumably by a Veltlin master. W. of the railway line is the high or late medieval **San Pietro.** In the semicircular apse wall paintings by an upper Italian master (1538), including a Wailing over the Body of Christ by saints over the early Renaissance frieze. AINO **Catholic parish church of San Carlo Borromeo** 1613 early baroque single-room building with narrower polygonal choir and three side chapels, including the passion chapel built in 1638 with a six-section dome. I

Posieux: remarkable Gothic cloister of the abbey church.

the dome excellent mid-17C wall and ceiling paintings by a Lombardy master. To the W. **priest's house** of 1622 with the road running through it.

Posieux FR

11 □ C1

1 km. from Posieux **Abbey Notre-Dame de Hauterive** (Altenryf). Cistercian abbey, founded in 1138 as a daughter monastery of Clairvaux by Guillaume de Glânc, who ended his days as a monk here. The monastery was dissolved in 1848 and was revived by the Cistercians in 1939. The monastery church was built between 1150 and 1160, the somewhat later monastery was completely rebuilt in the 18C. **Abbey church Notre-Dame-de-l'Assomption.** Very fine example of Cistercian architecture, showing clearly the structure and austerity of the early buildings of the Order. Church with nave and three aisles with transept and rectangular choir; the nave and crossing are vaulted with broken arches, the transepts have transverse vaults. The façade dates from the 13C, the Gothic choir from 1323–8, the N. chapel and polygonal apse from the same period. The windows in the nave were enlarged in the 18C. In the N. aisle tomb with recumbemt figure of Ulrich von Treyvaux, d. 1350. Main altar and carved choir stalls of 1472–86. S. of the church **cloister,** one of the finest in Switzerland. Three walks have survived, dating from the 12&14C. Tomb of the knight Konrad von Maggenberg, who died

Prangins: Reformed church, an early neoclassical building with false façade.

c. 1270. The monastery buildings form a homogeneous whole with the church and date from the 18C; work was directed from 1751–69 by the architect J.-P. Nader. Above the abbey is the **former St.Loup chapel,** now a private house and the **former monastery guest-house** of 1732.

Pralong VS

See HEREMENCE

17 □ E3

Prangins VD

10 □ C4

Reformed Church of 1761. Interesting rectangular building with rounded corners. False façade with 1860 bell tower incorporated. **Château,** built in the first half of the 18C for the banker Louis Guiguer on the site of a medieval château of the lords of Prangins. The building consists of a central section with two wings and has four corner towers.

Prato-Leventina TI

13 □ C4

Catholic parish church of San Giorgio,

Pratval: Schloss Rietberg in a dominant position above the Domleschg.

first mentioned in 1210, rebuilt in the 17&18C incorporating older parts which are still visible. The church has retained a very fine Romanesque tower with six storeys, probably 12C. 17C stucco in the choir and chapel.

Pratteln BL

2□A3

The **Reformed parish church of St. Leodegar,** a single-aisled building with polygonal choir in the middle of a group of houses, was sacked in 1468, rebuilt, and extended in 1642. The **Schloss,** a former moated Burg, is essentially 13C, extended after 1468, 1557&8 and in the late 17C. Once seat of the Lords of Eptingen, the Schloss was used as a patrician country seat until the 18C. Now *Heimatmuseum* (local history).

Pratval GR

9□A5

Above the village **Schloss Rietberg.** The residential wing, essentially 17C, is in front of the 12C keep. In the courtyard cistern tower with baroque dome.

Praz-Vully FR

6□C4

In the village interesting group of houses, including the spacious **maison Chervet,** which dates in part from the 16C, and the **maison Burnier** dating from the mid 18C, with a 1573 door.

Prugiasco: Romanesque San Carlo in Negrentino, a church with two apses.

Prugiasco: interior of San Carlo with Romanesque and Gothic paintings.

Pregny GE

16□E:

Château Tournay (Chemin Machéry), o medieval origin, rebuilt in the 17&18C Voltaire lived here from 1758 – 60. L **Reposoir,** on the other side of the railwa line, 18C country house with a French garden. **Château de Penthes** (18 Chemin de l'Impératrice), former fortified house, rebuilt in the 18&19C, now *Musée des Suisses à l'étranger* (museum of the Swiss abroad).

Preonzo TI
19 □ D1

Catholic parish church of Santi Simone e Giuda, originally medieval, rebuilt 1533 and altered in the 17C; partially Romanesque tower. On the façade remains of frescos, 1627. In the choir and side chapels interesting 17C stucco and paintings. 1662 high altar.

Prez-vers-Noréaz FR
11 □ B1

Château, now a savings bank. The stately home was built after 1746 for N. Féguely, the Vogt of Illens. Rectangular building with mansard roof; there is a flight of steps in front of the façade. By the church **barn** with 1876 neoclassical stone façade. SEEDORF **Château,** stately home built in 1769 for N.J.E. von der Wied, the Vogt of St.Aubin. Main façade with flight of steps and a triangular gable.

Prilly VD
10 □ E3

Reformed church, built 1765&6 by Rodolphe de Crousaz to designs by Gabriel Delagrange. Rectangular building with polygonal apse and elegant baroque-neoclassical façade with a tall square bell tower.

Promontogno GR
See STAMPA   14 □ B4

Prugiasco TI
13 □ D4

Above the village near the NEGRENTINO alpine pasture **Catholic church of San Carlo,** originally dedicated to St.Ambrose, one of the most important Romanesque churches in Switzerland, first mentioned 1214. The building has two aisles opening into two semicircular apses, the older aisle dates back to the 11C, the other one is smaller, and probably dates from the 13C, the separate tower was added in the 12&13C. The main apse has dwarf arches and a Romanesque relief of a peacock by the window reveal. In the interior notable wall paintings; on the W. wall of the N. aisle an 11C fresco showing Byzantine influence with the Ascension of Christ between the Apostles. In the N. apse Majestas Domini and Apostles, on the N. wall 15C Crucifixion and Madonna; the paintings are ascribed to Seregnese. In the S. aisle early 16C paintings, probably by Antonio da Tradate, in the apses Coronation of the Virgin and scenes from the Life of Mary, on the W. wall Battle of Paribiago with St.Ambrose. In the village **Catholic parish church of Sant'Ambrogio,** built *c.* 1700.

Pully VD
10 □ F3

Reformed church (St-Germain). Polygonal choir and N. chapel in the late Gothic style built in the 16C, nave renewed in the 20C. In front of the church **priory,** used as a parish hall, late Gothic former barn, renovated in the 18&18C. Under the priory car park remains of a **Roman villa,** probably 2C. *Musée de Pully:* local history collection.

Punt-Chamues-ch,La GR
14 □ E2

Chamues-ch is a long ribbon village, whereas La Punt is a typical bridge village at the foot of a pass, with many stately homes belonging to the von Albertini family. **Reformed church** in Chamues-ch. Rebuilt in 1505 by Bernhard von Poschiavo. Buttressed nave with narrower straight polygonal choir, both with net vaulting. Wall paintings by two painters, including the master of Pontresina, 1495.

La Punt: Reformed church (1680) with polygonal choir surmounted by a tower.

La Punt: Casa Mereda with living quarters and barn under the same roof.

In La Punt **Reformed church,** small 1680 baroque building with narrower polygonal choir in the tower. **Casa Mereda,** No. 22. built 1642. Battlemented longitudinal building with living quarters and barn under a common saddleback roof.

Quarten SG

K8☐F2

Community on the S. and N. bank of the Walensee. In the village of Quarten **Catholic parish church of St.Gallus,** rebuilt 1860-2 by Felix Wilhelm Kubly. In the hamlet of OBERTERZEN, E. of Quarten, the **Neue Kapelle,** built 1968&9 by Paul Scherrer. **Ruined Burg Bommerstein** on an outcrop of rock near Mols on the SE corner of the Walensee, built by the lords of Montfort, destroyed by the men of Glarus in 1386. In MURG memorial for the German freedom fighter Heinrich Simon, who drowned in the Walensee; it was designed by Gottfried Semper and made by Luigi Chialiva.

Quinto TI

13☐B4

Catholic parish church of Santi Pietro e Paolo, first mentioned 1227. As is shown by the excavations still visible under the choir, the church probably dates from the pre-Romanesque period. The fine six-storey tower has survived from the 12C predecessor building. The church was rebuilt in 1681 using materials from the old building. Rococo stucco by J.Mosbrugger in the choir vault, 1748, carved 1691-4 by Paolo Pisoni and Carlo Zezio, 1701 side altars from the studio of P.Pisoni, on the N. altar early 16C late Gothic Madonna. Outside the village on the road from Catto DEGGIO **San Martino chapel,** probably built on the site of an earlier church. Single-aisled building with rectangular choir, with walls decorated with blind arcades. In the interior fragmentary 15C frescos with traces of Romanesque painting underneath them.

Radelfingen BE

6□D3

Reformed church. The tower of this Gothic building has Roman pillars as the central support of the belfry opening. In the interior late Gothic wall paintings. **Priest's house** (1630) with wooden gallery.

Rain LU

7□E2

The **Catholic parish church of St. Jakobus der Ältere,** built 1853–4 to Anton Blum's design; it is the last example of the Singer-Purtschert scheme (▷ Ruswil), although the influence of neoclassicism is beginning to show.

Ralligen BE

12□A2

Schloss. The former vine house of the Augustinian monastery of Interlaken was largely built in the early 17C. The many mansards come from an extension built in 1900.

Ramiswil SO

2□A5

The **mill** built in 1596 has a façade painted with marks of ownership, coats-of-arms, mill wheel and triangular gable.

Ramosch/Remüs GR

15□B2

Reformed church. Late Gothic single-isle church with net vault in the nave and cellar vaulting in the polygonal choir, over Carolingian hall with three apses built

Ramisvil: old mill (1596) with lavishly decorated gable façade.

Ramosch: ruined Burg Tschanüff, remains of a massive 13C castle.

by Bernhard of Poschiavo in 1522. Wall tabernacle (1522) with aedicule (with a representation of the Last Judgement) dating from the early Renaissance period. At the entrance to the Val Sinestra **ruined Burg Tschanüff.** Heavily fortified Burg complex built 1256. Slender keep with high entrance in the fourth storey, given up at the end of the 18C.

Vna In the hamlet *Heimatmuseum* with ethnographic collection. **Mottata.** Remains of bronze and iron age settlements with outlines of houses in plan. Finds from the Laugen-Melau culture.

Ramsen SH

3□C1

Catholic parish church of St. Peter

Rancate: the Züst Pinacoteca has a collection of paintings by Tessin artists.

Rapperswil: Schloss, a late 12C foundation by the lords of Rapperswil.

und Paul. In 1928&9 Otto Schweri replaced the choir of the old church built 1796–1804 with a transept and a new choir. **Hofgut Bibermühle.** This idyllic old house on the Rhine with a mill business once belonged to the town of Stein am Rhein, but has been privately owned for more than a hundred years. The 1529 main building is late Gothic. The fresco on the S. façade (town arms of Stein am Rhein) dates from the early 17C. **'Schloss'** or Junkernhof in Wiesholz. Early 17C country seat of the Schaffhausen Peyer family with baroque interior.

Rancate TI

19 □ D5

Catholic parish church of Santo Stefano, first mentioned 1528, rebuilt 1771–6. Single-aisled baroque building with semicircular choir and dome over the crossing. In the choir marble high altar of 1758 and painting of the Martyrdom of Stephen, 1775. In the rosary chapel N. of the choir fragments of 16C paintings, on the S. wall of the nave fresco of the Madonna, 15C. By the church *Pinacoteca cantonale Giovanni Züst,* collection of paintings.

Rapperswil SG

8 □ C1

The town was founded *c.* 1200 by the lords of Rapperswil, partially destroyed in 1350 by Rudolf Brun, Mayor of Zürich and has belonged to the canton of St.Gallen since 1803. Three sets of buildings run S. from the Schloss hill down to the lake; the first row is the present Hintergasse, with its high arcades the prettiest little street in Rapperswil. Parallel to it runs the Marktgasse, also with buildings on both sides. The E. end of the 13C wall passes through the present Hauptplatz, now the centre of the Old Town. As the peninsular site only allows expansion to the E. the group of buildings around the present Engels- or Halsplatz was incorporated into the town wall as early as the 14C; this wall survived into the 19C. **Catholic parish church of St.Johannes,** originally 13C; after a fire in 1883 the church was rebuilt by Xaver Müller, who retained and raised the old towers. N. of the church is the two-storey late Gothic **cemetery chapel,** *c.* 1489. The **Heilig Hüsli,** probably 16C, is roughly 330 ft. into the lake; it was part of the wooden bridge built in 1358, which was pulled down and replaced by the Steindamm in 1878. **Capuchin monastery** in the W. of the peninsula, built 1606, much altered since then. **Schloss Rapperswil,** built late 12C, later seat of the Austrian and from 1458 the Confederate Vogts. Triangular complex in rubble masonry with palas, five-sided clock tower, square keep and round powder tower in the N corner. Substructure pre-1200, superstructure *c.* 1354. **Rathaus,** rebuilt *c.* 1470 tower 1614&15, Altered after 1866 and 1895. The building in the main square goes back to a watchtower from the earliest period of the town's history. **Hau Landenberg** (Breny-Haus) on the N. Herrenberg. Tower early 13C, residential sec tion late 15C. The Burg-like comple originally secured the NE corner of th

town. **Alter Sternen** in the Engelplatz, built 1568, later redesigned in the baroque style. **Bleulerhaus** (16 Hintergasse), built 1606 by Uli Stierli, imposing late Gothic stone building on massive pillared arches. The **Heiliggeistspital** on the Fischmarktplatz was founded in the 13C and was originally intended to house pilgrims and the needy; rebuilt in neoclassical style by Felix Wilhelm Kubly in 1843&4.
Museums. In the *Heimatmuseum* (Breny-Haus) Roman finds and Rapperswil art. The *Burgenmuseum* in the Schloss shows Burg types in Switzerland; also in the Schloss is the *Polenmuseum,* dedicated to the memory of the Polish uprising against the Russians in 1863. The *Stadtbibliothek* (municipal library) in the Haus zum Pfauen in the Hauptplatz has facilities for public functions.

Raron/Rarogne VS

18☐B1

Raron was the cradle of the mighty dynasty of the lords of Raron from the 12C; they were dependent on the bishop of Sion and played a major role in the Valais until 1419. On a rocky plateau above the village vidame **tower,** built in the 12C, step gables 16C. It was used as the seat of the lords of Raron, who traditionally held the right of vidame, and was acquired by the community in 1528. Next to it used to be a second tower, square, and of formidable dimensions: 66 by 66 ft.; it was built in the 13C for the steward of Raron and destroyed in 1417. The architect Ulrich Ruffiner used its walls in 1508–16 when building the late Gothic **Catholic parish church of St. Romanus.** In a second phase of building the nave was covered with pointed net vaulting supported by two pillars. Nave and choir contain numerous carved keystones and decorative painting, 1518. On the N. wall of the nave large wall painting, 1512 of the Last Judgement. On the triumphal arch 16C Crucifixion; neo-Gothic altars. A section of the Schloss ring wall survives in front of the church. By the S. wall of the church is the grave of the poet Rainer Maria Rilke, who lived in Valais

Raron: parish church of St. Romanus on a rocky hill above the village.

from 1921 and died in 1926 in a clinic near Montreux. In the N. old **priest's house** of 1537. In the village **Maxenhaus,** built in 1548 for Stefan Maxen, Vogt of Evian; the two-storey loggia was built in the 17C. On the street which leads to the Schloss, **Zentrigenhaus,** building with step gables, built in 1536 by U.Ruffiner for J.Zentrigen.
ST.GERMAN **St. German,** probably of Romanesque origin, first mentioned 1300, rebuilt in the 19C. Old sections still visible in the exterior, 16C crypt.

Rathausen LU
See EBIKON   7☐E3

Ravecchia TI
See BELLINZONA   19☐D2

Rebstein SG
4☐B3

Reformed church, built 1782 by Joh.Jakob and Joh.Ulrich Haltiner. **Catholic parish church of St. Sebastian.** Fortress-like building, 1950–60 by Fritz Metzger. **Haus Burg,** now a home for young girls, built *c.* 1580. **Haus zum**

Regensberg: small town founded 1244–6 on a picturesque hill site.

village has a series of very fine **wooden farm buildings,** including stables, barns and storehouses on stilts; the oldest date from the 17C.

Regensberg ZH
2☐F4

This compact little town in the E. foothills of the Lägern was founded in 1244 and has retained its medieval appearance. The main part of the town consists of the **Schloss** (once seat of the Freiherren of Regensberg) and two distinct sections: the fortified **Oberburg** and the **Unterburg,** which lay outside the fortifications. The keep of the Schloss is circular, an unusual design for the area. The residence was rebuilt in the 16C and used as the seat of the Landvogts. Since 1883 the Schloss has housed a reformatory.

Reckingen: clothed skeleton in the ossuary by the church.

Äckerli, built in 1831, possibly by Joh. Ulrich Haltiner. Fluted wooden pilasters on the gable side.

Rechthalten FR
11☐D1

Catholic church of St. German, first mentioned in the 12C, rebuilt 1764, single aisle with polygonal apse. Fine wooden Pietà (copy) on the N. side altar. Nearby **cemetery chapel,** 1553. The **priest's house** dates from 1697.

Reckingen VS
12☐E4

Catholic parish church de la Naissance de la Vierge, built 1743–5 in baroque style. Single-aisled buiding with porch and polygonal apse. Stucco decoration and painted medallions dating from 1745. 18C baroque high altar. Side altars 1745, carved pulpit 1766, 18C organ. S. of the choir **ossuary,** contemporary with the church. Altar 1700, clad skeletons in the glass cases. By the church **parish hall,** former priest's house, built 1753. The

Rehetobel AR
4☐A3

In the centre of the village 18C **timber houses.** The **Reformed church** was built in 1890–2 on the site of a baroque church. In Achmühli W. of Rehetobel **covered wooden bridge,** built 1701. Second **wooden bridge** in Oberach, built 1739 by Ulrich Grubenmann and sons.

Reichenau-Tamins GR
9☐A4

Reformed church, built in 1494 with

polygonal choir and rib vaulting. The nave and galleries were extended and the vestibule added in 1840; wooden tunnel vault 1920. **Schloss Reichenau,** built *c.* 1616, main section rebuilt in 1819 by Ulrich von Planta. Three-storey neoclassical main building, decorated with slight projections and a triangular gable. To the N. farm buildings, to the W. baroque gardens.

Reichenbach BE

12 □ A3

The timber buildings in the **Dorfstrasse** date largely from the 18C and have decorative carved and painted façades. **Gasthof Bären** of 1542 with typical late Gothic rod ornamentation on the corbels. RÜDLEN The **'Alte Kaplanei'** (old chaplaincy) is one of the oldest buildings in the Frutig valley (pre-1500). A clear sign of its age is the so-called Heidenkreuz (heathen cross) on the gable; this has nothing to do with heathen practices; popular speech has always used the word to express great age and strangeness, as in Heidenhaus and Heidenwölbi; there is a Heidenwölbi (a self-supporting vaulted wooden ceiling) in the interior of the building.

Reichenbach bei Bern BE

See ZOLLIKOFEN
6 □ E4

Reiden LU

7 □ C1

Former Commandery of the Knights of the Order of St.John, on the hill by the church. The existing buildings of the Burg of the Order founded *c.* 1280 date largely from the 16-18C.

Rennaz VD

11 □ B5

In the centre of the village is **château Grand-Clos,** a house built in 1760 for the Gaillard family. The rectangular main

Rennaz: Grand-Clos house, an elegant 1760-3 building with a large garden.

building is framed by servants' quarters and farm buildings.

Ressudens VD

See GRANDCOUR
6 □ B5

Reute AR

4 □ B3

Reformed church of 1687&8. Font dated 1687, pulpit and gallery 1688, painted ceiling 1706.

Reutigen BE

12 □ A2

The **Reformed church St.Maria** is a late Gothic single-aisle building with choir tower. The interior is decorated with paintings dating mainly from *c.* 1450-60, in particular those on the S. wall.

Rhäzüns GR

9 □ A5

Catholic parish church of St. Mariä Geburt, built 1697. Octagonal nave with side chapels, polygonal choir. N. of the church **St.Apollonia chapel.** Reversal of the ground plan of the parish church on a smaller scale, built 1721. **Former parish church of St.Paul.** Single-aisle church altered in the 15C with choir of equal width. Wall paintings of 5 different

Rhäzüns: Feiertagschristus, 2nd half of the 14C, in St. Georg.

Rheinau: 1720–3 baroque high altar in the former monastery church.

periods, including fragments of life-size individual figures by the Waltensburg master (second quarter of the 14C) on the S. wall. N. of the village **St. Georg.** Flat-ceilinged Romanesque hall with rectangular Gothic choir. Wall paintings by the Waltensburg master, 1st half of the 14C: in the choir four Evangelists around the face of Christ, 12 Apostles, Annunciation and Coronation of the Virgin, Adoration of the Magi and Crucifixion. On the chancel arch miracle and sufferings of St. George, on the N. wall fight with the dragon. Under that Feiertagschristus and St.George legend by the Rhäzüns master, 2nd half of the 14C. Cycle on the W. and N. wall (Old Testament and Life of Christ) and on the S. wall (Passion with Pentecost and the Last Judgement) by the same artist. E. of the village **Schloss Rhäzüns.** Present building predominantly 15&16C. Late 14C wall paintings: Tristan legend and bear-hunting.

Rheinau ZH

3□A2

Former Benedictine abbey. The abbey was founded in the Carolingian period and first mentioned in 844; it suffered heavily

in the 16&17C Wars of Religion. The former collegiate church was almost completely rebuilt in the early 18C, while the monastery buildings, which have been a sanatorium for more than a hundred years, were unified in the 19C. The monastery on an island in a loop of the Rhine and the little town of the same name are uniformly late baroque. **Former collegiate church of St.Maria.** The interior of the church was carefully renovated in the late 70s and is one of the finest specimens of high baroque in Switzerland. It is a pilastered hall with galleries; the new design, realised in 1704–11, was the work of Franz Beer, who after Rheinau also built the monastery church of ▷ St.Urban. He took over the late Gothic tower in the S. corner of the façade from the earlier building; it had been built by Hans Wellenberg in 1572-8. Beer added an identical tower in the N. corner. The tops of the towers are surmounted with angels blowing trombones. In the interior perspective choir screen by Hans Jörg Allweiler and Franz Scheuermann of Konstanz (1731&2) separates the four-bay lay church from the monks' choir (transept) and from the adjacent two-bay sanctuary. The pilasters in the nave have side altars in front of them; these strengthen the effect of perspective towards the high altar. The baroque high altar dates from 1720 – 3 and is the work of Judas Thaddäus Sichelbein. The ceiling frescos are by Francesco Antonio Giorgioli (1708&9), the stucco is by Franz Schmutzer of Wessobrunn (1708–10). The choir stalls, 1707–10 and the main organ-casing by J.T.Sichelbein are other notable features. **Former monastery buildings.** The numerous buildings in the spacious complex include the old *convent buildings* (1628–32), the new E. convent wing with sacristy and library (1711 – 17), the St. Magdalena chapel, also called **'Spitzkir-che'** (1587&8), the abbot's building (1604–18), the men's guesthouse (1675&6, W. extension 1726 – 34), the women's guesthouse (1585–8, E. wing with theatre 1740–4) and the farm buildings with the Zürich State cellars. **Ecumenical mountain church of St.Nikolaus.** This church on a hill was rebuilt in 1578&9 after the collapse of the earlier building. **Haus Wellenberg.** Late Gothic house of 1551. **Haus zur Post** (also Haus Waldkirch, 1602). Step gable building with round staircase tower. **Covered Rhine bridge** (1804, Blasius Baltenschweiler). **Roman watchtower** in the Köpferplatz (2nd half of the 4C). 1C BC Celtic rampart; parts of the town moat and town wall have survived.

Rheineck SG

4☐B3

The centre of the little town consists of the two rows of houses which make up the Hauptstrasse; it originally had a gate at each end (has survived). **Catholic parish church of St. Theresia.** This rotunda with dome and apse was built by Otto Linder in 1932&3 as one of the first modern churches in Switzerland. The **Rathaus,** 1553–5, with rococo panelling in the council chamber was renovated in 1876 and 1929&30. The wall paintings in the Ratssaal are by Heinrich Herzig, 1929. **Former Amtssitz of the Landvogts** (No 8). Three-storey 17C building with two oriels on mask corbels. **Löwenhof,** on the N. edge of the town. This Schloss-like

Rheineck: Löwenhof, a Schloss-like baroque building dating from 1746–8.

baroque monumental building was built 1746–8 for the merchant Giovanni Heer. Three-storey rectangular building with mansard roof and ridge tower, pilasters and scroll gables on the street façades. Fine interior staircase, French gardens and pavilion with flight of steps at the rear. **Custerhof,** built 1750–3, cantonal school of agriculture since 1896. Baroque building with oriel on mask corbel on the N. narrow façade, rococo stucco in the interior. **Altrheineck ruined Burg,** mentioned 1163, later Vogt's seat, given up in the late Middle Ages. The W. wall of the keep has survived.

Rheinfelden AG

2☐B3

The town founded by the Zähringen family in 1130 is the successor of a much older river-bank settlement. Rheinfelden blossomed as an independent town under the empire; it became part of Switzerland along with the Austrian Frick valley in 1803. **Old Town and fortifications.** The town wall has survived almost intact between the **Obertorturm** in the S. and the **Kupferturm** or **Storchennestturm** in the E. At the NE end of the wall on the bank of the Rhine is the triangular **Messerturm** or **Diebsturm,** which also survives from the 15C. **Old Catholic Church of St.Martin.** This late Gothic basilica with nave and two aisles dating from 1407 is influenced by the architecture

Rheinfelden: 1407 St.Martin, redesigned in the baroque style in 1769–71.

of the Mendicant Order. Radical alterations were made in 1669 (choir vaulting) and also in 1769–71 (baroque interior). The rococo stucco is by Martin Fröwis, the wall and ceiling paintings are by Franz Fidel Bröchen. **Chapel of the Order of St. John.** Rheinfelden was the seat of a commandery of the Order of St.John. The late Gothic chapel (1456&7) with nave with flat ceiling, polygonal choir and tower with steep saddleback roof was deconsecrated in 1806. It has numerous wall paintings, including a last Judgement of the Schongau school (*c.* 1490). In the Ratsstube are 16 Renaissance cabinet panels. **Roman watchtower** near the Pferrichgraben (about 3 km. NE of the town); presumably 4C. *Fricktaler Museum.* Collection on the history of the region.

Richensee LU
See Hitzkirch   7☐E1

Richental LU
                                               7☐C2

The **Catholic parish church of St. Cäcilia** was built in 1803–7 by Niklaus and Josef Purtschert and is a typical baroque country church of the ▷ Ruswil type. The **Blum granary,** dated 1736, in the 'Gugger' is lavishly carved and painted.

Richterswil ZH
                                               8☐B1

Reformed parish church. Neo-Gothic building by Jacques Kehrer (1902 – 5). **Mühlenen buildings.** Group of buildings around a mill which has existed from the 13C. The main section, a Gothic step-gable building with a Renaissance coffered ceiling dates from 1578. The complex was altered in 1949&50 and 1958 and fitted out as a home craft school. **Alt-Wädenswil ruin.** The medieval family seat of the Freiherren of Wädenswil was destroyed in the 16C as a result of a decision in the Diet. The remains were made subject to a conservation order in 1958.

Rickenbach SO
                                               2☐B5

St.Laurentius chapel, *c.* 1700. The furnishings are essentially baroque, including the Crucifixion in the choir arch; the statues of St.Laurence and the Madonna and Child are late Gothic. **Villa Tannenheim,** built to plans by Melchior Berri in neoclassical style. **Ruined Burg.** Mid-11C early stone building.

Rickenbach SZ
See Schwyz   8☐B3

Ried VS
See Bellwald   12☐D4

Rieden SG
                                               8☐D1

Catholic parish church of St.Magnus, built in neo-baroque style by Adolf Gaudy in 1912 with Jugendstil ornamentation. In the sacristy, monstrance (*c.* 1685-1700) by Georg Reischle.

Riehen BS
                                               2☐A:

Reformed parish church of St.Martin
Excavations revealed the foundations of

single-aisled building with two side-annexe rooms and semicircular apse, probably dating from the turn of the millennium. A first subsequent building can be placed in the mid 14C. The new building, completed in 1694, shows the tenacity of Gothic design. The **Catholic parish church of St. Franziskus** in the Pfaffenloh was built by Fritz Metzger 1949&50. The **Reformed Kornfeldkirche** was built in 1962 and designed by Max Ernst Häfeli, Werner M.Moser and Rudolf Steiger. The following three buildings were in the 11&12C fortified area which surounded the village church in a trapezium: the **Meierhof** was partially Romanesque and altered after 1662. The **Klösterli** belonged, along with the church, to the monastery of Wettingen from 1248; rebuilt from 1672. The **alte Gemeindehaus** was built on the site of the guard and courthouse in 1836 by Amadeus Merian to a design by Melchior Berri. The **Landvogtei,** built in several phases, was used by the monastery of Wettingen as a tithe barn and from 1522 became the seat of the town Landvogts. The **Wettsteinhäuser** in the Baselstrasse form a compact group around a courtyard; this residence belonging to the Basel mayor Johann Rudolf Wettstein also developed in stages. The old Wettsteinhaus, consisting of a front and a rear section, was built by Wettstein before 1650; he had been the Landvogt of Riehen until then. The 16C former Meielsche Gut was renovated in 1662 and included in the complex as the neues Wettsteinhaus. Today it is the *local and toy museum.* Between Riehen and Basel is the high baroque **Bäumlihof** country seat, 1686 and 1704; garden room with Régence décor, built *c.* 1738 and attributed to Johann Carl Hemeling. **Le Grandgut,** built between 1688 and 1692, altered *c.* 1770, was once part of a cour d'honneur. In the English garden is an orangery with exotic touches, after 1836. **Wenkenhof.** On one side of the cour d'honneur is the group of buildings known as the Alte Wenken, early 17C. The single-storey Neue Wenken was built as a pleasance with ballrooms in 1736 and gives on to a broad terrace and a French garden; it was raised in 1860, the building was

Riehen: Wenkenhof, the Alte Wenken, a farmhouse extended in the early 17C.

Riggisberg: Abegg-Stiftung; 11C Iranian woven silk.

restored and the English garden added in 1917&18.

Rifferswil ZH
8 □ A1

Dignified group of 18C **half-timbered houses** in Unter-Rifferswil.

Riggisberg BE
11 □ E/F1

Abegg-Stiftung. A collection founded by the industrialist Werner Abegg with an emphasis on textiles and medieval art. The museum includes an institute of art and a conservation studio. Open in summer.

Riom: the ruins of the castle, given up in the 19C, were restored in 1936.

Riva San Vitale: early Christian baptistery c. 500.

Ringgenberg BE

12 □ C2

Reformed church, built 1671 – 4 by building foreman Abraham I. Dünz in the **ruins** of a Burg founded *c.* 1240 by the Raron family. The façade tower is built of the masonry of the original keep. Early baroque interior.
GOLDSWIL **Church ruin,** W. of Ringgenberg. The foundation walls of a long

nave with W. annexe of the ruined Romanesque church of St. Peter have survived along with the tower, which is in good condition.

Riom/Reams GR

14 □ B2

Catholic parish church of St. Laurentius. Baroque complex (1677) with powerfully articulated façade. Below the village is the **Ream ruin,** a Burg built *c.*1200. Three-storey palas with seven-storey tower.

Risch ZG

7 □ F2

Catholic parish church of St. Verena, rebuilt 1680, incorporating the Gothic tower with steep saddleback roof between nave and choir.

Ritzingen VS

12 □ E4

Interesting village with 17&18C buildings. 1732 **St. Anna chapel** with altar by Anton Sigristen, 1740.
RITZINGERFELD Outside the village in the direction of Gluringen, **Madonna chapel,** built in 1687 in post-Gothic style, rebuilt in 1807–14 after avalanche damage. In the interior paintings by J.J.Pfefferle, 1808, high altar with carving by Joh. Ritz, 1690. The S. side altar is by the same master, the N. altar by Joh. and Andreas Ritz, 1713. Pulpit by Johann Sigristen, 1700.

Riva San Vitale TI

19 □ D5

Very old town, first mentioned in 774; one of the main ecclesiastical centres of the See of Como. In 1798 Riva set up an independent republic of the same name, but this only lasted for one month. **Catholic parish church of San Vitale,** mentioned 962, probably founded earlier; rebuilt 1756–9, façade 1865. By the church is the

baptistery which was once a part of it; this is the oldest surviving ecclesiastical building in Switzerland. The building dates from *c.* 500 and is on a square central ground plan, the octagonal interior has an octagonal drum dome. Originally the baptistery had an ambulatory, of which traces can still be seen. On the E. side 9C semicircular apse. In the interior of the baptistery original floor and in the centre an octagonal basin, let into the floor, designed for baptism by immersion; in the 9&10C it was replaced by the present font, a gigantic monolith. In the niches around the apse 12C paintings, in the apse traces of a 10&11C Crucifixion. At the S. end of the village **San Rocco chapel,** founded in the 16C, altered in the baroque style in 1665; 18C altars. In the N. of the village **Catholic church of Santa Croce.** one of the finest Renaissance buildings in Switzerland, founded by G. Andrea Della Croce and built 1588–92 by the architect G.A.Piotti, known as Vacallo. Rotunda with drum dome; the tower incorporated into the building has the same lantern as the dome. In the interior eight columns support the moulded cornice on which the pilasters of the drum stand. 16C decoration and large paintings by Camillo Procacciani. By the church 16C **Palazzo Della Croce,** former residence of the family who founded Santa Croce. In the Piazza **Casa Communale** with arched portico, built in the late 16C for the Della Croce family. Numerous interesting **houses** in the village.

Rivaz VD

11 ☐ A4

On the Nationalstrasse **château Glérolles,** probably built in the 12C to protect the N. bank of lake Geneva against attacks from Savoy, subject to the bishops of Lausanne and to the Bernese from 1536–1798. The oldest surviving section is the rectangular keep, some of which was demolished in the 19C.

Rive-Haute VS

See LIDDES   17 ☐ C4

Roche: there is an organ museum in the former staging post.

Roche VD

11 ☐ B5

Former 16C **staging post** on the route to the Great St.Bernard, intended site of the Swiss *organ museum.*

Rodersdorf SO

1 ☐ E4

In the middle of this intact nucleated village is the **parish church of St. Laurentius** with Romano-Gothic tower. **Altermatthof.** This group of walled buildings shows Sundgau influence.

Roggwil BE

7 ☐ B1

There is a small *Heimatmuseum* (local history) in an 18C storehouse.

Roggwil TG

4 ☐ A2

Schloss Mammertshofen, SE of the

Roggwil TG: 13&16C keep of Schloss Mammertshofen.

village. Former seat of the Marschalls of Sankt Gallen, in the possession of the von Planta family since 1922. 13C keep in massive, uncut erratics. Overhanging 16C wooden upper storey. Residence altered *c.* 1695. NE building and castellated wall built 1852 by Johann Christoph Kunkler.

Rohr AG
2☐D4

Roman road in the so-called 'Suret'.

Rolle VD
10☐C3

This little town with a 13C château was founded in 1318 by Ludwig II of Savoy and has retained its original ribbon layout with a central street. **Château.** 1291, owned by Aymon de Salleneuve, in the 15C by the lords of Viry and after 1536 the Bernese. The building is shaped like a trapezium and has four corner towers. Only the round tower in the NW is 13C, the other parts were rebuilt in the 15&18C. Up in the town **Reformed church** (St.Grat), built 1519, renewed in the 18C. Medieval bell tower. In the Ruelle des Halles **Catholic church of St-Joseph,** built in neo-Gothic style in 1843. In the choir stained glass (1929) by Alexandre Cingria. 50 Grand-Rue, small 16C defensive building with castellated entrance. All the buildings in

Rolle: three-winged Château on a trapezium plan with four corner towers.

the Grand-Rue date from the 16C. On the **Ile de la Harpe** monument to Frédéric-César de la Harpe (1844).

Romainmôtier VD
10☐D1

Former Abbey of St-Pierre et St-Paul, one of the oldest and most important buildings in Switzerland. According to legend the monastery was founded in the 5C by St.Roman and St.Lupicin. When the abbey of St-Maurice was founded in 515 the Burgundian King Sigismund sent for monks from Romainmôtier. In 928 the monastery was presented to Cluny, which was a powerful influence from 994 thanks to St. Odilo of Cluny; Romanmôtier flourished until the 15C; in 1536 the abbey was dissolved as a result of the Reformation; it has been excavated and restored since 1896. The present **church** was under construction from the beginning of the 11C, first of all probably under St.Odilo of Cluny, on the foundation of 7C and 8C churches. The cruciform basilica has a nave and two aisles, and originally had three semicircular apses. It is a particularly good example of Burgundian architecture, a reduced copy of Cluny II. The vestibule was built in the 12C; the entrance is 14C; at the same time the ante-choir was rebuilt on a rectangular ground plan. The exterior of the church is articulated with simple Lombardy blind arches. In the vault of the porch 14C frescos, in the interior of the church 8C ambo with braided decoration and inscription. In the choir recumbent tomb figure of Prior Henri de Siviriez, 14C, and fragments of the tomb of Prior

Jean de Seyssel, d.1432. 15C choir stalls. In the N. chapel 15C frescos. On the S. side of the church remains of the **former cloister.** Opposite the church 14C **clock tower,** the former gate of the walls which protected the monastery buildings. These were rebuilt in the Bernese period. The tithe barn and the **former prior's house** have survived; the latter was altered in the 16&17C when it was the residence of the Vogts of Bern. By the tower house of the **lieutenant baillival** (Vogts' steward), building with half-hipped roof, built for Jean-Pierre Roy in 1684&5. **Maison Glayre,** built in the 16C for André Tachet and rebuilt in 1762.

Romainmôtier: the most important Romanesque monastery church in Switzerland.

Romainmôtier: carved capital in the chapel of St-Michel above the vestibule.

Romanshorn TG

4 □ A2

The present town was rebuilt on numerous occasions after fires and was much changed in the 19C by the development of navigation on Lake Constance (harbour installations, shipbuilding). **Ecumenical Old Church.** Remains of the walls of the earlier building mentioned in 779 were excavated by archaeologists from 1964. 10C sanctuary extended in the 14C and painted, other alterations 1505–10 and 1829. Tower first half of 15C, topmost section 1670. **Catholic church of St.Johann Baptist,** built 1911–13 by Adolf Gaudy in neo-Romanesque style. Tower based on St. Mark's, Venice. **Reformed church,** 1906–11 by Otto Pfleghard and Max Haefeli. Rotunda on cruciform ground plan, painting on the chancel wall by Elisabeth Thomann-Altenburger.

Romont FR

11 □ B2

The town was mentioned from the 12C and began to develop from 1240 when it was acquired by Peter II of Savoy and extended as an important military base. It was occupied by the Confederates in 1476, and came into the possession of Fribourg from 1536. **Château,** built in the 13C by Peter II, probably on the site of an older building; owned by the lords of Billens.

The ring wall on three sides and the round keep have survived from the original building. The present Schloss and the entrance are 16C. In the courtyard, at the foot of the keep, large water wheel, 1772. The *Musée du vitrail* (stained glass) has been housed in the château since June 1981. In the S. of the town **tour à Boyer,** a massive 13C round tower intended for the defence of the outer town. A large proportion of the Romont town wall has survived. It was built by Peter II of Savoy and maintained and repaired by the Vogts of Fribourg until it was given up in the last century. **Collegiate church of Notre-Dame-de-l'Assomption.** The first church, built between 1244 and 1296, was completely destroyed by the fire of Romont in 1434. The present late Gothic church was consecrated in 1451; the S. aisle of the earlier building was retained. It has a nave and two aisles and a rectangular choir; in front of the façade is a 14&15C narthex with a 1250 Majestas in the tym-

Romont: Notre-Dame collegiate church, a 15C late Gothic building.

Ronco: interior of the parish church with 17C stucco in the vaulting.

panum. The interior was partially redecorated in the late 19C and in 1938. Interesting 14&15C glass, also 12 Apostle windows by Alexandre Cingria, 1939. In the narthex 15C Ascension window, in the chapel sandstone Madonna, *c.* 1250. In the nave carved pulpit of 1520, in the S. aisle carved tomb of the knight Jean Maillard, 16C. On the triumphal arch 15C Crucifixion. In the choir, separated from the nave by a 1478 screen (1478), fine choir stalls (1466–9) carved by Rodolphe Pottu. Some old buildings survive in the town. By the château **Restaurant de la Croix-Blanche**, 16C. In the Grand-Rue **Hôtel du Cerf**, 16C, completely altered in the 19C.

Ronco (Ascona) TI
19☐B2

Catholic parish church of San Martino, originally medieval, first mentioned 1498, altered in the 17C; single-aisled building with rectangular choir. Choir frescos by Antonio da Tradate, 1492, including labours of the months; in the vaulting 17C stucco, marble high altar with picture of St. Martin by A.Cisei 1860–70. In the nave 17&18C altars, In the piazza **Santa Maria delle Grazie chapel,** 1712 baroque building; frescos by G.Antonio Felice Orelli in the dome.

Ropraz VD
10☐F2

Reformed church, single-aisled church with polygonal apse altered in 1761. In the choir 1764 painted coats-of-arms. 1674 pulpit.

Rorbas ZH
3☐A3

Gasthof Adler. 16C half-timbered building, altered 1810.

Rorschach SG
4☐A/B3

Catholic parish church of St. Kolumban und Konstantius, rebuilt 1438, much altered in the 17C. Nave extended and altered 1782–86 by Joh. Haag, façade 1886 by Aug. Hardegger. The **former Benedictine monastery of Mariaberg** on the hillside S. of the town is one of the most important late medieval monastery buildings in Switzerland. It has three main sections and a cloister was begun in 1487 under the builder Erasmus Grasser. On the W. façade old entrance with paradise. In the N. walk of the cloister stellar vaulting, otherwise net vaulting. The vaulting in the chapterhouse is lavishly painted (1564–8). The **Kornhaus,** a dominant building by the harbour, was

Rorschach: late Gothic cloister of the former Benedictine monastery of Mariaberg.

high medieval, the residence building, which contains the St. Anna chapel, is Gothic. **Schloss Wartensee,** on the E. slope of the Rohrschachberg, was originally the seat of the Sankt Gallen Wartensee estate oficials. In the 19C the complex was rebuilt in neo-Gothic style, the E. wing burned down in 1885 and was again rebuilt. The only medieval section to have survived is the W. tower. **Schloss Wartegg** dates from 1557 and in 1860 was the home of the exiled Louise von Bourbon-Parma; much altered in the 18&19C. The Schloss chapel, built in 1707 as a Loreto chapel and refurbished in neo-Romanesque style in 1873 is now a daughter-church of the Rohrschach parish church.

built 1746–8 by Giov. Gaspare Bagnato and originally provided grain for the abbey area; it has been owned by the town of Rorschach since 1908. Symmetrical baroque building with twelve axes and rusticated corner pilaster strips. Central projection with triangular gable, side projections with curved gables. Hall with three aisles on the ground floor. On the Hauptstrasse some notable buildings: the **Rathaus** (No. 29), built 1681-9, S. wing 1747, has a two-storey stone oriel on the street side. The **Falken** (No. 31) also has a two-storey stone oriel and is contemporary with the Rathaus. **Haus Weber** (No. 33) has a lavishly carved double oriel with figures on the corbels, dated 1650. The **Kettenhaus** (No. 39) was rebuilt 1786–94; it has a façade articulated with pilasters and a central mansard gable. The **Engelapotheke** (No. 43) is baroque with mansard gable, built after 1761. The **Haus Brugger** (No. 48), built 1581 and altered early 18C, has a carved wooden oriel. The Mariabergstrasse, built 1774–8 to connect the town and the governor's residence, is lined with late baroque family seats, and contains the **Amtshaus** (No 15., 1790).

Rohrschachberg SG
4☐A/B3

St. Anna-Schloss, originally Burg stables of the Lords of Rohrschach. The keep is

Röschenz BE
1☐E/F4

The village. The houses in this farming village, which has survived intact, have their roof edges to the street and the village square in typical Laufental style.

Rossinière VD
11☐C4

In the upper part of the village **Reformed church** (Ste-Marie-Madeleine), mentioned since 1316 and rebuilt in 1645. In the choir 15C wall tabernacle and remains of frescos, 1645 pulpit. Pretty group of chalets in the village square. **Chalet Rosset** is of the Bernese type, built 1660 –70, with inscriptions on the façade and a carved frieze. On the lower side of the square **Grand-Chalet,** one of the largest and finest wooden buildings in the canton, built 1754 for Jean-David Henchoz. The building has 113 windows, the main façade is decorated with carved friezes, inscriptions and paintings.

Rossura TI
13☐C4

S. of the village **Catholic parish church of Santi Lorenzo ed Agata,** single-aisle building with polygonal choir, first mentioned 1247, but probably older. On the interior W. wall on the right paintings by Cristoforo and Nicolao da Seregno, 1463, on the N. wall paintings of the Last Supper, the Scourging of Christ, various saints, 15C.

Röthenbach i.E. BE
7□B5

WÜRZBRUNNEN Former **pilgrimage church,** rebuilt after the fire of 1494. The Gothic wooden ceiling dates from that time. The interior was painted in the baroque style in 1779.

Rothenburg LU
7□E3

BERTISWIL **St. Maria** is an essentially Romanesque church (11&12C); 1504 tower with steep saddleback roof and slightly later polygonal choir. Mid-16C frescos in good condition.

Rothenturm SZ
8□B3

Rothenturm came into being as a result of centuries of border conflict between Schwyz and the monastery of Einsiedeln. It was built on the site of a fortified wall built by Schwyz in the early 14C; the surviving **tower** was a part of this.

Rougemont VD
11□D4

Reformed Church. Former St-Nicolas, part of a Cluniac priory founded c. 1073 –85 and dissolved in 1555. The Romanesque church is late 11C or early 12C. It has a cruciform ground plan with a nave and two aisles. The choir was built 1585 –7 to replace three semicircular apses; roof and bell tower date from the 17C; modern interior. By the church, on the site of the former priory, is the **château,** built by the Bernese in the 16C, rebuilt 1756 and

Rossinière: carved frieze on the main façade of the Grand-Chalet, 1754.

Rougemont: former Cluniac priory of St-Nicolas and 16C Château.

restored after a fire in 1974. A fine core of 17&18C timber houses has survived in the village; their façades are decorated with carved friezes, inscriptions and paintings. Opposite the Cheval Blanc inn is a 1688 **storehouse** with fine door fittings.

Rovana TI
See CEVIO   19□A/B1

Roveredo GR
19□E2

Roveredo consists of various core settlements on both sides of the Moesa and has an impressive number of striking 16&17C houses; in the Marktplatz **casa Zucalli, casa della Grida** (courthouse) and the **casa di Mazio. Catholic parish church of San Giulio,** impressive medieval building. **Catholic church of La Madonna del Ponte chiuso.** The 1665 new building is an early example of the baroque pilaster scheme which developed to such heights in S. Germany.

Roveredo: parish church of San Giulio with post-Romanesque bell tower.

Rovio: Romanesque wall painting in the apse of San Vigilio chapel.

Rovio TI

19 □ D4

On the edge of the village **Catholic parish church of Santi Vitale ed Agata,** mentioned 1213, altered in the 18&19C. Fine marble high altar. On a hill W. of the village **San Vigilio chapel,** 11C single-aisled Romanesque building with semicircular apse, exterior articulated with pilaster strips and blind arches. In the apse Romanesque wall paintings showing Byzantine influence, including Christ Enthroned. On the road to Arogno **Santa Maria Assunta chapel,** small 17C baroque rotunda; 18C vestibule; 1709 marble altar. The village has narrow alleys and interesting **houses,** some of which are decorated with 17&18C stucco and frescos. In the Dorfplatz **Casa communale,** an important 19C building.

Rüderswil BE

7 □ A4

Settlement made up of isolated farms with fine **Emmental houses.** The typical farmhouse of the region has been of the Ständerbau type since the 17C and has the residential section and kitchen facing S. or SE. The simple houses have two rooms; the one at the front is a living and dining room, and the rear one generally the sleeping quarters. Some are semi-detached houses each with two rooms on either side of a communal kitchen, and were formerly occupied by two families. The kitchen also serves as the entrance. Example: **Haus Rothenbühler** of 1775. The early 18C **Krämerhaus** has sayings from the Bible painted on its upper storey.

Rüdlen BE

See REICHENBACH   12 □ A3

Rüdlingen SH

3 □ A3

Schaffhausen exclave in Zürich territory on the Rhine with striking half-timbered buildings. The **Gasthaus Stube** is very early 16C and the **Gasthaus Rebstock** dates from 1657.

Rue: Château above the Broye valley founded by the counts of Geneva.

Rüeggisberg: ruins of the Cluniac priory dissolved in 1528.

Rue FR

11 □A3

The lords of Rue, first mentioned 1152, were vassals of the counts of Geneva. In 1260 the town came under the jurisdiction of Savoy and in 1538 under that of Fribourg. The **château** is on a rocky outcrop above the town. It was built in the 12C, destroyed in 1237 and rebuilt by the Savoyards in the late 13C. The oldest part is the square keep, which commanded the only access to the little plateau. The residential section was built on old foundations in 1618–30. Below the château **Catholic church of St-Nicolas,** first mentioned in the 14C, rebuilt in the 18C and altered in the 19C. By the church is the 16C **maison Dupraz.** Some interesting buildings have survived in the village; in the main street covered **fountain** with 1849 basin.

Rüediswil LU

See Ruswil 7 □D3

Rüeggisberg BE

6 □E5

Former Cluniac priory. First Cluniac monastery foundation in German-speaking territory. A building dating from the period of the foundation was probably replaced by the Romanesque church after 1100; only the N. transept and parts of the crossing remain. The foundations indicate a typical Cluniac choir. Small *museum* in the cloister.

Oberbütschel is NW of Rüeggisberg and has a unified appearance with about ten farms. In the centre of the hamlet is a 17C **Hochstudhaus** with a low, hipped shingle roof. The buildings for retired farmers and storehouses are two-storey half-timbered Ständer buildings with semicircular decoration under the gables and arcades at the side.

Rümikon AG

2 □F3

Roman watchtower in the 'Sandgraben'; 4C AD.

Rümlang ZH

3 □A4

Reformed parish church. The present building dates from 1471. The squat choir tower dates from the 14C. Late Gothic symbols of the Evangelists in the choir vault.

Rümligen BE

6 □F5

Schloss. Samuel Frisching had the Burg built by the Freiherren von Rümligen altered into a baroque Schloss *c.* 1710.

Rümlingen BL

2 □B4

The **Reformed parish church St.Georg**

Ruswil: interior of the parish church, built 1781–3 using the so-called Singer-Purtschert scheme.

was frequently altered from the 13C to the 17C and with the ossuary (1609) and the priest's house (1667) it makes a fine ensemble in the middle of the village.

Russikon ZH

3 ☐ C4/5

Reformed parish church. Late Gothic choir with paintings. Crown of tower and baroque pulpit 1792.

Russin GE

16 ☐ D2

Reformed church (St-Laurent); some parts 10C. **La Grand'Cour,** Route des Molards, country house built 1670; façade with covered gallery with two rectangular side towers. **Château,** Chemin de la Croix de Plomb, 18C country house.

Russo TI

19 ☐ B2

Catholic parish church of Santa Maria Assunta, founded 1365, altered in the baroque period. 15C Christopher fresco on the façade, 17&18C interior. In the village square **casa Bezzola,** 18C building with arcade.

Ruswil LU

7 ☐ D3

Catholic parish church of St. Mauritius, rebuilt 1781 – 3 by the Vorarlbergers Niklaus and Jakob Purtschert; tower designed by Jakob Singer. This building is the finest example of the Singer-Purtschert scheme for late baroque country churches in Lucerne: ceiling with shallow vaulting, pilasters, diagonal niches linking nave and choir, usually two-storey galleries over the entrance, balcony-like loggias in the choir. The **priest's house,** built 1635–55, contains a ballroom with 1564 early baroque panelling. W. of Ruswil in Buchholz **St. Gallus und Erasmus chapel** of 1662 with ornamental panelled ceiling, the altars are probably by the Tüfel family of carvers. RÜEDISWIL. The late Gothic **St. Ulrich und Afra chapel** NW of Rüediswil has late 16C side altars with unusual Renaissance retables.

Rüti ZH: late Gothic painting on the choir arch of the Reformed parish church.

Rüthi SG

4□B4

The **Catholic parish church St. Valentin** is N. of the village on a hill in the plain, the so-called Valentinsberg. Altered or rebuilt *c.* 1519, new nave and baroque modification 1734, lengthened 1880. Tower probably medieval.

Rüti ZH

8□C1

Reformed parish church. The present church was built from 1771–3 by Heinrich Vogel, who used parts of an earlier Premonstratensian monastery. The choir

arch has paintings dated 1492 and attributed to Hans Haggenberg. **Former Amtshaus.** The building dates from 1706&7 and is by the church on the site of the W. wing of the former Premonstratensian monastery, which burned down.

Rüti bei Büren BE

6□E2

Reformed church St. Katharina. Gothic building with Romanesque walls also containing bricks from a nearby Roman settlement. The lavish wall paintings in the interior include material from the Paupers' Bible.

Rütli UR

8□A4

Meadow in the woods by the Urnersee; according to tradition the inhabitants of the valleys of Uri, Schwyz and Unterwalden met here in 1291 and made the pact which led to the liberation of the nucleus of the Swiss confederation from Habsburg rule. To protect it from being used for building the site was purchased in 1860 with contributions from the Swiss people and school children and presented to the Confederation as the inalienable property of the nation.

Rüttenen SO

6□F1

Kreuzen The church was founded in 1639 by mayor Johann von Roll. The representation of the Holy Sepulchre in the choir is at the end of a Way of the Cross; the Calvary still survives in the nearby wood. Below in the gorge where, according to legend, St.Verena used to live, is the **Einsiedelei St.Verena** with two chapels and her hermit's cell. The present building is essentially 17C.

S

St-Aubin FR

6☐B5

In the square in the upper part of the village **Catholic parish church of St-Aubin,** mentioned since the 11C, rebuilt early 16C, renovated 1949–51, bell tower 1630. Nave, two aisles and polygonal apse, fine Gothic rib vaulting. In the choir Gothic tabernacle and lavabo. Nearby **château,** a rectangular building with corner towers, polygonal staircase tower in the façade, dated 1631.

St-Aubin NE

6☐A5

Reformed church. An earlier church, mentioned in 1176 and dedicated to St. Albinus, has disappeared. The present façade tower is 15&16C, nave and choir date from 1637 and the S. section from 1811. 2 Rue de la Reusière, 16&17C **house,** three storeys with wooden gallery.

St-Barthélemy VD

10☐E2

Château on the hill opposite the village, former seat of the lords of Goumoëns. The originally medieval building has a polygonal and a square tower.

San Bernardino GR

See Mesocco   13☐E/F4

St-Blaise NE

6☐B3

Reformed church (St-Blaise) in the Gothic style, built in the 15&16C on the foundations of a Romanesque building. Façade tower with round-arched portal under a 1516 pointed arch. Grand-Rue. **Hôtel du Cheval Blanc,** 16C windows

St-Barthélemy: the Château is now a home for children in need of care.

Sta. Domenica: lavish baroque stucco in the Catholic church.

in the N. façade; **house** No. 23, built in 1649 and 1701 in two sections around a polygonal staircase tower. **Maison neuve,** 1 Rue de la Gare, 1660, heavily restored in the 19C, door with baroque decoration in the staircase tower. In the upper part of the village **maison de la Dîme** (tithe house), 5 Rue de la Dîme, with hexagonal staircase tower and main door 1581. 1 Chemin de la Mureta, 16C or 17C **house,** Renaissance window with three apertures and frieze with carved heads.

Ste-Croix VD

5☐E4

Below the Vuiteboeuf road **Roman road;** marks made in the rock by wheels can still be seen.

Sta.Domenica GR

13☐E5

Catholic parish church of Santa

St. Gallen: the old town developed in a circle around the monastery precinct.

Domenica. Baroque N.-orientated pilastered hall with rectangular choir and a gallery in the S. bay (1664–72). Tripartite semicircular windows with cornices. Medieval tower with two baroque storeys. Carved 1679 high altar, dense stucco in the chapel niches by Giovanni Broggio, 1974 –9.

St. Gallen SG

3☐F4

Economic centre of E. Switzerland and capital of the canton of the same name. The name comes from the monastery founded by St. Gallus, *c.* 612. The town itself developed near the abbey from a free religious foundation. After the Hungarian invasion of 926 a first ring wall was built around the monastery precinct, in the 15C the Irer suburb N. of the old settlement was brought within the fortifications. The first reference to St. Gallen as a town with the right to hold markets was in 1170. It

is not known when the town became independent, but gradual emancipation from the monastery began from 1180 under the protection of the king; this led to an alliance with the peasants rebelling against the monastery in the Appenzell War 1401 – 8. In 1454 the town concluded an perpetual alliance with the six members of the Confederation. The town was in favour of the Reformation, but the monastery asserted its rights in the surrounding area. Since the 14&15C the economic basis of the town's independence has been the linen trade. In the late 18C the manufacture and embroidery of cotton fabrics were added. In 1803 St.Gallen became the capital of the newly-founded canton, in 1805 the Helvetic Council decided to dissolve the monastery. The canton includes the whole of the Land Appenzell; it stretches in the SW to Rapperswil and in the S. well beyond the Walensee, while the valley of the Rhine forms a natural frontier in the E. In the N. the canton touches Lake Constance. The present town of St. Gallen shows all the signs of a long period of growth, but despite the removal of the town walls between 1808 and 1879 the circular boundaries of the high and late medieval town are still visible in an aerial photograph.

MONASTERY AREA AND TOWN CENTRE The historic germ of the town is the area around the present Gallusplatz, bordering on the SW section of the monastery precinct. This, the largest square in the old town, and the Gallusstrasse have to some extent retained their late Gothic character. The rows of old buildings are set like the shell of a nut around the square and the monastery, with the wedge of the Marktstrasse driven through them roughly from N. to S. The Spisergasse and the Multergasse were the most important medieval thoroughfares. The former is dominated by late Gothic buildings, the latter has mainly *c.* 1900 Jugendstil buildings. **Collegiate church of St. Gallus und Otmar.** Built 1755–6 on the site of earlier medieval buildings. Nave and rotunda 1755–60 by Peter Thumb, choir 1761 by Johann Michael Beer of Bildstein. The E. façade is the joint work of Beer, Brother Gabriel Loser and Josef Anton Feuchtmayer. The interior decoration was supervised by Christian Wenzinger, the stucco is by Johann Georg and Mathias Gigl of Wessobrunn. Thorough restoration 1961–7. The church is a long, symmetrical building with central rotunda. In the E. twin-towered façade with concave tower axes and convex central section; the sculptures on the gable are copies by Alfons Magg (1934); the originals by Feuchtmayer and Joh. Jak. Oechslin (1844) are in the Brunnenhof. Plain side and W. façades, rotunda with curved gable and Mansart roof. On the rotunda façade sculptures by Christian Wenzinger, who was also responsible for the Immaculata on the apsidal W. façade. E. and W. crypt, the latter early medieval, the former altered in 1767. Over the nave bays shallow pendentive domes, in the aisles groin vaults, pendentive dome with 8 pillars over the central space, surrounded by the calottes of the ambulatory. Stucco reliefs in the dome spandrels and on the pillars by Christian Wenzinger. Ceiling paintings in the E. apse by Josef

The powerful E. façade of the twin-towered Collegiate church.

J.Wannenmacher's dome painting in the Collegiate church.

Keller, 1809&10, in the choir by Josef Wannenmacher (partially painted over by Orazio Moretto in 1819 – 21), in the rotunda, the nave and the W. apse by Christoph Wenzinger. Choir screen by Joseph Mayer to 1771 design by Franz Anton Dirr. The curved choir stalls with three rows (1763–8) are the last work of Josef Anton Feuchtmayer. 1808–10 high altar by Josef Simon Mosbrugger. In the *church treasure* 16 – 18C altar vessels. **Stiftsgebäude.** The numerous medieval buildings were rationalised in the 17C, and extended and further unified in 1755–69. Of the older buildings the medieval round tower in the SE corner and the Karltor (1569) have survived. In the W. section,

Collegiate library with inlaid floor.

built 1758&9 by Peter Thumb father and son is the **Stiftsbibliothek** with two-storey library. Ceiling paintings 1762&3 by Josef Wannenmacher, stucco by Johann Georg and Mathias Gigl. In the manuscript room stuccoed tunnel vault and inlaid wall cupboards. The E. section with the **Herz-Jesu chapel** in the lower storey was raised later. The **Hofflügel** (alte Pfalz) E. of the church was extended in 1674 by Daniel Glattburger; the W. section is now used as a bishop's residence. W. of the passage to the Brunnenhof on the ground floor is the **Gallus chapel** (1666), above it **Hofkapelle**, dedicated 1676. **Neue Pfalz**, now government building, E. of the Klosterplatz, built 1767–9 by Ferdinand Beer. The **Zeughaus** forms the N. side of the square, built 1834 – 44 in neo-Renaissance style to plans by Felix Wilhelm Kubly. The adjacent two-storey **Kinderkapelle** of 1842 – 4 was also designed by Kubly. **Reformed church of St. Laurenzen,** founded mid 12C. The new building was started in 1413 by Johann Murer, continued by Michael von Safoy and consecrated in 1422. Rebuilt 1851 by Christoph Kunkler in co-operation with Ferd. Stadler to Johann Georg Müller's design. W. façade, portals, windows and top of tower are neo-Gothic, the statues on the W. flying buttresses are

by Johann Georg Oechslin (1850). The church is a pillared basilica with nave and two aisles with supplementary two-storey longitudinal sections dating from the 16C, with open arches below and galleries above. Neo-Gothic furnishings. **Stadthaus** (14 Gallusstrasse), formerly called Grosses or Halbes Haus. Built 1589 in Renaissance style; the curved gables are 18C. The **Zum Greif** house, 22 Gallusstrasse, has a carved baroque oriel with scenes from the Old Testament (*c.* 1680). Wooden or stone oriels are particularly common in the whole Lake Constance area and were built in St.Gallen well into the 20C. Examples: **7 Bankgasse,** with corner oriel, built 1578, altered 1615. **Haus zum Pelikan** (15 Schmiedgasse), built 1707, wooden oriel supported by male figures. **Zur Stärke house** (21 Schmiedgasse), rebuilt 1619, with stone oriel. **House** (6 Hinterlauben), late Gothic with stone oriel, rebuilt 1581 on original foundations. **Schlössli** (42 Spisergasse), rebuilt 1586 – 90, with two semicircular tower-like oriels and two façade oriels; painting on the staircase and the third floor. **Zum Schwanen house** (10 Kugelgasse). Lavishly carved oriel (*c.* 1590) with corbels in the form of swan and tritons; mythological scenes in the relief panels. Many of the buildings in the **Multergasse** have late 19C and Jugendstil oriels, for example No 10, built in 1907 by Wendelin Heene. **Zum Goldapfel house** (8 Hinterlauben), three-storey late baroque building dating from 1775; pilaster-framed portal with flattened arch and cartouche with house emblem above it. Inside staircase with wrought-iron rail, rococo stucco. **Kleine Engelburg** (18 Marktgasse). Façade stucco *c.* 1760, figures of Hermes and Fortuna on the cartouches. IRERVORSTADT **Reformed parish church of St. Mangen,** founded 898, rebuilt *c.* 1100, late Gothic tower 1505, renovated 1839 and 1946. Early Romanesque cruciform building, baroque pulpit 1658. **Former Dominican convent of St. Katharina.** The convent was founded in 1228 and dissolved 300 years later. The cloister dates from 1504–7, the church was altered in 1685, then used as a Reformed church. **Kaufhaus or Waaghaus** am

Bohl, built as a merchants' hall or weigh house in 1584, renovated 1962&3. The **Haus zum Goldenen Schäfli** (5 Metzgerstrasse), built after 1484 and altered in 1629, is the only guild building to have survived in St.Gallen (former guild of butchers); late Gothic ceiling with beams in the Wirtsstube.

OUTSIDE THE FORMER WALLS In the NE suburbs **Catholic parish church of St. Fides,** built 1777 in baroque style by Joh. Ferd. Beer; tower raised in 1874, extended in the W. in 1954&5 by Hans Burkard. **Catholic parish church of St.Maria** in Neudorf, built in 1913 by Adolf Gaudy in neo-baroque style. **Reformed church** in Heiligkreuz, built in 1913 by Curjel and Moser; neo-baroque building with some Jugendstil elements. **Capuchin convent Notkersegg,** rebuilt 1666, partially modernised in 1967. **Hauptpost** (1910–14) by Otto Pfleghard and Max Haefeli. **Hauptbahnhof,** by A. von Seenger, 1911–14. A new shopping area grew up in the **Leonhardstrasse,** the W. continuation of the Multergasse; the buildings date largely from 1880-1920. **Broderbrunnen** in the Leonhardstrasse 1894 by August Bosch. **Hochschule für Wirtschafts- und Sozialwissenschaften** on the Rosenberg, built 1960 – 3 by Walter M.Förderer, Rolf G.Otto and Hans Zwimpfer. The exposed concrete building is decorated with reliefs, sculptures and wall paintings. **Neues Stadttheater,** E. Vorstadt. Exposed concrete building, built 1966&7 by Fred Cramer, Werner Jaray, Claude Paillard and Peter Leemann. **Haus zum Hechel** (5 Burggraben), now so-called Kantiheim, built 1611. **Neues or Historisches Museum,** built 1916-21 by Otto Beidler, Lebrecht Völki and Karl Adolf Lang. **Stadtbibliothek Vadiana,** built 1905 – 7 by Karl Mossdorf. **Kunstmuseum,** built 1877 by Christoph Kunkler. In Winkeln, SW of the town, **former papermill** (79 Kräzernstrasse), built 1604. **Haggenschlössli** in Bruggen-Haggen (94 Haggenstrasse), built 1642 – 4, N. extension 20C. The early 19C **Tröckneturm** was used by the dye industry . Group of bridges on the Sitter near Kräzern, including a **stone bridge** with neoclassical **toll house,** built 1807-11 by

Haus zum Greif with lavishly carved baroque oriel in Gallusstrasse.

Three-storey domed oriel at 7 Bankgasse.

Wooden oriel of the Haus zum Pelikan, supported by male half-figures.

Curjel and Moser's 1913 Reformed Heiligkreuz church.

The Tröckneturm (drying tower) was used by the dyeing industry in the 19C.

'Dairy festival with shaken bells', 1882, by Franz A.Heim, in the Kunstmuseum.

Hans Haltiner, and the **Fürstland-brücke,** a concrete bridge by Charles Chopard and S. Brunner (1937 – 40). **Wooden bridge** in Zweibruggen, built according to inscription in 1783 by Hansjörg Altherr von Speicher. Not far from here **wooden bridge** over the Wattbach, presumably 17C. **Wooden bridge** over the Urnäsch at its confluence with the Sitter, built by Hans Ulrich Grubenmann in 1780.

Museums. *Stiftsbibliothek,* with one of the most important collections of 7–12C Irish manuscripts, ivory tablets *c.* 900, plan of the monastery of St.Gallen *c.* 820. *Neues or Historisches Museum;* ethnographic, medieval and primeval collection. **Heimatmuseum im Kirchhoferhaus;** prehistoric finds from the Wildkirchli, Drachenloch and Wildmanniloch caves. *Kunstmuseum;* collection of 19&20C Swiss, German and French masters. *Industrie- und Gewerbemusuem;* products of the textile industry. *Stadtbibliothek Vadiana;* historic representations of St.Gallen.

St.Gallenkappel SG
8☐D1

Catholic parish church of St. Laurentius und Gallus, rebuilt 1754&5 in baroque style by Johann Jakob Grubenmann; 1756 ceiling painting by Josef Ignaz Weiss. **Cemetery chapel** N. of the church, consecrated 1667. No. 432 im Vorwaldi and No. 614 on the road to the hamlet of Geretingen: 17&18C **timber houses.**

St-Germain VS
See SAVIESE
17☐E1

St-Gingolph VS
11☐A5

Swiss-French double village. **Chapel of the Holy Family.** Small building with arcaded forecourt, built in 1677. Next to it the **parish hall,** former château, built in 1588 for the Du Nant de Grilly family; portal 1688. Built on to it is the house of **Rivaz de Nucé** with 1752 portal.

St. Gotthard TI
See AIROLO
13☐A3

St-Imier/St.Immer BE
6☐B2

The **former collegiate church of St-Imier** is an early Romanesque pillared basilica with slightly protruding transept and three apses. There is a Michael oratory on the first floor of the later façade tower. The main apse is directly on the crossing, which adds an antique touch. **Tour de la Reine Berthe**. This is the tower of St. Martin's church, pulled down in 1828. It is a Romanesque building in carefully hewn ashlar.

St. Johannsen BE

6☐C3

Former Benedictine monastery, founded *c.* 1100. The choir of the monastery church, rebuilt *c.* 1390, has groin and fan vaulting. In the *Lapidarium* is the oldest known grave slab of a medieval 'magister operis'.

St. Katharinental TG

See DIESSENHOFEN 3☐B2

St-Léonard VS

17☐E1

Priest's house, built in 1542 for the priest Jean Miles, altered in the 17C. **Maison Zen Ruffinen,** built in the 16C for E.J. Bandmatter, castellan of St-Léonard. On the right bank of the Lienne **Tournclette,** country house, built in the 16C for E.J. Bandmatter on the site of a medieval tower.

St. Margrethen SG

4☐B/C3

Reformed parish church, built in 1804, probably by Johann Ulrich Haltiner; single aisle, choir apex tower. **Catholic parish church,** built 1910 by Albert Rimli; neo-Gothic hall church with net vaulting. **Cemetery chapel of St. Margaretha,** former ecumenical parish church, built *c.* 1300. Sacristy probably 15C, wooden ceiling in the nave 17C. Three 1662–4 altars in the 'gnarled' style, 15&16C wall paintings. Ruined Burg **Grimmenstein** below Walzenhausen; the Burg was founded in the 13C and razed by

Sta. Maria: painted house façade in the Engadine style.

citizens of Konstanz in 1418. Parts of the keep and foundation walls of the palas have survived, portal reconstructed. **Vorburg,** below Grimmenstein. Originally residence of the Burg lords, seat of the Vogt of Gallen 1429–1546. Schloss-like building, much altered.

Sta. Maria GR

15☐B5

Cruciform ribbon village at the foot of a pass with many buildings clearly influenced by the Engadine style (▷ Guarda): e.g. **Haus Perl,** No 50, altered 1671, with polygonal oriel of the same period, and at the E. end of the village **casa Capol,** now an hotel, built 1651. Well-proportioned cubic building with Sulèr and vaulted rooms on the ground floor. **Reformed church,** rebuilt 1492 by Andreas Bühler. Unarticulated late Gothic single-aisle building with narrower polygonal choir. Tower with spire, presumed to have been built *c.* 1400 using parts of a Romanesque building. Wall

Sta.Maria di Calanca: the village is dominated by the church and the Torre di Santa Maria.

paintings: on the exterior St.Christopher and Mount of Olives scene, in the interior 7 Apostles over inscribed bands, *c.* 1492.

Sta.Maria di Calanca GR

19☐E1

Catholic parish church of Santa Maria Assunta. The church was redesigned in the 17C. Long hall-like nave (Romanesque, extended later) widening towards the almost square choir. Tower and choir date from the Gothic period. Lavishly painted 1606 coffered ceiling, polychrome stucco and painting in the choir (1626) and in the baldachins and on the choir arch wall (*c.* 1650). **Torre di Santa Maria.** Three-storey pentagonal 13C tower. The stairs are incorporated in the outer wall, the groin vaulting, unusual in a Burg, has survived in the upper storeys.

St-Maurice VS

17☐B2

This old Celtic settlement became an important military base on the road to the Great St. Bernard pass in the Roman period. The history of the town begins around 360, when Bishop Theodor endowed a chapel; it was dedicated to St. Maurice and the soldiers of the Theban legion who, according to legend, were martyred here in AD300. The abbey was founded *c.* 515 by the Burgundian King

Sigismund. The town was one of the preferred residences of the kings of the first and second Burgundian empires until the 9C. In the 11C St-Maurice was subject to Savoy, in the 13C its citizens were granted freedom. The town has been administered by Upper Valais since 1476.

Abbey, oldest Christian site in Switzerland. Excavations by Louis Blondel between 1944–9 revealed the history of the numerous sacred buildings which were built here over 16 centuries. First came the funerary chapel of Bishop Theodor, and five churches were built on the sacred spot between the 5&11C. The entrance tower of the latest building, Romanesque, built 1017–31 and destroyed in 1614 has survived, although it has been much altered. The basilica was rebuilt in 1614–27, at right angles to the rock instead of parallel to it. With the convent buildings it was destroyed by fire in 1693. It was rebuilt in the early 18C and altered again in the 19C. It had to be restored in 1946–9 after the rock fall of 1942. The present building has a nave and two aisles, numerous E. side chapels and a polygonal choir. The interior is essentially 18–20C. In the choir baroque high altar, 1727 by D.Mathey-Doret, 1706 choir stalls. In the antechoir 8C Carolingian ambo. *Church treasure,* among the richest in Europe, especially in the field of medieval gold work. Notable items are: a sardonyx vessel, the Theoderich shrine, a water jug presented by Charlemagne, a head reliquary of St. Candidus and the shrines of St.Maurice and St.Sigismund. The abbey buildings by the church are 18C, the college dates from 1892 and 1913–15. **Catholic parish church St-Sigismond** 1712–17. Three-aisled baroque building with polygonal choir. Baroque side altars, 19C interior. 9 Avenue du Simplon, **Hospice St-Jacques,** 1695 building with 1726 chapel. 79 Grand-Rue, **maison de ville,** elegant two-storey building on 1727 – 32 arches. No. 54, **maison de la Pierre,** built in the 18C for Louis Macognin de la Pierre. It consists of two sections connected by three-storey arcades with wrought-iron balustrades. No. 50 **maison de Bons,** built 1710–20 for Louis de Bons, pretty internal staircase with wrought-iron banister. N. of St-

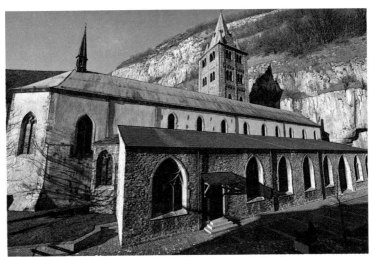

St-Maurice: the abbey church, originally 11C, has been much altered.

Maurice, in the Monthey direction, **château** and **bridge.** The site of the château, which commands access to the upper Rhône valley, has certainly been fortified since ancient times. In the 13C the Savoyards built a château here, and this was rebuilt towards the end of the 15C under Bishop Jost von Silenen and in 1523 under the direction of Ulrich Ruffiner. The building in front of the château dates from 1843, the dominantly placed round tower was built in 1830 by General Dufour. The stone bridge over the Rhône was built in 1491 by Jean Paniot.

VEROLLIEZ According to tradition this is the place were St.Maurice and his companions were martyred. **St-Maurice chapel,** endowed 1662 and renovated in 1742. 1751 rococo altar.

St. Moritz GR

14 ☐ D3

ST.MORITZ DORF **Reformed church,** rebuilt 1932 by N.Hartmann with 1897 neo-Gothic tower. The **leaning tower,** a relic of the former parish church of St. Mauritius, has a polygonal upper storey dating from 1672 on a Romanesque

substructure. 19&20C hotel buildings, including the **Palace Hotel,** built in 1892 –4 by Chiodera and Tschudy.

ST.MORITZ BAD **English church,** built in the late 19C in neo-Romanesque style; there are other historicist buildings around it. **Indoor pool,** 1966–8 concrete building by Obrist and Theus. *Engadiner Museum,* built 1906 by Nikolaus Hartmann. Historical and ethnographic collection with numerous panelled rooms. *Segantini-Museum,* built 1909, with works by Giov. Segantini, including the triptych Werden-Sein-Vergehen (Becoming-Being-Passing).

St. Niklausen OW

7 ☐ E5

St. Niklaus chapel. The 'Heidenturm' and the choir with interior fresco cycle dating from 1370–80 have survived from a church first mentioned in 1357. The name 'Heidenturm' implies a design alien to the area. The wooden ceiling in the late Gothic nave consists of 100 medallions depicting scenes from the Old and New Testaments and head-and-shoulders portraits of saints; other medallions in the choir. The paintings date from 1703&4

St. Moritz: Segantini monument by Leonardo Bistolfı, c. 1900.

St. Moritz: panelled room from Brail, 1580, in the Museum engiadinais.

and give an insight into popular piety in the baroque period.

St. Pantaleon SO
2 □ A4

The essentially Gothic **church,** the horseshoe-shaped **courtyard** of 1756 and

the **dairy** of 1684 are ranged around the parish garden in a picturesque group.

St. Peterinsel BE
See TWANN   6 □ C3

St. Peterzell SG
3 □ E5

The **Catholic parish church of St. Peter,** a former monastery church, was built in 1722; plain baroque with façade tower. The **Mary chapel** S. of the choir dates from 1620, the **priory building,** at right angles to the choir, was built in 1764. The **Rote Haus,** built in 1716, has baroque paintings on the façade. The **timber houses** in the Kirchplatz and in Rüti, E. of St. Peterzell, are typical of the area.

St-Pierre-de-Clages VS
17 □ D2

Former priory and church of St-Pierre. The priory, first mentioned in 1153 as a daughter foundation of the abbey of St-Martin d'Ainay in Lyon, was dissolved in 1580. The church was probably built in the early 12C and is one of the finest Romanesque buildings in Valais. Hall church with nave and two aisles with three semicircular apses. A fine octagonal bell tower in the Cluniac style was built over the crossing in the late 12C. The interior is very austere, the aisle vaults are 17C. The former priory is S. of the church; its foundations are Romanesque. In the village, in the Chamoson direction, interesting group of 16&17C stone houses.

St-Prex VD
10 □ D3

This little town was founded in 1234 by the chapter of Lausanne. The town was originally fortified; it was planned as a triangle, with a central street which once led to the lake. Only the **entrance gate** has survived of the ring walls; bell tower and clock date from the 18C. The square main tower and the residence, very much altered since the 16C, are all that is left of the **former château** by the lake. Outside the village **Reformed church** (St-Protais), first mentioned 885. The present 12&13C building has one aisle with rectangular choir and entrance tower. The excavations of 1977–9 have revealed evidence of several building phases; a first church was built in the 4&5C over a Roman building.

St-Romain VS
See AYENT   17☐E1

St-Saphorin VD
10☐F3

St-Pierre-de-Clages: early Romanesque former priory church.

The **Reformed church** (St-Symphorien) was built in 1520–30 over a medieval church, which was itself on the site of a 1–2C Roman building. Hall church with polygonal choir, 1530 Renaissance stained glass. On the right of the main entrance is a Roman milestone from the period of the Emperor Claudius built into a pillar, on the left a Roman altar with inscription. In the village, one of the most beautiful in the canton, a 16C **priest's house** with arcade, **Auberge de l'Onde** with 1750 inn sign and an 1812 **pierre à sabot** in the wall of the Place du Peuplier giving traffic regulations for coachmen.

St-Saphorin-s.-Morges VD
10☐D2

Château, built 1725 for General François-Louis de Pesmes. Impressive three-storey residence. There is a protruding semicircular staircase tower on the courtyard side. In the church by the château fine **grave slab** of General des Pesmes. In the village 16C **de Mestral estate.**

St. Stephan BE
11☐E4

The church of **St. Stephan** is a copybook example of rural church architecture in the Bernese Oberland. The essentially Romanesque nave has had wooden tunnel vaulting since the 17C. Tower and choir are late

Gothic, the latter with bas-relief carving on the ceiling. **Haus Perren** in Grodei is a typical Simmental Ständer-Blockbau. The building dates from 1672 and has a markedly symmetrical façade with carved and painted friezes.

St-Sulpice VD
10☐E3

Reformed church (St-Sulpice), founded in the 11C and presented to the abbey of Molesms in France between 1098 and 1111; Molesms founded a Cluniac priory here, which was dissolved in the 15C. The transept of the church with 12C crossing tower and three 11C apses are still standing. The side wings of the transept have tunnel vaulting, the crossing has a drum dome. Fragmentary wall paintings in the central apse. S. of the church former chapterhouse, restored 1971.

St-Triphon VD
See OLLON   17☐B1

St. Urban LU
7☐B1

Former Cistercian monastery of St. Urban, dissolved 1848, now sanatorium. The monastery founded in 1194 first flourished in the 13C, to a large extent through the export of decorated bricks.

St-Ursanne: Doubs bridge of 1728 leading to the Porte St-Jean.

St-Sulpice: Reformed church, once part of the former Cluniac priory.

St-Ursanne: Romanesque collegiate church with façade tower (1142).

lavishly carved choir stalls (1701–7) were the joint work of Peter Fröhlicher (columns), Viktor Wüest (reliefs) and Rochus Frey (figures in the Coronation). The sections of the monastery completed in 1733 are laid out in a symmetrical manner reminiscent of princely residences.

St-Ursanne JU

1 ☐ C / D5

St. Urban: gilded wooden rococo pulpit in the monastery church.

These bricks were also used for their own buildings, as shown by the late medieval monastery wall, which has survived in part. The 18C baroque building is by Franz and Johann Michael Beer. The **monastery church,** built 1711–15, is a Vorarlberg pilastered hall, so-called because the architects came from this area. In the interior Louis XVI stucco, probably by Franz Schmuzer of Wessobrunn. The

This picturesque little **town** developed from the monastic settlement which grew up around the hermitage of the Irish monk Ursicinus. The arrangement of the buildings shows clearly how the town wall used to run; it also shows the division between the concentrically planned 12C church town and the straight streets of the town of shopkeepers and craftsmen which came into being in the E. after the fire of 1403. The three town gates were rebuilt in the 16&17C. The **porte St-Pierre** at the E. entrance to the town has medieval substructure and a pavilion-style roof with bell turret (1552 and 1665). It is complemented in the W. by the **porte St-Paul** (Porte de Porrentruy), completely rebuilt in 1664. The S. entrance is the **porte St-Jean,** which also protects the **Doubs bridge,** built in 1728 to a heavy antique design (Nepomuk statue 1st half 18C). The **collegiate church** is a Romanesque pillared basilica without transept. Under the 12C choir is the hall crypt, which once contained the bones of St.Ursicinus. Despite its late date the nave is modelled on the Romanesque churches of Burgundy and the Franche-Comté. Façade tower rebuilt 1442. The S. portal is based in design and style on the Galluspforte of the Münster in Basel. Christ, accompanied by Peter and Paul, 7 angels and the figure of a founder are represented in the tympanum. Mary and Child and St.Ursicinus are enthroned in the niches. **Hôtel de Ville,** rebuilt 1825. The ground floor hall with round pillars and rib vaulting were part of the earlier building.

San Vittore: 13C collegiate church redesigned in the baroque period.

San Vittore GR
19☐E1

Collegiate church of Santi Giovanni e Vittore. The nave of the former hall church (13C) was raised in the baroque period to form a pillared basilica with nave and two aisles and narrower chancel. The belfry and pyramid roof of the Romanesque church were added at the same time. **San Lucio chapel.** The chapel consists of a rotunda on a rock with a chapel 10 ft. below it. The blind arches and high embrasure windows suggest that the rotunda dates from the Carolingian period. **Palazzo Viscardi,** built 1548, rebuilt 1680 -90 by Giov. Viscardi. It houses the *Museo Moesana* with collections of late Gothic sculpture and gold work.

St.Wolfgang FR
See DÜDINGEN   6☐C/D5

St.Wolfgang SO
2☐A5

Late Gothic **chapel** with high altar in pure

high Renaissance style. **Ruined Burg Neu-Falkenstein.** The fortress was probably founded in the 12C by the lords of Bechenburg-Falkenstein. A second, self-contained complex was built to the W. of it, separated from the original building by a moat. The round keep indicates Burgundian influence and thus a later building date.

St.Wolfgang ZG
See HÜNENBERG   7☐F2

Saanen BE
11☐D4

Reformed church of St. Mauritius, built in 1444-7 to a late Gothic design. Striking tower with wooden belfry. The wall paintings in the choir depict scenes from the Old Testament, the Life of Mary and the Maurice legend (*c.* 1470).

Saas Balen VS
18☐C2

Old parish church of Mariä Himmelfahrt, interesting baroque building, built 1809-12 by J.J.Andenmatten. Round nave, semicircular apse and a small vestibule. Interior stucco decoration and altars date from the 18C.

St. Wolfgang SO: ruined Burg Neu-Falkenstein above the valley.

Saanen: detail from the fresco in the Reformed church (Theban Legion).

Sachseln: interior of St. Theodul with black marble.

Saas Fee VS

18□C3

Chapel zur Hohen Stiege and Kreuzweg. Interesting sequence of 15 chapels, built 1707–10 in the style of the Sacri Monti in N. Italy, with carved and painted episodes from the Lives of Christ and the Virgin. The chapel was built at a height of 5764 ft. by A.Ruppen in 1747 and enlarged in 1747. Very fine high altar with 17C Mary statue.

Saas Grund VS

18□C3

Trinity chapel, built 1735 – 6 by J.P.Andenmatten. 1682 high altar and 18C side altars.

Sachseln OW

7□E5

The **Catholic parish church of St. Theodul** is at the end of a sweeping pilgrimage road lined with stately houses; the church was rebuilt as a result of the increased importance of the Brother Klaus pilgrimage by Hans Winden in 1672–84. It is an early example of baroque architecture in German-speaking Switzerland and has a most impressive interior dominated by the contrast between the black marble load-bearing parts of the building with the other surfaces in white marble. In the **ossuary** built on to the Romanesque tower is the old slab (1518) from the original grave of Brother Klaus, who is now buried under the altar in the main church. The **Peter Ignaz von Flüe house** in the Dorfstrasse, built 1784, houses the *Museum und Archiv Bruder Klaus von Flüe.* The **St. Katharina chapel** has the date 1628 on its late Renaissance portal and a lavishly gilded altar contemporary with the building. The **Alte Krone,** a three-storey half-timbered building of 1673&4, is built very lavishly in a style unusual for the area. The **Brunnmatt** house, built in 1750 for Landammann Walter von Flüe, is a typical high-gabled farmhouse of the type found in the Swiss interior; its excellence has been enhanced by the white plaster added at a later date. There are also numerous characteristic houses and storehouses in Ewil, SW of Sachseln.

Safien GR
13☐F2

Typical Walser settlement consisting of scattered farms. In Safien itself **Reformed church,** late Gothic single-aisled building with narrower choir built 1510 by Andreas Bühler; in THALKIRCH **Reformed church** (1441), choir 1503, choir vault with grisaille painting, lath ceiling and 1757 vestibule.

Sage,La VS
See EVOLENE 1/☐F3

Sagne,La NE
6☐A3

Reformed church, a fine late 15C Gothic building on the site of a St. Catherine chapel mentioned in 1351. The church is entered through a façade tower; the interior portal is decorated with very simple sculptures, including a Madonna and Child. Nave and two aisles with pentagonal choir and rib vaulting, numerous vaults with carved keystones. Typical Jura houses and farms in this village and in La Miéville, Le Crêt, Les Coedres and La Corbiatère.

Sagogn GR
13☐F1

Catholic parish church of St. Mariä Himmelfahrt. Nave with three bays, square choir, and transept with two E.-facing chapels. Built in 1634 with 1449 Gothic tower. Ceiling and wall paintings by Giov.Batt.Macholino 1639, the choir altar and stucco altars in the transept chapels date from the same period. **Haus Bundi,** dated 1597, with central corridor parallel with the roof beam and stone spiral staircase. **Castelli-Haus,** 14C tower-

Saignelégier: 16C Préfecture with added prison tower.

like E. section with residential rooms added *c.* 1670. W. on the triangle of land between Vorderrhein and Laaxertobel are remains of the **Schiedburg** complex; it dates back to the late antique period and commanded the Lukmanier route. **Bregl da Haida,** foundations of a 5C single-aisle church with N. annexe and Carolingian apse, perhaps the Columban church mentioned in the will of Bishop Tello in 765.

Saignelégier JU
6☐B1

The **Préfecture** used to be the official residence of the prince bishop's Landvogt. The massive hipped roof building with adjacent prison tower dates from the late 16C. LES CERLATEZ, SE of Saignelégier, has a row of typical **Freiberg Jura houses.** Living rooms, work rooms and stables are accommodated under a single roof. These 17&18C stone buildings with broad supports offer very little resistance to the wind.

Saillon VS
17☐C/D2

First mentioned 1052 as a château of the bishop of Sion. The little town was under Savoy rule until 1475 and was one of the most important trade and military bases in the Valais. The town is on a rocky outcrop above the Rhône and originally had a château and heavy fortification built by Peter II of Savoy. The **town wall** of 1257&8 was strengthened in the W. by an impressive round tower, the so-called **tour**

Saillon: Tour Bayart and remains of a 13C Savoy Burg.

Bayart, built 1260&1 by Pierre Meinier. It was intended as a refuge in time of siege. The walls, which still surround the town today, are fortified with semicircular towers and pierced by three gates. The château itself was destroyed in 1475. In the village **Catholic parish church of St-Laurent,** 1740, single-aisled baroque building with polygonal apse. Next to it is the **priest's house,** built in the 13C on the site of a former Saint-Jacques hospice. On the plain outside the village **St-Laurent chapel,** former church of Saillon, first mentioned in the 13C. Only the choir, which has been turned into a chapel, has survived.

Salenstein TG

3 ☐ D2

Schloss Arenenberg, once the home in exile of the family of Louis Napoleon, with interiors in the style of the first and second Empires. Core of the building 1546 – 8, acquired and altered in 1817 by ex-Queen Hortense of Holland. The future Emperor Napoleon III was brought up here and became an honorary citizen of the Thurgau here in 1832. Now *Napoleon memorial.* **Schloss Salenstein,** seat of the Schenken of Salenstein, mentioned in 1092. Of the original two fortresses Burg Obersalenstein with 11C sections has survived. It has been much altered, partially in the English neo-Gothic style. **Schloss Eugensberg,** built in 1821 in Empire style for Eugène de Beauharnais, the former viceroy of Italy. The extensions of

Salenstein: Schloss Arenenberg houses a Napoleon memorial collection.

1916 and the round temple in the park were by Johann Rudolf Streiff and Georg Schindler.

Salouf/Salux GR

14 ☐ B1

Catholic parish church of St. Georg. Late Gothic building with stellar vaulting by Petrus von Bamberg *c.* 1500. Winged altar of the Ulm school dating from the same period. Late 14C paintings on the N. wall: scenes from the Childhood of Christ and the Passion. **Former Capuchin hospice** (now priest's house), built *c.* 1750. At the foot of the Piz Curver is the **Ziteil pilgrimage church** (7677 ft. above sea level), where Our Lady appeared to a shepherd in 1580. Rebuilt 1959.

Samedan GR

14 ☐ D2

Reformed parish church, built *c.* 1682. Single-aisled building in the shape of a trapezium with galleries on three sides and shallow apsidiole, 1771 campanile. Delicately articulated façade. **Reformed church of St. Peter.** Late Gothic, (1492 by Andreas Bühler) with narrower polygonal choir (1491 by Steffan Klain), Romanesque tower *c.* 1100. On the floor 17&18C grave slabs. In the Plazett **Planta-Haus,**

Samedan: one of the 33 tomb slabs in St. Peter.

N. section extended *c.* 1600, S. section 1760. This stately home with a lavish interior now houses the *Planta-Stiftung* with Rhaeto-Roman library. **Haus Krone,** built *c.* 1650; fine panelled room in the upper storey. **Parish hall,** built 1750, central section emphasised by flight of steps, round-arched doorway and balcony. **Prison tower,** 12C former keep.

Sargans SG

9 □ A2

The fire of 1811 destroyed the whole of the town within the ring walls with the exception of the church and the chaplaincy. In the post-1811 Old Town between the Obertor and the Untertor the neoclassical Gallatihaus, now **Rathaus,** and the **Broderhaus,** a plain house with farm buildings, are particularly fine. **Catholic parish church of St.Oswald und Cassian** in the SW of the town, rebuilt 1709. Lower part of the tower of the earlier Gothic building, raised 1892, steep saddleback roof 1934. **St.Sebastian chapel** auf Splee, SE of the Schloss, dating from

Sargans: Schloss in a dominant position above the village.

1502. **Mary chapel** in the hamlet of Vild on the main road to the Schollberg, consecrated 1606. The antechoir and nave were added in 1628 and 1684, with the result that the original chapel became the sanctuary. **Schloss Sargans,** family seat of the counts of Werdenberg-Sargans. Mentioned 1282, partial collapse in 1459, rebuilt from 1460. After the Confederation acquired the County of Sargans in 1483 it was the seat of the Landvogt until 1798; the rear Burg was demolished after 1860. In the possession of the Sargans community from 1899. Cubic palas in the W., high medieval keep in the S. In the E. ruins of the rear Burg, in the courtyard octagonal fountain basin of 1651. In the keep is the **Sarganserländische Heimatmuseum:** local history collection, early historical finds and Gonzen mine museum. Remains of a Roman farm have been excavated in the Malerva.

Sarmenstorf AG

2 □ E5

Catholic parish church Heilig Kreuz. Late baroque single-aisled church (nave 1778–80 by Vitus Rey, choir and tower 1784–86 by Jakob Singer) with rococo interior. The church and the **ossuary chapel** (1780) and the **priest's house** (1744&5) form a compact and pleasing group. **Roman villa** in Murimooshau, SE of the village; the remains of the bath-house of a 1C or 2C villa were put under a preservation order in 1929. **Neolithic grave mound** in the Zigiholz E. of the village.

Sarnen: the twin-towered façade of St.Peter was not completed until 1881.

Sarnen: 1752 shooting lodge on the Landenberg Burg hill.

Sarnen OW

7☐E5

Principal town of the half-canton of Obwalden. When Obwalden joined the Confederation in 1291 Sarnen, which came into being in 1210, became the political centre of the section of Unterwalden 'ob dem Kernwald'. In 1403 Obwalden, along with Uri, undertook to protect the Leventina, but was not involved in the Confederate conquests in the Tessin in 1500. Some families who made their fortunes by mercenary services to France pursued francophile policies in the 17&18C, and this continued when Obwalden became the first inner Swiss canton to accept the Helvetian constitution in 1798. In 1815 the valley community of Engelberg became affiliated with the canton of Obwalden. After the defeat of the Sonderbund, to which Obwalden belonged, the cantonal constitution was altered in 1850 to provide for political as well as ecclesiastical communities.

Visible from afar on a hill above the village of Sarnen is the **Catholic parish church of St. Peter,** first mentioned 1036; the present church was built in 1739–42 by Franz and Johann Anton Singer using some parts of a Romanesque building, for example the foundations of the two diagonally placed towers. The spacious hall has lavish stucco. By the church is the

ossuary, built *c.* 1500; the ceiling, lavishly decorated with painted bas-relief carvings, is by Peter Tischmacher of Uri, 1507. In the Dorfplatz **village chapel of Maria Lauretana,** rebuilt 1658–62; the tower comes from the earlier building of 1556. Neo-Renaissance façade 1865–6, designed by a former Swiss guard. The **village fountain** with Brother Klaus statue was erected in the Dorfplatz in 1604 and frequently restored. Towards the lake is the **St. Andreas nunnery** with convent buildings (1616–18) and the church which was built later; also the **Benedictine college** with Jakob Singer's convent building of 1745–50, the massive 1890 grammar school and some modern buildings, including the 1964–6 **St.Martin.** The baroque **Rathaus** was built 1729–32 on the foundations of a 1551 building and now houses the 15C 'Weisse Buch von Sarnen' ('White Book of Sarnen'), the oldest source-book on the Swiss struggle for liberation. Its contents include an illustration of the conquest of **Burg Landenburg,** which used to stand on the hill opposite the Rathaus. Only the **Hexenturm** (witch's tower) remains of the early 13C Burg complex. The ruined fortress has been the meeting-place of the Obwalden Landesgemeinde since 1646. On the Burg hill is the **Schützenhaus,** built in 1752 by Just Ignaz Imfeld; it is a rococo building with central section and wings; next to it is the **arsenal.** At the foot of the hill is the **Wirtshaus Landenberg,** in essentials 16C Gothic. The **Haus am Grund,** half stone and half wood, was built 1588&9 for Landamman Marquard

La Sarraz: tomb of Franz I of La Sarraz in St-Antoine chapel.

Imfeld incorporating a former medieval keep. The street façade is articulated by small protruding roofs over the windows. The **Haus im Grundacher** consists of family accommodation and guest house joined by a gatehouse almost as high as the main roofs. Parts of the building are 16C, but most of it was added in 1737. The *Heimatmuseum* (local history) is housed in a former **barracks** built in 1599 at the edge of the village on the road to Lucerne (open April to October).

Sarraz, La VD

10 □ E1

Château, presumed to have been founded in the 11C by Adalbert von Grandson, rebuilt in the 13C. The Bernese destroyed the fortress in 1475 and 1536. The château was restored by the de Gingins family, who owned it until 1863. Now *museum.* Two towers in the S. façade by the gate have survived from the medieval building; the one on the right was originally the keep. The ring walls were destroyed when the gardens were laid out in the last century. **St-Antoine or Jaquemart chapel,** built 1360–70. In the interior, *tomb* of Franz I of La Sarraz, who died in 1363 according to the inscription. The dead man is represented naked and in a state of decomposition, being eaten by toads and worms.

Satigny GE

16 □ D2

Reformed church (St-Pierre-ès-Liens), well-known as a Benedictine priory from the 10C. The high Gothic choir of the present building is 13C, nave and façade date from the 18C. N. of the church 15&16C Gothic residence; to the S. the priest's house built in the 18C on the ruins of the priory.

Sattel SZ

8 □ B3

Catholic parish church of St. Peter und Paul, altered on several occasions in the 18C. Nearby the massive 1830 **priest's house.**

Savagnier NE

6 □ B3

Reformed church of 1651&2, single-aisle building with square choir and façade tower. Bas-relief in the frame of the S. portal.

Savièse VS

17 □ E1

Large parish including several hamlets. ST-GERMAIN **Catholic parish church of St-Germain,** founded in the 11C, new building by Ulrich Ruffiner in 1523, enlarged in the 19–20C. The originally late Gothic building has a nave and two aisles with splendid net vaulting and a rectangular choir. Late Gothic bell tower on Romanesque foundations. 18C altars and 1684 font. Mosaics and stained glass by Ernest Biéler, 1934–47. By the church **parish house,** 1580.

Savièse: St-Germain with 1687 carved door.

Savognin GR

14☐B2

The three old parts of the village, each with a baroque church, can still be made out, despite the unrestrained proliferation of tourist buildings. **Catholic parish church of Mariä Empfängnis,** built 1632–41, exterior still rooted in the Gothic style. Baroque single-aisle church with two transept-like side chapels in front of the choir arch and narrower polygonal choir. Wall paintings: in the nave Life of Mary among other things, in the choir scenes from the Old Testament. High altar, 1750. **Catholic church of St.Michael,** rebuilt 1663. The baroque idea of combining a longitudinal building with a rotunda was adapted to add a polygonal choir to the octagonal nave with dome and lantern and two rectangular side chapels. 1693 stucco. **Catholic church St. Martin.** Rebuilt 1677 on a Greek cross plan with widened transept arms and a polygonal apse. The Romanesque tower of the earlier building is incorporated in the N. façade corner. Tunnel vaulting on continuous beams with lunettes and oval crossing dome. Paintings 1681 by Carlo Nuvolone: Paradise in the dome, framed by the gates of the New Jerusalem. Over the left side altars miraculous image of Mary with saints, on the right Crucifixion. *Sala Segantini;* temporary exhibitions in the season.

Savognin: St. Martin has important paintings in the interior.

Volkskundliches Museum (ethnography); permanent exhibitions in a typical Oberhalbstein farmhouse, opening was planned for 1983. **Padnal.** 1800–800 BC bronze age settlement. Some houses have survived so well in outline plan that a partial reconstruction of the settlement was possible. Bronze age copper mining.

Sax SG
See SENNWALD   4☐A5

Saxon VS
17☐D2

On a hill above the village are ruins of the **château de Saxon.** The local lords were known from the beginning of the 13C; they sold Saxon to the Savoyards *c.* 1266. Count Philipp had new fortifications built in 1279; only the round keep has survived. Below the keep is the **St-Maurice chapel,** mentioned in 1153 as a daughter institution of St-Pierre-de-Clages. The building consists of a Romanesque nave and a late Gothic choir, which was rebuilt *c.* 1530–40. In the 19C Saxon became an important thermal spa. By the cantonal road is the former **Casino** of the spa.

Schaffhausen: the Munot, 16C refuge castle above the town.

Schaffhausen SH

3☐B2

Schaffhausen is set immediately above the impassable Rhine waterfall and has long been a crossing point over the Rhine. The increasing importance of long-distance trade in the high Middle Ages led to its development as a centre of craft, trade and industry, and to its becoming a sovereign canton of the Confederation. All goods transported on the Rhine have to be reloaded in Schaffhausen to avoid the rapids. The settlement was subject to the counts of Nellenburg, who acquired the town's right to mint in 1045. Four years later Eberhard von Nellenburg endowed the Bendictine abbey of All Saints, which shortly afterwards took over the govern-

ment of the flourishing town. The citizens did not achieve independence until 1218: town and monastery received the freedom of the empire, which was interrupted by a period of subjugation to Habsburg Austria between 1330 and 1415. After achieving freedom again Schaffhausen sought association with the Confederates. From 1411, (and indeed until the collapse of the Old Confederation in 1798) it had been subject to increasingly aristocratic rule by the guilds. After a test of strength in the Swabian war, which Schaffhausen fought on the side of the Confederates, it was accepted into the Confederation as a canton with full privileges in 1501. In 1529 Schaffhausen accepted the Reformation. The town tried to acquire territory in the E. (Hegau) and in the W. (Klettgau), but with only modest success. In the Helvetic Revolution Schaffhausen ceased to exist as an independent canton and was not reinstated until the Mediation of 1803, with the addition of Hemishofen, Ramsen and Stein am Rhein. Its favourable site and the centuries-old tradition of craft and trade helped Schaffhausen to become involved in the industrial revolution at the most suitable moment. A black day in the recent history of the town was the American bombing of April 1 1944, which not only killed 40 people but also destroyed much of cultural value.

TOWN CENTRE The core of the cantonal capital Schaffhausen, the **Old Town,** has hardly changed in size since the 14C. It is triangular in shape, with the Rhine bank as hypotenuse and the Schwabentor at the apex; the Grabenstrasse and the Bahnhofstrasse form the W. boundary, and the Bachstrasse is the E. edge. Within this triangle there is an unusual concentration of fine buildings. The disastrous fire in 1372 destroyed almost all the high medieval buildings, with the exception of the stone churches. For this reason the streets are dominated by late Gothic, baroque and rococo architecture; the façades are particularly rich, with over 150 full oriels and 100 half oriels. The old **fortifications** were largely pulled down in the 19C. The **Munot** has survived, in size it is unique in Switzerland; it is set on a hill on the E. edge of the Old Town and was a refuge castle with a striking round tower with pointed top. The fortress was built 1564 –8 and was secured to the N. by a wide ditch; two sections of the old town wall guarantee access from the Old Town. The other surviving towers are the **Obertorturm** in the W. (mentioned in 1273 as a residence tower, raised in 1463, top section built 1513), the **Schwabentorturm** in the N. (mentioned 1370 as a new tower) and the **Frontwagturm** (rebuilt after collapse in 1747; 1564 astronomical clock taken over from the earlier tower). **Reformed Münster church** (formerly monastery church of All Saints). This Romanesque columned basilica with three aisles was built *c.* 1100 on the site of an earlier church; it follows the Cluniac scheme of transept, square choir and flat ceiling. Alternate red and bluish-green sandstone round arches. In the nave remains of a

Reformed St. Johann, tower with battlements (1350) of the former Hochwacht.

Romanesque loggia in the Old Abbey of the former Benedictine monastery of Allerheiligen.

Romanesque meander frieze have survived, and there are 15C frescos in the choir. The five-storey Romanesque bell tower by the choir dates from *c.* 1200. Unsuitable accretions were stripped out of the Münster interior in 1958, and it has largely been restored to its original design. The portal doors were designed by Otto Charles Bänninger (1957–9). **Reformed parish church of St.Johann.** The church is presumed to have been founded in the 11C; it was rebuilt with a nave and two aisles in the 15C and in the Middle Ages two further aisles were added; in this period it was the 'people's church' of Schaffhausen; in Switzerland only the Münster buildings in Basel and Bern are wider. The bell tower dates from 1350; on top of the fourth storey the castellations of the former guard house can be seen. The nave and the two inner aisles have flat ceilings, whilst the outer aisles have rib vaulting; these outer aisles end to the left and right of the choir with endowment chapels of the Löw and Täuber families respectively. Some late Gothic wall paintings have survived. **Former Benedictine abbey of All Saints.** The monastery buildings are 11C in their core but were considerably extended in the 13–16C; with the Münster (see above) they form an impressive Romano-Gothic complex. Since 1928 the abbey, extended in 1935–8 with new buildings by Martin Risch, has housed the *historisches Museum* (very full prehistoric collection; cultural, social and economic history of Schaffhausen) and a *painting collection.* The W. wing of the museum was destoyed by bombing in 1944 and rebuilt in 1946. The great cloister, the contents of which include the the famous **Schillerglocke** (bell) of 1486 (its inscription is said to have inspired Schiller to write his 'Das Lied von der Glocke', is adjacent to the S. façade of the Münster. To the E. are the **St.Anna chapel** (12C, choir added 1522) and the Klosterhof (herb and spice garden). This is complemented in the W. by the Pfalzhof, bordered in the N. by the old abbey. The new abbey of 1484 is connectd with the Old Abbey by a passageway. N. of the Münster is the former Helferei (altered 1526) now a music school, and the final section of the church complex to the E. is the former **Kornschütte** (grain store, now **municipal library**), dating from 1554. FROM THE MUNOT TO THE OBERTOR The Freier Platz, the Vordergasse and the Oberstadt form an E.-W. axis which splits the Old Town into a N. and a S. section. At the foot of the Munot is the **Freier Platz**, which is directly by the landing stage, the most striking building is the 1785–7 **Güterhof**, a warehouse with inner courtyard. The **Vordergasse** with its baroque and rococo atmosphere is probably the most handsome street in the town. Among the many notable buildings the finest are: the **detached house zur Wasserquelle und zur Ziegelburg,** Nos. 26–8, medieval seats of the Am Stad and Trüllery families, made coherent by the addition of a fine rococo façade in 1783.

Rococo façade of the Wasserquelle and Zieglerburg double house.

1654 Renaissance oriel of the Haus zum Sittich.

Apotheke zum Glas, No. 47, late rococo façade of 1763. **Zunfthaus Schmiedstube,** No. 61, very lavish Renaissance-style doorway by Lorenz Schreiber (1653). **Haus zum Ritter,** No. 65, probably the best-known painted house in Schaffhausen. The façade, which originally included two noble houses, was remodelled in 1566 and painted in 1568 – 70 in the Renaissance style by Tobias Stimmer with allegorical figures, and scenes from antique mythology and Roman history. The heavily damaged frescos were removed and some of them are on show in the All Saints museum; the façade was repainted in 1938&9 and in 1943 (side wall) by Carl Roesch as a free copy of the original. **Rathaus.** The double building built in 1408–12 (the W. section is over the Rathausbogen, a vaulted passageway) was damaged in the bombing of 1944 and restored. Its interior includes the Grossratssaal with a monumental, temple-like wooden portal by Felix Buggi, Balthasar Rothpletz and Mathias Gaissenbock (1624). The striking mechanism of

Detail of C.Roesch's façade painting on the Haus zum Ritter (1938&9).

Clock with chimes above the portal of the Grossratssaal in the Rathaus.

the clock above the portal is particularly unusual: on the hour a Schaffhausen goat hits the bell. Behind the Rathaus is the 17&18C **Staatsarchiv** with a wrought iron rococo courtyard portal. The S. flank of the Fronwagplatz is dominated by the **Fronwagturm** and the **Herrenstube** (formerly the place where the nobility gathered); both were redesigned in rococo style in 1747&8 and decorated to complement each other (Herrenstube by Thomas Spleiss, tower by Johann Konrad Spengler). The continuation of the E.-W. axis is the **Oberstadt,** in which the **Haus zum Steinbock** is outstanding. The late Gothic building was the butchers' guild hall until the Reformation, then an inn until 1646, a private house from then. The façade was redesigned *c.* 1750 with lavish rococo stucco by Johann Ulrich Schnetzler and a trapezium-shaped oriel.

NORTHERN OLD TOWN The most striking square is the **Fronwagplatz;** its S. features (Fronwagturm and Herrenstube) have already been mentioned. One large building is particularly striking: the so-called **Grosse Haus,** (No. 24). Two sections of the semi-detached house, extended and lavishly decorated in 1685 – 7, run through to the Krummgasse; the S. section leads through an arcade to a rococo pavilion. The impressive baroque box-shaped oriel is on the façade on the square side; it is dated 1685 and bears the coat-of-arms of Hans Konrad Peyer-Im Hof. The **Vorstadt** leads, as a continuation of

the square, to the N. apex of the Old Town, the Schwabentorturm. The **Haus zum Goldenen Ochsen,** built *c.* 1600 and provided with an impressive Renaissance façade in 1609, has what is probably the most ornate oriel in the town, with allegorical representations of the five senses. The frescos in the upper storey probably also date from *c.* 1610. Striking 1595 Renaissance doorway. E. of the Vorstadt are the connected streets Karstgässchen-Am Platz-Safrangasse. The finest features here are the **Haus Drei Könige** (7 Karstgässchen) with its lavish rococo façade of 1746, and the three Peyer merchant houses built in the 16C in the cemetery of the dissolved Franciscan monastery. **Haus zur Fels,** 13 Am Platz, 1547 – 9, late Gothic façade with 17C elements and 16 – 18C interior; **Haus Freudenfels,** 8 Safrangasse, 1547-9, baroque façade, 18C interior; **Haus Safran,** 6 Safrangasse, 1551-6, altered 1622; oriel added 1686, lavish 17&18C interior. The **Stadthaus** (2 Krummgasse, previously Haus Freudenquelle) was built as the family seat of Hans Konrad von Ziegler-Peyer *c.* 1730 on the site of the demolished Franciscan church. The baroque building has stucco ceilings (some rococo) and ceiling paintings (Johann Ulrich Schnetzler, 1733). The dominant feature of the streets at the foot of the Munot, alongside the Bachstrasse, is the **Zunfthaus Gerberstube.** The house was rebuilt in 1599 on the site of an older guild hall and

Magnificent oriel, 1609, on the Haus zum Goldenen Ochsen.

redesigned with early rococo elements in 1708–10. The interior, with guild hall on the 1st floor and state room on the 2nd floor, was decorated for the most part by Ulrich Schnetzler (1733–7).

SOUTHERN OLD TOWN The so-called Beckenstube climbs W. from the Allerheiligen church and monastery buildings towards the Herrenacker. The most important building in the Beckenstube is the **Altes Zeughaus,** now **Regierungsgebäude** (government building), of 1617 (modern interior 1912 –14. The massive step gable-façade is considered an exemplary Swiss Renaissance building. The **Herrenacker,** where mystery plays were acted in the Middle Ages and which later became a parade ground, is the largest square in the Old Town. It is also the site of the **Stadttheater,** built by Karl Scherrer and Paul Meyer in 1954-6. Important buildings are the **Haus zum Korallenbaum,** No. 2, with one of the first uniform late baroque façades with central portal oriel, and the former municipal **Kornhaus or Kaufhaus** (corn or merchants' hall), No. 15, with three-storey Renaisssance façade. The **Neustadt** runs in a N.-S. direction; the most unusual building in it is the **Haberhaus,** originally a grain store of

1592–3 with an open, arched Gothic columned hall on the ground floor (since the 1943 renovation).
OUTER AREAS AND SUBURBS **Haus zum Fäsenstaub** (2 Steigstrasse), Empire country house of 1820 – 2. **Wirtschaft Schützenhaus** (inn, 1 Rietstrasse), rebuilt in 1686 using earlier parts, restored after a fire in 1957; numerous baroque heraldic reliefs. **Vorderer Stokarberg** (65 Kometsträsschen), summerhouse (*c.* 1740) with elegant room painted in 1743. **Sonnenburggut** (19 Sonnenburggutstrasse), Schloss-like building, presumably late 16C, altered 1871; interior largely 17C. **Belair** (65 Randenstrasse), 16C enlarged in the 18C; now Youth Hostel. **Schloss Herblingen,** former seat of Schaffhausen Obervogts with a building history going back to the 12C, radically altered in the 18C (privately owned). **Alte Post Herblingen.** 17C half-timbered building. BUCHTHALLEN Charming village (part of the town) with notable half-timbered buildings.
Museums. *Museum zu Allerheiligen* (▷ Text). *Museum Stemmler,* zoological collection of the taxidermist and collector Carl Stemmler.

Schafisheim AG

2□D5

15C Residence and hunting lodge of the Lords of Baldegg, radically altered in 1605&6 (privately owned).

S-chanf GR

14□E2

Reformed church. Late Gothic (1493) with net vaulting in the nave and stellar vaulting in the choir. Wall tabernacle contemporary with the building with ogee arch and finial. A feature of the village is a number of Perini family houses, including **Chesa Juvalta,** No. 29, built 1662. On the façade sgraffiti of mermaid and dragon, prism oriel and unusual knocker, room with inlaid panelling. In the hamlet of Chapella (in the Cinuos-chel direction) is a **former hospice,** once on

Schänis: Carolingian slab in the crypt of the former collegiate church.

an important site at the foot of a pass, with the ruined church of **St. Ulrich und Nikolaus.** The tower and the walls of the nave (*c.* 1200) have survived, along with the 1524 choir walls. The surrounding wall and the hospice buildings are Romanesque, with the exception of the Gothic N. section.

CINOUS-CHEL **Houses** Nos 258 and 262 have ornamental and figurative 17C sgraffito decoration.

Schänis SG

8☐D2

Former collegiate church of St. Sebastian, now parish church. Essentially Romanesque pillared basilica with hall crypt, built in the 11C partly over the remains of the walls of an earlier building. Tower and choir late Gothic, 1486–1507, the church was redesigned in the baroque style in 1780–1; in 1910–12 the church was renovated and a neo-baroque W. transept with vestibule was added by Adolf Gaudy, neo-Gothic sacristy 1910. The tympanum relief on the W. façade dates from 1911; in

the crypt guilloche slabs and pillars in Vintschgau marble, early 9C, the best surviving specimens in Switzerland, and remains of Romanesque relief sculpture. **Former collegiate building,** now an old people's home. Rebuilt *c.* 1048, burned down and rebuilt in 1610, redesigned in the baroque style by Michael Beer in 1649. S. wing rebuilt 1782–5; the cloister was pulled down in 1812. **Gallus tower,** remains of the Gallus chapel which burned down in 1824. Only surviving round Romanesque tower in Switzerland, probably 12C **Selinerhaus,** on the S. side of the village square. Rebuilt 1610, redesigned in neoclassical style in 1800; Louis XVI portal.

MASELTRANGEN At the foot of the Steinegg, N. of Schänis, the **Catholic parish church of St. Johannes Nepomuk,** a neoclassical country church built in 1791, renovated and extended in 1963 by Hans Burkard. A **fortress** of the Hallstatt period dating from the 5C BC has been excavated in the **Gasterholz.** The complex is covered by remains from a later, Celtic civilisation. On the **Biberlikopf,** the nagelfluh rock above Ziegelbrücke, a **Roman watchtower** of the Augustan period has been revealed. It was extended as a defence installation in the First World War.

Scharans GR

9☐A/B5

The core of this village on the edge of the 'old Schyn' has survived well. **Reformed church,** rebuilt 1490. The nave with net vaulting is by Andreas Bühler, the choir by Steffan Klain. The steep-roofed wooden belfry built on Romanesque stonework is contemporary with the main building. Late Gothic wall tabernacle with inscription 'Meister Steffan' and Bernhard von Poschiavo's stonemasons' marks. In the S. part of the village **Haus Gees,** built *c.* 1540 on the site of an episcopal dairy. 1605 façade painting by Hans Ardüser with characteristic scrollwork and intertwining flowers. Coats-of-arms of the three Confederations and of the builder. **Haus Buchli-Balzer,** built 1668, with façade

Scharans: Reformed church, 1490, with Romanesque tower and open belfry.

Schiers: Reformed church of St. Johann, single-aisled, 1519–22.

–22, nave ceiling and gallery 1926. In the parish garden two earlier 5C and 6C buildings have been marked out in outline with stone slabs.

painting. **Parish house,** built 1978, architect Monika Brügger.

Schattdorf UR

8 □ B5

Catholic parish and pilgrimage church of St. Maria, built 1729–34 on the site of a 13C chapel. The high altar is by the Upper Valais master Jodok Ritz, who also worked in other churches in the valley. By the church is the oval **ossuary,** which is roughly contemporary with it. **Crivelli chapel,** endowed in 1654 by Colonel Sebastian Crivelli, ambassador at the court of Philip IV of Spain, as a family funerary chapel.

Scherzligen BE

See THUN   11 □ F1

Schiers GR

9 □ C3

Reformed church of St. Johann. Late Gothic with flying buttresses, built 1519

Schinznach-Bad AG

2 □ D4

Bad Schinznach. These buildings, the oldest of which are 17C, were the site of the foundation of the Helvetian Society in 1761.

Schinznach-Dorf AG

2 □ D4

Reformed parish church. The single-aisle church with flat ceiling and rococo stucco replaced an earlier church in 1779; the Gothic tower of the earlier building was incorporated. S. of the tower is the 1650 Gothic Erlach chapel with lavishly decorated memorials to General Johann Ludwig von Erlach (1595–1650) and his wife.

Schlans GR

13 □ D1

Catholic parish church of St. Georg,

Schlans: Epiphany picture on the W. façade of St. Georg, c. 1515.

Schlatt AI: Haus Burg, presumed to be the oldest house in Innerrhoden.

rebuilt 1671 using parts of the earlier building. Wall paintings on the tower: Feiertagschristus and Gregorian mass, late 14C; on the W. exterior wall Epiphany picture and St.George scene, Lombardy work, *c.* 1515.

Schlatt AI

4 □ A4

Catholic filial church of St. Joseph, built 1911 by August Heidegger, neobaroque pulpit with 18C pictures of the Evangelists. In Unterschlatt is a so-called **Zythus** (house with a clock on the façade). In Lank, S. of Schlatt, **Haus Burg,** former dairy of the abbots of St.Gallen, considered the oldest secular building in rural Innerrhoden.

Schlatt ZH

3 □ C4

Reformed parish church. The late-Gothic country church is presumed to have been built in the early 16C. It and the massive **priest's house** form an impressive group. The priest's house was a residence of the nobility in the high Middle Ages and was radically altered in 1583 and 1748&9.

Schleinikon ZH

2 □ F4

So-called 'Zythüsli', small 1777 half-timbered building with bell turret.

Schleitheim SH

3 □ A1

The town's success in the 18&19C was based on gypsum mining, and this shows in some of the buildings; the history of gypsum mining is covered in the **Gipsmuseum** in Schleitheim-Oberwiesen. **So-called brewery.** This large building with residential and farm sections dates from 1748. Room with painted panelling and Régence stucco ceiling. **So-called Kätterlihus.** The baroque building of 1740 was named after Katharina Wanner, the wife of the man who commissioned it. Ceiling painting and portraits by Johann Melchior Eggmann.

Schlosswil BE

6 □ F4

Schloss. The central building is the 124 ft. high 12C keep; its walls are up to 11 ft. thick. The country house around it was built after the fire of 1546.

Schmerikon SG

8 □ D1

Catholic parish church of St. Jost, rebuilt 1775 – 81 by Jakob Andreas Gubelmann incorporating the late Gothic tower; nave rebuilt and upper part of the tower renewed by August Hardegger in 1905–6. **Haus zum Hirzen** (Schlössli), built *c.* 1610 – 20 by Heinrich Keller.

Schlosswil: the Schloss was built after 1546 around the 12C keep.

Schmitten GR: Gothic wall painting in the apse of St. Luzius.

Gabled building with polygonal staircase tower, Gothic portal in the tower.

Schmidigenhäusern VS

See **Binn**   12 □ D5

Schmitten FR

6 □ D5

Catholic church of St. Joseph, built in the late 19C in neo-Romanesque style, contemporary interior. In the centre of the village very fine 1830 farmhouse (No. 8), charming example of the typical Sensler style of building, façade with semicircular decoration under the gables (Burgundian arch).

Schmitten GR

14 □ C1

Catholic parish church Allerheiligen, built *c.* 1480, redesigned in the baroque style in 1706. Single-aisle church with narrower polygonal choir and massive 1522

entrance tower, probably part of a former defensive building. **St. Luzius church,** Romanesque single room with semicircular apse. Wall paintings from the second half of the 15C, including a Christ in Majesty and patron saint of the church surrounded by Apostles. **Dorfmuseum** with ethnographic collection.

Schöftland AG

7 □ C/D1

Reformed parish church. Early medieval graves of the founders containing grave goods were discovered in 1664 in this church, which is now Gothic-baroque (radically altered in 1682). **Schloss.** Early baroque Bernese house of 1660, now seat of the local administration.

Schöllenen UR

13 □ A2

Gorge of the Reuss between Göschenen and Andermatt, made passable in the 12&13C; this was the essential requirement for the opening up of the Gotthard route, which began to replace the old Bünden passes. The 16C **Häderlis bridge** at the lower end of the gorge has survived from the old pack route. Higher up, now under the modern bridge carrying the main road, is the **Teufelsbrücke** (devil's bridge), built in 1830 to replace a narrower, older bridge, which could not carry post coaches. The older bridge collapsed in 1888; the Russian General Suvorov captured it to enable his troops to pass over the Gotthard when he attacked Switzerland from Upper Italy in 1799. There is a memorial to this crossing of the Alps hewn into the rock below the bridge.

Schönengrund AR

3 □ F5

Church and community founded in 1720; Schönengrund then developed as a typical ribbon village. **Reformed church,** built in 1720 by Laurenz Koller and David Jeger, tower altered 1884.

Schönenwerd: 11C former collegiate church in the Lombard style.

Schötz: Hunkeler farmhouse in Buttenberg, 1750.

Schönenwerd SO

2☐C5

The **former collegiate church of St. Leodegar** is an 11C early Romanesque basilica with three apses. In the baroque period the two original façade towers were replaced with a single central tower. The interior masonry is original, though it is now clad with rococo stucco. Cloister renewed 1610. In the Villa Felsgarten, formerly occupied by the Bally family is a *shoe museum*. The *Museum Bally-Prior* has a mineralogical and local collection.

Schongau LU

7☐E1

OBERSCHONGAU **Former parish church of St. Maria und Ulrich.** The 1500 Gothic building was redesigned in the baroque style by Jeremias Schmid *c.* 1700. There is a ceiling decorated with heraldic devices in the **priest's house.**

Schönholzwilen TG

3☐E3

Reformed church. Single room, built 1714 to Ulrich Grubenmann's design, tower altered 1867.

Schötz LU

7☐C2

Catholic parish church of St. Mauritius, neo-Romanesque building by Wilhelm Keller. The **pilgrimage church St.Mauritius und Stefan** on the S. edge of the village is a slender 1660 building still in the Gothic style. *Wiggertaler Heimatmuseum* with prehistoric finds from the Wildweilermoos; ethnographic *Museum zur Ronmühle* (both with limited opening hours or by appointment).
BUTTENBERG The **Hunkeler farmhouse** is a Blockbau dating from 1750.

Schübelbach SZ

8☐D2

Catholic parish church of St.Konrad und Ulrich. The present building dates from 1602–5, 1769 baroque interior.

Schupfart AG

2☐C3

'Herrain' Burg mound. This artificial hill N. of the village is thought to go back to a medieval fortification.

Schüpfheim LU

7☐C4

Catholic parish church of St.Johann und Paul. Niklaus Purtschert's last work, dating from 1804–8; the interior shows early neoclassical restraint. *Entlebucher*

Schwarzenburg: Reformed church with unusual shingle-clad tower.

Schwellbrunn: this beautifully sited village has been a health resort since the 19C.

Schwende: St.Martin (1928&9) harmonises with its surroundings.

Heimatmuseum (local history; irregular opening times).

Schwanau SZ

8☐A3

Island in the Lauerzersee. **St. Joseph chapel,** built 1684 as part of a hermitage, rebuilt *c.* 1810. The **ruins** of a 12&13C Burg Schwandau suggest that the buildings were on a considerable scale.

Schwanden GL

8☐D/E4

Reformed church, built 1753 by Jakob and Johann Ulrich Grubenmann on the site of a 1341 building. In Thon, on the Schwändi road, a **group of houses,** all built in the first half of the 19C for members of the Blumer family.

Schwarzenberg LU

7☐D3

EGENTHAL **Mary chapel,** built 1517. The ceiling picture showing the driving of witches out of the valley during a cattle plague dates from the period of baroque redesign *c.* 1753.

Schwarzenburg BE

11☐E1

Reformed church of Maria Magdalena. The 1463 square choir has a conical shingle-roofed bell tower. This unusual extension is contemporary with the nave, rebuilt in the 17C. **Schloss Schwarzenburg** was built 1573–5 as seat of the Bernese Oberamtmann, after the Grasburg (▷ Wahlern) became too dilapidated to serve this purpose. There are squat square towers on either side of the former entrance to the Schloss courtyard.

Schwellbrunn AR

3☐F5

The highest village in Appenzell, 3169 ft. above sea level; it has developed into a health resort since the late 19C. Typical ribbon village; the original 17&18C wooden gabled houses have largely survived. **Reformed church** of 1648, tower altered 1763 by Ulrich Grubenmann, extension to the W. 1877&8. **House** (No.14) 17&18C, NE extension 1790, 1843 neoclassical entrance. **Fabrikantenhaus** (No. 72) of 1797. Blockbau with three-centered arch over the sandstone portal, moulded string course, ogee-arched gable.

Haus Vorder Au (No. 487), 1737, partly panelled, partly shingled farmhouse. The only example in Appenzell AR of cladding with façade panelling and decorated boards in all storeys.

Schwende AI

4 □ A4

Catholic parish church of St.Martin. In Alfred Gaudy's 1928&9 new building Jugendstil elements are mixed with neo-baroque features. Processional cross *c.* 1500 with *c.* 1320 reliefs. **Pilgrimage chapel of Maria Hilf** in Ahorn, built in 1937 by Johann Hugentobler. The *Sammlung Hermann Fässler* in the Weissbadstrasse shows Appenzell painting. S. of Schwende in the Wildkirchli rock caves is the former **St. Michael hermitage,** founded in 1658 and dissolved in 1853. Much visited in the Romantic period, lived in for a few days by the poet Josef Victor von Scheffel, now an inn.

Schwerzenbach ZH

3 □ B5

Reformed parish church. Neoclassical church building by Hans Conrad Bluntschli the Younger (1812–14).

Schwyz SZ

8 □ B3

Principal town of the canton of Schwyz, from which Switzerland took its coat-of-arms and its name. Kaiser Frederick II declared the town subject only to the Holy Roman Emperor in 1240, but this was challenged by the Habsburgs and the people of Schwyz had to fight to assert their independence. They entered into various agreements with the valleys of Uri and Unterwalden until 1291, in 1315 they won a victory in Morgarten, and repulsed an Austrian punitive expedition. Schwyz played a leading role in the subsequent consolidation of the Confederation; at the same time the old Land Schwyz began to acquire the surrounding provinces of

March, Einsiedeln, Höfe and Küssnacht. In the Reformation Schwyz remained Catholic. In 1798 the canton failed to stem the French invasion. In 1833 the canton was temporarily divided, as inner Schwyz was still occupied to the emancipation of the outer provinces. It was not until 1847, when the Sonderbund, of which Schwyz was a member, was defeated, that a breakthrough to a modern cantonal constitution became possible. The centre of Schwyz is the **Hauptplatz,** laid out after the fire of 1642, with four major streets leading from it. On the N. side the square is dominated by the terrace on which the **Catholic parish church of St.Martin** stands; it was built 1769–74 by the brothers Jakob and Johann Anton Singer. The plain sides are complemented by the simple façade with three axes in the Herrengasse. The characterisic feature of the hall with nave and two aisles is the emphasis on the effect of the whole space at the expense of the side aisles, and the light, late baroque stucco. The **Kerchel,** the two-storey ossuary, was built in 1512–18 by the church at the N. end of the cemetery its time. Above the two-aisled lower building is the St.Michael chapel; its late Gothic vault paintings are lit by tracery windows. On one of the four main streets leading out of the Dorfplatz is the **Büeler chapel** of 1683, named after its founder and dedicated to Our Lady of the Sorrows. The finest feature of the building is the stucco, not only in the interior but also on the façade and the ceiling of the porch. **Klösterlein im Loo.** Built 1586&7 for the Capuchins who had been founded shortly before, extended as a closed community in 1895, when the monastery was taken over by the 'Daughters of the Sacred Heart'. Shortly after the building of the Klösterlein im Loo the Capuchins moved into the **Capuchin monastery** in the Herrengasse, which had been completed in 1620. **Dominican convent of St.Peter am Bach**. The monastery was founded in 1274 and rebuilt with church and guesthouse in the 17C. In the interior of the church are three late baroque altars with lavish figure decoration. In the Hauptplatz is the **Rathaus,** built 1642–5 on the site of a 1593 building. The 1891

Schwyz: the interior of St.Martin makes a festive impression.

The Kerchel, a pleasing ossuary with a St. Michael chapel in the upper storey.

The domed turrets were added to the Ital-Reding house c. 1663.

Palais von Weber, a wide building with mansard roof dating from 1738–40.

façade paintings are by a painter of the Munich school. The finest room is the small Ratssaal with lavish Renaissance panelling; in the former large Ratssaal is a series of pictures of Swiss Landammänner. In the medieval **Archivturm** (archive tower) is the *Museum* with a collection on the history of the canton; until 1936 important documents on the history of the Confederation were stored here, but they are now in the **Bundesbriefarchiv,** built in 1934–6. The mural 'Bundesschwur' (oath of confederation) by Heinrich Danioth is on the gable façade of the modern building. In the main hall is a wall painting by Walter Clénin; exhibits here include the two Bundesbriefe of 1291 and

1315. The **Zeughaus,** built 1711–17 as a corn store, has been used as an arsenal since 1802. Opposite the Zeughaus is the **Alte Spital,** now parish hall, built in 1752. Parts of the façade painting are a reminder of the original function of the building, for example St.Rochus and St. Jakobus, the patron saints of the sick and of pilgrims, on the N. side of the building. One of the oldest surviving private buildings is the **Haus Bethlehem,** which goes back to the 16C; it is a wooden building, with a two-storey arcade on each of the longer sides. The **Ital-Reding-Haus** is on the same site; it was built in 1609, extended in 1663 and given several baroque features. It is a mixture of traditional farmhouse architecture and the architecture of the baroque town house, which was now required by the local families who has become rich and enhanced their status in the pursuit of foreign wars. The architectural development of the Schwyz town house in the 17&18C is determined by this gradual transformation from town house influenced by the local farmhouse to the palais influenced by Italian and French models. Thus the 1604 **Grosshaus** is still a late Gothic gabled building; its defensive character is emphasised by the fact that it is built in stone and by its imposing size (staircase added mid 17C). The **Redinghaus** in the Schmiedgasse, built 1614-17 around a central courtyard, is even more strongly influenced by baroque models; its characteristic curved gable was added at the end of the 17C. The move away from the gabled house orientated towards the S. with a central corridor running from W. to E., which was typical of the region, is first carried through logically in the **Ceberghaus** built in 1686. The entrance is now placed in the S; the roof is broken by a Mansart storey running round the entire house. The Ceberghaus also had a high, crenellated wall, since pulled down, which gave the house a fortress-like appearance; different from this was the **Maihof,** built shortly before 1700 and later altered, which clearly expressed the wish to build a palais rather than a Schloss. This idea is carried though in the **Palais von Weber-von Müller.** This two-storey house with Mansart roof and corner projections on the main façade has a central room overlooking the garden on the French model; the garden and farm buildings are laid out in a strictly symmetrical pattern. Similar outside, but simpler in plan is the **Hettlingenhaus,** built in 1760-70, the seat of the Hedlinger family, who moved here from Winterthur at the time of the Reformation. The building replaced a wooden one, which belonged to the nearby **Steinstöckli.** The medal coiner Johann Carl Hedlinger lived in this house dated 1593 from 1750.

RICKENBACH SE of Schwyz is the much-altered 17C **Haus Immenfeld,** which is near **Haus Waldegg,** built *c.* 1600; Haus

Immenfeld has a porch with lavish stucco. On the path by the Hoftor is the **St. Antonius family chapel** of 1687. In the wood above Rickenbach was a medieval hermitage in the Tschütschi; a chapel was built on its site in 1670-2.

Scona TI
See OLIVONE   13☐D3

Scuol/Schuls GR
                                               15☐A3

Both Oberschuls and Unterschuls have picturesque streets with typical Lower Engadine buildings (▷ Guarda). In Unterschuls **Reformed church.** This late Gothic single room was built in 1516 by Bernhard von Poschiavo. Choir and nave have stellar vaulting; gallery, pulpit and windows are all contemporary with the building and all have tracery. At the foot of the church hill is Unterschuls with its village squares. They are bordered by numerous stately Engadine houses decorated with sgraffiti, paintings, coats-of-arms, wrought-iron balconies and ornate Sulèr doors. In the Brunnenplatz is the so-called monastery of **Chà Granda** (originally 16C). The masonry and timber arcades were added in the course of alterations in 1704; now *Heimatmuseum* (local history).

Sedrun GR
See TAVETSCH   13☐C2

Seedorf FR
See PRES-VERS-NOREAZ   11☐B1

Seedorf UR
                                               8☐A5

St.Lazarus convent, endowed in 1197 by the Lazarite Order, refounded by Benedictine nuns in 1559. The present buildings came into being in 1682-6. In 1695&6 the **church** was built, probably to designs by the Einsiedeln monastery architect Caspar Mosbrugger in co-operation with Johann Jakob Scolar. This is firstly distinctive for its dome, which shows Italian influence,

Scuol: the Reformed church on the rocky hill above the Inn dates from 1516.

and secondly for its lavish interior stucco, giving a feeling of great spaciousness to the interior of the church, which is in fact quite small. On the plain leading to the lake is the **Schloösschen A Pro,** built in 1556 –8 for the knight Jakob A Pro. The family originally came from Prato in the Leventina valley and became rich in the 16C; as an outward sign of their prosperity they commissioned the little Schloss; even at the time of building the moat and crenellated walls were purely decorative. The Schloss was often seriously neglected; in the 19C it was used as a priest's house for a time, probably because of its proximity to the **Catholic parish church of St. Ulrich,** a 17C baroque building.

Seelisberg UR
8□A4

Pilgrimage chapel of Maria Sonnenberg, built 1666. High altar and choir screen baroque, side altars 19C. On the road to Bauen is the **Schlösschen Beroldingen,** the seat of the family of the same name, whose Uri branch has died out. It is probably on the site of an earlier building of c. 1530; the chapel was added in 1546 by Josua von Beroldingen in memory of his acceptance into the Order of the Knights of the Holy Sepulchre in Jerusalem.

Seengen AG
2□E5

Reformed parish church. This oc-

Seedorf UR: Italian stucco in the St.Lazarus monastery church.

tagonal neoclassical church by Jost Knopp dates from 1820–1. There is a similar building in the parish of Meisterschwanden. **Schloss Hallwil.** Moated Schloss on two islands in a system of artificial ditches. The two islands are connected to each other by a drawbridge, and a stone bridge leads from the E. island to the mainland. The oldest parts of the building (substructure of the keep, palas on the rear island) are high medieval, the residence, corn store, gatehouse and ivy tower are late medieval. Both islands walled. The Schloss, once the seat of the Lords of Hallwil, houses a **Wohnmuseum** (domestic museum). **Schloss Brestenberg.** Early baroque Herrenhaus of 1625 with later extensions; now hotel and restaurant.

Seewen SZ
8□B3

Old catholic village and pilgrimage church of Our Lady. The interior of this church built in 1642–4 was altered in 1772–5 and provided with late baroque stucco and ceiling paintings.

Seewis GR
9□B3

Reformed church. Late Gothic single

Seengen: Schloss Hallwil, an impressive moated Burg with domestic museum.

Semione: ruins of Serravalle, a medieval castle.

room of 1487, nave redesigned in the baroque style in 1758. In the Klus is the ruined **Burg Fracstein,** a 12C cave fortress. Above Schmitten is the ruined **Burg Solavers,** a former citadel church, extended as a feudal castle in the 11C. It contains the remains of the medieval **Liebfrauenkirche.**

Segno TI
See CAVAGNAGO   13 □ C5

Sembrancher VS
17 □ C3

Catholic parish church of St-Etienne, of medieval origin, rebuilt 1786; late Gothic bell tower with lunette spire. Nave and two aisles and rectangular choir, 1686 side portal with baroque Pietà and carved door. Fine baroque choir stalls. In the church square **maison Luder, 1765.** The village has a series of fine stone houses and wooden utility buildings. On the W. edge of the village 17C **Notre-Dame des Sept-Joies chapel,** baroque altar. On a rock in the S. of the village ruins of the **château de Sembrancher** or **d'Entremont,** founded in the 12C and destroyed in 1575, also the **St-Jean chapel,** built in a former tower and first mentioned in 1460.

Semione TI
13 □ D5

Catholic parish church of Santa Maria Assunta, first mentioned 1207, rebuilt 1731 – 6. The Romanesque bell tower has survived of the earlier church; it probably dates from the 11C. 18&19C interior. By the church an **ossuary,** baroque fresco on the façade, interesting 15C frescos by the Seregneses in the interior. N. of the village ruins of the **castello di Serravalle,** presumed to have been built c. 1162–8 by a member of the Torre family. In 1176 Frederick I Barbarossa spent four days in the castle. After his defeat at Legnano, Serravalle was destroyed by the Milanese in 1181. The castle was rebuilt and destroyed again in 1402. The surviving ruins show the extent of the castle precinct; in the N. the ruins of the keep and the palas, which was connected to the courtyard; the round pillars are visible. A defensive tower from the ring wall has survived. By the castle is the **Santa Maria del Castello chapel,** first mentioned in 1339, choir and vestibule 16C. On the W. façade 15C fresco, in the choir paintings (1587) by Giovanni Battista Tarilli and wrought-iron choir screen, 1691.
NAVONE **Santa Maria Bambina chapel,** small octagonal baroque building with vestibule, built in 1667; in the interior paintings with scenes from the life of the Virgin Mary.

Sempach LU
7 □ D2

This little town was founded by the Habsburgs c. 1220 and until the level of the lake dropped in 1806 it was directly at its side; the village has remained compact and attractive, however. Parts of the ring wall and two towers have survived of the fortifications; in the SE corner of the defence system is the so-called **Hexenturm** (witches' tower), a rectangular building with 13C crenellations, and at the S. entrance to the town the 16C **Luzernertor** (gate). **Catholic parish church of St. Stefan,** built 1827–9 as a neoclassical version of the Singer-Purtschert scheme (▷ Ruswil). In the *church treasure* is a Gothic tower monstrance. On the road to Hildisrieden is the **battle chapel of St. Jakob,** built in memory of the victory of the Confederates over the Habsburg-Austrian army on the spot where Duke Leopold fell. The chapel was consecrated just one year after the battle of 1386 and is painted with a picture of the battle after Hans Rudolf Manuel dating from 1551, and also coats-of-arms or names of the fallen. The **Rathaus** is a 17C half-timbered building; the first floor was originally a cloth hall. The exhibits in the *Museum* include cantonal shields by Jakob Wägmann.

KIRCHBÜHL NE of Sempach is **St. Martin,** built *c.*100 over Roman walls. The church contains the fullest and oldest fresco cycle in the canton. The surviving outline drawings include a procession of saints in the courtly Gothic style of the early 14C. The painting of the choir was done as soon as it was rebuilt *c.* 1583. The furnishings include three late Gothic shrine altars.

Sempach: St. Jakob chapel in memory of the battle of 1386.

que style. **Gasthaus Schlössli,** built in 1551 as a residence and altered in 1735; painted panelled ceiling on the first floor. Ruined Burg **Hohensax,** on a spur of rock W. of Sax. This first great castle in the Rhine valley was founded in the 12C and destroyed by the Appenzeller in 1446. **Burg Forstegg** N. of Salz, built *c.* 1200, Palas burned down in 1894. The **Zeughaus** in front of it dates from 1625.

Sent GR

15□B3

Dignified nucleated village with several squares; notable **farmhouses** with sgraffiti, oriels, façade painting (influenced by the nearby Tyrol) and curved rococo gables. **Reformed church,** built 1496, presumably on the walls of an earlier building. Late Gothic single-aisle church with narrower polygonal choir, probably by Andreas Bühler. Nave and choir have stellar vaulting, window with Flamboyant tracery. Stepped buttresses all around the exterior, neo-Gothic tower by Nikolaus Hartmann the Elder, 1899. Late Gothic wall tabernacle with crenellations, pulpit with bas-relief decoration, 1712. On the W. edge of the village **ruined church of St. Peter,** built in the 12C. Romanesque single room with broad nave and the only semicircular apse in ashlar in Graubünden. Tower with blind niches and round-arched windows.

Sennwald SG

4□B5

The **Reformed parish church** was destroyed in the Swabian war, rebuilt *c.* 1500 and altered in 1753 by Joh.Ulrich Grubenmann; late Gothic building with polygonal choir. The **Haus Leuener** and the **Haus Raduner** have saddleback roofs with a shallow slope; the right hand section of the former is built of stone. There are other **wooden houses** in Frümsen, SW of Sennewald.

SAX The **Reformed parish church,** a late Gothic building, was rebuilt *c.* 1500; the nave was later redesigned in the baro-

Sent: ruined church of St. Peter with surviving Romanesque tower.

Le Sépey: 17C wooden storehouse in the hamlet of La Forclaz.

Seon AG
2 □ D5

Hallstatt grave mounds in the Fornholz and the Niederholz, researched in the early 30s.

Sépey, Le VD
11 □ C5

There are interesting groups of 17&18C **wooden houses** in this hamlet and in La Forclaz. The buildings have substruc-

Sierre: the Château de Chastonay has panelled rooms.

tures in masonry and façades with carved decoration and engraved or painted inscriptions. The storehouses in La Forclaz are 17C, and those in Le Sépey 18C.

Sessa TI
19 □ C4

Catholic parish church of San Martino, first mentioned 1288, altered 1609 – 30. High altar with lavishly decorated monumental tabernacle by Antonio Pini, 1662. 17&18C stucco in the chapels. Pulpit with 17C sculptures and font of 1658&9. **Catholic village church of Sant'Orsola,** built in 1601 in Renaissance style. In the interior, stucco high altar with paintings of St. Ursula. Interesting buildings in the village. On the piazza former **courthouse** with portico and arcade, 16C painting. Nearby **house** with arcade, façade fresco with Crucifixion.

Sevelen SG
9 □ B1

Reformed parish church, rebuilt *c.* 1500, nave burned out in 1892. Much altered building; the masonry is probably late medieval. The **priest's house,** a gabled building, is probably 16C in its

Signau 347

essentials; altered in the 18&19C. On the **Geissberg** W. of Sevelen traces of a neolithic settlement with tools and weapons of the so-called Horgen culture have been discovered.

Sevgein GR

13 □ F1

Catholic church of St. Thomas. Baroque single-aisled building with polygonal apse and transept-like side chapels 1687–91 with lavish decoration. The late Gothic choir of the earlier building is now used as the sacristy. **Holy Sepulchre chapel,** built 1679.

Siblingen SH

3 □ A1

Reformed parish church. The church is essentially 13C but was greatly enlarged in 1641. Remains of a Gothic wall painting depict a larger-than-life St. Christopher and other subjects.

Sierre/Siders VS

17 □ F1

From the 11C Sierre was in the possession of the bishops of Sitten and was administered by vidames and later by castellans. In those days the present town was simply a modest settlement. Originally the town and fortifications were further S. on the four hills Géronde, Goubing, Plantsette and Alt-Siders, each with a château. In the Rue du Bourg **Catholic parish church of Ste-Catherine.** Single-aisle baroque building of 1649 with polygonal apse. In the choir 18C stucco and 1696–1713 choir stalls, 19C altar with baldachin, glass 1924 by Edmond Bille and 1946 by Paul Monnier. **Church of Notre-Dame-des-Marais** (Mary of the Marshes), built 1422 and enlarged 1524 by Ulrich Ruffiner. 16C frescos on the main façade, in the interior tabernacle by Ruffiner, 1528. In the Rue du Bourg, near the station, **Hôtel Château-Bellevue,** built 1658-66 by J.-F. de Courten, castellan of Sierre,

completed in 1732 and altered in the 20C. The building has a central section with arches on two storeys and two side sections defended by towers. **Château des vidames,** built in the 16C by the de Chevrons, vidames of Sierre. Massive square tower with four machicolated corner turrets, completely altered in the interior. No. 3, **maison de Chastonay,** built 1636–45 for J.-F. de Courten; façade with arches and an elegant oriel. No. 30, **maison Pancrace de Courten,** 1769 private house, façade with broken gable. In the suburb of Glarey **château de Chastonay,** built 1718–34 for J.E. de Chastonay, castellan of Brig; baroque building with ground floor arcade and square corner tower. In the N. of the town Rue du Manoir, **château de Villa,** built in the 16C for the de Platea family, enlarged in the 17C for the Preux family. The oldest section in the E. has a hexagonal staircase tower. Now a little *musée de la viticulture* (wine-growing). In the vineyard SE of the town **tour de Goubing,** square residence tower, built in the 13C for the Lords of Albi.

GÉRONDE The site of the oldest settlement, occupied in Roman times. The episcopal château and the settlement used to be on the N. side of the hill and were abandoned in the 13C. In the S. was the Romanesque **St-Félix chapel,** now in ruins. **Church and convent of Géronde,** founded in the 13C, now used by the Bernadines of Collombey. The convent has been much rebuilt and was recently badly damaged by fire. The church (St-Martin) has a heavily restored Romanesque bell tower and a late Gothic choir. In the interior two Roman votive steles and fine choir stalls dating from *c.* 1400.

Signau BE

7 □ A4

The baroque **Reformed church** has a square tower with wooden belfry and polygonal spire. The **priest's house** was built in 1738 in the style of a baroque, Bernese country house. A wooden bridge (mid 19C) connects the church hill with the village; the streets have unbroken rows of houses. **Moserhaus,** Ständerbau of 1756 –60, broad, shingled, half-hipped roof. The open roof space was originally used for drying freshly-dyed fabric. The **Krämerhaus,** built in the mid 18C, is also a Ständerbau with arcades, and has a hipped roof with gables decorated with semicircular timbers. The two **farms in the Liechtgut** (1828 and 1835–8 respectively) form a compact group of Emmental buildings with attached 'Stöckli' (quarters for farmers in retirement). The central 'Stöckli' has an arcade with carved supports and panelling.

Sigriswil BE

12 □ A2

Reformed church of St.Gallus, rebuilt with a baroque interior by Abraham I.Dünz after a fire in 1671–91. The tower, remains of paintings in the interior and a font dated 1506 remain from the earler building. The **priest's house** of 1679 is a half-timbered building with hipped roof.

Silenen UR

13 □ B1

Catholic parish church of St. Albin, built 1754–6 on an eminence above the Reuss valley. The smooth main façade with three arches giving access to a vestibule was added at a later date. The broad aisle has ceiling paintings by Josef Ignaz Weiss. The wooden central section of the **Steinhaus** on a slope behind the church is set on a massive stone base; the side walls are entirely without windows. In a more southerly part of the village on the old Gotthard route is the 11&12C von Silenen **residence tower.** The von Silenen family moved from the Zürich Fraumünster abbey to administer their lands in Uri in the mid 13C, but later settled in the Valais and in Lucerne, and so their tower fell into disrepair. By the tower is the **Nothelferkapelle** (chapel of the Auxiliary Saints); there are pictures of the 14 saints in the interior, with formulations for the invocation of protection against the dangers and illnesses named (the frescos

were painted in 1925 on the basis of older wall paintings).

Sils im Domleschg GR

14 □ A/B1

Palazzo, now parish house, built 1740. Severely symmetrical cubic building with high hipped roof and gable light. Behind it is a baroque garden with rising terraces reminiscent of Italy, with steps and corner pavilions. N. of the village **St. Cassian burial chapel.** Single-aisle church, probably medieval, with a tunnel-vaulted rectangular choir off the central axis. N. of that **Schloss Baldenstein.** Keep c. 1200, extended in three phases in the 16&17C, partially altered after a fire in 1877. S. of the village **Burg Ehrenfels,** a youth hostel since restoration in 1934. SW of this is the **Hohenrätien Burg ruin,** former feudal castle of the Lords of Hochrialt, at present under restoration. Restored buildings include the former mother church on the left side of the valley, **St. Johannes,** with its campanile (14C). **Carschenna;** rock drawing, probably Bronze Age: concentric circles, dishes, sun motif and animal motifs.

Sils im Engadin GR

14 □ C3

Reformed church of St. Lorenz. Late Romanesque single-aisled building with narrower rectangular choir. In Sils-Maria **Nietzsche-Haus,** collection including memorabilia of the philosopher.

FEX-CRASTA **Reformed church,** Romanesque, with semicircular vaulted apse. Wall paintings (1511): in the apse Throne of Grace with symbols of the Evangelists, Loreto picture, female saints and Man of Sorrows, including St. Anne with the Virgin and Child and Apostles. Annunciation on the choir arch wall.

Silvaplana GR

14 □ D3

Reformed church. Late Gothic single

Silenen: baroque interior of St. Albin, 1754 -6.

Sils i.D: ruined Burg Campell at the mouth of the Schyn gorge.

room with stellar vaulting using parts of the original building, polygonal choir 1491 by Steffan Klain. Paintings on the N. wall by the same artist as those in ▷ Sils-Fex (*c.* 1491): St.Anne with the Virgin and Child, Magdalene, votive picture.

Simplon VS

18 □ D1/2

The Simplon pass, in regular use since Roman times, became more important in the 17C at the time of Kaspar Jodok of Stockalper. The present road was built for Napoleon by the Geneva engineer N.Céard. At the summit of the pass **hospice,** started in 1801 by order of Napoleon, completed in 1831 by the canons of Great St. Bernard. By it is the Simplon eagle, a memorial to the 1939–45 mobilisation, executed by E.Baumann. On the far

Silvaplana: Reformed church, a late Gothic single room with steep roof.

side of the pass, below the road, **former Stockalper hospice,** founded by the Order of St.John in 1235, rebuilt in 1666 by Kaspar Jodok of Stockalper. An imposing square building with a belfry.

SIMPLON DORF **Catholic parish church St. Gotthard,** baroque building, 1725. 16C wall tabernacle in the choir, high altar 1725, side altars 1729, probably from the studio of Anton Sigristen. 17C painting of the rescue of Moses from the river, attributed to Salvatore Rosa.

Sins AG

7 □ F2

Catholic parish church of Mariä Geburt. The oldest church of the Freiamt (after Muri) has survived in the form of a single-aisle church built by Paul Rey 1746–53; the polygonal choir is by Niklaus Hurschler. The substructure of the bell tower is late Gothic (1493). The interior is partially neoclassical. **Former Amtshaus** of the little town of Meienberg, which no longer exists (destroyed 1386 in the Sempach war). 1575, with residence tower and 1765 painted wooden façade.

Sion/Sitten VS

17 □ E2

Principal town of the Valais. There is evidence of civilisation in the Rhône valley from the neolithic period; the names Sedunum (Sion) and Octodurus (Martigny) prove the presence of various Celtic tribes from the Iron Age. In the Roman

Sins: former Amtshaus in Meienberg with residence tower, 1575.

period the Valais, with Martigny as capital, formed the entire province of the Poeninine Alps. Christianity came to the region at a very early stage. The first bishop, Theodor, is known to have been in Martigny *c.* 381. In the 5C the area was occupied by the Burgundians and became part of their kingdom, from 534 it was subject to the Franks. In 888 Rudolf I founded the second Burgundian empire in St-Maurice. After 1032 the Valais was part of the Holy Roman Empire and subject to the Bishop of Sion, but Savoy opposed him from the 11C; it conquered Lower Valais and held it until 1477. The Burgundian Wars enabled the bishops to reconquer Lower Valais, which was given to Upper Valais in 1477. In 1630 the patriots compelled the bishop to renounce his territorial claims, and joined the Catholics. The revolution of 1698 caused the fall of the Republic of Upper Valais; Lower Valais declared itself independent. In 1810 the area was annexed by Napoleon and made part of his empire as the Département du Simplon. In 1815 Valais joined the Confederation. The earliest evidence of civilisation in the town of Sion dates from the neolithic period (3500 BC), as excavations in the town have shown, especially at the so-called Petit-Chasseur. It was occupied by the Celtic Seduni tribe, and like the whole valley came under Roman domination. As the seat of a bishop the town became the political and ecclesiastical capital of the Valais in 565–85, and has remained so ever since.

VALÈRE **Château and collegiate church of Notre-Dame-de-Valère.** It is presumed that the hill was the site of a Celtic oppidum. The precise date of the

château is not known, but it has been mentioned since 1049. Valère was an extended fortress with a church and several houses within the town walls. The top of the hill is surrounded by 12&13C defensive walls, with three towers and a single crenellated entrance on the N. side. The residential buildings are on the N. side of the hill; the oldest are 13C. The church was also fortified; the bell tower was used as a keep. **Collegiate church of Notre-Dame,** important 12&13C Romano-Gothic building. Three-aisled church with vestibule and semicircular apse with polygonal superstructure. A 13C rood screen divides the nave from the choir and also shows the break between the Romanesque and Gothic sections. The Romanesque choir was altered in the Gothic period and vaulted; remarkable 12C carved capitals in the choir and fourth bay of the nave. In the apse 15C wall paintings, on the high altar fine statue of Mary in marble, also 15C. In the antechoir carved choir stalls (1662 –4) with reliefs of scenes from the Life of Christ. In the S. transept are the original wings of the Jesse altar triptych and a fine collection of old Byzantine and oriental fabrics. In the S. aisle are the 15C grave of bishop Wilhelm III of Raron and wall paintings ascribed to Peter Maggenberg, 1435. On the W. wall 14C organ, one of the oldest in the world, painted panels by Peter Maggenberg, 1435. The **château buildings** now house the *Musée de Valère* The reception hall is notable; it is known as the Caminata, and has 15C wall paintings from the studio of Konrad Witz. In the **Calendes building** is a large hall with 15C wall paintings. Below the château **Tous-les-Saints** chapel, a small Romano-Gothic building dating from 1325.
TOURBILLON It is probable that there was also a fortified Celtic settlement on this hill, as there was on Valère. The present **château** was built *c.* 1294 for Bishop Boniface of Challant in order to be able to defend the town against the Savoyards. It was also used by the bishops as a residence and was damaged on many occasions in the 14&15C, then restored in 1447 and destroyed by fire in 1788. The ruins of the fortress include remains of the crenellated ring wall and, on the esplanade, parts of

Sion: the town is protected by two hills with castles, Valeria on the right.

Wall painting, c. 1440, in the Notre-Dame-de-Valère collegiate church.

the square keep and the 1447 **St-Georges-et-St.-Grat chapel.**
Town Centre The medieval town grew up on a terrace below the Valère hill. It had

a ring wall which grew with the town from the 11C onwards. The only remaining part of the last town wall, built in the 12C, is a round tower in the Avenue Riz, the **tour des sorcières** (witches' tower). **Cathedral Notre-Dame-du-Glarier.** The only part of the 12C church to survive the fire of 1418 was the bell tower; the present building is 15C. In 1947 the choir was enlarged and altered. The late Gothic building is cruciform, with three aisles. The fine five-storey entrance tower has round-arched windows. In the choir are a *c.* 1505 winged altar, and Renaissance stalls by M.Pfauw (1622&3). In the St-Barbara chapel S. of the choir: 1474 Gothic triptych, perhaps of Bernese origin, altered in 1636, tombstone of Walter Supersaxo, d.1482, late Gothic screen. In the S. aisle tomb of Bishop Andreas von Gualdo, d.1437, Crucifixion group over the recumbent figure. In the chapel N. of the bell tower 1621 font. The *cathedral treasure* includes important medieval gold work. By the cathedral **Catholic church St. Theodul,** built by Ulrich Ruffiner in 1514&5 in the Flamboyant style and completed in the 17&18C. The 1960–4 excavations are still visible under the nave. They show a series of churches; the oldest was

Tour des Sorcières, all that remains of the 12C town fortifications.

15C Notre-Dame-du-Glarier cathedral with massive Romanesque tower.

built in the Middle Ages over Roman buildings. The present building has a nave and polygonal choir with fine stellar vaulting and carved keystones. There is a half-figure of an angel at the foot of each of the pillars of the triumphal arch. In a wall niche in the S. aisle is a fine 15C Pietà. Opposite the cathedral **episcopal palace,** a large rectangular building dating from 1839&40. By the cathedral square 19C **chapterhouse** and **vicariat,** a 17C baroque building. In the Place de la Planta **palais du gouvernement,** 1838 neoclassical building. 7 Rue de Conthey, **maison Supersaxo,** built 1503 – 5 by Georg Supersaxo, altered in the 17&18C. On the second floor is a large room with fine ceiling lavishly carved by Jacobinus Malacrida, 1505, with a large central relief depicting the birth of Christ. 8 Rue de Savièse, **maison Barberini,** built late 18C, fine façade with stone double portal, balcony with wrought-iron grille above it. No. 16 **maison de Wolff,** 18C baroque building with stucco arms on the gable. 16 Avenue de Ritz **maison de Courten** of 1538 with Gothic windows and corner turrets.

Late Gothic ceiling by Jacobinus Malacrida in the Supersaxo house.

OLD TOWN **Vidommat,** former seat of the vidames of Sitten, mentioned since the 11C. The present step-gabled building was frequently altered and now houses the school of applied art. Next to it is **la Majorie,** now the *Musée des beaux-arts,* mentioned since the 13C, seat of the bishop from 1373–1788. The present building was created by Ulrich Ruffiner in 1536. It is reached via a curtain wall with crenellated tower and a round staircase tower. N. of the Majorie 14C **tour du chien** (dog tower), a fragment of the fortifications which connected Tourbillon with the Majorie. 1 Rue du Collège, **maison de la Diète** built in the 17&18C for bishop Adrian V of Riedmatten. Massive building with broken gable and coat-of-arms over the door. No. 14, **maison de Platea,** group of 16&17C buildings, recently restored; inner courtyard with wooden galleries. No. 16, **maison des Soeurs de l'Hôpital,** 17C. **Catholic college church** of 1806–10. Next to it **theatre,** seat of the bishop from 1788, rebuilt in the 19C. 3 Ruelle de la Lombardie, **Ancienne pharmacie,** built in 1547 for the pharmacist Joh. Uffenbort. In the vestibule interesting paintings of the expulsion from Paradise. Rue du Grand-Pont, **Hôtel de Ville,** built in 1657–65 on a square plan, façade with bell tower and astronomical clock by M. Spaeth, St. Gallen, 1667. Fine carved wooden door dating from 1657. Roman inscriptions in the vestibule, including that of the praetor Pontius Asclepiodotus with christogram, the oldest Christian inscription in Switzerland, dating from 377. Fine carved doors on the first floor. Behind the Hôtel de Ville **maison Penaudier,** a late Gothic building. 4 Rue du Grand-Pont, **casino,** built 1863 by E. Vuillod. **Fontaine du Lion,** 1610–13. No. 17 **maison Riedmatten,** elegant residence dating from 1813–18. No. 29, **maison Ambüel,** built in the 17C, altered in the 18C, painted façade, arcaded courtyard. In the Avenue St-François **Capuchin monastery,** rebuilt 1968–8. The 17C monastery church was rebuilt in 1947&8. In the interior paintings dating from 1948 by Gino Severini.

MONTORGE In the Savièse direction **ruins** of château de Montorge, built in the 13C by the counts of Savoy and destroyed in 1417.

LES AGETTES In the hamlet **chapel of the Visitation,** built 1680–4, with a pretty 17C wooden house next to it.

MAYENS-DE-SION **Chapel of Notre-Dame-du-bon-Conseil,** built 1770. In the interior Way of the Cross, engravings by Domenico Tiepolo, 1749, and collection of votive pictures. In the environs **Chalet Rion,** former summer residence of bishop Franz Josef Supersaxo, built 1716. Wooden building with stone tower.

Sion: 'Maternité à Hérémence' by R. Dallèves, Musée des beaux-arts.

Museums. *Musée archéologique du Valais;* important collection of finds from the canton. *Musée cantonal des beaux-arts;* collection of works by Valais artists. *Musée cantonal de Valère;* lavish collection on the art and history of Valais.

Siselen BE
6☐D3

St. Silvester, built in the early 16C to a late Gothic design. The tabernacles in the choir are in the same style. Horseshoe-shaped **priest's house** of 1633 and 1737.

Sisikon UR
8☐B4

There has been a **chapel** since the 16C on the spot (Tellsplatte) where William Tell is said to have escaped from Landvogt Gessler's boat by leaping on to the shore. The chapel was rebuilt to the original design in 1879&80; the interior dates from the same years; the frescos by the Basel painter Ernst Stückelberg have become famous.

Sissach BL
2☐B4

The **Reformed parish church of St. Jakob** was rebuilt in 1525&6 over several previous buildings. The carved wooden

Sisikon: frescos by E.Stückelberg (1879&80) in the Tell chapel.

Sissach: Schloss Ebenrain is a lavishly decorated 18C house.

ceiling in the nave and the net vault in the choir distinguish the building from other rural churches of the period. **Schloss Ebenrain,** built 1773 – 5 to Samuel Werenfels' design is one of the most ambitious baroque country houses in the area; the house is lavishly appointed, the courtyard has a rococo railing and the grounds are landscaped in the English style. Several refuge castles were built in the 10C as a protection against invading Hungarians, Saracens and Normans; there are traces of some of these high fortresses on the **Sisacherfluh** and the **Burgrain.** *Heimatmuseum* (local history) Zunzgerstrasse.

Soazza GR

13 ☐ F5

Nucleated Misox village on a little hill above the Moesa. The cubic **stone buildings** with stone slab roofs have survived in good condition. **Catholic parish church of San Martino** Early baroque single-aisled church with polygonal choir and side chapels by the entrance, built in 1639 using parts of an earlier building. The nave has a painted wooden coffered ceiling, the choir has vault stucco by a local artist (late 17C). Tower with dome on an octagonal base, 1639, 1503 Renaissance wall painting on the entrance façade. In the NW corner **ossuary,** rectangular building with arched entrance and a painted coffered ceiling, *c.* 1700. **Madonna Addolorata chapel,** built in 1751. The nave with pendentive dome and the choir of equal width with half dome create a rotunda-like baroque impression of space, especially as the choir wall is more of a connection than a division. The building has a porch on the same roof-tree and a triangular turret. In the village proper is **San Rocco,** rebuilt 1633. It is similar to the parish church in appearance and concept; the stucco decoration on the choir vault is by the same artist as that in the church. Above the village is the **Ospizio,** former home of the Capuchin mission. Cubic building with steep stone roof, now priest's house. 1686 wall paintings: in a niche of the courtyard entrance the Infant Jesus is passing a nail from the cross to St.Francis and a lily to St.Antony. In the interior niches of the garden wall representations of the Passion.

Soglio GR

14 ☐ B4

Terraced village high above the valley floor. A number of palaces tower above the closely-built houses. At the front on the slope is the **Reformed church,** now baroque. It contains numerous epitaphs of the Salis-Soglio family, who also commissioned the impressive palaces in the village. The modest **casa alta** (1524, rebuilt 1680) is the oldest house still standing in Salis. In 1554–73 the **casa Gubert** was built in the E. of the village; it is essentially a Renaissance building. On the N. edge of the village is the **casa Battista,** dating from the first half of the 17C (now a hotel). The principal façade axis is emphasised by the portal and the central

Soglio: tightly packed village on a terrace above the valley.

windows set in pairs. At the heart of the building is a two-storey hall with gallery. Behind this is a baroque terraced garden with mediterranean vegetation, which was a decisive influence on many Bünden gardens. To the E. are the **Stallazzo**, **casa Max** (both 1696) and the **casa Antonio** (*c.* 1740), which also has gardens.

Sogn Gagl GR
See MEDEL   13☐C2

Solduno TI
See LOCARNO   19☐C2

Solothurn SO
                                             6☐F2

The town first set up a mayor and eleven-man council in 1182, with the support of the Zähringen family. As the noble families began to die out from the mid 14C a struggle began between Bern, Basel and Solothurn for the feudal inheritance, in the course of which Solothurn secured its present ragged cantonal area. Although it took part in most Confederate campaigns from the Sempach war onwards, Solothurn was not accepted into the Confederation until 1481. The Reformation found many supporters in country areas, but finally Solothurn remained true to the old faith. The establishment of the French embassy in 1530 determined the politics of the town for about 260 years. Mercenary service and billeting created a new wealthy upper class. In 1798 Solothurn was the first canton to accept the Helvetian constitution. The

Patriziat finally abdicated at the Volkstag of Balsthal on the 22 December 1830.
TOWN AND FORTIFICATIONS After the 4C Alemannic invasions the Gallo-Roman 'Vicus Salodurum' shrank to a castrum N. of the present Wengi bridge. Remains of the **castrum wall** can still be seen in the Löwengasse and on the Westring by the passage to the Friedhofplatz. On the site of the early medieval Stadtburg E. of the castrum is the **Zeitglockenturm;** this dates from the first half of the 12C and is the oldest building in the town. In the 15&16C the astronomical clock with moving figures was added. Part of the **medieval town wall** with three half towers has survived on the Nordring. The **Krumme Turm** (crooked tower) remains of the fortifications S. of the Wengi bridge; it is so-called because the top of the tower sits awkwardly on the irregular pentagonal substructure. The **Bieltor** is the W. entrance to the town. The lower section probably dates from the Zähringen era; the present 'Bernese dome' was added after much alteration in the early 19C. The four corner towers of the ring wall and the E. gate were rebuilt in the 16C. The **Baseltor,** built in 1504–35, is a square gatehouse tower with two massive round side towers. The round towers were copied in 1534 in the NW corner of the Old Town in the **Buristurm** and in the 1548 **Riedholzturm,** at the NE corner. In front of the latter tower is the trapezium of the **Riedholzschanze,** with parapet and defensive ditch. This and the demilune by the Krummer Turm made up the baroque fortifications, which had 11 bastions including the older towers. Building of the fortifications started in 1667 under the direction of Francesco Polatta and was halted in 1727. The little streets with crane gables are typical of Solothurn.
OLD TOWN N.BANK **St. Ursen cathedral,** begun in 1762 by Gaetano Matteo Pisoni of Ascona and completed in 1773 under the direction of his nephew Paolo Antonio. St. Ursen is the first neoclassical church in Switzerland. The interior stucco by Francesco Pozzi matches the strict rationality of the articulation. The rich *cathedral treasure* includes the so-called Hornbach Sacramentary, a

Solothurn: the Old Town presents an image of remarkable unity.

Reichenau manuscript dating from *c.* 983. **Jesuit church,** built in 1680 – 9 and presumably designed by Brother Heinrich Mayer, who also worked on the ▷ Lucerne Jesuit church. The façade has lateral sections to give a greater impression of size in the narrow street. The interior emancipated itself from the basilical pattern of the Lucerne church: by omitting the clerestory windows the building became a baroque pilastered hall. The stucco, some three-dimensional, is by Tessin artists. **Old Catholic church,** former church of the Franciscan monastery. The monastery was founded in 1280 and a new church was built 1426–36 in the simple Gothic style of the Mendicant Order. The nave was transformed into a neoclassical hall without direct light in 1822. The monastery buildings date from 1664. The **St.Peter chapel** was the burial place of the Theban legionnaires Urs and Viktor, martyred in Solothurn *c.* 300. Alteration and rebuilding have turned it from an early Christian mausoleum into the present post-

Gothic building. **Rathaus.** The square tower remains from the first building phase *c.* 1476; it used to have a Gothic spire. In 1623 Gregor Bienkher began to incorporate the tower into a mannerist façade, completed 1711. In the N. staircase tower is a spiral staircase with cantilevered inner spiral. The **parish hall** at the upper end of the St.Urban-Gasse is a mixture of architectural styles and was the home of Louis von Roll, the founder of the famous ironworks. **Ambassadorenhof.** Franz Beer (▷ St. Urban) designed a new residence for the French Embassy after an earlier building burned down in 1717. The **Zeughaus,** built 1610–14 in early baroque style houses the *Militärmuseum* with a fine collection of weapons and uniforms. The **Landhaus** (1722) was, as the name suggests, a landing stage for river traffic. The **Stadttheater,** built in 1676, used to belong to the Jesuits. **Palais Besenval,** at the N. end of the Kreuzackerbrücke. Built in 1701–6 to plans by a French architect for mayor Johann Viktor Besenval. Schloss

W. façade of St. Ursen cathedral with monumental steps.

Stucco by Tessin artists in the interior of the Jesuit church.

Waldegg (▷ Feldbrunnen), also built for Besenval, combined local and foreign elements, but the Palais is a direct copy of the French hôtel. **Haus von Roll,** NW of the cathedral. The oldest parts of this patrician house date from the early 17C. The trompe l'oeil pictures in the Rittersaal are by Wolfgang Aeby. F. of this is the **Mauritiusbrunnen** (fountain), 1556, with figure by Hans Gieng of Fribourg. The figures on the **Simsonbrunnen,** (1543) the **St.Georgsbrunnen** (1548) and the **Gerechtigkeitsbrunnen** (justice fountain, 1561) are by Laurent Perroud, partially based on models in Bern and Fribourg. The façade of the **Haus Dr.Reinert** (11 Gurzelngasse, 1692) has a baroque façade richly decorated with pilasters, ashlar pilaster strips and lunettes with 'gnarled' and shell ornamentation. The **Hotel Krone** opposite the St.Ursen steps is a neoclassical building dating from 1772.

VORSTADT **Spitalkirche zum Heiligen Geist,** rebuilt 1734–6 to designs by the French architect Joseph Abeille in Régence façade. In the interior late Gothic Bearing of the Cross. The **Alte**

Rathaus with Gothic central tower and side pavilions dating from 1623–1711.

Bürgerspital, mentioned in the 13C, was rebuilt at the same time as the church. **Bürgergemeindehaus** opposite the Spitalkirche. Built in the 15C as a hospice, redesigned as an orphanage 1726–33. There are remains of the medieval town wall in the courtyard of the 1756 prison. GREEN BELT AND OUTER SUBURBS **Reformed church,** built by Armin Meili in neoclassical style. Four new monasteries were built in the outskirts of the town in

The early baroque Zeughaus now houses a military museum.

Von Vigier summer residence, a Türmlihaus in a walled park.

the first half of the 17C. **Capuchin monastery.** The late 16C church was enlarged in 1629 in post-Gothic style. The high altar picture is by the Antwerp painter Gerhard Seghers. The **Loreto chapel** N. of the monastery church contains a copy of the miraculous image of Loreto. **Convent of the Visitation,** built 1676–93 around four courtyards. The baroque church has a trefoil ground plan. **Convent Nominis Jesu.** In the choir of the post-Gothic church is a monumental crucifix dated 1461. **Convent of St. Joseph** on the road to Basel. The late-Gothic church of the Clares convent built 1644–54 has survived. The green area around the bastions was used in the 19C for public buildings in the historicist

style: **Konzertsaaal,** built 1897–1902 by Edgar Schlatter in neo-Gothic style. The **Kunstmuseum** was built at the same time and under the direction of the same architect; it bears a marked resemblance to the work of Gottfried Semper. The 1575 **Cartierhof** (1 St. Niklausenstrasse) followed the local trend by adding corner towers *c.* 1680 and thus becoming a so-called 'Türmlihaus'. The barn was built in 1508. **Sommerhaus von Vigier** (Untere Steingrunbenstrasse), built 1618 –22. This 'Türmlihaus' with its hints of the French château and gardens in the style of Le Nôtre is a clear example of the influence French culture on the 'ambassadors' town'. **Aarhof** (Hans-Huber-Strasse), built 1619 but with a Gothic staircase tower. **Zetterhaus** (39 Bielstrasse), built *c.* 1640 for mayor Johann von Roll. Connected with it is the **Zentralbibliothek** by the Pfister brothers. Opposite is the *Staatsarchiv.* **Episcopal palace** in Baselstrasse. 17C baroque country house. House altered and English garden laid out behind under the direction of Karl Ludwig von Haller. Diagonally opposite the Hallerhaus is **Schloss Steinbrugg** (priests' seminary). It was built 1670 – 2 to a Parisian design for Johann Josef von Sury. A avenue of lime trees leads from the rear gardens to the Aare. **Schloss Blumenstein,** built *c.* 1725 for Maria Franziska von Stäffis-Mollondin in Régence style houses the town's *historisch-antiquarische Sammlung* (historical-antique collection) and gives an insight into French domestic culture.

Museums and collections. *Zentralbibliothek* and *Staatsarchiv* (central library and state archive) by the Zetterhaus. **Kunstmuseum;** the finest items in the collection are the upper Rhenish 'Madonna im Rosenhag' and the 'Solothurn Madonna' by Hans Holbein the Younger. **Historisches Museum Schloss Blumenstein** (▷ text). **Naturmuseum,** Klosterplatz. *Kosciusko-Museum,* 12 Gurzelngasse: memorial to the Polish general. **Altes Zeughaus** (▷ text). **Lapidarium** (collection of stone monuments) in the loggia of the Jesuitenkirche and in the Kollegium in Goldgasse.

Solothurn: 'Akt liegend', 1908, by Félix Vallaton, in the Kunsthaus.

Somvix GR

13 □ D1

Haus Meissen (No. 20), built 1570 with late 16C façade painting. In Sogn Benedetg above Somvix **St. Benedikt chapel.** Single-aisle church with choir of 1522 and baroque wooden tunnel vault in the nave. On the W. wall Last Judgement, *c.* 1435.

Sonvico TI

19 □ D3

Catholic parish church of San Giovanni Battista, first mentioned 1375, rebuilt in the 15C, choir 1600. Single-aisled building with four side chapels and polygonal apse. Hall with columns on the S. side of the nave. Fine 17C stucco in the choir, paintings by Domenico Caresano on the walls, 1614, 15C Gothic crucifix on the altar. 15C frescos on the W. wall. Above the village **Santa Maria di Loreto chapel,** founded 1636. Above the village **Catholic church of San Martino sul Colle,** first mentioned 1146, probably 11C. Single-aisle Romanesque building with shallow-vaulted semicircular apse and three-storey tower. In the interior remains of late Gothic and baroque paintings. DINO **Catholic church of San Nazario,** first mentioned 1146 and altered 1879, Romanesque tower. In the nave 12C Romanesque wall paintings showing Byzantine influence with the Emperor Nero and three soldiers. In the N. chapel detached Crucifixion fresco ascribed to Bernardino Luini.

Sonvilier BE

6 □ B2

Erguel ruin. This fortress of the Lords of Erguel was built in the 11C and acquired in the 13C by the prince bishops of Basel and was then further fortified. The striking round keep survives; the holes for the beams in the various storeys are clearly visible. **Auberge La Grande Coronelle.** The dairy built in 1621 has a vaulted kitchen with massive round pillars. Small *Musée d'histoire naturelle* in the collège.

Soral GE

16 □ D2

Catholic church of St-Pierre-ès-Liens, neoclassical church built in 1831. In the lower part of the village 18C **covered well.**

Sornetan BE

6 □ D1

Reformed church, built 1708. The baroque interior designed to emphasise the importance of preaching has a wooden panelled roof. The choir stalls and the carved pulpit are notable features.

Soubey JU

6 □ C1

St-Valbert is a late Gothic single-aisled church dating from 1632 with façade tower and rare stone roof. The furnishings include staues of the church patron (18C) and the Madonna (15C).

Speicher AR

4 □ A3

Reformed church. Rebuilt by Konrad Langenegger in 1808–10 to a design by Johann Heinrich Tobler. Rectangular neoclassical building with chamfered corners, tower in the central rear axis. Font, pulpit and clock case 1809 – 10 by the Mosbrugger brothers. **'Alter Herbrig'** of 1654, moved and placed on its present site (No. 161) on a masonry base in 1705, rebuilt 1791. **Hotel Krone** (No. 57), 1690, rebuilt as a neoclassical hip-roofed building 1828 – 30. **Former Landammann-Zuberbüler-Haus** in the upper village (No. 61), built 1747 by Johannes Grubenmann, rebuilt 1815. Portal in the Régence style, interior Régence stucco, probably of the Wessobrunn school.

Speiz BE

12 ☐ A2

Schloss church of St.Kolumban. According to the so-called Strättlig chronicle Spiez was endowed by King Rudolf II of Burgundy (d. 937) along with eleven other churches, and subject to the mother church of Einigen. Certainly some of the churches mentioned by the chronicler are essentially early Romanesque (▷ Einigen, ▷ Amsoldingen, ▷ Scherzligen, ▷ Wimmis). The Spiez church is a pillared basilica with crypt and without transepts and as such most like the Amsoldingen chruch, although the Spiez crypt has no pillars or buttresses, and is oval, which is unique in Switzerland. The late Romanesque (presumably *c.* 1200) frescos in the tunnel-vaulted choir show the Ascension of Christ in schematic form. There is a late Gothic representation of the Throne of Grace in the apse conch. **Schloss.** Earliest section 10C (lower part of the keep), often enlarged. Until 1516 seat of the von Bubenberg family, then acquired by the von Erlach family, who lived here until 1875. It now houses a *Wohnmuseum* (domestic museum). There is fine 1614 early baroque stucco by Tessin artists in the Festsaal.

Splügen GR

13 ☐ F3

Nucleated village on the roads to two passes; it consists of terraced groups of

Spiez: the Schloss church dates from the turn of the millennium.

houses on the sunny side of the slope; there was a village fire in 1716. **Reformed church,** baroque single room with polygonal choir by Peter Zurr, built 1687 – 9. **School and parish hall.** Stone building with hipped roof, built 1716 for Paul von Schorsch. Mezzanine floor with round windows, staircase tower, vaulted corridors. Rheinwald *Heimatmuseum* (local history). **Schorsch-Albertini houses,** built 1717 – 19 by Christ. von Schorsch. Upper house with diagonal roof tree, corner ashlars and brightly marbled gable profile. **Bodenhaus,** built 1722, hotel since 1822. Cubic stone building with round-windowed mezzanine and hipped roof. **Ruine zur Burg,** defensive tower dating from the 2nd. half of the 13C.

Stabio TI

19 ☐ D5

In the Kirchplatz **Catholic parish church of Santi Giacomo e Cristoforo,** first mentioned 1104, rebuilt in the 16&18C, extended and vestibule added

Splügen: the Schorsch-Albertini houses, an impressively tall building dating from 1717 –19.

Stalden: the Embda tower was once the seat of the lords of Stalden.

1920–30. Interesting 17C figures with the Body of Christ in the S. chapel. By the church **Brotherhood chapel of Santa Maria di Caravaggio,** baroque building, 1760.

Stadel ZH

3 ☐ B3

Leuenbrunnen (lion fountain). Octagonal late Renaissance fountain (1636) with lavishly decorated column: lion masks, coats-of-arms, seated lion bearing shield.

Stäfa ZH

8 ☐ B1

Reformed parish church. Single-aisle church with early neoclassical stucco by Johann M.Zobel, rebuilt 1688&9; interior altered 1788. **Ritter houses** in UERIKON, medieval lord's residence, much altered 1520–30. Ritterstube with Renaissance beam ceiling by Ludwig Nöggi (*c.* 1530). The **Ritterhaus chapel** is presumed to date from 1315; the late Gothic choir was added in the 15C.

Stalden VS

18 ☐ B2

In the upper village **tour de Embda,** square residence tower, probably 13C, former seat of the lords of Stalden. **Catholic parish church St-Michel,** first mentioned 1535, rebuilt 1777. Single-aisled baroque building with polygonal choir, 16C bell tower. Baroque Apostle statues in the nave, 18C altars and decoration. By the church **priest's house,** fine wooden building on stone substructure with portal of 1676. Interesting group of very old houses in the street opposite the church. NEUBRÜCK **Stone bridge** by Hans Pinella, 1599, and Kapelle Mariä Unbeflecke Empfängnis (chapel of the Immaculate Conception) dating from the 18C.

Stammheim ZH

3 ☐ C2

Beautiful farming village in the Zürich wine-growing area with numerous half-timbered buildings in excellent condition; divided since 1652 into the independent parishes of Oberstammheim and Unterstammheim, each with a picturesque centre. **Reformed parish church** (Unterstammheim). Choir and tower 1515–17, nave rebuilt in its present form 1779&80. Adjacent to the W. the 1779

Stammheim: Gasthof Hirschen in Oberstammheim, a splendid half-timbered building.

Stampa: Late Roman 'bathtub' grave, cut precisely into a block of granite.

priest's house. Gallus chapel (Oberstammheim), 12C, altered c. 1320 and 1485, with high Gothic wall paintings c. 1320 (Creation, Fall of Man, Youth and Passion of Christ, St. George and St. Eligius). **Unterstammheim parish hall.** 1531 half-timbered building rebuilt in 1717. Cycle of 16&17C coats-of-arms in the panelled parish room. **Oberstammheim parish hall.** 1737 half-timbered building with parish room. **Gasthof Hirschen** (Oberstammheim), 1684 half-timbered building with three-storey oriel (1730). Lavish 18C interior. **Alte Kanzlei** (Oberstammheim), 16C half-timbered building.

Stampa GR

14☐B/C4

Reformed church of San Giorgio, built 1694. Hall church with two bays with narrower polygonal choir. Lunette glass 1935 by Aug.Giacometti of Stampa: entry into

Jerusalem. **Ciäsa Granda,** built 1581 by Giov. della Stampa. Four-storey building with round-arched portal in rectangular frame, chamfered window reveals and lavatory channel in the W. wall. Now *Museo della valle* (June to October) with historical collection and works by Giov., Aug. and Alberto Giacometti. The stone **Maira bridge** of 1699 leads to Coltura, where the **Palazzo Castelmur** (June-October) is to be found: 19C neo-Gothic with wall paintings and rococo and Biedermeier paintings. In Palü W. of Stampa on the river Maira **late Roman 'bathtub' grave,** hewn out of a block of granite. It is the only grave of its kind in Switzerland and suggests a tribe living in the Como region.

BORGONOVO Long ribbon village E. of Stampa, on the Julier and Septimer roads, which have been used since Roman times; the buildings show Engadine and Italian influence.

ISOLA on the Silersee. **Haus Perico-Baldini,** built 1672 as an Alpine summerhouse. Wall paintings (1687) on themes from ancient mythology.

PROMONTOGNO **Reformed church Nossa Donna,** first mentioned 988, mother church of the Bergell, given up in the 16C, reinstated 1863. Romanesque single room, raised in the 19C, with semicircular apse, campanile c. 1100, 11C font. **Ruined Burg Castelmur,** mentioned as guardian of the valley from 831, in the 12C in the possession of the lords of Castelmur, collapsed after 1500.

Stans NW

7☐F4

Principal town of the half canton of 'Unterwalden nid dem Kernwald', known as Nidwalden since the 19C. Stans was first mentioned in 1124 and started to develop as a town in the 13C; this development was interrupted by its joining the Confederation in 1291. The Diet met in Stans in 1481 to discuss the division of the spoils of the Burgundian War and the admittance of Fribourg and Solothurn to the Confederation. The quarrelsome delegates were finally united by the 'Stanser Verkommnis'

Stans: St. Peter, an important example of early Swiss baroque.

Black marble rococo pulpit inside St. Peter.

(Agreement of Stans) formulated by Brother Niklaus of Flüe. In the 16&17C Nidwalden achieved equal status in the Confederation with Obwalden. In 1798 Nidwalden was one of the few cantons to reject the new Helvetian constitution; the punitive campaign by the French which this unleashed on September 9 1798 created devastation on a level without parallel in Switzerland. In 1847 Nidwalden was involved in the Sonderbund.

The Stans **Dorf- und Rathausplatz** was laid out after a fire in 1713 and has a unity which bears all the marks of 18C planning. In the square is the **Catholic parish church of St. Peter**, built 1641–7. The basilica with nave and two aisles is a very early example of Swiss baroque. The massive Romanesque church tower was part of a 12C building. By the church is the two-storey **ossuary** of the 16C **Capuchin monastery**, endowed in 1583 by Knight Melchior Lussy, rebuilt 1683. By the gate is a memorial (1956) to Lussy (1529–1606), commander of foreign armies, statesman, and envoy to the Council of Trent as a protagonist of the Counter-Reformation in Switzerland. Pestalozzi founded his famous orphanage in the **St. Klara convent**, built 1799 after the French invasion. The **Rathaus**, built 1714&15 by Josef Aebi on the foundations of a 1484 building, houses a collection of portraits of Nidwalden Landammänner. **Altes Zeughaus** (now state archive), built 1666. A 1700 building, originally a **salt and corn store** in the Stansstaderstrasse is now the *Historisches Museum*. **Rosenburg** (Höfli), built in the 13C as the seat of the steward of the monastery of Murbach-Luzern. In the 16C the present Schloss-like building and outbuildings were built on the old foundations. A large proportion of the former magnificent furnishing is now in the Schweizerisches Landesmuseum in Zürich. **Breitenhaus**, built in 1790 by Niklaus Purtschert on the French model as a country house. Lavishly decorated main portal on the S. narrow side. **Obere Turmatt**, built 1729 as a country house for Ritter Remigi Keyser; in contrast with this stone building the **Untere Turmatt**, the 16C family seat, is built of wood. In the present suburb of Oberdorf is the **Winkelriedhaus** (Lussyhaus), which was owned by the family until 1524 and passed to Melchior Lussy in 1560. In the 16C extension of much of the building; the gatehouse, decorated with frescos on all sides, dates from after 1600. In Wil, E. of Stans on the

The Rosenburg is presumed once to have had a moat.

Aa is the Nidwalden **Landesge-meindeplatz,** first mentioned in 1398; it has a low, rectangular wall around it. The Landesgemeinde (annual assembly of the citizens of the canton) is held here on the last Sunday in April. Nearby is the **Alte Kaserne** (old barracks), now Zeughaus (armoury) built in 1775 as a corn store.

Stansstad NW

7☐E/F4

Stansstad, an important harbour and strategic passage for invasion of the Obwalden and Nidwalden valleys, had extensive fortifications as early as the 13C, including the **Schnitzturm** by the harbour, which survived until it burned down in 1798.

Staufen AG

2☐D5

Reformed parish church of Staufberg. The church, the priest's house and the sexton's house form a unified group on a small hill within sight of Schloss Lenzburg. Romano-Gothic nave and late Gothic choir. Excellent stained glass in the Soft Style *c.* 1420.

Steckborn TG

3☐D2

The town developed from a forced-labour

Stansstad: Schnitzturm, part of the medieval fortifications.

farm of the monastery of Reichenau and was granted its charter in 1313. The town walls were built at this time and have largely survived; they form two arms of an obtuse-angled triangle and lead from the church to the lake, where stone age bank settlements have been discovered. Formerly non-denominational, now **Reformed church of St.Jakob.** Rebuilt 1766&7 by Franz Anton Bagnato, baroque choir tower pulled down in 1833–5 and replaced with a neoclassical façade tower designed by Ferdinand Stadler assisted by Gustav Alb. Wegmann. **Rathaus.** Rebuilt 1667 using the stone base of the earlier building by master of works Schwederle; octagonal staircase tower in the gable façade. **Turmhof** on the bank of the lake, built as a fortified base by Abbot Diethelm von Castell *c.* 1320. Altered 1583 and 1613, merchants' hall added in 1648. **Schloss Glarisegg,** 1772–4 by Franz Anton Bagnato. *Heimatmuseum* in the Turmhof with primeval, Roman and Alemannic finds.

MAMMERN **Schloss,** former Amtshaus, altered after 1621 by the Lords of Roll; 1772&3 rebuilt and S. wing added. Schloss chapel, 1749&50 by Michael Beer of Blaichten, with early rococo trompe l'oeil painting by Franz Ludwig Herrmann. **Neuburg ruin,** NE of Mammern. Remains of buildings begun by Ulrich III of Altenklingen; demolished by the monas-

Staufen: stained glass in the Soft Style in the Staufberg church.

Steckborn: trompe l'oeil painting in the Mammern Schloss chapel.

tery of Rheinau, the owners of the Schloss at the time.
KLINGENZELL **Pilgrimage church of Mariahilf,** SW of Klingenzell. Viewpoint over the lower lake and the Rhine on the former Celtic-Roman road from Eschenz to Pfyn. Endowed by Walter V von Hohenklingen; priory burned down in 1957. Chapel on cruciform plan, built 1704&5 by Johann Dobler, 18&19C interior.

Steffisburg BE
12☐A1

Reformed church, rebuilt 1682 by Abraham I.Dünz. The Romanesque tower has a wooden belfry with spire. The **priest's house** is a baroque hip-roofed building of 1738. SE of the centre of the village are the **Hochhüser.** The smaller is a stone building with a saddleback roof and Gothic profiled windows. The larger Höchhus next door was probably built c. 1480 by Schultheiss Heinrich Matter; it has a massive hipped roof and is a link between the farmhouse and country house styles. **Inneres Ortbühlgut,** W. centre of the village. The 18C country seat was rebuilt in 1794 by Carolus von Sinner to a neoclassical design. In the place called 'In der Erlen' 18C **storehouse.**

Stein AR
3☐F5

18C village centre with church separated by a spur running NE from the 19&20C section of the village. **Reformed church,** built in 1749 by Jakob and Hans Ulrich Grubenmann, renovated 1832 by Enoch Breitenmoser. **Haus Burg** (No. 238) am Sonder, built in the 16&17C on the remains of a fortified residence tower, wooden house with gable. **Schaukäserei,** (711 Dorf) cheese exhibition with specialist restaurant.

Stein SG
8☐F2

Reformed church, 1497 late medieval building renovated in 1929; N. tower with steep saddleback roof. **Catholic church of St. Jakob,** built 1927&8 by Wilhelm Schäfer; rococo pulpit c. 1770.

Stein am Rhein SH
3☐C2

This little medieval bridge and monastery town has survived largely unchanged and

Stein am Rhein: church and former monastery of St. Georgen on the Rhine.

Ballroom of abbot D. von Winkelsheim with grisaille and wooden ceiling.

is considered an almost perfect specimen of its type. It started to develop from a fishing and farming settlement at the end of the Untersee when the Benedictine monastery of St. Georgen auf dem Hohentwiel moved to Stein in 994. The fortifications were first mentioned in 1094. The abbey was first under Zähringen rule, later under the Freiherren of Klingen, who adapted the old fortress above the town as Burg Hohenklingen and named themselves after it. Stein was granted a charter in 1267, and in 1457 the freedom of the empire, but in 1484 it came under Zürich, which introduced the Reformation in 1525 and secularised the monastery. From 1803 Stein was part of the canton of Schaffhausen. American bombing caused some damage on February 22 1945. The town developed in a W. direction from the bridgehead with monastery, church and market; the Hauptstrasse runs parallel to the Rhine and marks the division into N. and S. parts of the town; on the left bank of the Rhine is the Vorderbrugg quarter with remains of a Roman citadel and the church auf Burg.

Of the **medieval fortifications** the W. **Untertor** (destroyed in the 1945 air raid, rebuilt with old stone in 1948), the Obertor on the N. side and the Diebsturm or Hexenturm in the SW, along with parts of the town wall have surivived. A 17C star redoubt was blown up in the 19C. **Reformed church (and former monastery church) of St. Georgen.** This Romanesque columned basilica with nave and two aisles was built in the 11C or early 12C on the site of an older church. Until the Reformation the originally twin-towered building was the monastery church, with monks' choir and sanctuary. In 1583&4 it was altered as a Reformed church: the nave was extended by two pairs of pillars to replace the monks' choir. On the N. side the present late Gothic tower was rebuilt. Several frescos have survived in the sanctuary, including a larger-than-life St. Christopher (13C), scenes from the history of the monastery with a model of the former monastery on the Hohentwiel and other 15C representations. There are also 15C wall paintings in the Liebfrauenkapelle on the N. side of the choir. **Reformed parish church of Burg.** This is the oldest church in the canton (mentioned 799); it stands on a rise in the centre of a Roman citadel built in 294; sections of wall have survived. The present church has a Gothic choir with belfry and a nave dating from 1671. The choir contains a late Gothic cycle of pictures dating from 1466 –9. **Former Benedictine abbey of St. Georgen.** The originally Romanesque complex was altered in the 14C and then again in the 15C in the Gothic style and had a final period of success just before the Reformation. Fine features are the lavishly painted abbot's lodgings and particularly the Festsaal of Abbot David von Winkelsheim with its famous grisaille work by Thomas Schmid, Ambrosius Holbein and the monogram master CA. Among the scenes in early Renaissance style the pictorial representation of the Zurzach mass is outstanding. The monastery buildings are open to the public and house a *Heimatmuseum* (local history). **Rathaus.** The upper storey of the building (1539–42) was altered 1745&6 and decorated with historicist façade paintings by Carl von Haeberlin and Christian Schmidt in 1898 – 1900. The *Rathaus treasure* includes fine gold and silver work and panes of glass with cantonal arms of the 13 Old Places by Carl von Egeri (1542) and other panes with the arms of friendly towns. Adjacent to the Rathaus is the **Haus zum Steinbock,** with the former **St. Agatha chapel** on the ground floor; the building now houses the Stadtarchiv (town archives). **Painted houses.** There are many extremely attractive houses painted in baroque and later styles; the finest are in the Rathausplatz area. The following are particulary noteworthy: **Gasthaus Roter Ochsen,** late Gothic façade with 1615 oriel, painting of the same date by Andreas Schmucker (allegorical pictures and scenes showing Marcus Curtius in the forum in Rome, death of Lucrece, David and Goliath, Wise and Foolish Virgins. **Haus zur Vorderen Krone.** façade altered in the 18C with baroque painting of 1734. Interior hall with 13 wall paintings (biblical themes, Swiss history and morality), presumed to be by Andreas Schmucker. **Haus zum Weissen Adler.** Early Renaissance façade painting, ascribed to Thomas Schmid (*c.* 1520): extremely lavish work with fables, scenes from Boccaccio's 'Decameron' and two parables from the 'Gasta Romanorum'. Other striking houses are the **Haus zum Chupferberg**, now Heimatwerk (local craft workshop), the **Haus zum Lindwurm** (Empire façade), the **Haus zum Hirzli** (half-timbered building with gable),

Stein am Rhein: façade painting on the Haus zum Weissen Adler.

the **Haus Vetter** in the Choligasse (half-timbered with gable) and the 1739 **Haus Neubu** in Bärengasse, built as a private house and office, with a particularly lavish rococo interior. **Burg Hohenklingen.** The oldest parts (residence tower) are probably 11C and the whole Burg is in good condition. The palas with Rittersaal dates from the 13C. The Burg has housed a restaurant since 1865.

Steinach SG
4☐A2

The **Catholic parish church of St. Jakobus Major und St. Andreas** is a baroque building with vestigial transepts, built 1742-6 by Joh.Jak.Grubenmann and altered in 1770 by Joh.Ferd.Beer. The **Gredhaus** was built in 1473 as the St. Gallen corn store, rebuilt 1557 – 61. **Ruined Burg Steinach** S. of the village. Former seat of the lords of Steinach, in disrepair since the 19C.

Steinebrunn-Egnach TG
3☐F3

Alte Kapelle of St.Gallus, chapel on the Amriswil-Arbon road. Built in the 13C, altered 1674, 1743 and 1842. Chapel, cemetery, beneficiaries' house (half-timbered, 1743) and the half-timbered farmhouse opposite form an attractive group.

Steinen SZ

8☐B3

Catholic parish church of St. Jakob.
The walls are Gothic, the interior was
redesigned in the baroque style in 1660–
70. **Ossuary** (1517) with late Gothic
wooden ceiling.

Stettfurt TG

3☐D3

Schloss Sonnenberg in a setting with
fine views. Mentioned 1242, rebuilt 1595
using parts of the former building by Matthias Höbel for Josef Zollikofer, from 1678
administrative building of the monastery
of Einsiedeln. Step gable building with
corner towers, central façade tower on the
valley side and courtyard in the W. In the
upper storey 18C stuccoed and painted
stateroom.

Stierva/Stürvis GR

14☐B1

**Catholic parish church of St. Maria
Magdalena.** Late Gothic single room
with polygonal choir, built 1520&1 by
Lorenz Höltzli. The nave and choir have
the most elaborate net vaulting in
Graubünden. Late Gothic winged altar
from an Ulm studio, sacristy door with
bas-relief friezes of the same period. W. of
the church three-storey **residence tower**
c. 1200, former seat of the lords of Stierva.

Stuckishaus BE
See BERN   6☐E4

Studen BE

6☐D2/3

Remains of the Roman ribbon settlement
Petinesca can be seen W. of the village.
At the foot of the Jäissberg is a late Roman
gatehouse, with a complex of residential
buildings excavated 1898–1904 adjacent
in the N. The **Gumpboden temple pre-**
cinct is higher up in the Sudenwald. It
contains six square temples, three smaller
cult buildings and a priest's house. The
buildings date from the 1&2C BC and are
within pre-Roman ramparts, of which the
'Keltenwall' to the W. has survived in the
best condition. (▷ Bellmund).

Stuls/Stugl GR
See BERGÜN   14☐C1

Suhr AG

2☐D5

Reformed parish church. The oldest
church, discovered in 1956, was built in
the pre-Carolingian period over a Roman
temple. The present church is late Gothic
with a single aisle, choir and tower (1495)
with a steep saddleback roof.

Sumiswald BE

7☐A/B3

Reformed church of St. Maria. This
church of the Teutonic Order was built
1510 – 12 to a late Gothic design. The
16&17C glass depicts the founders and
patron saints. **Spittel,** former house of the
Teutonic Order. Endowed 1225 in order to
establish a hospice here. The present castle of the Order is largely the result of
reconstruction after a fire in 1730.

Sundlauenen BE

12☐B2

The **Beatushöhlen** (caves) are open to the
public, who are allowed to go down about
3300 ft. About 5 miles of caves have been
explored, but the whole system is much
larger. The *Hermitage of St. Beatus,* held
by legend to have driven a dragon out of
the caves, was a popular place of
pilgrimage in the Middle Ages. The saint
was presumably one of the Irish monks
who came to Switzerland in the 6C.

Sur En GR
See ARDEZ   15☐A3

Surcasti GR

13 ☐ E2

The **Catholic parish church of St. Laurentius** is on a rocky spur between Glenner and Valserrhein, on a spot which was settled in the late Iron Age. Rebuilt 1520, single room with narrower polygonal choir and late Gothic stellar vaulting, perhaps by Andreas Bühler. Nave redesigned in the baroque style and side chapels added *c.* 1774. Late Gothic crucifix on the choir arch, relief from the same period beside it. The keep of a 12C Burg (probably originally an early medieval church Burg) with half-hipped roof serves as the bell tower. In the village itself is the baroque **St. Joseph chapel** (1689), with choir and choir arch wall painted by Jacob Soliva in 1723.

Sursee: late Gothic Rathaus with staircase tower and step gables.

Sureggio TI

See Lugaggia 19 ☐ D3

Surpierre FR

11 ☐ A1

Château. The Nobles of Surpierre were mentioned from the 12C; in the 13&14C the village belonged to the Lords of Cossonay, who may have built the château. The present complex is 16C, and includes a massive 14C square tower.

Sursee: Capuchin monastery on the NE edge of the town dating from 1606–8.

Sursee LU

7 ☐ D2

This town founded by the Kyburgs in the 13C is almost rectangular in plan, but the streets form an irregular pattern. Two towers of the fortifications have survived. The **Untertor** at the exit to Basel, rebuilt 1674, a cubic block with pyramid roof and stone gables. The **Schützenhaus,** built at the same time as the gate, houses a *weapon collection,* opened on request by the Stadtverwaltung (town administration). At the S. corner of the fortifications is the **Diebsturm** or **Hexenturm** (thieves' or witches' tower). The **Catholic parish**

church St. Georg was built 1638–41 by Jakob Berger in late Renaissance style, an unusual design for sacred buildings in the region. The high altar in early Italian neoclassical style has figures by Johann Baptist Babel. The considerable **church treasure** shows that Sursee was the centre of 17&18C gold work (opened on request). The late 15C two-storey **ossuary** has a Gothic wooden ceiling in its upper room. The **Capuchin monastery** on the road to Aarau dates from 1606–8 and was endowed by mayor Michael Schnyder. The *museum* here deals with the history of the Capuchins in Switzerland. The **Rathaus,** built 1539–45 by Jakob Zum

Susch: Planta residence tower with baroque dome by the Reformed church.

with ceiling painting by Josef Anton Messmer. Next to it is the **St.Urbanhof,** dating from the mid 16C in its present form; it accommodates the *Heimatmuseum Sursee* (local history). Opposite the Rathaus **Haus Beck,** built 1631 for mayor Ludwig Schnyder of Wartensee, a late Renaissance building.

MARIAZELL At the N. end of the lake **pilgrimage church Mariazell,** mentioned 1353 and rebuilt 1657 as a plain, rectangular building with polygonal choir. In the interior altars by Hans Wilhelm Tüfel with three-dimensional figures in theatrical arrangements. On a tongue of land near Mariazell the **ruined Zellmoos church,** presumed to date from the early 11C.

Steg of Prismel, retains only the N. round tower of the 1482 building. Polygonal staircase tower, windows and step gable are evidence of the building's late Gothic origins. The baldachin niche in the E. corner was still used as a pillory in the 18C. In the council chamber above the former merchants' hall, wall panelling and coffered ceiling by the Tüfel family of carvers. N. of the church are the monastery's two administrative buildings, The **Murihof** was rebuilt 1707–10. Louis XVI ballroom

Susch GR
9□F5

Reformed church, built *c.* 1515. Late Gothic with single aisle, stellar vaulting, organ and gallery in the choir 1770. By the church **Planta residence tower** with Gothic windows and baroque onion dome.

Susten VS
See LEUK   18□A1

T

Tafers FR

11 □ D1

Catholic church of St. Martin, first mentioned 1148. The present building includes a nave and ante-choir of 1786–9 and a late Gothic choir with 16C polygonal bell tower. In the interior, on the N. side altar, fine wooden 15C Pietà, baroque statues in the choir. By the church **chapel of St. Jakob,** (1769) frescos by Jakob Stoll on the façade. **Former ossuary** of 1753 with 16C Crucifixion. **Sexton's house** in the church square, fine building typical of the area, built in 1780 as a school house. The façade is decorated with carvings and inscriptions. Now *Heimatmuseum des Sensebezirks,* ethnographic collection including votive pictures.

Tafers: 15C wooden Pietà in St. Martin.

Tamins GR
See RICHENAU-TAMINS

9 □ A4

Tarasp GR

15 □ A3

Schloss Tarasp, probably built in the 11C by the Lords of Tarasp. The keep, the N. building, the campanile and the chapel are medieval. The S. residential buildings were rebuilt in the 16&17C. Present interior largely 1907 – 16. Romanesque **Schloss chapel of Joh. Battista** with semicircular apse. *Museum* in the Schloss. Numerous hotels built at the turn of the century are evidence of Scuol-Tarasp-Vulpera's development as a spa; they include the **Kurhaus** in Bad Tarasp, built 1860-4 by Felix Wilh. Kubly and the **Hotel Waldhaus,** built in neo-Renaissance style 1896&7 by the Bünden architect Nikolaus Hartmann the Elder.

Tarasp: impressive 11 – 17C Schloss in a dominant position.

Tavannes BE

6 □ D1

Catholic church, built 1929&30. Mosaic Resurrection by Gino Severini over the portal. The interior is by A. Blanchet, P.-Th. Robert, M. Feuillat and A. Cingria. **Pierre Pertuis.** The Romans were undeterred by the problem of cutting through a rock S. of the town when building the road; an inscription in the

Tenna: detail from the Passion cycle in the Reformed church, c. 1400.

Tesserete: San Stefano (1444) with Romanesque bell tower.

town names the Duumvir and Helvetian Marcus Dunius Paternus as the builder responsible.

Tavetsch GR

13 □ C2

SELDRUN **Catholic parish church of St.Vigilius.** 1691 baroque building with 1702 high altar by Joh.Ritz. In the S. chapel 1515 late Gothic winged altar.
CAMISCHOLAS **St. Anna chapel,** built 1658, 1517 Gothic winged altar.

TSCHAMUT **St.Nikolaus chapel,** altered 1658, with late Gothic wooden ceiling.

Tegerfelden AG

2 □ E3

Ruined Burg. Former seat of the Lords of Tegerfelden, first mentioned 1113.

Tenna GR

13 □ F1

Reformed church. 14C single room, choir with stellar vaulting and 1504 late Gothic wooden ceiling. Wall painting *c.* 1400: Passion cycle on the N. wall, on the S. wall Epiphany and saint bishop.

Territet VD
See MONTREUX

11 □ B4/5

Tesserete TI

19 □ D3

Catholic priory church of Santo Stefano, first mentioned in the 12C, rebuilt 1444 and altered in the 18C. The fine Romanesque tower of the first church has survived; it is probably 13C, and is now incorporated in the façade. The interior is lavishly decorated: in the choir behind the altar 16C paintings including the stoning of Stephen, 1568 Renaissance choir stalls, paintings on the walls, 1770 –80. In the side chapels lavish stucco and 17&18C altars. In the first and third S. chapels 15C frescos. Fine 14C **Crucifixion** on the tower.

Teufen AR

4 □ A4

Second largest community in Ausser-rhoden. Ribbon village with originally unified square; much altered in the 19C, however. **Reformed church.** Rebuilt 1776 – 8 by Hans Ulrich Grubenmann. The 1777 rococo stucco is ascribed to Peter Anton Mosbrugger, rococo pulpit 1777&8. **Parish hall** opposite the church, built

1837&8 by Felix Wilhelm Kubly in neo-Renaissance style. The **school house** next door (1837–40) is also by Kubly and in the same style. Early 18C **priest's house** (No. 272), in the Hörli, probably the former home of the architect Johann Ulrich Grubenmann. **Zeughaus** (No. 83), built 1853–5 by Jakob Schefer under Kubly's direction in Florentine Renaissance style. **'Althus'** in the Lortannen NE of the village, 1539. Building with a shallow saddleback roof with its gable side to the street, one of the two oldest dated houses in Ausserrhoden. The *Grubenmann-Sammlung* in the 'old station' is dedicated to the memory of the Grubenmann family of architects. **Covered wooden bridge** 1862 by Remigius Seif over the Rotbach E. of its confluence with the Goldibach. **Wooden bridges** over the Sitter and the Wattbach NW of Teufen. **Wonnenstein convent.** Capucine convent of Mariä Rosengarten, in NIEDERTEUFEN, W. of Teufen. Subject to Innerrhoden from 1608, founded as a Beguine convent in 1397, Capuchin reform accepted *c.* 1590. Monastery and church rebuilt 1687.

Thal SG

4☐B3

The **ecumenical parish church of Our Lady,** first mentioned 1163, was rebuilt *c.* 1494 and altered 1770–80. Renewal of nave vault and tower 1904; ceiling painting and rococo stucco 1770&80. The **Trüeterhof,** a half-timbered building at the W. end of the village, was built *c.* 1570 and rebuilt in the 17C; wine press dated 1573 in the cellar. **Schlösschen Kruft or Klingelburg.** This slender half-timbered building with rear tower is probably medieval; altered in the 17C. **Rosentürmli,** 18C gabled building with half-timbered extension and staircase tower. **Schloss Risegg** in Staad-Buchen, NW of Thal, is a medieval foundation. The cubic building with five round corner towers was rebuilt in 1605 (now an old peoples' home). **Schloss Greifenstein,** group of buildings on the N. slope of the Buchberg dating from the third quarter of the 16C; Burg-like square consisting of residence

Thalheim: ruined Burg Schenkenberg with dominant keep.

and diagonally- placed gatehouse and servants' quarters with crenellated wall.

Thalheim AG

2☐D4

Ruined Schenkenburg. Habsburg fortress with large rooms on a wooded hill above the village, presumed to date from the early 13C, seat of the Schenken of Schenkenberg. Bernese from 1460, bought in 1918 by the Aargau Society for the Protection of the Homeland; the extensive ruins were made safe in 1931–8.

Thalkirch GR
See SAFIEN   13☐F2

Thalwil ZH

8☐A1

Reformed parish church. Late neoclassical building dating from 1846&7, rebuilt in 1943–6 after a fire. Glass by Max Hunziker (1945&6).

Thayngen SH

3☐B1

Reformed parish church. Built 1500–4 on the site of a 12C church destroyed in the Swabian War. The tower on the N. side

of the choir was built almost like a fortress
and has arrow slits. **Former Gasthaus
zum Adler.** Built 1711&12 by Hans Josef
Vetter; painted rococo panelling 1770, in
the so-called Goethezimmer. **Former
Gasthaus zum Rebstock.** This building,
until 1803 the official seat of the repesen-
tatives of the Konstanz cathedral chapter,
was mentioned in the Middle Ages. In
1701 the large farm section as added.
Former Gasthaus zum Sternen. 1792
neoclassical building. **So-called Schloss
or Oberhof.** Irregular gabled building
(1593–1604, staircase tower 1615), built as
the summer residence of Vogtsherr Hans
Im Thurm. Interior partially rococo.
Dorfbrunnen (village fountain) by the
church. Original column and basin dated
from 1614; a copy was erected in 1935.
Prehistoric site at Kesslerloch The
Kesslerloch cave is, along with
Schweizersbild, the most important Swiss
palaeolithic site. The objects found are in
the Allerheiligen Museum in Schaffhausen.

Therwil BL
1 ☐ F4

The **Catholic parish church of St.
Stephan** (1637–31, interior redesigned in
the rococo style in 1781) and **Anna chapel**
(probably 1669) are made into a unified
group by a courtyard wall.

Thierachern BE
11 ☐ F1

Reformed church St.Martin, built 1707
by Abraham I.Dünz as a baroque single
room. 15C interior wall paintings have survived from its mid-15C Gothic
predecessor.

Thierrens VD
10 ☐ F1

Reformed church (St-Martin).
Originally medieval building with partially Romanesque nave and Gothic choir
with fragments of 15C paintings.

Thun BE
11 ☐ F1

Town The name of the town is derived
from the Celtic 'dunum', meaning fortified
hill or castle. This suggests that the
Schlossberg was settled in the early Christian period. The Old Town at the foot of
the hill is laid out on a long axis, following the Zähringen scheme. It was extended
to the N. and on the Aare island from the
12–14C. The **Burgitor,** the **Chutzen-
turm** and the **Grabenturm** have survived
from the fortifications. The **Hauptgasse**
is lined with houses with their roof sides
to the street and arcades. Raised footpaths
over the cellars, the former stables.
Rathaus, built 1589, rebuilt 1685. The
building has arcades on the ground floor.
Schlossberg **Reformed church of St.
Mauritius,** built 1738 to Johann Paulus
Nater's design. The baroque church
designed to emphasise the importance of
preaching has a 14C polygonal façade
tower. The frescos in the vestibule (c. 1430)
represent the Annunciation, Adoration of
the Magi and Crucifixion. In the vault
symbols of the Evangelists. The 1748 epitaph of Beat Ludwig von May in the interior is by the Prussian court sculptor
Johann August Nahl the Elder. **Schloss,**
built after 1191 by Berchtold V of Zähringen, the only fortress of this family to
have survived intact. The keep with four
corner towers is not unlike a Norman castle, which is explained by the fact that Berchtold von Zähringen had relatives in W.
France. The Kyburgs raised the castle and
the Bernese added the steep hipped roof.
The *Historisches Museum* is accommodated
in the interior. W. of the Burg is the late
Gothic **Amtsschloss** (1429) of the mayors
of Bern. The *Kunstsammlung der Stadt
Thun* (art collection) is in the **Thunerhof,**
built 1870–5 by Adolf Tièche.
Scherzligen on the W. bank of the Aare
by the lake. The **Reformed church of
St.Mariä** is a Romanesque single room
with 14C polygonal choir and side tower.
(For history of the foundation ▷ Spiez).
The majority of the wall paintings are mid
15C, by a Bernese painter called Peter.
Like much contemporary stained glass,

Thun: 12C Schloss with a large hall in the residence tower.

Scherzligen: detail from the Passion, c. 1450, in the Reformed church.

especially that in the Münster in Bern, their subjects are largely architectural. Alfred de Rougemont had the area S. of the church made into an English park *c.* 1840 and also commissioned **Schloss Schadua** to replace the medieval house in 1846–52. The Schloss was designed by the French architect Pierre-Charles Dusillon and is a good example of the 19C tendency to mix styles: Tudor sections alternate with French Renaissance design. **Wocher-Panorama,** W. of the Schloss. The circular picture, painted in 1808–14 by Marquard Wocher then mounted on linen, is a lifelike representation of Thun in the Biedermeier period.

Thunstetten BE

7□B2

Reformed church of S.Johannes der Täufer. The 1745 baroque building con-

Thunstetten: the 18C Schloss has a high hipped roof.

tains parts of the 13C Gothic former church of the Knights of the Order of St. John. The commandery attached to it, the present **priest's house,** was altered in the 17&18C. **Schloss,** built 1714&15 for Hieronymus von Erlach, imperial Field Marshal, Landvogt of Aarwangen and later mayor of Bern. The baroque country seat designed by the French architect Joseph Abeille follows the prevalent scheme of a corps de logis between main courtyard with kitchen buildings and a symmetrical garden terrace. In the ballroom paintings by Johannes Brandenburg of Zug.

Thusis GR

14□A1

The village is divided into an old section and the new village built after the fire of 1845, with late neoclassical buildings with Italian-looking roofs. **Reformed church.** Typical building (1506) by Andreas Bühler of Kärnten. Late Gothic single aisle with stellar vaulting and integral polygonal choir, tower with octagonal top and onion dome added after the fire of 1727. Opposite the 1981 Rathaus is **Haus Rosenroll,** built 1634. It was largely destroyed in the fire of 1845. The portal with rounded arch, the three-aisled vestibule and the stuccoed saletta have survived. In front of it is the **Via-Mala-Brunnen** with a lion sculpture (1953) to commemorate the building of the Via Mala in 1473. N. of it is the Schlössli with baroque façade and scrolled gable, built in 1670 for Silvester von Rosenroll and extended after the fire of 1727.

Thusis: stellar vaulting in the Reformed church of 1506, pulpit 1628.

Tiefencastel: St. Stefan, 17C baroque building, façade painted 1931.

Tiefencastel GR

14☐B1

Catholic parish church of St. Stefan.
Baroque 1650–2 single-aisled church orientated towards the W. on a Latin cross plan. Interior by Misox artists, high altar 1655 by Tyrolean artists.

Tinizong/Tinzen GR

14☐B1

Catholic parish church of St. Blasius, built 1643–63 by Paolo Torello. Baroque single room with two transept-like side chapels and polygonal choir. Late Gothic winged altar by J. Kändel.

Tobel TG

3☐D3

Commandery of the Knights of the Order of St. John, built 1228 by Diethelm I of Toggenburg in expiation of the crime of fratricide. Church demolished 1706 and rebuilt on the hill by the old defensive tower. Commandery rebuilt 1744 by Gaspare Bagnato. Much altered and extended after 1809, cantonal penal establishment until 1973.

Toffen BE

6☐F5

Schloss. Hans Georg von Werdt had the existing Burg rebuilt as a baroque country house *c.* 1671. Its medieval origins show only in the irregular disposition of the buildings. Renaissance panelling in the 1633 'carved room', late-17C pressed leather wallpaper in the Pokuliersaal (drinking room) and rococo paintings in the summer room are of interest.

Torello TI

See CARONA 19☐D4

Torny-le-Grand FR

11☐B1

In the upper part of the village **château,** square building with Mansart roof, built in the 18C for the Diesbach-Torny family.

Tinizong: shrine in the triptych in St. Blasius, 1512.

Torny-le-Grand: 18C Schloss, mansard roof.

Toffen: medieval Schloss, rebuilt in baroque style c. 1671.

Torre TI
13☐D4

Above the village is the **Catholic parish church of Santo Stefano,** rebuilt 1732; elegant 12&13C Romanesque tower. 16&17C paintings on the interior W. wall. By the church 1897 **villa.** In the village **casa Baltera** with 1495 fresco of the Madonna and Child.

Torre (Mendrisio) TI
See MENDRISIO 19☐D5

Tour-de-Peilz, La VD
11☐A4

Reformed parish church (St-Théodule), mentioned from the 12C, rebuilt in the 16&18C. Part of the former town wall forms the N. wall of the church; the entrance in the façade tower was originally a town gate. By the lake **château,** built between 1251 and 1257 by Peter II of Savoy,

destroyed 1476 by the Bernese and rebuilt from 1747. Parts of the two round towers date from the Savoy period. By the church **fontaine de la liberté** with bust by Gustave Courbet.

Tour-de-la-Trême, La FR
11☐C3

On a rock by the road 13C tower for the defence of the little village founded by the Counts of Gruyère and mentioned since 1271.

Trachselwald BE
7☐A3

Village in good condition with Emmental houses all facing S. The **Reformed church** was rebuilt 1685 to a design by Abraham I. Dünz. The interior has ornamental painting. A medallion in the centre of the ceiling gives a trompe-l'oeil view of stone balustrade and sky, a motif based on Mantegna's Camera degli Sposi in Mantua. **Schloss.** The oldest parts of the much altered former imperial Burg are the tufa keep and the part of the palas on the courtyard side (2nd half of the 12C). Staircase tower (1641) probably by a Prismell artist.

Tramelan BE
6☐C1

LE CERNIL Hamlet N. of Tramelan with **Jura houses** of the Freiberg type. The 17&19C farmhouses have shallow saddle

Torre: baroque Catholic church of Santo Stefano with slender Romanesque tower.

La Tour-de-Trême: the massive medieval tower was used for defence.

roofs and round-arched barn gates. Wood was used for parts of the oldest buildings, which is unusual above 2,600 ft.

Travers NE

5□F3

Reformed church (St-Côme), first men-

Trachselwald: 1641 staircase tower of the Schloss.

tioned 1228. The single-aisled building with rectangular choir was rebuilt 1569, the tower dates from 1632. By it is the **Schloss,** an extensive 17&18C residence. **Bridge** over the Areuse, stone bridge with four arches, 1665.

Treib UR

8□A4

Old refuge harbour, fortified from the 14C. The **Haus an der Treib** was first mentioned in 1482, rebuilt 1659, originally

Treytorrens: Reformed church and Château, both medieval.

Trin: the village is dominated by the former fortress church of Hohentrins (on the right).

used by sailors surprised by the Föhn on Lake Lucerne. The Gasthof was an asylum for delinquents fleeing capture and on numerous occasions accommodated smaller Diets.

Treytorrens VD

11 □ A1

Reformed church (St-Jean-l'Evangéliste), single aisle and rectangular choir with pointed groin vaulting, Flamboyant portal. By it **château** originally medieval, with late Gothic windows.

Triengen LU

7 □ D1

WELLNAU The **Heiligkreuz chapel** is a 1639 post-Gothic building. Lavishly carved 1633 pulpit.

Trimbach SO

2 □ B/C5

Froburg ruin. Seat of the Lords of Froburg, destroyed in the earthquake of 1356. Excavations revealed remains of 10C wooden buildings and signs of prehistoric settlement.

Trin GR

9 □ A4

Reformed church. Unified late Gothic building of 1491, pulpit 1680. E. of the village **former Hohentrins fortified church.** built *c.* 750, extended as a feudal castle in the Middle Ages. The **St. Pankraz Burg chapel** is said to date from the pre-Carolingian period.

Trogen AR

4 □ A3

Capital of the half-canton Apenzell-Ausserrhoden since the division of 1597. It alternates with Hundwil as the seat of the local administrative council. The Dorfplatz is surrounded by stately stone buildings with houses with wooden gables between them; the surrounding streets have plainer wooden buildings. Trade and building in the 17–19C were dominated by the Zellweger family. The 1779–82 **Reformed church** on the NE edge of the Dorfplatz is the work of Hans Ulrich Grubenmann and stands at the point of transition from late baroque to neoclassicism. Rectangular building with integral polygonal choir, main façade with false three-storey columned section and curved gable. Interior gallery on the W. and N. walls. Stucco marble pulpit and rococo stucco 1781 by Andreas Mosbrugger. Ceiling painting presumably by Joseph Müller. The **parish and community centre** on the S. corner of the square was built 1760–3 by Johannes or Hans Ulrich Grubenmann for Jakob Zellweger. Interior rococo stucco by Andreas or Peter Anton Mosbrugger and Steckborn tower stove dating from *c.* 1762. The **Rathaus** to the right of the church is a cubic neoclassical building built 1803–5 by Konrad

Trogen: Reformed church and dignified 18C houses, visible for a long distance.

Trubschachen: 1738 Himmelhaus; the façade is decorated with sayings.

Langenegger. Landamman portrait gallery in the ballroom. **Arsenal** in the Alte Landstrasse by Joh. Hohener, 1824. Former **Zellwerger double palace** (Nos. 5&6) in the Dorfplatz by the church. Right half 1747, presumably by Johannes Grubenmann, in the interior Régence stucco *c.* 1747, probably by a Wessobrunn master. Left half, 1787–9 by Hans Jörg Altherr, with rococo stucco by a Mosbrugger team. **Gasthaus zur Krone** (No. 3), built *c.* 1727 with rococo painting, 1767. The present **girls' boarding school** (No. 43) W. of the square was built *c.* 1650 and is thus the oldest building in the Dorfplatz. The **Zellerwegersche Fünfeckpalast** consists of five sections of unequal length around an inner courtyard. Interior ceiling stucco by Jos. Simon Mosbrugger and neoclassical tower stove. The **Sonnenhof** (now Café Ruckstuhl) S. of the Dorfplatz is presumably by Johannes Grubenmann, 1761. The **Honnerlagsche double palace** (Nos. 116&17), 1763, in the Niederen is also ascribed to Joh. Grubenmann. The **Türmlihaus** in the Schopfacker (No. 74)

was built 1788 for a manufacturer. S. of Trogen is the **Pestalozzi village** founded in 1946 for war orphans of various nationalities.

Trub BE

7☐B4

A typical Emmental farming village with Ständerbau houses. **Reformed church of St. Johannes Ev.**, largely rebuilt 1641–5. The baroque interior also dates from this period: font, wooden pulpit with inlay, communion table and some coats-of-arms.

Trubschachen BE

7☐B4

The **Gasthof Bären** (1698) and the **Himmelhaus** (1738), both Ständerbauten, are decorated with ornamental façade painting and sayings. The **Gasthaus zum Hirschen** is an 1872 half-timbered building. The *Heimatmuseum* is housed in a former **storehouse** (1785) and a house for a retired farmer (1783). An exhibition pottery is planned in a nearby farmhouse. Between Trubschachen and Bärau is the **Ramsen bridge** built in 1793, a single-span wooden bridge with double trapezoid suspension.

Trun GR

13☐D1

Catholic parish church of St. Martin. Baroque single room with narrower polygonal choir and two chapel niches (1662), Romanesque tower. The 1660 high altar was altered in the rococo style in 1766. **St. Anna chapel.** baroque building with polygonal choir, 1704. Wall paintings by Otto Baumberger in the vestibule (1924); they represent the establishment (1424) and the last renewal (1778) of the Confederation. They refer to the unification of the individual valleys in the Grey Confederation, which was sealed here under an old sycamore (the present tree is a scion of the original one). Meetings of the Confederation took place in the *Landrichtersaal*

Trun: St.Anna chapel, baroque (1704) with Tuscan porch.

Tschlin: Reformed church (1515) with late Gothic stellar vaulting in the interior.

of the **Disentiser Hof** at the W. end of the village. It houses the *Kulturhistorisches Museum*. Above Trun is the **pilgrimage church of St.Maria Licht.** The original church (1663) consisted of the ante-choir and polygonal choir, the nave with wooden tunnel vault was built 1683.

Tschamut GR
See TAVETSCH   13 □ B2

Tschlin GR
                                       15 □ B2

Reformed church. Late Gothic single room with polygonal choir larger than the nave on one side, built 1515 using the nave walls of an earlier building, perhaps by Bernhard von Poschiavo. Early 16C late Gothic wall painting: on the S. wall of the choir Mary Magdalene opposite a saint bishop, on the E. wall of the nave Sebastian and saints, including James. On the choir arch apex Veronica sudarium, on the W. wall scenes from the life of St.Blasius. In front of the church **Donna-Lupa fountain,** 1960.

Tschugg BE
                                        6 □ C3

Steigerhaus. The existing vine house was extended in 1756 as a horseshoe-shaped rococo country house. The painted octagonal interior is notable.

Tübach SG
                                        4 □ A3

Catholic parish church of Mariahilf, rebuilt 1744 – 6, presumably by Johann Jakob Grubenmann. Tower and two-storey sacristy 1767&8 by Johann Ferdinand Beer. **Franciscan nunnery of St. Scholastika.** The Romanesque-Byzantine church was built 1905&6 by August Hardegger.

Tuggen SZ
                                        8 □ D2

Catholic parish church of St.Erhard, built 1733–43 on the site of a church men-

tioned since *c.* 700. Unusually fine interior
dating from the same time as the building.
The medieval **Grynau Schloss tower** at
the Linth crossing is a reminder of Tug-
gen's former role as a centre on an important road.

Tumegl/Tomils GR

9 □ A5

**Catholic parish church of Mariä
Krönung.** 1486 late Gothic building with
rib vaulting in the nave and stellar vaulting
in the polygonal choir, which is narrower
than the nave, tower from an earlier
building with 1678 spire. Paintings from
two periods: late Gothic fragment *c.* 1490
(Holy Kindred) in the third bay of the N.
wall and 1597 painting. 1490 late Gothic
winged altar. Below the village on a rocky
outcrop **Schloss Ortenstein.** The individual residential sections are set around
the central 12C defensive tower; the late
Gothic **chapel** *c.* 1500 is ascribed to Andreas Bühler.

Turbenthal ZH

3 □ C4

Reformed parish church. 1510–12 late
Gothic building, altered in 1703 and 1765.
The tower was rebuilt in 1903&4. Three
keystones with coats-of-arms in the choir
vault. **Former Gasthaus Hirschen** in
HUTZLIKON. A baroque half-timbered
building used as the welfare institution of
a weaving mill. **Breitlandenberg Burg
ruin.** The foundations of the keep and a
gatehouse of the early 14C Burg have
survived.

Turtig VS

18 □ B1

WANDFLUH Stations of the Cross and

*Tumegl: Schloss Ortenstein, with a central
tower.*

Chapel of the Mater Dolorosa, 17C
baroque building, enlarged 1770–80. Altar
by Joh. Ritz, 1695.

Twann BE

6 □ C3

The beautiful village of Twann was known
for its wine in the Middle Ages. The main
street is lined with wine-growers' houses,
some of which have Gothic profiled windows. The rendered buildings have protruding roofs with skylights and hoists.
Reformed church of St. Martin.
Originally Gothic church altered in the
baroque style in the early 17C. In the interior notable early baroque carved choir
stalls (1666) and wooden inlaid pulpit. The
Fraubrunnenhaus houses Dr. Carl Irlet's
lake village collection.
    ST.PETERINSEL **Former monastery.**
Parts of the Romanesque walls of the
Cluniac priory founded in 1127 have survived in the present building (a Gasthaus
since 1919). Jean-Jacques Rousseau stayed
here in 1765, and there are memorabilia
concerning him in a room in the S. wing.

U

Ueberstorf FR

6 □ D5

In the middle of the village there is a massive **schloss** with a polygonal staircase tower, probably built in 1505 by the Englisberg family; now privately owned.

Ueberstorf: Schloss with seven-sided staircase tower, 16C.

Uebewil FR
See DÜDINGEN

6 □ D5

Uerikon ZH
See STÄFA

8 □ B1

Uerkheim AG

7 □ C1

Reformed parish church: In 1520 a choir with strikingly lavish stonework was added to the original Romanesque nave.

Uesslingen TG

3 □ C3

Uesslingen: former charterhouse of Ittingen dating from the 16–18C.

The **chapel of St. Sebastian** is first mentioned in 1461 but is in fact older; it was later rebuilt several times. Wall paintings with a Passion cycle, saints and Majestas Domini from around 1300, stylistically related to the Manesse codex. **Former Carthusian monastery of Ittingen:** Founded in 1152 as an Augustinian priory, rebuilt in several stages from the mid 16C, dissolved in 1848. *Former monastery church,* built in 1549–53. Sanctuary of 1703 by Johannes Mosbrugger to plans by Caspar Mosbrugger. Choir stalls by Chrysotimus Fröhli from 1703 onwards; rococo decoration of 1763 by the stucco artists Joh. Georg and Mathias Gigl, sculptor Mathias Faller and painter Fritz Ludwig Herrmann. *Former convent buildings* with small and large cloister, on the outer walls of which there are still 7 monk's houses, funded in part by Ludwig Pfyffer of Altishofen. Cultural centre since 1982.

Ufenau SZ

8 □ C1

Island on Lake Zurich. Site of a Roman temple as early as the 1 or 2C, on the site of which the 12C Romanesque **church of St. Peter und Paul** now stands. On the outside of the church is the tombstone of the knight Ulrich von Hutten (1488–1523), who found sanctuary here during the Reformation ('Hutten's last days' on Ufenau, described in a poem by Conrad Ferdinand Meyer). **Chapel of St. Martin,** also known as the Reginlinden chapel ater the mother of St. Adalrich, who settled here in the 10C. Built in 1141 it contains wall paintings from various different centuries.

Unterägeri: neo-Gothic church of the Holy Family with statues on the façade by L. Keiser.

Uhwiesen ZH
See LAUFEN-UHWIESEN   3☐B2

Uitikon ZH
                                      2☐F5

Reformed parish church: This single-aisled church with choir and ridge-turret was rebuilt in 1625–6. Glass-painting by Heinrich Müller (1961).

Umiken AG
                                      2☐D4

Reformed parish church: This Romanesque-Gothic complex with saddle-roofed tower forms an integral part of a group of buildings around an inner court with the **priest's house,** built in 1752–5, probably to plans by Giovanni Gaspare Bagnato, and the **priest's barn** of 1760.

Unterägeri ZG
                                      8☐A2

Catholic old parish church of Maria Immaculata, built in 1718–19; the tower stands on foundations of an earlier building from the 16C. **Catholic parish church of the Heilige Familie,** built to plans by Ferdinand Stadler, 1857–60. In the sacristy is a monstrance donated by Louis XV of France in 1728, after the community of Oberägeri had received a similar piece from the Imperial house of Austria.

Unterbäch VS
                                      18☐B1

In the hamlet of Bachtolen is the **Catholic parish church of the Holy Trinity** from 1558, rebuilt in the 17&18C. Single-aisled building with a polygonal apse containing wall tabernacle of 1558, high altar with Coronation of the Virgin Mary by Joh. Ritz, 1697. Above the triumphal arch is a Crucifixion by Joh. Ritz; side altars attributed to Peter Lagger, c. 1740–50.

Untereggen SG
                                      4☐A3

Catholic parish church of St. Maria Magdalena, built in 1782–4 by Johann Ferdinand Beer. Baroque building with a narrow polygonal apse, stuccos probably by Peter Anton and Andreas Mosbrugger.

Unterkulm AG
                                      2☐D5

Reformed parish church: In the square-ended choir, dated around 1300, early 14C frescos were discovered during interior renovations in 1967–8: Apostles, St. Martin and St. Fridolin, Majestas Domini, Christ in Judgement, Holy Trinity and Coronation of the Virgin Mary.

Unterlunkhofen AG
                                      2☐F5

Hallstatt burial mounds in 'Bärhau', E. of the village. The finds are now in the Swiss National Museum.

Unterschächen UR
                                      8☐C5

Catholic church of St. Theodul, built in baroque style in 1681–4 on the site of an older chapel. Rococo stucco inside. The **ossuary,** consecrated in 1701, contains baroque wall paintings.

Untervaz: Rappenstein cave Burg, 1200, in ruins since the 16C.

Urnäsch: 'Schöner' Klaus in the museum of Appenzell customs.

mouth; *c.* 1200. SE of the village are the **ruins of Neuenburg castle:** A four-storeyed 14C residential section with wells in the courtyard.

Unterseen BE

12☐B2

Small town founded by the barons of Eschenbach in 1280. A feature of the town are the 17–19C wooden houses with medieval style rows of windows. The Gothic **church** was altered in baroque style under Abraham I. Dünz in 1674.

Untersiggenthal AG

2☐E3

Ruins of Freudenau castle: Ruins of a tower and walls on the banks of the Limmat.

Untervaz GR

9☐B3

Catholic parish church of St. Laurentius, rebuilt in 1848. Hall church incorporating a polygonal choir. The wooden figure of the Virgin Mary and the reliefs of St.Barbara and Mary Magdalene are from a late Gothic winged altar of around 1500. **Reformed church:** Simple baroque building with integral, straight-ended choir, built in 1696–1700; carved pulpit from the same period. SW of the village are the **ruins of Rappenstein castle:** A cave with a wall built across the

Unterwasser SG

See **Alt St.Johann** 8☐F2

Uors GR

13☐E2

Chapel of San Carlo Borromeo: Medieval nave with polygonal apse of 1616, painted by Hans Jak. Greutter (1616). The painting on the N. aisle wall dates from the middle of the 17C.

Urnäsch AR

3☐F5

Rectangular village square, lined with church and timber buildings from the 17&18C. The **Reformed church** was founded in 1417 as the daughter church of Herisau and rebuilt on the old foundation walls after the village fire of 1641. Tower increased in height in 1866–7. In the **village hall** there is a banner with Appenzell or Urnäsch bears and the Apostle Philip, *c.* 1400. The 18C **Haus im Bindli, (No. 632)** built in the 18C, is a timber frame building with a masonry cellar. The **Zürchersmühle,** first documented in 1599, is a wood frame building with roofs over windows and portals, burned down in 1784 and rebuilt in 1786. *Local history museum,* concentrating on local customs.

Uster: the Schloss has been much altered and has a massive central tower.

Utzenstorf: Schloss Landhut, the only moated castle in the canton of Bern.

Ursins VD

5☐F5

Reformed church: Built on the site of a Roman building, probably a temple. The ancient building is still visible up to a height of about 3 ft.

Uster ZH

3☐B5

Reformed parish church: Monumental-classical building by Johann Volkart (1823–4) on the site of an 11C Romanesque church. Reached up a wide flight of steps and gabled portico. **Schloss:** The tower dates from the 11C, the residential section from 1751-2. Alterations were carried out in 1853 and 1918. **Gujer house or Kleinjogg house** in the district of **Wermatswil.** House of the peasant philosopher Jakob Gujer ('Kleinjogg'), who was popular in the 18C. Timber frame building of around 1750 with paintings. **Kleinjogg fountain** by Walter Hürlimann (1941).

Uttwil TG

3☐F3

17 - 19C **half-timbered buildings** . **Schloss,** probably 17&18C, altered in 1822 and 1934. From 1918-20 it was the home of the architect Henry van de Velde.

Utzenstorf BE

6☐F2

Reformed church of St. Martin, built in late Gothic style in 1522, incorporating older parts. Next to it is the baroque **priest's house** of 1744. **Schloss Landshut:** This moated castle, first mentioned in 1253, was largely rebuilt in the 17C. Today it houses the *Swiss museum for hunting and the protection of game,* as well as a *granary museum.*

Utzigen BE

6☐F4

Schloss Utzigen was built in Italian late Renaissance style in 1664 for Samuel Jenner. Extending southwards is a terraced area with flanking pavilions, 1741.

Uznach SG

8☐D1

Town laid out in an oval with an outer and an inner ring lined by houses. **Catholic parish church of St. Maria,** rebuilt in 1867-9 by Wilhelm Keller, alteration and new front tower by Hans Burkard, 1940. **Catholic church of the Holy Cross.** A late Gothic church with an integral polygonal choir built in 1494 - 1505 on the site of several earlier Carolingian and Romanesque churches; reworked in baroque style in 1775; tower with steep saddle-roof. **Zum Hof;** this gabled timber frame inn was built around 1734. The **Linthhof,** built as a hotel in 1834, is a late classical building with a columned portico and transverse gable; now a business. The **Tönier house** by the parish church houses a *regional collection* with finds from the Hallstatt period and documents on the town's history. **Ruins of Uznaberg castle,** on the height above the Aabach gorge to the right, mentioned in 1234 as the ancestral seat of the Counts of Toggenburg, destroyed in the first Zurich war.

Uzwil SG
3 □ E4

Niederuzwil: The **Catholic parish church of Christkönig** is a basilican building, built by Karl Zöllig in 1933–4; glass-painting by August Wanner.
Oberuzwil: The **Reformed church** was built in 1765–6 by Joh. Ulrich Grubenmann, the steps date from 1858. The hall church with a front tower contains rococo stucco, probably by Peter and Andreas Mosbrugger.

V

Vaas VS

See **Lens**   17 □ E1

Val-d'Illiez VS

17 □ A2

Saint-Maurice The Catholic parish church was recorded as early as the 13C and was rebuilt in 1687 as a single-aisled church with a square-ended choir and a bell tower above the porch which is still partly medieval. It contains locally made 18C altars. The **priory** beside the church was built in 1711.

Valangin NE

6 □ B3

The first lords of Valangin were mentioned 12C but by 1215 their fief had passed to the counts of Aarberg, the cadet line of the counts of Neuchâtel, and they continued to hold it until 1592. It was the Aarbergs who built the **château** and the walls, with their nine semicircular towers, in the 13 –16C. The residence, 15C with later additions, is trapezoid in form and is flanked to the SW by a square tower. Today it is a *regional museum*. The **village** extends to the north of the walls and the main street is lined by two rows of 16–18C houses and ends in a gateway with a 15C tower. The **Reformed church** is the former collegiate church of Saint-Pierre, which was built in 1500–5 outside the village. Late Gothic in style, it lost part of its nave in 1840, and its main façade was rebuilt at about the same time. It contains the tomb of its founders, Claude d'Aarberg and Guillemette de Vergy, whose effigies were heavily restored in the 19C, and numerous tombstones. Beside the church is the **Maison Touchon** (1588), with a polygonal staircase tower and Renaissance windows.

Val-d'Illiez: St-Maurice, façade tower with unusual spire.

Valchava GR

15 □ B5

Late Gothic **Reformed church** with a trapezoidal choir. The E. wall of the **parish hall** has two overhanging floors with the painted arms of the Three Leagues. **Haus Melcher,** No. 21, built about 1800. The *Museum of the Valley* in the 18C Chasa Jaura.

Valendas GR

13 □ F1

The long, single-aisled **Reformed church** has a polygonal choir that is narrower than the nave (1481). There are several substantial 17C houses in the village, including, on the square (fountain, 1760), the **Graue Haus** of 1663.

Valeyres-sous-Rances VD

5 □ E5

A beautiful village which has retained an interesting collection of dwellings and, on

Valangin: 15C Château, remains of an extensive fortress.

Valchava: two-storey painted oriel on the parish house.

Valeyres-s.-Rances: late Gothic Reformed church with 16C bell in the ridge turret.

a hill outside the village, the **Reformed church of Saint-Jacques**. This was originally Romanesque but was rebuilt in the 14&15C and has a late Gothic portal. The **Maison de la Dîme,** a vast 17C building with a Bernese roof, stands above the village. In the village's centre there is the **Maison Bonstetten** and, beside the road, the **Vieille Auberge,** a 16C building with late Gothic windows. To the E. of the village is the enormous **Manoir,** which still retains 16C sections.

Vals GR

13 ☐ E2

The Catholic **parish church of St.Peter und Paul,** which was rebuilt in 1646, stands on a picturesque square. It is a baroque building with a vaulted nave and a polygonal choir that is narrower than the nave and which contains the high altar by Antoni Sigrist (1738–9). To the E. is the **Lady Chapel,** the polygonal apse of which is from the preceding late Gothic church. Inside, in its original place, is a late Gothic triptych of the Ulm school. To the west is the **Chapel of St.Anthony,** built 1688. The **Gandahaus** contains a museum devoted to the popular traditions of the Walser.

CAMP **Pilgrimage church of Mariä Schmerzen.** A baroque single-aisled church with a square-ended choir and a side chapel in the bell tower. In the choir there is a miraculous image of the Virgin (the original is in Vienna) and a collection of ex-votos, including ones by Jakob Soliva and Antoni Sigrist.

Valsainte, La FR
See CERNIAT

11 ☐ D2

Vaulruz FR

11 ☐ B3

Château. The lordship of Vaulruz dates from the end of the 13C and the castle, which may have existed at this time, was rebuilt on several occasions. Surrounded by ramparts, it occupies a vast square and is dominated by a tower in the NW corner.

Vaumarcus: Château with tower-like sloping buttress dating from the 15C.

Vaz: 1678–80 Catholic St.Luzius church in Lain with painted façade.

The residence probably dates from the Fribourg period, after 1538.

Vaumarcus NE

6 ☐ A5

The **château,** which is recorded as far back as 1285, belonged first to the lords of Vaumarcus, then to the counts of Neuchâtel and then to a bastard line of this family. In 1476, after the battle of Grandson, it was burnt by the Swiss and it then passed to the Bonstetten and the Büren. The old castle, supported by a sloping buttress, was rebuilt after 1476. The new château dates from 1773.

Vaz/Obervaz GR

14 ☐ B1

A commune made up of several scattered hamlets.
LAIN **St.Luzius** A single-aisled baroque church (Catholic) with a rectangular choir that is narrower than the nave (1678–80). It contains a number of fine items, including, by the door, two triptychs in the late Gothic South German style dating from 1509 and *c.* 1520.
MULDAIN **St.Johann Baptist.** A baroque church with a side chapel and a rectangular choir that is narrower than the nave (1673–6), stucco by the Broggio brothers.

Veltheim AG

2 ☐ D4

Schloss Wildenstein. A castle with twin towers founded by the early Kyburgs at the entrance to the Schenkenbergertal. Both keeps are 14C but the living quarters were added later.

Venthône VS

17 ☐ F1

This interesting village has numerous fine 15&16C houses and towers belonging to noble families. The single-aisled Catholic parish church of **Saint-Sébastien** was built in 1633–67 and has a polygonal apse. The W. portal has a carved doorway, the S. portal a stone one. Inside, its decoration and furnishings are 17C baroque. Beside the church is the **tower** which is now the parish hall but which in the 13C was owned by the lords of Venthône, the representatives of the bishop of Sion, passing in 1421 to the lords of Rarogne and in 1600 to the citizenry. The tower, which is a fortified house built in the late 12C or early 13C, was extensively altered in the 15&17C. In the village, the **Tour Vareilli,** which is today the priest's house, is a 13C square residence which was owned by the Vareilli family in the 14C. The upper parts were destroyed in the 17C and it was re-roofed. The Platea family has owned the

Verscio: detail of the late Gothic frescos in San Fedele.

château in the hamlet of Anchettes since 1436, although the present building is mainly 17C.

Vercorin VS
17□F1

The former church of **Saint-Boniface** was founded in the 12–13C but was completely rebuilt in 1704, although the bell tower is still partly Romanesque. The **château** is a large wood and stone chalet built in 1777 for A.-P. de Courten but since the 19C it has been owned by the Chastonay family. To the side is the chapel of **Saint-Louis,** which was built in 1784 and contains the rococo altarpiece by Johann Melchior Wyrsch.

Verdasio TI
See Intragna   19□B2

Vermes JU
1□F5

The church of **Saint-Pierre et Saint-Paul,** was built in 1722 and enlarged 1783. Inside, the ceiling and the window surrounds are decorated with rococo stucco. To the SW lies the **Château de Raymontpierre,** a late-16C fortified manor. The late Gothic castle may be compared to those of Greifenstein (▷ Staad-Buchen) and A Pro (▷ Seedorf UR).

Vérolliez VS
See St-Maurice   17□B2

Verrières, Les NE
5□D4

Standing outside the village, on the road leading to the border, is the late Gothic **Reformed church** built in 1517. The nave and choir are rib vaulted and the apse has three windows with Flamboyant tracery.

Versio TI
19□B/C2

San Fedele. The Catholic parish church; the original 13 or 14C church was rebuilt and partially incorporated into the octagonal baroque church of 1743 – 8; beautiful marble altars and balustrades. To the right of the entrance is the choir of the original church, which has a vault with 15C late Gothic frescos; detached Romanesque frescos on the wall and a 17C baroque altar.

Vers-L'Eglise VD
1□C5

Reformed Church. (Saint-Théodule), built 1456 but altered in the 18C. The bell tower rises above the porch, which houses a collecting box (1756) and which leads into a single-aisled church with a polygonal choir.

Vevey VD
11□A4

The Vibiscum of the Romans became, in the Middle Ages, one of the most important of the Vaudois towns and was controlled in turn by the bishops of Lausanne, those of Sion, the dukes of Savoy and finally, until 1798, by the Bernese. Today, it is an industrial centre and resort. The **Reformed church** (Saint-Martin) was first mentioned in 1472 but the present Gothic church was built in three phases: the two-bayed choir in the late 13C; the porch and bell tower, with its balustrade and four projecting bartizans, in 1496 and

Vevey: Cour-au-Chantre, a dignified building dating from 1736.

Vevey: the Nestlé headquarters: glass and concrete.

Vezia: Villa Negroni, a two-storey 18C building.

1511; and the three aisles and the chapels in 1522-3 by the master builder François de Curtine. S. of the choir there is a neo-Gothic porch (1896). Inside the keystones and consoles are carved, the pulpit dates from 1787, the stained glass from 1900 and 1945 and a mosaic by Ernest Biéler from 1941. The **Reformed church** (Saint-Claire, on the square of the same name) belonged to a convent of the Poor Clares founded in 1425. In 1776-83 it was rebuilt in the style of the time by N. Sprüngli, who added a neoclassical portal on the S. side. The **Russian church** (Eglise Russe, rue des Communaux) was built at the expense of the Shouwaloff counts in 1878.

Notre-Dame-de-l'Annonciation is a neo-Gothic church built in 1869-72 by Emile Vuilloud. **Hôtel de Ville,** 1709-10, enlarged in 1751; the façade has a balustraded balcony and a pediment with a clock. 19C buildings link the Hôtel de Ville to the originally medieval **Tour Saint-Jean,** once the bell tower of the chapel of the former hospital. In front of it is a **fountain** (1778). Rue du Simplon, the **Cour-au-Chantre,** now the Préfecture, was built in 1746. Rue d'Italie 43, the **château** is built on the site of a castle, altered in the 18C, when it was the residence of the Bernese Landvogts. It now houses the *Musée du Vieux Vevey* and the *Musée de la Confrérie des Vignerons.* The *Musée Jenisch,* rue de la Gare, was built in 1897 in neoclassical style. Every 25 years, the 19C **Grand Place,** is the setting of the Fête des Vignerons (wine growers' festival); the **Grenette** of 1808, the old grain market, and the neo-Gothic **Château de l'Aile** or **Couvreu,** built in 1840. In an alley E. of the square is **Le Castel,** the house built in 1830-40 by Mme. Warens, the friend of J.-J. Rousseau. In the Avenue Nestlé there is the **Batiment Nestlé,** the company headquarters built in 1958-60 by the architect Jean Tschumi. 21, Route de Lavaux is the **Villa Le Lac,** which Le Corbusier built for his parents in 1923. Rue du Centre, **Fontaine du Guerrier** (1678); rue d'Italie, **Tour de l'Horloge** (1840) and the **fountain** of Michel V. Brandouin.

Vex VS

17☐E2

Originally 12&13C, the church of **Sainte-Sylve** is near the graveyard. The nave and bell tower are partly Romanesque; the square choir was rebuilt on 1498. The village has some beautiful chalets with decorated fronts.

Veyras VS

17☐F1

At Muzot, a 13C **tower house** built by Guillaume de Blonay, a vassal of the

Vico Morcote: Catholic church (1625–7) with lavish interior decoration.

Vicosoprano: San Cassanio dates from c. 1000.

bishop of Sion. It has a 16C roof and stepped gable. Rainer Maria Rilke, the poet, lived in it in 1921–6.

Vezia TI

19 ☐ D4

The **Villa Negroni,** a vast, rectangular residence built in the 18C, with a courtyard surrounded by outbuildings, stands by the cantonal road. Beside it is an exotic garden with the 8C chapel of **Santa Maria delle Grazie.**

Viano GR
See BRUSIO 14 ☐ D4

Vico Morcote TI

14 ☐ D4

The single-aisled **Catholic parish church of Santi Fedele e Simone** was built in 1625–7, incorporating parts of a medieval church. It has four side chapels and rectangular choir surmounted by an octagonal cupola. Baroque façade of 1720. An ornately painted and stuccoed interior, the choir has frescos from 1625, an 18C

Vicques: remains of a large Roman farm dating from the mid to late 3C.

high altar, and a fine, early-16C carved triptych of the Virgin and Saints, attributed to Rodari, on the S. wall of the nave.

Vicosoprano GR

14 ☐ C4

Originally the centre of the Val Bregaglia. Its tightly packed houses display a mixture of Alpine and urban Italian features. The single-aisled early baroque Reformed church of the **Santa Trinità** has a rib-vaulted nave, whereas the narrower choir has a fan vault. The rococo pulpit and the marble communion table both date from 1760. The **Reformed church of San Cassiano** was probably built in 1003 but its present appearance is the result of 15&17C rebuilding. The aisle is rib-vaulted but the polygonal choir has an articulated barrel vault. The pulpit is from *c.* 1680. **Pretorio,** built 1583, with sgraffiti depicting Temperance and Justice. E. of the semicircular portal there is an old pillory with an iron collar. A four-storeyed 13C round tower, known as the **Senwelenturm,** is incorporated in the building. Further E., the **house** at No. 41, built in 1577, with sgraffiti (lute players and duel). Above the doorway are the arms of the Three Leagues and the Prevosti family. The **Torre Salis** is medieval.

Vicques JU

1 ☐ E5

Near the **church,** which was rebuilt in 1925, are the remains of a Roman estate (villa rustica).

Vidy VD
See LAUSANNE

10 ☐ E3

Vigens GR

13 ☐ E2

The **Catholic parish church of St. Florinus** was rebuilt in 1500 and it is now late Gothic, with a stellar vault and buttresses the length of the polygonal choir and nave. Triptych (1516) by Jörg Kendel. There is a carved pulpit with blind tracery by the entrance to the choir.

Villa GR

13 ☐ E2

The main square is ringed by substantial houses, including the **Schloss Demont** of 1666. The **Catholic parish church of St. Vinzenz** at Pleiv was originally the mother church of Lugnez, with a choir from about 1500 and a nave of 1661. The high altar (1724) is by J.Ritz and there is a Renaissance altar (1630) by Hans Jakob Greutter on the N. wall of the choir. The chapel of **St. Sebastian und Rochus,**

Villa GR: central picture on the triptych of 1630 in the church of St. Vinzenz, Pleiv.

built 1587, is a single-aisled Gothic church with a triptych by Hans Ardüser of 1601.

Villa TI
See GORDEVIO

19 ☐ C2

Villarzel VD

11 ☐ B1

At one end of the village is the small medieval **Reformed church** mentioned in 1450. It is single-aisled; has a rectangular choir and a bell tower by the façade which is crowned by a pediment. The core of the adjacent **tower** is 13C but it was rebuilt under the Bernese.

Villeneuve VD

11 ☐ B5

'The new town of Chillon' was founded in 1214 by the counts of Savoy in order to consolidate their position on Lake Leman. The medieval plan, with a single axis formed by the main street, has survived, although the street is now lined by two rows of 18&19C houses. Remains of the SE fortifications still exist by the church; on the other side, Villeneuve enjoyed the natural defence of the lake, which, in the Middle Ages, extended right up to the houses. The **Reformed parish church** (Saint-Paul) pre-dates the Savoyard foundation and is first mentioned in 1166 as a dependency of the Cistercian abbey of Hautcrêt. The date of the present church's building is unknown but the nave and side aisles are Romanesque; the Cistercian type rectangular choir may date from 1220, whilst the bell tower and porch are in part 15C. Near the station, the **Hôtel de Ville** was originally a hospital founded by Aymon de Savoie in about 1236. The present, neo-Gothic building dates from 1874 –6 and incorporates the former chapel of **Notre-Dame**; the only remnant of the 13C hospital; 16C bell tower to the side.

Villeneuve: the Reformed church is a Romanesque hall with nave and two aisles.

Villette VD

10 □ F3

The **Reformed parish church** (Saint-Saturnin) is a 13&14C building that was restored in 1924. The bell tower with its dormer windows rises above the choir, which contains 14&15C frescos. At the entrance to the village is the house of the 16C Bernese Landvogts.

Villette VS

See **BAGNES**

17 □ D3

Villmergen AG

2 □ E5

Catholic parish church of St. Peter und Paul. A neo-Gothic hall church with a rib-vaulted nave built in 1863 – 6 by Wilhelm Keller.

Vilters SG

9 □ A2

The **Catholic parish church of St. Medardus** was rebuilt in 1785-7 with the help of the convent of Pfäfers. The high altar has trompe l'oeil paintings. The neighbouring priest's house dates from the

Villette VD: Landvogt's house, a late Gothic building with half-hipped roof.

same period. The **mill** S. of the church has a frescoed Crucifixion, dated 1766.

WANGS The **Catholic parish church of St. Antonius Eremita** was rebuilt in neo-Romanesque style in 1880-2. Excavations on the **Severgall** hill have unearthed prehistoric, early historic, Neolithic, Bronze Age, La Tène and Roman finds.

Vincy VD

See **GILLY**

10 □ C3

Vinelz BE

6 □ C3

A village of timber framed houses and a fountain of 1780 that has been preserved

Visp: church of the Three Kings, a baroque building with a Romanesque tower.

intact. The baroque single-aisled **Reformed church of St.Maria** retains some Romanesque portions. The paintings inside are late Gothic.

Vionnaz VS

17☐B1

The **bell tower and porch** (1581) of a now vanished church stands in the graveyard; portal of 1650. Opposite is the **Casa Barberini,** an old fortified house with a 17C square tower.

Vira-Gambarogno TI

19☐C2

The decorated fronts of some houses were painted in 1970.
FOSANO The medieval chapel of **S.Maria di Loreto** was altered in the 18&19C. The choir has late Gothic (16C) frescos by Antonio da Tradate.

Visp/Viège VS

18☐C1

Inhabited since antiquity, Visp fell under the control of the bishop of Sion in the 12C. Over the centuries it was devastated on several occasions and the town fiercely resisted the French in 1799. The **Catholic church of the Hl. Drei Könige** (Magi), the former church of the citizens, dates back to the 11&12C and was rebuilt in 1710–30. Now baroque, it is single-aisled and has a rectangular choir, although it re-tains a fine six-storeyed Romanesque bell tower. In the choir, which stands above the crypt, there is a stuccoed high altar by G.B. Rappa (1720), the remains of baroque frescos and a late Gothic wall tabernacle. The three-aisled crypt is possibly Romanesque in origin but now dates from the 15C. The **Catholic parish church of St.Martin** of 1650–5 was totally rebuilt in 1950; only an elegant, arched portal surviving from the original church. The façade has a carved 17C doorway. The medieval town lies to the N. of the modern one and retains an interesting array of 16&17C buildings, as well as the remains of the old ramparts. Beside the citizens' church is the step-gabled **Haus Inalbon** built in the 16C for Simon Inalbon. 5, Martinsplatz is the **Haus Burgener,** which has two storeys of galleries and was built in 1699 for J.J. Burgener. The Spittelgasse contains the 16C former **hospital,** which was altered in the 18C, has a machicolated gateway. At the end of the Treichweg stands the **Lochmatterturm,** the former residence of the Meier, a square tower built in the 12&13C with later additions.

Visperterminen VS

18☐C1

In the forest above the village is the **Marienkapelle,** a pilgrimage chapel and Way of the Cross. The ten chapels which line the Way date from the 18C and house painted wooden statues from the same period. The Chapel of the Visitation was founded in 1679 and has frequently been rebuilt; inside it has a high altar of 1665, 17C altars in the chapels and numerous 17&18C ex-votos; fine painted organ of 1619.
NIEDERHÄUSERN A pretty village with a fine group of wooden houses and other buildings. 18C baroque chapel of **St. Barbara.**

Vissoie VS

17☐F2

The **Catholic parish church of Sainte-**

Euphémie, recorded as far back as the 12C, was rebuilt in 1808; bell tower of 1784. There is a 17C Crucifixion on the triumphal arch; 18&19C altars. The chapel of **Notre-Dame-de-Compassion** was built in 1668 on the site of the castle of the lords of Anniviers. which was known from the 13C onwards. The 13&14C **Tour de la Cour Neuve** is the former residence of the vassals of the bishop of Sion.

Vnà GR
See Ramosch   15☐B2

Vollèges VS
17☐C3

The **Catholic parish church of Saint-Martin,** mentioned in the 12C, rebuilt in the 17C; late Gothic bell tower with porch; baroque nave and polygonal choir; 18C side altars. Interesting 16&17C houses in the upper part of the village.

Vouvry VS
11☐B5

Saint-Hippolyte, the Catholic parish church, stands on a hill dominating the village. It is a centrally planned neoclassical church built in 1820. The bell tower and porch of the earlier, 15C church stands to the N. and a stone portal to the S. Interesting 15C stained-glass windows.Porte Du Scex A four-sided château with a square tower (founded 1597, rebuilt 1674-6), it stands beside the cantonal road and once controlled the narrow passage between the Rhône and the mountains.

Vrin GR
13☐E2

The **Catholic parish church of the St. Mariä Geburt und St.Johann** is a single-aisled baroque church dating from 1689–94 with a polygonal choir that is narrower than the nave and side chapels which form a transept; and a free-standing bell tower. It was designed by Antonio Broggio, an art-

Vufflens-le-Château: the Château, a massive 14&15C building.

ist from the Val Mesolcina. The high altar (1710) is attributed to Johann Ritz; the *ossuary* has a frieze of death's heads.

Vuarrens VD
10☐E/F1

Reformed church. Medieval, altered in the 18C, single-aisled with a massive bell tower above the choir. The façade bears carved Romanesque elements.

Vufflens-la-Ville VD
10☐E2

The **Reformed church** of Saint-Etienne was originally Romanesque but it was altered in the 15C; then, in 1777, its orientation was altered and a bell tower and porch were added. Remnants of the earlier church are visible on the walls of the nave and there are carved medieval fragments inside.

Vufflens-le-Château VD
10☐D3

Château. A fine example of brick military architecture inspired by the castles of northern Italy. It was built by Henri de Colombier, the vassal of the duke of Savoy, between 1395 and 1430. The dominant feature is a massive square keep flanked by four similar towers. The residential section is rectangular with four semicircular corner towers and faces the keep across an in-

Vuippens: former 17C Château, now a farmhouse.

ner courtyard. Machicolations run around the entire castle.

Vuippens FR

11 □ C2

The old single-aisled **Catholic church of Saint-Sulpice** has a rectangular choir and was rebuilt in the 18C and again in 1859 –62 after a fire. In the old village the former **château,** now a farm, is a massive rectangular building with mullioned windows and a rectangular staircase tower. It was built in the early 17C for the Boccard family but the tower may be from an earlier building. To the side stands the **new château,** which was built to administer the area by the canton of Fribourg. It stands on the foundations of the old castle of Vuippens, which was known from as far back as the 13C.

Vullierens VD

10 □ D2

The beautiful classical **château** which stands to the S. of the village was built for Gabriel-Henri de Mestral in 1706–12. It has a central section flanked by two lower wings, with pedimented façades. The main courtyard has a wrought-iron gate and is bounded by the outbuildings.

WY

Wädenswil ZH

8 □ B1

A vast agricultural commune on the left shore of Lake Zürich with numerous substantial houses in the centre of the village and farms around the edge (especially the Wädenswiler Berg). The **Reformed parish church** is a large, rectangular, galleried building built by Johann Ulrich Grubenmann in 1764–7. The bell tower on the broad W. front is preceded by a projecting section. The rococo stucco of the interior is by Peter Anton (I) Mosbrugger. **Haus zur Gerbe.** Neoclassical house, 1814–15. **Haus zur Hohlen Eich.** (hollow oak) A timber-framed house which contains a *local museum*. **Haus Auf Bühl,** another timber-framed house in three sections with a painted front and carved coats-of-arms (1717).
HALBINSEL AU (peninsula) The neo-baroque **Schlossgut Hintere Au** was designed by Johann Albert Freytag in 1928–9 and occupies the site of a country house built in 1651 for General Johann Rudolf Werdmüller.

Wagenhausen TG

3 □ C2

The small former **Benedictine monastery** was founded by Tuoto von Wagenhausen in 1083 and granted to the monastery of Allerheiligen, Schaffhausen. The former monastery church is now the **Reformed parish church.** Built in 1083–7, the pillared basilica lacks transepts and ends in three apses in Lombard style. The nave has a flat ceiling; the rectangular form of the main apse dates from the 16C. The N. aisle collapsed in the 17C. Along the S. front are the Romanesque cloister and chapterhouse. There is a plague sarcophagus in the cloister.

Wagenhausen: 11C former Benedictine monastery.

Wahlern: Grasburg ruin on the cliff bank of the Sense.

Wahlern BE

11 □ E1

The late Gothic **Reformed church of St. Maria Magdalena und St. Jakobus** was built in about 1511. The choir has a net vault and traceried windows. NW of Wahlern, high above the Sensetal, are the ruins of the **Grasburg.** The surviving buildings date from the 12–15C. After passing through the remains of an outwork, with a house built about 1300 to the N., the route leads to the castle courtyard, where, in the 13C there was a small core of dwellings, service buildings and a chapel. On the W. part of the summit, separated from the rest of the castle by a ditch, stands the main fortress, which held in turn by the Zaehringens, Kybourgs, Habsburgs and Savoy—a mark of its strategic importance. In 1423 it became a joint possession of the cities of Berne and Fribourg. It began to fall into ruins in 1572 (▷ Schwarzenburg).

Walchwil ZG

8□A3

The single-aisled **Catholic parish church of St.Johannes der Taufer** was built in 1836-8 on a square ground plan and is strongly influenced by the church of Arth.

Wald AR

4□B3

The **Reformed church** of 1686-7 has a balustraded gallery and an inlaid early baroque wooden pulpit dated 1686. The **Wirtshaus Harmonie** has a portal dated 1764. It is a gabled Appenzell style house but it lacks a weaver's cellar. The **Geschaftshaus Walser & Co.** was built in 1778 and has a hipped roof with gables at the sides.

Wald ZH

8□C1

The **Reformed parish church** was rebuilt by Jakob Grubenmann in 1757 using the existing choir of 1508-10 and an even older bell tower. Major alterations were made in 1784 (enlargement) and 1890 (building of a bell tower). The **Haus zur Roten Schwert** (red sword) is in the area known as BLATTENBACH. It is a former hostel for pilgrims travelling to Einsiedeln (1621).

Waldenburg BL

2□B5

The Froburgs founded this small town in the about the middle of the 13C. Protected by walls to the N. and S. it commands the narrows of the valley and lies at the foot of their citadel, which was built at the end of the 12C. The Oberes Tor (upper gate) dates from the 13C and 1593. The **Reformed parish church** is a former granary which was converted in 1833-42. The late Gothic **presbytery** was a noble's house prior to 1573.

Waldenburg: ruin of the Froburg fortress, burned down in 1798.

Waldkirch SG

3□F4

The **Catholic parish church of St. Blasius** has a late medieval choir and a nave that was rebuilt in 1720-2 by Hans Caspar Glattburger and Johannes Pfister. The interior by Johann Ferdinand Beer dates from 1783; extended W. and restored in 1942. The **Restaurant Kreuz** is a timber-framed house built in 1688 by B.Burgstaller.

BERNHARDZELL E. of Waldkirch, the **Catholic church of St.Johannes Baptist** (1776-8) was designed by Johann Ferdinand Beer and is one of the few pure, cruciform, centrally planned churches in Switzerland. The cupola has a Mansard roof. The bell tower is from the previous church. The paintings on the ceiling (1778) are by Franz Ludwig Herrmann, the stucco by Peter Anton Mosbrugger, the high altar by Franz Anton Dirr.

Waldstatt AR

3□F5

Waldstatt developed around the church, along two stretches of the cantonal road. The **Reformed church** was built in 1720-1. The height of the bell tower was increased and the nave rebuilt to its original design in 1874 by Sebastian Sturzenegger; it was extended to the W. in 1934-5 by Ulrich Watt. **Bürgerhaus,** No. 192 of 1793; remains of a small building from 1521 in the cellar. Louis XVI portal; wooden panels on the façade dating from

Walenstadt: St. Georg chapel at Berschis, high above the valley.

Waltalingen: Schloss Girsberg with medieval tower in Guntalingen.

1830. A room with the original furniture. **Bauernhaus Unterwaldstatt,** No.333, dated 1601, shows the transition from the older type of farmhouse roof with two slopes at a shallow angle to the later form; a gable with two steeper slopes.

Walenstadt SG

8☐F2

The **Catholic parish church of St. Lucius und Florinus** lies outside the old walls of the town. Nave and transept probably late medieval; choir largely rebuilt in 1881–2. Rubble carried down by the Seez delta extends right up to the round portal of the Romanesque bell tower (*c.* 1200). The chapel of **St.Wolfgang,** rebuilt 1741, consecrated 1753; high altar of 1745 with a Gothic Pietà from the first half of the 15C. The **Grosse Haus** extends from the Gässli to the old fosse which surrounds the town. The W. part is early 16C, the E. end 1633. Opposite is the **Zugen-bühlerhaus,** 17C. The **Merklihaus,** in the lower town, is by the old gate; the ground floor corridor has a Gothic stone doorway dated 1534. The **Of-fizierscasino,** a neoclassical house built in about 1830–40.
TSCHERLACH SE of Walenstadt, the chapel of **St.Johannes Evangelist,** built in 1641 as a dependency of the church of Flums; Coronation of the Virgin from the same period on the high altar.
BERSCHIS The chapel of **St.Georg** stands on a rocky ridge facing Grpplang. The oldest chapel in the region, it was part of a fortified church from the high Middle Ages, deriving in turn from a fortified late

Roman settlement. The S. section and the apse are probably from the 1st millennium. The twin aisles and the vaulting are 11&12C. **Refuge** on the Raischiben, prehistoric.

Wallbach AG

2☐B3

4C **Roman observation tower** at Stelli, N. of the village.

Wallenried FR

6☐C5

The vast 18&19C **château,** formerly owned by the Castella family, lies below the high road.

Walperswil BE

6☐D3

The **church of St.Andreas** contains a carved, inlaid baroque pulpit (1707). The two-storeyed priest's house is 16&17C and has a staircase tower and wooden galleries.

Waltalingen ZH

3☐C2

The small 13C Reformed chapel of **St. Antonius** was altered in the 14&16C. Inside there are numerous late Gothic frescos (15C). **Schloss Schwandegg** has a 13C tower and a 17C residence; The hall has fragments of grisaille paintings.

Waltensburg: martyrdom of St.Sebastian, c. 1350, in the Reformed church.

Wangen a. A: 16C covered wooden bridge.

GUNTALINGEN The feudal Schloss Girsberg was rebuilt after a fire in 1756–9; fine rococo decoration inside with stucco and also several stoven.

Waltensburg/Vuorz GR

13 ☐ E1

The single-aisled **Reformed church,** built in about 1100, late Gothic alterations, has a narrow square choir. *Wall paintings* from three periods: those in the nave are by the Waltensburg master, a representative of the courtly early Gothic who worked mainly in the territories of the Barons of Vaz, Rhäzüns and Belmont. The painted area is divided into four horizontal bands, the outer ones depicting tapestry motifs typical of the artist, the inner ones being reserved for figurative scenes. On the N. wall there is a Passion cycle, which must be viewed from left to right above and from right to left below. Then, higher up, come St. Luke and St. Florinus, together with other saints; the cycle continuing on the E. wall with St.Sebastian; the martyrdom of St.Sebastian below and episodes from the life of St.Nicholas. In the other corner of the triumphal arch there are the Apostles John and Thomas, above, and Conrad and Ambrose below. The choir was painted in about 1450 in the International Gothic style. Outside, on the W. wall, there is a cycle devoted to St.Margaret from the 2nd half of the 14C. E. of the village is the ruined **Jörgenberg castle,** which began as a fortified church in the early Middle Ages and became the largest castle in the Oberland. Below the road to Brigels is the

three-storeyed ruined 12C castle of **Kropfenstein,** which is cut into the rock.

Walzenhausen AR

4 ☐ B3

Reformed church, 1638. **Capuchin monastery of St.Ottilia** at Grimmenstein, mentioned in 1378 as a Beguine house, on the present site from 1424 onwards; church and monastery rebuilt 1724. Early baroque (1668) altars in the church; treasury with baroque items; stucco from 1724 in the monastery.

Wangen an der Aare BE

7 ☐ A1

The medieval **heart** of the town is laid out on an almost square plan, with the corners being occupied by the castle, the bridge gate, the chancellery and the clock tower, the tower and the priest's house. The church originally stood outside the town in the locality of Pfrundmatte. Because of its bridge, Wangen was an important stage on the Basel-Bern road. The present wooden **covered bridge** was largely built in 1552 but two earlier bridges crossed the Aare at the same point. It has five spans but in 1967 the wooden piers were replaced by concrete ones clad in wood. The **Reformed church of the Hl. Kreuz und St. Maria** was rebuilt in 1825, although the Gothic choir with its wall paintings was retained. The frescos on the E. wall depict St. Christopher, the lives of St. George and St. Ulrich with the angel

Wartau: impressive ruined Burg on a dominant hill site.

Wattwil: 17&18C Capuchin convent of Maria.

(third quarter of the 14C. The S. wall has an Annunciation of about 1470–80. The **priest's house,** a former Benedictine priory, is a fortified corner building with a hipped roof. The medieval **castle** was completely transformed under Landvogt Beat Fischer from 1680 onwards, although the Landvogt Im Hof had already built a large staircase tower in 1632. The baroque paintings on the ceiling of the second floor are from the workshop of Joseph Werner. The parish hall houses a modest *local history collection.*

Wängi TG
8□D3

The **Catholic church** built by Fritz Metzger in 1957–8 has mosaics and stained glass by Johann Jakob Zemp and sculptures by Kurt Brunner. The chapel has a window by Heinrich Stäubli.

Wangs SG
See VILTERS
9□A2

Wartau SG
9□A/B2

The ruined castle of **Wartau** was mentioned in 1261 as the home of the lords of Wildenberg; the five-storeyed keep and the four-storeyed residence survive. On the N. side there is a raised gateway. The late Gothic Reformed church of Gretschins was rebuilt in 1493 by Stoffel Wetzel, bell tower with a steeply sloping roof above the doorway S. of the choir.

AZMOOS The neo-Gothic **parish church**

was built in 1891–2 by August Hardegger. The neoclassical **Rathaus** (since 1918), with its pilastered façade, was built as a house for the Sulser brothers in 1802–4.

Wartensee LU
See NEUENKIRCH
7□E3

Wasen VS
See BITSCH
12□C5

Wassen UR
13□B2

Standing on the summit of a steep hill, the **Catholic church of St. Gallus** forms a landmark for anyone taking the train up the Gothard and in fact it can be viewed from three different angles as the tunnel twists round the mountainside. Built 1734 – 5, the church has richly inlaid wooden altars by the Upper Valais cabinet-maker Jodok Ritz. In the Meien valley there are the remains of the **Meienschanze,** a fortress completed in 1712 by Pietro Morettini, a follower of Vauban, the well known French military architect. He was also responsible for planning the 'Urner Loch' (the hole of Uri) in the Schöllenen gorge, the first road tunnel in the Alps (1707–8).

Wattwil SG
8□E1

The **Reformed church** was rebuilt by Wilhelm Kubly in 1845–8; subsequently restored and refaced inside in 1969. It is a late neoclassical building with a nave that

Weinfelden: early baroque Gasthaus zum Trauben with fountain (1931) in front of it.

is broader than it is long, with a pedimented, projecting façade and three porticoed entrances. The bell tower rises above the choir. The walled Capuchin monastery of **Maria der Engel** is almost fortress-like. Its church was built by Father Joseph Metzler and was consecrated in 1622. The nave for the faithful and the new vault of the choir date from 1780, the porch from 1893; most of the convent buildings from 1730–82. The timber framed **Haus Merkur** (21 Ringstrasse) has a masonry ground floor and gabled sides. The 17C timber framed **Haus Mohren** (No. 71) at Bunt was altered at the end of the 19C and has baroque wall paintings on the second floor. The **old people's home** (No. 77), a former factory built by Andreas Hartmann in 1893, with Biedermeier style alterations being made to the roof in 1827. Note the doorway. No. 1247 Scheftenau is a gabled house on a masonry base. **Burg Iberg** was built by Heinrich von Iberg in about 1240 and rebuilt after the damage it suffered in the Appenzell war (1405). The living quarters were demolished in 1835, the roof and parapet walk are new.

Weesen SG

8☐E2

The 13C **Catholic church of the Heiligkreuz** on the Bühl, to the W., has late Gothic alterations and ones from 1630 – 40, a rectangular nave, a narrow choir, a W. bell tower and a polygonal wooden ceiling. The Catholic parish church of **St. Martin** at Autis, E. of Weesen, was rebuilt in *c.* 1500 and in 1823–4 the nave was again rebuilt and the choir altered. The buildings of the **Dominican convent of Maria Zuflucht,** founded *c.* 1260, rebuilt *c.* 1690, form a square and the church faces W. Together with the church of the Heiligkreuz and the late Gothic **'Schlössli'**, the gabled, late Gothic former **Kaplanei** (chaplaincy) SE of the Bühlterrasse, forms a splendid, homogenous group of buildings.

Wegenstetten AG

2☐C4

The mid-18C **Catholic parish church of St.Michael** with its rococo decoration was built by Giovanni Gaspare Bagnato; late Gothic bell tower (1487).

Weggis LU

7☐F3

The **chapel of Allerheiligen,** built 1623, has a porch and bell turret; late Renaissance frescos inside. Hôtel du Lac, neoclassical, 1838.

Weinfelden TG

3☐E3

Weinfelden played an important part in the liberation of Thurgau in 1798 and in the Constitutional movement in 1830-1. The centrally planned cruciform **Reformed church,** with its bell tower above the crossing, was built by Otto Pfleghard and Max Haefeli in 1902-3 and successfully blends the neo-Romanesque with art nouveau. In the centre of the village, the early baroque **Gasthaus zum Trauben** (1649) has figured prominently in the canton's history and in 1798 it was from its steps that Thurgau's independence was proclaimed to the popular assembly. The neoclassical **Hafterhaus,** opposite, is by Rudolf Hoffmann (1836-8). E. of the Reformed church, the **Scherbenhof,** called after its owner, Jakob Scherb, since 1630. The main building was burned down in 1889. It is half timbered, with a turret, galleries and a portico, altered in 1823–5. It was here that the earliest legal manuscript in Old German, the 'Schwabenspiegel' of 1287, was discovered. To the N., on the Ottenberg, stands the **Schloss** which was the seat of the Kyburg's Weinfelden representatives in 1180. 12C keep with battlements from 1870; the living quarters were rebuilt in 1860, the chapel is late Gothic. The 16C **Landhaus Bachtobel,** also on the Ottenberg, has mansard roofs and Biedermeier additions from *c.* 1820. The service buildings contain shafts from presses over 30 ft. in length (1584 and 1729).

Werthenstein: chapels and cloister in the former Franciscan monastery.

Weissenbach BE
11 □ E3

The **Haus Seewer** (1705) is an early example of carved wood decoration.

Weisslingen ZH
3 □ B4

Wettingen: former monastery church with lavish 17&18C interior.

The late Gothic **Reformed parish church** has a carved wooden ceiling (1509) by Peter Kälin. 14C bell tower.

Wellnau LU
See Triengen   7 □ D1

Wenslingen BL
2 □ C4

The village square is one of the finest in the Oberbaselbiet.

Wermatswil ZH
See Uster   7 □ D3

Werthenstein LU
7 □ D3

Standing on a crag above the Emme are the pilgrimage church of **Unserer Lieben Frau** and the former **Franciscan monastery.** The post Gothic church was built

in 1608–13 by Anton Isenmann, who was responsible for the Hôtel de Ville in Lucerne. On the other hand the additions of 1621 display Gothic, Renaissance and baroque features. These chapels, which were named after the founders—the Pfyffer family — contain carved and painted altars in the German late Renaissance style. The cloister of the monastery founded in 1630 displays the southern tendencies of Lucerne architecture in its Tuscan arches. At the foot of the hill there is a covered **wooden bridge** dating from 1710.

Wettingen AG
2 □ E/F4

The former **Cistercian abbey** was founded in 1227, suppressed in 1841 during the Kulturkampf, and then used as a school from 1847 onwards and a cantonal school from 1976. The *church* was originally an early Gothic basilica with a nave and two aisles, a transept and a rectangular choir. The decoration is the work of south German rococo masters (*c.* 1750), although the choir stalls are late Renaissance and have wood carvings by Hans Jakob. The cloister, which forms part of the *abbey buildings,* has been altered in late Gothic style and has a considerable amount of stained glass (late Romanesque to the baroque). The abbot's house has sumptuous late Renaissance decoration.

Wetzikon ZH
3☐C5

Dating from the high Middle Ages, the **schloss** was originally moated and had two towers. The W. tower was adapted as living quarters in 1614–17 and the E. one was destroyed in 1832.

Wichel VS
See FIESCH   12☐D5

Widnau SG
4☐B3

The neo-baroque **Catholic parish church of St.Joseph** was built in 1903 by Albert Rimli, with a ceiling painted by Siegfried Herforth in 1939.

Wiedlisbach BE
7☐A1

Founded by the counts of Froburg in *c.* 1240, the small town, with its rectangular layout, developed around a square, as in Aarberg. However, this was later built up and ther are now two streets of houses where the square used to be. In the 'Hinterstädtli' a **corner tower** still stands from the fortifications. The **Katharinenkapelle,** founded in 1338, is decorated with late Gothic scenes from the lives of St.Catherine and St.Dorothea, the Passion and the Martyrdom of the Ten Thousand. The **granary** houses a *regional museum.*

Wiesendangen: wall paintings in the choir of the Reformed church, c. 1480.

Wienacht-Tobel AR
4☐B3

The **Catholic chapel of Hl. Bruder Klaus** was built by T.Niess in 1963.

Wiesen GR
14☐C1

The single-aisled **Reformed parish church,** built 1490–9, has a narrow, polygonal choir and a flat, late Gothic ceiling with painted friezes and mouldings. The choir has a net vault.

Wiesenberg NW
7☐F4

The **pilgrimage church of St.Maria** was built in 1754 on the site of a 14C hermitage. Rococo stucco inside.

Wiesendangen ZH
3☐C3

The late Gothic **Reformed parish church** was built in 1480 on the site of a much earlier church. In the choir there is a major collection of wall paintings (21 panels) attributed to Hans Haggenberg. Restored in 1967, a section of the paintings has been severely damaged. The **schloss,** which was once moated, dates back to the 12C and was restored in 1965–7, having ceased to be a feudal castle by the 15C.

Wil: small medieval town with remarkable buildings.

Wigoltingen TG

3 □ D3

The **Reformed church** has a Romanesque nave and a 14&15C bell tower; a stellar-vaulted choir and a sacristy and N. aisle of 1504.

Wikon LU

7 □ C1

The keep of what was once the **castle** of Wikon, on the Marienberg, is today surrounded by the new buildings (1965–7) of a girl's school.

Wil SG

3 □ D4

Founded in the second half of the 12C by the Toggenburgs, the town passed to the abbey of St.Gallen following the family's fratricidal strife in 1226. Since 1831 it has been the main town of the district.

The **old town** of narrow, sloping streets stands on a hill in the middle of a valley. It comprises an inner ring of houses bet-

ween the Marktgasse, the N. part of which is lined by picturesque arcades, and the Kirchgasse, and an outer oval of buildings which give it the air of a fortress. Although, with the exception of the NW Schnetztor, the actual walls and gates were demolished in 1835. Mentioned in 1333, the **Catholic parish church of St.Nikolaus** has a choir that was rebuilt in 1429 and a nave in 1478. The interior underwent neo-Gothic alterations in 1866 and then in 1933–4 Erwin Schenker and Paul Truniger again altered the interior, extended the late Gothic church, with its nave, two aisles and narrow, polygonal choir, to the W. and built a new bell tower. On high ground N. of the town stands the **Hof,** a late-12C castle that was rebuilt in the 15&16C, with a massive hipped roof. Although the garden room has late Gothic wall paintings by Hans Haggenberg (1479), the interiors of the castle are mostly 17&18C. The Hof, which contains a local museum, is connected to the town gate by the late-15C **Haus zum Toggenburg,** which was originally the residence of the governor of the abbey. The **Gerichthaus** (86 Marktgasse) has three arches borne by round pillars. Built in 1795, the four-storeyed **Baronenhaus,** with its hipped roof, turrets and arcaded

Marktplatz front, is the most important neoclassical residence in the canton of St. Gallen. The E. side has a rusticated terrace with pillars. SE of the town, the Dominican convent of **St.Katharina** was built in 1605-7 under the direction of father Jodokus Metzler. The church has three Régence altars. E. of Wil there is a Capuchin monastery that was built in 1654-6 and enlarged and modernized in the 20C. The **Rudenzburg** (35 Toggenburgerstrasse) was built in 1774 by the Reichsvogt Josef Pankraz Grüebler. It has a hall with rococo polychrome stucco by Peter Anton Mosbrugger.

Wila ZH

3☐C4

The 13C **Reformed parish church** was enlarged in the 15C and in 1612. Gothic wall paintings, including some by Hans Haggenberg, were covered over in 1903.

Wilchingen SH

2☐F2

Wilchingen, a Klettgau wine growing village, has altered little in appearance and one of its features are the covered, partly vaulted passages which run between the houses, connecting the alleyways. The **Reformed parish church** has a timber ceiling and panelled walls. Heinrich Peyer's new church (1676) stands on a hill that was once fortified and replaces an earlier church, only the bell tower of which survives. The **presbytery** is part of these old defences. The oldest parts are 16C; with alterations made in 1780-2.

Wildegg AG

See **MÖRIKEN-WILDEGG**   2☐D4

Wilderswil BE

12☐B2

The baroque single aisled **Reformed church of St.Michael** was built in 1659 but retains Gothic sections from the earlier church. A covered **wooden bridge** spans

the Lütschine and has a double trapezoidal frame (1738). To the N. of the town is the ruined medieval castle of **Unspunnen,** which now comprises a round keep, an upper and lower residence and a courtyard. The meadow at the foot of the castle was the setting of the famous Hirtenfeste in 1805 and 1808; rural festivals organized by Niklaus Friedrich von Mülinen, president of the Cantonal Council.

Wildhaus SG

8☐F1

Built by Johann Ferdinand Beer, the baroque **Catholic parish church of St. Bartholomäus** has a bell tower rising above the choir and ceiling paintings by Jakob Josef Müller (1776). The **Zwinglihaus,** one of Switzerland's oldest wooden houses, was the birthplace of the reformer Huldrych Zwingli (1484-1531). It has a gable, a shallow sloping roof and the late Gothic ceiling has round beams.

Wilen OW

7☐E5

The **chapel of St.Michael** was built in 1700-2. The Gothic doorway which leads from the choir to the sacristy (two floors) survives from an older, 16C building.

Willern VS

See **BINN**   12☐D5

Willisau LU

7☐C2

Founded in the 13C, the town was destroyed by fire on four occasions, assuming its present form after the last one, in 1704. Parts of the medieval fortifications survive, including sections of the wall and, at the W. end of the Hauptgasse, the **Obertor** (upper gate, 1551); the Untertor has been rebuilt. The neoclassical **Catholic parish church of St.Peter und Paul** was rebuilt in 1804-10 by Josef Purtschert and the Romanesque bell tower above the façade is crowned by a baroque dome. A

Wildhaus: 15C birthplace of the reformer Huldrych Zwingli.

Willisau: Catholic parish church, a neoclassical building by J.Purtschert.

Wimmis: early Romanesque church with the impressive Schloss above it.

massive, two-storeyed bell tower was built above the choir in 1928-9. The early baroque pilgrimage chapel of the **Heiligblut** (1674-5) stands in front of the Obertor. Like the chapel at Herigswald, it has scenes from the Bible painted on its wooden ceiling. The former **Landvogteischloss** was built in 1690-5 on the site of the Hasenburg, the castle of the family said to have founded the town. The **Altes Kaufhaus** (old shop) in the Hauptgasse is a baroque building of c. 1720 with an archaic stepped gable.

Wimmis BE

12□A2

In the upper part of the village there is a group of Bernese Oberland style houses from the late 17C. The 10&11C early Romanesque **Martinskirche** is one of the Lake Thun churches (▷ Amsoldingen) and has three aisles, each ending in an apse. Inside, there are mid-15C wall paintings. The **schloss,** probably founded c. 1100 by the barons of Weissenburg, took on its present form when altered in the 17C.

Windisch AG

2□E4

Reformed parish church replaced an early Christian bishop's church in about 1300. The walls and ceiling of the choir, built c. 1400, bear late Gothic frescos. **Abbey of Königsfelden.** In 1311 Elisabeth, the widow of Albrecht I (who was assassinated by his nephew Johann von Schwaben at Windisch) founded a convent of the Poor Clares and a Franciscan monastery. The abbey passed to Bern in 1415 and was secularized in 1528, following the Reformation. It became a residence of the Landvogts and then, in 1804, a mental hospital. Much of the original structure was demolished in 1868 – 71 when enlargements were being made, however, the late medieval **abbey church,** has survived and has a famous choir with 11 high Gothic **windows** (1325-30). Both in form and content, this array of glass is an expression of the Franciscan spiritual universe. A crypt beneath the E. end of the nave houses the tombs of 11 Habsburgs. The

Windisch: stained glass (Wailing over the Body of Christ) in the Königsfelden monastery church.

Winkel: part of the Roman farm excavated in Seeb.

Roman military camp and the **colony of Vindonissa.** In *c.* AD 17 the Romans built a camp to the W. of a Helvetian village which was to continue in use until *c.* 400, its importance fluctuating with the changes in Imperial policy towards the Germans. A civil colony grew up to the E. of the camp and from the 6C Vindonissa was a bishop's seat. Since 1896 systematic digs have been carried out and the finds

are now in the *Vindonissa-Museum,* Brugg. On the site itself, there are sections of the wall, with the remains of a gate near the abbey of Königsfelden, and the remains of the largest Roman **amphitheatre** in Switzerland.

Wingreis BE
6 ☐ D3

The **Thormanngut** is a 16C country house which was enlarged in the 17&18C. On the first floor the row of windows rises in a series of steps.

Winikon LU
7 ☐ C/D1

The church of Mariä Himmelfahrt was built in 1699–1702 and decorated in rococo style. The varied choir stalls were probably once in the choir of the abbey of St.Urban.

Winkel ZH
3 ☐ A4

The 1&2C AD **Roman villa of Seeb** covers some 690 x 1310 ft. Excavations (1958–70) have uncovered the foundations of a villa, two houses, a farm, a workshop, a well house and four other buildings.

Wintersingen BL
2 ☐ B4

The **Reformed parish church,** which was rebuilt by Daniel Hartmann in 1676, stands on high ground, S. of this straggling, wine growing village. The **presbytery** (1662) is at the entrance to the village.

Winterthur ZH
3 ☐ B3

The site of the Gallo-Roman colony of Vitudurum, which includes a Roman fort first mentioned in AD 280, is occupied by the village of Oberwinterthur, which has been part of the city of Winterthur since

The Stadthaus (1865–9) is an important historicist building.

Winterthur: shopping arcade on the ground floor of the Rathaus.

1922. The city proper lies a mile or two SW and was founded by the Kyburgs in 1170. From 1180 onwards it was held by the Oberwinterthur church and in 1467 the Habsburgs pledged what was by then a market town to Zurich, which lies some 15 miles away. Its subsequent history has been one of continuous competition, sometimes hard pressed, with its more powerful neighbour, Zurich, which jealously guarded its privileges. It was this rivalry that was the catalyst for Winterthur's astonishing industrialization during the 19C, following the removal of protectionist barriers and national unity. This economic growth was matched in the cultural sphere, as can be seen from the numerous impressive buildings and by the private patronage of music and the plastic arts—patronage which established Winterthur as the cultural centre its still is. The original heart of the city is the quarter around the cathedral (formerly the church of St.Laurentius) and the extremely long, but rather narrow, Marktgasse. By the 13C the outer quarters to the E. and W., around the present Obertorgasse and Untertorgasse, were part of the fortified city. The town fortifications were destroyed in the last century and only the much altered round tower in the Technikumstrasse, which flanks the old S. wall, survives. The walls have been replaced by a circular boulevard, lined by public buildings and parks, ringing the old town, which retains its compact character. In 1922 Oberwinterthur, Töss, Steen, Veltheim and Wülflingen were incorporated in Winterthur,

although they still retain something of their village like atmosphere.

OLD CITY The **Reformed town church.** A chapel of St.Laurentius existed in the 11C but the present church, a basilica with two bell towers, a nave and two aisles, no transept and a square choir, dates from various periods. The nave was rebuilt in 1501-18, the choir post-dates a town fire in 1313, the N. bell tower is 14C and the S. one dates from 1486-90, with a baroque upper section by Hans Conrad Frey (1659). In 1853 – 6 Ferdinand Stadler altered the church in neo-Gothic style and Paul Zehnder's wall paintings, which are of uncertain artistic worth, are the product of the 1923 – 30 renovation. The neoclassical **Rathaus** was built by Johann Ulrich Büchel in 1782-4 and the council chamber has a stuccoed ceiling by Lorenz Schmid. Josef Bösch altered the building in 1872-4, most notably by adding a shopping arcade running between the Marktgasse and the Stadthausgasse. The Moorish-Gothic **Waaghaus,** built in 1503, has four large ogee arches and now, after a thorough restoration, serves as a local library and exhibition centre. The early neoclassical former Oberes Spital or Altes Stadthaus has a panelled passageway and hall built by Diethelm Schneider in 1790. The former **Unteres Spital,** a large neoclassical building (1806 – 14) by Salomon Sulzer the younger, is now an old people's home. The **Haus zur Geduld** is a substantial house with an early baroque façade and a baroque stuccoed ceiling with joists. It is in fact composed of two houses, one on the Marktgasse (1690) and one on the Stadthausstrasse (1717). In 1921–2 it

Haus zur Pflanzschule, an early neoclassical country house with mansard roof.

'The Pissevache Falls', 1815, by J.J.Biedermann, in the Kunstmuseum.

was turned into a private club with a restaurant. The **Haus zum Adler,** an elegant baroque house (1763-4) near the Obertor, is now the police station. The former **barracks** is an imposing timber and masonry building by Salomon Sulzer the elder (1765); baroque portal. The **Haus zum Hinteren Waldhorn** was the house of the painter Hans Haggenberg, who came from Winterthur, and he decorated every floor with sgraffiti (1490-4), which survive in part. The late neoclassical **Gewerbemuseum** (arts and crafts) in the Kirchplatz was built by Ferdinand Stadler in 1849-52. There are numerous fine fountains, including the Justitia- and Florabrunnen.

OUTER AREAS The **Stadthaus** (1865-9, extended 1932-4) is one of Gottfried Semper's major works and his extensive use of Greek motifs is an example of the historical style. The S. façade is in the form of a Corinthian temple and is approached by a monumental staircase. The galleried great hall is three storeys high and is used for concerts. The **Stadthausbrunnen** before the S. façade was inspired by the fountains of Rome. The **Stiftung Oskar Reinhart,** built by Leonhard Zeugheer in 1838-42 as an industrial school, has a neoclassical façade with statues of Zwingli and Pestalozzi (Johann Ludwig Keiser), Conrad Gessner and Johann Georg Sulzer (Johann Jakob Oechslin). Much altered in 1941-50, the building houses an important collection of works by Swiss and German artists. The **Kunstmuseum** and **Stadtbibliothek** is a neoclassical building

(1912-16) by Robert Rittmeyer and Walter Furrer. The **Haus zum Balustergarten** (or Barockhüsli), a late baroque pleasure house (*c.* 1740) with painted panelling, stands in the town park. The new **Theater am Stadtgarten** by Frank Krayenbühl was opened in 1979. The **Bezirksgebäude** (administrative building) is a neo-Renaissance building (1876-9) by Ernest Jung, with a further storey being added in 1925. The **Heimatmuseum im Lindengut** is a neoclassical house (1787, probably by Franz Ignaz Krohmer) with splendid wall paintings (Christoph Kuhn, Johann Rudolf Schellenberg, Caspar Kuster) and baroque stoves of the Winterthur school (Pfau, Erhart, Graf). The **Haus zum Pflanzschule** is a neoclassical country house (1771-2) with a main façade of dressed brick. Built in 1853 and enlarged twice, the **Villa Flora** houses the private Hahnloser art collection (not open). Theodor Gohl built the neo-Renaissance **Technikum (HTL)** in 1874-5. Since 1970 the *Oskar Reinhart Collection* (masterpieces of European art given to the Confederation in 1958) has been open to the public in **Villa am Römerholz.**

OBERWINTERTHUR The 12C **Reformed parish church** is a pillared Romanesque basilica which stands on the site of an early medieval church in the area of the camp of Vitudurum. The walls of the nave are adorned with splendid early Gothic frescos: the life of Christ, the life of St. Arbogast, the church's patron, images of other saints and a Virgin of the Cloak. The

Winterthur, Schloss Hegi, a medieval castle.

Winterthur: Schloss Wülfingen, a 17C building with step gable.

church was carefully restored in the 1970s. The **Hollandhaus,** the oldest parts of which are 12C, and the **presbytery,** a half-timbered house, c. 1750, stand in the centre of the village. **Schloss Hegi** is a moated castle with a 12C tower, and 15C living quarters and service buildings. It contains a *historical museum* and a youth hostel. **Schloss Mörsburg** retains an old keep which may date from the early Middle Ages, although this is not certain. The stuccoed chapel is early Gothic and the castle itself houses the *collection of the historical and archaeological society.*
VELTHEIM The oldest section of the present **Reformed parish church** dates from 1358 (nave); the choir from 1482 and the bell tower from 1498. The choir vault has frescos by Hans Haggenberg (c. 1482). WüLFLINGEN **Schloss Wülflingen** (1644 –5), the early baroque seat of a lord of the manor, has splendid interior decoration. baroque 'Herrenstube' with carved panels and a coffered ceiling; other rooms have rococo paintings by Christoph Kuhn; panels painted by Kuhn, Salomon Landolt, Heinrich Freudweiler and others. The

Rosenzimmer has grisaille paintings, probably by Hans Conrad Kuster (1763). There are some splendid stoves from Winterthur and Zurich workshops. Only the tower of the ruined castle of **Alt-Wülflingen** survives; it occupies the site of a Celtic refuge. Dissolved in 1525, all that remains of the ruined convent of **Mariazell** on the Beerenberg, a centre of medieval mysticism, are the foundations. The large, three winged **hospital** was built in 1818–24 as a spinning mill. There is a pedestrian walkway over the Töss by Robert Maillart and Walter Pfeiffer (1934).
Museums and Collections. *Kunstmuseum* (25 Museumstr.): an important art collection, 16–20C. The *Oskar Reinhart Collection 'am Römerholz',* see text. *Stiftung Oskar Reinhart* (6 Stadthausstrasse): Romantic and Realist paintings, as well as ones from other 18–20C movements. *Uhrensammlung Kellenberger* (clocks, Rathaus). *Museum Lindengut* (8 Römerstr.): local arts. *Technorama der Schweiz,* opened in 1982, devoted to the history of technology.

Wislikofen AG
2☐F3

The **former priory and parish church of St. Oswald** comprises an impressive group of buildings; and the church (façade probably to plans by Giovanni Gaspare Bagnato, c. 1730), priory and priest's house date from about 1690 in their present form. During the 1970s the buildings were restored and now house a Catholic meeting place and an adult training centre.

Wittenbach SG
4☐A3

The baroque, single-aisled **Catholic parish church of St. Ulrich** was built in 1675 by Daniel Glattburger to plans by father Maurus Heidelberger, and extended in 1724 and 1812. The rectangular choir is narrower than the nave and a bell tower stands at one end. The ceiling was painted in 1812 by Josef Keller. The long, groin-vaulted chapel of **St. Johannes Nepomuk** was built in 1758 by Johann Pfister. E. of the church, **Schloss Egg** was originally a farm belonging to the abbey of St.Gallen; rebuilt 1624, altered several times.

Wittnau AG

2 □ C4

There are Bronze Age and Hallstatt **fortifications** on the Wittnauerhorn, together with a late Roman wall. The ruined 11C castle of **Homberg,** the seat of the counts of Homberg, was destroyed by an earthquake in 1356.

Wohlen AG

2 □ E5

The neoclassical **Catholic parish church of St.Leonhard** was built in the form of a temple by Niklaus Purtschert (1804–7).

Wohlen BE

6 □ E4

The **Reformed church of St.Eusebius** at Unterwohlen was built in 1678 by Abraham I Dünz; Romanesque elements, Gothic bell tower, open bell chamber.

Wolfenschiessen NW

7 □ F5

The **Catholic parish church of St. Martin** was built in 1775–7 by Johann Anton Singer and its layout is of the so-called Singer-Purtschert type, which is common in the Lucerne area (▷ Ruswil). Nearby is the cell of brother Konrad Scheuber, who moved here in 1867. Dörfli, to the S., has a 13C **tower** occupied by a lord of Wolfenschiessen and a chapel of **St. Sebastian und Rochus** (1620), dedicated to two plague saints, and with a massive bell tower beside the entrance. In the Aa valley there are several large houses, including the **Höchhus** built in 1586 for the fourth wife of the knight Melchior Lussy. It is a perfect example of a 16C lord's house

Wolfenschiessen: 1586 Höchhus with ridge turret.

from central Switzerland, combining, for the first time, a steep roof with a tall gable and a room for entertaining in the attic storey (access on request). Further S., on the slope overlooking the valley, is the mountain village of Altsellen, with the 15&17C chapel of **St.Joder.**

Wolfhalden AR

4 □ B3

The **Reformed church** of 1652 has a bell tower by its façade with a steeply sloping roof. Neoclassical galleries. 18C **Haus zur Blume.**

Wolfwil SO

7 □ B1

The single-aisled Catholic parish church of **Maria Himmelfahrt** dates from 1616 but has an earlier, post-Gothic choir. The priest's house also displays Gothic features (windows). Built by Paolo Antonio Pisani in *c.* 1780 **Gasthaus zum Kreuz** was once a private residence; French garden.

Wolhusen LU

7 □ D3

The neo-Romanesque **Catholic parish church of St. Andreas** is by Wilhelm

Keller. Dance of Death in the **ossuary** (1661); the skulls are real.

Wollerau SZ
8☐B2

The **Catholic parish church of St. Verena** was rebuilt in 1781-7 by Niklaus Purtschert. The interior, with the linking of the choir and nave, is typical of his style (▷ Ruswil). **Weisses Haus,** a late-16C stone house with a step gable.

Worb BE
6☐F4

The late Gothic Reformed church of **St.Mauritius** was built in 1500 and has Renaissance windows decorated with figures and coats-of-arms. Mentioned in 1130, the barons of Worb were the first owners of the **schloss,** which then passed to the lords of Kien and then to the Diesbach and von Graffenried families. It was completely rebuilt in 1535 following a fire, the oldest surviving parts being in the residence. The 17C baroque living apartments house a *collection of peasant glassware,* whilst the rooms of the piano nobile are decorated with painted linen hangings. **Schloss Neu-Worb,** baroque, built after 1743 for the Graffenried family.

Wuppenau TG
3☐E3

The neo-Gothic **Catholic church of St. Martin** was built in 1890-7 by August Hardegger; altered in 1967-8 by Hermann Schmidt.

Würenlos AG
2☐F4

Benedictine convent of Fahr. Now baroque in appearance, the convent has long been connected with the abbey of Einsiedeln, and since the Act of Mediation of 1803 it has been situated in an Aargau enclave within Zurich territory, *c.* 7 km.

Würenlos: frescos on the N. façade of the Fahr monastery church.

from Würenlos. The *convent church,* in its present form, dates from 1743-6, the bell tower from 1689. The interior is richly painted, for the most part by the Ticino artists Giuseppe and Gian Antonio Torricelli, with other works by Franz Anton Rebsamen. The *covent buildings* are by Caspar and Johann Mosbrugger (1689-1701) and Paul Rey (1730-4).

Wurmsbach SG
See JONA
8☐C1

Würzbrunnen BE
See RÖTHENBACH I.E.
7☐B5

Wynau BE
7☐B1

The **Reformed church of St.Mauritius** is a pillared basilica with a nave and two aisles standing on the site of an early medieval sanctuary. The pointed triumphal arch separates the Romanesque nave from the Gothic choir. Frescos of *c.* 1400.

Wynigen BE
7☐A3

The core of the **Reformed church** is medieval but it was altered by Abraham Dünz in 1671. It still has a Romanesque bell tower and a late Gothic ceiling with beams. Baroque grisaille paintings. The **presbytery** (1630) has late Gothic painted windows.

BRECHERSHÄUSERN A hamlet of wooden

Yverdon: 13C Château on the 'carré savoyard' pattern, keep on the left.

Yverdon: 1779 Villa d'Entremonts, country house in a park.

farmhouses with hipped and half-hipped roofs (17&18C).

Yverdon VD

5☐E/F5

Eburodunum, a settlement founded by the Celts, became the site of a Roman castrum that was destroyed by the Alemanni in the 5 or 6C. The medieval town was founded by Peter II of Savoy in 1260. In 1536 Yverdon fell to Bern and then from the 18C onwards it became a well known spa. The **château** is a fine example of the Savoyard square (square ground plan, round corner towers, massive SE keep) and was begun in 1260-1 by the master builder James of St.George. Partly destroyed in 1475, it was restored in the 16C and became the residence of the Bernese Landvogts. In 1805-25 it housed Enrico Pestalozzi's Institute. The Place Pestalozzi has the **Reformed church** (Notre Dame), built in 1753-7 on the site of a Gothic church by the Geneva architect Jean-Michel Billon; the late Gothic bell tower (1608-10) survives from the earlier church. The modern one is trapezoidal in plan and has a beautiful baroque façade with a curving pediment and sculptures forming an allegory of Faith—to a design by the Bernese architect Jean-Auguste Nahl. Inside, there are galleries on three sides and fine stalls (1499-1502) by Claude Chapuis and Bon Bottolier; numerous

carved 17&18C tombstones. The **Hôtel de Ville,** near the church, was built in 1767 - 73 by A.-D. Burnand. Its façade is preceded by a pedimented portico. What was the Hôtel de l'Aigle, built 1776 to the plans of Béat de Hennezel, is now the **Préfecture. Pestalozzi Monument,** 1889, by A.Lanz. 17 Rue du Four is a house built in 1791, carved front. No. 25 was built in 1751. **A la reine Berthe** (Rue du Pré) is 16C with Gothic windows. 10 Rue du Lac, the **Cercle d'Yverdon,** dates from 1777, Ionic pilasters on the façade. No. 6 is 18C, mask on the door. No. 4 was built in 1790 for General Frédéric Haldimand; it is a vast house with arcades and a Louis XVI façade. The **Caserne** (barracks) on the river Thièle incorporates a tower from the now vanished town walls. The **Casino** in the Place d'Armes was built in 1898. Opposite there is a **school** built in neo-Renaissance style in 1897. 14 Rue de la Plaine, the **Banque Piguet,** is a large 18C building. In the Rue des Jordils near the cemetery there is a monument on the site of the Roman castrum. The **Villa d'Entremonts,** towards Lausanne, was built in 1779 for D.-P. Barthélemy of Treytorrens. Louis XVI in style, the main façade has a portico with a double staircase. Beside it is the old bath house built in 1729 by J.-G. Martin and Guillaume Delagrange; 19C rotonda.

Museums. *Musée du Vieil-Yverdon,* local history and ethnography. *Maison d'Ailleurs,* devoted to science fiction.

Z

Zell LU

7 □ C2

The late baroque **Catholic parish church of St. Martin** was built in 1801 –3 by Josef Purtschert; ceiling frescos by Josef Anton Messmer. The **parish house** has a walled garden and corner pavilions, along the lines of the houses of the nobility. The **Schacherhof** is a mid-19C house with a hipped roof and displaying Bernese influence.

Hüswil The **Grossmatt granary** (1769) has a richly carved door.

Zell ZH

3 □ C4

Reformed parish church. Zell's first church was built around 700, and all the succeeding ones have been built around the tomb of a hermit. The present one is a late Gothic single-aisled building from the end of the 15C. The bell tower above the choir has fine mid-14C wall paintings.

Zenbinnen VS

See Binn

12 □ D5

Zernez GR

9 □ F5

This village of square buildings with gently sloping roofs owes its uniform appearance to a fire in 1872, after which it was rebuilt. The **Reformed church** has a nave of three bays with a narrower polygonal choir (1607–19) and a bell tower from the preceding church (c. 1200) with a baroque spire. Above the entablature there is an articulated tunnel vault. There are sumptuous early baroque stuccoes and an escutcheon with the arms of the founder, Rudolf von Planta, on the chancel arch. To the S., the chapel of **St. Sebastian**

Zernez: Reformed church, choir gallery, 1741, with pierced wooden parapet.

(vaulted 1490) has late Gothic wall paintings in the choir: St. Anne with saints on the E. wall; Church Fathers and the Apostles on the diagonal walls; a Virgin on the end wall and a Crucifixion with saints on the W. wall. Further S., below these churches, is **Schloss Wildenberg,** which is arranged around a court, with a projecting, fortified corner tower dating from 1280. The staircase and upper floor has Louis XVI decoration. The *Nationalparkmuseum* is devoted to the natural sciences.

Ziefen BL

2 □ A4

The village, which was originally two distinct settlements, extends along the Hintere Frenke. A farming and wine growing community, it enjoyed a certain amount of economic prosperity as a result of the lace industry in the 19C. S. of the village, in the **Reformed parish church of St. Blasius,** which has been altered on several occasions, there are fragments of a high Gothic cycle of wall paintings (c. 1350).

Zihlschlacht TG

3 □ F3

The **chapel of St. Nikolaus und St. Magdalena** lies to the SE at Degenau-Bildegg. It has a 12C nave and apse and a sacristy from 1614. Inside there are late Reichenau school wall paintings dating from the time of the chapel's building.

Zihlschlacht: Romanesque chapel in Degenau-Blidegg; the half-timbered porch dates from 1698.

Zillis: detail of the painted Romanesque wooden ceiling in the Reformed church.

Zillis GR
14☐A1

Reformed church of St. Martin has a late Gothic polygonal choir. Outside, on the W. wall, there is an enormous St. Christopher from *c.* 1300. Inside, there is the oldest completely painted and preserved *wooden ceiling* in the West (*c.* 1150). 153 painted panels with mouldings are fixed to the beams of the roof by a system of T-shaped attachments. Twin longitudinal and transverse friezes emphasise the axes. The border panels contain sea monsters and fishermen, symbolically linked by lines representing water. In the corner panels the four angels of the Last Judgement personify the winds. The central cycle should be read starting in the choir from east to west and tier by tier from south to north. Introduced by the Kings of the Old Testament, it depicts the Life of Christ, ending with the Crown of Thorns. The last seven panels are devoted

to the Life of St.Martin and are probably the work of his companions. The style of the tempera painting on the plastered panels and mouldings clearly shows the influence of book illumination in Bavaria and Northern Italy. The *Schamser Talmuseum* (Tgea da Schons) is an ethnographic collection in a 16C peasant's house with a passageway leading to the barn.

Zimmerwald BE
6☐F5

The former restaurant of the Pension Beau-Séjour, where the socialist Zimmerwald conference was held, now houses a *wind-instruments museum*.

Zizers GR
9☐B3

The present **Catholic church of St.Peter und Paul** is a 15C single-aisled church with a narrower polygonal apse. It stands at right-angles to the earlier Romanesque church (old choir in the bell tower). The Rosary Chapel was vaulted in about 1686; rococo decoration, including three altars from 1767. The **Reformed church** is also single-aisled, but has a long, straight-ended choir, which is staggered on the S. side. In its present form it dates from 1711; carved pulpit from the same period. **Unteres Schloss.** Powerful square covered with a hipped roof, with a domed, octagonal tower centrally positioned at the front. **Oberes Schloss.** Late-17C, a three-storeyed, square building with flights of steps and a balcony on the mezzanine floor. Inside, there are wall paintings (*c.* 1750) and Régence stuccoes (1725).

Zofingen AG
7☐C1

Even before the foundation of the village by the Froburgs at the end of the 12C, the church of St.Mauritius existed as a possession of the Lenzburgs. A collegiate church until 1528, it now stands in the centre of a rectangular town of narrow streets and vast squares. The **old town** dates back to the high Middle Ages and has been kept separate from the new quarters, although it does possess some imposing baroque buildings. All that survives from the medieval fortifications are two towers and a section of wall. The **Reformed Stadtkirche.** The oldest parts of the former collegiate church of St. Mauritius are still Romanesque, although it was extensively altered in the 14&15C and the choir was rebuilt in 1513-17. The present bell tower dates from 1646-9. The central bay of the choir has a twelve-part stained-glass window (Crucifixion, Entombment, Resurrection) from *c.* 1400. **Rathaus.** An impressive town hall with a double outside staircase, built in 1792 – 5 to plans by Niklaus Emanuel Ringier. The interior is Louis XVI and has stucco ceilings by Franz Georg Rust. Former **Lateinschule** (Latin school). A three-storeyed late Gothic building by Antoni Stab (1600-2). Today it is the town library and archive. The **Neuhaus** was built in 1770 by Johann Jakob Ringier for a wealthy citizen and has an ornately decorated façade; now a bank. The **Städtisches Museum** is a neo-Renaissance building (1901 – 2) by Emil Vogt and stands outside the old town; it houses *historical collections.* On the E. slope of the Heitersberg there are two **mosaic floors** from a Roman villa of the 2C.

Zizers: 17C lower Schloss with domed façade tower.

Zofingen: late baroque Rathaus with domed porch.

lake, built in 1599. Inside, there are painted 17&18C beams.

Zollikofen BE

6☐E4

Schloss Reichenbach was built in 1688 for Beat Fischer, the founder of the Bernese postal system. The baroque paintings in the court room are from the first phase of building, whereas the stuccoes of the stairwell and the upper floor date from the enlargement of 1719.

Zollikon ZH

3☐A5

Haus zum Traubenberg, a large timber-framed country house on the edge of the

Zuckenriet SG
See Niederhelfenschwil   3☐E4

Zug ZG

8☐A2

This town was first mentioned in 1242; it was founded by the counts of Kyburg and inherited by the Habsburgs in 1283; it became an important base in their struggle against the Waldstätte. The Austrian army destroyed at Morgarten in 1315 assembled here. In 1352 Zug was besieged by the Confederates, who wished to secure the route to Zürich, and compelled to join the Bund. While the rural districts of

Zug: the semicircle of the late Gothic Old Town on the bank of the lake.

The medieval castle, altered and raised in the 16C, is a historical museum.

Late Gothic 'Königspforte' on the façade of the Catholic church of St. Oswald.

Façade of the Brandenberghaus with wall paintings of 1710.

Aegeri, Baar and Menzingen have always been been able to claim considerable independence, Zug asserted its rights over Walchwil, Hünenberg, Cham, Risch and Steinhausen. In 1415 the town was granted freedom from the Empire. Zug remained Catholic at the time of the Reformation, and subsequently threw in its lot with the inner Swiss cantons. The present canton was formed in 1803 and Zug became the capital. In 1847 Zug was part of the Sonderbund. The canton has been heavily industrialised in the 19&20C.

Old Town and outer walls. The oldest part of the town is on the lake, amd originally consisted of three streets runn-

ing parallel to the shore; in 1435 the outermost row of houses sank into the lake. Four towers and parts of the connecting walls remain of the 16C curtain wall to the N. and E. of the town. The **castle,** once the official seat of the Kyburg and Habsburg Landvogts, has housed the *historisches Museum* of the town and canton of Zug since 1982. **Catholic church of St. Oswald,** built 1478–83 by Hans Felder the Elder, extended as a basilica with nave and two aisles in 1511, nave raised and vaulted in 1545. 'Königspforte' in the main façade with lavish decorative carving (before 1500): left and right above the portal are St. Oswald and St. Michael, in the centre is the Virgin Mary, and above that St.Anne with the Virgin and Child. A little above the town is the **parish church of St. Michael,** built by the architects Curjel and Moser in 1898 on the site of a Gothic church. Adjacent is the **funerary chapel of St.Michael** of 1513–15. Late Gothic wooden ceiling with carved bas-reliefs by Hans Winkler. The **Liebfrauenkapelle** was mentioned in 1266; it was originally part of the curtain wall. **St. Verena chapel,** built in 1705, probably to Johann Caspar Mosbrugger's design, on a Latin cross plan. The **Capuchin monastery,** built on a raised site 1595–7, can be reached from the town via the covered Kapuzinerstiege. **Convent of Maria Opferung.** Convent building 1607&8 by Jost Knopflin; the neoclassical tunnel vault in the church (1626–9) was added c. 1790. The **Rathaus,** 1505, is late Gothic; the Ratssaal in the upper storey has very lavish carving dating from 1507. The Renaissance portal of 1617 and the wall and ceiling panelling in the Kleiner Ratssaal are later. The massive baroque gabled **Stadtbauamt** was built in 1710–22 as a guild school. **Brandenberghaus.** Dated 1540, with baroque façade paintings of 1710. The double **Münz** (mint) building, 1580 (Obere Münz) and 1604 (Untere Münz), presumably built by Jost Knopflin, was the residence of the Master of the Zug mint. The building also housed the town mint and treasury. By the Münz in the **'Gloriettli',** a triangular rococo pavilion dating from 1772. **Zurlaubenhof,** just outside the town, built 1597–1621 by Jost Knopflin. This house has the largest private state rooms in inner Switzerland; it was the seat of the influential Zurlauben family, who were important officers in the service of the French from the 16–18C. By the Zurlaubenhof is the **St.Konrad chapel,** built in 1623.

Zuoz GR

14 ☐ E2

This is the principal town of the Upper Engadine, and had a Carolingian settlement; it was originally episcopal territory,

Zuoz: 18C Haus Poult, incorporating a medieval residence tower.

came under Planta rule in the 13C and was burned down in the Swabian War in 1499. **Reformed parish church.** Buttressed late Gothic single-aisled church with much narrower polygonal choir built using parts of the earlier building by Bernhard von Poschiavo in 1504. Romanesque tower incorporated into the N. wall of the choir; the belfry and spire are later. Windows 1929–33 by A. Giacometti 1929–33 and Jan Kasty 1957. **Catholic chapel of St. Katharina,** rebuilt simply in 1510 using the old nave walls; stellar vaulting in the choir. Secularised **chapel of St. Sebastian,** built c. 1250. On the end wall of the square choir with groin vault late Gothic wall paintings, late 15C: St. Sebastian and St.Antony. Half figure of Mary, church fathers, Christ in Majesty and heads and shoulders of Christ and the Apostles. The nucleated village has numerous patrician and farm buildings, many of which were formerly part of castles (20 authenticated examples), including **Haus Paul Willy,** No. 84. In the centrally-placed village square are the **Oberes and Unteres Planta-Haus,** redesigned c. 1760. In the Oberes Haus, with massive façade, are decorative wall paintings and panelling (second half of the 16C). The Unteres Haus has steps with a rococo stone balustrade and is connected to the **Dorfturm** (rebuilt 1555). Below the street is the **Weisses Kreuz,** built in 1570, with painted coat-of-arms frieze of the same period. In the Plazett **Haus Poult,** extended c. 1730, with a residence tower incorporated into the central section, which is set slightly behind the line of the building.

Zürich ZH

3□A5

The first traces of human habitation in what is now the largest and economically strongest Swiss town can be traced back to the La Tène period (refuge castle on the Üetliberg). Under the Romans the Lindenhof, on the left bank of the Limmat, was fortified from the second decade BC, and in the 4C AD a many-towered citadel was built, and lasted well into the early Middle Ages. The Gallo-Roman village of Turicum developed into a flourishing high-medieval town, with settlements on both bank of the river. They crystallized on the left bank around the convent of Fraumünster, founded in 853 by Ludwig the German, and on the right bank around the Grossmünster, an Augustinian foundation on the site of a much earlier church. Zürich was an imperial residence towns; the emperor stayed in the Lindenhof, in the Pfalz built in the 9C by Ludwig the German, replaced by Otto I with a Romanesque building in the 10C. Government of the town passed gradually from the abbess of Fraumünster to mayor and council, first under the Zähringen regime, but as a town with freedom from the empire from 1218, when the dynasty died out. The two ecclesiastical foundations also achieved independence at this time. The aristocratic regime of nobles and merchants was brought down by a coup d'état by Ritter Rudolf in 1336; he established a guild constitution which gave equal rights to craftsmen. Zürich was at the height of its powers economically, culturally and also in the religious sphere in the 13C. In 1351 it joined the Confederacy, and stayed within it, despite a temporary estrangement in the Old Zürich War. Zürich, along with Bern and Lucerne, soon became one of the most important towns in the Confederacy, and after acceptance of the Reformation as preached by Huldrych Zwingli, who worked in Zürich from 1519, it became the unchallenged leader of the Reformed areas of the country. Cultural development was inhibited for a time by the rigidity of the Reformers, but trade and crafts flourished, particularly under the in-

Zürich: the Grossmünster, a 12&13C Romanesque galleried basilica.

Seated figure of Charlemagne (c. 1460) in the crypt of the Grossmünster.

fluence of numerous religious refugees from France and Italy. In the 18C Zürich again became a cultural centre on the European plane with the writers and critics Bodmer and Breitinger, the poet and theologian Lavater and the educationalist Pestalozzi. After the French invasion of 1799 Zürich was the football in two major battles between the French and the

The State Archive was established in the choir of the Predigerkirche in 1917.

Late Gothic moated church and early neoclassical Helmhaus; behind them is the Grossmünster.

Austrians and then the Russians. In the first half of the 19C the aristocratic government was replaced by a democratic regime which accorded equal rights to the surrounding rural areas. From 1830 Zürich was a centre of liberal ideas in a largely reactionary Confederacy, and was a major force in the establishment of the federal state in 1848. The citizens of Zürich, freed

from protectionism, quickly created a centre of industry, trade, transport and finance which was accorded world-wide recognition.

Until the 17C Zürich remained within the confines of the two old parts of the town, the smaller on the left bank and the larger on the right; strict building regulations have maintained the appearance of these two areas. The complex defensive system of entrenchments and ditches was set up in 1642, and made the secure city centre a popular place for the patrician families of the 17&18C to build their houses. From the middle of the 19C the defensive walls and entrenchments were largely removed and the ditches filled in. This allowed the free development of inner city areas, particularly around the Hauptbahnhof and the Bahnhofstrasse. Fringe communities were incorporated into the town in two stages, in 1893 and 1934, and this finally established Zürich as a major city; some of the these communities have maintained the character of villages. OLD TOWN, RIGHT BANK **Grossmünster.** It is assumed that there was a Christian church on the right bank of the Limmat in the 7C. Little is known about the origins of the Münster, but it was probably a Carolingian foundation. The foundations and the crypt of the present building date from before 1100. The Romanesque basilica with nave and two aisles and columns was built in stages in the 12&13C. The towers were raised and spires added 1487–92; the present distinctive domes were built after a fire, 1781–7. Both the exterior, with its equestrian statue of Charlemagne (copy, original in the crypt) and the interior, with capitals in the Lombardy and Catalan styles, are of considerable architectural interest. The wall paintings largely disappeared at the time of the Reformation; fragments remain in the arches of the nave, and there are complete paintings in the Zwölfbotenkapelle (14C Judge of the World; late-13C Last Supper and Washing of the Feet; Christ and Apostles *c.* 1300), in the S. tower (13C Last Judgement) and in the large crypt with three aisles (legend of Felix and Regula, late 15C, school of Hans Leu the Elder). The bronze reliefs on the N. main portal (Biblical scenes, 1950) and on the

The Rathaus was built in 1694–8 under the direction of Ratsherr H. Holzhalb.

Hall of the Carpenters' guild with twin arches and central oriel.

S. portal (Reformation scenes, 1935-8) are by Otto Münch. The interior of the Grossmünster was restored in 1980. Adjacent to the Grossmünster in the NE is the Grossmünsterschulhaus of 1850 (which now houses parts of the theological faculty) and which contains the **cloister,** (c. 1200). In the W. and S. walks are originals, in the other two walks mainly copies and imitations of Romanesque sculpture (plants, animals, legendary beings, masks, human forms). The Münster complex also includes the neo-Gothic **Grossmünsterkapelle** by Johann Jakob Breitinger (1858&9) and the **Münsterterrasse,** with the shops built in 1838&9 by Aloys Negrelli. **Predigerkirche.** The former Dominican monastery was first mentioned in 1231, and dissolved in the Reformation in 1524; the monastery buildings W. of the church burned down in 1887; the central library was built on the site in 1915-17. The Predigerkirche itself was completed in 1269 and the architecturally important Gothic choir was added in the 14C. This was separated from the church at the time of the Reformation and used for the storage of corn; in 1917 extra floors were put in and the building was equipped to house the state archives. The rest of the church was much altered in 1663, as it threatened to collapse; the pseudo-antique stucco dates from 1610. **Wasserkirche.** Excavations have revealed a church with nave and two aisles dating from c. 1000. A church with one aisle was consecrated in 1288. The present church,

The Grimmenturm in the Neumarkt is a 13C early Gothic residence tower.

late Gothic, and designed to emphasise the importance of preaching, was the work of Hans Felder the Elder (1479 - 84). The island was joined to the mainland by the extension of the Limmatquai in 1839. In 1791-4 Hans Conrad Bluntschli built the adjacent **Helmhaus** on the site of earlier secular buildings. The early neoclassical building with with arcaded hall is now used for exhibitions. **Rathaus.** The characterful rectangular building with columned portal was built 1694-8 over the tunnel vault of the old Rathaus; it has late Renaissance and early baroque elements. It houses the cantonal and town administrations and a fine state banqueting hall. **Hauptwache.** Neoclassical building with portico and triangular gable by Hans Caspar Escher (1824–5). The building now looks rather isolated; the adjacent Fleischhalle was pulled down in 1962. **Haus der Museumsgesellschaft** (Limmatquai 62). The arcades were added to the ground floor of Ferdinand Stadler's building (1866–8) in 1965&6. There are numerous *guild buildings* in this part of the town: **Zunfthaus zur Schmiden** (Marktgasse 20). Gothic corner house altered in 1520 by the addition of a guild hall; partially rebuilt in the 19C. Coffered ceiling on the second floor with motifs from the Nuremberg World Chronicle. **Zunfthaus zur Zimmerleuten** (Limmatquai 42). Mentioned in 1295 as a meeting place of the Constaffel (association of noblemen), rebuilt 1659–62. Gothic hall (restaurant) and Grosser Saal with stucco ceiling dating from 1659 (second floor). **Zunfthaus zur Saffran** (Limmatquai 54). Rebuilt 1719-23. Guild hall with fine door on the first floor, coffered ceiling and Corinthian window column. **Gesellschaftshaus der Schildner zum Schneggen** (Limmatquai 64). Rebuilt 1864-6 by Leonhard Zeugheer and Georg Lasius. There are many fine houses in this part of the town, especially the **Haus zum unteren Rech** (Neumarkt 4), high medieval building, altered in 1497, 1534 and 1879, completely renovated in the nineteen-seventies and now town archive; the **Grimmenturm** (Neumarkt), early Gothic residence tower, restored 1964–6. **Haus zum Napf** (Napfgasse 6). Late Gothic façade; Renaissance rooms with panelling and coffered roof on the first floor, Gothic hall with beamed ceiling and Régence décor on the second floor, on the third floor 17C banqueting hall with stucco ceiling. **Brunnenturm** (Obere Zäune 26). Mentioned in 1340, baroque door with coats-of-arms. **Haus zur Engelburg** (Kirchgasse 27). Built 1599-1604, fine stucco ceiling on the first floor. **Haus zum Kiel** (Hirschengraben 20). Built in 1716 with early neoclassical interiors; mythological and allegorical stucco by Valentin Sonnenschein, landscapes with ruins by Johann Heinrich Wüst. **Haus zum Lindengarten**

Remains of the Frauenmünster cloister with frescos by Paul Bodmer (1921–41).

(Hirschengraben 22), built 1725, altered in 1899; panelling and Renaissance stucco ceilings. **Wettingerhäuser** (Limmatquai 36 and 38). The three houses owned by the monastery of Wettingen from 1240 and 1332 were much altered in 1840.

OLD TOWN, LEFT BANK **Fraumünster.** King Ludwig the German handed the Fraumünster over to his daughter Hildegard in 853; the abbess of this community, which was free of the Empire, also ruled the town until the high Middle Ages. The last abbess, Katharina von Zimmern, convinced by Zwingli's ideas of reform, handed the convent buildings and other possessions over to the town in 1522. The neo-Renaissance and neo-Gothic **Stadthaus** took over the site in two stages, 1885-7 and 1899-1900; only parts of the *cloister* between the church and the Stadthaus have survived (fresco cycle by Paul Bodmer, 1921 – 41). Excavations undertaken from 1953 revealed the six phases of the Fraumünster church. The earliest building was a Carolingian basilica with three apses but no towers, little smaller than the present church. Major rebuilding took place in the second half of the 13C and lasted for about two centuries. The Münster was then an imposing twin-towered basilica with nave, two aisles and a transept, combining Romanesque and Gothic design. The E. façade, facing the river, was dominated by a large rectangular choir. Only three storeys of the S. tower survive, and it is no loger recognisable as such. The originally undecorated W. façade was altered in 1911&12 by Gustav Null in neo-Gothic style, with portal and tracery windows. Spire and belfry of the

St. Peter, a baroque galleried hall with late Romanesque choir tower.

Zur Meise Guild Hall, an outstanding baroque building by David Morf.

N. tower date from 1728–32. The nave was never vaulted in stone, but has neo-Gothic wooden rib vaulting dating from 1713. There are impressive keystones in the vaults of the transept. The three tall, narrow windows in the E. choir wall and the two windows in the side wall were replaced with modern stained glass by Marc Chagall in 1970 (prophet window, law window, Zion window and Christ window). In 1978 Chagall also replaced a rose window in the transept. Only fragments of the wall paintings survived the Reformation. **Reformed parish church of St. Peter.** The oldest church in Zürich was until the Reformation the only lay priests' church in the town. Four churches have stood on the moraine mound below the Lindenhof, which has been fortified since Roman times. Excavations in 1970–4 revealed: a small Carolingian single-aisled church, c. 800, extended in the late 9C; an early 13C late Romanesque church with a choir tower; a late Gothic church with a choir tower on its predecesor's foundations, c. 1450; The nave was extended in 1705&6, and the renovation of 1970–4 returned the church to this state. The church has galleries, and is divided into a nave and

three aisles by two rows of Tuscan columns set one above the other. Tunnel vaulting. The interior has fine stucco. The choir, separated by a wooden choir screen, was restored to its late Romanesque condition in 1970–4. The wall paintings discovered at the time were restored to as large an extent as possible. The church square (**Peterhofstatt**) makes a fine setting for the church, and is surrounded by fine houses: the **Haus zur Armbrust** (St. Peterhofstatt 6) was the home of the man who is probably the best-known incumbent of St. Peter's, the theologian Johann Caspar Lavater (1741–1801; Lavater room on the second floor). **Augustinerkirche.** This church, built at the end of the 13C, was secularised in 1525: the choir was separated and used as a mint. In 1842 celebration of the Catholic mass was permitted in the nave; the church was handed over to the Old Catholics after the schism of 1873. In the thirties the Old Catholics rebuilt the mint as a parish hall. The nave of the old church had been rebuilt in the neo-Gothic style in 1843&4, but was largely returned to its former condition in the renovation of 1958&9. On the left bank the two **guild houses** in the Münsterhof are important: **Zunfthaus zur Meise.** Rebuilt in 1752–7 by David Morf for the vintners' guild in fine rococo style. This fine building now houses the *ceramic collection* of the *Schweizerisches Landesmuseum.* **Zunfthaus zur Waag.** Built in 1636&7 on the site of an earlier building and much altered since. Baroque portal 1636, guild hall with late Gothic windows on the third floor. The houses near the so-called **'Schipf'** on the E. slope

Schipfe houses, extended in the 17&18C.

of the Lindenhof are also impressive. Some of the excavations of the Roman citadel and later imperial palace in the Lindenhof are open to the public. The **Freimaurerloge** built in 1852 by Gustav Albert Wegmann is a striking feature.

Two-storey inner courtyard of the Eidgenössische Technische Hochschule built in 1861–4.

KREIS 1 RIGHT BANK (not including Old Town). **Französische Kirche** (Hohe Promenade). 1900–2, built by Benjamin Recordon in neo-Romanesque style. The numerous school and university buildings in this area include: **University.** Built 1911–14 by Karl Moser; asymmetrical buildings with courtyard and a massive tapering tower. **Eidgenössische Technische Hochschule.** Built in 1861 –4 by Johann Caspar Wolff to designs by Gottfried Semper. The wings and oval dome were added in 1914–25 by Gustav Gull. The ETH is the most important Swiss historicist building. **Observatory of the ETH** (Schmelzbergstrasse 25); built 1861–4 by Gottfried Semper. **Alte Kantonsschule.** Built by Gustav Albert Wegmann in 1839–42 under the influence of Schinkel. **Hirschengraben-Schulhaus.** Neo-Gothic brick building by Alexander Koch (1893). Important cultural buildings in this area are the **Kunsthaus** (Jugendstil building 1907–10 by Karl Moser, first extension 1925&6 by Karl Moser, second extension 1955-8, third extension 1972), the **Opernhaus,** a neobaroque building by Ferdinand Fellner and Hermann Helmer (1890&1), and the former **Corso-Theater** in the Bellevue-Platz, built 1899–1900 by Hermann Stadler and Jakob Emil Usteri in neo-baroque style (rebuilt 1934). Conspicuous among the patrician houses because of its

The Haus zum Rechberg is a lavishly decorated rococo building dating from 1759 –70.

sloping site is the **Haus zum Rechberg** (Hirschgraben 40), built in 1759–70 in rococo style by David Morf for guild master Johann Caspar Werdmüller. The house stands in a symmetrical garden, and has lavish stucco, ceiling and wall paintings, linenfold panelling, grisaille and stoves. **Haus zum Neuberg** (Hirschgraben 56– 60). Group of houses built in 1733 and rebuilt in 1818; birthplace of the Zürich statesman Alfred Escher. **Stockargut** (Sempersteig 2). Stately home with outbuildings and garden, built c. 1630, rebuilt 1690&1. Ballroom with ceiling paintings on the second floor. **Haus zum Krönli** (Hirchengraben 42). Built in 1739 and altered in 1823 and 1901; lavish panelling in the upper storey. **Haus zum Oberen Schönenberg** (Schönberggasse 15), built

in 1665, once the home of Johann Jakob
Bodmer; the upper storey now houses the
Thomas-Mann-Archiv. **Haus zum Son-
nenhof** (Stadelhoferstrasse 12), built in
1643 for mayor Salomon Hirzel, with fine
doors and rococo grille. **Haus zum
Garten** (Rämistrasse 18). The old 17C
building was radically altered in 1720; fine
stucco ceilings. **Villa Ehrenfels**
(Rämistrasse 26), neoclassical building of
1837.
Kreis 1 left bank (excluding Old
Town). **Synagogue** (corner of
Nüschelerstrasse/Löwenstrasse), built in
Moorish style by Alfred Chiodera and
Theophil Tschudy. **Hauptbahnhof.** Hall
construction by Jakob Friedrich Wanner
(1865–71). In the Bahnhofplatz in front of
the main portal **Alfred-Escher-Denkmal**
by Richard Kissling (1889).
Schweizerisches Landesmuseum.
Built in neo-Gothic style to look like a large
castle in 1893–8 by Gustav Gull. Other important public buildings are the **Amtshäuser I-IV** of the town administration
on the site of the former monastery of
Oetenbach. Amtshaus I was built in 1765
–71, and was an orphanage until 1911.
From 1911–14 it was altered by Gustav
Gull, and the same architect built the other
Amtshäuser in stages from 1903–1919.
They are neo-Gothic buildings, connected
by a bridge over the Uraniastrasse. In the
area between the Hauptbahnhof and the
lake some business and banking buildings
are of interest: **Geschäftshaus Oscar
Weber** (Bahnhofstrasse 75), built in 1899
by Richaed Kuder and Albert Müller,
rebuilt 1912&13 and 1928. **Geschäftshaus Jelmoli** (Seidengasse 1), early iron
skeleton-frame building by Hermann
Stadler and Jakob Emil Usteri (1897);
much altered. **Geschäftshaus Peterhof
und Leuenhof** (Bahnhofstrasse 30). Early
reinforced concrete building with
historicist façade by Otto and Werner
Pfister (1913 – 16). **Schweizerische
Kreditanstalt** (Paradeplatz). 1873–6 by
Jakob Friedrich Wanner with neo-
Renaissance and neo-baroque features.
Schweizerische Nationalbank
(Börsenstrasse 10). Iron and glass building
by Heinrich Ernst (1893). **Block Stad-
thausquai 1** by Adolf Brunner (1887–9).

Of the few older buildings the **Haus zum
Grossen Pelikan** (Pelikanplatz 5) is striking; built in 1675 and extended in 1683 as
the town house of a silk merchant, with a
magnificent interior.
Kreis 2 **Reformed church in Enge.**
Built on a high site 1892 – 4 by Alfred
Friedrich Bluntschli, cross-in-square plan
with a side tower; the steps were added in
1925&6. **Bahnhof Enge,** built 1925–7 by
Otto and Werner Pfister; semicircular arches and ashlar pillars. **Kantonsschule
Freudenberg** (Gutenbergstrasse 15). Jacques Schader's modern school (1958–61)
blends harmoniously with the surrounding
park. **Tonhalle and Kongresshaus.** The
old Tonhalle was built 1893–5 by Ferdinand Fellner and Hermann Helmer; parts
of it were pulled down in 1938 and
replaced with the new Kongresshaus by
Max E.Haefeli, Werner M.Moser and
Rudolf Steiger. **Geschäftshaus
Bleicherhof** (Bleicherweg 18), skeleton
building by Otto R.Salvisberg. **Ver-
waltungsgebäude Zürich-Versiche-
rungen** (Mythenquai 2) by Gottfried
Julius Kunkler (1899 – 1901) with
decorative sculpture by Gustav Sieber and
Arnold Hünerwadel. **Rotes Schloss**
(General Guisan-Quai 20–22). Large block
in 9 sections in red brick with French
Renaissance features, built 1891 – 3 by
Heinrich Ernst. **Weisses Schloss**
(General Guisan-Quai 32–36). Block of six
houses with French Mannerist features,
1890–3 by Heinrich Honegger-Näf. There
are a number of fine patrician houses in
Kreis 2: **Muraltengut** (Seestrasse 203).
Built 1777–82 by Johann Werdmüller (gardener's house in the park *c.* 1780). Built
in imitation of French state buildings; interior altered 1924; owned by the city of
Zürich since 1944. It is used for formal
receptions and temporary exhibitions.
Belvoirgut (Seestrasse 125). Neoclassical
building by Hans Caspar Escher (1826–
31) with portico on the street side and a
pillared porch on the SE façade. **Villa
Wesendonck** (Gablerstrasse 15). Late
neoclassical town house by Leonhard
Zeugheer (1853–7). **Freigut** (Parkring 31),
built in 1772 by Johann Meyer, lavish rococo interior. **Villa Rosau** (Glär-
nischstrasse 10). Neoclassical building by

The Rote Schloss, a late-19C residencce.

The PTT communications centre in Zürich-Herdern.

Ferdinand Stadler (1843; altered 1967&8). A remarkable product of the surge of building activity in the inter-war years is the so-called **Werkbundsiedlung Neubühl** in the Nidelbadstrasse in Wollishofen, the collective work of architects Max E.Haefeli, Carl Hubacher, Rudolf Steiger, Werner M.Moser, Emil Roth, Paul Artaria and Hans Schmidt, 1930–2. KREIS 5 **Hardturm** (Hardturmstrasse 136). 12C residence tower with 17C extensions. **Kunstgewerbemuseum und -schule** (Ausstellungsstrasse 60). Functional building in Thirties style by Karl Egender and Adolf Steger (1930–3; extended in 1961 by Eduard Del Fabro and Bruno Gerosa). **Bernouillihäuser** (Hardtrumstrasse 200–394). Unusual terraced living accommodation by the architect Hans Bernouilli (1925). KREIS 6 **Catholic Liebfrauenkirche** (Weinbergfussweg), built in imitation of the early-Christian-Romanesque tradition by August Hardegger (1893&4); cycle of paintings by Fritz Kunz. **Beckenhof** (Beckenhofstrasse 31 – 5). Estate with several buildings and English park: Lehenhaus (17C), Kleines Herrenhaus (*c.* 1720), Grosses Herrenhaus (*c.* 1740; lavish interior), Gartenpavillon (*c.* 1735). The Beckenhof now houses the *Pestalozzianum*. KREIS 7 **Alte Kirche Fluntern** (Gloriastrasse 100). Single-aisled church by Heinrich Notz (1762); paintings by Paul Bodmer (1934). **Alte Kirche Witikon** (Loorenstrasse). Single-aisled church mentioned in 1270 and altered in the 17C; elevated site. **Reformed Kreuzkirche** (Dolderstrasse/Car-

menstrasse), domed building by Otto Pfleghard and Max Haefeli (1901 – 5). **Catholic Antoniuskirche** (Neptunstrasse 60) by Karl Moser (1908). Massive neo-Romanesque building with Jugendstil portal. **Catholic church of Mariä Krönung** (Carl-Spitteler-Strasse) by Justus Dahinden (1965); pyramid tower. **Christian-Science-Kirche** (Merkurstrasse 4) by Hans Hofmann (1938). **Former Haus zum Sonnenbühl** (Zürichbergstrasse 2 – 8). Now houses numerous departments of the university, originally built as offices by Gottfried Semper (1866 – 8). **Hirslandenmühle** (Forchstrasse 244–8). 16C buildings, mill with overshot water wheel. **Landhaus Kreuzbühl** (Hohenbühlstrasse 1) by Johann Meyer (1760). **Villa Wegmann** (Hohenbühlstrasse 9) by Alfred Friedrich Bluntschli (1887 9). **Flats at Doldertal 17 and 18** by Alfred Roth and Marcel Breuer (1936). KREIS 8 **Reformed church of Neumünster.** Monumental neoclassical church by Leonhard Zeugheer (1836 – 9; partially rebuilt 1911&12). In the choir 'Tranfiguration' by Konrad Zeller (1840) and 'Gethsemane' by Rudolf Münger (1912). **Villa Patumbah** (Zollikerstrasse 128). Built in 1883–5 by Alfred Chiodera in an astonishing mixture of styles. **Villa Egli** (Höschgasse 4). Neo-Gothic country house by Alexander Koch (1899–1902). KREIS 9 **Alte Kirche Albisrieden** by Hans Conrad Stadler (1816–17). **Alte Kirche Altstetten** (Pfarrhausstrasse). Built in 1761 on the site of medieval predecessors; tabernacle dating from *c.* 1500. **Reformed church Altstetten** by Werner M.Moser

Zürich: late Gothic residential wing of the 'Hirslandenmühle'.

The Kreuzbühl Landhaus is a square building with a steep mansard roof.

(1939–41) **Städelihus** (Dachslernstrasse 20). 13C or 14C timber building.
Museums and collections. *Kunsthaus* (Heimplatz 1); important 15–20C art collection. *Stiftung Sammlung E.G. Bührle* (Zollikerstrasse 172); private collection of French, Dutch and Italian art. *Schweizerisches Landesmuseum* (Museumstrasse 2); largest historical museum in Switzerland, also museum of cantonal history. *Graphische Sammlung der ETH* (Künstlergasse); collection of old and modern prints. *Museum Bellerive* (Höschgasse 3); important collection of non-European art. *Völkerkundemuseum der Universität* (Pelikanstrasse 40); large ethnographic collection. *Zoologisches Museum der Universität* (Künstlergasse 16). *Wohnmuseum Bärengasse* (Baärengasse 22); domestic museum.

Zurzach AG

2□E3

This was an important bridge over the Rhine in Celto-Roman times (Forum Tiberii) and later flourished as a place of pilgrimage and site for fairs; it is now known for its thermal springs. In spite of its importance Zurzach has never been granted a charter, and yet it has an astonishing number of fine buildings; it consists essentially of two streets. **Collegiate church of St. Verena.** This church, once the centre of a cult of St. Verena, is in two distinct but harmonious sections: the 10C Romanesque nave (redesigned in the baroque style by Giovanni Gaspare Bagnato, 1733&4) leads to a Gothic choir with tower (1294–1347) over the grave of St. Verena (Verena sarcophagus in a Gothic crypt). **So-called Upper Church,** formerly parish church of St. Maria, renovated in 1944 and deconsecrated for use as a function room. Single aisle and polygonal choir of 1517–18 over a crypt-like former ossuary. Stucco by Lucius Gambs (1763). **Reformed parish church.** Unorthodox octagonal church by Matthias Vogel (1717). **Roman citadel of Tenedo and early Christian church** on the Kirchlibuck. Excavations in 1903–5 and 1954&5 revealed large sections of wall, and also the foundation walls of a 5C early Christian church with apse and font.

Zuzgen AG

2□C3

Old Catholic parish church of St. Georg. Late baroque church built 1737–9 to plans by Giovanni Gasparo Bagnato. The high altar of 1739 has pictures by Hans Negele of Waldshut.

Zweisimmen BE

11□E3

Reformed church of St.Maria, built in the mid 15C. Interior and exterior late Gothic frescos, showing connections with

Zursach: Gothic hall crypt under the choir of the collegiate church of St. Verena.

Zwingen: Schloss with 14C keep and 16&17C palas.

Swabian painting (Strigel studio). On the W. façade St. Christopher, the Annunciation and St. George and the Dragon (*c.* 1500). In the interior, scenes from the legend of the Virgin Mary and the Life of Christ in the nave (*c.* 1470–80). In the choir sequence of Apostles and Angel with Censer (*c.* 1500) The *Simmentaler Heimatstube* in the old primary school has a modest collection of furniture and agricultural and domestic implements.

BLANKENBURG The simple baroque **Schloss** was built in 1767 on the site of a medieval castle. **Haus Rieder** im Betelried was built in 1746 and is decorated with carved friezes and painted baroque flower motifs. There is a dragon's head among the carvings on the S. façade.

Zwingen BE

1 □ F4

The **Schloss** associated with the Freiherren von Ramstein is surrounded on three sides by the river Birs. A wooden bridge leads from the outworks to the main castle; the keep is 14C and the palas built around it dates from the 16&17C.

Glossary

A

Abbey: An independent monastery of Benedictines or regular canons under an abbot or abbess.

Acanthus: Decorative element found especially on ▷ Corinthian capitals; it developed from the stylized representation of a thistle-like leaf.

Aedicule: Wall niche housing a bust or statue; usually with a ▷ gable, ▷ pillars or ▷ columns.

al secco: ▷ fresco.

Altar: Greek and Roman sacrificial table. The Lord's table in the Christian faith. Catholic churches often have several side altars as well as the high altar.

Ambo: Stand or lectern by the choir screen in early Christian and medieval churches; predecessor of the ▷ pulpit.

Antependium: Covering for the front of the altar.

Apse: Large recess at end of the ▷ choir, usually semicircular or polygonal. As a rule it contains the ▷ altar.

Apsidiole: A small apsidal chapel.

Arcade: A series of arches borne by columns or pillars. When the arcade is attached to a wall (and is purely decorative) it is called a blind arcade.

Arch: A curved structure of support employed in spanning a space; *Basket arch:* flattened round arch; *ogee arch:* arch with lower part concave and upper part convex (S-shaped); *pointed arch:* arch with pointed top; *round arch:* semicircular arch.

Architrave: Main stone member on top of the columns; lowest part of the ▷ entablature.

Ashlar: Squared building stone.

Archivolt: The face of the arch in Romanesque and Gothic portals; often more than one.

Atrium: In Roman houses a central hall with an opening in the roof. In Christian architecture a forecourt usually surrounded by columns and known as a paradise.

Aula: Main hall of a school or university.

B

Baldachin: Canopy above altars, tombs, statues, portals etc.

Baluster: Short squat or shaped column.

Baptistery: Place of baptism; may be a separate building.

Barbican: gatehouse in front of medieval fortifications, usually round with embrasures.

Baroque: Architectural style from *c.* 1600–*c.* 1750; distinguished by powerfully agitated interlocking forms.

Bartizan: A small corner turret projecting from the roof of a building.

Base: Foot of a column or pillar.

Basilica: Greek hall of kings. In church architecture, a type of church with a nave and two or more aisles, the roof of the nave being higher than the roofs above the aisles.

Basket arch: ▷ Arch.

Battlements: Upper part of a defensive wall, with protective shield-like structures alternating with ▷ embrasure-like spaces.

Bay: Vertical division of a building between pillars, columns, windows, wall arches etc.

Biedermeier: Period of art history, particularly in the German-speaking countries, from *c.* 1815 to *c.* 1850.

Blind arcade: ▷ Arcade.

Blind tracery: ▷ Tracery.

Blockbau: Wooden building with load-bearing walls constructed of horizontal timbers (opposite: ▷ Ständerbau).

Bossed ashlar: ▷ Ashlar rounded on its visible side.

C

Calotte: Half dome with no drum.

Capital: Topmost part of a ▷ column. The shape of the capital determines the style or ▷ order.

Campanile: Bell tower, usually freestanding.

Carré Savoyard: Square castle with protruding round towers at the corners, one of which serves as the keep.

Cartouche: Decorative frame or panel imitating a scrolled piece of paper, usually with an inscription, coat-of-arms etc.

Cenotaph: Monument to dead buried elsewhere.

Choir: The part of the church in which divine service is sung. Shorter and often narrower than the nave, it is usually raised and at the E. end. In the Middle Ages the choir was often separated from the rest of the church by a screen.

Citadel: Fortified area for the garrison in Roman times.

Clerestory: Upper part of the main walls of the nave, above the roofs of the aisles and pierced by windows.

Coffered ceiling: A ceiling divided into square or polygonal panels, which are painted or otherwise decorated.

Column: Support with circular cross-section, narrowing somewhat towards the top; the type of column is determined by the ▷ order. ▷ Pillar.

Conch: Semicircular recess with a half-dome.

Cornice: Projecting upper limit of a wall; topmost member of the ▷ entabulature of an ▷ order.

Corinthian order: ▷ Order with richly-decorated ▷ capitals; the ▷ base has two or more tiers and is similar to that of the ▷ Ionic order.

Crossing: The intersection of the ▷ nave and ▷ transept.

Crowning: The topmost part, often carved in wood or stone, of a Gothic winged altar.

Crypt: Burial place, usually under the ▷ choir.

Curtain wall: Outer wall of a castle.

D

Deesis: Representation of Christ enthroned with Mary and John the Baptist.

Dom: Episcopal church, cathedral.

Dome: Most common types: *Drum dome:* Pendentive dome with a cylindrical or polygonal insertion (tambour, drum) between the ▷ pendentives and the dome proper. *Pendentive dome:* circular dome on a square base. A dome is usually crowned with a ▷ lantern.

Donjon: Large tower in a castle combining ▷ palas and ▷ keep.

Doric order: ▷ Order in which the columns have no ▷ base and a flat pad-shaped ▷ capital.

E

Entablature: Upper part of an ▷ order; made up of ▷ architrave, ▷ frieze and ▷ cornice.

Epitaph: A memorial to the dead set into a pillar or wall.

F

Feiertagschristus: Representation of Christ as Man of Sorrows, surrounded by agricultural implements or craftsmen's tools, suggesting that Christ continues to be wounded when men work on Sundays.

Finial: Small decorative pinnacle.

Flamboyant: Late Gothic design prevalent in France, especially in ▷ tracery.

Fresco: Pigments dispersed in water are applied without a bonding agent to still-damp lime plaster. As the mortar dries the pigments are adsorbed into the plaster.

Frieze: Decorative strips for the borders of a wall. The frieze can be two- or three-dimensional, and can consist of figures or ornaments.

G

Gable: The triangular upper section of a wall, normally at one end of a pitched roof, though it may be purely decorative.

Gallery: Intermediate storey; in a church it is usually for singers and the organ. Arcaded walkway.

Grisaille: Painting in various shades of gray.

Groin vault: Vault in which two ▷ tunnel vaults intersect at right angles. The simple groin vault is to be distinguished from the ▷ rib vault, in which the intersecting edges are reinforced by ribs.

H

Half timbering: Beams are used as supporting parts with an infill of loam or brick.

Hall church: In contrast to the ▷ basilica, nave and aisles are of equal height, no ▷ transept.

Heidenhaus: Often popularly used, along with 'Heidenwölbi' and 'Heidenstock' to describe buildings of antiquated or foreign design which are therefore associated with alien beliefs (Heiden=heathen).

I

Incrustation: Coloured stone ornaments set into walls or façades.
Intarsia: Inlaid work in wood, plaster, stone etc.
Ionic order: ▷ Order in which the columns stand on a ▷ base of two or more tiers; the ▷ capital has two lateral ▷ volutes.

J

Jamb: Vertical part of arch, doorway or window.
Jugendstil: A style which took its name from the Munich magazine 'Jugend' (Youth); it avoided old forms and created new ones based on natural objects. At its height 1895–*c.* 1905.

K

Keep: Main tower of a castle; last refuge in time of siege.
Keystone: Stone at the apex of an arch or vault, often carved or painted.

L

Landvogt: Governor, head of a regional administration.
Lantern: Small turret with windows on top of a roof or dome.
Loggia: Pillared gallery, open on one or more sides, often on an upper storey.
Loreto chapel: Chapel in imitation the house of the Virgin Mary, transported according to legend from Nazareth to Loreto, near Ancona, in Central Italy.
Lunette: Semicircular panel above doors and windows, often with painting or sculpture.

M

Machicolation: Small openings in a projecting battlement or gallery for dropping liquids or objects on the enemy.

Mandorla: Almond-shaped niche containing a figure of Christ or Mary enthroned.
Mensa: Flat surface of the altar.
Mezzanine: Intermediate storey.
Münster: Minster, an abbey or monastery church; sometimes applied to cathedrals or other great churches without such connections.

N

Nave: Central aisle of church, intended for the congregation; excludes choir and apse.
Net vault: Vault in which the ribs cross one another repeatedly.

O

Onion dome: Bulbous dome with a point, common in Austria, Bavaria and Switzerland; not a true dome, i.e. without a vault.
Order: Classical architectural system prescribing decorations and proportions according to to one of the accepted forms: ▷ Corinthian, ▷ Doric, ▷ Ionic etc. An order consists of a column, which usually has a base, shaft and capital, and the entabulature, which itself consists of base, frieze and cornice.
Organ front: Decorated screen on an organ.
Oriel: Projecting window on an upper floor, often a decorative feature.
Ossuary: Building for storage of bones removed from graves, often with a chapel.
Ottonian art: Art in the reigns of King Otto I, II and III (936–1002). Kings and church dignitaries encouraged and financed artists.
Outworks: The outer defences of a large castle.

P

Palas: Living quarters of a castle.
Paradise: A church forecourt, usually surrounded by columns.
Pedestal: Base of a column or statue.
Pendentive: The means by which a circular dome is supported on a square base; concave area between two walls and the base of a dome.

Peristyle: Continuous colonnade surrounding a temple or open court.

Pfalz: Palace of medieval kings and emperors, who had no permanent residence, but moved from place to place.

Pietà: Representation of the Madonna with the body of Christ on her lap.

Pilaster: Pier projecting from a wall; conforms to one of the ▷ orders.

Pilaster strip: Pilaster without a base and capital; a feature of early Romanesque buildings.

Pillar: Supporting member like a ▷ column, but with a square or polygonal cross-section; does not conform to any ▷ order.

Portico: Porch supported by columns, often with a pediment; may be the centrepiece of a façade.

Predella: Substructure of the altar; painting along the edge of a large altarpiece.

Presbytery: The part of the church reserved for officiating priests.

Prior: In the Benedictine or related Orders deputy to the abbot in an abbey, or house superior in a priory; head of the monastery in the Dominican and Carthusian Orders.

Pulpit: Raised place in a church from which the sermon is preached. May be covered by a ▷ baldachin or ▷ sounding board.

R

Refuge: Fortress used by the population in time of war in the Middle Ages.

Régence: French development of ▷ rococo.

Reliquary: Receptacle in which the relics of a saint are preserved.

Respond: An attached shaft.

Retable: Shrine-like structure above or behind the altar.

Ridge turret: Slender belfry on a roof ridge, common in the towerless churches of the Cistercian and Mendicant Orders.

Rib vault: ▷ Groin vault.

Rocaille: Ornaments adapted from the shell motif; chiefly late Renaissance and ▷ rococo.

Rococo: Style towards the end of the ▷ baroque (1720 – 70); elegant, often dainty; tendency to oval forms.

Rood screen: Screen between the ▷ choir and the ▷ nave, which bears a rood, or crucifix.

Roofs: See page in German edition

Round arch: ▷ Arch.

Rustication: Massive blocks of stone separated by deep joints.

S

Sgraffito: Scratched-on decoration.

Soft Style: Description of the late Gothic (c. 1390 – 1430) style of painting and sculpture noted for its gentle line.

Sounding board: Canopy above a pulpit with an acoustic and an artistic function.

Spandrel: The part of a vault between two adjacent ribs; concave area between two walls and the base of a dome.

Ständerbau: Building method in which the load-bearing walls are constructed with vertical supports.

Stellar vault: Vault in which the ribs are set in a star pattern.

Stepped gable: Gable which decreases in width towards the top in stepped stages.

Stucco: Plasterwork, made of gypsum, lime, sand and water, which is easy to model. Used chiefly in the 17&18C for interior decoration.

T

Tabernacle: Receptacle for the consecrated host.

Tambour: ▷ Dome.

Terracotta: Fired, unglazed clay.

Tracery: Geometrically designed stonework, particularly used to decorate windows, screens etc.

Transept: The part of a church at right angles to the nave.

Triforium: Arcaded wall passage looking on to the nave, between the arcade and the clerestory.

Tunnel vault: Simplest vault; continuous structure with semicircular or pointed cross-section uninterrupted by cross vaults.

Tympanum: The often semicircular panel contained within the lintel of a doorway and the arch above it.

V

Vestibule: An anteroom integrated into the W. façade of a church.

Vidame: Representative of the local lord or bishop.

Volute: Spiral scroll on an Ionic capital; smaller scrolls on Composite and Corinthian capitals.

W

Wall passage: Defensive passageway in the upper part of a ▷ curtain wall.

Welsche Haube: ▷ Onion dome with many curves, usually on a tower.

Westwork: Properly a transverse building in the W. of Carolingian and Ottonian churches with a vestibule in the lower storey and a chapel with side galleries open on the inside in the uppper storey; any fortress-like two-storey W. section in medieval churches.

Roofs

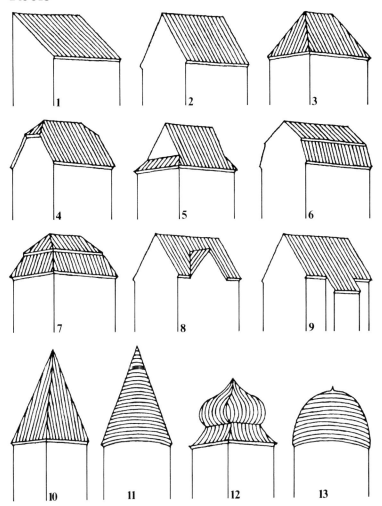

1 Lean-to roof
2 Saddleback or gable roof
3 Hipped roof
4 Half-hipped roof
5 Gambrel roof
6 Mansard saddleback roof
7 Mansard hipped roof
8 Dormer roof
9 Slipped roof
10 Pyramid or tent roof
11 Conical roof
12 Onion roof
13 Domed roof

Farm buildings in Switzerland

This pictorial map shows the types of building predominant in the various regions of the country.

1. Living and working areas with shallow-pitched roof, predominant in the Ketjen and plateau areas of the Jura (La Chaux-de-Fonds, NE, 1614.

2. Living and working areas with steep gable roof covering some of the yard, N. Swiss half-timbered building (Allschwil, BL, 1746).

3. Farmhouse in solid masonry (Hölstein, BL).

4. Living and working areas with steep gable roof, half-timbered, NE Switzerland (Tägerwilen, TG).

5. Multi-purpose building with formerly thatched hipped roof and very low eaves (Muhen, AG).

6. Main farm building in the central Mittelland (Nennigkofen, SO, 1740).

7. Multi-purpose building with hipped roof, gabled gallery and vehicle entrance on the mountain side, most common in the Emmental region (Konolfngen, BE, 1842).

8. Multi-purpose building in the Seeland and central Fribourg (Liebistorf, FR, 1734).

9. Farm building in central W. Switzerland (Carrouge, VD).

10. Solid stone building with very shallow gable roof, typical of the canton of Genève (Bardonnex, GE, 1634).

11. Pre-alpine Blockbau (Champéry, VS, 1778).

12. Pre-alpine Blockbau, longitudinally divided into living and working quarters (St. Stephan, BE, c. 1650).

13. So-called 'Paarhof' in the W. Northern Alps, with parallel living quarters and stable (Grindelwald, BE, 1777).

14. Farm buildings in the N. pre-alpine region (Baar, ZG).

15. Farmhouse in the E. pre-alpine region with living quarters orientated towards the sun and working building set at right angles. (Fischental, ZH, 1785).

16. Grisons farmhouse and stable (Luzein, GR, 1691).

17. Alpine farm buildings (Obersaxen, GR).

18. House in the Valais Alps. Blockbau with kitchen section in masonry (St-Jean, VS, 1667).

19. Living and working quarters with small Blockbau room in a solid masonry Engadine house (Lavin GR, 1725).

20. Plain stone building, some dry stone (Sonogno, TI, 1840).

21. Masonry farmhouse and stable (Poschiavo, GR).

22. Enclosed farmstead in S. Ticino (Rancate, TI).

From Atlas of Switzerland, Table 36, Farmhouses and farmyards, 1965 edition. Editor: Prof. Dr. Ed. Imhof. Expert advice: Max Gschwend. Reproduced by permission of the Bundesamt für Landestopographie, 15.12.81.

Map of Switzerland in 19 sections
showing the places covered in the guide

Numbers refer to individual maps

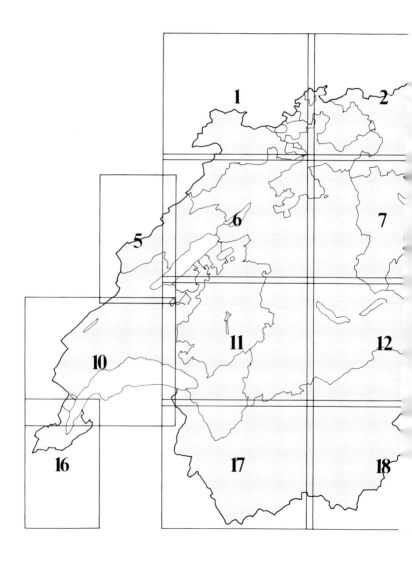

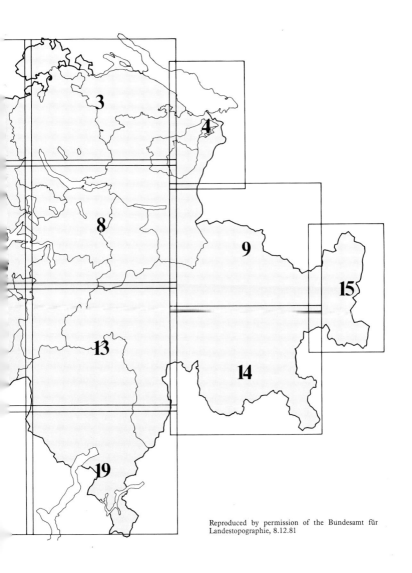

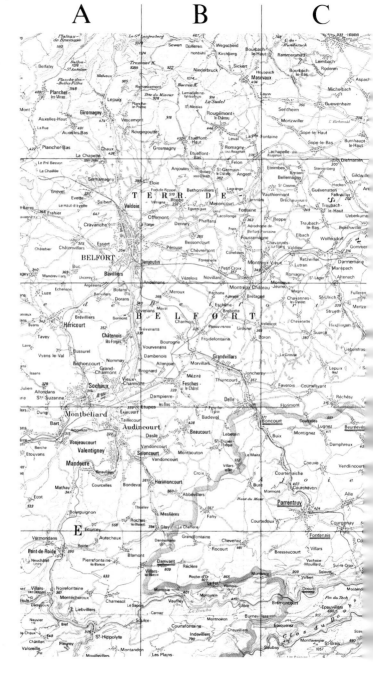

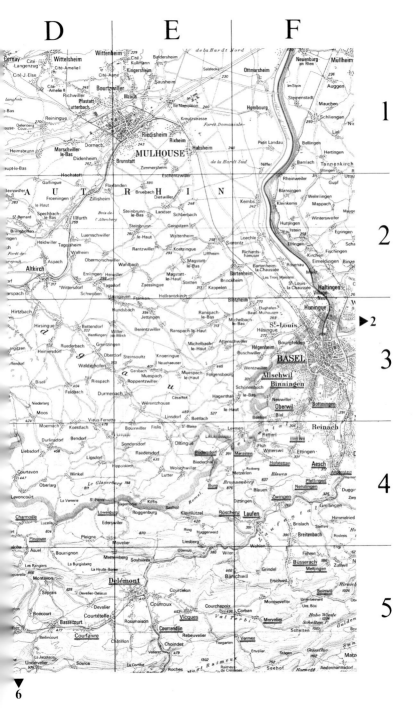

A   B   C

2

Müllheim   Badenweiler   Schönenberg   Utzenfeld   Gschwend

Vögisheim   Lipburg   Sehringen   Brandeck   Kühlenbronn   Böllen   Aitern   Schönau-Schwarzwald   Tunau   Prag   Innerleng

Feldberg   Blauen   Friedrichsheim   Hof Fröhnd   Herrenschwand   Hochkopf

Obereggenen   Käsacker   Kaltenbach   Hohwidderf   Raich   Elbenschwand   Ob. Hepschingen   Stadel   Todtmoos Weg   Rütte

Niedereggenen   Vogelbach   Wies   Hohenegg   Ehrsberg   Hohemuttlen   Todtmoos

Feuerbach   Sitzenkirch   Malsburg   Hochblauen   Pfaffenberg   Häg

Kandern   Hohe-Stückhaus   Tegernau   Gresgen   Adelsberg   Zell im Wiesental   Mambach   Rohren K.   Todtmoos-Glashütte   Freiwaldkap.

Riedlingen   Endenburg   Kirchhausen   Atzenbach   Wehrhalde

Uttnach   Heuberg   Holzen   Hammerstein   Munzenberg   Eichholz   Wieslet   Hausen-en Wiesental   Riedichen   Gersbach   Todtmoos-Au

Egisholz   Schlächtenhaus   Enkenstein   Hohe Möhr   Glashutten   Grossherrischwand

Maugenhard   Egerten   Nebenau   Kl. Weitenau   Weitenau   Raitbach   Rütte   Metrlen

Wollbach   Rechberg   Langenau   Kürnberg   Lang Eck   Hornberg

Egringen   Wittlingen   Hägelberg   Schopfheim   Fahrnau   Hasel   Niedergebisbach   Altenschwand   Segete

Schallbach   Rümmingen   Hauingen   Steinen   Eichen   Glashutten   Hogs

Binzen   Rötteln   Haagen   Höllstein   Maulburg   Wiechs   Filenkos   Wehr   Hutten   Hotting

Tumringen   Brombach   Husingen   Hoh Flum   Bergalingen   Rickenbach

Otlingen   Lörrach   Adelhausen   Nordschwaben   Enkendorf   Willaringen

Fullingen   Weil a. Rh.   Stetten   Dinkelberg   Minseln   Hinterdorf   Dossenbach   Jungholz

1 ◀   Waidhof   Eichsel   Riedmatt   Schwörstadt   Oflingen   Wieladingen   Hanne

Riehen   Inzlingen   Hagenbach   Karsau   Forst   Brennet   Egg   Rippolingen   Oberhof   Harpolingen

Christchona   Degerfelden   Nollingen   Riburg   Forstzelgli   Wallbach Baden   Eggberg   Niederhof

Bettingen   Aubrübg   Rheinfelden   Warmbach   Seline   Möhlin   Wallbach   Säckingen   Murg

Grenzach   Wyhlen   Herten

Birsfelden   Kaiseraugst   Rheinfelden   Magden   Zeiningen   Mumpf   Stein   Stein AG   Sisseln   Kai

Schweizerhalle   Augst   Munchwilen   Eiken   Kaister

Muttenz   Pratteln   Giebenach   Olsberg   Maisprach   Obermumpf   Frick

Münchenstein   Arisdorf   Buus   Zuzgen   Hellikon   Schupfart

Horn   Frenkendorf   Füllinsdorf   Herzberg   Wintersingen   Wegenstetten   Oberfrick

Arlesheim   Schauenburg-Bad   Liestal   Nusshof   Rickenbach   Hemmiken   Wittnau   Choraberg

Dornach   Scharten   Gempen   Nuglar   Lausen   Sissach   Gelterkinden   Ormalingen   Rothenfluh   Anwil   Oberhof   Wölflinsw

St Pantaleon   Seltisberg   Itingen   Böckten   Tecknau

Hochwald   Duggingen   Buren   Lupsingen   Bubendorf   Zunzgen   Thürnen   Diepflingen   Wenslingen   Kienberg   Benke

Ziegelschurer   Ziefen   Ramlinsburg   Tenniken   Rünenberg   Oltingen   Wasserf   Hard

Himmelried   Seewen   Lampenberg   Hölstein   Wittinsburg   Rumlingen   Zeglingen   Salhöchi   Salhöchi

Roderis   Rechtenberg   Arboldswil   Niederdorf   Diegten   Kanerkinden   Buckten   Häfelfingen   Ramsach   Rohr SO   Obererlinsbach   Erlins

Bretzwil   Reigoldswil   Titterten   Wisenberg   Burgflue   Stüsslingen

Nunningen   Lauwil   Bennwil   Oberdorf   Dietisberg   Wisen   Bad Lostorf   Lostorf   Niedererlinsbach   Aar

Zuliwil   Chilchli   Liedertswil   Waldenburg   Läufelfingen   Unt. Hauenstein   Eptingen   Froburg   Mahren   Niedergösgen   Epp

Gestenberg   Wassertalen   Hint. Egg   Rehhag   Beichen   Ifenthal   Hauenstein   Trimbach   Winznau   Schönenwerd

Hirnichopf   Obererswil   Phasenung   Belchenflue   Homberg   Ölten   Obergösgen   Gretzenbach

Ob. Hauenstein   Schöntal   Allerheiligenberg   Starrkirch   Däniken   Ober

Ramiswil   Langenbruck   Rickenbach   Wil   Dulliken   Eich   Kölliken

Guldental   Brunnersberg   Mümliswil   Holderbank SO   Hägendorf   Wangen   Engelberg   Gretz

Balsthal   St Wolfgang   Egerkingen   Hochi Flue   Rothacker   Walterswil   Sunnenberg

Laupersdorf   Hangen   Oberbuchsiten   Kappel   Born SO   Gunzgen   Aarburg   Oftringen   Strigel   Safenwil

Matzendorf   Anerholz   Roggen   Neuendorf   Boningen   Kungoldingen   Uerkheim

mannsdorf   Härkingen   Rothrist   Mühlethal

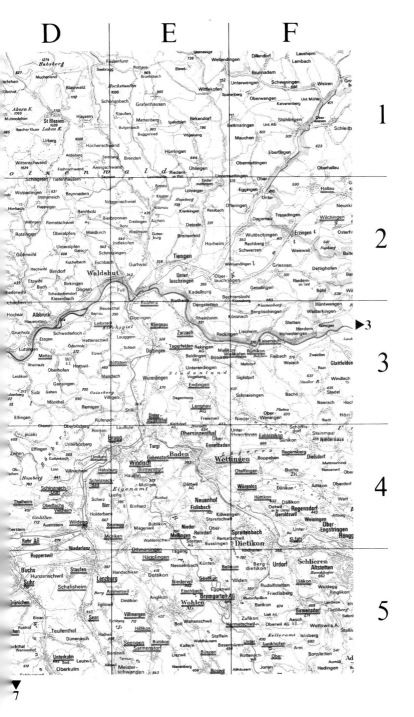

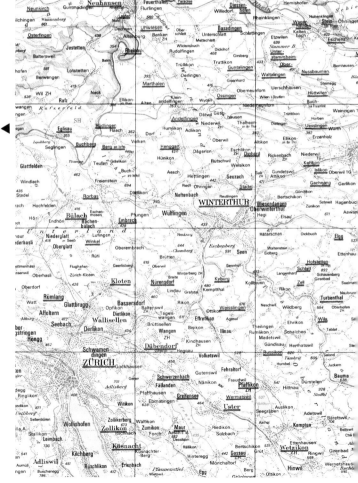

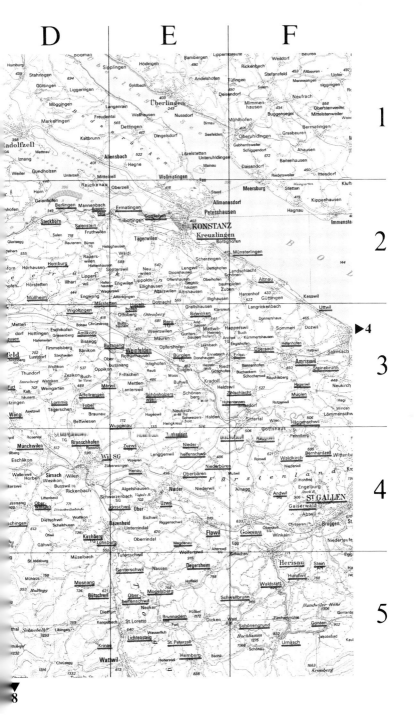

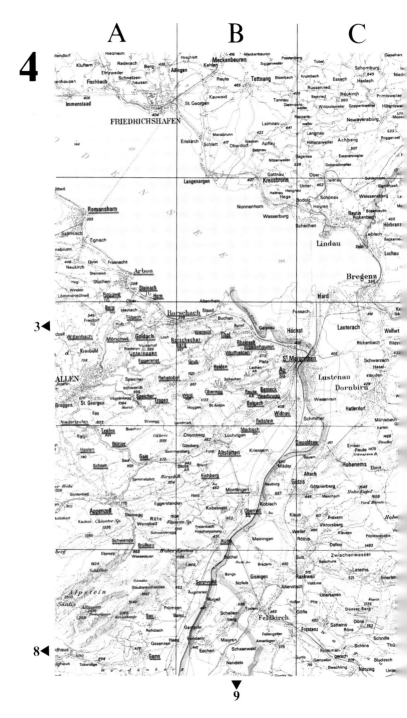

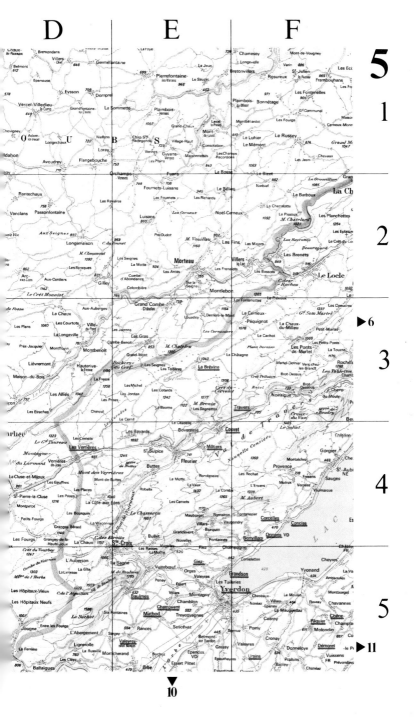

de-Chaux St-Hippolyte Chauvillers Clos d' Scou
Châtillon Fleurey Indevillers Montfavergier St-Brais 880
Valoreille Moudlevillers Montandon 790 Soubey 476 1057
  390 Les Plains- Les Sairains
Vaucusotte et-Grands-Essarts Les Enfers Montfaucon La Combe 860
aine Blanchefontaine Trévillers 826 Pré-Petitjean Lajoux
420 Orgeans Thiébouhans Ferrières- Fessevillers Les Pommerats 1072 1924 Les Genev
Maurice Les Bréseux M. Miroir le-Lac Goumois 633 Le Bémont Prédame
attenans- 985 Belfays Les Montbovats 1784
vare Le Froilais 777 Maîche Cernay- Damprichard 978 Saignelégier Rouges-Terres
Mont-de-Vougney Les Corneux l'Église 964 Charmauvillers Muriaux Les Cerlatez Le Cerisi
n 886 La Segnotte La Vierge Le Noirmont LesGenevènez La Chaux- Tramelan
St-Julien Les Écorces Charquemont La Goule Le Emibois Le Roselet des-Breuleux
le Russu 865 Essarts-Cuenot 971 Les Reussilles 917
Frambouhans Les Fourneaux 863 1043 Les Barrières Les Vacheries Les Breuleux r o i t
Les Fontenelles Les Bréuleux Le Creux-des- Mont-Tramelan Le Jean-Bren
306 Gd Communal 1227 Le Boichet Biches Les Enfers 1283 Cortébert Corgémont
725 Maisons-Dessous Creux- Le Peuchapatte Cernaux-Veusil Mont Crosin Cormoret Courtelary Les Bo
Cernaux Monnots de-Charquemont Cernaux-Godat 1034 Les Bois Mont Soleil 701
sey 965 Grand Mont Fournet- Biaufond St-Imier Villeret La Blanche Les P
874 1067 Blancheroche 611 La Joux d'Abel 1291 Met-du-Milieu- Mont Sujet
Les Jean- Chevaux Le Valanvron La Ferrière Sonvilier de-Bienne 1982
Le Groseiller Grand Combe Les Bulles 1066 989 Renan Les Pontins Le Chasseral Mont Sujet
1085 1048 La Chaux-de-Fonds Les Bugnenets Lamboing

Le Barboux Belleval Nods Duesse Les Combes
châtelard Les Planchettes 1278 Les Convers La Joux du Plâne Le Pâquier 885 Montagne de Diesse Prêles
1027 1264 Derrière-Pertuis 1153 La Côty 835 La Praye Ligneres 826
Recrettes Les Éplatures 991 Le Grand Combe Le Vieux-Prés 802 Ligerz
eauregard Le Crêt-du-Locle 1283 Mont d'Amin 1417 Villiers 736 Londel Schlossberg St-Petersinse
Brenets Vue des Alpes St-Martin Cernier Dombresson 1270 Combes La Neuveville
376 La Corbatière 1422 Chézard Savagnier Le Grand- Le Landeron Lüsche
La Sagne-Église Têre-de-Ran Fontainemelon Fontaines Chaumont Enges Cressier St-Johannsen 433 Erlach
Le Locle La Sagne Les Hauts-Geneveys Saules 1080 Frochaux Gals Vipeiz
hes Le Crêt Pradières Vilars Chaumont Cornaux Wavre Jolimont 563 Tschugg Ob Budik
1337 Les Coeudres M. Racine 751 Boudevilliers Ferein- 1087 St-Blaise Thielle Brütleten
Gd Som Martel 1439 Les Geneveys- Valangin Hauterive Epagnier Gampelen 478
aux- sur-Coffrane La Coudre Marin
nieu Petit-Martel 1009 Coffrane Montmollin Peseux 580 Monruz Tannelhof Ins S Grosses
Les Petits-Ponts La Tourne Rochefort 758 Corcelles Neuchâtel Witzwil 653
Les Ponts- 1170 Les Grattes Cormondrèche Serrières La Sauge Bellechase
de-Martel Vers-chez- Les Tablettes Chambrelien Auvernier Cudrefin Montet Mont Vully Sugiez
Dessus les-Brandt 1788 Bôle Colombier 582 Lugnorre Nant Gat
Brot- Champ- Baudry Champmartin Môtier Praz 429
Dessous du-Moulin Perreux Mur Muntelier Münchenwiler
Creux- 1359 de Chabrey Villamand Murten Burg BE
du-Van Boudry Bevaix Cortaillod Montmagny Bellerive Meyriez 152 Cressier
alia 475 Portalban 435 Salavaux BE
Châtillon Constantine Faoug Courgevaux Münchenwiler
Gorgier CANTON DE VAUD Clavaleyres 358 Cousshberg
ontalchez Chez-le-Bart Villars-le-Grand Chandossel Courlevon Klein- BE
e 468 Les Friques Courtepin Villarepos gusc
778 St-Aubin 439 Gletterens St-Aubin Avenches Wallenried Gross-
Frezera NE Chevroux Vallon Missy Donatyre Cormérod Courtaman
Vaumarcus Sauges Forel Grandcour Ressudens Domdidier Courtion Courtepin 570 Barbere
FR Rueyres-les-Prés Dompierre Oleyres Misery Courtillens La Corbaz Barb
Concise Estavayer-le-Lac 448 Autavaux FR 443 Russy Cournillens Cutterwil Losey
Font Montbrelloz Morens Chandon Grolley Belfaux
Châbles Lully FR Sévaz Bussy Corsalettes 583 Givisiez
Cheyres FR 525 Frasses près Payerne la-Ville Nierlet- 650
Bollion Montet Corcelles Léchelles les-Bois Corminboeuf
Yvonand Granges- 500 Cugy FR Payerne 458 Montagny Prehaux

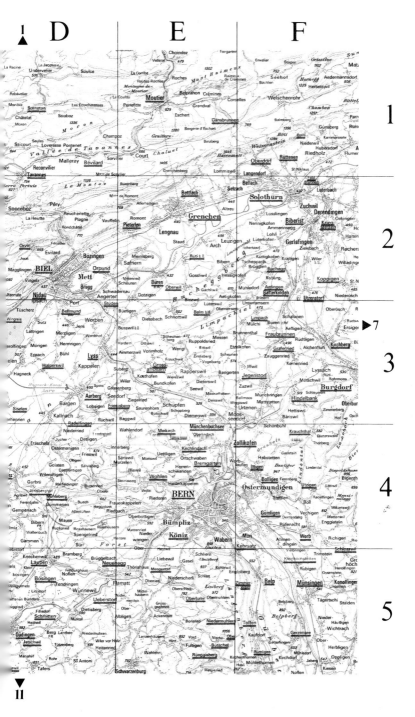

A B C

Lauupersdorf Hongen Oberbuchsiten Gungen SO Aarburg Strigel Safenwil Holziken
Matzendorf Dünnern Roggen Neuendorf Harkingen Boningen Rothrist Küngoldingen Uerkheim
rmannsdorf Müli Onsingen Niederbuchsiten Gland Strengelbach Zofingen Naudod Sc
Hüttelh Wolfsberg Walden Kestenholz Wollfwil Fulenbach Riken Vordemwald Riedt Adelboden Bottenwil Williberg
Farnern Rumisberg Oberbipp Niederbipp Holzhausen Murgenthal Wikon Mosersagi Atte
erg Dettenbühl Schwarzhausern Wynau Agerten Glasbütten Brittnau Reidermoos
ersrohr Wiedlisbach Stalten Aarwangen Mumenthal Roggwil Schürberg Grood Reiden Rei
Attiswil Walliswil b.Bipp Batzenwil St. Urban Sagen Pfaffnau Langnau b.R Latte
Flumenthal Berken Hard Langnau Uflikon D
Wangen Walliswil b.W. Graben Bützberg Langenthal Richenthal Dagmersellen
Wangenried Heimenhausen Thunstetten Rögglswil Unter- Inn. Fronhofen Altishofen Nebikon
Deitingen Röthenbach a.H Steckholz Arpolingen Egolzwil Wauw
Subingen Inkwil Wanzwil Forst Ober- Busswil Albüron Ebersecken Schötz
gen Oekingen Etziken Bolken Niederönz Bleien- Gutenburg Grossdietwil
Haften Horriwil Aesku Oberönz Thörigen Rütschelen Ghünn Melchnau Zell Ohmstal Kot
Rechterswil Hersiwil Steinhof Bollodingen Madiswil Linden Mattenbach Reisiswil Fischbach
Heimiswil Seeberg Ochlenberg Kleindietwil Wyssbach Gondiswil Alberswil Etti
Willadingen Grasswil Spych. Leimiswil Biseck Gettnau Gr
en St. Niklaus Riedtwil Oschwand Ursenbach Bruggenwald Huswil Willisau-Stadt Wolfteg
Alchenstorf Breitenegg Rohrbach Auswil Hofstetten Oste
Niedergrosch Rumendingen Leggiswil Ferrenberg Waltersswil Rohrbach-graben Ufhusen
Rüdtswil Oeschenbach Chaltenegg Huttwil Rueffswil Breiten Sta
Ersigen Bickigen Kappelen Ob.Hüferdingen Daiwil Schülen Menz
Bütikofen Hirschbrunnen Dürrenroth Nyffenegg Hergiswil b.Willw Rehrmoos
Heimiswil Affoltern i.E. Wyssachen Eriswil Hofstatt Albach Opferse Twerenegg
gdorf Mützigen Oberwald Wasen i.E. Chalberweid Luthern Menzberg
Oberburg Busswil Egg Ruegsbach Muzi Ahorn Lüthernbad Doppl
erberg Hof Oschwand Hasle Ruegsau Trachselwald Grünen Churzenei Hinterarni Ob. Scheidegg Redbad Fontann
Lützelflüh Grünen Ramsei Rotenbuel Luderenalp Höchänzi Napf Adtisberg
Goldbach Schafhausen Chaipers Geisssrütflue Brandboden Hause
Bigenthal Leopoldsbühnenegg Tal Schwanden Ranflüh Schynen Brambodfen Anc
Oberg-goldbach Zollbrück Finzenhus Fankhaus Fontannen
Menzi reinegg Hameg Aspi Mutzlenberg Egg Ei Brandboden
Vikartswil Landiswil Lauperswil Witenbach E. Schüpfheim
renwil Walkringen Hamismatt Moosegg Emmenmatt Chnuzbrugg Längenbach Treub Michelsschwand
stein Arni Blasenflue Langenegg Turner Leho Chu
Biglen Oberthal Signau Langnau i.E. Bärau Längengrund
chigen Schlosswil Ried Moschberg Mutten Hohwacht Trubschachen Escholzmatt
Gross-hochstetten Zäziwil Oberhofen Steinen Aschau Huptenboden Kroschen-brunnen Reichlen Ronigmos
Heroldswil Runatenen Horn Wiggen E
Konolfingen Mirchel Bowil Blappach Schwarig Flühli
ruellen Oberhünigen Rütenen Marbach Hilferen F.
chi Niederhünigen Martisegg Chapp Eggiwil Heidbuel Pfyffer Hohwald
hautigen Ruegsegg Chapfschwand Zichlett Marbach Hilferental
chtrach Churzenberg Linden Jassbach Siehlen Wachtbuel Steingut
Oberdiessbach Heimenschwand Wachsetboden Schallenberg Str. Loshütenberg Hengst Habchegg
erbligen Falkenflue Schangnau Schibenguistüli
Doppligen Brenzikofen Buchholterberg Heimenegg Oberei Bleiken Bumbach Salwidili

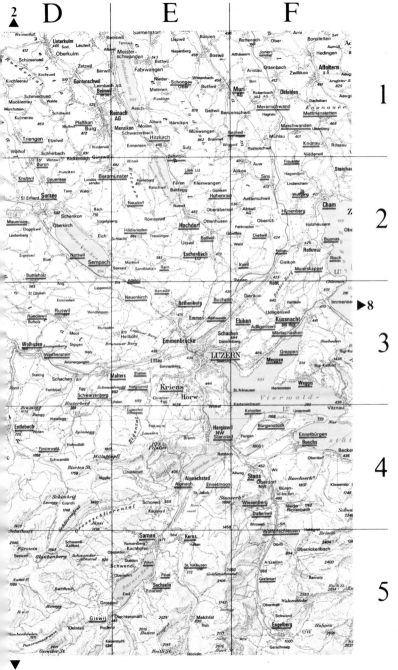

8

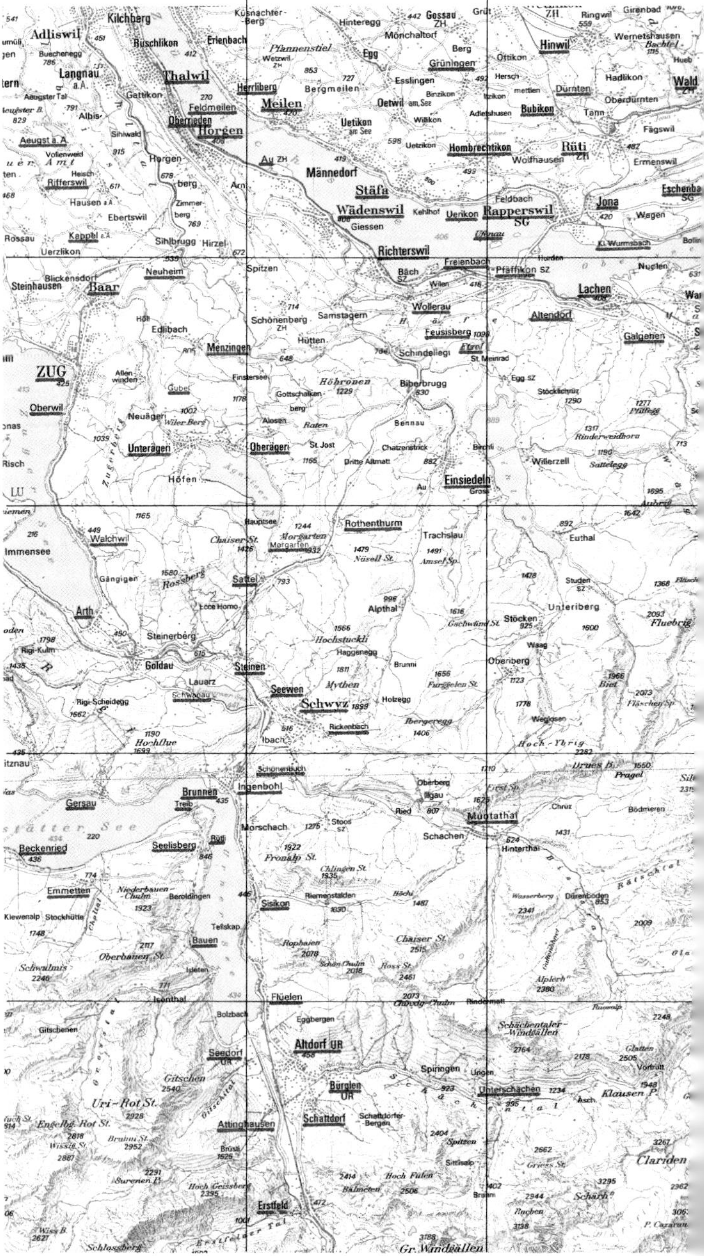

A   B   C

7 ◀

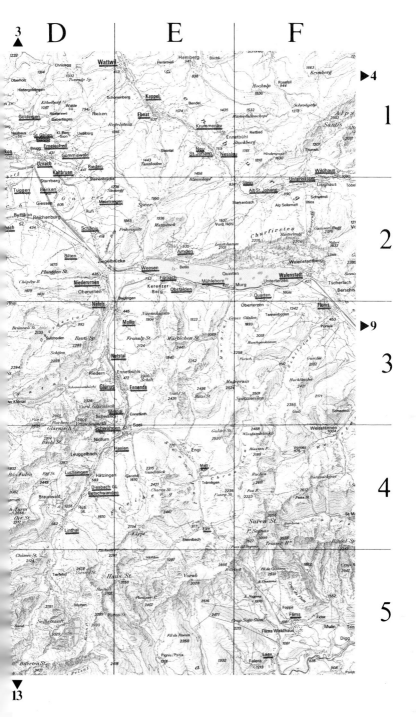

9

A 4 B C

8◄

13◄

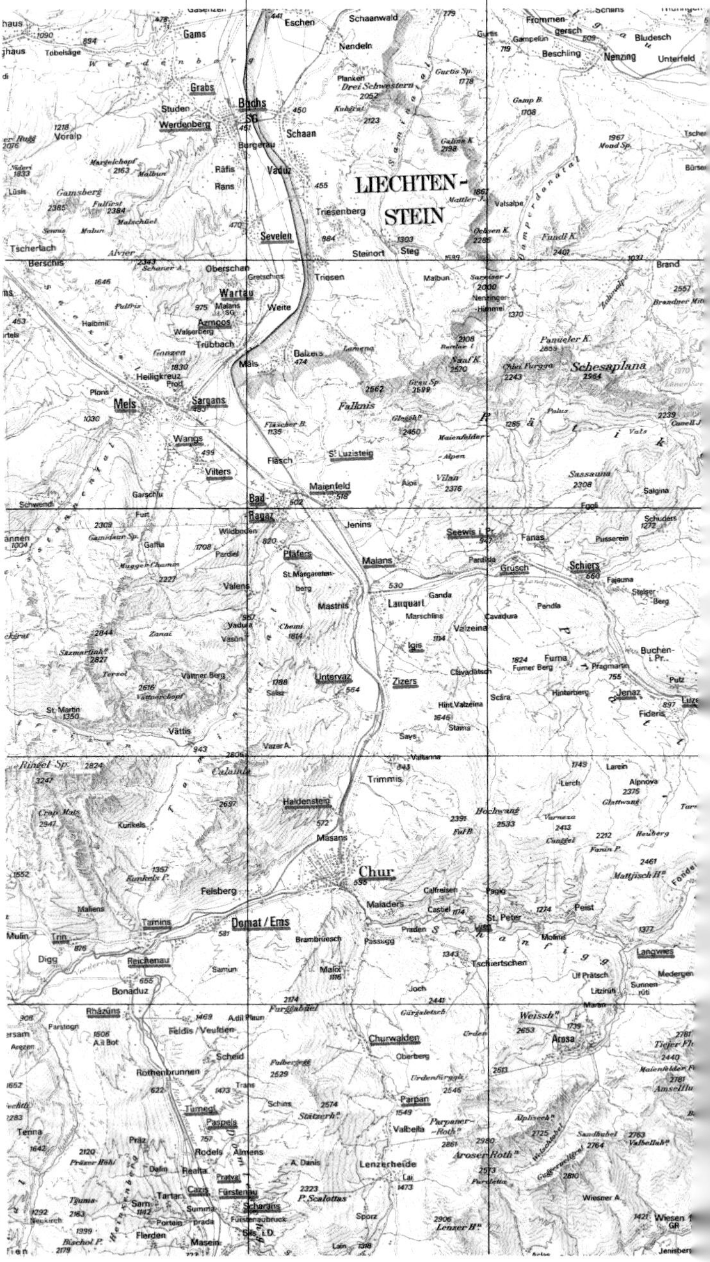

Gams
Eschen
Schaanwald
Nendeln
Frommen
Bludesch
Beschling
Nenzing
Unterfeld

Grabs
Buchs SG
Werdenberg
Studen
Voralp
Schaan
Kühtriet

Drei Schwestern
2052

Gamp B.
1908

Räfis
Vaduz
Rans

LIECHTEN-
STEIN

Triesenberg
Valüna

Sevelen

Triesen
Steinort Steg
Malbun

Berschis
Oberschan
Gretschins
Wartau
Malans
Weite
Azmoos
Trübbach
Mäls
Balzers
Lareina

Fläsch
St. Luzisteig
Alpen
Villan

Pusueler K.
2653

Schesaplana
2964

Falknis
2562
Gonzen
Sargans
Wangs
Vilters

Mels

Bad Ragaz
Maienfeld
Jenins

Vättis
St. Martin
Valens
Pfäfers
St. Margarethenberg
Mastrils
Malans

Seewis i. Pr.
Fanas
Grüsch
Schiers

Lanquart
Marschlins
Igis
Valzeina

Jenaz
Fideris

Untervaz
Zizers
Says

Trimmis

Calanda
Haldenstein
Masans

Chur

Felsberg
Domat/Ems
Maladers
Passugg
St. Peter
Molinis

Tamins
Trin
Reichenau
Bonaduz

Rhäzüns
Feldis/Veulden
Scheid
Rothenbrunnen

Churwalden
Oberberg

Arosa
Weissh.

Parpan
Valbella

Tomils
Paspels
Rodels Almens
Realta

Lenzerheide
Lai

Praden
Tschiertschen
Langwies
Medergen

Scharans
Fürstenaubruck
Sils i. D.
Masein
Flerden

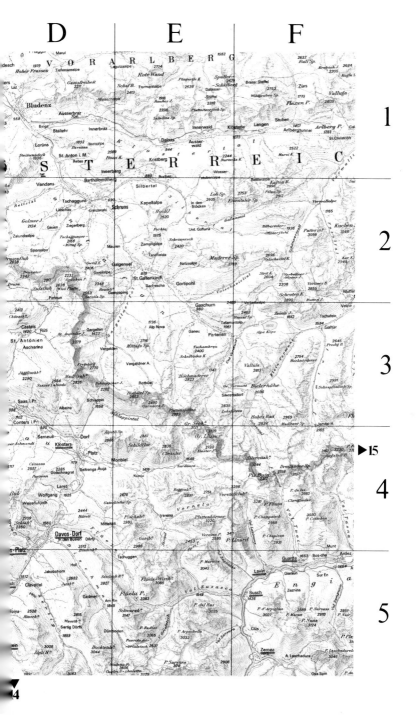

Champagnole   Lent   Gillois   Froroz   Cerniébaud   952   Rondefontaine   Gellin   921   Maison du Bois   Rochejean

Bourg- de Sard   Sirod   629   1237   Sarragepis   Les Villedieu

ize   Treffay   Arsure Arsurette   St-Sorlin   Les Pontets   933   Mouthe   Le

816   Syam   Crans   329   Bief des Maisons   Reculfoz   Le Crouzet   Petite Chaux   Les Sapeaix

udioux   762   Les Chalesmes   1206   Le Cros Mont   Châtelblanc   La Chaux-Neuve   1185   Petit Risoux

La Perrena   1014   Grand Crêt   1419   Les Charbonnières   Le Pc

Chaux- des Crotenx   Les Planches- en Montagne   Foncine- le Haut   Le Cernois   Le Séchey   1014

Pont de- la Chaux   728   Sur- la Côte   1270   Le Lieu   973   L'Abbaye   Hau- Mol-

Entre Deux Monts   Morillon   Foncine- le Bas   Le Mont Noir   1221   1378   Le Solliat   Vers-chez- Grosjean

la Boissière   Fort- du Plane   812   Le Marichet   La Golisse   Le Sentier   Les Bioux

Chaux- lu Dombel   Pont de Lemme   Le Voisinal   Les Thavennins   Chapelle- des Bois   1076   1679   Mont Tendre

Les Chauvettes   Les Prés Hauts   L'Orient

Chaumusse   St-Laurent- en Grandvaux   Les Martins   1079   Les Mortes   Le Brassus   1036

507   La Combe- de Morbier   La Roche- Bernard   1289   Pré Derrière Bas du Chenit   1530   Moulin de Bière

Les Poncets   Col de la Savine   993   Les Marais   1020   1447   Col du Marchairux   Bière

Les Mussillons   Combe- Froide   Bellefontaine   698

Abbaye- de Grandvaux   1156   Morbier   Bois d'Amont   1077   1494   Crêt de la Neuve   M. Chaubert   1082

Tancua   Les Lattes   736   Morez   Gimel

Les Mouillés   La Mouille   1299   913   1545   St-George   St-Oyens   Sa

Lézat   Gros Crêtel   Mont Sâla   1532   1763   Marchissy   821   Longirod   Essertines- sur Rolle

La Doye   Bois du Bouez   Mont Pelé   1568   Le Noirmont   896   Mo

Les Repentys   Les Arcets   Les Rousses   Le Vaud   Burtigny   Tartegnin

856   Longchaumois   M. Fion   1282   1114   1152   La Cure   Arzier   Bassins   Gilly

Prémanon   1228   St-Cergue   Les Muids   Bursins   Luins   Vinzel   376

Les Charnières   1416   C. de la Givrine   1041

Haut Crêt   1119   Labagno   1677   1308   Genolier   Begnins   Bursinel

rénois   Forêt de la Prusse   La Barillette   La Dôle   Givrins   Vich   Dully

Chaux Barthod   1435   Coinsins   Gland

Lamoura   Bonmont   Gingins   Grens   Trélex   Quillier   Promenthoux

lain Monts   Chéserex   Prangins

Lajoux   1511   La Rippe   Borex   Eysins   Nyon

1171   Col de- la Faucille   Vésenex- Crassy   Crassier   Yvoire   401

Laisia   1255   Mijoux   1320   La Pailly   Villard   Divonne- les-Bains   Crans   Nernier   Messery

Montrond   1614   Vésancy   Arbère   494   Céligny   Essert   Che

Gex   Bogis   Bossey   GE   Chens- sur Léman

Mijoux   1398   Mourex   Chavannes- des Bois   755   M. Mourex   Founex   Sous Estr-

res   1687   Tougin   Grilly   Commugny   Tougues   Massongy

Colomby de Gex   Echenevex   Cessy   Sauverny   Chavannes- les Foix   Tannay   Coppet   Véretre   Douvaine

Lélex   834   Naz   Seghy   Vesancy   Mies   429   Ballai-

Col de Crozet   1485   Avouzon   Brégny   Ecogia   Hermance   Loisin

Crozet   Chevry   Bossy   Veigy   Chamberi   Marcorens   Moget

1719   Forêt de la Neige   Villeneuve   Prégnin   Moens   Ornex   Collex   Versoix   Anières   Corsier   Foncenex   Brens

717   Reculet   Sergy   Pailly   Privessin   Genthod   Collonge   Machilly   52

Allemogne   480   St-Genis   Ferney- Voltaire   Bellevue   Bellerive   St- Maurice   440   Gy   Monniaz   St-Cergues

Thoiry   Meyrin   Le Grand- Saconnex   Chambésy   Vésenaz   Meinier   Juss-

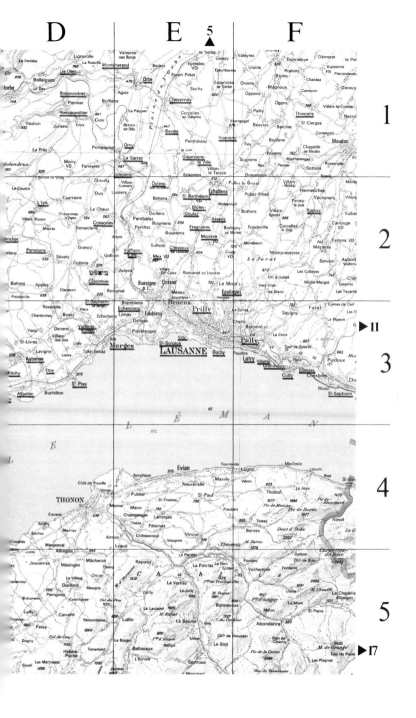

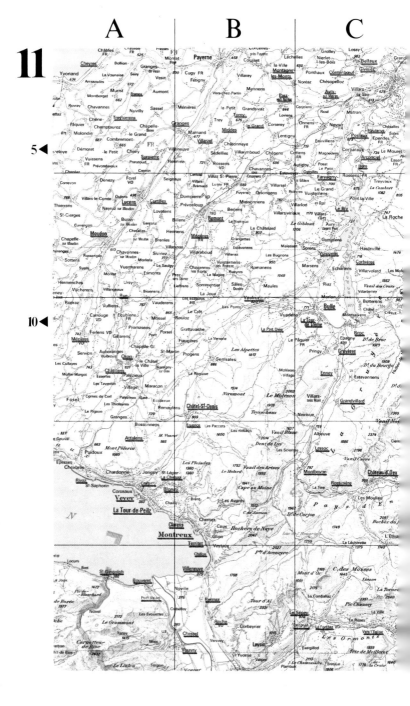

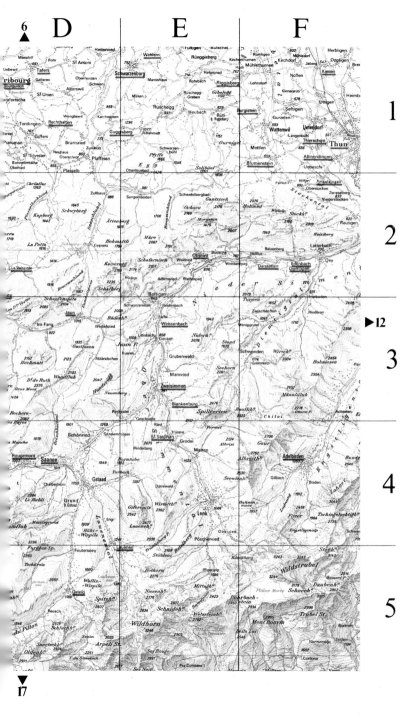

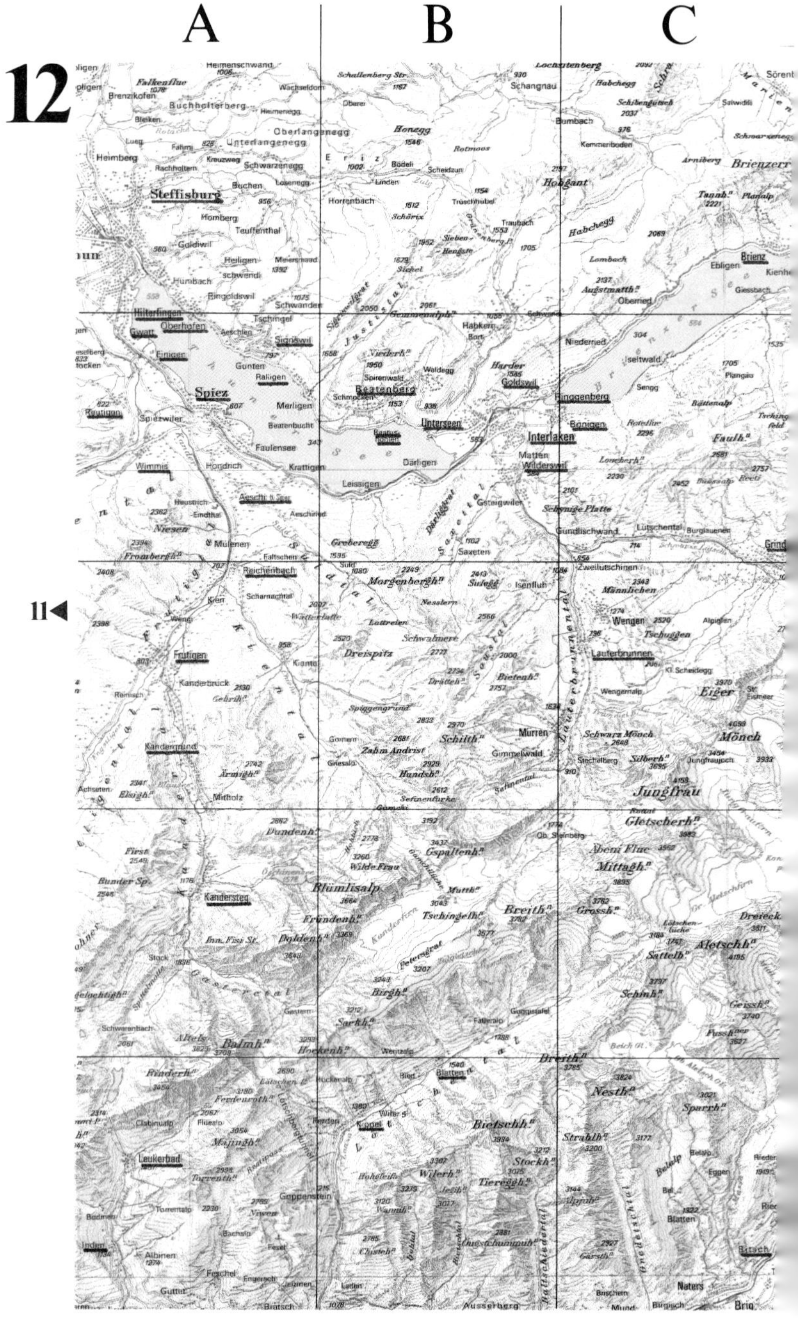

Heimenschwand

Falkenflue

Brenzikofen
Buchholterberg
Blatten

Bleiken
Oberlangenegg
Untanlangenegg

Heimberg
Steffisburg
Buchen
Homberg
Teuffenthal
Goldiwil
Heiligen-
schwendi
Hünibach
Ringoldswil
Schwanden

Hilterfingen
Oberhofen
Sigriswil
Gunten
Ralligen
Spiez
Merligen
Beatenbucht
Faulensee
Krattigen
Leissigen

Wimmis
Hondrich

Niesen

Fromberghn

Reichenbach
Scharnachtal

Frutigen
Kanderbrück

Kandergrund

Kandersteg

Schallenberg Str.
Schangnau
Röthenbach
Bärau

Hohgant

Habchegg

Arnberg
Brienzerr

Tanah
Planalp
Brienz
Ebligen
Giessbach

Goldswil
Ringgenberg
Bönigen

Interlaken
Matten
Wilderswil

Saxeten

Gündlischwand
Lütschental
Burglauenen
Grind

Zweilütschinen

Morgenberghn
Sulegg
Isenfluh
Wengen
Tschuggen
Lauterbrunnen
Wengernalp
Eiger
Mönch

Mürren
Gimmelwald
Schwarz Mönch
Silberhn
Jungfraujoch
Jungfrau

Schlith
Zahm Andrist

Gletscherhn
Ebni Flue
Mittaghn
Grossh
Dreieck

Aletschhn
Sattelhn
Schinhn

Blümlisalp
Fründenhn
Doldenhn
Birghn
Sackhn
Hockenhn
Breithn

Kandersteg
First

Bunter Sp.

Leukerbad
Torrenthn

Rinderhn
Ferdenrothn
Majinghn

Bietschhn
Stockh
Tieregghn

Nesthn
Sparrhn
Strahlhn

Baltschieder
Eggen
Blatten
Bitsch

Naters
Brig
Brigerbad

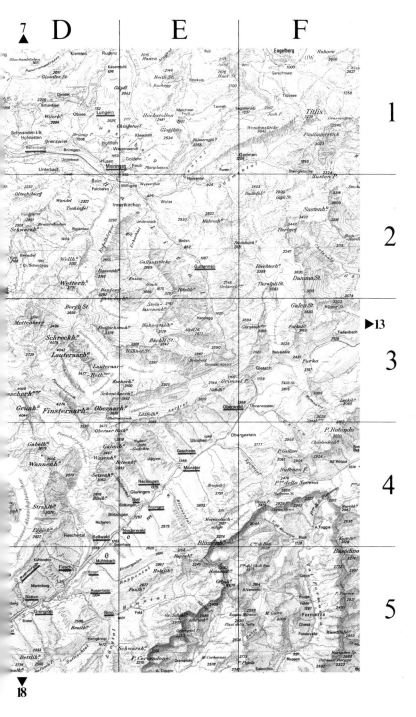

A B C

13

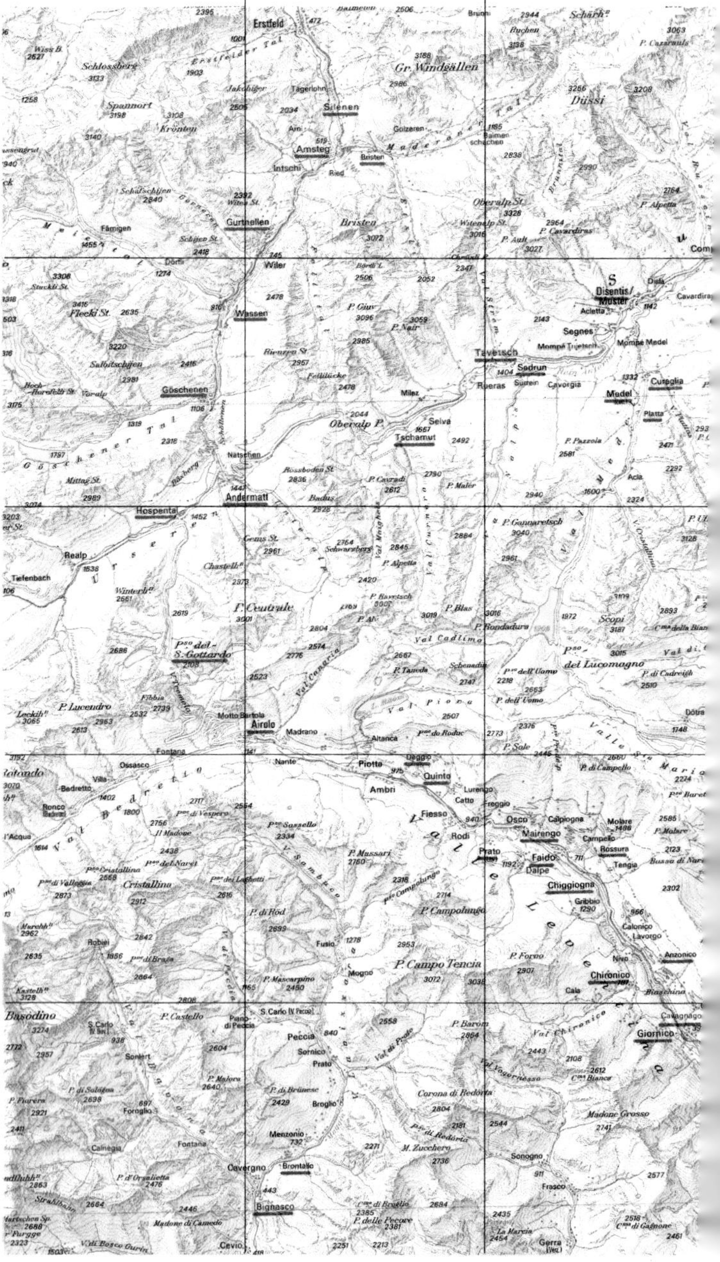

Erstfeld
Erstfelder Tal
Schlossberg
Spannort
Krönten
Gr. Windgällen
Düssi
Silenen
Amsteg
Intschi
Bristen
Maderaner Tal
Oberalp St.
Gurtnellen
Fämigen
Meiental
Wiler
Wassen
Flecki St.
Salbitschijen
Göschenen
Göschener Tal
Tavetsch
Sedrun
Rueras
Disentis/ Muster
Segnes
Medel
Curaglia
Oberalp P.
Tschamut
Selva
Andermatt
Hospental
Realp
Tiefenbach
Urseren
P. Centrale
P.so del S. Gottardo
P. Lucendro
Airolo
Madrano
Val Cadlimo
Val Piora
P.so del Lucomagno
Scopi
Fontana
Ossasco
Bedretto
Villa
Val Bedretto
Ronco
Cristallina
Nante
Piotta
Quinto
Ambri
Fiesso
Rodi
Prato
Faido
Osco
Mairengo
Chiggiogna
Valle Leventina
P. Campolungo
Fusio
Mogno
P. Campo Tencia
Chironico
Robiei
Basòdino
P. Castello
S. Carlo
Peccia
Sornico
Prato
Broglio
Menzonio
Cavergno
Brontallo
Bignasco
Cevio
Val Bavona
Corona di Redorta
M. Zucchero
Val Chironico
Giornico
Madone Grosso
Sobrio
Frasco
Gerra

12◀

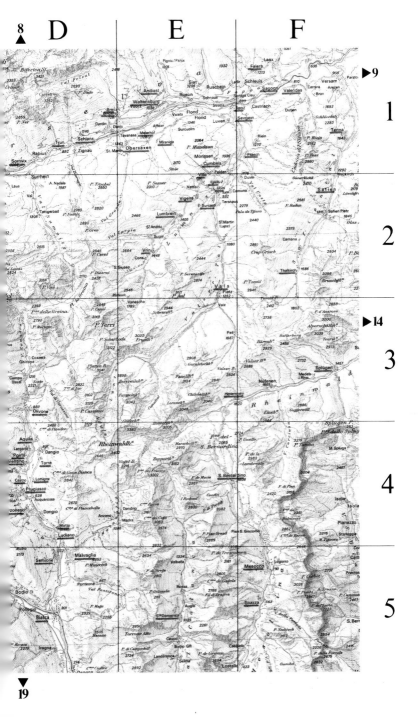

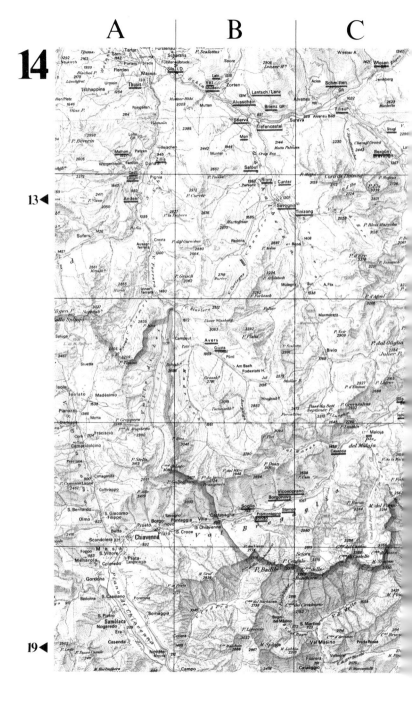

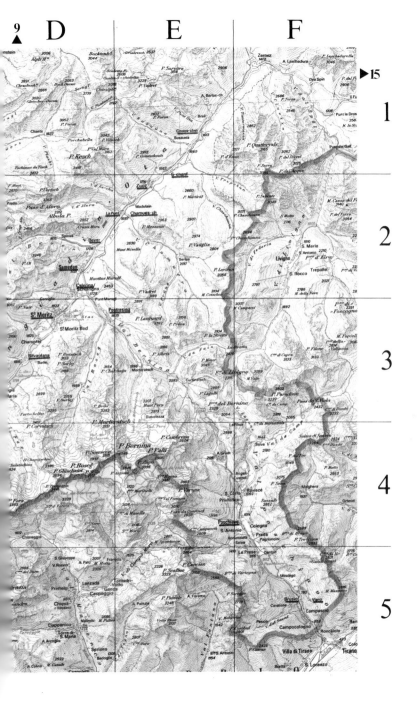

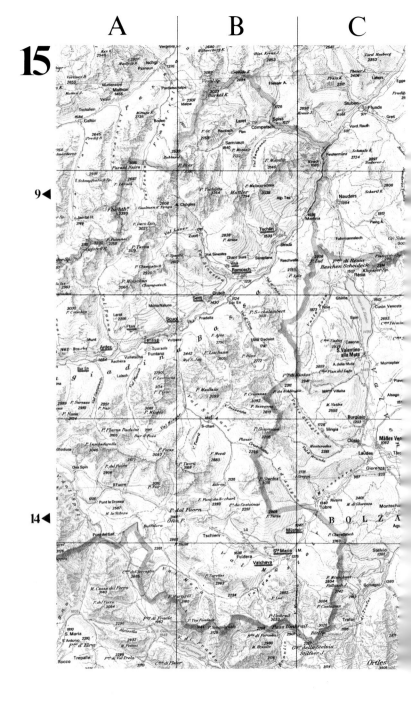

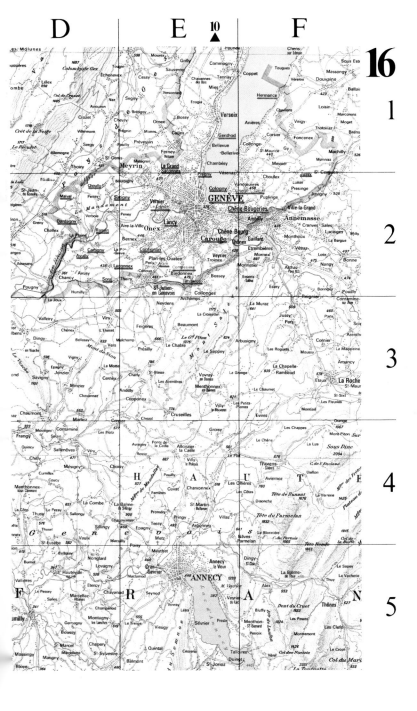

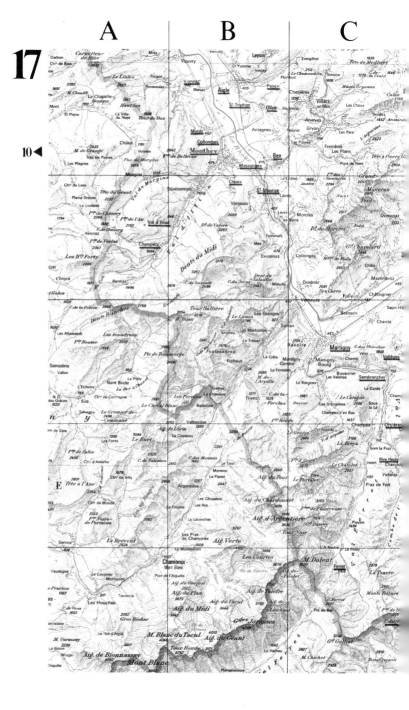

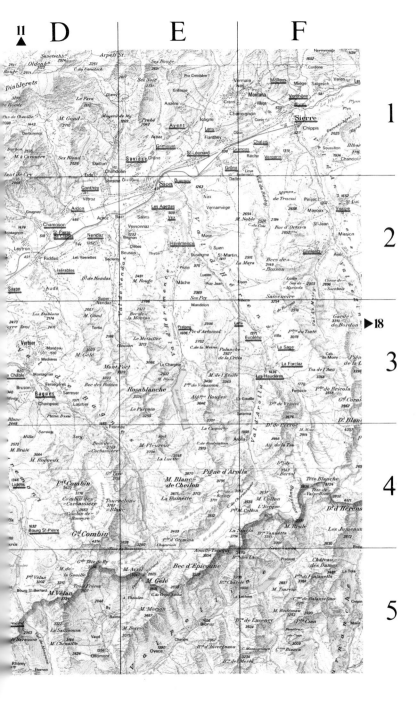

Leuk · Feschel · Guttet · Erschmatt · Bratsch · Gampel Steg · Niedergesteln · Laden · Hohtenn · Raron · Ausserberg · Baltschieder · Eggerberg · Brigerbad · Görsth · Brischen · Bodmen · Mund · Bügisch · Naters · Brig · Gamsen · Glis · Ried

Susten · Turtmann · Agarn · Unterems · Ergisch · Ried · Eischoll · Turtig · Visp · Eyholz · Glish

Plyn · Oberems · Unterbäch · Bürchen · Zeneggen · Stalden · Gebidem · Spitzhörnli · Tschenh · Visperterminen

Illhorn · Meretschalp · Bella Tola · Chandolin · Brunethn · Ginals · Moosalp · Törbel · Stalden · Staldenried · Alter Spitz

St. Luc · Meidpass · Meiden · Gruben · Augstbordh · Embd · Hannigalp · Gspon · Ochsenh · Galeh · Bösh

Pte de Tourtemagne · Blumatt · Jungtal · Grächen · Esten · Simelih · Fletschh

Roc de Boudri · Furggwärgh · Roth · Festih · Ried · Distelh · Roth · Laggenh

Fredih · Mottec · Turtmann H. · Barrh · St. Niklaus · Fäschh · Jegih

Les Diablons · Breith · Mattsand · Balfrin · Lammenh · Saas Balen · Trift

Zinal · Steinberg · Herbriggen · Balfrin · Tamatten · Weissmie

Tête de Milon · Brunegg · Dürrenh · Trift · Saas Grund · Trifth

Bordon · Bish · Weissh · Randa · Dom H. · Nadelh · Saas Fee · Portjen

Pigne de la Le · Besso · Weisshorn H. · Dom · Schalih · Täschh · Mittaght · Langflue · Saas Almagell · Almagellh

Zinalroth · Mettelh · Täsch · Leiterspitzen · Alphubel · Botanna H. · Sopa

Trifth · Rothorn H. · Zermatten · Täschalpen · Sattelspitz · Allalinh · Stellih

D. Blanche · Ob. Gabelh · Trift · Ried · Oberroth · Rimpfischh · Jazzih

Pte de Zinal · Unt. Gabelh · Zermatt · Spitzi Flue · Strahlh · Spechh

Zmutt · Zum-See · Findeln · Flue · Steinchalchh · M. Moro · pta

Schwarzsee · Riffelalp · Rotboden · Stockh · di Jazzi · Battel

Matterh · M. Cervino · Rifelberg · Gornergletscher · Weissgrat · Macugnaga · Staffa · Borca

Hérens · Trockener Steg · Jägerh · Alter Belvedere · Pestaren

Jumeaux · Plan Maison · Theodul P. · Theodulh · Dufour Sp. · P. Nero · E. dei Vitti

Bräuil · Golliet · Testa Grigia · Breith · P. Bianco · Pallone dei

Gran Sometta · Zwillinge · Monte Rosa · Pta Gruber · Fillar

La Tola · Liskamm · Piramide Vincent · Cma di Faller · P. Montevecchio

Singlin · Rocca di Verra · Cap. Quintino Sella · Pta Vittoria · A. Vigne · A. Faller · Cma Piffimo · Rima

Crepin · M. Baisetta · A. Narda · M. Mare · M. Rosso · A. Salza · Stolemberg · Cma d'Olen · M. Taglinferro

Valtournanche · Gd Tournalin · St. Jacques · M. Bettaforca · A. Cortlys · Olivel · Cma d'Olen · S. Giuseppe

Chenell · A. Champsec · A. di Nana · Frachey · Pta Straling · Piannmisura · Alagna-Valsta · Cma Carnera

Bec de Nana · Le Gd Dent · Champoluc · M. Roth · Orza · Riva · Pennnisura

Chamois · Testa Grigia · Cunéaz

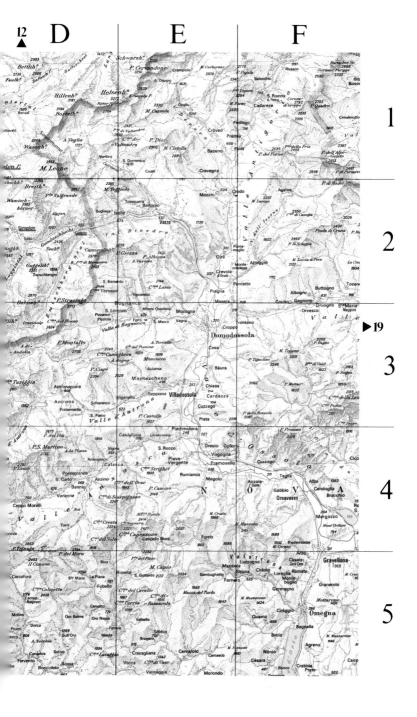

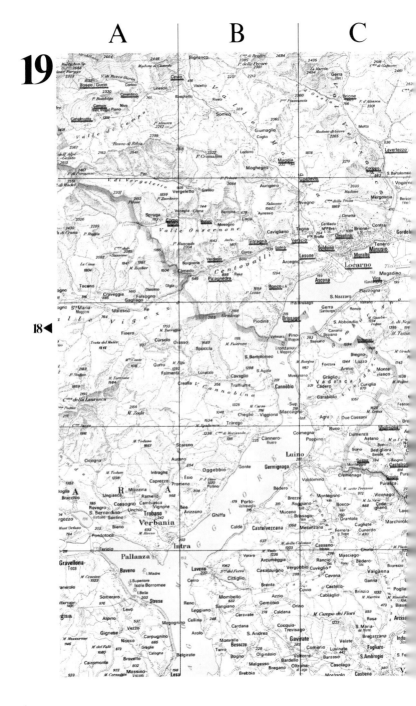

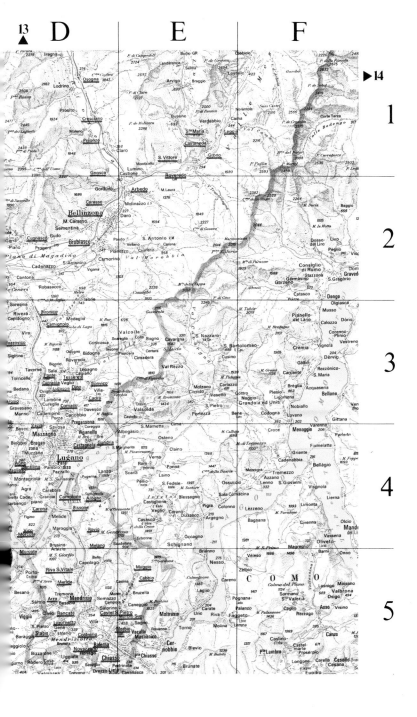

Luxembourg